THE UNITED NATIONS AND THE MAINTE-NANCE OF PEACE AND SECURITY

THE BROOKINGS INSTITUTION

The Brookings Institution is an independent organization engaged in research and education in the social sciences. Its principal purposes are to aid in the development of sound public policies and to provide advanced training for students in the social sciences.

The Institution was founded December 8, 1927 as a consolidation of three antecedent organizations: the Institute for Government Research, 1916; the Institute of Economics, 1922; and the Robert Brookings Graduate School of Economics and Government, 1924.

The general administration of the Institution is the responsibility of a self-perpetuating Board of Trustees. In addition to this general responsibility, the By-Laws provide that, "It is the function of the Trustees to make possible the conduct of scientific research and publication, under the most favorable conditions, and to safeguard the independence of the research staff in the pursuit of their studies and in the publication of the results of such studies. It is not a part of their function to determine, control, or influence the conduct of particular investigations or the conclusions reached." The immediate direction of the policies, program, and staff of the Institution is vested in the President, who is assisted by an advisory council, chosen from the professional staff of the Institution.

In publishing a study the Institution presents it as a competent treatment of a subject worthy of public consideration. The interpretations and conclusions in such publications are those of the author or authors and do not necessarily reflect the views of other members of the Brookings staff or of the administrative officers of the Institution.

The United Nations and the Maintenance of International Peace and Security

By
LELAND M. GOODRICH
and
ANNE P. SIMONS

THE BROOKINGS INSTITUTION
WASHINGTON, D.C.

Printed in the United States of America
George Banta Publishing Company
Menasha, Wisconsin

Preface

I<small>N THE</small> summer of 1951, the Brookings Institution began a series of studies on the United Nations. The series was initiated by the late Dr. Leo Pasvolsky who, until his untimely death on May 5, 1953, was Director of the International Studies Group at the Institution. The general plan for the research was formulated in the winter of 1949-50 when many proposals for changes in the United Nations system were being widely discussed in the United States. Much of the public discussion indicated the need for a systematic analysis of the issues arising from the experience with the United Nations system and for a careful evaluation of the immediate and ultimate implications of the various courses of action being proposed. To assist in meeting this need, became, therefore, the central purpose of the Brookings studies.

While this research has been under way, new developments have further affected the attitude of many Americans toward the United Nations. Paramount among these have been the difficulties encountered in dealing with aggression in Korea and in trying to achieve a settlement of the situation there, within the broader context of the whole Far Eastern situation. Some American pressures for changes in the United Nations system are increasing and may reach a climax in the autumn of 1955 when the General Assembly is expected to consider the question whether to convoke a conference for the purpose of reviewing, and possibly revising the Charter. In these circumstances, it is hoped that the Brookings studies will be of special value in contributing to better public understanding of the problems that will be involved.

The studies are being published in seven volumes, of which this is the first to appear. Although these volumes form a related series, each of them constitutes a separate study of a major feature of the United Nations system. The order given below is not the actual order of publication, but it represents the logical arrangement of the series.

One volume is entitled *A History of the United Nations Charter*. It will present, from the American point of view, the evolution and negotiation of the Charter as part of the developing United

v

Nations system during the period from 1940 to 1945. A major purpose of the volume will be to show the principal ideas and proposals considered by the United States Government in reaching its final position on the specific provisions of the Charter.

Three volumes will analyze and appraise the principal activities and organizational problems of the United Nations and its related agencies since the Organization came into being in January 1946.

One of these, entitled *The Organization and Procedures of the United Nations,* will cover the general organizational development of the United Nations. It will be concerned both with particular organizational problems in each of the principal organs—the General Assembly, the Security Council, the Economic and Social Council, The Trusteeship Council, the International Court of Justice, and the Secretariat—and with some of the general problems encountered, such as the interpretation of the Charter, the definition of domestic jurisdiction, and the question of membership.

The second of these, the present volume, which is entitled *The United Nations and the Maintenance of International Peace and Security,* deals with methods and processes for maintaining peace and security through the United Nations. It covers the procedures that have been developed under the Charter for the peaceful settlement or adjustment of disputes and situations, the use of collective measures in threats to or breaches of the peace, and the regulation of armaments, and seeks to evaluate these methods and processes in light of the conditions in which the United Nations has had to function.

The third, entitled *The United Nations and Promotion of the General Welfare,* will cover the major activities undertaken by the United Nations in response to the insistent pressures that, during the postwar period, have brought to the fore issues in the field of general welfare. The work of the Organization and its related agencies in dealing with problems of international co-operation in economic and social affairs, in the promotion of human rights, and in the advancement of dependent peoples, will be analyzed, and the efforts made to harmonize conflicting national views in solving these problems will be appraised.

Another volume in the series will deal with *Regional Security and the United Nations.* It will analyze and appraise the history and activities of the principal regional security, collective defense, and other similar arrangements that have developed within the framework of the United Nations Charter. The volume will describe how and why the arrangements came into existence and the manner in which they have functioned, and will analyze some of the problems raised by their establishment and operation, both within the scope of the individual groupings and in relation to the broader United Nations system.

A sixth volume, entitled *Proposals for Changes in the United Nations,* will present a description and analysis of the principal proposals advanced by governments and by private groups and individuals for changes in the United Nations system. The analysis will include a review of the major arguments advanced both for and against particular proposals, the impact of the proposals on the United Nations, and their implications for United States policy.

The final volume, entitled *The United States and the Future of the United Nations,* will attempt an over-all appraisal of the United Nations system from the American point of view. This volume, which will be based primarily on the studies in the other six volumes, will present general conclusions and recommendations regarding such changes as may appear to be desirable in the United Nations Charter or in the organization and functioning of the system.

A special word should be said regarding the conclusions in the present volume. They are those of the authors, who have been free to express their views based on their analysis and appraisal of the facts that they have examined. Similar freedom will be exercised by the authors of other studies in the series. The general conclusions and recommendations presented in the seventh volume of the series will take into account the conclusions reached in the other volumes, but they will be formulated from the point of view of the United Nations system as a whole and of United States policy with respect to it.

Leland M. Goodrich, Professor of International Organization and Administration at Columbia University, and Anne P. Simons, formerly of the staff of the General Political Section of the Department of Security Council Affairs, United Nations Secretariat, collaborated in the preparation of the present volume. They acknowledge with gratitude the assistance of Aleksander W. Rudzinski, Harold J. Taubenfeld, and John S. Gibson in making some of the background studies for various chapters in Parts Two and Four of this volume, and the assistance of Charles J. Moore and Leonard Wainstein, who prepared a special study on the regulation of armaments that provided some of the essential background for the chapters in Part Five. A. Evelyn Breck, with the assistance of Medora Richardson, edited the final manuscript, and Virginia Angel prepared the index.

The authors and the Institution also acknowledge with gratitude the many thoughtful comments and constructive suggestions made by several present and former officials in both government and international organizations who responded to inquiries or read drafts of various sections of the manuscript. Their courtesy and willingness in making their expert knowledge and experience available have aided in clarifying many difficult points and issues. Although custom precludes the citing of these persons by name, the Institution greatly appreciates the individual assistance of each of them.

The studies on which this volume is based were essentially completed under the direction of Dr. Pasvolsky. After his death, Robert W. Hartley was assigned the responsibility for bringing the entire research project to completion, and the manuscript for the present volume was prepared under his direction. We have had the benefit of continuing consultation with Ernest A. Gross, James N. Hyde, Joseph E. Johnson, C. Easton Rothwell, and Willard L. Thorp, who comprise an informal group, organized during the summer of 1953, to advise on the direction of the project, and to whom the Institution is heavily indebted for many helpful suggestions.

Finally, I wish to express on behalf of the Institution grateful appreciation to the A. W. Mellon Educational and Charitable Trust of Pittsburgh for the generous grants that have made possible this series of studies on the United Nations system. The conclusions and recommendations of these studies have been reached, however, wholly independently of the Mellon Trust, which is not to be understood as approving or disapproving the views expressed in this and the other volumes in the series.

ROBERT D. CALKINS
President

Contents

PART FOUR: ACTION WITH RESPECT TO THREATS TO THE PEACE, BREACHES OF THE PEACE, AND ACTS OF AGGRESSION

CHAPTER XIV

CHAPTER XV

PART FIVE: THE REGULATION OF ARMAMENTS

CHAPTER XX

CHAPTER XXI

CHAPTER XXII

PART SIX: CONCLUSIONS

CHAPTER XXIII

APPENDIXES

Introduction

THE United Nations was created for the primary purpose of maintaining international peace and security. To that end, the Charter provided a system for the peaceful settlement or adjustment of disputes and situations, the use of collective measures in threats to or breaches of the peace, and the regulation of national armaments.

With a view to the peaceful settlement or adjustment of disputes and situations, the Charter prescribed obligations to be assumed by Member states and the procedures to be followed by them, by the Organization, and by agencies acting under its authority, in dealing with disputes and situations that might arise. In planning the United Nations, it was accepted from the outset that the Organization would be primarily an international instrument for political adjustment. Therefore, the success of the system was deemed to depend fundamentally on the degree to which the Organization would be able, as was stated in Article 1(1) of the Charter, "to bring about by peaceful means, and in conformity with the principles of justice and international law, adjustment or settlement of international disputes or situations which might lead to a breach of the peace."[1]

In case of a threat to or a breach of the peace, the Charter provided specifically for the use of collective measures, including armed force, by the Organization itself and by Member states or groups of them acting under its authority. The purpose of such measures was stated in Article 1(1) to be "for the prevention and removal of threats to the peace, and for the suppression of acts of aggression or other breaches of the peace." Those who planned the Charter believed, however, that the arrangements and procedures for the use of these measures especially had to take account of the distribution of political, economic, and military power in the postwar world. Hence, the concept evolved of centering in the major nations re-

[1] The full text of this article and the texts of all other articles of the Charter of the United Nations to which reference is made in this study are given in App. B.

sponsibility for the decisions to use collective measures by giving those nations permanent membership and special voting privileges in the Security Council.

To achieve the regulation of armaments, the Charter vested in the Organization responsibility for developing principles and formulating detailed plans for submission to its Member states. Such regulation would have the objective, in the words of Article 26, of promoting "the establishment and maintenance of international peace and security with the least diversion for armaments of the world's human and economic resources." This objective originally was envisaged, however, as one that could be attained only after a permanent basis for international peace and security had been established.

In light of the trend of international events since the Organization came into being in 1946, questions have been raised regarding the practicability, under present and foreseeable conditions of world affairs, of the United Nations system for the maintenance of international peace and security, despite the attempts that have been made to adapt the functioning of the system to postwar conditions. Some now believe that the system might be made more effective by amendment of the Charter, or that, if amendments are impossible, a formal review of the Charter, for which provision is made in Article 109, should be undertaken with a view to exploring the possibilities of strengthening the system by further adaptation of it. Others would prefer, however, to keep the existing system because either they hope that in time world conditions will improve to a point where the system can function more effectively, or they believe there is little chance of making changes in the Charter that will strengthen the system.

It is the purpose of this volume to aid in a better understanding of these issues by analyzing and appraising the functioning of the United Nations system for the maintenance of international peace and security. Attention is thus concentrated on the activities of the United Nations in the peaceful settlement or adjustment of disputes and situations, the use of collective measures in threats to or breaches of the peace, and the formulation of plans for the regulation of armaments. These are not, however, the only activities of the Organization that aid in achieving the goal of international peace and security. The Charter also provides that the United Nations shall undertake a wide range of activities "with a view," as stated in Article 55, "to the creation of conditions of stability and well-being which are necessary for peaceful and friendly relations among nations based on respect for the principle of equal rights and self-determination of peoples." An analysis and appraisal of these other activities, however, is reserved for another volume in this series.[2]

Although this study covers those activities of the United Nations that are most directly related to the maintenance of international peace and security, it does not deal in any systematic and detailed manner with the several regional security and collective defense arrangements that have been concluded under the relevant provisions of the Charter. Account is taken, however, of such arrangements in so far as their development and functioning have had direct and significant consequences in the operations of the United Nations. But as the study is concerned with activities carried out through the Organization itself in maintaining peace and security, a detailed analysis and appraisal of the regional security and collective defense arrangements is also reserved for another volume.[3]

The scope of this volume is further narrowed by two other arbitrary exclusions. First, although the analysis is concerned especially with the operations of three principal organs of the United Nations —the Security Council, the General Assembly, and the International Court of Justice—in the maintenance of international peace and security, relatively more attention has been given to the operations of the Council and the Assembly than to those of the Court. Not only have the operations of the Council and the Assembly been more central to the maintenance of international peace and security but also the role these two organs should play and the manner in which they should perform their functions in this field have been the subject of greater controversy. Second, important related matters such as membership in the Organization, representation in its organs, and the voting procedure of the Security Council are dealt with only incidentally, because questions relating to the structure and procedures of all organs are given detailed consideration in another volume.[4]

A final limitation on the scope of the present volume, which must be noted, arises from the time period it covers. No attempt is made to trace the evolution of the provisions of the Charter prior to and during the San Francisco Conference because this development is

---

[2] *The United Nations and Promotion of the General Welfare.*
[3] *Regional Security and the United Nations.*
[4] *The Organization and Procedures of the United Nations.*

narrated in another volume in this series.[5] The present study is concerned with the eight-year period from January 1946, when the Organization formally came into being, through December 1953. In a few instances, however, brief references have been made to developments during 1954 that occurred after the study was largely completed.

This volume is divided into six parts. As a background for the main body of analyses, Part One sketches in broad outline the development, under the impact of changing world conditions, of the United Nations system for the maintenance of international peace and security. It opens with a brief description of the system as it was created by the Charter that emerged from the negotiations at the San Francisco Conference. Next, it reviews some of the principal factors in the postwar world that affected the development of the United Nations—the bipolarity of power around the United States and the Soviet Union, the ideological conflict between them and the states associated with them, the failure to achieve the peace settlements, the development of atomic weapons, the cold war, and the rise of Asian and African nationalism. This part closes with a summary account of the work of the United Nations since 1946 in the maintenance of international peace and security, with special attention being given to its role in dealing with disputes and threatening situations.

The next three parts of the volume are devoted to an analysis and appraisal of the work of the Organization in handling disputes and threatening situations. No attempt is made, however, to give a case history of every dispute and situation that has been considered by the United Nations. Nor is the record analyzed in terms of what the Organization accomplished or failed to accomplish in handling particular cases. The analysis concentrates instead on the problems that the Organization has faced at various stages in the handling of disputes and situations, the considerations that have influenced the choice of the course of action that has been followed, and the nature and adequacy of the processes that have been developed in order to achieve the declared purpose of the United Nations.

Part Two deals with the initial consideration of questions by the organs of the United Nations. It covers the manner and the circumstances in which questions have been submitted to the Security

[5] *A History of the United Nations Charter.*

Council, the General Assembly, and the International Court of Justice; their preliminary examination with a view to deciding whether and how the particular organ will deal with them; and the procedures for dealing with certain other preliminary matters such as the participation in the discussions of states not members of the organ, the issue of competence, and the clarification of facts and issues.

Part Three covers the methods used or recommended by the United Nations for peaceful settlement and adjustment. It deals, first of all, with recommendations of general principles for the maintenance of international peace and security and the promotion of international political co-operation. Recommendations for the adjustment of particular situations are then considered with attention being given to their preparation, content, and implementation. Finally, this part deals with the recommendation and the use of the various procedures of pacific settlement: direct negotiations between the interested parties, mediation, conciliation, arbitration, and judicial settlement.

In Part Four an analysis is made of the work of the United Nations in dealing with situations in which a threat to the peace, breach of the peace, or act of aggression has occurred or has been alleged to exist. Consideration is first given to the conditions under which a formal determination has been made of the existence of such a situation and the consequences of that decision. This is followed by an analysis of practice in the use of provisional measures to avert or end hostilities. The preparation, organization, and use of collective measures—both military and nonmilitary—are then examined. Among the specific problems considered are: the extent of advance preparations for the taking of such measures; the circumstances and the manner in which collective measures have been initiated; their organization and direction; and the conditions and manner of their termination.

The experience with the formulation of plans for the international regulation of armaments is analyzed in Part Five. The postwar development of atomic and other weapons of mass destruction and the rapid deterioration of relations between the Soviet Union and the Western powers have given a new and growing importance to the attempts of the United Nations to fulfill its responsibilities in this field. The results of these efforts and the lessons to be drawn from the experience are the focal points of this analysis.

In Part Six, the final one, the work of the United Nations in the peaceful settlement of disputes and situations, the use of collective measures, and the regulation of armaments is summarized and appraised. The yardstick applied is the extent to which the United Nations has through these activities contributed to the maintenance of international peace and security. But the appraisal is not only concerned with the degree of success achieved; it also seeks to make clear the limitations under which the United Nations has operated, and which have conditioned its effectiveness. In making this appraisal, it has been borne in mind, however, that the operations of the United Nations cannot be fairly judged by the standards that are usually applied in evaluating the effectiveness of national governments, for the Organization has few of the essential attributes of a government. The United Nations is primarily an instrument for facilitating co-operation among national states for purposes on which they have commonly agreed, and its record can be evaluated only on that basis. If such evaluation shows that failures in the maintenance of international peace and security have been due to inherent weaknesses of the United Nations, then it will be appropriate to examine what changes need to be made in the Organization to make it a better instrument for fulfilling the great purpose for which it was created.

PART ONE

THE DEVELOPMENT OF THE UNITED NATIONS SYSTEM

CHAPTER I

The San Francisco Charter

THE United Nations represents the second major effort in the twentieth century to achieve the goal of a better world through a general international organization of states. Like the League of Nations, the United Nations is an organization based on the principle of the free co-operation of its Members and having as its primary purpose the maintenance of international peace and security. Its Charter provides for a system of obligations, organs, and procedures similar to those of the League of Nations, as it actually developed in practice.[1] In the course of twenty years of active functioning, the League of Nations came to be in many respects a quite different organization from what the text of the Covenant suggested. Similarly, since its establishment, the United Nations has greatly changed.

Background of the Charter

The Charter of the United Nations, which was signed at San Francisco on June 26, 1945, was the product of the joint efforts of many minds.[2] The major part of the technical preparation was done in the United States Department of State. The United States Government was primarily responsible for getting the major allied powers in the Second World War to accept the idea of establishing a general international organization for the maintenance of international peace and security. The Moscow Declaration of October 30, 1943, committed the United States, the United Kingdom, the Soviet Union, and China to the establishment of such an organization and to the principle of joint action in the maintenance of international peace and security. The Dumbarton Oaks Proposals contained the agreed suggestions of these four powers for the Charter of such an organization and, together with further agreed proposals of the sponsoring

[1] See Leland M. Goodrich, "From League of Nations to United Nations," *International Organization*, Vol. 1 (February 1947), pp. 3-21.
[2] For a detailed account of the evolution of the Charter see the volume in this Brookings series, *A History of the United Nations Charter*.

governments, provided the basis for discussions at the San Francisco Conference.

Although putting the Charter in its final form was the work of all who participated in the San Francisco Conference, there is no denying the fact that the sponsoring governments and France, and more particularly the United States and the Soviet Union, exercised decisive influence. This influence was quite openly recognized at the time. No one was prepared to argue that the United Nations could succeed without the full participation of these governments. But the smaller states did exercise an important influence on the work of the Conference, and the Charter as it emerged differed in many respects from that which the sponsoring governments had initially proposed.

To be sure, the Charter was an international agreement, a treaty concluded by the signatory states. It was, however, more than an ordinary treaty. It was the constitution of an international political organization, created to assist in achieving certain common purposes on which all were agreed. It could not be regarded merely as a series of restrictive clauses and be expected to accomplish its purposes. It had to be capable of development and adaptation to changing circumstances. This view of the Charter as providing for an adaptable and developing system of international co-operation based on certain common purposes and principles was well expressed by Lord Halifax of the United Kingdom Delegation at San Francisco, when he said:

Mr. President, the purposes and the principles in Chapters I and II [Articles 1 and 2 of the Charter] seem to me and to my Delegation of the highest importance. I think they introduce a new idea into international relations, for instead of trying to govern the actions of the members and the organs of the United Nations by precise and intricate codes of procedure, we have preferred to lay down purposes and principles under which they are to act. And by that means, we hope to insure that they act in conformity with the express desires of the nations assembled here, while, at the same time, we give them freedom to accommodate their actions to circumstances which today no man can foresee.[3]

Underlying Assumptions

Those who drafted the Charter made certain assumptions that must be understood if the nature of the system for the maintenance

[3] U.N. Information Organizations and U.S. Library of Congress, *Documents of the United Nations Conference on International Organization*, Vol. 6 (1945), p. 26. (Hereinafter cited as *UNCIO Documents*.)

of peace and security that they proposed to establish is to be comprehended. Some of these assumptions received explicit statement in the Charter itself; others were implicit in the provisions of the Charter. They may be summarized as follows: (1) The maintenance of international peace and security is the most important single objective of the United Nations, because on its achievement depends not only the possibility of economic and social advancement for the peoples of the world but also the survival of modern civilization. (2) The maintenance of international peace and security, however, must be viewed in a broad perspective as requiring common action not only in dealing with threatening disputes and situations but also in creating political, economic, and social conditions favorable to peace throughout the world. (3) At the present stage of world political development, the organization of this common action must take the form of voluntary co-operation between governments, not of action dictated by a world government. (4) Within such a cooperative system, the primary responsibility for taking action to maintain international peace and security in specific situations must be assumed by the great powers, acting in accordance with the purposes and principles to which all are committed. (5) Peace-enforcement action must be taken on the basis of agreement by these powers as serious conflict between them would endanger the existence of the Organization and threaten a world war. Such action must not, however, be taken without due regard for the interests of smaller states because otherwise their confidence in the Organization would be destroyed. (6) Although the powers responsible for the defeat of the Axis powers should undertake initially the drafting and enforcement of the terms of the peace settlements, the new Organization should assume primary responsibility for maintaining peace and security on the basis of these peace settlements once the major powers relinquish their special responsibilities.

The authors of the Charter fully recognized how important it was to the full success of the new Organization that the great powers co-operate in carrying out its purposes and principles. In fact, it was recognized that without this co-operation the peace-enforcement provisions of the Charter, especially the provisions of Chapter VII, would not be workable. In his report to the President on the work of the San Francisco Conference, Secretary of State Stettinius said: "It was taken as axiomatic at Dumbarton Oaks and continued to be the view of the Sponsoring Governments at San Francisco, that the cornerstone of world security is the unity of those nations which formed the core of the grand alliance against the Axis."[4] Not only was it believed that such unity was essential to the success of the United Nations; it was also argued that only through this kind of co-operation could the best interests of the great powers themselves be protected. Thus Secretary Stettinius, in his report, further stated: "We cannot base our national policy solely on independent action. We can support our interests effectively in Europe and Asia only by patient consultations through which we will extend the area of agreement among the great powers. Only by such discussions will our influence be felt."[5] Nevertheless, there was recognition of the difficulties that stood in the way of such co-operation and a reluctance on the part of many to make the future success of the Organization wholly dependent upon it. This reluctance found expression in provisions of the Charter such as those relating to the functions and powers of the General Assembly.

It was not alone co-operation among the great powers in dealing with important questions before the United Nations that was assumed to be necessary to the success of the Organization. Agreement on the terms of peace to be imposed on the defeated enemy powers was viewed as equally essential. If agreement could not be reached on the terms of the peace settlements and the measures necessary for their implementation, the basis for effective co-operation within the United Nations would be greatly weakened.

Purposes of the Organization

Although the maintenance of international peace and security was declared to be the primary purpose of the United Nations, the authors of the Charter were not satisfied with such a general statement. Instead, they undertook to define in somewhat greater detail, and with attention to the methods to be followed, the substance of this purpose. Thus paragraph 1 of Article 1 declares that one purpose of the United Nations is:

To maintain international peace and security, and to that end: to

[4] U.S. Department of State, *Charter of the United Nations, Report to the President on the Results of the San Francisco Conference*, Publication 2349 (June 26, 1945), p. 68. See also, the report of the British Government to Parliament, Cmd. 6666, Misc. No. 9 (1945), pp. 16-17.

[5] U.S. Department of State, *Charter of the United Nations, Report to the President . . .*, p. 68.

take effective collective measures for the prevention and removal of threats to the peace, and for the suppression of acts of aggression or other breaches of the peace, and to bring about by peaceful means, and in conformity with the principles of justice and international law, adjustment or settlement of international disputes or situations which might lead to a breach of the peace.

Closely related purposes, set forth in paragraphs 2 and 4, are "to develop friendly relations among nations based on respect for the principle of equal rights and self-determination of peoples, and to take other appropriate measures to strengthen universal peace" and "to be a center for harmonizing the actions of nations in the attainment of these common ends." Also related is the purpose, expressed in paragraph 3, to achieve international co-operation in economic and social matters. As stated by Secretary Stettinius:

> The purpose to maintain international peace and security is not wholly expressed . . . in the procedures for pacific settlement, preventive action and enforcement measures. The Organization also has the purpose and is empowered to take positive and affirmative action in bringing about the conditions essential for peace throughout the world and for its enjoyment.[6]

Duties and Obligations of Members

The Charter lays down certain principles for the guidance of Members in their relations with each other and of the organs of the United Nations. These principles establish duties and obligations that Members are expected to fulfill in good faith. By Article 2(3) all Members undertake to "settle their international disputes by peaceful means in such a manner that international peace and security, and justice, are not endangered." This obligation is repeated in substance in Article 33, where the particular purpose is to emphasize the priority to be accorded to peaceful means of the parties' own choice. However, by the terms of Article 33, this obligation applies only to a dispute "the continuance of which is likely to endanger the maintenance of international peace and security." Here is an indication of the special concern of the Charter with international peace and security, as distinguished from law and justice. Although the San Francisco Conference agreed to the insertion of the words "and justice" in paragraph 3 of Article 2, the primary concern of the Charter, as of the Dumbarton Oaks Proposals, continued to be the maintenance of peace and security.

[6] *Ibid.*, p. 37.

Under the terms of Article 2(4), Members undertake to "refrain in their international relations from the threat or use of force against the territorial integrity or political independence of any state, or in any other manner inconsistent with the Purposes of the United Nations." This permits the use of force by a Member when authorized by an organ of the United Nations, and in those cases where the Charter expressly allows it by way of exception, as under Articles 51 and 53. It was clearly intended to make unlawful the independent use of armed force by any Member except in self-defense against aggression.

Article 2(5) requires every Member to give full support to the United Nations in any action it takes and to refrain from giving assistance to any state against which the United Nations is taking preventive or enforcement action. The Charter places on Members the obligation to carry out decisions of the Security Council "in accordance with the present Charter." It was not intended, however, that this should have the effect of making a recommendation by the Council a binding decision. Recommendations made by the Council under Articles 36, 37, 38, and 39, in the performance of its function of peaceful settlement, are, notwithstanding the provision of Article 25, to be treated as recommendations only, and not as legally obligating Members to carry out their terms.

Furthermore, under the Charter as drafted, Members are under no obligation to take enforcement measures of any kind in case of a threat to the peace, breach of the peace, or act of aggression until the Security Council has taken decisions specifying the measures to be applied. This is in contrast to the provision of Article 16 of the Covenant of the League of Nations, which required the immediate application of economic and financial sanctions against a Member resorting to war in violation of the Covenant.[7] Under the Charter system, however, in case of flagrant aggression, the Security Council is expected to take enforcement measures without delay and to the full extent required by circumstances.[8] Members of the Council, therefore, have the duty so to act as to make the Council effective in the discharge of its responsibility. In the performance of this duty, they undertake to act in accordance with the purposes and principles of the United Nations.

[7] The full text of this article and the texts of all other articles of the Covenant of the League of Nations to which reference is made in this study are given in App. A.

[8] *UNCIO Documents,* Vol. 12, p. 507.

Functions and Powers of the Organs

The Charter provides for six principal organs. Of these, four are substantially and directly concerned with the maintenance of international peace and security—the Security Council, the General Assembly, the International Court of Justice, and the Secretariat. These four organs have functions roughly corresponding to the four recognized functions of any government—executive, legislative, judicial, and administrative. As a matter of fact, with respect to the relations of the Council and the Assembly, the Charter carries the differentiation of functions considerably further than the Covenant of the League of Nations.

The Charter expressly provides that the Security Council is to have "primary responsibility for the maintenance of international peace and security." As the great powers enjoy special membership and voting prerogatives in the Council, the effect of the Charter provision is to place "primary responsibility" on the great powers that are the permanent members of the Council. The special responsibility of the permanent members is given explicit recognition in Article 106, which provides that pending the conclusion of agreements under Article 43 necessary to the exercise of the responsibilities of the Council under Article 42, these members shall consult with a view to joint action on behalf of the Organization to maintain international peace and security. The adoption of these provisions at San Francisco marked a return to the nineteenth century idea of the "Concert of Great Powers," with an important modification. Under the Charter the "concert" was to function within a larger association of states and with the smaller states having clearly defined rights and responsibilities. Although the Charter thus places primary responsibility for the maintenance of international peace and security on the Council, it does not make this responsibility exclusive. It defines the powers of the Assembly in such general terms as to permit a considerable development of its role in the maintenance of international peace and security.

The Dumbarton Oaks Proposals definitely envisaged a limited though important role for the Assembly in the maintenance of international peace and security, largely that of discussing, formulating, and recommending general principles of international co-operation and considering questions not involving any immediate danger to peace. The Council was envisaged as the organ that would

normally deal with specific disputes and situations entailing a substantial threat to the maintenance of international peace and
security.[9] In fact, the provisions of the Dumbarton Oaks Proposals
were criticized on the ground that they gave too much power to the
Council and the great powers and did not give sufficient prominence
to the Assembly and the role of the smaller states.[10]

At the San Francisco Conference, a number of attempts were made
to broaden the functions and powers of the Assembly. The adoption
of Articles 10 and 14 became particularly significant in this connection. Under the former, the Assembly was empowered to "discuss
any questions or any matters within the scope of the present Charter
or relating to the powers and functions of any organs provided for
in the present Charter" and to make recommendations with respect
to such matters to Members of the United Nations or to the Council
or to both. By the terms of Article 14, the Assembly was expressly
empowered to "recommend measures for the peaceful adjustment of
any situation, regardless of origin, which it deems likely to impair
the general welfare or friendly relations among nations, including
situations resulting from a violation of the provisions of the present
Charter setting forth the Purposes and Principles of the United
Nations."

Although the Charter as finally adopted seemed to go some way
toward breaking down the differentiation of functions and powers
between the Council and the Assembly that the Dumbarton Oaks
Proposals envisaged, it still contained certain provisions emphasizing the uniqueness of the functions and powers of each organ in
dealing with peace and security matters. Any question "on which
action is necessary" was to be referred by the Assembly to the Council either before or after discussion.[11] Moreover, while the Council
was performing its Charter functions with respect to any dispute or
situation, the Assembly was to refrain from making any recommendation with respect to it.[12] The detailed provisions of the Charter
relating to pacific settlement of disputes, action with respect to

[9] Such disputes and situations might have a considerable range of seriousness.
They must at least be so serious that their continuance would be "likely to endanger the maintenance of international peace and security." They might constitute threats to or breaches of the peace.

[10] Arthur H. Vandenberg, Jr. (ed.), The Private Papers of Senator Vandenberg
(1952), Chaps. 10 and 11.

[11] Art. 11 (2).

[12] Art. 12 (1).

threats to the peace, breaches of the peace, and acts of aggression, and regional arrangements were almost without exception drafted on the assumption that the Council would be the United Nations organ primarily concerned. The Charter contained few provisions dealing explicitly with the powers of the Assembly or the procedures to be followed in the exercise of these powers.

In testifying as the Department of State expert before the Senate Committee on Foreign Relations, during the hearings on the Charter, Dr. Leo Pasvolsky defined the respective functions of the Council and the Assembly in the following words:

There is one basic concept which had to be agreed upon very early in the game, and that was whether or not the General Assembly and the Security Council, which obviously would be the principal organs of this Organization, would have the same functions and the same powers and would differ from each other only in the sense that when the Assembly is not in session the Council exercises all of its functions. The League of Nations was built very largely on that concept.

Those who worked on the Dumbarton Oaks document and those who worked on the same subject in San Francisco were very definitely of the opinion that experience had shown that it was well to separate the functions; that, particularly in the new Organization, there are two primary sets of functions that would have to be performed by the Organization.

In the first place, there is the function related to the maintenance of peace and security; that is, the function of doing everything possible to bring about peaceful adjustment of disputes that arise, of removing threats to the peace when threats arise, and of suppressing breaches of the peace, if in spite of the preventive action, peace should be broken. It was the opinion that those comprise one great function of the new Organization.

The second great function of the Organization, it was thought, was the creation of conditions which would be conducive to the maintenance of peaceful relations among nations, which would make for stability, friendship, and good neighborliness.

It was thought that as between those two functions, the first one should be given to the Security Council as its primary responsibility; that the second function should be given to the General Assembly as its primary responsibility. The second function, obviously, involves a very wide and complicated field of activity, the field of economic, social, and related problems and relationships. So it was thought that if the General Assembly were given the function of having primary responsibility in that vast and all-important field, it would then be the agency, being the fully representative body, for bringing about conditions in which the use of force as the ultimate sanction would be less and less necessary. After all this Organization will have to be judged not by the amount of force that it will use in maintaining peace and security, or the frequency with which it will use force, but precisely by how infrequently and how little it will be necessary to use force as the ultimate sanction in the maintenance of international peace and security. Hence the General Assembly is given here the functions of creating these indispensable conditions for orderly international living.[13]

Later, with particular reference to the terms of Article 14 and its bearing on the respective functions of the Assembly and the Council, Dr. Pasvolsky said:

Article 14 is, from the point of view of the General Assembly, the counterpart of the primary function assigned to the Security Council. The Security Council has primary responsibility for dealing with situations which relate to the maintenance of international peace and security. Article 14 gives the General Assembly the function and power of recommending measures for the peaceful adjustment of any situation regardless of origin which it deems likely to impair the general welfare or friendly relations among nations. . . .

The criterion here is a criterion of impairment of the general welfare or friendly relations among nations; and there are included here situations resulting from a violation of the provisions of the present Charter setting forth the purposes and principles of the United Nations. This is the first place we come to where specific use is made of the Chapter on Purposes and Principles in order to lay down the guiding rules of action and behavior for the Organization and its Members.

Under the terms of this provision the General Assembly has the power to make recommendations as to measures which should be taken for the peaceful adjustment of any such situation which is likely to impair the general welfare or friendly relations among nations, irrespective of whether or not such a situation may threaten international peace and security. If the situation is of such a nature that it may threaten international peace and security, then articles 11 and 12 apply, and the General Assembly, instead of taking action itself, would have to refer the situation to the Security Council. But if a question of the maintenance of international peace and security is not involved, then the General Assembly is completely free to perform this vastly important function of helping the world to operate on the basis of stability and justice and fair dealing.[14]

In addition to distinguishing between the functions of the Council and those of the Assembly in the political field, the Charter makes an important distinction between the powers and procedures of the Council and those of the Assembly, a distinction logically related to the composition and functions of the two organs. The Council, vested with the executive function, is limited to making recommendations when engaged in seeking the peaceful settlement

---

[13] *The Charter of the United Nations,* Hearings before the Senate Committee on Foreign Relations, 79 Cong. 1 sess. (July 1945), pp. 243-44.

[14] *Ibid.,* pp. 249-50.

and adjustment of disputes and situations or the regulation of national armaments, but it is given the power to take decisions committing Members to the use of specific measures of coercion when confronted by a threat to the peace, breach of the peace, or act of aggression. The obligation, however, of any Member to take military measures is to be defined and limited by an agreement concluded under Article 43 specifying the forces, facilities, and other assistance to be placed at the disposal of the Council. Furthermore, the power of the Council is subject to the restraint that no decision can be taken—and this applies to all substantive decisions, whether recommendations or orders—without the concurrence of the permanent members.

The Assembly, on the other hand, is not given the exceptional powers vested in the Council, nor is it subject to the same voting restrictions. The powers of the Assembly are limited, no matter how urgent the question with which it may be called upon to deal, to discussion and recommendation. As already noted, the power of recommendation is not to be used when it may interfere with the discharge by the Council of its special responsibilities. It can, therefore, through discussion, always inform and assist in forming opinion, but under certain circumstances, out of deference to the Council, it is required to refrain from exercising its full influence. Moreover, it can be fairly said that the provisions of the Charter reflect a view, which was initially quite widely held, that the Assembly would normally limit its activity to questions of a general nature. In the exercise of its powers, the Assembly is not subject to such restrictions as are placed on the voting procedure of the Council to protect the interests of the great powers. Decisions may be taken by a simple majority or a two-thirds majority, depending on their importance, and each Member is entitled to a vote. Clearly such a voting arrangement would have been unacceptable to the great powers, and probably to the "middle powers," if the Assembly had been given more authority than power to recommend.

Brief mention must be made of the functions and powers of two other principal organs, the Secretariat and the Court. The Secretary-General, the chief administrative officer of the Organization, is empowered to bring to the attention of the Council any matter that in his opinion may threaten the maintenance of international peace and security. It was clearly intended by those who wrote the Charter that the Secretary-General should have a more important political role than his counterpart in the League of Nations.[15] The International Court of Justice, composed of fifteen judges elected by the Security Council and the General Assembly voting concurrently, is by the terms of the Charter "the principal judicial organ of the United Nations."[16] It decides any dispute submitted to it by agreement of the parties or submitted by one party if the Court has compulsory jurisdiction. In addition, either the Assembly or the Council may request the Court to give an advisory opinion on any legal question.

Means and Procedures

The authors of the Covenant of the League of Nations believed that the maintenance of international peace and security could best be achieved by the qualified outlawry of war and the use of collective measures against aggression, by encouraging the peaceful settlement of disputes, by limiting and reducing national armaments by international agreement, and by emphasizing respect for law and justice in international relations. From the provisions of the Charter, it can be inferred that its authors had somewhat different views regarding means and priorities as a result of their interpretation of the experience of the League and that of the Second World War. They recognized the importance of developing and encouraging the use of peaceful methods of settlement and adjustment, including the use of judicial procedures for the settlement of legal disputes. They were, however, less inclined to stress the legal approach to questions relating to the maintenance of international peace and security and placed more emphasis on economic and social co-operation to promote conditions favorable to international peace and security. They were inclined to the view that the agreed limitation and reduction of armaments was to be achieved as part of a total system of armament regulation that would also assure the availability of adequate force for deterring and suppressing aggression. They recognized the need for "outlawing" the unauthorized use of armed force and went beyond the provisions of the Covenant in this respect. They saw, in the light of the experience of the League, the necessity for taking effective preventive action in advance of an actual breach

---

[15] U.S. Department of State, *Charter of the United Nations, Report to the President* . . ., p. 148.

[16] Art. 92.

THE SAN FRANCISCO CHARTER

of the peace. Furthermore, taking account, as they thought, of the realities of power politics, they were unsympathetic toward "automatic sanctions" to be applied indiscriminately against any transgressor and were inclined to the view that collective measures to keep the peace must be organized around the facts of the special interests and superior power of certain states that had made major contributions in defeating the Axis powers.

Thus those chiefly responsible for the drafting of the Charter came to favor a system that purported to harness responsibility to power, placed the emphasis on the availability to the United Nations of adequate forces and facilities for keeping the peace, encouraged states to settle their disputes by peaceful means of their own choice, and accorded to the organs responsible for the maintenance of international peace and security a wide range of discretion in the choice of particular measures to be taken to achieve the desired ends. Yet it was recognized that this discretionary power must be subject to certain limitations in order to make its use generally acceptable. It was understood and emphasized that the members of the Security Council in discharging their responsibilities should be guided by the purposes and principles of the Charter.[17] In addition, Chapters VI and VII of the Charter prescribe in some detail the manner in which the Council is to perform its functions.

The Council is to be concerned with the settlement or adjustment of disputes and situations only to the extent that their continuance "is likely to endanger the maintenance of international peace and security."[18] In no case may the Council do more than recommend the methods or terms of settlement. In case a threat to the peace or a breach of the peace is claimed to exist, the Council "shall determine" its existence. The Council is authorized under Article 40 to call upon the parties to take provisional measures to prevent the aggravation of the situation. The coercive measures that may be taken to maintain or restore peace are limited to those covered by Articles 41 and 42. Moreover, a Member is required to use armed force only to the extent it has expressly agreed to do so by special agreement under Article 43, and before the Council calls upon a Member not represented on the Council to use such force, it must invite the Member to participate in the decision.

It is significant that the detailed provisions of Chapters VI and

[17] Art. 24 (2).
[18] Arts. 34, 36, and 37. Exception is made in Art. 38.

VII of the Charter regarding methods and procedures apply almost exclusively to the Council. This reflects in part the importance of the role contemplated for the Council in comparison with that of the General Assembly. It also reflects the unwillingness of the architects of the Charter, particularly those representing the smaller states, to vest unrestricted discretionary power in the Council.

The Charter system for the maintenance of international peace and security adopted at San Francisco was widely viewed as a substantial improvement over the League of Nations system. Nevertheless, one important reason for this view had little relation to the intrinsic provisions of the Charter itself. This was the hope, amounting almost to a belief, that the United Nations would be able to function with the advantage, denied to the League from the beginning, of the active participation and co-operation of the great powers that were primarily responsible for victory in the war about to be ended. The importance to the full success of the United Nations of this participation and co-operation and the evidences of such co-operation at San Francisco seemed to blind the eyes of many United Nations supporters to the stark realities of world politics. It soon became clear, however, that the forces of division and dissension were stronger than the forces of unity and co-operation, and that the United Nations, under conditions of political and economic dislocation, ideological conflict, great power struggle for supremacy, and revolutionary upheaval, could not achieve its purposes in the way that its more enthusiastic supporters had hoped.

CHAPTER II

The Postwar World

THE KIND of international organization that was established for the maintenance of international peace and security was determined to a large extent by political conditions and expectations existing at the time the Charter was being prepared. The way in which the United Nations developed in the years that followed was equally influenced by changes that took place in these conditions and expectations as a result of the revival of basic conflicts in the national attitudes and purposes of the Member states, the inability of governments to agree on the problems of peacemaking once the compelling pressures of common military objectives had been removed, and the emergence of dynamic forces and problems of adjustment the full nature and implications of which had not been foreseen.

The Hope of Postwar Unity

The Charter system for the maintenance of international peace and security was based on the assumption that, in their own best national interests, the powers that had been primarily responsible for prosecuting the war to the point where final defeat of the Axis powers was a certainty would co-operate through the United Nations in the maintenance of international peace and security on the basis of agreed peace settlements. Experience in the actual conduct of the war provided only limited support for such an assumption, because the Soviet Union had been a suspicious and extremely cautious ally, reluctant to co-operate in military matters on anything like the terms of mutual trust and confidence that had characterized relations between the United States and the United Kingdom. Nevertheless, the Soviet leaders, by their willingness to discuss and assume commitments with respect to the handling of postwar political issues, had given some evidence that their suspicions could be overcome in part at least by a demonstration on the part of the United States and the United Kingdom of their willingness to collaborate on terms of sympathetic understanding and equality. In fact, the commitments that the Soviet leaders had been willing to undertake gave some support to the idea that the postwar unity of the victorious powers was an assumption on which the future peace might with some confidence be organized.

In signing the Declaration by United Nations of January 1, 1942, the members of the anti-Axis coalition had agreed to accept the "common program of purposes and principles" embodied in the Atlantic Charter, to prosecute the war to a successful conclusion, and not to make peace separately. At Moscow, in the fall of 1943, the foreign ministers of the United States, the United Kingdom, and the Soviet Union had agreed to a declaration, later adhered to by China, under which the signatories declared that their "united action" would be continued for the organization and maintenance of peace and security, that they would act together in all matters relating to the surrender and disarmament of a common enemy, that they recognized the necessity of establishing at the earliest practicable date a general international organization for the maintenance of international peace and security, and that, for the purpose of maintaining international peace and security, pending the establishment of such a general system, they would consult together with a view to joint action on behalf of the international community.[1]

At Teheran in December 1943, the heads of the governments of the United States, the United Kingdom, and the Soviet Union repeated their determination to continue to work together and recorded their conviction that this would result in enduring peace. They also recognized their initial responsibility to arrive at a peace settlement that would "command the good will of the overwhelming mass of the peoples of the world." At Dumbarton Oaks in the summer and fall of 1944, this collaboration became more specific when representatives of the four governments signatory of the Moscow Declaration conferred and agreed on proposals for the charter of the proposed general international organization.

In the meeting at Yalta in February 1945, President Roosevelt, Prime Minister Churchill, and Premier Stalin made further progress, at least so it appeared, in the implementation of the concept of postwar unity of the major allied powers. Agreement was reached

[1] U.S. Department of State, *Toward the Peace, Documents,* Publication 2298 (1945), pp. 4-8.

on the voting procedure in the proposed Security Council and on holding a United Nations Conference in San Francisco for drafting the United Nations Charter. There was also agreement on the principles to be applied in the treatment of Germany, and on the principles and procedures to be followed in the rehabilitation and reconstruction of those countries liberated from the domination of Nazi Germany or which had accepted the role of Axis satellite states.[2] The three heads of government reaffirmed their "common determination to maintain and strengthen in the peace to come that unity of purpose and action which has made victory possible and certain for the United Nations in this war." In reporting on the work of the Conference to Congress, President Roosevelt expressed the confident view that "never before have the major Allies been more closely united—not only in their war aims but in their peace aims. And they are determined to continue to be united with each other—and with all peace-loving nations—so that the ideal of lasting world peace will become a reality."[3]

President Roosevelt appears to have been aware of the difficulties in the way of maintaining and strengthening co-operation among the principal victors. Nevertheless, he was convinced that such co-operation, based on unity of purpose and mutual confidence, was necessary to the achievement of a peaceful world. In spite of discouraging experiences, he appears to have been hopeful to the end of his life that, with patience and determination, Soviet co-operation with the Western powers could be achieved.[4] At least on the surface, the San Francisco Conference in the spring of 1945 and its results seemed to justify this hope. The Conference, however, did little to strengthen the spirit of co-operation, and before the year was out, little was left of it but the memory. The substance had largely disappeared under the impact of mounting fears and distrusts, conflicting interests and ideologies, and the uncertainties and confusion of the postwar world.

Growth of Bipolarity of Power

The basic power situation in the world at the conclusion of the war and the conditions governing its future development were such

[2] U.S. Department of State *Bulletin,* Vol. 12 (Feb. 18, 1945), pp. 213 ff.
[3] *Ibid.* (Mar. 4, 1945), p. 321.
[4] Edward R. Stettinius, Jr., *Roosevelt and the Russians* (1949), Chap. 16.

as to be unfavorable to the functioning of the kind of "concert" that the framers of the Charter had envisaged. During the nineteenth century and down to 1914 international politics had been largely dominated by a small number of great powers. The number varied, as did the methods by which these powers exercised their influence and the relative importance of each. Their number and their approximation to each other in strength and influence made it impossible for any one to achieve an unchallenged supremacy. Furthermore, even allowing for such groupings as occurred for reasons of defense and increased power—the Triple Alliance and the Triple Entente, for example—effective power never became completely polarized into two dominant, mutually antagonistic groups. Great Britain never formally relinquished its right of independent action. The United States, rapidly forging to the front as one of the greatest of the great powers, deliberately abstained from formal commitments. Japan, although bound to Great Britain by a treaty of alliance after 1902, did not consider this an obstacle to the pursuit of an independent course of action.

The First World War, however, profoundly affected these power relations. One of the reasons for the failure of efforts to keep the peace in the interwar period was the inability of statesmen to reconstitute power relations on an acceptable basis and effectively to tie the formal structure of the League into such a reconstituted system of balanced power relations.

But if the effect of the First World War on the system of power relations was serious, the effect of the Second World War was catastrophic. Germany, which had come to be the strongest power in Europe in the 1930's, was destroyed for the time being as an independent political entity and was placed under the military occupation of the victor nations. The neighboring countries that had been brought under the effective control of Germany before or during the war were freed of that control, but in several cases their political status was left uncertain. To a less degree this was also true of Italy, which, although it was left with a government, was forced to relinquish colonial areas and other territories that it had brought under its control. In the Far East, the military defeat of Japan resulted in the collapse of its "New Order" and created problems similar to those in Europe of determining the political future of countries liberated from Japanese military control. As many of them had not been fully independent, even before the war, and as native aspirations for independence from foreign control had been greatly strengthened by the war experience, the problems of reconstruction in this part of the world were in some respects more difficult than in Europe.

The effects of the Second World War were not limited, however, to the defeated Axis powers. Some of those that shared in the final military victory, gained acceptance as permanent members of the Security Council (the mark of great power status), and participated in the drafting of the peace treaties were gravely weakened by the war ordeal. France, which suffered the ignominy of military defeat and German occupation of its territory, emerged from the war militarily weak and politically divided, its economy dislocated and its national spirit confused and enfeebled. In addition, during the Second World War, the control of metropolitan France over its colonial empire was temporarily destroyed or greatly weakened, and efforts to reassert this control encountered the strong resistance of nationalist forces. Thus France had become less capable of playing an independent and influential role in world politics than after the First World War and found itself dependent on outside aid, particularly from the United States.

The United Kingdom came out of the war with a record of great achievement. Its national spirit was strong and its prestige as a staunch defender of liberty and democratic values was high. Nevertheless, victory had been won at a terrific cost. British economic resources had been largely exhausted, and without external aid on a large scale, the achievement of economic recovery seemed impossible. The development of weapons of mass destruction and of means of delivering these weapons quickly over great distances destroyed its capacity for independent self-defense and made it seem more necessary than ever to have the friendship and support of the United States. Furthermore, the United Kingdom was no longer able to finance the military policies and programs needed to maintain the Empire and protect British interests on a world-wide basis. A policy of retrenchment was dictated by the stresses and strains to which the Empire was subjected as the result of Japanese occupation of colonial territories in the Pacific area and the strength of nationalist movements for independence.

As a consequence of such considerations, the postwar British Labor Government, with general support from the people, gave India, Pakistan, Burma, and Ceylon complete self-government, stepped up the rate of progress toward self-government in other parts of the Empire, and drastically reduced the policy commitments of the United Kingdom, notably in the Eastern Mediterranean and the Middle East. This retrenchment was facilitated by the readiness of the United States to increase its commitments in certain of these areas. A close working co-operation between the United States and the United Kingdom therefore became an essential element of British foreign policy and gave assurance that on most questions of importance the United Kingdom would not adopt an attitude fundamentally different from that of its stronger ally.

Although the Republic of China was included, on insistence of the United States, in the exclusive group of powers that were to have a primary responsibility for the making and the maintenance of international peace, its condition at the conclusion of the war with Japan was such as to raise real doubts regarding its capacity to play that role. The war with Japan, which had been going on since 1937, lack of effective leadership, the internal struggles between the Communists and the Nationalists, and failure or inability to cope effectively with the rapidly deteriorating economic situation had left China with little capacity to put its own house in order or to resist such pressures as might be exercised from the outside. Although the agreements reached at Yalta between Roosevelt and Stalin involved substantial Chinese concessions to the Soviet Union, they did hold out the hope that the Nationalist Government would be allowed to develop internal strength and stability over a period of time without being called upon to deal with foreign interference in its affairs. The Sino-Soviet agreements of August 1945 appeared to give support to this hope. It soon became clear, however, that the Nationalist Government would be unable to establish its authority throughout China by its own efforts. Efforts of the United States Government to get the Communists and the Nationalists to stop fighting and support a common government were without avail. By the end of 1946, it was clear that China, instead of becoming a stabilizing influence in eastern Asia, was to be a major power vacuum with the Communists and the Kuomintang struggling for power from within and the United States and the Soviet Union competing for dominant influence from without.

At the end of the Second World War, therefore, two powers, and two powers only—the United States and the Soviet Union—appeared to have the actual and potential capabilities of effectively defending their interests by their own efforts and of following independent policies in their relations with other states and with each other. Although they had been allies in the war against the Axis, differences in their accepted values, their historical experiences, their economic and political systems, their guiding principles and purposes, their general outlooks on the world made intimate association unlikely and placed serious obstacles in the way of co-operation. The fact that they were thrown into close contact with each other in many unsettled areas under conditions of great stress and strain made co-operation even more difficult. The awesome fact of the atomic bomb, the circumstances in which it was developed and used, the profound ideological conflict and suspicions and distrusts of long standing probably made it impossible.

The Ideological Conflict

The ideological conflict between the United States and the Soviet Union and those states associated with them dates from the Bolshevik Revolution of 1917. The government that was set up by the revolutionary Bolsheviks and that in time became firmly established and generally recognized as the government of the Soviet Union was based on ideas and values that were antagonistic to the ideas and values generally accepted in the Western democracies. This incompatibility between the Russian revolutionary regime and the liberal constitutional system of the United States was an important reason for the refusal of the United States Government to recognize the Soviet Government until 1933.

During the initial period of outside hostility when the revolutionary ardor of the Communist party was still strong, the leaders of the Communist party and the government of Russia sought to stimulate revolutionary activity throughout the world through the Communist International, the Comintern. After Stalin's assumption of undisputed power, the emphasis of Communist policy in Russia came to be placed on the development of Soviet strength rather than revolutionary activity. Nevertheless, the Comintern continued to function, and its activities were viewed with strong suspicion by non-Communist countries.

Following the German attack on the Soviet Union in June 1941,

Stalin and the other Soviet leaders emphasized the patriotic aspect of the struggle and the identity of the "democratic purposes" of the Soviet Union and the other countries fighting the Axis powers. In May 1943, the Presidium of the Executive Committee of the Communist International adopted in Moscow a resolution providing for the dissolution of the organization. Among the reasons given for this action were the need for greater flexibility of organization in order that Communist parties in different countries might have greater freedom in determining their courses of action and the desire to expose "the lie" that Moscow was seeking to interfere in the affairs of other nations. This action was received with wide approval, particularly in the United States, and accounted in part for the considerable improvement in relations between the United States and the Soviet Union during the war.

The official dissolution of the Comintern and other conciliatory acts were not successful, however, in creating general acceptance of the idea that Moscow had ceased to be the planning and operational center of a world Communist movement. There was still strong evidence that national Communist parties took their cue from Moscow and were being used to serve its purposes. Furthermore, even the men in the Kremlin and the party theoreticians were not prepared to deny a fundamental conflict between the Communist system and the capitalist system. Although Stalin and others did argue for peaceful coexistence, there were enough authoritative suggestions of the inevitability of armed conflict to cause many to believe that the basic ideological conflict between Moscow and the Western democracies was incapable of peaceful resolution.

With the growing distrust of Soviet good faith as the result of failure to live up to Stalin's promises at Yalta and other evidence that the Soviet leaders were pursuing expansionist policies, there was an increasing tendency in the West to find the primary explanation of Soviet action in the desire of the Communist leaders to impose their ideology and their totalitarian system on the rest of the world and to discount whatever legitimate concern the Soviet leaders might have had for the national security of the Russian state. At the same time the Soviet leaders professed to see in the policies and actions of the Western powers a concerted attempt on the part of the capitalists to destroy communism and impose their system on the peoples of the world. Especially in official propaganda, whether through radio broadcasts or speeches in the General Assembly,

Moscow stressed the ideological motif. Soviet propaganda emphasized the alleged abuses of the capitalist system in the West—its
exploitation of the masses, its denial of basic economic and social
rights, and its war-mongering proclivities—and called attention to
specific provocative acts, particularly of the United States, which,
so the Communist leaders argued, indicated the desire of the reactionary forces to impose their system on the peoples of Asia and
Eastern Europe who had at long last been given the benefit of the
only true democracy. On the other hand, the Western democracies,
especially the United States, attempted to show how communism
in practice was the instrument of Russian expansionism and meant
the denial of basic human rights, the complete subordination of
the individual to the state, and the subjection of millions of people
to a totalitarian system based on exploitation of the many by the
few and of necessity committed to attempting to extend its power
by force.

Emphasis on the conflict of ideas by both parties to the cold war
tended to create the impression, especially in the United States,
that the conflict was primarily an ideological one. As the experience
of the past has indicated—the religious wars of the seventeenth
century, the struggle between Islam and Christianity, and the
French Revolution and its aftermath—such conflicts do not lend
themselves easily to peaceful adjustment. Differences become sharp-
ened and accentuated, logical incompatibilities are stressed, and
moral positions are taken that imply that any departures from them
are essentially immoral and therefore to be condemned. Little room
is left for compromise and accommodation.

During the war, there was some indication of relaxation of the
ideological conflict. In the discussions at San Francisco, the struggle
for men's minds, which later was to become so open, was largely
subordinated to efforts to maintain a united front. After San Francisco and even during 1946, disagreements between the Soviet
Union and the Western powers were becoming more numerous and
disturbing, and mutual suspicion and distrust were obviously on
the increase, but the ideological note was still being lightly struck.
During the second part of the first session of the General Assembly, for example, the debate on disarmament noticeably lacked
the vituperative and propagandistic qualities that were to characterize later discussions of disarmament and similar subjects.

It was in the course of 1947 that the ideological conflict began to receive its major emphasis and that the incompatibility of Communist and Western democratic ideas and regimes came to be the dominant note. The announcement of the establishment of the Cominform in October 1947 signaled renewed emphasis by Moscow on the revolutionary and subversive activities of Communist parties throughout the world acting under instructions from a central Moscow-controlled organ. Countermeasures on behalf of the Western democracies, especially the United States, emphasized communism as the enemy. It is significant, for example, that President Truman publicly declared that the North Korean attack of June 25, 1950, made it "plain beyond all doubt that communism has passed beyond the use of subversion to conquer independent nations and will now use armed invasion and war."[5]

The problems associated with the making and maintenance of peace after the Second World War have been difficult and would have been hard to resolve in any case as the experience of past wars and efforts at peacemaking have amply shown. But there can be little doubt that the ideological conflict, which has become interwoven with the conflict of more traditional national interests, has made infinitely more difficult the accommodation and adjustment of divergent interests and policies.

Implications and Effects of the Atomic Bomb

The explosion of the first atomic bomb at Alamagordo in July 1945, followed by its use in August with devastating effect at Hiroshima and Nagasaki, introduced a new factor into the international politics of the postwar world, the full implications of which are only now being realized. But it was not only the bomb itself that produced an impact on international politics; it was also the circumstances under which the bomb was developed and used, and the power that it gave its sole possessor. Superimposed on the fears and rivalries resulting from the bipolarization of power and the ideological conflict, the fear of the atomic bomb helped to create a situation of unparalleled tension.

The development of the atomic bomb had been largely an American enterprise, although the British and Canadians had shared

[5] U.S. Department of State *Bulletin*, Vol. 23 (July 3, 1950), p. 5.

on a restricted basis. This development had been a closely guarded secret, although it is now known that through espionage the Russians were able to get important information that those responsible for the development of the bomb had sought to deny to them. Once the bomb had proved a decisive factor in ending the Second World War, the question inevitably arose of future peacetime policy and more particularly of the extent to which the United States would share its secret with other powers, including the Soviet Union.

Henry L. Stimson, who as Secretary of War had had a major responsibility for the development and use of the bomb, clearly recognized the importance of the bomb to future United States relations with the Soviet Union. Mr. Stimson believed that these relations might be "irretrievably embittered" by the way in which an approach to the Soviet leaders was made. "If we fail to approach them now," he wrote in September 1945, "and merely continue to negotiate with them, having this weapon rather ostentatiously on our hip, their suspicions and their distrust of our purposes and motives will increase."[6]

It is impossible to say whether the subsequent course of relations between the Soviet Union and the United States would have been different if such a direct and immediate approach had been made. There is little to suggest that it would have been. Responsible Soviet leaders had already shown an unwillingness to carry out in good faith commitments that they had entered into at Yalta. They apparently were not impressed by President Truman's assurance, contained in his Navy Day address of October 27, 1945, that "in our possession of this weapon, as in our possession of other new weapons, there is no threat to any nation."[7]

When the United States Government, after consultations with the Canadian and United Kingdom governments, was ready to discuss the atomic bomb at Moscow in December 1945, the Soviet leaders gave no evidence of particular interest or sense of urgency, although they were willing to join in sponsoring the proposal to establish the United Nations Atomic Energy Commission. Possibly they had already committed themselves to a course of rivalry instead of co-operation, hoping that by developing the bomb them-

---

[6] Mr. Stimson attached great importance to this statement. See "Memorandum for the President, 11 September 1945," in Henry L. Stimson and McGeorge Bundy, *On Active Service in Peace and War* (1948), pp. 642-46.

[7] U.S. Department of State *Bulletin*, Vol. 13 (Oct. 28, 1945), p. 656.

selves they would be able to counter the power of the United States and would be in a better position to defend and promote Soviet-Communist interests and objectives; or perhaps they had not yet reached a decision whether a co-operative course should be followed. Once the United Nations Atomic Energy Commission met in June 1946, it became clear that neither of the two great powers was approaching the problem of the international control of the atomic bomb in a spirit of mutual confidence and trust. Rather each displayed complete distrust of the motives and purposes of the other and manifested a desire to retain freedom of decision in matters of vital concern to itself.[8]

With the announcement by President Truman in 1949 that the Soviet Union had exploded an atomic device and the subsequent development and explosion of infinitely more powerful and destructive thermonuclear devices by both the United States and the Soviet Union, it became clear that to the initial distrusts and suspicions was now added the mutual fear of atomic attack and the sudden destruction of vast centers of population and industry with no real assurance of effective protection. It is, of course, possible to hope that the initial impact of the atomic bomb—and its successors —may be reversed once governments generally, including those of the United States and the Soviet Union, come to believe that no one can possibly gain any advantage, and that unbearable risks are being run, if the race in atomic armaments is allowed to continue. Nevertheless, up to the present, it must be recognized that the existence of the atomic bomb has been an important factor in obstructing the achievement of great power unity.

Failure of Peacemaking

The most important single feature of the postwar international situation has been the failure of the victors, especially the United States, the United Kingdom, and the Soviet Union, to achieve a satisfactory peace settlement and adjustment of their mutual relations. The Napoleonic wars were brought to an end with the conclusion of a comprehensive peace settlement at Vienna, which largely defined the basis of international relations in Europe during succeeding decades. The First World War was in like manner

[8] See below, Chap. XXI.

immediately followed by a series of peace treaties and other agreements, constituting for all practical purposes one settlement, which included in addition to the usual provisions, the Covenant of the League of Nations. This was intended by the peacemakers to be the means by which the peace was to be kept during the postwar period. The fighting of the Second World War has now been ended for nearly a decade, yet peace treaties acceptable to the major victor nations have not been concluded with the two major Axis powers, and agreements have not been reached on other features of a new political order to take the place of that destroyed by the war.[9]

The delay in the conclusion of peace treaties was not in reality a matter of deliberate decision on the part of those responsible for the conduct of the war, especially the Government of the United States. The view appears to have been taken by some officials early in the war that there should be a "cooling-off period" between the end of fighting and the actual conclusion of treaties of peace.[10] Subsequently, however, the disadvantages of such a course came to be generally recognized. Delay was in fact made necessary by the decision of the major allies to insist on the unconditional surrender of the enemy states. Particularly in the case of Germany, where at the time of surrender no effective government existed, it was impossible to conclude a peace treaty within a relatively short period of time. Whether delay in peacemaking was a matter of deliberate choice or the necessary result of other decisions, it made all the more necessary a measure of continuing collaboration among the major victor nations over a fairly extensive period of time in which the urgencies that had produced the wartime coalition had largely disappeared.

It was apparently assumed, by responsible United States leaders at least, that, if the general principles of such collaboration were laid down by agreement during the war, the self-interest of the victorious powers would lead them to collaborate in the application of these principles once the war was over. Such agreement had been recorded in the Declaration by United Nations of January 1, 1942, the Moscow and the Teheran agreements, the Yalta agreements, and the Charter of the United Nations. One necessary con-

[9] For the history of efforts at peacemaking, see Redvers Opie and Associates, *The Search for Peace Settlements* (1951).
[10] Sumner Welles, *The Time for Decision* (1944), pp. 370-71.

dition of such collaboration, however, was lost sight of once the actual fighting was over. That was the maintenance of a military power relationship in each of the areas where new political arrangements had to be made that would impress upon each interested power the importance in its own national interest of living up to the principles to which it had committed itself. Unfortunately, the United States allowed its military strength in Europe to be dissipated before the necessary peace settlements could be achieved. Even in the Far East, where the United States had played the decisive part in the defeat of Japan, the unwillingness of the United States Government to maintain its military strength pending final peace settlements was a significant factor in the general deterioration of political conditions in that area.

Before the end of the fighting in Europe, there were clear indications of the difficulties that lay ahead in the way of peacemaking. Although agreement had been reached at Yalta in February 1945 on the general principles to be applied in the political reconstruction of the liberated areas, more particularly the territories of Poland and Yugoslavia, even before President Roosevelt's death there was evidence that the Soviet Union was acting in disregard of its promises in Poland and was seeking to impose a Communist-controlled regime on that country. With the surrender of Germany and the completion of the work of the San Francisco Conference, it soon became apparent that the victor nations would not be able to reach agreement quickly and easily on the terms of a general European settlement. The intention of the Soviet Government to proceed, in disregard of its promises at Yalta, to organize Eastern Europe in accordance with its own security and power requirements became increasingly clear. Allied co-operation in the political reconstruction of Poland, Rumania, Hungary, and Bulgaria became at most a formality, with Soviet armed forces, Soviet diplomats, and local Communists co-operating closely to ensure the establishment of Communist-controlled regimes.

Agreement was reached at Potsdam in August 1945 on the general procedures to be followed in the negotiation of the peace treaties. However, the first session of the Council of Foreign Ministers held in London in September and October to consider peace treaties with Italy, Rumania, Bulgaria, Hungary, and Finland, ended in a deadlock over what appeared to be a strictly procedural matter. This was regarded by some observers as a turning point in great power relations. Former Secretary of State Byrnes later referred to it as a test of strength, and also as "a test of whether we really believed what we said about one world and our desire to build collective security."[11] John Foster Dulles, who participated in the meeting as a Republican spokesman, later saw the incident in a more momentous light. To him it marked the end of an epoch, the epoch of Teheran, Yalta, Potsdam. It marked the ending of any pretense by Soviet Communists that they were friends of the Western Powers. It began the period when Soviet hostility to the Western Powers was openly proclaimed throughout the world.[12]

At Moscow, in December 1945, the Foreign Ministers were able to reach agreement on the procedures to be followed in the conclusion of peace treaties. This seemed at the time to be encouraging progress. The appearance of success, however, was possible only because certain areas of disagreement and potential conflict were not seriously explored. The conference had little more than adjourned when open disagreement broke out between the Soviet Union and the Anglo-American powers over the situation in Iran. Before withdrawing its military forces in accordance with the 1942 agreement, the Soviet Government sought to achieve a favored position in Northern Iran. Believing that the Iranian complaint to the Security Council over alleged Soviet intervention had been inspired by the United States and the United Kingdom, members of the Soviet bloc countered by bringing complaints to the attention of the Council concerning the presence of British troops in Greece and Indonesia. Thus from the beginning the suspicion and distrust that characterized relations between the Soviet Union and the Anglo-American powers in the making of the peace infected the atmosphere and procedures of the Security Council.

The major victor nations did, however, find it possible to reach agreement during 1946 on the terms of peace treaties with Italy, Bulgaria, Hungary, Rumania, and Finland. These negotiations saw concessions on both sides. In negotiating the Italian treaty, the Soviet Union recognized the superior bargaining position of the West and, except for Trieste, finally conceded that Italy and its colonies fell within the sphere of dominant Western influence. On the other hand, the Western powers recognized the dominant position of the Soviet Union in Eastern Europe and largely accepted the

[11] James F. Byrnes, *Speaking Frankly* (1947), p. 105.
[12] John Foster Dulles, *War or Peace* (1950), p. 30.

Soviet proposals for peace treaties with Bulgaria, Hungary, Rumania, and Finland. With regard to Germany and Austria, it was
clear that agreement would be difficult to reach as neither Moscow
nor the West was willing to recognize the dominant influence of the
other in this area.

But the struggle for advantage in Central Europe did not come to
a head as the direct result of any development there. It assumed
cold war proportions only after cold war had been declared on
another and closely related front, the Balkans. During the war,
Stalin had recognized that Greece fell within the British sphere
for purposes of political reconstruction, and the British had played
a leading role in installing a Greek Government in Athens after
liberation. By late 1946 it had become clear that the Communists,
with the support of the Soviet Union and the satellite states, were
challenging the British-supported government. In December, the
Greek Government requested that the Security Council consider
the situation. In late February 1947, the British Ambassador in
Washington informed the United States Government that after
March his government would be unable to continue its financial
and military support to Greece. Under these circumstances, on
March 12, President Truman made the historic statement to Congress in which he expressed his belief that "it must be the foreign
policy of the United States to support free peoples who are resisting attempted subjugation by armed minorities or by outside
pressures." He requested, and Congress appropriated, $400 million
for military and economic aid to Greece and Turkey.

The reaction of the United States to Soviet pressure southward in
the Balkan and Middle East areas came at a time when the United
States was reconsidering its whole policy toward the Soviet Union.
The limits of concession in order to achieve agreement had been
reached. It was now deemed necessary to find effective means to
check the further expansion of Communist influence. The economic crisis of Western Europe, which had been in large part the
reason for British withdrawal from Greece, seemed to require a
comprehensive program of economic aid to create conditions of
economic and political stability and strength in the area. The outlines of this new policy were presented by Secretary Marshall in
June 1947. In the months that followed, the details of such a
program were worked out and put into effect. The refusal of the
Soviet Union to participate and its insistence that Eastern European countries should likewise refuse to take part were indicative

of the serious view the Soviet leaders took of the program. It can fairly be said that the Truman Doctrine and the Marshall Plan of economic aid marked the beginning of the cold war between Moscow and the West, a struggle characterized by the use of practically all means short of armed force by the Soviet Union to extend its influence in areas of weakness and by the adoption of such countermeasures by the Western powers as seemed necessary to contain this pressure. Central Europe was one, and generally regarded as the most important, of these areas.

After vetoing the participation of Soviet satellites in the Marshall Plan, the Soviet leaders announced in October the creation of the Cominform as a means of co-ordinating the activities of Communist parties in nine European countries. In February 1948 the Communists executed a coup in Czechoslovakia, which brought that country effectively under Soviet control. During the following month, the United Kingdom, France, and the three Benelux countries signed the Brussels Pact with United States approval. Also in late March 1948, the Soviet representative, by quitting an Allied Control Council meeting in protest against alleged violation by the Western powers of agreements on Germany, signaled the collapse of control machinery for that country. In June, delegates of the Western powers meeting in London announced agreement on recommendations to their governments looking toward the economic unification of Western Germany and the establishment of a West German Government. Shortly afterwards, the Berlin blockade was instituted by the Soviet Union, which then proceeded to establish a Communist-dominated East German government. In July, negotiations were started for the conclusion of a North Atlantic mutual-defense treaty, which was signed in April 1949, and large-scale American military aid to Europe soon followed. It is unnecessary to detail further with the course of events that saw the division of Europe into two armed hostile camps, with the line of division extending across Central Germany through Austria to the Adriatic.

In the Far East, hostilities came to an end under conditions seemingly more favorable to the United States. The Government of China was friendly, although insecure. The Soviet Union by reason of the Yalta agreements and the 1945 treaty of alliance had agreed to recognize it and give it support. Japan was occupied by United States armed forces. Although Moscow gave evidence of dissatisfaction with the military occupation policies being followed, there was little that it could do by way of effective protest. Furthermore, the Soviet Government was prepared to recognize the special interests of the United States, as in the former Japanese mandated islands, in return for continued support by the United States of the territorial concessions made to the Soviet Union at Yalta.

Only in Korea was there serious and open conflict from the beginning between United States and Soviet policies and objectives. Here the postwar division of the country at the thirty-eighth parallel, initially for the purpose of receiving the surrender of Japanese forces, had been perpetuated by the inability of the United States and the Soviet Union to agree on the conditions under which Korean independence was to be achieved. By 1949, this conflict had not only become intensified in Korea through the establishment of two rival Korean governments, but it had extended to China where the Communists with Soviet support were in the process of ejecting the American-supported Nationalist Government. The North Korean attack in June 1950, which President Truman interpreted as having implications of Communist aggression beyond the limits of Korea, marked the Far East as a generally recognized major arena of East-West conflict. The Japanese Peace Treaty, concluded in 1951 despite strong Soviet and Chinese Communist opposition, was a major move in the effort to organize the Far East on a non-Communist basis.[13]

Asian and African Nationalism

Although the tensions and conflicts associated with the cold war have taken the headlines and undoubtedly have been of major importance in shaping the course of postwar politics, the emergence of organized nationalist movements in Asia and Africa reflecting the desire for independence and economic betterment is a phenomenon that may in the long run have equally great significance. Before the war, the world was largely dominated by the culture of Western Europe and the Western Hemisphere. With a few important exceptions, the countries of Asia and the Middle East were either colonies or states theoretically independent but still subject to some important practical limitations on their sovereignty. The number of independent states on the continent of Africa was

[13] The conclusion by the United States of mutual defense treaties with Australia, New Zealand, Japan, the Philippines, and the Republic of Korea were further steps in this effort.

even smaller and the prospect of any considerable increase more remote. Particularly in Asia, but to a certain extent in Africa as well, the war served as a powerful stimulant to nationalism. When the time approached for considering the conditions of a peaceful and stable world to follow the war, it was necessary to take cognizance of nationalist demands and to relax substantially the external, chiefly European, controls that previously existed.

It is significant that of the fifty states that signed the Charter of the United Nations at San Francisco, twelve were Asian or African states,[14] and of these nine had only recently achieved or were in the process of achieving their independence and full autonomy in the management of their own affairs. It is also significant that of the nine states admitted to membership from 1946 to 1954 six were Asian or African states with similar backgrounds and experience. Many of the most important questions affecting international peace and security that have arisen since the war have had their origin in, or at least have been affected by, the aspirations of the peoples of these two continents for independence and recognition as equals.

Having recently been subject to foreign rule, in most instances by West European countries, the peoples and governments of these Asian and African states have been distrustful of the West and susceptible to many of the claims of Communist propaganda. They have been primarily concerned with making their own independence secure and improving their own conditions, and with seeking to obtain for other subject peoples the independence that they themselves so greatly prize. With these interests and attitudes, they have been unwilling to line up with either East or West but have preferred to follow an independent course, which they are convinced is most likely to further their own interests. For example, when the question of Chinese Communist intervention in Korea was before the General Assembly in 1950 and 1951, an Asian-Arab bloc of thirteen members was largely instrumental in inducing the Assembly to explore possibilities of peaceful settlement before taking the drastic action that was desired by the United States. The Asian and African members have also by and large emphasized the role of the United Nations as an instrument of political, social, and economic development and change. They have made frequent appeals to the United Nations for this purpose. They are not inclined

[14] Excluding the Union of South Africa where the governing class is European in origin.

as much as the West to stress the role of the United Nations in guaranteeing the *status quo* against violent change, and they are much less interested than the West in the military defense of the free world against communism. Stating the proposition in another way, the particular interests of the Asian and African states have by and large inclined them to favor a mediatory role for the United Nations in the cold war.

Impact of Postwar Developments on the United Nations

These developments of the postwar period have, of course, greatly affected the functioning, and indeed the nature, of the United Nations system for the maintenance of international peace and security. Brief mention will be made here of the more significant of the effects produced.

The questions with which the United Nations has been chiefly concerned have been of a different kind than was generally expected at the time of the San Francisco Conference. There, it was hopefully assumed that the Allied powers would be able to agree among themselves on the conditions of peace, including the political and economic reconstruction of areas occupied by Axis forces during the war. The primary role of the United Nations was consequently to be the maintenance of international peace and security within the framework provided by the peace settlements. This has not been the fact. Many questions have been brought before the organs of the United Nations that have directly involved the conflicts of the great powers in connection with peacemaking. Furthermore, as the result of the emergence of strong nationalist movements in Asia and Africa and the desire of the parties to the cold war to win the support of the peoples and emerging states of this area, much of the attention of the United Nations has been given to assisting in the birth of new states and the orderly development of institutions of self-government.

In still another respect, the nature of the activities of the United Nations has been different than envisaged at San Francisco. In writing the Charter, the reduction and limitation of armaments was treated as a matter of less importance than assuring the availability to the Security Council of armed forces and facilities needed for enforcement action. The explosion of the atomic bomb changed this. From the first session of the General Assembly, the United Nations has been concerned, as was the League of Nations, with questions of the limitation and control of national armaments, with the important difference that the potentialities of atomic weapons has seemed to make the problem a much more critical one.

The respective roles of the Council and the Assembly have been profoundly altered by developments since 1945. The impasse between the Soviet Union and the Western powers, made apparent in the United Nations by repeated failures of the permanent members of the Council to agree, led the United States and other Members in sympathy with its purposes to make increasing use of the Assembly to perform those functions that had originally been regarded as the special province of the Council. This extended to the use of the Assembly to deal not only with disputes and situations the continuance of which might endanger the maintenance of peace but also with threats to the peace or actual breaches of the peace, which the Charter explicitly reserved for action by the Council. This tendency to develop and strengthen the role of the Assembly was further accentuated by the interest that the smaller powers had in building up the Assembly where all had equal votes and the veto did not operate. The Asian and Arab states particularly saw in the Assembly the means by which they could bring strong pressure to bear on the Western powers in the interest of the eventual independence of subject peoples. Furthermore, the Assembly was a more effective body than the Security Council for conducting a propaganda battle and exercising psychological and political pressure.

Finally, the operating methods and procedures used by the United Nations in carrying out its function of maintaining peace and security have been greatly affected by postwar developments. The impasse in great power relations and the failure to conclude agreements under Article 43 have largely eliminated the possibility of decisions being taken by the Council that would obligate Members to take particular measures to maintain or restore peace. Consequently, one of the distinctive features of the United Nations, in comparison with the League of Nations, has disappeared. One result is that the Council, no less than the Assembly, has found itself practically limited to making recommendations, even when dealing with threats to or breaches of the peace. Thus, in dealing with the North Korean attack in 1950, the Council recommended measures to be taken. Furthermore, the manner of carrying out these measures actually resembled the pattern of sanctions taken by the League of Nations against Italy more than the pattern for which the Charter provides in some detail.

The discussions and actions of the Council and the Assembly, particularly in dealing with matters bearing on East-West relations, have frequently been directed to gaining tactical advantages, to building up support for national positions, to exercising pressure on the "enemy" in the cold war, rather than to establishing the bases for agreement and facilitating such agreement. National positions are stated in extreme terms. Terms of abuse are commonly used. Members have pressed for votes, not because votes represented progress toward agreement but rather because they might embarrass or weaken the position of the other side. The tone of the discussions in the Assembly and the Council has thus been set by the conflicts and divisions that have existed instead of by a common desire to achieve some satisfactory accommodation in the interest of international peace and security.

The inability of the Council to deal with threats to and violations of the peace, along with the increased threat of aggression resulting from the cold war, has convinced many Members of the United Nations that the only effective international guarantees of peace and security are to be found in special security arrangements, concluded under Article 51 or Article 53 of the Charter. As a result there has been a substantial development of such arrangements, as exemplified by the Inter-American Treaty of Reciprocal Assistance, the North Atlantic Treaty, the bilateral agreements concluded by the Soviet Union and its satellites, and the agreements concluded by the United States and countries in the Western Pacific area. Although these agreements have been entered into under the permissive clauses of the Charter, they clearly reflect a decline of confidence in the general security provisions of the Charter, which even the Korean experience has not reversed. The adoption by the Assembly of the "Uniting for Peace" resolution in November 1950 showed that some Members desired to develop effective methods of dealing with breaches of the peace through the Assembly, but there has been no evidence that states generally are willing to take these efforts seriously as substitutes for limited security arrangements of a more tightly knit character.[15]

[15] The full text of the "Uniting for Peace" resolution to which frequent reference will be made in this study is given in App. F.

CHAPTER III

The Record of the United Nations

IN THE performance of its role in the maintenance of peace and security, the United Nations has been profoundly affected by the dynamic forces of world politics. A world organization such as this one, based on the principle of sovereign equality of its Members and therefore largely at the mercy of their policies, cannot escape the influence of its political environment. The important question is whether the Organization, in spite of its weaknesses and its susceptibility to the influence of its environment, does have some influence on that environment and on the relations among its Members. A survey of the record of the United Nations suggests that the influence has been real, and that, in spite of many failures and disappointments, the Organization has made a substantial contribution to the maintenance of international peace and security.

The First Year

When the Security Council and the General Assembly first met in London in January 1946, relations between the Soviet Union and the United States and Great Britain had already seriously deteriorated. The failure of the Soviet Union to carry out the Yalta agreements regarding the liberated countries of Eastern Europe had produced rising doubts in the West regarding the good faith of the Kremlin. The first meeting of the Council of Foreign Ministers in London had ended in October 1945 in a deadlock viewed by some of the participants as marking a decisive turning point in great power relations. The Moscow Conference in December had produced some agreement, it is true, but more significant were the issues that were left unsettled.

It soon became clear that the meetings of the Security Council and the General Assembly were not to be immune to these divisive influences. The same statesmen who had been unable to reach agreement in meetings of the foreign ministers and who had lost confidence in each other's good faith could not be expected to work together in the Council and Assembly in the spirit of unity for which the authors of the Charter had hoped. If tension in the Assembly was at first kept at a less explosive level and was slower in becoming manifest, this was largely due to the general agreement to postpone consideration of substantive questions until the second part of the session in September 1946. In so far as the Council was concerned, the only chance of keeping distrust, suspicion, and open conflict from invading its premises was by excluding from its agenda all questions on which the permanent members were in serious disagreement. This would have left the Council—supposedly in continuous session —with very little to do and might have resulted in serious loss of prestige not only for the Council but for the United Nations as well.

There was, however, little inclination on the part of the British and American governments at least to shield the United Nations from the realities of the growing conflict between Moscow and the West. The first substantive matter to be brought to the attention of the Council late in January 1946 was the complaint of the Iranian Government regarding Soviet interference in the internal affairs of Iran. Although there is no evidence that this was done at the in-stigation of either London or Washington, the Western powers were not inclined to discourage the Iranian Government from taking this action. Moscow, however, appears to have viewed the Iranian com-plaint as being directly inspired by the United Kingdom and the United States.

Two days after the submission of the Iranian complaint, the Soviet Union and the Ukraine, in separate requests asked that the Council consider the dangers resulting from the presence of British troops in Greece and Indonesia. Thus the Council in the very be-ginning was called upon to deal with questions that brought into the open the growing distrust that characterized East-West relations. This had a permanent effect on the operating processes of the Council because the procedural decisions that were taken under conditions of tension and urgency provided the procedural pattern for the future. The Council thus was denied the opportunity calmly to consider its rules of procedure before being pressed into action.

The pattern of conflict of these early days was the one that dominated Council proceedings throughout the first year, even when the Council was not dealing with questions that affected directly the relations between the Soviet Union and the Western democra-cies. In early February 1946, the Syrian and Lebanese governments brought the continued presence of British and French troops in their countries to the attention of the Council. Without too much difficulty, a formula was found that was acceptable to the parties directly concerned, but the Soviet Union vetoed it because it did not go far enough in indicting the British and French governments. In April, the Polish Government requested that the Council consider the Spanish situation as a threat to international peace. This quite obviously represented a further effort on the part of the Soviet Government to embarrass and divide the West. The reluctance of the United States and the United Kingdom to go as far as France desired in bringing pressure to bear on the Franco regime was well known. After the Soviet Union had blocked the kind of moderate action by the Council that the Western powers were prepared to accept, the matter was later brought before the Assembly, which adopted a resolution acceptable to a substantial majority of the Members.

In August, the Soviet Union resumed its attacks in the Council on the Western powers. The Ukrainian Government requested that the Council consider the threatening situation in Greece, resulting from the alleged reactionary activities of the Greek Government and the presence of British troops. This complaint was considered at great length but inconclusively.

In early December, the Western democracies resumed the initiative when the Greek Government itself requested that the Council consider the situation resulting from aid allegedly given by the northern neighbors of Greece to guerrilla forces operating in Greek territory and endangering the public order and territorial integrity of the country. In the debate that followed, the members of the Soviet bloc took the line that the trouble was due wholly to the internal situation in Greece and violently opposed the suggestion that there was any outside interference on their part. The Soviet Union and Poland, however, did join in supporting a resolution providing for a commission to conduct a full inquiry and report to the Council. This appeared superficially at least to be a hopeful omen of co-operation in contrast to the disagreements that had characterized the earlier deliberations of the Council. Indeed, it led some to believe that the Soviet Union was moving toward a more conciliatory attitude. Another view was that the Soviet tacticians saw the possibility through an inquiry of bringing to light facts that would discredit the West.

In addition to conflict in the Council, the first year of the United Nations saw the beginning of a deadlock, which was later to prove unbreakable, in the Atomic Energy Commission. With encouraging unanimity, the Assembly had agreed in January to the establishment of a commission to consider the international control of atomic energy and to report to the Council. When the commission met the following June, the United States proposals were submitted first. In essence, they provided for international management as well as strict international control of the development and use of atomic energy, including a system of inspection and sanctions intended to give adequate protection against violation. The Soviet proposals provided for the prohibition of the production and use of atomic weapons and the exchange of technical information, without any provision for enforcement acceptable to the United States. Subsequent discussions in the commission indicated that there was no willingness on either side to retreat substantially from positions initially taken.

When the Assembly met in late October, the political debate became largely focused on the question of disarmament. After an extended and involved discussion, initiated by the Soviet Union, an omnibus resolution was unanimously adopted that tied together numerous approaches to the general problem of the limitation of armaments, including the international control of atomic energy, the limitation and reduction of conventional armaments, and the conclusion of military agreements under Article 43 of the Charter. This debate was the forerunner of subsequent discussions in the Assembly, usually initiated by the Soviet Union, in the course of which the opposing forces of East and West maneuvered for favorable verbal positions.

Although the first year of the United Nations significantly reflected the growing breach between the Soviet Union and the Western powers, there were some concrete indications of a desire on the part of these powers to use the United Nations as a means of reaching agreement. The establishment of the United Nations Atomic Energy Commission and the adoption of the resolution of the Assembly on the principles governing the regulation and reduction of armaments seemed to reflect such a desire. Furthermore, the decision of the Council of Foreign Ministers to place the independence and integrity of the Free Territory of Trieste under the guarantee of the Security Council and to request the Assembly to make recommendations regarding the final disposition of Italian colonies if the Council of Ministers were unable to agree within a year—decisions that were included in the Italian peace treaty—indicated a willingness on the part of the major powers to use the United Nations to supplement and strengthen their own efforts in the making of peace.

In the popular mind, the most dramatic symbol of East-West conflict in the United Nations has been the frequent use of the veto in the Council. Because the veto has been used almost exclusively by the Soviet Union, it has come to symbolize Soviet obstruction and non-co-operation. By the time the Assembly met in late October 1946 for the second part of its first session, the Soviet Union had already, by a negative vote, thwarted the will of the necessary majority on at least ten occasions. As was to be the repeated experience at future sessions, consideration of the veto problem by the Assembly led to no solution, for the use of the veto reflected a fundamental political condition—non-co-operation between the Soviet Union and the Western democracies.

Although the dominant political development in the United Nations during its first year was undoubtedly the deepening antagonism between East and West, there were already indications of another development that was to affect significantly the role and functioning of the Organization. In the course of consideration by the Council of the Lebanese and Syrian complaint, it became apparent that certain of the Arab and Asian states, with considerable support from the Latin American republics as well as from the Soviet bloc, were prepared to look to the United Nations to further their own nationalist aspirations, which in many instances might be satisfied only at the expense of the Western powers. The Indian complaint to the Assembly against the treatment of Indians by the Government of the Union of South Africa did not raise this issue directly, but it did represent a demand on the part of the Asiatic peoples for equality, and therefore had far-reaching implications for Western colonialism.[1] It was also quite clear at this early time that the Communists were prepared to exploit the nationalistic aspirations and grievances of colonial peoples for the purpose of embarrassing and weakening the Western democracies and that they saw in the organs and procedures of the United Nations convenient instruments for this purpose.

---

[1] As the Union of South Africa has repeatedly pointed out, the persons referred to are not Indian nationals but are South African nationals of Indian origin. Throughout this study, the term "Indians" has been used for convenience.

The Beginning of the Cold War

The veto was used but once in the Security Council from late September 1946 to July 1947. The Soviet Union employed it on March 25 to defeat a British proposal in the Corfu Channel dispute. Nevertheless, this period was in fact one of rapidly increasing tension between the Soviet Union and the Western powers, highlighted by such events as: the growing split over the treatment of Germany; the approval, despite Soviet opposition, of the United States control plan by the Atomic Energy Commission in December 1946; increasing alarm over the situation in Greece and the consequent announcement of the Truman Doctrine on March 12, 1947; the inability of the permanent members of the Council to agree on the appointment of a governor of the Free Territory of Trieste; the report of the Military Staff Committee on April 30 showing that the great powers were unable to agree on the implementation of Article 43; and Secretary Marshall's proposal of economic aid to Europe on June 5.

Late in May 1947, the Commission of Investigation completed its report on the Greek situation, which was considered by the Council during the following two months. On July 29, the Soviet Union vetoed a United States proposal for the acceptance of the majority report and its implementation. It then became clear that the Council could not be used effectively for the purpose of protecting the Greek Government against efforts being made, with the direct aid of the Communist-dominated northern neighbors of Greece, to overthrow it by force and establish a Communist-controlled regime. At the same time, it was also becoming clear that the negotiations that had been carried on for over a year between the Soviet and United States military commands in Korea were not making any progress toward a satisfactory agreement. Meanwhile the United States Government had announced, in the Truman Doctrine, a policy of containing threatened Communist expansion by assisting those prepared to help themselves. But the military means at its disposal were limited as a result of the drastic reduction of United States armed forces since the war, and the conclusion appears to have been reached that the United States should concentrate its major effort in Western Europe, and look to the United Nations for assistance in meeting the Communist threat in those areas considered of less vital direct concern. The ever-present threat of a Soviet veto in the Council, however, largely removed any possibility of effective United Nations action through that organ. There remained the General Assembly, with large and vaguely defined powers, but not originally envisaged as well equipped to play an important role in the maintenance of international peace and security.

When the Assembly met in September 1947, it was called upon, at the request of the United States Government, to consider both the Greek question and the question of Korean independence. The United States proposed that a special committee of the Assembly should be established to perform certain functions when it was not in session, so that the Assembly would be better equipped to discharge the increased responsibilities it was being asked to assume.

The second session of the Assembly marked an important turning point in the work of the United Nations. The Assembly, despite strong opposition from the Soviet Union, assumed responsibility, after the Council had failed in its efforts, for dealing with a situation that some Members considered to be a major threat to international peace and security. The Assembly also assumed the responsibility for finding the solution to a problem on which the United States and the Soviet Union had become hopelessly deadlocked. Thus at this session, the Assembly assumed functions that had hitherto been reserved for the Council or for the great powers themselves, which led to recognition by Members that changes in the organization and procedures of the Assembly would be necessary if it was to perform these new functions satisfactorily. Although the Council retained important responsibilities, including those that the Charter specifically vested in it to the exclusion of other organs, the Assembly henceforth assumed an increasingly important role in dealing with disputes and situations when the major interests of East and West were in conflict. In dealing with these matters, the Assembly became subject to strong pressure from the Western powers to take action that would assist in the containment of Communist expansion and the weakening of the Soviet bloc.

The issues confronting the United Nations in this critical year, however, were not alone questions involving the East-West conflict. It also became apparent that one of the important functions that the United Nations would be called upon to perform would be to assist in the orderly development of independence and freedom from external control in areas where peoples had been subjected to some form of foreign rule and where nationalism had become a strong and vital force. In particular, the United Nations had a responsibility under its Charter to see that such development took place without endangering or disturbing international peace and security. Three situations brought to the attention of the United Nations during 1947 called for action along these lines.[2] The first was the Palestine situation, which the United Kingdom submitted to the Assembly for the stated reason that it regarded the Council as "an imperfect instrument" for achieving an agreed settlement. In early July, the Egyptian Government requested the Council to consider charges that the United Kingdom by the continued presence of its troops in the Suez Canal Zone and its policies in the Sudan was endangering peace in that area. Later during the same month, the Indian and Australian governments requested Council consideration of the situation in Indonesia resulting from the breakdown of agreements that had been reached and the outbreak of hostilities between the Netherlands and Indonesian forces.

The year 1947 also saw a great increase in the strength of the forces seeking independence for the more advanced of the Asian and African peoples. In August, India and Pakistan became fully independent states, and India immediately assumed a leading role in the movement for the independence and equality of Asian and African peoples. The action of the Council in the Indonesian case and of the Assembly in Palestine did much to encourage the belief that the United Nations had an important function to perform in this connection. Those who with increasing insistence were to demand that the United Nations take a leading part in advancing independence and equality among subject peoples were not equally willing to commit themselves in the East-West conflict to the cause of freedom as understood by the Western democracies. This may have been due to the fact that the Western democracies were not prepared to give unqualified support to the demands of Asian-African nationalists.

The Cold War Since 1947

Since the decisive events of 1947, the cold war has been the dominating force in international relations. Inevitably, it has con-

[2] The Korean problem in a sense fell in this same category, but as it was presented to the General Assembly, the most important single aspect was the deadlock between the United States and the Soviet Union over the implementation of the principle of Korean independence "in due course."

ditioned and to a large extent determined the activities of the United Nations. Those Members of the United Nations whose concerns and energies have to such a large degree been absorbed in this conflict could hardly be expected to divorce their United Nations policies and activities from its demands. This is not to say, however, either that the United Nations has been the exclusive or even principal arena of conflict, or that, even for those Members principally concerned with the cold war, the United Nations has not had significant functions to perform other than to support one side or the other in this struggle.

The role of the United Nations in the cold war has been differently viewed by the non-Communist nations. Their attitudes have been determined by many considerations, including the degree of seriousness with which they view the threat of Communist expansion and their affinity to the values and culture patterns of the West. To many Asian and Arab states just emerging from colonial status or some measure of economic and political subordination to the West, the dangers of Western imperialism have seemed no less real than the threat of external Communist aggression. Furthermore, they have viewed the proper means of coping with the Communist danger in a different way from the West. Their influence has been exercised to restrain the use of the United Nations to serve the purposes of one side or the other in the cold war. They have been more concerned with its use for avoiding war and assisting in the political, economic, and social development of underdeveloped areas.

During 1948, the United Nations exercised its main influence in the cold war by the activities of its Special Committee on the Balkans in Greece and the observation of elections by the Temporary Commission in South Korea. The Security Council was asked by Chile to investigate the part played by Soviet authorities in connection with the Communist coup in Czechoslovakia, but by using the "double veto" the Soviet representative killed this initiative. In August, the Council considered inconclusively a Yugoslav complaint that the United States and United Kingdom had violated the treaty of peace with Italy by certain financial measures adopted in their zone of Trieste.

Although the Berlin blockade had been instituted in late June, it was not until late September that the situation was brought to the attention of the United Nations. At that time, the United States, the United Kingdom, and France joined in asking the Council to

take action under Article 39, for the primary purpose of putting
pressure on the Soviet Union to end the blockade. The Soviet Union
was opposed to any consideration of the matter by the Council, apparently convinced that it could force the Western powers out of
Berlin. Although the United Nations provided the atmosphere and
the physical setting that permitted agreement finally to be reached
for the lifting of the blockade and the holding of a meeting of the
Council of Foreign Ministers, it was not asked by the parties to
undertake the peaceful settlement of outstanding differences. Nor
did the informal efforts of other members of the Council succeed in
bringing about such a settlement.

Until June 1950, the general pattern of United Nations action with
respect to the cold war continued largely unchanged. So far as
Western and Central Europe were concerned, the Western powers
continued to rely primarily on their own individual resources and
on collective arrangements, which, although in form subordinated to
the United Nations, were outside its framework. In April 1949, the
North Atlantic Treaty was signed by twelve Western powers, and
this was immediately followed by an agreement among the United
States, the United Kingdom, and France on an Occupation Statute
for Western Germany. The draft constitution of the future German
Federal Republic was approved in May by the occupation authorities, and civil government in Germany became operative in September. To counter this action, the establishment of a "German Democratic Republic" in Eastern Germany was announced in October.

Following the entrance into force of the North Atlantic Treaty in
August 1949, attention was immediately given to its implementation.
Passage by Congress and presidential approval of the Mutual Defense Assistance Act in early October were followed by the opening
of negotiations for mutual defense assistance agreements between
the United States and other North Atlantic Treaty powers. Quite
clearly, in the matter of the organization of peace and security in
Western and Central Europe, the Western powers were not attaching
much importance to the United Nations. Nor were the Soviet Union
and its satellites any more interested in its use.

In other areas, however, the United Nations was viewed as having more importance. In the Balkans, the Western powers continued their efforts through the General Assembly to assist Greece
in resisting pressures from the north. By the end of 1949, the situation was greatly improved from the Western point of view, partly

because of the activities of the Assembly and its Special Committee on the Balkans, but principally because of effective United States military and economic aid and the defection of Yugoslavia from the Soviet bloc. The Assembly was also utilized in 1949 for the purpose of publicizing and publicly condemning alleged infringements of human rights by Bulgaria, Hungary, and Rumania in violation of the treaties of peace.

In the Far East, the United Nations continued to provide the means of steady pressure on the Soviet Union to consent to a solution of the Korean problem along the lines of the resolution of the Assembly in November 1947. The partial implementation of this resolution had resulted in the continuation of a divided Korea, with the Republic of Korea, declared by the Assembly to be the only lawful government, exercising effective control south of the thirty-eighth parallel, and the People's Republic of Korea, recognized by the Soviet Union, in effective control north of the parallel. At its fourth session in 1949, the Assembly extended the functions of its Commission on Korea to include reporting on any threats to or violations of the peace along the northern frontier of the Republic. Furthermore, with the situation in China undergoing rapid change as the result of Chinese Communist successes in the civil war, the Assembly, in response to a request from the Chinese National Government, called upon all states to respect the independence and integrity of China and to abide by existing treaties.

Since 1947, the principal Communist initiatives in the United Nations have been taken at the annual sessions of the Assembly when members of the Soviet bloc have introduced proposals dealing with disarmament, the outlawry of atomic weapons, or the reduction of world tensions, which point an accusing finger at the Western powers, especially the United States, and give the Communist Members the opportunity to repeat their customary claims that Western capitalists, following the leadership of the United States, are bent on imposing their will on the peace-loving "democracies," even at the price of another war. The Western powers have invariably been successful in defeating these proposals or shaping them to suit their own purposes by obtaining the adoption of resolutions that point the accusing finger, by implication at least, at Moscow instead.

The North Korean attack on the Republic of Korea on June 25, 1950, was an important event, not only in the cold war but also in the relations of the United Nations to it. Up to this time, European developments had clearly overshadowed those in other parts of the world, and the role of the United Nations had clearly been a subordinate one. The North Korean attack, following on the victory of the Communists in China and the attitude adopted by the Soviet Union with respect to Chinese representation in the United Nations, focused attention on developments in the Far East, emphasized the danger of resort to violence on other fronts, and as the result of prompt appeal by the United States to the Security Council, gave the United Nations a new importance in the East-West struggle.

As a result of the United States initiative and its desire to keep its own action within a United Nations framework, the collective action undertaken to repel the North Korean attack took on the character of United Nations action. As a consequence, first the Council and then the Assembly assumed important roles in initiating and guiding the collective action that was undertaken. After the North Korean forces had been driven back of the thirty-eighth parallel in September 1950, the Assembly recommended in its resolution of October 7 a program for achieving an independent, united, and democratic Korea. Shortly thereafter, when Chinese Communist forces intervened, the Assembly undertook to achieve a cease-fire and political settlement by its resolution of December 14, and when that was found to be impossible on acceptable terms, the Assembly adopted a resolution on February 1, 1951, finding the Chinese Communists guilty of aggression and recommending the study of additional measures. After further efforts at peaceful settlement had failed and the intent of the Chinese Communists to drive the United Nations forces out of Korea became clear, the Assembly in May 1951 recommended the application of additional collective economic measures. Finally, both sides were found to be willing to undertake truce talks in late June and early July, and the negotiations were conducted by the United Nations Command with the Assembly playing a mediatory role of some importance in achieving an armistice agreement.

It was not only the United States and those Members more intimately associated with it in efforts to contain and weaken communism that made use of the United Nations in connection with the Korean incident. Once collective military action had been initiated, the Soviet Union and its allies proceeded to strike back through United Nations channels. The Council and later the Assembly were asked to consider complaints alleging United States aggression in

Korea and Formosa, United States bombing of Chinese territory, the mistreatment of prisoners of war, and the use of bacteriological warfare by United States forces.

It was in connection with the Korean incident, as compounded by subsequent Chinese Communist intervention, that the first determined and significant initiative was taken in the United Nations by the Arab-Asian bloc[3] to bring about an alleviation of the East-West conflict. Under the leadership of India, this group of Asian and African states, with special interests of their own and anxious to avoid not only war but any irrevocable commitment to either side in the struggle, exercised their influence to achieve a peaceful adjustment of the Korean problem and of great power relations in the area, on a basis that would assure to Asian peoples the maximum opportunity to determine their own future without interference from the outside. Although this initiative was not successful in modifying substantially the pattern of great power conflict, it did play a significant part in keeping hostilities limited and in bringing about the final conclusion of an armistice agreement putting an end to the fighting. These Members were not successful, however, in gaining recognition of a mediatory role in the political conference that was to follow the armistice.

Following the return of the Soviet representative to the Security Council after an absence of six months and the consequent blocking of further action by the Council, the Assembly took an important step in November 1950 by approving the "Uniting for Peace" resolution under which the Assembly, in future cases of aggression, would play the role that the Council had been able to perform in the initial stages of the Korean fighting. This was a significant impact of the cold war on the United Nations, and was a striking indication of the intent of the Western powers at the time to continue to use the United Nations as an instrumentality to check Communist expansion. When, however, efforts were made to implement this resolution by committing members in advance to provide properly trained and equipped military units, it became clear that it would be dangerous to rely on it too heavily. The recent trend would seem to be away from serious use of United Nations organs in dealing with any

[3] This group, referred to in this volume as the Arab-Asian bloc, does not have a consistent membership. It has usually consisted of those members of the Arab League that are Members of the United Nations, plus India, Pakistan, Burma, Afghanistan, Iran, and Indonesia, with Thailand, the Philippines, Liberia, and Ethiopia frequently associated.

alleged threats to the peace or acts of aggression, and greater reliance on limited mutual assistance and regional arrangements.[4]

In areas outside of eastern Asia, the United Nations has not been called upon since 1950 to deal with many disputes or situations resulting directly from the cold war. By the time the sixth session of the Assembly met in September 1951, the Greek situation had so improved that the Special Committee of the General Assembly was discontinued and the task of observation was turned over to the Peace Observation Commission. The Assembly did consider in the fall of 1951 a Yugoslav complaint that the Soviet bloc was conducting "aggressive pressure" against it. Also, in the same session a commission was established to investigate whether conditions for a free election existed in Germany, and the Assembly made an appeal to the great powers for the conclusion of a treaty with Austria. Apart from these actions, however, the Western prosecution of the cold war, except in its propaganda aspects, was outside the United Nations and chiefly through the North Atlantic Treaty Organization. As a result of the Korean incident, the armed forces of the North Atlantic Treaty powers were greatly strengthened, and the first moves were made to bring Western Germany into the military defense of Western Europe. As in the past, the members of the Soviet-dominated Communist bloc largely limited their use of the United Nations to general attacks on the West and claims that Western policies and acts were of such kind as to suggest deliberate intent to increase international tension and bring about another world war.

Emergent Nationalism

In addition to its role in the cold war, the United Nations has played a constructive and moderately successful part in limiting the use of violence for the achievment of independence by peoples hitherto subject to alien rule or to some serious limitation upon their sovereignty. Most of these situations have arisen within the African and Asiatic rimland extending from Morocco through northern Africa, south and southeastern Asia, to Korea. With the outbreak of hostilities in Indonesia in 1947, the Security Council, by following a course of action carefully calculated to avoid giving

[4] Since the handling of the Guatemalan complaint in the Security Council in June 1954 took place after the period covered by this study, it is not dealt with in this volume.

unnecessary offense to the Netherlands and at the same time recognizing the international consequences of continued fighting was successful, through its Committee of Good Offices, in getting the Netherlands and the Republic of Indonesia to sign agreements in January 1948. These agreements established a truce and set forth the principles that were to provide the basis for subsequent political discussions. As a result of the breakdown of these discussions and the resumption of hostilities in December 1948, the Council again had to consider ways and means of bringing violence under control. After considerable pressure was brought to bear on the Netherlands Government, the Council, through its newly constituted Indonesian Commission, was able to get the parties to consent to participate in a round table conference at The Hague on terms acceptable to the Council. The conference convened on August 23, 1949, and resulted in an agreement under which the Republic of Indonesia was recognized as independent. Subsequently, the Republic was admitted to the United Nations.

With respect to Korea, the role of the United Nations has been principally to reinforce one side against the other in the cold war, and to assist in suppressing aggression. A subsidiary role, and one of some importance, has been to assist in the establishment of an independent, unified, and democratic Korean state. As the United Nations Commission for Korea was quick to recognize, the difficulties in the way of successfully performing this task have largely come from the cold war, which has found expression locally in the mutual enmity of two Korean regimes.

The Indochinese situation, which in part at least was the outcome of an attempt on the part of native nationalists to overthrow foreign rule, has not been brought to the attention of a United Nations organ.[5] In view of the similarity of this situation to that in Indonesia, one is inclined to look for an explanation of this in the larger world situation. The fact that France was a permanent member of the Security Council and the Anglo-American belief that a strong and co-operative France was essential to the defense of Western Europe against Communist expansion were undoubtedly important

[5] After the period covered by this volume, the Security Council was asked to consider a situation arising from the fighting in Indochina. In May 1954, Thailand asked the Council to dispatch the United Nations Peace Observation Commission to Thailand on the ground that there was a danger that the fighting might spread to other countries in the area.

factors in the explanation. Confronted by French opposition, no one was prepared to take the initiative that Australia and India had taken with respect to Indonesia. But it is also important to note that, at least from the time of the North Korean attack, the Vietminh effort under Ho Chi Minh to overthrow French rule in Vietnam was identified in influential quarters with world communism more than with Indochinese nationalism. In fact, President Truman in his statement of June 26, 1950, made it quite clear that the United States Government regarded the Vietminh activities in Indochina primarily as a manifestation of Communist aggression, possibly not as flagrant as the North Korean but clearly of the same kind.

The weakening of British imperial authority as the result of the Second World War and the emergence of new independent states within the prewar limits of the Empire created other situations of international concern. The United Nations played an important role in easing the transition from dependence to independence, and in assisting in the solution of difficult problems that arose.

In 1947, the United Kingdom on its own initiative submitted the question of the future of Palestine to the General Assembly. Here the problem was not so much that of easing Palestine out from under British control as of determining the conditions under which the peoples of Palestine might achieve their independence without becoming involved in a bloody internecine struggle. The Assembly failed in its immediate objective to find conditions of independence acceptable to Jews and Arabs alike. Not only were the recommendations of the Assembly of late November 1947 unacceptable to the Arabs, but even before the termination of British authority on May 15, 1948, violence had broken out in Palestine between Arabs and Jews. This became open war after British withdrawal and with the proclamation of the independent state of Israel and the intervention of the neighboring Arab states. The Council finally was able in July to obtain the agreement of the parties to a permanent cease-fire. Subsequently, through the efforts of a United Nations mediator, armistice agreements were signed between Israel and the individual Arab states establishing the conditions of the permanent cessation of hostilities and providing machinery for their enforcement. But further United Nations efforts to achieve a political settlement were unsuccessful. Since the conclusion of the armistice agreements, the Council has found it necessary on numerous occasions to deal with alleged violations, and with other questions resulting from the deterioration of the situation.

With the granting of full dominion status to India and Pakistan in August 1947, serious disagreements developed with respect to the future status of certain territories, especially the princely states, which had previously enjoyed a special status in the British Empire. These disagreements arose in an atmosphere already charged with fear and hatred as the result of racial and religious conflicts. Two of these matters were brought to the attention of the Council: the Hyderabad complaint of Indian aggression, which was considered by the Council in September 1948 but without any action being taken; and the Indian charge that Pakistan was engaged in aggressive action in the state of Jammu and Kashmir, which had been submitted to the Council in the previous January. In dealing with the latter complaint and the countercharges of Pakistan, the Council concentrated its efforts on achieving a peaceful settlement of the dispute. A commission set up by the Council was able to report on January 1, 1949, that the parties had put into effect cease-fire orders. Efforts were made to obtain the agreement of the parties on conditions under which a plebiscite, to which both had agreed in principle, would be held. Working first through a commission and then through appointed individuals serving as United Nations representatives, the Council succeeded in narrowing the issues without, however, achieving full agreement.

Efforts of the British Government to re-establish its authority in Malaya after the war were met by strong native resistance, aided and abetted by the Communists. The enlightened policy of the British regarding colonial self-government was probably one reason no serious consideration was given at any time to bringing this situation to the attention of the United Nations. Burma, also a British colony before the war, was granted full independence in January 1948, but the Government had serious trouble establishing its authority throughout the country. Following the overthrow of the Nationalist Chinese Government on the mainland, Nationalist military units took refuge in Burmese territory near the Chinese border and, in the fall of 1952, the Burmese Government found it necessary to ask the assistance of the Assembly in dealing with this problem.

In the Middle East generally, considerable pressure was brought to bear on the Western powers, particularly the United Kingdom, to yield special economic, political, or military rights associated in the minds of the native populations with imperialism. As has been already noted, Egypt had asked the Council in 1947 to consider its charges against the United Kingdom. Although the question remained on the agenda of the Security Council, no further efforts were made in the following years to get United Nations action. British oil interests in Iran were faced with the confiscation of their properties as the result of nationalization measures instituted by the Mossadegh Government in May 1951. The United Kingdom submitted the case to the International Court of Justice and later asked the assistance of the Security Council. The net result of United Nations action in this case, however, was the acceptance of the *de facto* situation, leaving to the interested parties the task of working out an acceptable solution.

Nationalistic feeling against "Western imperialism" became particularly strong in the postwar period among the peoples of North Africa, largely Moslem, who saw in the defeat of Italy, the weakness of France, and the weakening of the British Empire opportunities for achieving independence. The future of the Italian colonies was first considered by the Council of Foreign Ministers and the Paris Peace Conference of 1946. When it proved impossible to work out any agreement in the Council of Foreign Ministers, a provision was put into the Italian Peace Treaty to the effect that, if within another year no agreement was reached, the whole question would be referred to the Assembly, which subsequently occurred in September 1948. The Asian and African Members thus found themselves in a strong position to influence decisively the final decision. The decision taken in the fourth session of the Assembly to give Libya full independence understandably received their full support but was accepted with some reluctance by the colonial powers, especially by France, which saw clearly the implications of this decision.

Nationalist leaders in Tunisia and Morocco naturally were encouraged by the decision. Their demands were supported by most Asian and African Members. An attempt on the part of members of the Arab League to have the Assembly in late 1951 consider the complaint of French violation of human rights in Morocco failed. In April 1952 the same states, supported by other Asian and African states, requested that the Council consider the alleged use of repressive measures by France in Tunisia. Opposition by France and the

United Kingdom and unwillingness on the part of the United States to antagonize or weaken France, in view of its key position in the anti-Communist coalition, resulted in the defeat of the proposal to include this matter in the agenda of the Council. An attempt on the part of Asian and African states in the summer of 1952 to have a special session of the Assembly summoned to consider the Tunisian situation failed for want of sufficient support. Both the Moroccan and Tunisian questions were submitted to the Assembly when it met in October 1952. After extended and heated discussions, it adopted resolutions calling upon the parties to continue negotiations and appealing to them to settle their differences in the spirit of the Charter. Efforts by the Asian and African members to obtain consideration of the Moroccan question by the Council in the spring of 1953, and to get stronger action by the Assembly on both the Tunisian and Moroccan questions again failed to receive the necessary support.

The activities of the United Nations in dealing with disputes and situations resulting from the emergence of nationalism in Asia and Africa have not been limited to the areas referred to above. In South Africa, a situation has developed where a small white minority, in order to preserve its position, has used its control of the government to impose restrictions on the civil, political, and economic activities of the nonwhite population. Two different complaints arising from these practices have been brought to the attention of the Assembly. The first was the complaint of India, already referred to, over the discriminatory treatment of Indians by the Government of the Union of South Africa, which has been considered repeatedly and indecisively since 1946. The second was a complaint first submitted in 1952 by thirteen Asian and African Members over the policies of segregation (*apartheid*) followed by the Government of the Union of South Africa. A commission of inquiry was set up, which reported to the General Assembly in 1953. The Assembly registered its disapproval of the policies being followed, and instructed the committee to continue its studies.

This brief summary does not exhaust the activities of the United Nations in dealing with problems resulting from the clash of nationalist aspirations on the part of Asian and African peoples and the conservative policies of the politically and economically more developed Western nations. In the discharge of its responsibilities for economic and social co-operation and the promotion of the well-being and development of non-self-governing territories, the United Nations has been very active.[6] What is of special significance here is that in the discharge of its responsibilities for the maintenance of international peace and security, acting in accordance with the broad purposes of the Charter, the United Nations has sought with considerable success to restrain the use of violence in conflicts between emerging nationalism and the defenders of the established order while exercising its influence on behalf of constructive solutions of basic problems.

The United Nations and a Legal Order

For the most part, the activities of the United Nations, in the maintenance of international peace and security, have been concerned with the two major conflicts of the postwar world: (1) the cold war resulting from the struggle between the Soviet-Communist nations and the Western democracies, and (2) the struggle of Asian and African peoples for greater independence and equality. Quite understandably in dealing with forces of such an elemental nature, it has been impossible for the organs of the United Nations to apply nonexistent legal standards or to apply legal rules when discontent with the existing order has been at the very basis of the conflict. It is therefore understandable that the approach of the United Nations to the questions that have come before it has generally been a nonlegal one.

In those cases where an attempt has been made to deal with such questions on a legal basis, the result has usually been a failure. Thus, in the Corfu Channel dispute, although the International Court of Justice successfully maintained its jurisdiction and gave a judgment on the merits of the case, Albania refused to carry out the judgment. In the Anglo-Iranian oil dispute, the Court was probably saved from a repetition of the same experience by its decision that it did not have jurisdiction in the case. In only one instance where a legal question has been raised in the course of the consideration of a dispute or situation by the Assembly or the Council has the Court been asked to give an advisory opinion. This was with respect to the procedure to be followed in the settlement of disputes regarding the interpretation of provisions of the peace treaties with Bulgaria, Hungary, and Rumania. On questions whether the Gen-

[6] See the volume in this Brookings series, *The United Nations and Promotion of the General Welfare.*

eral Assembly or the Security Council had competence to consider matters such as the treatment of Indians in South Africa and the Indonesian question, both the Assembly and the Council have insisted on making their own decisions without consulting the Court.

It is of significance that all the cases that have been brought before the International Court of Justice for judgment have been brought on the initiative of some state outside of the Soviet bloc and also outside the Asian-African bloc. In every instance the initiative has been taken by a European or Latin American state.[7]

The United Nations has made some modest progress in developing acceptable standards of international conduct. The Assembly has reaffirmed the principles of international law contained in the agreement that established the tribunal for the Nuremberg trials and has approved a declaration of human rights. Considerable progress has been made in the drafting of covenants of human rights. A Genocide Convention was approved by the General Assembly during its third session in 1948, and submitted to Member governments for ratification. In its second session, the Assembly established an International Law Commission to assist in the development and codification of international law. In spite of the emphasis in the United Nations activities on the political approach to the problem of maintaining international peace and security, there has been recognition of the importance of developing an adequate legal foundation. Peace and security on the basis of law have clearly been a serious objective of the United Nations.

In any review of the total activity of the United Nations, it is clear that the Organization has been an important instrument of orderly change. Although it has not been successful in eliminating all use of force or even bringing the use of force promptly to an end, it has had some success in keeping violence within limits. The Organization has not satisfied all demands made on it for the modification of the existing order, but it has been a means by which public opinion has been mobilized and pressure has been exercised in support of the goals set by the Charter. The United Nations has not imposed a new order of law and justice, but it has provided a framework of established organs and procedures for subjecting international conduct to a judgment based on defined purposes and principles.

[7] After the period covered by this volume, the United States instituted proceedings against Hungary and the Soviet Union before the Court in connection with the treatment of American aircraft and crew members.

PART TWO

THE INITIAL CONSIDERATION OF QUESTIONS

CHAPTER IV

The Submission of Questions

THE ESTABLISHMENT of a world-wide organization for the maintenance of international peace and security is predicated on the universal recognition of a fundamental assumption—that there is a sufficiently general and common interest in the maintenance of peace to justify states taking the initiative in disputes or situations in which they are not directly concerned to bring about the settlement or adjustment of the particular dispute or situation, or to restore peace if it has already been breached. The propriety of this initiative has not always been recognized. As late as the nineteenth century, states offering their good offices in the cause of peace were open to the charge of unfriendly intervention in matters of no concern to them. Consequently, the Hague Convention of 1899 for the Pacific Settlement of International Disputes contained a provision to the effect that the offer of good offices or mediation was never to be regarded as an unfriendly act. It is significant that the inclusion of this provision was considered necessary and that it was viewed as an advance of some importance in the cause of peace.

Down to the First World War, there was no assurance that states would take the initiative in the general cause of peace. In fact, states were not even under any general obligation to settle their disputes and differences by peaceful means. Furthermore, although the conference method had been used on a number of occasions to deal with disputes and situations with a view to peaceful settlement or adjustment, there was no assurance that such a conference would be held when the need arose.

The establishment of the League of Nations at the conclusion of the First World War brought a new approach to the handling of international disputes and threats to peace. Members of the League agreed to submit disputes "likely to lead to a rupture" to arbitration, judicial settlement, or inquiry by the Council of the League.[1] They recognized the right of either the Council or the Assembly of

---

[1] Art. 12 of the Covenant.

the League to deal "with any matter . . . affecting the peace of the
world."[2] They declared "any war or threat of war, whether immediately affecting any of the Members of the League or not," to be a
matter of concern to the whole League. They declared it to be "the
friendly right of each Member of the League to bring to the attention of the Assembly or of the Council any circumstance whatever
affecting international relations which threatens to disturb international peace or the good understanding between nations upon which
peace depends."[3] Thus the principle was firmly established and well
implemented that any dispute or situation that might threaten
international peace would be a matter of concern to all members of
the organized international community and not only to the states
directly concerned.

When the Charter of the United Nations was being written, it
was taken for granted that this principle would be accepted and
implemented. The provisions of the Charter recognize justice and
respect for law as worthy goals, but stress the maintenance of international peace and security as the primary objectives and define the
powers of the Security Council and, to a lesser extent, the General
Assembly, in these terms.

Provisions of the Charter

Under the provisions of Article 2(3) of the Charter, Members of
the United Nations are obligated to "settle their international disputes by peaceful means in such a manner that international peace
and security, and justice, are not endangered." If the parties to a
dispute, the continuance of which is likely to endanger the maintenance of international peace and security, are unable to settle it
by peaceful means of their own choice, they are required to submit
it to the Security Council.[4] Under the terms of Article 35, any
Member may bring any dispute, or any situation "which might lead
to international friction or give rise to a dispute" to the attention
of the Security Council or the General Assembly. But the Security
Council is expected to make recommendations only with respect to
those disputes and situations the continuance of which is likely to

---

[2] Arts. 3, 4.
[3] Art. 11.
[4] Art. 37 of the Charter.

endanger the maintenance of international peace and security.[5] The importance of the term "international" as employed in these articles is further emphasized in Article 2(7), which specifically states that Members shall not be required to submit to settlement under the Charter those matters that are essentially within their domestic jurisdiction.[6]

Although it was assumed that most questions would be submitted by Members of the Organization, the Charter does permit the submission of questions by states not Members of the Organization. Under Article 35(2), such a state may bring to the attention of the Council or the Assembly a dispute to which it is a party if it accepts in advance, for the purposes of the dispute, the obligations of pacific settlement provided in the Charter. The significance of the fact that this express permission does not extend to "situations" has been greatly reduced by the unwillingness of the Council in practice to distinguish between a "dispute" and a "situation."

In certain circumstances a matter may be brought to the attention of the Council by the Assembly or vice versa. The Charter envisages that questions relating to the maintenance of international peace and security may be brought to the Assembly by the Council and that the Council may request the Assembly to make recommendations with regard to disputes or situations with which the Council itself is dealing.[7] The Council is also authorized under Article 20 to convoke a special session of the Assembly.

Not only may the Assembly call the attention of the Council to situations that are likely to endanger international peace and security, but it is also authorized to make recommendations to the Council.[8] In addition, the Assembly is under an obligation to refer to the Council any questions relating to international peace and security upon which "action" is necessary, presumably enforcement action under Chapter VII of the Charter. One further provision concerning the submission of questions to the Security Council is found in Article 99, which authorizes the Secretary-General to bring to the attention of the Council "any matter which in his opinion may threaten the maintenance of international peace and security."

[5] Art. 38 provides an exception.
[6] The Covenant exempted disputes arising out of matters that by international law were solely within the domestic jurisdiction of a state. See Art. 15(8).
[7] Arts. 11 and 12.
[8] Arts. 10 and 11.

Disputes may also be submitted to the International Court of Justice. In fact, by declaration under Article 36 of the Statute, parties to the Statute may agree in advance to accept the jurisdiction of the Court "in all legal disputes" coming under the terms of that article and subject to such conditions as may be set forth in their declaration.[9] But only states may be parties in cases before the Court. The Court is "open" to all parties to the Statute, including not only the Members of the United Nations but also states not Members of the Organization that become parties on conditions "determined in each case by the General Assembly upon the recommendation of the Security Council." The Statute of the Court provides that the conditions under which the Court shall be open to states not parties to the Statute shall be determined by the Security Council, it being specified that the conditions shall not place such a state in a position of inequality before the Court.

The procedure by which disputes are submitted to the Court depends upon whether or not the Court is asked to exercise its compulsory jurisdiction. The compulsory jurisdiction of the Court may be invoked by application of one party to the dispute. If there is no claim that the Court has such jurisdiction, normally the dispute will be submitted by agreement of the parties, signified by a notification to the Court of such agreement.[10] In addition to the exercise of its jurisdiction over disputes, the Court may be asked by the Council or the Assembly to give an advisory opinion on a legal question that may arise in connection with a dispute or situation before either organ. This opinion is not legally binding upon either the organ asking it or the states directly concerned in the dispute or situation, but it is likely to be accorded great weight.

Origin of Submissions

Many of the questions considered by the Security Council or the General Assembly have been in the nature of disputes submitted by one of the parties to them. In other cases, it has generally been a state that has had some special responsibility or interest that has

[9] The full text of this article and the texts of all other articles of the Statute of the International Court of Justice to which reference is made in this study are given in App. C.
[10] For further discussion, see below, Chap. XIII.

brought the matter to the attention of the Council or the Assembly. Occasionally, however, questions have been submitted by states not directly concerned. It was Chile, for example, that requested an investigation by the Council of the Communist coup in Czechoslovakia. The consideration of nearly half of the questions in the Assembly and the Council has been initiated by one or more of the five major powers. Of the remaining questions, most have been submitted by one or more of the members of the Arab-Asian bloc.

Of the cases before the International Court of Justice through 1953, all except the dispute between Colombia and Peru were brought by European states outside the Soviet orbit, most of them by France or the United Kingdom. Except for one case submitted by Liechtenstein and one by Italy, all cases were submitted by Members of the United Nations.[11]

Non-Member States

Although the Security Council and the General Assembly have received innumerable appeals from states not Members of the Organization in the form of communications containing charges, accusations, and statements that it was the duty of the Council or the Assembly to take some particular action, there have been few instances in which such states have availed themselves of the opportunity accorded them under Article 35(2) of the Charter. Thailand, prior to becoming a Member of the United Nations, asked the Security Council to consider a dispute with France, but the matter was settled outside the Council.

Article 35(2) seems to require submission by a "state" that is a "party" to a "dispute" and has accepted for the purposes of the dispute the obligations of the Charter for pacific settlement. In some instances it has been, to say the least, doubtful that these conditions have been met. But there has been little discussion on this point. The Council considered, although inconclusively, charges brought by Hyderabad against India. Hyderabad, like Thailand, in bringing its complaint to the Council specifically accepted the obligations of pacific settlement laid down in Article 35(2). Throughout the discussion India contended that Hyderabad was not a "state" and was not therefore qualified to invoke Article 35(2).

---

[11] Liechtenstein, while not a Member of the United Nations, was a party to the Statute of the Court.

The Council also discussed in 1950 two complaints against the United States by the People's Republic of China: one concerning the invasion of Formosa, the other the bombing of Chinese territory. As the majority of the members upheld the right of the National Government to represent China in the United Nations, the People's Republic of China could scarcely have been considered a Member state. In view of the claim of the Peiping Government that it was the rightful representative of China in the United Nations, it is not surprising that it did not invoke Article 35 (2) of the Charter nor specifically accept the obligations for pacific settlement required by that article. This point was not discussed by the Council. The representative of the National Government of China, in arguing that the Government of the People's Republic of China had no right to bring any matter to the attention of the Council, stressed the nonrepresentative character of that regime.

Technically speaking, none of the questions that the General Assembly has considered has been submitted by a state that was not a Member of the United Nations. Two complaints, similar to those brought to the Council by the People's Republic of China, were included in the agenda of the Assembly in 1950. One, however, was brought to the Assembly by the Soviet Union. The second, the Soviet Union "supported," and at the suggestion of the United States, it was included in the agenda as a complaint by the Soviet Union.[12]

One reason the interpretation of Article 35(2) has not come up more frequently in the Council or the Assembly has been that usually some Member of the United Nations has assumed the initiative in submitting a question. India and Australia, for example, in 1947 brought the Indonesian question to the Security Council. And El Salvador asked the Assembly in 1950 to consider an appeal by Tibet concerning the invasion by the People's Republic of China.

Whether an appeal will be considered as coming within the provisions of Article 35(2) would seem to depend in large measure on the attitude taken by the Secretary-General, who has the responsibility for the circulation of documents and an important role in the preparation of the provisional agenda of the Council and the Assembly. In the original Rules of Procedure of the General Assembly, there was no specific provision for the inclusion on its agenda

[12] U.N. General Assembly, Fifth Session, General Committee, *Official Records*, 71st Meeting (Oct. 5, 1950), pp. 13-14.

of questions submitted by states not Members of the United Nations. It was considered that these matters would be brought to the attention of the Assembly by the Secretary-General who has the responsibility for drawing up the provisional agenda.

The original communications from Hyderabad in August 1947 asking the Secretary-General to bring to the attention of the Security Council "the grave dispute" between Hyderabad and India were circulated with a prefatory note by the Secretary-General to the effect that, not being in a position to determine whether the circulation of the documents was required by the Provisional Rules of the Council, he was bringing the communications to the attention of the Council for such action as it might desire to take.[13] While the Secretary-General, under the Provisional Rules is responsible for preparing the provisional agenda of the Council, his proposals must have the President's approval. Consequently, the President is in a position to exercise an important influence on any decision whether or not an appeal comes under the terms of Article 35(2). The manner in which the Tunisian question was brought before the Security Council is significant in this connection. In January 1952 (ironically, while France held the presidency of the Council), the Prime Minister of Tunisia addressed to the Council a letter citing Article 35(2) and bringing an alleged dispute with France to the attention of that organ. The communication was not circulated as a document of the Council, however, until the end of March,[14] just before Pakistan assumed the presidency and a group of Arab-Asian states asked that the Tunisian question be considered.[15]

An additional point that might be mentioned in connection with the submission of questions by states not Members of the United Nations is an interpretation given by one of the committees at the San Francisco Conference to the effect that former enemy states shall not have the right of recourse to the Security Council or the General Assembly until the Security Council has given them that right.[16] This statement has never been discussed in the United

[13] U.N. Docs. S/986 (Aug. 21, 1948), 998 (Sept. 12, 1948), and 1000 (Sept. 13, 1948). Rule 6 is the one to which reference is made. The full text of this rule and the texts of all other rules of the Security Council to which reference is made in this study are given in App. D.

[14] U.N. Doc. S/2571 (Mar. 31, 1952).

[15] U.N. Docs. 2574-84 (Apr. 2, 1952).

[16] U.N. Information Organizations and U.S. Library of Congress, *Documents of the United Nations Conference on International Organization*, Vol. 12 (1945), p. 560.

Nations. Those questions of direct concern to former enemy states have been submitted by Member states. For example, at the request of the Chancellor of the West German Government, France, the United Kingdom, and the United States asked that the Assembly appoint a commission to investigate whether conditions obtained throughout Germany for the holding of free elections. It should be noted, however, that the interpretation given at San Francisco regarding the rights of former enemy states applies only to the Assembly and the Council and not to the International Court of Justice. As noted previously, one dispute has been submitted to the Court by a former enemy state—Italy. Italy, although not a party to the Statute of the Court, filed a declaration accepting its jurisdiction, thereby complying with the resolution of the Security Council establishing the conditions under which the Court was open to states not parties to the Statute.

The Secretary-General

The Secretary-General has been most cautious in exercising his power under Article 99 of the Charter to bring to the attention of the Security Council any matter that in his opinion might threaten the maintenance of international peace and security. He has at various times intervened for the purpose of presenting to the Council his views on matters that the Council is considering, and he has on occasion mentioned the possibility that he might, on his own initiative, propose that the Council consider a particular dispute or situation. On the outbreak of hostilities in Korea in June 1950, the United Nations Commission on Korea suggested that the Secretary-General consider the possibility of bringing the matter to the attention of the Council. From his speech at the outset of the discussion in the Council, it was clear that had the United States not requested an emergency meeting of the Council to consider the question, the Secretary-General himself would have done so.[17]

Although the Charter contains no provisions authorizing the Secretary-General to bring matters to the attention of the General Assembly, the Rules of Procedure of the Assembly (like those of the Council) provide for the inclusion on the provisional agenda of items proposed by him. Most of the Secretary-General's proposals

[17] U.N. Security Council, Fifth Year, *Official Records*, No. 15, 473rd Meeting (June 25, 1950), p. 3. See also, Trygve Lie, *In the Cause of Peace* (1954), pp. 327-30.

have concerned matters of an organizational character. It was through his action, however, that the report of the United Nations Mediator for Palestine was included on the agenda of the third session of the Assembly. The major question of a "political" character that the Secretary-General on his own initiative has proposed was his twenty-year peace program. When this program was first circulated to Members in the spring of 1950, the Secretary-General indicated that he might ask the Council to consider it and also that he might submit it to the Assembly.[18] Within three weeks the Council was preoccupied with the outbreak of hostilities in Korea, and the peace program was not therefore submitted to it. At the request of the Secretary-General, however, the program was considered by the Assembly at its fifth session.

Other Organs

There have been only a few instances in which the consideration of a question by one organ of the United Nations has resulted from an initiative taken by another.[19] The General Assembly has on various occasions requested advisory opinions from the International Court of Justice, but the only question relating to an actual dispute or situation on which such an opinion has been sought concerned the obligations of Bulgaria, Hungary, and Rumania under the provisions of the peace treaties.[20]

The Assembly has made a number of recommendations to the Security Council concerning such matters as the regulation of armaments, the admission of new Members, voting procedure in the Council, and other questions of an organizational nature. In two situations the Assembly has addressed requests to the Council. The first resolution of the Assembly on the Spanish question recommended that the Council consider "adequate measures to be taken" should certain conditions not obtain in Spain, and at a later session the Assembly expressed "its confidence" that the Council would exercise its responsibilities under the Charter should the situation so require.[21] Neither of these resolutions was discussed in the Coun-

[18] *United Nations Bulletin*, Vol. 8, No. 12 (June 15, 1950), p. 511.

[19] For example, the Security Council or the General Assembly. It is, of course, to be understood that in order for either of these organs to take such an initiative, the question must have been submitted to it in the first place by one of the procedures already described.

[20] Res. 294 (IV), Oct. 22, 1949.

[21] Res. 39 (I), Dec. 12, 1946, and Res. 114 (II), Nov. 17, 1947.

cil. The Assembly request that the Security Council take certain measures in connection with the implementation of the plan for the partition of Palestine[22] was, however, considered at length.

The Assembly has considered a number of questions that have been previously discussed in the Council and subsequently brought to the Assembly as a result of the failure of the Council to reach a decision. Proposals that the Council request the Assembly to make recommendations on particular disputes or situations have been made, but none has been adopted. The Soviet Union vetoed a proposal to refer the question of Greek frontier incidents to the Assembly and also vetoed a proposed recommendation by the Council that the Assembly adopt certain measures on the Spanish question. Both of these questions were, however, brought to the Assembly independently by Member states. In the spring of 1948, when it had become apparent that the plan for the partition of Palestine, which the Assembly had adopted some months previously, could not be carried out by peaceful means, the United States suggested that the Security Council recommend to the Assembly the establishment of a temporary trusteeship for Palestine. The suggestion did not receive the support of the Council, but, on the initiative of the Council, a special session of the Assembly was convoked.

Form of Submission

A question is submitted to the Security Council or the General Assembly by means of a written communication that usually contains a specific request that the question be placed on the agenda.[23] In the case of the Council, there is often a request that a meeting be called to take up the question.

There are few rules concerning the form of submission. There has been considerable variation in the practice of the Council and the Assembly with regard to both the amount of information submitted at this initial stage and the extent to which the submitting state indicates what, in its opinion, is the nature of the question and the steps that the Council or the Assembly should take. Sometimes

---

[22] Res. 181 (II), Nov. 29, 1947.

[23] During the discussion of a question, Member states have on occasion attempted to raise a related question. Despite the fact that both the Council and the Assembly have generally been very liberal with regard to the matters considered relevant to questions on their agenda, they have in some instances insisted that the discussion of new matters was out of order and have required that separate requests be made for the inclusion of the matters in their agenda.

the letter of submission has merely set out the title of a proposed agenda item; in other cases, such as the Hyderabad complaint, the Berlin question, and the treatment of Indians in South Africa, a considerable amount of documentation has either accompanied or followed the initial request.

In both the Council and the Assembly, there has been some discussion concerning the desirability of requiring more information from the submitting state. It has been suggested that a state bringing a dispute or situation to the attention of the Council should submit evidence that it is of the nature described in Article 34 of the Charter and that the state should give an explanation of the steps that have been taken to comply with the requirements of Article 33 of the Charter.[24] The Assembly in 1949 adopted a new rule of procedure to the effect that "all items proposed for inclusion in the agenda shall be accompanied by an explanatory memorandum and, if possible, by basic documents or by a draft resolution."[25] The memorandum, but not the documentation or draft resolution, has been considered obligatory. This addition to the rules constituted some improvement over previous procedure. Both the Council and the Assembly might benefit, however, if more information were made available to them at this initial stage in their proceedings.

Under the Statute of the International Court of Justice, if a case is brought by means of a special agreement between the parties, the notification to the Court must indicate the subject of the dispute and the parties. If a case is brought by means of an application by one of the parties, the Rules of the Court require that the application must in addition, in so far as possible, specify the provision on which the "applicant founds the jurisdiction of the Court," state the precise nature of the claim, and give a succinct statement of the facts and grounds on which the claim is based.[26] Although such a rule would not be directly applicable to the Council and the Assembly, it would seem that the two organs could benefit by encouraging the submitting state to give a more precise indication regarding the nature of the question and the type of action desired.

[24] U.N. Docs. A/AC.18/49 (Mar. 18, 1948), and A/AC.18/17 (Feb. 10, 1948).

[25] Rule 20. The full text of this rule and the texts of all other rules of procedure of the General Assembly to which reference is made in this study are given in App. E.

[26] See Art. 40 of the Statute of the Court and Art. 32(2) of the Rules of the Court. The rules of the Court can be found in: International Court of Justice, *Charter of the United Nations, Statutes and Rules of the Court and Other Related Documents,* Court Publication Series D 1 (1947).

Nature of the Questions

States submitting questions to the Security Council have usually referred to Article 35 of the Charter, and often the Council has been requested to undertake an investigation in accordance with Article 34. In some cases, it has been alleged that a threat to the peace exists, as in the Berlin question, or that a breach of the peace has been committed, as in the Indonesian case. The Security Council has in a few instances been asked to exercise its powers under Chapter VII of the Charter. There have been occasional references to other articles. Egypt, for example, cited Article 37 in bringing its dispute with the United Kingdom to the Council. In a number of cases, the submitting state has cited its efforts to settle the dispute in compliance with Article 33 of the Charter before bringing it to the Council. There have been less frequent references to the Charter in the communications submitting questions to the General Assembly. Occasionally, a state has referred to the broad powers of the Assembly under Articles 10 and 14 or has alleged that there has been a violation of the Purposes and Principles of the Charter, but there has never been any reference to Article 35.

Many of the questions submitted to the Council and the Assembly have been in the nature of charges that one state is interfering in the internal affairs of another. There have been charges of direct intervention or aggression, as in the case of the complaint of aggression on the Republic of Korea, the complaint of the invasion of Tibet, the Hyderabad complaint, and the charges by the People's Republic of China of aggression by the United States. The Soviet Union was also charged with direct intervention in the affairs of Czechoslovakia in connection with the Communist coup in that country in 1948. The Council, during its first years of operation, considered a number of cases, such as the Iranian, Syrian-Lebanese, and Egyptian questions, in which the central issue was the presence of foreign troops on the territory of a Member of the United Nations. In other cases, the issue was an allegation of support being given by one state to forces working for the overthrow of the established government in another state. This was the basis of the charges made by Greece against Albania, Yugoslavia, and Bulgaria in 1946 and by Nationalist China against the Soviet Union in 1949. The principal charge made by India in bringing its dispute with Pakistan to the Council was the alleged support given by Pakistan to irregular forces in Kashmir. The Yugoslav complaint against the Soviet bloc in November 1951 was that these states were organizing and exercising aggressive pressure for the purpose of threatening its territorial integrity and national independence. The members of the Soviet bloc have repeatedly brought to the General Assembly a complaint that the United States was interfering in their internal affairs by organizing subversive and espionage activities.

In many cases it has been charged that a state by its actions is either failing to carry out, or acting contrary to, its obligations under international treaties or agreements. The question of the observance of human rights and fundamental freedoms in Hungary, Bulgaria, and Rumania was primarily a controversy over the alleged failure of the three states to carry out their obligations under the peace treaties. The basis of the Yugoslav complaint over Trieste in 1948 was that the United States and the United Kingdom were acting contrary to their obligations under the Italian peace treaty. Other cases involving alleged violation of international agreements were the Iranian complaint against the Soviet Union, the Anglo-Iranian oil dispute, the Berlin question, the Nationalist Chinese charges against the Soviet Union, the question of the treatment of Indians in South Africa, and the Indonesian and Hyderabad questions.

In addition to the charges of violation of specific treaties binding only on a limited number of states, there have been many instances in which violation of the Charter has been alleged. The two Charter provisions most often singled out in this connection have been those relating to the obligations of Members to refrain from the use or threat of force and the duty of Members to co-operate in promoting human rights and fundamental freedoms. The latter has been invoked repeatedly in connection with the racial policies of the Union of South Africa. The Moroccan question also was originally brought to the Assembly as a complaint of French violation of the principles of the Charter and the Universal Declaration of Human Rights.

Many of the questions that the United Nations has been called upon to consider have arisen in connection with the efforts to conclude peace settlements following the Second World War. In accordance with the terms of the Italian peace treaty, the Security Council was asked to accept certain responsibilities in regard to the Free Territory of Trieste, and the General Assembly was asked to decide the disposal of the former Italian colonies if the four powers (France, the United Kingdom, the United States, and the

Soviet Union) failed to arrive at an agreement. The United Nations has dealt with two questions arising from failure to reach an agreement on the terms of a peace treaty for Germany: first, the situation concerning the rights of the occupying powers in Berlin; and second, the request for a United Nations commission to investigate whether conditions obtained throughout Germany for the holding of free elections. In 1952, the Assembly was asked to consider an appeal to the signatories of the Moscow Declaration of November 1, 1943 for an early fulfillment of their pledges to Austria. The only issue dealt with by the United Nations as a direct result of failure to agree on a peace settlement for the Far East was the problem of the independence of Korea, brought to the General Assembly by the United States.

The use of the machinery of the United Nations for the purposes of achieving political adjustments has not, of course, been restricted to problems arising from the peace settlements. One of the most important questions that the United Nations has been called upon to consider was the problem of the future government of Palestine. The Moroccan, Tunisian, and Indonesian questions were all essentially problems of political adjustment.

Although the United Nations has been concerned primarily with specific disputes and situations, a number of questions of a more general nature have been submitted to the General Assembly. The discussions in the Assembly concerning general principles for the maintenance of international peace and security have arisen primarily in connection with proposals concerning the regulation of armaments. They have taken place on the basis of the reports from various subsidiary organs charged with responsibility for working out plans for the regulation of armaments and also on the basis of the "omnibus" proposals, which some member of the Soviet bloc has introduced at almost every session. These proposals, allegedly designed to remove the threat of a new war and to improve the friendly relations among nations, have been primarily concerned with the outlawing of atomic weapons and the limitation and reduction of other armaments. They have also covered such matters as war propaganda, the North Atlantic Treaty Organization, and appeals for the conclusion of a five-power peace pact.

Other discussions of a general nature have taken place during the consideration of various proposals for "strengthening" the United Nations system for the maintenance of international peace and security. Some of the more important of these discussions occurred when the Assembly was considering the reports of the Interim Committee, the Secretary-General's twenty-year program for achieving peace through the United Nations, the "Uniting for Peace" resolution, and the reports of the Collective Measures Committee. Another question with broad implications was the Mexican proposal, considered by the Assembly in 1948, of an appeal to the great powers to compose their differences.

As previously noted most of the questions brought to the United Nations have directly concerned either (1) the conflicts of interest between the United States and the Soviet Union and their respective allies, or (2) the efforts of the peoples throughout Asia, Africa, and the Middle East to establish and strengthen their independence.[27] There have been few issues arising out of these two basic conflicts that have not been discussed at some time in the United Nations, but there have been some notable exceptions. Down to the end of 1953, the situation in Indochina had not been brought to the United Nations nor had a few "colonial" disputes, such as the controversy between India on the one hand and France and Portugal on the other over the colonial possessions on the Indian sub-continent. Similarly, a few issues between the Soviet bloc and the West, such as the navigation of the Danube and the Dardanelles question, have not been considered.

In some cases, it has been clear that consideration by the United Nations would not help to achieve a settlement, and in others, states have apparently deemed it more to their advantage to proceed through channels other than the United Nations. For example, although the United Nations has been asked to consider a number of questions that have arisen as a result of the failure of the major powers to agree on the peace settlements, it has not been asked to play a direct role in working out settlements for Japan, Germany, or Austria. There have been numerous and acrimonious exchanges concerning the treatment of aliens behind the Iron Curtain and the shooting down of planes, and it has been suggested that some of these incidents and a few other disputes, such as the controversy between the United States and the Soviet Union over lend-lease, be submitted to the International Court of Justice. Clearly, the main obstacle to the consideration of these matters by the Court has been that the members of the Soviet bloc have not

[27] See above, Chap. III.

accepted the compulsory jurisdiction of the Court and have shown little inclination to submit questions to the Court or to agree to their submission.

To the end of 1953, no questions involving the relations between states that are members of an established grouping, such as the North Atlantic Treaty Organization, the Arab League, the Organization of American States, and the Soviet bloc, have been brought to the attention of either the Security Council or the General Assembly. It is scarcely surprising that disputes between members of the Soviet bloc have not been brought to the United Nations because conflicts of interest are not presumed to arise among them. It is significant, however, that the same has been true of other regional or limited-membership organizations. For example, the complaint of Costa Rica in December 1948 that its territory had been invaded by armed forces coming from Nicaragua was communicated to the President of the Council but was not placed on the agenda of the Council. Presumably, this was because of the receipt of a communication a few days later from the Chairman of the Council of the Organization of American States stating that initial steps to deal with the question had already been taken by that Organization. Since 1949, differences between the Dominican Republic and other Caribbean states have also been handled by the organs and procedures of that organization. The Security Council in accordance with Article 54 of the Charter was informed, however, of the action taken.

There are many reasons that questions involving relations between members of established groupings of states have not been submitted to the Assembly and the Council. In the first place, the Charter itself in Articles 33 and 52, encourages Members to settle their disputes through regional arrangements or by regional agencies.[28] Furthermore, members of such regional groupings—the Organization of American States is a good example—are in some instances obligated by the terms of the basic agreement to use regional organs and procedures that have been established. In addition, states that have common interests and attitudes sufficiently strong to induce them to enter into regional peace and security arrangements are likely to prefer the use of procedures that limit active

[28] For comment on the relationships between peaceful settlement under the United Nations and the Organization of American States, see U.N. General Assembly, Fifth Session, *Official Records*, Supplement No. 14, pp. 7-8.

participation in the working out of the settlement of their differences to states of similar interests and attitudes. Finally, decisive influence may be exerted by a leading member of a group to prevent disputes arising between members of the group from being brought before the Council or the Assembly when the special interests of that particular member may not be best served thereby.

In the International Court of Justice, however, the situation is largely reversed. The Court has been asked to consider: a conflict between two Latin American states; two cases involving states in the Western Hemisphere and Western European states; and a number of disputes between European states outside the Soviet bloc. Only one dispute has involved a member of the Soviet bloc. In three cases Western European states have submitted disputes with states in the Middle East. In contrast to the questions submitted to the Council and the Assembly, most of the disputes considered by the Court have involved states that normally enjoy friendly relations.

Circumstances of Submission

Without going into the background of the various questions that have been submitted to the United Nations, a few general observations may be made concerning the circumstances in which questions affecting international peace and security have been submitted to organs of the United Nations.

Underlying Reasons

There are many possible reasons for a decision to submit questions to the Security Council or the General Assembly. In many of the cases involving charges of interference by one state in the internal affairs of another, for example, it may be believed that the United Nations can make a contribution to the favorable settlement of the problem by applying pressure on the states concerned to desist from certain acts or to undertake certain measures. Again, in such questions as that of Palestine or of the disposal of the former Italian colonies, it may be hoped that the United Nations will be able to find a solution to a problem that the parties directly interested have been unable to settle by agreement among themselves. There may be a desire to shift some of the responsibility to the United Nations, or a state may wish to enlist the support of the international community in carrying out a program that it feels incapable of undertaking alone, as in the Korean question. The submitting state may wish to convince public opinion both at home and abroad of its devotion to the United Nations and its determination to seek a solution by every available peaceful means, considerations that possibly influenced the decisions to bring the Berlin and the Anglo-Iranian questions to the Security Council. A state may wish to get recognition by the international community of the seriousness of a situation, as in the Yugoslav complaint against the Soviet bloc. In those instances in which it is quite clear that neither the Council nor the Assembly can make any real contribution to a settlement, a state may hope that other Members on their own initiative will give it some support or it may feel that, after a demonstration of the recalcitrance and unreasonableness of the other party, it will appear more fully justified in pursuing a unilateral course of action.

All too frequently the Council and the Assembly have been asked to consider questions when it has been apparent that they could do little but register the moral indignation of Members by condemning the policies or actions of certain states. A few examples of this have been the questions concerning: alleged Soviet intervention in Czechoslovakia; the racial policies of the Union of South Africa; and the observance of human rights and fundamental freedoms in Bulgaria, Hungary, and Rumania. Of a similar nature have been those questions submitted by the states in the Soviet bloc in which it was clear that no action at all would be taken, and the Council or the Assembly was to be used merely as a propaganda forum.

Attitude of the Parties Concerned

In view of the nature of the questions submitted to the United Nations, it is understandable that the parties directly concerned have seldom agreed that the matter was suitable for consideration by the United Nations.[29] Even when disputes have been submitted to the International Court of Justice, the parties have usually been unable to agree on the terms of submission. The dispute over the

---

[29] The specific objections that have been raised to the consideration of questions are dealt with later in this study.

Channel islands was brought by means of a special agreement between France and the United Kingdom. Albania and the United Kingdom eventually agreed on the questions to be submitted to the Court in connection with the incidents in the Corfu Channel. Most efforts to work out special agreements have, however, been unsuccessful, and the majority of cases have been submitted by means of an application by one of the parties invoking the compulsory jurisdiction of the Court.

Even less often have the parties directly concerned concurred in the submission of a question to the General Assembly or the Security Council. With regard to the Security Council, although certain provisions of the Charter, such as Articles 37 and 38, seem to envisage a situation in which all the parties might join in submitting a dispute to the Council, there has never been such a submission. In fact, seldom have the parties agreed that any question was suitable for consideration by the Council or the Assembly. The outstanding exceptions have been the two matters brought to the United Nations in connection with the Italian peace treaty when France, the United Kingdom, the United States, and the Union of Soviet Socialist Republics jointly asked the Council to endorse the statute for Trieste and jointly brought the question of the disposal of the former Italian colonies to the Assembly. These same four powers, together with China and Canada, also joined in making proposals to the General Assembly in 1946 for the establishment of the United Nations Atomic Energy Commission.

Timing of Submission

In many cases a request for the consideration of a question by the Security Council or the General Assembly has been preceded by some decisive event, such as the outbreak of hostilities in Korea in 1950 or in Indonesia in 1947, the trial of church leaders in Hungary and Bulgaria in 1949, and the deposing of the Sultan of Morocco in 1953. Occasionally, questions have been submitted for the purpose of forestalling imminent action. The Anglo-Iranian case, for example, was submitted to the International Court of Justice by the United Kingdom in May 1951 in an effort to prevent Iran from carrying out the Oil Nationalization Act that had been enacted by the Iranian Parliament. The request by the United Kingdom that the Council consider the case later in September was likewise prompted by a desire to put pressure on Iran to revoke an expulsion order that was just about to go into effect. One reason the Nationalist Chinese charges against the Soviet Union were brought to the Assembly in 1949 was a desire to forestall recognition of the People's Republic of China.

Obvious difficulties are encountered when questions are submitted as a result of some decisive event or the imminent threat of some unilateral action. The atmosphere in which the discussions take place is apt to be highly charged, and the desire for prompt action may militate against a calm consideration of the best course of action based upon adequate information. Fortunately, perhaps, both organs are somewhat cumbersome in their operations, and neither has shown an inclination for precipitate action. The reluctance to restrict discussion in any way and the wide variety of opinion that has sought expression have made it almost impossible for either organ to act with any degree of promptness.

In most instances a question has been submitted to the United Nations only after a state has concluded that it is impossible to reach a solution by normal diplomatic means. A great many of the questions submitted to the United Nations have had a long history of unsuccessful efforts to reach an agreement. This is particularly true in regard to questions submitted to the International Court. The Ambatielos case between the United Kingdom and Greece, for example, involved charges dating back to 1919.

Questions submitted to the Assembly have often been the subject of exhaustive previous efforts at settlement. The United Kingdom brought the Palestine question to the Assembly in 1947 after repeated failures to work out a plan for the future of Palestine acceptable to the Jews and the Arabs. Lengthy discussions in the Council of Foreign Ministers and the meetings of their deputies on the question of disposing of the former Italian colonies preceded the submission of it to the Assembly. The problem of the independence of Korea was presented to the Assembly by the United States after a deadlock had occurred between the Soviet Union and the United States over the manner in which Korean independence was to be realized.

The Charter itself, of course, encourages states to make every effort to settle their disputes before bringing them to the Council. The obligation of prior effort has not been considered a bar to the submission of questions, but Members have on occasion protested that a state has not sought a solution by negotiations prior to submitting a question to the United Nations. There are good reasons for the Organization to encourage states to seek a solution of their disputes before bringing them to the United Nations, but it must be pointed out that one result of such a delay may be that, by the time the matter is considered in the United Nations, the situation may have become so aggravated and the positions of the parties so crystallized that it is exceedingly difficult for the Organization to bring about a peaceful settlement.

Considerations Influencing the Choice of Organ

In deciding whether to bring a question to the attention of one or another of the organs of the United Nations, a state must consider which organ is most likely to adopt the course of action desired or which will provide the most auspicious forum for the discussion of the question. The two principal factors that influence the choice of organ are: (1) the differentiation in the powers and functions of the organs, and (2) differences in their composition and methods of operation.

Under the Charter system for the maintenance of international peace and security, each of the organs, the Security Council, the General Assembly, and the International Court, has a distinct role to perform. The reasons a particular question is brought to one rather than another of these organs are to be found in large measure in the special role assigned to each under the Charter system.

The authors of the Charter assumed that the Security Council, which is given the primary responsibility for the maintenance of international peace and security, would be principally concerned with disputes or situations of a truly serious nature. They gave the Council special powers to deal with threats to the peace, breaches of the peace, and acts of aggression. Even though questions relating to the maintenance of international peace and security have been handled by the Assembly to a much greater extent than was expected, this special responsibility of the Council has continued to be recognized by the Members themselves and by the Assembly.

Almost without exception, in any case in which a threat to the peace is alleged to exist or a breach of the peace or act of aggression has allegedly been committed, the question has been submitted, at least initially, to the Security Council. The Assembly has recognized the special role of the Council in specific cases such as Palestine, when the Council was asked to take certain steps if a threat to the peace developed. Furthermore, under the "Uniting for Peace" resolution, which was largely directed toward enabling the Assembly to deal effectively with threats to the peace, breaches of the peace, and acts of aggression, it is contemplated that the Assembly will deal with such questions only if the Council, because of the lack of unanimity among its permanent members, fails to exercise its primary responsibility for the maintenance of international peace and security.[30] Again, because of the special responsibility of the Council under the Charter, the Anglo-Iranian question was submitted to it. The United Kingdom, in presenting the case to the Council, specifically cited Article 94(2) of the Charter and asked the Council, in accordance with that Article, to call upon Iran to comply with the preliminary measures indicated by the International Court of Justice.[31]

Many questions have obviously been submitted to the General Assembly because of its broad powers of discussion and recommendation. Some of the disputes and situations have not been of such a serious character that they would have been suitable for consideration by the Council in accordance with the theory of the Charter. Moreover, the specific authorization to the Assembly to consider general principles of international co-operation and the special role assigned to it in connection with the promotion of human rights and fundamental freedoms have accounted for the submission of a number of questions to the Assembly.

The Charter recognizes that as a general rule "legal disputes" should be submitted to the International Court of Justice. The compulsory jurisdiction clause, Article 36(2) of the Statute, indicates the types of disputes considered especially appropriate for submission to the Court. These include "all legal disputes concerning: (a) the interpretation of a treaty; (b) any question of international law; (c) the existence of any fact which, if established, would constitute a breach of an international obligation; (d) the nature or extent of the reparation to be made for the breach of an interna-

[30] Pt. A, Sec. A (1). See App. F.

[31] U.N. Security Council, Sixth Year, *Official Records*, 559th Meeting (Oct. 1, 1951), pp. 3 and 11 ff.

tional obligation." The principal considerations influencing the decision to submit a case to the Court have been (1) whether the submitting state considers the case a legal dispute, (2) the extent to which considerations such as national prestige, national security, or the requirements of the domestic political situation are decisive, and (3) whether the states concerned have accepted the compulsory jurdisdiction of the Court under Article 36(2) of the Statute or under other agreements. There is a certain advantage, especially for a state that is convinced that the law is on its side, in bringing a case to the Court rather than to the Council or the Assembly, because a decision by the Court is normally based on international law and is "binding" on the parties, while a decision by the Assembly or by the Council on terms of settlement may be in the nature of a compromise and is merely a "recommendation." For the most part, the disputes submitted to the Court have not concerned matters of great importance to the parties nor have they been of such a serious nature that international peace and security could be considered in any way endangered.[32]

In the course of the consideration of some questions by the Council or the Assembly, notably the question of incidents in the Corfu Channel, the Yugoslav complaint concerning Trieste, and the Nationalist Chinese charges against the Soviet Union, the opinion has been expressed that the issues were more suitable for consideration by the Court. In only one case has the Security Council recommended that a dispute be referred to the Court—the question of the incidents in the Corfu Channel—and this recommendation was made only after the Soviet Union had blocked a proposal of the United Kingdom for a finding by the Council itself. In other cases where a dispute, or at least some of the issues in dispute, might properly have been submitted to the Court but instead were brought to the Council or the Assembly, such as the Anglo-Egyptian question and the question of the treatment of Indians in South Africa, it has been clear that the submitting state did not desire to have the matter decided on strictly legal grounds. Although the Statute of the Court provides that the Court may decide a case *ex aequo et bono* if the parties agree, Article 38 of the Statute makes clear that in general it is the function of the Court to decide disputes "in accordance with international law." As noted previ-

---

[32] An outstanding exception is the Anglo-Iranian case.

ously, it has been primarily the Western European states that have submitted questions to the Court. The Members of the Soviet bloc, and, with few exceptions, the Arab-Asian states have shown little predilection to use the Court for the settlement of disputes.

There are many factors besides the role assigned by the Charter to the Council and the Assembly that influence the decision whether to bring a question to one or the other. In submitting a question to the Assembly, a state must consider whether it has a broad enough basis of support for its position to obtain the adoption of a resolution by the required two-thirds of the members present and voting. In submitting a question to the Council, a state must take into account that it may be impossible to obtain the adoption of the course of action it desires, either because at least seven members will not support its case or because one of the permanent members of the Council will exercise its right of veto on the proposal.

The most important factor influencing the submission of questions to the Assembly rather than to the Council has been the failure of the Council, because of the inability of the permanent members to agree, to perform the role originally envisaged for it under the Charter. Because the Charter provisions concerning the voting procedure of the Council permit a permanent member to prevent the Council from taking action, some questions have been transferred to the Assembly after the Council has failed to act. Other questions, which might have been brought to the Council, have been submitted directly to the Assembly because of the likelihood that a veto would block action by the Council.

Even aside from the point whether a permanent member of the Security Council will by its veto prevent action on a particular question, the failure of the permanent members to agree has had the added effect that the force behind a resolution that the Council adopts is considerably less than was originally intended by the drafters of the Charter. The failure to conclude agreements under Article 43 to make forces available to the Security Council has meant that the Council has not been in a position to order measures under Article 42. This has weakened the authority of the Council all along the line. Moreover, the practice of abstention, while it has allowed the Council to act in some cases where a permanent member is not willing to support a measure but does not desire to block action, has weakened the effectiveness of many recommendations by the Council, for it was originally assumed that such a recommendation would have great influence precisely because it had the support of all the permanent members.

In these circumstances, the broad powers of the General Assembly have taken on an added significance. The Assembly is, by the very fact that it is composed of all the Members of the Organization, the more appropriate organ for considering not only broad questions of international political co-operation but also any program that is primarily dependent for its implementation upon the actions of all the members of the international community. When the Security Council either cannot or does not wish to adopt, on behalf of the Members of the Organization, the binding measures that are open to it under Chapter VII of the Charter, there remains the possibility of exercising pressure through the combined efforts of the Members of the Organization acting on the basis of a recommendation by the Assembly. There are, of course, obvious advantages in having such a recommendation passed with the support of as large a portion of the membership as possible. Thus when the majority of the Council concluded that the Spanish question did not justify action under Chapter VII of the Charter, they attempted to transfer the question to the Assembly in order that the whole membership could join in support of a declaration on the question and a recommendation that Members terminate diplomatic relations with Franco Spain. It was felt that, even though the action could be taken by the Council itself, the Assembly was the more appropriate organ to adopt such a recommendation.

Despite the almost total lack of agreement among the permanent members of the Council, there have been relatively few questions, although admittedly they have been of great importance, that have been brought to the Assembly as a result of the failure of the Council to act. On the question of the Greek frontier incidents and the question of the intervention by the Chinese Communists in Korea, the proposals supported by the majority in the Council were vetoed by the Soviet Union, and the Soviet proposals were unacceptable to the other members. The majority considered it essential that the United Nations continue handling these two questions. Both were submitted to the Assembly, which was asked to carry out substantially the same program as the Council had been unable to adopt. Although the Assembly performed an important role in the subsequent handling of these two questions, in other cases, such as the charges by the People's Republic of China against the United States, the deadlock in the Council was merely repeated in the Assembly.

In a great many cases either the use of the veto has not prevented the Council from carrying out its program, or other procedures have been agreed upon for handling the question. The veto of proposals on the Indonesian and Palestine questions, for example, did not prevent the Council from continuing to seek a settlement along the lines previously adopted. The Syrian-Lebanese question and the Berlin question were settled directly by the parties concerned, and the question of incidents in the Corfu Channel was referred to the Court. In fact, only the veto in the Czechoslovak question resulted in the abandonment of further efforts to deal with the question.

In view of the use that the Soviet Union had made of its veto privilege, there was little reason to assume that the Council would be able to adopt any resolution unfavorable to the Soviet Union or to the states allied with it. Regardless of this fact, the Council was asked to take up a number of complaints against the members of the Soviet bloc, but it has had little success in dealing with them. In some cases, either immediate action was desired at a time when the Assembly was not in session, or action was called for under Chapter VII of the Charter. For these reasons, the complaint of aggression against the Republic of Korea was brought to the attention of the Council. The Berlin question, which from the point of time could have been brought to either the Assembly or the Council, was brought to the latter organ with a request for action under Chapter VII. The Western powers appear to have preferred to force the Soviet Union to account for its actions in the Council even though it was clear that it would be likely to veto any draft resolution put forward. It should also be noted that, even if the Assembly had adopted the type of resolution the Western powers desired, there is little reason to believe it would have had any effect on the situation.

Many questions directly involving the Soviet Union and its allies such as the Yugoslav complaint against the Soviet bloc, the Nationalist Chinese charges against the Soviet Union, and the observance of human rights and fundamental freedoms were brought directly to the Assembly. The submission of questions to the Assembly has been prompted not only by the realization that the Soviet Union was likely to veto any proposals in the Council but also because the submitting states wished to obtain as broad a support as possible for their positions. The question of free German elections and the problem of the independence of Korea, for example, were brought directly to the Assembly. In these two cases, the submitting states had a program that they wished the United Nations to carry out, a program that could be adopted by the Assembly, and one for which the support of the international community was desired. With psychological warfare assuming great importance in the cold war, the General Assembly as the highly publicized town meeting of the world has seemed to offer a much more promising forum than the Council for propaganda to influence public opinion. This has been an important consideration in many instances in influencing states to bring questions before the Assembly.

The Council, unlike the Assembly, is in continuous session, and there have been a few questions brought to it that might have been submitted to the Assembly had it been in session when the issue arose. This difference between the two organs is mitigated by the tendency of the Assembly to remain in session throughout an increasingly greater part of the year. It is, of course, always open to a state to request a special session of the Assembly although it is rather difficult to obtain the support of the majority of the entire membership for such a session, as is required.

On the other hand, some questions have been brought to the Assembly precisely because it either was in session or was soon to be in session. It is questionable, for example, whether the Indonesian question would have been brought to the Assembly had that organ not decided to hold a second part of its third session in the spring of 1949. The second Netherlands "police action" occurred in December shortly after the Assembly had adjourned. When the Assembly reconvened, the negotiations were not making much progress. At this point, Australia and India submitted the question to the Assembly in order to muster the pressure of the whole of the international community against the Netherlands. Shortly after the submission, an agreement was reached, and no action was taken by the Assembly. Had the agreement been reached earlier, it is probable that the Indonesian question would have remained the exclusive concern of the Security Council.

In theory, it would seem to be to the advantage of the small powers to bring questions to the Assembly, in which they constitute a majority, and to the advantage of the permanent members to submit questions to the Council. In practice, however, many questions have been brought to the Council by small powers, and all the permanent members of the Council have at one time or another submitted questions to the Assembly. Many of the smaller powers, however, consider it in their interest to continue to build up the role of the Assembly, for it is possible that on some questions they are more likely to obtain a sympathetic hearing in the Assembly than in the Council. The Latin American states, for example, are among the staunchest advocates of a predominant role for the Assembly and with the exception of the Czechoslovak question, which arose at a time when the Assembly was not in session, have submitted questions to the Assembly rather than to the Council. However, the natural suspicion that the small powers might be expected to harbor against a council under the control of the big powers has failed to develop in large measure because the Security Council has not been able to exercise much of the power assigned to it under the Charter.

A study of practice regarding the submission of questions to the organs of the United Nations raises two issues: (1) whether any changes should be made regarding the rights and obligations of states, and (2) whether any changes should be made in the procedure by which questions are submitted. With regard to the procedure of submission, it is possible that the handling of questions by the Security Council or the General Assembly might be improved if states were encouraged to submit more information, and more precise information, in connection with their requests for the consideration of questions. However, the experience of the Assembly since the adoption of the rule concerning the form of submission, does not indicate that this rule has had much effect on the handling of questions. Furthermore, although in a number of cases states have objected to the form in which a question has been submitted, Members have in general been reluctant to impose any technical requirements that might in any way restrict access to the Council or the Assembly.[33]

With regard to the "right" of submission, a study of the experience of the United Nations indicates that however desirable it might be to restrict the matters considered by the Council and perhaps by the Assembly to those of a serious nature that have proved to be

[33] In this connection see the discussion concerning the submission of the Ukrainian complaint against Greece. U.N. Security Council, First Year, *Official Records*, Second Series, No. 4, 53rd Meeting (Aug. 16, 1946), pp. 33-46.

incapable of settlement by other means, it does not appear that any effort to limit the right of Members to bring questions to the attention of the two organs would accomplish this purpose. It is difficult to see how any Member could be prevented from asking the Council or the Assembly to consider any question, and it is for the organ itself to decide whether or not it will accede to the request. The provisions concerning the submission of questions by states not Members of the United Nations are to some extent unclear, but they have caused surprisingly little difficulty. Some improvement might be made in the rather untidy practices followed in the handling of communications from such states, but this is a matter that must be considered within the context of the larger question of the relations of these states to the Organization.

In the light of the experience of the Council with Article 37 of the Charter, or rather the lack of experience, it is not likely that there would be much support for any effort to broaden the obligation of Member states to bring questions to either the Council or the Assembly. Moreover, as it is always open to any Member to request the consideration of a question by the Council or the Assembly, a modification of the obligation to submit questions seems unnecessary to improve the operation of the United Nations system.

Whether in a given situation a state should bring the particular matter to the attention of one of the organs of the United Nations is always a difficult question to answer. A Member merely wishing to obtain the support of the Organization for the policy that it is pursuing or intends to pursue may lay itself open to the charge that it is using the Organization for its own purposes, even though the Member and other Members may be of the opinion that those purposes are identical or at least consonant with the purposes and principles of the United Nations itself. On the other hand, if a Member proceeds with its own program without reference to the United Nations, it may find itself accused of "by-passing" the Organization.

It appears that if any improvements are to be made, they must be through the reconsideration by the Members themselves of the policies they will follow in submitting questions to the United Nations. Such a reconsideration, however, raises a fundamental question regarding the role that Members consider the United Nations should play in the maintenance of international peace and security.

CHAPTER V

The Decision to Consider a Question

ONCE a question has been brought to the attention of the Security Council or the General Assembly, the organ itself decides whether it will consider the matter. The first step has been for the organ to decide whether a particular question should be placed on its agenda. This preliminary decision assumes importance because, although it has not always meant that the question will be fully discussed, it has been considered a prerequisite to such a discussion. There has been considerable difference of opinion regarding the significance of this preliminary decision, the procedure by which it should be reached, and the criteria upon which it should be based.

Procedures for the Inclusion of Questions in the Agenda

In practice almost every question brought to the attention of the Security Council or the General Assembly has been included in its agenda. The decision has not, however, been automatic, and the discussions at this stage of the proceedings have often been lengthy and complicated. It may be useful to begin by examining briefly the procedure that each organ has followed.[1]

The Security Council

The Provisional Rules of Procedure of the Security Council do not deal extensively with the procedure by which the Council decides to consider a question, nor has the practice of the Council been wholly consistent. The rules make no distinction between the procedure for adopting the agenda of a particular meeting and that for including a new item in the agenda of the Council. When the Council meets, it has before it the provisional agenda for that meeting, which has been drawn up by the Secretary-General, approved by the

[1] For a further treatment of this subject, see the volume in this Brookings series, *The Organization and Procedures of the United Nations*.

President, and circulated to the members. The first item is the adoption of the agenda itself. Usually, the agenda includes items that the Council has already decided to consider, and in this circumstance it is generally adopted without discussion and without vote. But in many cases where the provisional agenda has included a new item, disagreements have arisen and, on occasion, it has taken a number of meetings for the Council to reach a decision.

Under the Provisional Rules of Procedure: "The Secretary-General shall immediately bring to the attention of all representatives on the Security Council all communications from States, organs of the United Nations, or the Secretary-General concerning any matter for the consideration of the Security Council in accordance with the provisions of the Charter."[2] The rules further provide that any item brought to the attention of members of the Council under this rule shall be placed on the provisional agenda. Although almost every communication is brought to the attention of members, it has not customarily been put on the provisional agenda unless the text has made clear that such action is necessary. Many resolutions of the General Assembly and communications concerning matters being handled by the Organization of American States, for example, have been circulated as Council documents but not placed on the provisional agenda.

The rules leave considerable discretion to the Secretary-General, but in the last analysis the President of the Council decides what the provisional agenda of any meeting shall contain. As became apparent when the representative of the Soviet Union was President of the Council in August 1950, the President, if he so desires, can formulate the provisional agenda in whatever way he wishes. In this instance, the provisional agenda was heatedly discussed during three meetings, and six votes were required before the Council could even adopt an agenda. Votes on the adoption of the agenda and on any amendment such as changing the wording of an item or the priority of items are procedural, and many decisions have been taken despite the negative vote of a permanent member.[3]

[2] Rule 6.

[3] In general, the vote has been taken on the inclusion of an item in the agenda. Occasionally, particularly in the early years, the Council voted on proposals to delete an item. The manner in which the agenda is put to the vote is of considerable importance because any decision by the Council requires seven affirmative votes.

The General Assembly

In accordance with the Rules of Procedure, the provisional agenda for a session of the General Assembly, which is drawn up and circulated well in advance by the Secretary-General, includes:

1. All items proposed by principal organs of the United Nations, as well as reports from those organs, and subsidiary organs of the Assembly;

2. All items proposed by any Member of the United Nations or by a non-member state under Article 35(2);

3. All items that the Secretary-General deems it necessary to put before the Assembly; and

4. All items the inclusion of which has been ordered by the Assembly at a previous session.[4]

The rules also provide for the circulation of a "supplementary list" covering items submitted after the provisional agenda has been circulated. Additional items "of an important and urgent character" may be placed on the agenda, even if submitted after the session has commenced. Usually, such items have been proposed during the course of the general debate that opens the session. However, sometimes they have not been brought to the attention of the Assembly until long after the session has begun. Efforts have been made with little success to cut down the number of additional items. Of the few items that the Assembly has refused to take up, two have been "additional items" brought to the attention of the Assembly toward the end of a session. The Rules of Procedure provide that additional items can be added to the agenda of a special session only by a two-thirds vote.[5] A proposal to follow the same procedure at regular sessions was, however, rejected.

The provisional agenda, the supplementary list, and the additional items are referred to the General Committee of the Assembly, which is composed of the President, the seven vice-presidents, and the chairmen of the main committees. One of the primary tasks of the General Committee is to make recommendations to the Assembly concerning the inclusion of items in the agenda and their allocation to the various committees. After a discussion of the report of the

[4] Rule 13.

[5] Under the rules adopted in accordance with the "Uniting for Peace" resolution concerning "emergency special sessions," additional items must concern threats to the peace, breaches of the peace, or acts of aggression. For text see App. F.

committee, the Assembly votes on the adoption of its agenda, and usually accepts the recommendations of the committee without change.[6]

There has been some disagreement and confusion concerning the proper role of the General Committee in relation to the consideration of the agenda, especially regarding the types of recommendations that the committee may make to the Assembly. The original Rules of Procedure were not specific on this point. During the first few sessions, it was established that the General Committee itself could not delete an item from the agenda but could only make a recommendation to that effect to the Assembly itself. The first time the committee recommended that an item *not* be included in the agenda was at the first special session in connection with the Arab request for the consideration of an item on the termination of the Palestine mandate. Some doubts were expressed that the General Committee could make such a recommendation because under the rules it was debarred from deciding any political question. The recommendation was, however, adopted by the Assembly. This action, which was exceptional, was taken because the majority of Members considered that the discussions should be limited to the single question for which the special session had been convoked.[7]

When in 1949 the Special Committee on Methods and Procedures considered what could be done to enable the Assembly to discharge its functions more effectively and more expeditiously, one of the subjects dealt with at length was the role of the General Committee.[8] The Rules of Procedure, as revised by the Assembly on the basis of the report of the Special Committee, indicate in greater detail the type of recommendations that the General Committee is to make. Under Rule 40, "The General Committee . . . shall make recommendations to the General Assembly with regard to each item proposed, concerning its inclusion in the agenda, the rejection of the

[6] There has been no consistent practice regarding whether a vote is taken on the inclusion of an item in the agenda or on a proposal not to include an item. This is of no great significance because the decision is taken by a majority of the members present and voting.

[7] Under the Rules of Procedure the provisional agenda for a special session is restricted to the items proposed in the request for the convocation of the session. Supplementary as well as additional items require a two-thirds vote for inclusion in the agenda.

[8] U.N. General Assembly, Fourth Session, *Official Records,* Supplement No. 12, p. 8.

request for inclusion, or the inclusion of the item on the agenda of a future session." These changes did not end the discussion on the proper role of the committee. When the committee recommended to the Assembly during its sixth session that "the consideration of the question of placing" the Moroccan question on the agenda be postponed, a number of representatives argued that this recommendation was not in accordance with the Rules of Procedure. The President held, however, that the rules enumerated some but not all of the recommendations the Committee might make. His ruling that the proposal was in order was upheld by a narrow margin, and the recommendation of the committee was accepted by the Assembly, also by a narrow margin.[9] This "postponement" was tantamount to a rejection of the request. A similar involved device for avoiding a discussion was employed in connection with the question of the invasion of Tibet when the General Committee itself decided to postpone considering whether to place the matter on the agenda.

Participation in Discussions

The Security Council has maintained that the adoption of the agenda is a "private" matter of business to be discussed and decided by the members of the Council alone. It has therefore refused to permit states not members of the Council to take part in discussions on this point. In 1946, the Council by a close vote decided against inviting the Ukraine to take part in the discussions on the inclusion in the agenda of a Ukrainian complaint concerning the situation in Greece.[10] The Council has never departed from this position, and in 1952 and 1953 it rejected, but by no means unanimously, proposals that certain Arab and Asian states be heard during the discussions on the inclusion of the Tunisian and Moroccan questions in the agenda of the Council.[11] In opposition to the practice of the Council, it has been contended with a good deal of logic that it is impossible for the Council to decide whether to include an item in

[9] U.N. General Assembly, Sixth Session, General Committee, *Official Records*, 76th Meeting (Nov. 9, 1951), p. 11, and U.N. General Assembly Sixth Session, Plenary, *Official Records*, 354th Meeting (Dec. 13, 1951), p. 269.

[10] U.N. Security Council, First Year, *Official Records*, Second Series, No. 6, 58th Meeting (Aug. 30, 1946), p. 156.

[11] U.N. Security Council, Seventh Year, *Official Records*, 576th Meeting (Apr. 14, 1952), p. 24, and U.N. Security Council, Eighth Year, *Official Records*, 624th Meeting (Sept. 3, 1953), p. 16.

the agenda unless it has heard the views of the states that have asked the Council to consider the question.

In the General Assembly the discussion on the inclusion of items in the agenda takes place in the General Committee and in the plenary meeting of the Assembly. All Members of the United Nations are, of course, represented at the plenary meetings of the Assembly; but under the rules, debate on the inclusion of any item recommended by the General Committee is limited. Furthermore, the Assembly has not permitted states not members of the United Nations to take part in discussions in plenary.

With regard to the discussions in the General Committee, Rule 43 specifically entitles any Member that has requested the inclusion of an item in the agenda to participate in the discussion on its request. No mention is made of the position of non-members. The General Committee has, however, been very liberal in permitting states to take part in its discussions. Not only states submitting questions to the Assembly but also those directly concerned have been given an opportunity to present their views. For example, when the General Committee was considering a request from Australia and India that the Indonesian question be placed on the agenda of the Assembly, the Netherlands and the Republic of Indonesia were heard.[12]

The Council and the Assembly are in slightly different situations in that items proposed for consideration by the Council have usually been questions of such general concern and seriousness that members are already familiar with them. Because the Assembly considers a wide range of matters, many of which are not urgent, it may need additional information before it can decide whether to place an item on its agenda. With limited time at its disposal, it must decide which items it will be able to handle during the course of any session and what priority should be accorded to these items. The Council, being in continuous session, has not faced these same problems.

So long as both organs follow the practice of granting almost every request for the inclusion of a question in their agenda, and so long as the discussions on the inclusion of items do not deal with substantive issues, there is little reason for hearing all the interested

[12] U.N. General Assembly, Third Session, Second Part, General Committee, *Official Records*, 60th Meeting (Apr. 8, 1949), pp. 40-43. Indonesia was not at that time a member of the United Nations.

parties at this stage in the proceedings. These two conditions have not always obtained, and should the organs revise their attitudes toward the inclusion of items, there would be some justification for hearing all parties, especially as one party may be represented on the Council or on the General Committee and thus enjoy an advantage.[13]

Limitation on Scope of Discussion

Opinions have differed regarding what matters may be appropriately discussed in connection with the inclusion of items in the agenda. As will be seen later, in a great many cases objections to the inclusion of items have raised substantive issues and also issues of competence. Practice has varied concerning the discussion of competence prior to the inclusion of an item in the agenda. The rules of procedure of the Security Council and the General Assembly do not preclude a discussion at this stage in the proceedings, and in view of the nature of many of the objections to the inclusion of items, it has often been impossible to avoid such a discussion. For example, the competence of the Assembly was discussed at length in connection with the inclusion in its agenda of the question of the observance of human rights and fundamental freedoms in Bulgaria, Hungary, and Rumania. The Council held a similar discussion concerning the inclusion of the Berlin question. In this case, the parties chiefly concerned were represented on the Council. In other cases, such as the Indonesian, Hyderabad, and Anglo-Iranian questions, the principal discussion on competence did not take place until after the questions had been included in the agenda and the parties had been invited to take part in the discussions.

In the Assembly, the further question has arisen regarding the proper range of discussion in the General Committee. Many Members not permanently represented on the committee, particularly in the early years, feared that the committee might obstruct access to the Assembly and for that reason sought to restrict its role. Rule 41 states that the General Committee shall not "decide any political question," and there has been general agreement that the com-

---

[13] Almost every question, for example, has been of direct concern to at least one of the permanent members of the Security Council, which by tradition have also been represented on the General Committee.

mittee itself cannot decide any question of competence, but considerably less agreement regarding whether a discussion on competence in the committee is in order. The Rules of Procedure state:

> . . . In considering matters relating to the agenda of the General As-
> sembly, the General Committee shall not discuss the substance of any item,
> except in so far as this bears upon the question whether the General Com-
> mittee should recommend the inclusion of the item in the agenda, the re-
> jection of the request for inclusion, or the inclusion of the item in the
> provisional agenda of a future session, and what priority should be accorded
> to an item the inclusion of which has been recommended.[14]

It is difficult to see how the General Committee can perform any
useful function in the organization of the work of the Assembly unless it is given considerable latitude in the range of its discussions
and recommendations. The role of the committee in relation to the
preparation of the agenda has become largely a formality. This is
illustrated by the growing tendency on the part of members to confine their remarks in the General Committee to "formal protests."
For example, the major arguments by South Africa against the inclusion of the *apartheid* question were made not in the General
Committee but in the plenary meeting during the debate on the
adoption of the agenda.

The handling of the *apartheid* question also illustrates the position of the majority of Members that the issue of competence should
be discussed and decided after the substantive question has been included in the agenda. During the discussion in plenary on the adoption of the agenda, the Union of South Africa introduced a proposal
that the Assembly, "having regard to Article 2(7) of the Charter,"
should decide that it was not competent to consider this item. The
ruling of the President that this motion was in order was overruled
by the Assembly, which proceeded to place the item on its agenda
and refer it to committee.[15] This vote is particularly significant because it has been seldom indeed that a President of the Assembly
has been overruled. The Assembly in this instance was reaffirming
the oft-stated position that the issue of competence should be discussed in the committee to which the item was referred.

There is one further point concerning the discussion of competence in connection with the inclusion of items in the agenda. It has

been realized that once the issue of competence is raised, it is difficult to avoid a full-scale debate. It is significant that few of the arguments against the inclusion of the Moroccan question in the agenda of the sixth session of the Assembly, and against the inclusion of the Tunisian question in the agenda of the Council were expressly based on grounds of competence, although there is reason to assume that these considerations were not without influence on the final decisions not to consider the two questions.

Proposals for Agenda Committees

Dissatisfaction with the procedures followed by the General Assembly and the Security Council has been voiced from time to time. It has been suggested that items proposed for inclusion in the agenda should be examined by a committee in advance of the meetings of the Council or the Assembly.

During the first year of the operations of the Council, the Netherlands proposed that the Council appoint a subcommittee of three *rapporteurs* to examine each complaint brought to the attention of the Council and to submit a preliminary report.[16] The Council could thereby avoid a preliminary discussion of the substance of the question and at the same time retain the means for rejecting baseless accusations. It was emphasized that the final decision on the inclusion or exclusion of an item would rest with the Council itself. This suggestion did not, however, recommend itself to other members of the Council.

In the case of the Assembly, the proposals for an agenda committee have been primarily directed toward expediting the work of the organ as a whole, and because political questions constitute only one part of the activities of the Assembly, many of the arguments supporting an agenda committee are not relevant to this study.[17] Members of the Assembly have not been in agreement regarding whether the proposed agenda should be examined by a small committee or by a committee of the whole. It is doubtful whether a small

[16] U.N. Security Council, First Year, *Official Records*, Second Series, No. 13, 67th Meeting (Sept. 16, 1946), p. 326, and *Ibid.*, No. 18, 72nd Meeting (Sept. 24, 1946), p. 460.

[17] U.N. General Assembly, Third Session, *Official Records*, Supplement No. 10; and U.N. General Assembly, Fourth Session, *Official Records*, Supplement No. 11 and Supplement No. 12, p. 8.

committee would enjoy the support of all the Members of the Organization, although the advantages of such a committee are obvious. The idea of a committee of the whole arose primarily in connection with the terms of reference of the Interim Committee, which was in fact authorized to carry out a preliminary examination of certain types of questions.[18] As most of the questions considered by the Assembly have been discussed at previous sessions and very often have been referred to other organs or special committees for study, a preliminary examination would be of limited usefulness. Furthermore "new items" have not usually been submitted sufficiently in advance of a session for a preliminary examination to be possible. Without a change in the attitudes of Members, an agenda committee could scarcely be any more successful than the General Committee in assisting the Assembly to function more effectively.

The principal arguments against the creation of an agenda committee have been that access to the Council or the Assembly would be obstructed and that debate would be restricted. Unless the majority of the members conclude that such restrictions are desirable, it is doubtful that any significant changes in the present system will be made.

Significance of the Inclusion of an Item in the Agenda

In January 1946, when the Security Council was faced with its first "dispute," the Council had not had time to consider its methods of operation or its rules of procedure. When the President asked whether there were any observations with regard to the inclusion of the Iranian question in the agenda, the Soviet representative stated: "If this item is placed on the agenda so that we may discuss whether the question should be considered, then I have no objection. . . ." The President replied that the inclusion of the item "would not deny to the Soviet representative the opportunity of being able to move in whatever direction he might wish."[19] The Iranian question was placed on the agenda of the Council, but the vagueness and confusion evidenced at this meeting regarding the significance of this preliminary decision have continued.

[18] Res. 111 (II), Nov. 13, 1947.
[19] U.N. Security Council, First Year, *Official Records*, First Series, No. 1, Second Meeting (Jan. 25, 1946), p. 16.

The Issue of Competence and the
Merits of the Complaint

Some members have considered that the inclusion of an item in the agenda is merely a formal act. This position has not been shared by those who consider that, before placing an item on its agenda, the Security Council or the General Assembly must be satisfied that certain criteria have been met; for example, that a situation exists that is of sufficient importance to warrant examination and that the matter falls within the scope of the powers and functions of the organ. The opinions expressed by the Soviet and Belgian representatives regarding the inclusion of the Berlin question in the agenda of the Council in 1948 are illustrative of the differences in attitude toward the significance of this preliminary decision. The Soviet representative stated that: "To approve an agenda means to recognize that it is appropriate, and that the questions to be included . . . are suitable and correspond to the competence of the body in question."[20]

The Belgian representative, alluding to the right of Members to call upon the Council stated:

When a Member State exercises that right, the Council is automatically seized of it. Consequently, the inclusion by the Council of the communication thus made on its agenda is merely a formality. The Council notes that the request in fact emanates from a Member State and that, consequently, it has been seized of it in a regular fashion. As such, the inclusion of the item on the agenda has no other significance. It does not imply any admission of competence on the part of the Council.[21]

In many cases, Members have stated that in voting to include an item in the agenda they were doing so with the understanding that this did not prejudice the question of competence. Prior to the decision by the Council to include the Hyderabad question in its agenda, nearly all of the members made statements to this effect. In this case, the situation was complicated by the fact that the dispute had been brought to the Council by Hyderabad, which was not a Member of the United Nations. Only the Chinese representative, however, felt that in these circumstances the inclusion of the item in the agenda might "prejudice a very important aspect" of the question. He stated:

[20] U.N. Security Council, Third Year, *Official Records*, No. 113, 361st Meeting (Oct. 4, 1948), p. 17.
[21] *Ibid.*, p. 16.

While it is true that placing a question on the agenda of the Security Council does not prejudge the merits of the question, . . . it is not equally true that placing the question on the agenda does not involve a certain view of the competency of the Security Council in regard to that question. . . . The admission of a question to the agenda does imply a certain view of the juridical status of the parties to a dispute. . . .[22]

Although there have been some statements to the effect that the Council or the Assembly, by placing an item on its agenda, has decided the question of its competence, in general the opposite view has prevailed. The majority of Members have maintained that this preliminary decision was not to be construed as a decision on the competence of the organ, or on the merits of the complaint. The implication of this position is that objections to the consideration of a question by the Council or the Assembly may be discussed after the question has been placed on the agenda. One reason for the increased opposition to the inclusion of items in the agenda has been that many states have felt they have not been given adequate opportunity to develop their objections to the consideration of questions before a full-scale discussion takes place. In the International Court of Justice, for example, if a preliminary objection is raised by one party regarding the jurisdiction of the Court, consideration of the merits of the case is suspended until this preliminary point has been resolved. Little attempt has ever been made in the Council or the Assembly to confine a discussion to the issue of competence and, in the light of the considerations that have to be taken into account in determining the competence of the two organs, it would indeed be difficult to do so.[23]

Relevance of Article 12

Article 12 of the Charter enjoins the Assembly from making recommendations, except at the request of the Council, on any dispute or situation with respect to which the Council is exercising its functions under the Charter. The Secretary-General is further instructed by this article to notify the Assembly of "any matters relative to the maintenance of international peace and security which are being dealt with by the Security Council. . . ." Under the interpretation given to this article, the Secretary-General's notification has covered all disputes and situations that have been placed

[22] *Ibid.*, No. 109, 357th Meeting (Sept. 16, 1948), p. 5.
[23] For more detailed treatment see below, Chap. VII, pp. 160-63.

on the agenda of the Council and have not subsequently been disposed of. [24]

The position that the limitation on the Assembly under Article 12 applies to all disputes and situations that are technically before the Council, even when it appears clear that the Council is not going to take any action on them, was emphasized by the action of the Council in removing the Spanish question and the question of the Greek frontier incidents from its agenda in order to permit the Assembly to act. However, the Assembly has not considered itself barred from adopting resolutions on disputes and situations merely because they are listed on the Secretary-General's notification. In April 1953 the Assembly adopted a resolution establishing a commission for an investigation of charges concerning the use of bacterial warfare by United Nations forces in Korea,[25] a question that had been considered inconclusively by the Council the previous July.

It has been generally recognized that Article 12 does not constitute any limitation on the competence of the Assembly to discuss a dispute or situation. There have been a few statements to the effect that the Assembly may not adopt *any* resolution on a dispute or situation before the Council unless the Council so requests, but it has not been considered that the prohibition was that extensive, because Article 12 specifically bars the Assembly only from making "recommendations." Resolutions were adopted by the Assembly on the Indonesian question while that question was being actively considered by the Council. However, the Assembly decided that it was not competent to adopt a Ukrainian proposal on the same question on the ground that it was in the nature of a "recommendation."[26]

It can be argued, although the argument becomes at times strained, that in such cases as Palestine and Korea, the Council and the Assembly were dealing with different aspects of the same question, the Council devoting its efforts to obtaining an end to hostilities while the Assembly, which had taken up both questions initially, remained responsible for working out a political settlement. Article 12 has not in fact raised any difficulties with regard to the concurrent

[24] Thus in 1953 the Security Council was presumably still considered to be dealing with the Iranian question, which had not been discussed in the Council since May 1946.

[25] Res. 706 (VII), Apr. 23, 1953.

[26] U.N. General Assembly, Fourth Session, Plenary, *Official Records*, 272nd Meeting (Dec. 7, 1949), p. 564.

handling of the Palestine question by the Council and the Assembly, although a few scattered objections were made by Arab delegates in 1948 that this article precluded recommendations by the Assembly on the military aspects of the question. Nor was the possible applicability of Article 12 discussed during the early fall of 1950 when the Security Council was still considering the "Complaint of Aggression upon the Republic of Korea," and the Assembly took up the "Problem of the Independence of Korea," an item that it had considered at three previous sessions. When the Assembly was later requested to consider the question of "Intervention by the People's Republic of China in Korea," a matter on which the Soviet Union had prevented the Council from taking action, the Council proceeded to remove the Korean complaint from its agenda in order that there would be no question regarding the competence of the Assembly to act.[27] The argument that the letter, or indeed the intent, of Article 12 has been strictly followed is not too convincing, although the Assembly has for the most part endeavored not to interfere with any efforts that the Council was actively making for the maintenance of international peace and security.

Greater significance has not been attached to the decision to include a question in the agenda because of the tendency of the Security Council and the General Assembly to include in their agenda every matter brought to their attention. From the few instances when the Council or the Assembly has refused to place a question on its agenda, one could hardly conclude that the decisions of the two organs have been based on any consistent criteria.

The Council refused to consider the following items proposed by members of the Soviet bloc: information on the presence of foreign troops in non-enemy countries (1946); the Assembly resolution on Franco Spain (1948); and unceasing terrorism and mass executions in Greece (1950). In 1950 when the Council had on its agenda the "Complaint of Aggression upon the Republic of Korea," the Council refused to consider as a separate item charges by the People's Democratic Republic of Korea and refused to approve a provisional agenda formulated by the Soviet Union that included an item "Peaceful Settlement of the Korean Question." The Council has also declined to place on its agenda two items brought to its attention by

[27] U.N. Security Council, Sixth Year, *Official Records*, 531st Meeting (Jan. 31, 1951), pp. 7-12.

a group of Arab-Asian states: the Tunisian question (1952) and the Moroccan question (1953).

The Assembly refused to place on the agenda of its first special session (1947) an Arab sponsored item on the termination of the Palestine mandate. Poland was unsuccessful in an attempt to get the Assembly in 1949 to take up a series of charges against the United States, principally concerning the case of Gerhart Eisler. A request by El Salvador for the consideration of the question of the invasion of Tibet was turned down (1950). Requests by a group of Arab-Asian states for the consideration of the Moroccan question at the sixth session of the Assembly (1951) and for the convocation of a special session in 1952 on the Tunisian question were refused, although both questions were placed on the agenda of the seventh session (1952). Finally, the Assembly refused in 1953 a request by the Soviet Union for the inclusion in its agenda of a report by the Secretary-General concerning one aspect of the Korean question.

The majority of the Members did not consider that the discussion of the above matters would be advisable. The converse of this proposition, however, does not hold true in all instances in which the Council and the Assembly have decided to place questions on their agenda. Many members have voted in favor of placing items on the agenda, not because they considered that a discussion was necessary or desirable, but merely because it seemed less desirable to attempt to block a discussion. It would seem reasonable to assume that if the majority of the Members were willing to place a matter on the agenda, they would be willing to afford the submitting state an opportunity to state its position, but even this conclusion has to be modified in the light of the refusal of the Council to permit the People's Republic of China to present its case concerning the alleged bombing of Chinese territory. Normally, however, the inclusion of an item in the agenda has been the signal for a full-scale discussion, although this has not necessarily meant that any action would be taken.

The Council has taken the position that, once a question has been placed on its agenda, it becomes in effect the "property" of the Council. The Council refused to remove the Hyderabad and Iranian questions from its agenda even when the parties themselves so requested. The position of the Council appears to have been prompted by a desire to protect parties from pressure to withdraw their complaints. In contrast, under the Rules of the International Court of Justice, proceedings are discontinued if the parties settle their dispute or agree not to go on with the proceedings. Furthermore, if the party instituting proceedings does not wish to proceed, as in the case brought by France concerning the protection of French interests in Egypt, the case is removed from the list of the Court unless the other party has already taken a step in the proceedings and does not agree to discontinuance.[28] However, as the majority of members argued in upholding the right of the Council to refuse to accede to the request by Iran for the withdrawal of its dispute with the Soviet Union,[29] the exercise by the Council of its powers under the Charter is not dependent upon the consent of the parties directly involved, nor are the responsibilities of the Council necessarily discharged when the parties themselves have reached an agreement.

Factors Influencing Decision to Consider a Question

The arguments raised against the inclusion of certain items in the agenda reflect a variety of attitudes toward the criteria to be applied. Briefly, the principal arguments have been: (1) that no dispute or situation of the nature described in the complaint exists; (2) that the question is not within the competence of the Security Council or the General Assembly; (3) that the Council or the Assembly should not take up the question because other procedures of settlement are available, have been agreed upon, or are being used for seeking a solution to the problem; and (4) that the consideration of the question would serve no useful purpose and might obstruct rather than facilitate a settlement. Members, on the one hand, have attempted to refute the objections and, on the other hand, have argued that the matters raised by these objections should be discussed after the item has been included in the agenda. For example, when a Member has claimed that a complaint is "completely without foundation," those supporting the inclusion of the question in the agenda have contended either that there is sufficient evidence to justify consideration or that, in order to de-

[28] Arts. 68 and 69 of the Rules of the Court.
[29] See, in particular, U.N. Security Council, First Year, *Official Records*, First Series, Supplement No. 2, p. 49.

termine whether a complaint is justified, it is necessary to place the question on the agenda and proceed with an examination of the charges. When a Member has argued that a matter is outside the jurisdiction of the Council or the Assembly, the counterargument has been either that the organ is competent or that the question of competence should be discussed after the inclusion of an item.

The Right of a Hearing

The primary factor operating in favor of consideration of questions by the Security Council and the General Assembly has been a broad acceptance of the general principle that access to the organs of the United Nations should not be restricted. Because of this reluctance to deny any Member an opportunity to present any question that in the opinion of the Member deserves consideration, both organs have included in their agenda almost every question brought to their attention. There have been a number of statements to the effect that either organ would be failing in its duty if it refused to consider such questions, but statements concerning the "obligation" of the Assembly have been less frequent and more qualified, probably because in fewer instances has there been an allegation of a possible "threat to the peace."

Many Members have expressed the opinion that the Council cannot or should not deny any Member the right to present its case when that Member contends that a dispute or situation exists that is likely to endanger the maintenance of international peace and security. Belgium has frequently maintained that when a Member makes an appeal to the Council based upon the provisions of the Charter, the Council cannot refuse to include the item in its agenda. Most of the Latin American members of the Council have supported this position. The Polish representative has also stated that the very fact that a Member of the United Nations has brought a matter to the attention of the Council indicates that the question is of sufficient importance to be considered. In 1946, in support of the inclusion in the agenda of the item proposed by the Soviet Union concerning information on armed forces, he expressed the opinion that "the question of whether or not we should adopt it on the agenda is not a problem, but that it is a simple duty of the Council to place on the agenda items which are brought before it by Members of the United Nations."[30] Also in 1946, the

---

[30] *Ibid.*, Second Series, No. 17, 71st Meeting (Sept. 23, 1946), p. 429.

United States representative made the following statement concerning the Iranian question: "When a Member of the United Nations advises the Council that a situation exists which is likely to threaten the peace and security of the world, we cannot deny to that nation the opportunity to be heard. . . ."[31]

The fact that certain questions have not been included in the agenda is sufficient evidence that Members have refused to accept the simple thesis that there is an obligation to consider each and every question submitted by a Member state. Many Members of widely differing political orientation have stressed that the decision whether to include a question in the agenda is within the discretion of each organ.

Application of Article 2(7)

Article 2(7) of the Charter provides that "Nothing contained in the present Charter shall authorize the United Nations to intervene in matters which are essentially within the domestic jurisdiction of any state. . . ." In a great many cases it has been argued that the Security Council or the General Assembly should not place a question on its agenda because it concerned matters essentially domestic in nature and its discussion in the United Nations would constitute interference in the internal affairs of the state or states concerned. The Soviet bloc has often and vociferously voiced this objection, particularly with regard to the consideration of the Czechoslovak question in the Council, and the question of the observance of human rights and fundamental freedoms in Bulgaria, Hungary, and Rumania in the Assembly. It has also been the basis on which the Union of South Africa, and other Members supporting its position, have argued against the inclusion in the agenda of the question of the treatment of Indians in South Africa and the *apartheid* question. Neither a member of the Soviet bloc nor the Union of South Africa has been successful in its efforts to exclude matters from the agenda on the ground of Article 2(7) of the Charter. Nor did the Council consider that similar arguments justified the exclusion of the Anglo-Iranian question. On the other hand, the domestic jurisdiction principle appears to have been one of the main grounds on which the Council declined to consider the Soviet-sponsored item on unceasing terrorism and mass

[31] *Ibid.*, First Series, No. 2, 25th Meeting (Mar. 26, 1946), p. 13.

executions in Greece,[32] and the basis on which many Members have voted against the consideration of the Moroccan and Tunisian questions.

The principal argument against the thesis that Article 2(7) precludes the inclusion of a question in the agenda of the Council or the Assembly has been that the organ must discuss a matter before it can decide that it is essentially within the domestic jurisdiction of a state. Members have been especially zealous in upholding the broad powers of discussion in the Assembly. As one of the presidents of the Assembly has stated:

> . . . The right of discussion provided for in Article 10 of the Charter was one of its most important provisions. There was no question or problem which came within the scope of the Charter and which concerned its aims, its principles or any one of its provisions which could not be discussed by the General Assembly. If any question could be covered by an Article of the Charter, that question could no longer be held to be a matter essentially within the domestic jurisdiction of a State.[33]

Whether or not Article 2(7) can be considered as a limitation on the power of the Assembly or the Council to discuss a question depends upon the interpretation given to the word "intervene." There has been considerable difference of opinion on this point. The majority of Members have taken the position that discussion cannot be considered as intervention. The United States has stated that "discussion could not normally be construed as intervention within the meaning of Article 2 (7)."[34]

On the other hand, the members of the Soviet bloc have contended that the Council or the Assembly may not discuss a complaint that concerns matters essentially within the domestic jurisdiction of a state. Other Members of the Organization, although differing with the Soviet Union regarding matters that are essentially within the domestic jurisdiction of a state, have maintained the same position: that Article 2(7) does preclude the discussion of certain questions by the Council or the Assembly. The most vigorous exponent of this thesis has been the Union of South Africa, which

[32] U. N. Security Council, Fifth Year, *Official Records,* No. 35, 493rd Meeting (Aug. 31, 1950), p. 30.
[33] Australian Representative Evatt. U.N. General Assembly, Third Session, Second Part, General Committee, *Official Records,* 58th Meeting (Apr. 6, 1949), pp. 15-16.
[34] U.N. General Assembly, Third Session, Second Part, Plenary, *Official Records,* 189th Meeting (Apr. 12, 1949), p. 12.

has argued that "the right of discussion can only result from the competence of the organ to concern itself with a matter."[35] During the consideration of the *apartheid* question, the South African position received some support from other Members of the Organization, notably, the United Kingdom, France, and Australia, all of whom argued that discussion does constitute "intervention" within the meaning of Article 2(7).[36] Similar arguments were also raised in connection with the discussion of the Tunisian and Moroccan questions. The increase in the number of statements favoring this position can be attributed not only to the nature of the questions that have been brought to the Council and the Assembly during the last few years but also to the increasing concern of some Members with the tendency of United Nations organs to discuss and to adopt resolutions on a wide variety of questions without, in the opinion of those Members, giving adequate consideration to the provisions of Article 2(7) of the Charter.

Possible Danger to International Peace and Security

In discussions in the Security Council, the argument has often been made that no dispute or situation existed that in any way threatened international peace and security, and therefore no question required consideration. During the discussions on the inclusion of the Moroccan question on the agenda of the Council, the representative of the United States, in a decided departure from positions previously taken by his government, explained that he would vote against placing the matter on the agenda because the situation in Morocco did not endanger international peace and security. A similar position was taken by the representatives of Denmark and the United Kingdom, the latter basing his arguments more directly on the application of Article 2(7) of the Charter.[37] On the Spanish question, one reason the Council refused to accede to a Ukrainian request for consideration in 1947 of the resolution of the Assembly

[35] See in particular U.N. General Assembly, Sixth Session, Plenary, *Official Records*, 341st Meeting (Nov. 13, 1951), p. 84.

[36] U.N. General Assembly, Seventh Session, Plenary, *Official Records*, 381st-82nd Meetings (Oct. 17, 1952), pp. 53 ff., and U.N. General Assembly, Seventh Session, *Ad Hoc* Political Committee, *Official Records*, 14th-15th Meetings (Nov. 12-13, 1952), pp. 71-88.

[37] For the discussion, see U.N. Security Council, Seventh Year, *Official Records*, 619th-24th Meetings (Aug. 26-Sept. 3, 1953).

on Spain appears to have been the belief that the situation was not sufficiently serious to warrant action.[38]

In some cases it has been argued that no "dispute" existed. In March 1946, for example, the Soviet Union objected to consideration by the Council of the Iranian question on the ground that an agreement had already been reached between Iran and the Soviet Union (in accordance with a previous resolution of the Council) and that therefore there was no "dispute" for the Council to consider. The Council, despite Soviet objections, decided to place the question on its agenda in order to examine the matter further.[39] The Council also refused to place on its agenda a Soviet-sponsored item concerning information on the presence of foreign troops in territories of states other than ex-enemy, a matter that the majority of members of the Council did not feel was a "situation" such as the Charter envisaged for consideration by the Council.[40]

Application of Article 107

The Soviet Union has contended that agreements concluded between the major allies in the Second World War establishing the procedures for handling the problems of peacemaking precluded the submission of these matters to the United Nations. In this connection, the Soviet Union has cited Article 107 of the Charter, which reads: "Nothing in the present Charter shall invalidate or preclude action, in relation to any state which during the Second World War has been an enemy of any signatory to the present Charter, taken or authorized as a result of that war by the Governments having responsibility for such action." On these grounds the Soviet bloc has objected to the consideration of the Berlin, Austrian, and Korean questions and the item concerning free elections in Germany—all matters brought to the United Nations because the major powers had failed to reach agreement on them. Similarly, the Soviet bloc has raised objection to the consideration of questions arising from the peace treaties, such as the observance of human rights and fundamental freedoms in Bulgaria, Hungary, and Rumania, and the suggestions for the revision of the Italian treaty.

[38] U.N. Security Council, Third Year, *Official Records*, No. 90, 327th Meeting (June 25, 1948), p. 9.
[39] U.N. Security Council, First Year, *Official Records*, First Series, No. 2, 26th Meeting (Mar. 26, 1946), p. 27.
[40] *Ibid.*, Second Series, No. 18, 72nd Meeting (Sept. 24, 1946), p. 460.

One of the clearest statements of the Soviet position was made in opposition to the consideration of this last question. The representative of the Soviet Union stated:

This proposal contravenes the United Nations Charter, which excludes from the competence of the United Nations all measures by allied Powers in relation to countries with which they were at war. . . .

The Charter clearly leaves no doubt that under Article 107 questions such as that of the Peace Treaty with Italy are not subject to discussion by the General Assembly. [41]

The most extensive discussion of Article 107 occurred in the Security Council in connection with the Berlin question and in the General Assembly on the proposal to appoint a commission to investigate conditions for holding free elections in Germany. The Soviet Union argued that the four powers had entered into agreements concerning the manner in which these problems were to be handled, that the questions fell within the jurisdiction of the Council of Foreign Ministers, that they could not therefore be considered by the United Nations, and that in bringing these questions to the United Nations, the United States, France, and the United Kingdom were violating their agreements with the Soviet Union. The attitude of the majority has been that the purpose of Article 107 was to enable the governments primarily responsible for the defeat of the Axis powers to take whatever action was necessary to the conclusion of hostilities and the working out of the peace settlements, but that the article was not intended to prohibit the Assembly or the Council from dealing with questions arising from either the peace treaties or the failure of the powers to conclude such treaties.

One of the clearest statements of the majority position was made by the United Kingdom representative in answer to the Soviet objection to the consideration of the request for a commission to investigate conditions for holding free elections in Germany. According to the summary report of the meeting he argued that:

There was nothing in the Charter to preclude the Assembly from dealing with such a request; Article 107 of the Charter was purely permissive in that it permitted certain action by the Allied Governments with regard to ex-enemy states which might otherwise be contrary to the Charter. Its sole effect was therefore to rule out complaints about such action if the complaints were based on the ground that it was contrary to the Charter.

[41] U.N. General Assembly, Second Session, Plenary, *Official Records,* 90th Meeting (Sept. 23, 1947), p. 277.

It did not rule out complaints based on other grounds, such as breaches of international law or of a specific treaty or undertaking, still less, of course, proposals in the United Nations for dealing with an ex-enemy state in a certain way.[42]

Although neither the Council nor the Assembly has admitted the validity of the Soviet argument that Article 107 bars the consideration of such questions, a few Members have been sympathetic to the view that problems of postwar peace settlement should be handled by other means and have felt that, for reasons of expediency, such questions should not be considered in the United Nations. Moreover, it is not clear whether the majority would consider that Article 107 might not in certain circumstances preclude the discussion of a question. The statement by the United Kingdom referred to above appears to admit the possibility that a complaint from an ex-enemy state would in some circumstances be inadmissible.[43]

Possibility of Settlement by Other Means

During the discussion on the adoption of the agenda, there have been occasional references to the obligations of parties under Article 33 of the Charter "first of all" to seek a solution of their disputes by peaceful means. It has been contended that a question should not be included in the agenda because other means of settlement have not been attempted or have not been exhausted. This was the argument that the Soviet Union made, unsuccessfully and not very forcefully, against the inclusion in the agenda of the Council of the question of the incidents in the Corfu Channel.[44] That the Security Council or the General Assembly in principle should not interfere so long as there is a reasonable chance that the parties concerned may themselves be able to reach a settlement is a proposition in harmony with the provisions of the Charter. The arguments that the Council or the Assembly should not include a question in its agenda because a settlement was being or should be sought by the parties by means of their own choice has, how-

[42] U.N. General Assembly, Sixth Session, Ad Hoc Political Committee, Official Records, 15th Meeting (Dec. 4, 1951), p. 76.

[43] See also Chap. IV, above.

[44] U.N. Security Council, Second Year, Official Records, No. 6, 95th Meeting (Jan. 20, 1947), p. 114.

ever, been used primarily as a justification for refusing to take up questions on which, for various political reasons, Members do not wish to take a stand.

The principal argument advanced against the taking up by the Council of the Tunisian question in 1952 was that the consideration of the question at that time would obstruct rather than advance the possibility of a satisfactory solution being reached through negotiations.[45] It is interesting to note that while France contended that, as a settlement had been reached, there was no necessity for the Council to take up the matter, many of the other members of the Council, who refused to vote for the inclusion of the item in the agenda, stated that discussion in the Council would interfere with negotiations being carried out. One of the arguments raised against the inclusion of the Moroccan question in the agenda of the sixth session of the Assembly—and there were very few arguments put forward—was that a solution should be sought through direct negotiations and that the Assembly should not take up the question "at that time."[46] An attempt was made to justify the refusal to place the question of the invasion of Tibet on the agenda of the Assembly on the grounds that the status of the matter was "unclear" and that it still appeared possible that a settlement would be reached by peaceful means.[47] The reluctance to consider this complaint, however, for the most part was a result of apprehension regarding the position that the People's Republic of China might take on a number of issues, especially the Korean problem.

Validity of the Charges

The contention that there is no substance to a complaint brought to the attention of the Security Council or the General Assembly has been put forward in a great number of cases. The records of the Assembly and the Council are replete with statements that charges are "spurious" or "completely unsubstantiated," and that their submission to the Council or the Assembly is a "mere propaganda maneuver." This has been the position of mem-

[45] U.N. Security Council, Seventh Year, *Official Records,* 574th-76th Meetings (Apr. 4, 10, and 14, 1952).

[46] U.N. General Assembly, Sixth Session, Plenary, *Official Records,* 354th Meeting (Dec. 13, 1951), pp. 243-69.

[47] U.N. General Assembly, Fifth Session, General Committee, *Official Records,* 73rd Meeting (Nov. 24, 1950), p. 20.

bers of the Soviet bloc with regard to almost all charges made against them. Their contention that these charges should not be included in the agenda has not received support, however, from the other Members of the United Nations.

The argument that a complaint is "completely unfounded" has been raised in opposition to the inclusion in the agenda of various questions brought to the Council and the Assembly by the members of the Soviet bloc, and it may be considered as a ground on which some of the Soviet charges have been excluded from the agenda. Usually, however, these complaints have been included and have been discussed, although sometimes quite briefly. This has been in large measure because of the willingness of the United States to permit discussion of all charges by the Soviet bloc and to use the Assembly and the Council as forums for replying to these charges. United States representatives have on numerous occasions stated that they "welcomed" an inquiry by the United Nations into Soviet charges inasmuch as the United States had "nothing to hide."[48]

It can be argued that the United States can ill afford to adopt any other position and has little reason to fear that either organ will adopt a course of action that the United States does not approve. Furthermore, a defeat by an overwhelming vote in the United Nations of Soviet proposals condemning the United States seems to be considered as a great moral victory. Although it may be in the best interests of the United States to demonstrate its willingness to defend itself against Soviet charges in the United Nations, it is questionable whether in every instance these discussions further the purposes of the United Nations. There appears to be an increasing realization that the purposes of the United Nations are not served by the discussion of "unsubstantiated" complaints, but there seems to be little likelihood that the situation will improve unless the Members refuse to allow the United Nations to be used as a propaganda forum and will themselves abstain from submitting to the United Nations questions to the solution of which the Organization can make little if any contribution.

Benefits of Full Discussion

Closely related to the above-mentioned objections to the consideration of questions has been the view frequently expressed that

[48] See, for example, U.N. General Assembly, Sixth Session, General Committee, *Official Records,* 78th Meeting (Nov. 27, 1951), p. 21.

a discussion will serve no useful purpose. Members have been especially concerned lest such discussions interfere with efforts to obtain peaceful settlements. The opposition to the consideration of the possible termination of the Palestine mandate at the first special session of the General Assembly, for example, was based on the view held by the majority of Members that a full discussion should be deferred until the next session when the Assembly would have a report from its special investigating committee. In the Indonesian case, there was opposition to discussion by the Assembly on the ground that this might interfere with the efforts being made by the Security Council and its commission to obtain a peaceful settlement.

Since 1950, a considerable number of complaints have been brought to the United Nations concerning matters peripheral to the hostilities in Korea. Some of these have come up for consideration at inopportune times, and Members have expressed apprehension that the discussion might further obstruct the solution of the Korean question. For example, in October 1953 while talks were being held concerning the holding of a political conference on the Korean question, the United States asked the Assembly to consider the "Question of Atrocities by the North Korean and Chinese Communist Forces against United Nations Prisoners of War in Korea." The members of the Soviet bloc charged that this was an obvious attempt to raise fresh complications detrimental to the peaceful settlement of the problem. Although voting in favor of placing the matter on the agenda, other members questioned the timeliness of dealing with the matter.[49] During this same session, the Soviet Union requested the inclusion in the agenda of a report by the Secretary-General submitted in compliance with the resolution of the Assembly of the previous month on the convening of the political conference. It was obvious that the Soviet Union desired by this means to reopen the question of participation in this conference. The request was rejected, the members apparently agreeing with the United Kingdom that the Korean question was already on the agenda and that the discussion of this interim report would serve no useful purpose and might in fact hinder or delay the setting up of the political conference.[50]

[49] U.N. General Assembly, Eighth Session, Plenary, *Official Records*, 457th Meeting (Nov. 11, 1953), p. 287.
[50] *Ibid.*, 440th Meeting (Sept. 22, 1953), p. 77.

Attitudes of Major Groups

The positions of the major groups in the United Nations toward the inclusion of questions in the agenda of the Security Council and the General Assembly might be summarized briefly as follows:

The members of the Soviet bloc, as has been pointed out, have almost without exception objected to the consideration of any charges made against them, but they have seldom objected to the consideration of other questions. An exception was the Soviet vote, in which only Yugoslavia concurred, against consideration of the Anglo-Iranian question by the Council. This was an example of the firm Soviet policy of backing the Arab-Asian states in their controversies with the Western European states.[51]

Most, but not all, of the questions submitted by the members of the Soviet bloc to the Council or the Assembly have been included in its agenda, occasionally over some opposition. The efforts of the Soviet bloc to exclude questions have received very little support from other Members, although in the voting on the inclusion of some questions, such as the observance of human rights and fundamental freedoms in Bulgaria, Hungary, and Rumania, there have been a large number of abstentions. In only one case, the question of the invasion of Tibet, has the opposition of the Soviet Union to the consideration of a question been concurred in by the majority.

The members of the Arab-Asian bloc have seldom taken a position in opposition to the consideration of any question in the Council or the Assembly, although some of them have abstained from voting on the inclusion of items relating to the cold war. Most of the questions submitted by the Arab-Asian states have been included in the agenda. Where there has been opposition to the consideration of these questions, it has come mainly from the Western states.

The Latin American states have generally supported the consideration of every question by the Council or the Assembly, although they have voted with the United States to exclude a few items proposed by the Soviet bloc. The success of the Arab-Asian

---

[51] In 1947 in a rare demonstration of non-solidarity, the Soviet bloc split over the inclusion in the agenda of the first special session of the item on the termination of the Palestine mandate, but the Soviet bloc supported the efforts of the Arab-Asian bloc to get consideration of the Tunisian and Moroccan questions and the charges against the Union of South Africa.

bloc in getting items on the agenda of the Assembly has been in large measure because of support received from the Latin American states.[52] The failure to obtain this support resulted in defeat on three issues, (1) consideration of the Moroccan question at the sixth session; (2) inclusion in the agenda of the first special session of the item on the termination of the Palestine mandate; and (3) convocation of a special session on the Tunisian question.

The members of the Western bloc (for this purpose the members of the North Atlantic Treaty Organization plus Australia, New Zealand, and the Union of South Africa) have taken a more restrictive position with regard to the inclusion of items in the agenda, although in contrast to the Soviet bloc they have objected to the consideration of very few questions. It was the support given to France by those members of the Security Council that were also members of the North Atlantic Treaty Organization that resulted in the refusal by the Council to consider the Tunisian and Moroccan questions. The Western bloc was also the center of opposition in the Assembly to the three Arab-Asian requests. Furthermore, of the few abstentions or negative votes cast against the inclusion in the agenda of the Assembly of the Indonesian question and the various charges against the Union of South Africa, most were by the members of the Western bloc.

The original policy of the United States favoring the consideration of almost every question brought to the Council and the Assembly has undergone modification in the last few years, although the United States has in general continued its policy of not opposing the consideration by the United Nations of charges brought directly against the United States. The United States has been highly successful in obtaining support for the positions it has taken with regard to the consideration of questions. No question has ever been placed on the agenda of either organ in the face of opposition by the United States. Every question that has been excluded from the agenda has failed to obtain this support. There was considerable apprehension, even outside the Arab-Asian bloc, regarding the United States opposition to the consideration of the Tunisian and Moroccan questions. The United States did not oppose their consideration at the seventh session of the Assembly, where it was clear

[52] The two Latin American members on the Security Council voted in favor of the inclusion of the Tunisian question on the agenda, but split on the Moroccan question.

that the Arab-Asian bloc would be able to get enough votes to place these two matters on the agenda. Whether the United States can successfully follow a more restricted policy toward the consideration of questions in the United Nations will depend upon whether it can enlist the support of those smaller nations that have on the whole been very reluctant to limit access to the organs of the United Nations.

The major question that arises from the examination of the practices of the Security Council and the General Assembly with regard to the inclusion of items in the agenda is whether the two organs have been too free in deciding to place on their agenda for consideration almost every question brought to their attention. Considering the nature of some of these questions and the inconclusive character of some of the discussions, one might criticize the liberal policy that has been followed. An unfortunate result of this policy has been that any effort to adopt a more restrictive attitude meets with bitter opposition.

It seems unlikely that the Members of the Organization can agree on a series of criteria to govern this initial decision. There would scarcely, for example, be agreement regarding what, if any, matters should be ruled out as coming essentially within the domestic jurisdiction of a state. Any effort by the Council to exclude questions on the grounds that the possibilities of settlement have not been exhausted or that there is no potential threat to international peace and security might only encourage states to adopt more rigid and adamant positions in negotiations outside the United Nations. A solution would seem to lie largely in a reconsideration by both the Assembly and the Council of the manner in which they will handle the questions brought to their attention, a matter that will be considered at greater length later in this volume. Instead of including almost every question in the agenda and then proceeding to a full discussion, a procedure might be followed along the lines of one that, as has been noted, was suggested by the Netherlands. Either before or immediately after a question is placed on the agenda, a preliminary examination might be undertaken to explore possible ways of handling the matter. In this way the Council and the Assembly might be able to devise a more satisfactory procedure for handling objections to their jurisdiction.

Even if no changes along these lines were to be made, it would seem that the rules of procedure and the practices of the two organs with regard to the inclusion of items in the agenda deserve reconsideration. There is always a danger that extensive and precisely formulated rules will interfere with the flexibility of the Council and the Assembly. However, the procedure of the two organs could undoubtedly be improved by clarification of, additions to, and changes in, the existing rules. The question of possible changes in the procedure by which questions are brought to the attention of the Security Council and the General Assembly has already been considered.[53] It might also be worthwhile to restudy the procedures for handling communications, drawing up the provisional agenda, and adopting the agenda.

Changes in procedure will not of course remove from the realm of politics the basic question of what matters the Council and the Assembly should consider. In the end, any significant changes will be brought about only if Member states reconsider their attitudes toward what questions they themselves will bring to the Council and the Assembly and what questions they will support for consideration by the two organs.

[53] See above, Chap. IV.

CHAPTER VI

Participation of Non-Members in Consideration of Questions

IN THE proceedings of the Security Council and the General Assembly, recognition has been given to the principle that interested parties should be given an opportunity to present their views before any decision is taken that might affect their interests. The hearing of interested parties has also been one of the methods utilized by the two organs for obtaining information on which to base their decisions. By associating the parties with the decision-making process, it has been hoped that their co-operation would be obtained in the satisfactory solution of the question.

Article 31 of the Charter provides that a Member of the United Nations not represented on the Council may participate in the discussion of any question when the Council considers that the interests of the Member are specially affected. Under Article 32, the Council is obligated to invite any state that is a party to a dispute being considered by the Council to participate in the discussions. Participation of a state not a Member of the United Nations, however, is subject to the acceptance by that state of the conditions laid down by the Council.

The practice in the United Nations has been similar to that followed by the League of Nations.[1] There is, however, an important distinction between the approaches of the two organizations. Although in the practice of the League a state was invited to sit as a member of the Council, in the United Nations the invited state merely "participates" in the discussions; it has not, for example, been accorded the right to vote.[2]

[1] Cf. Arts. 31, 32, and 44 of the Charter and Arts. 4 and 17 of the Covenant of the League of Nations.

[2] For discussion of the decision not to give regular voting rights to ad hoc participants see the volume in this Brookings series, A History of the United Nations Charter.

Practice of the Security Council

The Security Council has been very liberal in inviting states to participate in its discussions. Usually, invitations have been extended by the president of the Council as the result of a request, but not all requests have been granted, nor have requests been considered prerequisites to invitations. On occasion, the Council has issued an invitation on its own initiative. The decision has been considered "procedural," and a number of invitations have been extended despite the negative vote of a permanent member.

Usually the invitation has been issued immediately after the Council has decided to place the question on its agenda. Efforts, primarily by the Soviet Union, to link the decision to include a question on the agenda with a decision to extend an invitation have been unsuccessful. In some cases a request has not been received until a later stage in the proceedings, or the Council itself has postponed its decision regarding the issuance of an invitation until such a later stage. For example, the majority of the members of the Council were anxious that immediate action be taken with regard to the outbreak of hostilities in Indonesia in 1947. Because a proposal to invite the Republic of Indonesia to participate in the discussions would have been the subject of extensive debate, the Council adopted its initial resolutions and postponed until later the question of an invitation to the Republic.

Invitations to Member States
Not Members of the Council

Although a Member of the United Nations not represented on the Security Council may be invited under Article 31 or 32 of the Charter to participate in the discussions of the Council, the Council has usually issued its invitations under Article 31 or without specific reference to either article.[3] The Council has given a broad interpretation to the phrase "specially affected" as used in Article 31. Members bringing questions to the attention of the Council,[4] as

---

[3] The reason for this has been the reluctance of the Council to decide that any question before it is a "dispute." Such a decision may have other important implications, particularly with regard to the application of Art. 27, which governs the voting procedure in the Council. The decision might well require a lengthy Council debate. For further discussion on this point, see below, Chap. X.

[4] See Rule 37 of the Provisional Rules of Procedure.

well as Members against which charges have been levied, have been invited to participate in the discussion of those questions. On occasion, Members represented on subsidiary organs have been invited to take part in the discussions of the Council relating to the work of such organs. Canada, for example, as a permanent member of the Atomic Energy Commission, was invited to take part in discussions of the Council on the work of the commission.

Under Article 31, it is for the Council to decide whether the interests of a Member are "specially affected," but in practice it has been sufficient for a Member to make a claim to that effect. On only one occasion, the original request from the Philippines in connection with the Indonesian question, did the Council hold that the indications of special interest adduced by a Member were not adequate grounds for an invitation, and, even in this case, the Council later reversed its decision. Members themselves have interpreted the phrase "specially affected" broadly and have seldom failed to ask to be heard on questions that concerned them. For example, the Netherlands, India, the Philippines, Pakistan, Burma, Australia, and Belgium were invited to participate in the discussions of the Council on the Indonesian question (the latter two by reason of their membership on the Committee of Good Offices of the Council).

Invitations to Non-Members
of the Organization

Although the Security Council has had little difficulty in reaching decisions to invite Members of the United Nations to participate in its discussions, the question of the participation of states not Members of the Organization has occasioned some of the most lengthy and bitter debates in the Council. The tendency of the Council to avoid any action that might be construed as a specific application or interpretation of any article of the Charter has been especially apparent with regard to Article 32. Seldom has Article 32 been specifically cited as the basis for any of the numerous invitations to such states. Occasionally, the Council has issued invitations to these states under Rule 39 of its Provisional Rules of Procedure, which provides that the Council "may invite members of the Secretariat or other persons, whom it considers competent for the purpose, to supply it with information or to give other assistance in examining matters within its competence." More often invitations have been issued without reference to either this rule or to Article 32.

The Council is under an obligation to extend invitations under Article 32, but the application of the article requires that the following conditions obtain: (1) the invitation must be extended to a "state"; (2) the state must be a party to a "dispute"; and (3) it must have accepted the "conditions" the Council has laid down.

The interpretation to be given to the term "state" for the purpose of applying Article 32 has been discussed in the Council on a number of occasions, most extensively in connection with the proposal in 1947 to invite the Republic of Indonesia to participate in the discussion of the Indonesian question. During this debate a number of members of the Council stated that in view of the fact that their governments had not recognized the Republic they could not vote in favor of an invitation. In support of the proposed invitation, attention was drawn to the *de facto* recognition that had been accorded to the Republic by the Netherlands and by other Members of the United Nations. It was argued that the application of Article 32 did not require that a state possess all the attributes of sovereignty and that the intent of the article was that both parties to a dispute should be given an opportunity to present their views. Immediately prior to the approval of the invitation, the President of the Council announced that he was putting the proposal to a vote "without any definition or determination of the sovereignty" of the Republic of Indonesia and with the understanding that every state retained "complete liberty either to recognize or not to recognize the sovereignty or independence" of the Indonesian Republic.[5]

This precedent was an important one. The President's statement has been frequently cited in other discussions, primarily in statements asserting that an invitation by the Council or the Assembly does not imply any "recognition" of the sovereignty of a state not a Member of the Organization or of the representational claims of a nongovernmental organization. The Council continued to follow the liberal policy established in the Indonesian case during succeeding years. An invitation was extended to the representative of Hyderabad, for example, to take part in the discussion of the Hyderabad question without debate on the status of Hyderabad, although its status was later discussed in the Council at some length.

[5] U.N. Security Council, Second Year, *Official Records*, No. 74, 181st Meeting (Aug. 12, 1947), p. 1940.

The question of the status of an entity not a Member of the Organization was raised again in 1950 in connection with various Soviet proposals to invite the representatives of the People's Democratic Republic of Korea and the People's Republic of China to participate in the discussions of the Council. One ground on which the proposed invitation to the North Koreans was rejected was that the General Assembly had already declared that the Republic of Korea was the only lawfully established government in Korea. The situation with regard to the People's Republic of China was complicated by the fact that the Council was closely split, with some members having recognized the Communist regime as the government of China while others continued to recognize the National Government. Since the Council upheld the right of the latter to represent China, it was argued that no invitations could be extended to the Communist regime under Article 32 of the Charter. Proposals to extend invitations without specific reference to Article 32 of the Charter failed of adoption, although they were supported by a majority of the members of the Council—the five members who had recognized the Central People's Government plus France. The Council finally decided to issue its invitations under Rule 39 of its Provisional Rules of Procedure. Even then the United States representative felt it necessary to state that his government did not recognize any such government as the Central People's Government.

The members of the Council, with the notable exception of the Soviet Union, have held that Article 32 is applicable only when the question under consideration is a "dispute." It has been generally agreed that it is for the Council itself to decide whether a dispute exists. One of the first questions that arose in connection with the participation of states not members either of the Council or of the Organization was how the Council could obtain the views of such states before it reached a decision on this preliminary point. For example, the Council agreed that the states concerned should be heard before it reached a decision whether the question of the Greek frontier incidents was to be considered a "dispute," and invitations were extended to the two Members of the United Nations, Greece and Yugoslavia, under Article 31. As this article does not apply to states not Members of the United Nations, the Council decided to invite Albania and Bulgaria "to enable the Security Council to hear such declarations as they may wish to make." At the same time it was decided that should the Council later find that the matter was a "dispute," the two representatives would be invited "to participate in the discussions." Such invitations were later extended.[6]

The distinction between a dispute and a situation was a matter of considerable concern to the members of the Council during the first year of its operations, but in succeeding years the subject was seldom discussed. For example, the Council invited Hyderabad and Albania, respectively, to participate in the discussions of the Hyderabad question and the question of the incidents in the Corfu Channel without any preliminary determination that these were "disputes." In 1950, the extent of the obligation of the Council under Article 32 was again raised, primarily in connection with the Soviet proposal to invite representatives of the People's Democratic Republic of Korea to participate in the discussions on the Korean question. Here the central point of the controversy was the distinction to be made between the procedures of the Council under Chapters VI and VII of the Charter. The Soviet representative drew attention to the traditional practice of the Council in hearing both sides of any controversy and further maintained that the Council in refusing to invite the North Koreans was violating Article 32 of the Charter. This position was opposed by the majority of the members of the Council who maintained that the Council was under no obligation to issue the invitation because the question under consideration was not a "dispute" but a "breach of the peace." As the representative of India pointed out:

. . . We are not investigating or considering a dispute; we are in the midst of enforcement action to suppress a dangerous breach of the peace. The two things are quite distinct. The Security Council has, in fact, a dual function under the Charter; it investigates disputes under Chapter VI of the Charter and it takes action with respect to breaches of the peace under Chapter VII. It is only when it is considering disputes that Article 32 of the Charter applies. . . .[7]

In accordance with Article 32 not only must the question under consideration be a "dispute" but also the state not a Member of the Organization must be a *party* to the dispute. This was one of the grounds on which the Council rejected proposals that East Indonesia and Borneo be invited to participate in the discussions on

[6] U.N. Security Council, First Year, *Official Records*, Second Series, No. 24, 82nd Meeting (Dec. 10, 1946), p. 559, and *Ibid.*, No. 26, 84th Meeting (Dec. 16, 1946), p. 613.

[7] U.N. Security Council, Fifth Year, *Official Records*, No. 36, 494th Meeting (Sept. 6, 1950), p. 15.

the Indonesian question. The same point was raised in opposition to the original Soviet proposal to invite the People's Republic of China to take part in the discussions on the Korean question.

This interpretation of Article 32 has not, however, meant that the Council has refused to hear the views of states not Members of the Organization in connection with various questions that have not been considered disputes. In 1946, while the Council was considering the Ukrainian complaint concerning Greece, Albania submitted a request under Article 32. There was considerable difference of opinion in the Council regarding whether an invitation could be extended to Albania in view of the fact that the question had been submitted as a "situation." It was in these circumstances that the first suggestion was made that the Council resort to Rule 39 of its Provisional Rules of Procedure. Despite the reluctance of some members of the Council, it was decided to invite Albania, not to participate in the discussions, but to make a "factual statement" to the Council. Since then, Rule 39 has been specifically cited in a number of invitations. It was under this rule, for example, that the People's Republic of China was invited "to be present" during the discussion by the Council of the Special Report of the United Nations Command concerning the presence of Chinese Communist military units in Korea.[8]

Invitations were also extended under Rule 39 to the Republic of Korea in connection with the Korean question and to the Jewish Agency for Palestine and the Arab Higher Committee during the initial consideration by the Council of the Palestine question. When the Council took up the Czechoslovak question, Jan Papanek, who had represented Czechoslovakia at the United Nations prior to the 1948 coup, was invited under Rule 39 to present to the Council information at his disposal. The rule was also the basis for an invitation to the representative of Hyderabad to take part in the discussion on the validity of his credentials. Mention might also be made at this point of the practice that the Council has developed of inviting members of commissions to attend discussions in the Council, usually for the purpose of formally presenting the report of the commission. At various times during the discussions of the Palestine problem, the Council questioned such officials as the United Nations Mediator, the acting mediator, and the Chairman of the Truce Supervision Organization.

[8] *Ibid.*, No. 62, 520th Meeting (Nov. 8, 1950), p. 8.

Consideration has also been given in connection with the application of Article 32 to the "conditions" that the Council should lay down for the participation of states not Members of the Organization. Such states invited under Article 32 have been asked to accept the same obligations as imposed by Article 35(2) of the Charter.[9] In the case of the Greek frontier incidents, the Council, employing the phraseology of this article, requested Albania and Bulgaria to accept for the purposes of the dispute the obligations of pacific settlement provided in the Charter. This same condition was applied to Albania in the case of the incidents in the Corfu Channel. It appears that a state not a Member of the United Nations in accepting the invitation of the Council has been considered to have accepted the "conditions" contained therein. Often such states have announced their acceptance of these obligations even before the Council has extended the invitation. The Council has been reluctant to specify just what these obligations entail. In fact, the matter has seldom been discussed.[10] It should be noted that the Council has not attached the same conditions to invitations extended under Rule 39. The Republic of Korea, for example, was not asked to accept the obligations of pacific settlement in connection with the Korean question. Nor was there any discussion on this point in connection with the various proposed invitations to the People's Democratic Republic of Korea and the People's Republic of China.

The Position of Invited Representatives

It has been frequently asserted that it is the aim of the Security Council in extending invitations under Articles 31 and 32 to place all parties on the same footing regardless whether they are members of the Council or Members of the United Nations. In practice a member of the Council does enjoy certain privileges. Some, like precedence in the order of speaking, are of no great significance; others, such as the right to vote except in so far as the abstention clause of Article 27 applies, are important. It has not been clear from the practice of the Council whether an invited representative has

---

[9] See above, Chap. IV.

[10] This matter was, however, considered in the International Court of Justice in connection with the contention of the United Kingdom that Albania was obligated to accept the jurisdiction of the Court in the Corfu Channel case. See below, Chap. XIII.

the right to raise points of order or to make proposals concerning the procedure the Council should follow. The Provisional Rules of Procedure accord to Members of the United Nations who are not members of the Council the right to submit proposals and draft resolutions.[11] No mention is made, however, of the position of states not Members of the United Nations. Proposals by invited representatives are put to the vote only at the request of a member of the Council. Many such proposals have been voted upon, including one by the People's Republic of China, but on occasion proposals have failed to obtain sponsorship by a member of the Council.

It has been contended that invited representatives may not take part in certain procedural discussions of the Council. As pointed out previously, such representatives have not been permitted to participate in the discussions concerning the inclusion of items in the agenda. It has also been argued that they may not take part in the "drawing up of the agenda" or in the discussions on the postponement of the consideration of a question or the deletion of an item from the agenda.

There has been a certain amount of inconsistency concerning participation in discussions on the establishment of commissions of investigation. The Council decided to exclude invited representatives from a discussion concerning the functioning of the commission dealing with the question of Greek frontier incidents, presumably on the grounds that the Council was not discussing the dispute itself and that the obligation under Article 32 did not therefore apply. The invited representatives had, however, taken part in the earlier discussions on the establishment of the commission. On the other hand, the Council decided against inviting the People's Republic of China and the People's Democratic Republic of Korea to participate in discussions on proposals to set up commissions to investigate the charges against the United States concerning the bombing of Chinese territory and the use of germ warfare in Korea.

Various statements have been made that a representative invited under Rule 39 may not introduce proposals, may not raise points of order, and in fact may not intervene in the discussions except at the request of the Council. In some cases a speaker has withdrawn from the Council table after having concluded his statement, but in each case the terms of the invitation itself have indicated the very limited degree of participation being granted. The restriction

[11] Rule 38.

has not been merely a consequence of the fact that in these particular cases the invitation of the Council had cited Rule 39 rather than Article 32 of the Charter, for in other cases representatives invited under this rule have continued to take part in the discussions. It was on this point, whether the initial invitation under Rule 39 to the Republic of Korea entitled the Korean representative to take part in the subsequent discussions in the Council, that the Council argued for the whole month of August 1950. The Soviet representative was unsuccessful in his attempt to exclude the Korean representative from the discussions. At a later stage the Soviet representative again objected without success to the presence of the representative of the Republic of Korea during the discussion of a complaint submitted by the North Korean authorities.

The difficulties that can arise from any attempt to restrict the participation of invited representatives to the discussion of certain aspects of a question were illustrated by the situation that developed at a later stage in the Korean discussions. Under the terms of the invitation of the Council, the participation of the representative of the People's Republic of China was to be restricted to discussion of the Special Report of the United Nations Command on the presence of Chinese Communist military units in Korea. Because of this restriction the invitation was declined, but it is difficult to see how the restriction would have been applied had the invitation been accepted. As pointed out by the President of the Council, the report was not a separate agenda item, and other members of the Council supported the President's opinion that the representative would be permitted to express his views on the whole problem of Korea.

It does not seem that representatives invited under Rule 39 have in fact enjoyed a less privileged position than that accorded to representatives invited under Article 32. It appears that the main difference has been that an invitation under Article 32 has been considered as an implied recognition by the Council of the right of the representative to take part in discussions, while an invitation under Rule 39 has been merely a recognition by the Council of the desirability of hearing the views of the representative.

Practice of the General Assembly

Neither the Charter nor the Rules of Procedure of the General Assembly contain any provisions concerning participation in the discussions of the Assembly. The Assembly has been very liberal in giving interested parties an opportunity to present their views. On this point the practice of the Assembly has been similar to that of the Security Council, and the problems that both have faced have also been very much alike.

As in the Council, most invitations to participate in discussions have been extended as a result of a request, most requests have been granted, and occasionally the Assembly has issued invitations on its own initiative. Usually, the invitation has been extended at the outset of the discussion by the chairman of the committee to which the particular question has been referred. The participation of invited representatives has been restricted to discussions in committee. Occasionally, they have taken part in the work of subcommittees, but they have not been permitted to participate in the plenary meetings of the Assembly.

In most cases, invitations have been extended to states not Members of the United Nations that have a direct interest in the matter being discussed and whose co-operation is necessary to a satisfactory solution of the question. Generally, there has been agreement that these parties should be heard. Invitations were, for example, extended with little discussion to Austria in connection with the Austrian treaty question and to representatives of East and West Germany (and both sectors of Berlin) in connection with the proposed appointment of a commission to investigate whether conditions obtained throughout Germany for the holding of free elections. In some cases where the status of an entity not a Member of the United Nations has been the subject of controversy, proposed invitations have been rejected. The Assembly refused to hear representatives of the Provisional Democratic Government of Greece and the People's Democratic Republic of Korea. A proposal to invite the Bey of Tunis to send a representative to attend meetings on the Tunisian question was also rejected, but by a narrow vote.

The committees of the Assembly have shown a propensity for using different phraseology in their invitations, but it does not appear that these variations have had much significance. Although the invitation to Jordan "to participate" in the discussion of the Palestine question was broadly phrased, and the participation of Italy in the consideration of the question of the Italian colonies was by the terms of the invitation restricted to an initial statement and such other interventions as the committee itself requested, it does not appear that Italy played any less active role than did Jordan.

Although the point has been raised from time to time, in only one instance has the Assembly purposely extended a restricted invitation. At its second session, the Assembly sought to follow the precedent of the Council and make the participation of Albania and Bulgaria in the discussion of the Balkan question conditional on the acceptance by those states of the "principles and rules of the Charter." Both governments stated that they could not consent to having their right to submit views subjected to any conditions whatsoever. The committee of the Assembly then decided to hear statements from the representatives of the two states and requested them to place themselves at the disposal of the committee to reply to any questions put to them.[12] At subsequent sessions proposals that Albania and Bulgaria be invited to "participate" in the discussion of the Balkan question were always rejected, and invitations similar to those adopted at the second session were extended. As a result, during the discussions the chairman of the committee interrupted the Albanian representative to point out that, in accordance with the terms of the invitation, he should confine himself to answering questions.

As in the Council, qualified invitations to participate in the discussions of the Assembly appear to have been prompted primarily by attitudes toward the right of a hearing. The representative of Chile, for example, in submitting an amendment to a Soviet proposal to extend an invitation to the People's Republic of China explained that it was not his desire "to limit the opportunity of the Communist representatives to be heard," but that it should be made clear that they would not be considered as representing "a government recognized by the United Nations as having the right to a seat in its councils."[13]

Although invitations of the Council have been extended for the most part to "states," in the committees of the Assembly there have been a number of occasions when organizations, not possessing governmental powers, have been given an opportunity to present their views. This has resulted in part from the nature of some of the questions brought to the Assembly. For example, in order to

[12] U.N. General Assembly, Second Session, First Committee, *Official Records*, 62nd Meeting (Sept. 27, 1947), p. 31.
[13] U.N. General Assembly, Fifth Session, First Committee, *Official Records*, 406th Meeting (Nov. 24, 1950), p. 384.

reach decisions regarding the disposal of the former Italian colonies, the Assembly considered it desirable to have information on the views of the inhabitants of the areas. These views were obtained not only through the dispatch of a commission of investigation but also through hearings in the committees of the Assembly. During the discussions, close to a dozen organizations from Libya, Eritrea, and Somaliland were given the opportunity to present their views.

In other cases, it has been recognized that, if too liberal a policy were adopted, the entire time of the Assembly might be taken up with hearing the numerous organizations that wished to be heard. It is doubtful whether the hearings have been particularly useful and whether the organizations are sufficiently representative to give the Assembly a clear picture of any situation. Members have been reluctant to support proposals such as: to grant a hearing to a representative of the "Palestine Arab Refugees"; to permit a South African professor to make a statement on the *apartheid* question on behalf of the African National Congress; and to invite the Vatican and the Christian Churches to present their views regarding the observance of human rights and fundamental freedoms in Bulgaria, Hungary, and Rumania.

One method that the Assembly has adopted in dealing with requests from organizations has been to establish a subcommittee to recommend what organizations should be heard. This procedure was followed in dealing with the question of the former Italian colonies. A similar subcommittee was established at the first special session during the discussion of the Palestine question. In this case, the Assembly decided to hear the Jewish Agency for Palestine and the Arab Higher Committee. The subcommittee recommended that no other hearings be granted in view of the fact that a special committee was being sent to Palestine and would be able to hear any organizations that desired to present their views.

The procedure followed by the Assembly during the initial consideration of the Korean question in 1947 is worth noting. The Soviet Union proposed that the "elected representatives of the Korean people" be invited to take part in the consideration of the question. One of the principal issues in dispute between the Soviet Union and the United States, however, was precisely who was qualified to represent the Korean people. Thus, the Assembly adopted an "amendment" to the Soviet proposal establishing a commission "to observe" that the Korean representatives were "in fact duly elected by the Korean people."[14] The commission served as a sort of credentials committee, and, on the basis of its report, the Assembly invited the Republic of Korea to take part in its subsequent debates and rejected proposals to invite representatives of the People's Democratic Republic of Korea.

The question has arisen on other occasions whether hearings could be dispensed with when the sending of a subsidiary organ of the Assembly to the area is contemplated. In most cases the interested parties have been heard before a commission has been established. The Assembly, however, like the Council, rejected a proposal that the People's Republic of China and the People's Democratic Republic of Korea be invited to take part in the discussions concerning the appointment of a commission to investigate the germ warfare charges.

Hearings Before the International Court of Justice

The Statute of the International Court of Justice and the Rules of the Court contain extensive provisions concerning the position of states parties to a dispute before the Court. There are in addition provisions under which states that are not parties may be permitted "to intervene." Under Article 62 of the Statute, should a state consider that it has an interest of a legal nature that might be affected by the decision in the case, it may request permission to intervene. Under Article 63, any state that is a party to a convention the construction of which is in question has a right to intervene in the proceedings, but, if it uses this right, it is bound by the construction given in the judgment. Moreover, "public international organizations" may either on their own initiative or at the request of the Court supply information relevant to a case before the Court.[15]

In practice, there have been few occasions for applying the elaborate provisions concerning third party intervention.[16] The only case in which a state other than a party to the dispute has requested permission to intervene was in connection with the dispute between Colombia and Peru over the asylum granted by the former to Haya de la Torre. One of the points at issue was the interpreta-

[14] Res. 112 (II), Nov. 14, 1947.
[15] See Rules of the Court, Art. 57.
[16] *Ibid.*, Arts. 64-66.

tion of the Havana Convention on Asylum of 1928. Cuba, a party to the Convention, requested and, despite the objections of Peru, was granted permission to intervene in the proceedings.

Article 66 of the Statute of the Court also provides for the submission of written and oral statements by states and international organizations in connection with the consideration by the Court of requests for advisory opinions. The Secretary-General of the United Nations and several states signatories of the peace treaties with Bulgaria, Hungary, and Rumania, presented statements to the Court during proceedings on the request for an advisory opinion on the interpretation of the treaties. In addition, the Court has admitted statements from the International Labor Organization, the Organization of American States, and an organization entitled the International League for the Rights of Men.

Any significant changes in the practices of the Security Council and the General Assembly with regard to participation in their discussions of states not Members of the United Nations depend in large measure on changes in attitudes toward the broader questions of what are the proper functions of the two organs, and how their business should be conducted. Were the two organs to decide to exercise a stricter control over the conduct of their discussions, the liberal practices with regard to the hearing of such states would no doubt be altered. But it is scarcely logical to restrict the participation of these states as long as the two organs continue to regard themselves as performing the functions of diplomatic conferences and do not even attempt to confine their discussions to matters that are directly relevant to the questions under consideration.

With regard to the basis on which invitations should be extended, Articles 31 and 32 do, of course, establish criteria for the Security Council. The practices of the Council and the Assembly, however, show that decisions with regard to the participation of states not Members of the United Nations, like decisions on other matters, are based primarily on political considerations. It is doubtful that there would be much advantage in including either in the Charter or in the rules of the two organs additional provisions regarding the criteria to be applied.

A plea can be made for more consistency and less ambiguity. The tendency to regard an invitation as some kind of reward for good behavior may be seriously questioned. As the primary purpose of the discussions that take place in the organs is to assist the Council and the Assembly in reaching conclusions, little if any advantage is to be gained by excluding parties directly involved in a controversy from participation in the discussions of the United Nations, even though it seems clear that their co-operation will not be forthcoming or that they may use the opportunity to present irrelevant propaganda statements. Regardless whether the North Koreans and the People's Republic of China had by actions in disregard of the United Nations forfeited any "right" they might have had to take part in the discussions in the Council and the Assembly, it could be argued that the refusal to give them a hearing made the tasks of the Council and the Assembly more difficult.

CHAPTER VII

Procedures for Clarifying Issues

ONE OF THE initial tasks that the Security Council and the General Assembly face in the consideration of a particular dispute or situation affecting international peace and security is the clarification of specific issues. This is not merely a matter of "fact-finding," as in most instances either the "facts" are well known, or, in addition to questions of fact, there are important issues of a legal or political nature that need clarification if the organs of the United Nations are to act intelligently. In contrast to the Statute and Rules of the International Court of Justice, the Charter and the rules of procedure of the Council and the Assembly provide little detailed guidance regarding procedures to be followed. The practices of the two organs have been determined to a large extent by considerations of a practical nature. Normally, the initial step is a general discussion in the organ concerned, in the course of which the interested parties explain their positions and other states are afforded the opportunity to present their points of view. It is therefore necessary to begin by considering the procedure of discussion in the Council and the Assembly.

Procedure of Discussion[1]

Neither the Security Council nor the General Assembly has in practice made any distinction among the procedures for considering the various kinds of questions brought to its attention. The Council has discussed disputes, threats to the peace, and questions of an organizational nature in much the same way. The Assembly has differed even less in its approach to the wide variety of matters brought to its attention. The procedures followed by both organs have been determined to a large extent by the special circumstances of each case.

[1] For a further discussion of the procedures of the Security Council and the General Assembly, see the volume in this Brookings series, *The Organization and Procedures of the United Nations.*

There has been little attempt to work out a pattern for the consideration of particular categories of questions.

The Security Council

As soon as the Security Council has placed a question on its agenda and has decided who shall be heard, it has usually proceeded to a full-scale discussion. Usually, the discussion has been initiated by the state that has brought the matter to the attention of the Council. If the question has involved charges against another state, the second state has usually been given the opportunity to make an immediate reply. These replies have contained counter-charges, denials of the allegations, and, very often, denials of the competence of the Council to deal with the question. In some cases, the accused state has confined its remarks to denials of competence and has refused to take part in the subsequent discussions. Once the parties have stated their views, there has usually been a general discussion in which the other members of the Council take part.

Generally, after the consideration of a question has begun, the Council has continued its discussions until a decision or a deadlock has been reached. These discussions have often extended over a considerable period of time. As the Council is in continuous session, it can time its discussions to developments in the situation, and, occasionally, it has decided to suspend discussions in order to give its members more time to formulate their positions or to await further developments. The "suspension" of a discussion may have the result, and may in fact be designed for the purpose, of terminating the consideration of the question. For example, in May 1946 the Council "adjourned" consideration of the Soviet-Iranian question until a date in the near future, and in October 1951, the Council adjourned the discussion of the Anglo-Iranian question in order to await a decision of the International Court of Justice. In neither case did the Council return to a consideration of the matter.

The suggestion has been made that the proper course for the Council to follow is to place a question on its agenda, discuss it, and then dismiss it if action by the Council is not considered appropriate, but this pattern has seldom been followed. When the Greek question was first brought to the attention of the Council in February 1946, the members of the Council agreed that no action was necessary and eventually agreed on the dismissal of the case by a statement of the President; but this was an exceptional action. Usually, the Council has merely ceased to discuss a question when, either after general discussion or after voting on proposals, it has become clear that the members of the Council are divided regarding what, if any, action should be taken.

The General Assembly

As has already been pointed out, the General Assembly usually accepts the recommendations of the General Committee concerning the inclusion of items in the agenda. The recommendation of the General Committee regarding the main committee to which a question should be referred is likewise generally followed. Under its Rules of Procedure, the Assembly may decide to discuss a question without referring it to a committee, but this procedure has seldom been considered appropriate for the consideration of "political" questions. In a few cases where a lengthy discussion has not seemed necessary, the Assembly has dealt with questions directly in its plenary meeting. The Secretary-General's twenty-year peace program, for example, was not considered in committee. When the Soviet Union made charges concerning the treatment of prisoners of war in Korea, on the eve of the Christmas adjournment of the 1952 session, the Assembly decided to place the matter on its agenda, listened to the statement of charges in plenary meeting, and then voted down the Soviet draft resolution. This is one of the few occasions when the Assembly has foregone a lengthy discussion of a question in favor of a procedure designed to dismiss charges with the utmost dispatch.

In view of the fact that each Member of the United Nations is represented on each of the main committees, it would seem to make little difference in which committee a matter is discussed. However, the reference of a question to a committee does constitute an indication by the Assembly regarding the essential nature of the question. Furthermore, the approach of the various committees differs to some extent. Occasionally, there have been differences of opinion on the question of reference. For example, during the second part of the first session of the Assembly, there was a lengthy debate on whether the question of treatment of Indians in South Africa should be referred to the First (Political) Committee or the Sixth (Legal) Committee, an issue that was finally resolved by establishing a joint committee of the two for the consideration of the question.[2]

Once the Assembly has decided on the allocation of items, the committee itself must decide on the priority to be accorded to the various items on its agenda. This decision has been considered of importance. An item placed at the end of the list is not likely to receive careful consideration, or may even, because of a heavy schedule, be postponed to a future session. In addition, the discussions and recommendations on one item have not been unrelated to action on other items, for the position of a Member on one question may be directly influenced by the support it has received or hopes to receive on another question with which it is particularly concerned.

The discussion of a question in a committee of the Assembly is initiated in the same manner as in the Security Council in that the state submitting the question has usually been permitted to speak first for the purpose of presenting its case. As in the Council, in cases where charges have been made against other states, the replies have usually contained countercharges, denials of allegations, denials of competence, and even refusals to take part in the discussions. In contrast to practice in the Council, debates in the committees of the Assembly have usually been more formal in nature because the opportunity for immediate reply is more limited. With sixty potential speakers and a time schedule to meet, it is also necessary for a stricter control to be exercised over debate. The degree to which this has been successful has depended in large part upon the skill of the committee chairmen in guiding discussion. Also, in contrast to the Council, it is much more difficult for the Assembly to time its discussions to the development of the situation, because questions are taken up in succession, and once a discussion has begun, it has usually continued without interruption until a vote is taken.

The pattern of discussion in the Assembly was established originally on the premise that it would be in session for only a few months of the year. The sessions of the Assembly have, however, become increasingly prolonged. Thus a question may not be discussed until long after it has been submitted, by which time the

[2] U.N. General Assembly, First Session, Second Part, General Committee, *Official Records,* 19th Meeting (Oct. 24, 1946), pp. 70-73; U.N. General Assembly, First Session, Second Part, Plenary, *Official Records,* 46th Meeting (Oct. 31, 1946), pp. 930-31.

situation may have changed considerably. In September 1950, for example, the United States asked the Assembly to take up the question of Formosa, but by the time the matter came up for consideration, the situation in the Far East had so radically changed that the United States did not press for a discussion of the matter.

Once a committee has concluded its consideration of a question, it makes a report to the Assembly containing the recommendations, if any, that it considers the Assembly should adopt. As a rule, the recommendations of the committee have been adopted by the Assembly without change. However, as a decision can be taken in committee by a simple majority, while the adoption by the Assembly of a resolution on an "important question" requires a two-thirds majority, some committee recommendations have failed to obtain the necessary support in plenary.

The original tendency of the Assembly to adopt some kind of resolution on every question on its agenda has been reversed to some extent in recent years. There have been a variety of reasons for this, including the increased difficulty of getting sufficient support for a resolution, the realization that in some cases the appropriate procedure is merely to dismiss a charge by voting down proposals, and the feeling in many cases that the objectives of the Organization have been adequately served by a discussion without any resolution being adopted.

The procedures of discussion in the Council and the Assembly give the states directly concerned in a dispute or situation the opportunity to state their positions fully and freely. Also they afford Members the opportunity to express their views on the issues that may be raised. They therefore serve the useful purpose of helping to elucidate the issues that may be involved, whether legal, factual, or political, and may contribute to the publicizing of the facts of a situation, to the mobilization of public opinion, and to the formation of a consensus in support of a particular point of view or a concrete proposal. It is not, however, so clear that these procedures are well suited to facilitate agreement among the parties whose consent is necessary to any final settlement. The question might be raised whether the degree of publicity that has characterized the procedures has not at times obstructed agreement.

It was often the practice of the Council of the League of Nations to discuss questions in private and then hold public meetings for the purpose of announcing decisions. In contrast, there has been a great emphasis from the beginning in the United Nations on the full discussion of all issues in open meeting. A state bringing a question to the United Nations for the purpose of giving publicity to the actions or policies of another state, or a party to a dispute hoping to mobilize the support of the international community for its position, will naturally tend to prefer full public discussion of its complaints. In some circumstances this may be the best procedure. A public discussion or the possibility thereof may produce sufficient pressure on an intransigent party to bring about necessary concessions. In those cases where there is a disparity of power between the disputants, the pressure of public opinion may become an equalizing factor. Experience with the handling of the questions of Iran, Syria and Lebanon, and Indonesia illustrates the value to the weaker party of a mobilized public opinion. There can be little doubt that the Council discussions of these questions in themselves made an important contribution to the eventual settlements. However, these public discussions may not in all cases be the most effective method for reaching a settlement, and even in those instances where they prove necessary, it would seem that they might well be postponed until after a preliminary effort at conciliation has been made.

It is precisely on this point that the difference between the approach of the League of Nations and that of the United Nations in handling political questions becomes most apparent. Although the League almost invariably devoted its initial efforts to working out solutions acceptable to the parties concerned, the United Nations has not, except in a few instances, made any such effort.

Initial Efforts to Work Out Agreements

That delicate political negotiations cannot be carried out under the eye of a television camera and that an agreement between the interested states is more likely to be reached before rather than after public discussion have not gone completely unrecognized in the United Nations. The General Assembly in 1949 recommended that the Security Council "examine the utility and desirability" of following a practice similar to that employed by the Council of the League, which appointed *rapporteurs* to act as conciliators for the cases brought before it.[3] This practice, the Assembly suggested, "allowed private conversations among the parties and the *rapporteur* and avoided the crystallization of views that tends to result from taking a stated public position." The procedure that the Assembly recommended was as follows: After a dispute or situation was brought to the attention of the Council, and not later than immediately after the opening statements by the parties, the parties should be invited to meet with the President of the Council, and an attempt should be made to agree on a representative on the Council to act as *rapporteur* or conciliator for the case. If this step were taken, the Council should abstain from further action while efforts at conciliation were undertaken. The *rapporteur* was to report "in due course" to the Council.[4]

The members of the Council expressed general agreement with the principle involved. It was pointed out, however, that its application in a specific instance would depend upon circumstances, and that the Council should not therefore lay down a rule that the procedure be automatically applied. The Council decided to take note of the resolution, and "should an appropriate occasion arise, to base its action upon the principles contained therein."[5] It might be argued that "no appropriate occasion" has arisen in recent years. In any case, although the possibility has been discussed in private negotiations, the Council has not followed this approach in dealing with any of the questions it has considered since the resolution was adopted.

There have been many cases in which the Council and the Assembly have recognized that the most appropriate procedure is to attempt to work out an agreement between the parties directly concerned. Both organs have on occasion established special subsidiary organs for the purpose of assisting the parties in working out agreements, but it is seldom that any such effort at conciliation has been made during the initial stage of the handling of a question.[6]

The handling of the India-Pakistan question provides one of the few examples of resort to this procedure. In January 1948, immediately after the initial statements by the parties, the Council

[3] For comments on the *rapporteur* system see F. P. Walters, *A History of the League of Nations,* Vol. I (1952), p. 87 and U.N. Doc. A/AC.18/68 (June 29, 1948).

[4] See Res. 268 (III), B, Apr. 28, 1949.

[5] U.N. Security Council, Fifth Year, *Official Records,* No. 14, 472nd Meeting (May 24, 1950), pp. 2-16.

[6] See below, Chap. XII.

adopted a suggestion by the United Kingdom that conversations between the parties be held under the auspices of the President.[7] The outcome of these initial conversations was encouraging. At the next meeting the Council adopted a resolution, introduced by its President, that had been drafted as a result of his conversations with the parties and had the approval of both India and Pakistan. The Council endorsed a continuance of the conversations. Unfortunately, although the six members of the Council who took part in the conversations agreed on the course of action to be followed, full agreement of the parties was not obtained. At a later stage, the Council again suspended consideration of the India-Pakistan question in order that a further effort might be made to work out with the parties a "mutually satisfactory basis for dealing with the problem."

As the Charter itself stresses the serious nature of the questions to be handled by the Council, it is to be expected that in most cases a dispute or situation will have reached an advanced stage by the time it is brought to the Council. It might be presumed that the Assembly, being authorized to deal with matters of a less serious nature, would have a greater opportunity to exercise a conciliatory influence at an early stage in the development of a controversy. Unfortunately, it is difficult to adapt the machinery of the Assembly to this type of activity.

In 1948, the Interim Committee proposed the following addition to the Rules of Procedure of the Assembly in order that preliminary negotiations with the parties might be undertaken before a full discussion of a question:

Where any question has been placed on the agenda under Article 11, paragraph 2, of the Charter of the United Nations, the representatives of the parties shall, before or immediately after the opening statement and in any case before the item is referred by the General Assembly to its appropriate committee, be invited by the President to meet under his direction for the purpose of reaching agreement as to the facts underlying the question and of conciliation.[8]

But the Assembly decided to refer this proposal back to the Interim Committee for consideration within the context of its studies on

---

[7] U.N. Security Council, Third Year, *Official Records*, Nos. 1-15, 229th Meeting (Jan. 17, 1948), p. 128.

[8] U.N. General Assembly, Third Session, *Official Records*, Supplement No. 10, p. 34.

the procedures of the Assembly. No further effort has been made to obtain its adoption, or to apply this approach to any of the questions considered by the Assembly.

In some instances, the Assembly has made a deliberate effort to obtain an agreement among the parties concerned before proceeding to the adoption of a resolution. For example, many subcommittees have been charged with the task of attempting to work out agreed resolutions. These subcommittees have been in a sense "drafting committees," but, in the larger sense, they have represented an effort to conciliate differing viewpoints.

The procedure followed in handling the Palestine question at the second session of the Assembly is of some interest in this connection. Recognizing that this question would require extensive discussion, the Assembly did not refer it to the First Committee but set up an additional committee, the *Ad Hoc* Committee on the Palestinian Question. The *Ad Hoc* Committee in turn established three subcommittees: one to work out a detailed plan for partition; a second to work out a plan for an independent unitary state; and a third "conciliation" group that "would try to bring the parties together." This group was not successful in its efforts, although the chairman assured the committee that the group "explored the ground from every possible point of view."[9] When the report of the *Ad Hoc* Committee was considered by the Assembly in plenary, there was some criticism to the effect that no effort had been made to work out a solution acceptable to the parties and that the terms of reference and the composition of the two subcommittees were such that it was inevitable that their proposals would not provide a basis for agreement. Confronted by a small margin of support for the partition plan, the negative attitude of the United Kingdom toward the plan, and indications of a conciliatory attitude on the part of certain Arab representatives, some delegations appeared willing to support a further effort to work out a solution that would be acceptable to all the interested parties. Nevertheless, after agreeing to a twenty-four hour postponement, the Assembly proceeded to adopt the resolution recommending partition.

On a few occasions, the Assembly has suspended its discussion so an effort might be made to find a solution acceptable to the parties concerned. While the Balkan question was being considered

[9] U.N. General Assembly, Second Session, Plenary, *Official Records*, 128th Meeting (Nov. 29, 1947), pp. 1413-14.

in the fourth session, for example, the First Committee deferred its discussions in order that a conciliation group might attempt to work out an agreement among the parties.[10] At a crucial point during the consideration of the Korean question in the fifth session, shortly after the military intervention of the People's Republic of China in Korea had been brought to the attention of the Assembly, the Assembly established the "Group of Three" to "determine the basis on which a satisfactory cease-fire in Korea" could be arranged.[11] The unsuccessful efforts of this group and the resulting action taken by the Assembly are dealt with later, but the matter is referred to here as one of the few instances in which the Assembly has interrupted its discussions in order to obtain a clarification of the positions of the parties directly concerned before taking action.[12]

Mention might also be made of the procedure followed by the First Committee during the discussions on disarmament at the sixth session of the Assembly. Debate in the committee was suspended so the Soviet Union, France, the United Kingdom, and the United States might meet under the auspices of the President of the Assembly to formulate agreed proposals. Although no agreement was reached on the substantive issues involved, there was agreement on the establishment of a new commission.[13]

The very nature of many of the questions brought to the attention of the Council and the Assembly makes it unlikely that any real solution will be reached merely through consultations with the parties. However, except when a matter is really urgent, little can be lost through an initial effort to work out an agreement. The advantages of such an effort are numerous and obvious. It provides an opportunity for a clarification of the positions of the parties, and even if no agreement is reached on the substance of the question, an agreement may well be reached on the procedures to be followed. Particularly in those cases—and there have been an increasing number of them—where one of the parties objects to the consideration of a question by the Council or the Assembly, a procedure of informal consultation may indeed accomplish more than a full-scale debate and discussion.

[10] U.N. General Assembly, Fourth Session, First Committee, *Official Records*, 276th Meeting (Sept. 29, 1946), p. 11. For a similar effort made during the third session, see United Nations Press Release BAL/480.

[11] Res. 384 (V), Dec. 14, 1950.

[12] See below, Chap. XIX.

[13] See below, Chap. XXI.

Initial Steps to Prevent Deterioration of a Situation

In the United Nations, as in the League of Nations, it has been recognized that it is extremely difficult, if not impossible, to proceed with the consideration of a situation if, at the same time, it is deteriorating because of the unilateral actions of one or more of the interested parties. Therefore, in some cases an initial effort has been made to obtain the agreement of the parties to take certain measures or to abstain from certain acts that might be prejudicial to a solution of the question.

The initial action of the Council of the League of Nations when a dispute was submitted to it was the dispatch of a message stressing the desirability that the "governments concerned should take whatever steps may be necessary or useful to prevent anything occurring in their respective territories which might prejudice the examination or settlement of the question by the Council."[14] A similar approach occasionally has been employed by the United Nations. For example, even before the India-Pakistan question was considered by the Security Council, the President of the Council addressed an appeal to the parties to refrain from any steps likely to result in the aggravation of the situation and thereby render "more difficult any action by the Security Council."[15] Whereas the above-mentioned practice of the League of Nations was followed in connection with all disputes, in the United Nations the practice of calling upon the parties to take provisional measures to prevent the aggravation of a situation has been followed primarily in cases where hostilities have appeared imminent or have already broken out.[16]

Under Article 41 of the Statute of the International Court of Justice, the Court is authorized "to indicate, if it considers that circumstances so require, any provisional measures which ought to be taken to preserve the respective rights of either party." Under the Rules of the Court, a request for such interim measures of protection is to be given priority and regarded as a matter of urgency.[17] The indication of provisional measures is a rather exceptional pro-

---

[14] U.N. Doc. A/AC.18/68 (June 29, 1948).

[15] U.N. Doc. S/636 (Jan. 6, 1948).

[16] The concept of "provisional measures" under the Charter system, as well as the nature and effect of such measures taken by the United Nations to avert or bring an end to hostilities are dealt with at length in Chap. XV, below.

[17] See Art. 61.

cedure. There has been only one case in which the Court has been requested to exercise this authority. Shortly after the United Kingdom submitted the Anglo-Iranian Oil Company case to the Court, and before the hearings on the case had begun, the United Kingdom requested the Court to indicate certain interim measures of protection. The President of the Court immediately telegraphed the Iranian Government suggesting the avoidance of all measures "which might render impossible or difficult the execution of any judgment which the Court might subsequently give and to ensure that no action is taken which might aggravate the dispute. . . ."[18] The Court then proceeded to indicate the provisional measures to be taken by Iran and by the United Kingdom, measures which differed to some extent from those the United Kingdom had requested.[19]

The extent to which procedures for preventing deterioration of a situation can be successfully employed at the initial stage in the consideration of a question is in part dependent on the information available. Of even more importance, however, is the need for convincing the states concerned that their compliance with such measures will not in fact prejudice their own positions and that these initial steps will be effectively followed up.

Procedures for Obtaining Information

At the outset of the consideration of a question, the Security Council and the General Assembly face the problem of obtaining information necessary to intelligent and effective action. Obviously, the main source of information is the statements of the parties directly concerned and the written documentation they supply. As already pointed out, the amount of information at the disposal of the Council and the Assembly at the outset of the discussion of a question has varied considerably.[20] Sometimes when a state is bringing a question to the attention of the Council or the Assembly, it has submitted extensive documentation. Parties directly concerned have occasionally submitted further written memoranda. For example, the United Kingdom presented a lengthy memo-

---

[18] *I.C.J. Reports, 1951,* p. 91.
[19] *Ibid.,* pp. 90-94.
[20] See above, Chap. IV.

randum on "The Political History of Palestine under British Mandate," and on the question of the disposal of the former Italian colonies, the report of the four-power Commission of Investigation was made available to Members. Generally, however, little emphasis has been placed on the availability of adequate documentation. Texts of treaties, laws, or diplomatic correspondence have seldom been circulated unless one of the parties directly concerned has included such materials in its own memoranda.

It is interesting to contrast the practices of the Security Council and the General Assembly of the United Nations with those of the League of Nations. Under the Covenant, the parties to a dispute submitted to the Council or the Assembly of the League under Article 15 were required to communicate to the Secretary-General "statements of their case with all relevant facts and papers." Furthermore, the Secretary-General of the League was directed to make "all necessary arrangements for a full investigation and consideration" of the dispute. It was the practice of the Secretary-General of the League, in connection with questions brought to the attention of the Council and the Assembly of the League to present a report covering the factual situation.[21] The only time the Secretary-General of the United Nations has followed a similar practice in placing information at the disposal of Members was in connection with the Palestine question. A special library was established, and two special volumes covering factual background material were prepared.

Occasionally, during the course of the consideration of a dispute or situation, specific requests for information have been addressed to the interested parties. After the opening statements on the Berlin question, for example, the President of the Security Council on behalf of the six "neutral" members, addressed a series of questions to the four occupying powers. France, the United States, and the United Kingdom replied to these questions at a later meeting. The Soviet Union, however, because it denied the competence of the Council to deal with this question, refused to do so. At one point during the consideration of the Palestine question by the Council, a questionnaire was addressed to the Arab states, the Jewish authorities in Palestine, and the Arab Higher Committee.[22] It is seldom, however, that such systematic attempts to obtain information have been made.

[21] See Walters, *op. cit.*, Vol. I, p. 87.
[22] U.N. Doc. S/753 (May 18, 1948).

Both the Security Council and the General Assembly have established special committees or commissions for the specific purpose of obtaining information on which the Council or the Assembly can base its decision.[23] Customarily, a resolution adopted by the Council or the Assembly has included a request for a report on the implementation of the resolution. Such reports from Members and from the special subsidiary organs, often established to assist in the implementation of resolutions, provide a basis for any further action. On occasion specific requests have been addressed to such special subsidiary organs for information on some aspect of a question.

The Assembly in a few cases has also requested other principal organs of the United Nations to study and report on some aspect of a question. At one point during the discussion of the Palestine question, for example, the Assembly asked the Trusteeship Council to study "suitable measures" for the protection of Jerusalem and to submit proposals thereon to the Assembly. Later, at the same session, the Assembly adopted a resolution based on the proposals of the Council.[24] Again during its fifth session, the Assembly requested the Economic and Social Council in consultation with the specialized agencies "to develop plans for relief and rehabilitation" in Korea.[25] Later during this same session, after a study of the report of the Council, the Assembly established the United Nations Korean Reconstruction Agency.[26] One of the functions assigned to the Interim Committee of the Assembly, when it was established in 1947, was to study and report on questions referred to it by the Assembly. Very few questions have been handled in this way largely because the refusal of the Soviet Union to recognize the validity of the committee deprived it of much of its importance.

Clarification of Legal Issues

Some of the Members of the United Nations have expressed the opinion that inadequate consideration has been given to the handling of issues of a legal nature that arise during the discussion of questions affecting international peace and security. In both the Security Council and the General Assembly, attempts have been

---

[23] These fact-finding bodies are discussed below, Chap. VIII.
[24] Res. 185 (S-2), Apr. 26, 1948, and Res. 187 (S-2), May 14, 1948.
[25] Res. 376 (V), Oct. 7, 1950.
[26] Res. 410 (V), Dec. 1, 1950.

made, however, to establish special procedures for handling such issues.

One of the first steps taken by the Council was the establishment of the Committee of Experts. Its original function was to consider Rules of Procedure for the Council, but it was contemplated that this committee might serve as a body to which legal issues could be referred. The committee has also been asked to consider: the issue that arose during the consideration of the Iranian question concerning the right of a party to withdraw a complaint; the conditions under which states not Members of the United Nations might become parties to the Statute of the International Court of Justice; the relations between the Security Council and the Trusteeship Council with regard to strategic trusteeships; and the credentials of members of the Council. On the whole, however, the Security Council has made little use of the committee, and it has not met since 1950.

The discussions in the Assembly concerning the handling of legal issues have for the most part revolved around two points: (1) the use of the advisory opinion procedure of the International Court of Justice, and (2) the use of the Sixth (Legal) Committee of the Assembly to clarify legal questions for the other main committees of the Assembly. During the consideration of specific issues, some thought has also been given to the possibility of referring questions to the International Law Commission or to special *ad hoc* committees. At one point the Assembly established a special committee to study the handling of legal and drafting questions. On the basis of the report of this committee the Assembly recommended: "When a Committee considers the legal aspects of a question important, the Committee should refer it for legal advice to the Sixth Committee or propose that the question should be considered by a joint Committee of itself and the Sixth Committee."[27] Moreover, it was recommended that the advice of the Sixth Committee be sought on any resolution that requested an advisory opinion from the Court or that referred a matter to the International Law Commission. However, the committees of the Assembly have generally continued their practice of not following any special procedures for dealing with legal issues that arise during the consideration of questions affecting international peace and security.

[27] Res. 684 (VII), Nov. 6, 1952.

In contrast to the Council of the League of Nations, the Security Council and the General Assembly, in dealing with disputes and situations, have made little use of the advisory function of the Court. In 1947, the Assembly adopted a resolution encouraging greater use of the Court. The Assembly recommended that organs of the United Nations should "from time to time, review the difficult and important points of law within the jurisdiction of the International Court of Justice which have arisen in the course of their activities and involve questions of principle which it is desirable to have settled, including points of law relating to the interpretation of the Charter of the United Nations" and should refer them to the Court for advisory opinions.[28]

The Council has never requested an advisory opinion from the Court, and the Assembly has done so in only one instance in connection with the handling of a dispute or situation. This was in the handling of the question of the observance of human rights and fundamental freedoms in Hungary, Bulgaria, and Rumania. This request to the Court was made after certain of the signatories to the peace treaties with these three states had failed to obtain any cooperation in instituting the procedures for peaceful settlement laid down in the treaties.[29] The questions on which the opinion of the Court was asked were: (1) whether a "dispute" existed within the meaning of the terms of the peace treaties; (2) if so, whether these states were obligated to carry out those provisions of the treaties relating to the appointment of representatives to commissions for the settlement of disputes. In the event of an affirmative answer to the above, and if the three governments did not then appoint representatives, the Court was asked whether the Secretary-General had the authority under the treaty to appoint the "third" member of the commission on the request of the other party, and whether such a two-member commission would be competent under the treaty to make a binding decision in the settlement of a dispute. The Assembly abandoned its efforts to bring about a settlement of the question after the Court had answered affirmatively the first two questions, after Bulgaria, Hungary, and Rumania continued to refuse to appoint representatives to the commissions, and after the Court had given a negative answer to the question concerning the authority of the Secretary-General.

[28] Res. 171 (II), Nov. 14, 1947.
[29] Res. 294 (IV), Oct. 22, 1949.

A request for an advisory opinion from the International Court of Justice may be intended to assist the Security Council or the General Assembly in deciding on the course of action it should follow, or it may be simply a means of gaining time and avoiding the necessity for an immediate decision. An alternative procedure for getting legal assistance might be to set up a committee of legal experts to advise the Council or the Assembly on the point at issue as was done by the Council of the League of Nations in the Aaland Islands case. A request for an advisory opinion may also be primarily designed to assist the parties themselves in reaching a solution of a dispute. There have been suggestions both within and outside the United Nations, that the parties to a dispute should join in asking the Security Council or the General Assembly to request an opinion from the Court on some legal issue involved. In such a case the Council or the Assembly would be acting as an intermediary because the parties themselves cannot directly make such a request to the Court.

Many of the issues of a legal nature that have arisen in connection with the consideration by the Council and the Assembly of questions affecting international peace and security have related to the competence of the two organs to act generally or to act in particular ways. Especially is it true that most of the discussion regarding the procedures to be followed in handling legal issues has been concerned with matters of competence. It is therefore necessary to give special consideration at this point to the manner in which the Council and the Assembly have dealt with challenges to their competence.

Procedures for Dealing with Challenges to Competence[30]

Challenges to the competence of the Security Council and the General Assembly have taken three principal forms: (1) objections to the consideration of a question; (2) objections to the adoption of any resolution on a question; and (3) objections to the adoption of a particular proposal. The first two of these have been very closely related. Whenever a state has objected to the consideration of a

[30] It should be noted that this section does not deal with the substance of the objections that have been raised concerning the jurisdiction of the Council and the Assembly but only with the way in which these objections have been handled.

question, it has usually objected to the adoption of any resolution on that question. Occasionally, however, states have admitted that the Council or the Assembly could discuss a question but have maintained that the adoption of any resolution on that question would be out of order. The third form of objection is of a slightly different character. The contention is not that the subject matter of the question under discussion is *per se* outside the jurisdiction of the Council or the Assembly, but that the organ lacks the authority to adopt some particular course of action. Thus on grounds of competence, a state may support one resolution but not another, or may merely object to some specific provision within a draft resolution.

The objections to the competence of the Council and the Assembly have been: (1) that the Council or the Assembly cannot consider a particular question or adopt a particular resolution because of the limitations imposed by Article 2(7) of the Charter; (2) that Article 107 of the Charter precludes the United Nations from dealing with certain matters concerning the peace settlements; (3) that the Assembly cannot make recommendations regarding matters specifically reserved for the Council under Chapter VII of the Charter; (4) that the Assembly cannot make a recommendation on a particular dispute or situation because of the limitations imposed by Article 12 of the Charter; (5) that the Council cannot adopt a recommendation on a particular dispute or situation either because its continuance does not endanger the maintenance of international peace and security, or because the Council has not made a finding to this effect; (6) that the Council cannot in a particular situation exercise its powers under Chapter VII of the Charter because there is no threat to the peace, breach of the peace, or act of aggression, or because the Council has made no determination to that effect; (7) that the powers of the Council are limited to those specifically stated in the Charter and that nowhere in the Charter is the Council authorized to take the particular action proposed; and (8) that the powers of the Assembly are limited in like manner.

When a state has merely objected to the adoption of a particular proposal, the objection has been made during the discussion and voting on that proposal. Objections to the consideration of a question, or to the adoption of any resolution thereon, have been raised, however, at many stages. As has been pointed out,[31] in the Council

---

[31] See above, Chap. V.

the objection has sometimes been made during the discussion on the inclusion of a question in the agenda, and it has usually been repeated at the outset of the general discussion. Often it has been raised again each time the Council has considered the question and each time a draft resolution has been put to the vote. For example, the Indonesian question was discussed by the Council over a period of three years. Innumerable resolutions were adopted, but the Netherlands never abandoned its original contention that the action of the Council was a violation of Article 2(7) of the Charter.

In the Assembly, objections to the consideration of questions have usually been raised first in the General Committee during the discussion of the agenda, again in plenary during the discussion of the report of the General Committee, again in the committee to which the question is referred, and finally in plenary when the committee report is considered. If, as has often been the case, the same question is considered at a later session, the same objections are normally raised at each of the stages of discussion.

Preliminary Consideration of the Issue

There has not been complete agreement regarding when the issue of competence should be considered. The majority of Members have taken the position that discussion of this point should take place after the inclusion of the item in the agenda. The point then arises whether it is appropriate and possible to discuss issues of competence in advance of the consideration of the merits of a particular question. This procedure has been supported particularly by those states that have argued that "discussion" constitutes intervention within the meaning of Article 2(7) of the Charter. The representative of the Union of South Africa, for example, unsuccessfully attempted on a number of occasions to persuade the Assembly to discuss the issue of competence before discussing the Indian complaint concerning the question of the treatment of Indians in South Africa.

The provisions of the Charter and the Rules of Procedure of the General Assembly neither suggest nor preclude the possibility of treating the issue of competence as a preliminary question. The rules of the Assembly provide that "any motion calling for a decision on the competence of the General Assembly to adopt a proposal submitted to it shall be put to the vote immediately before a vote is taken on the proposal in question." There is a similar rule concerning the order of voting in the committees of the Assembly.[32] The contention of South Africa that in accordance with this rule the Assembly must vote on proposals concerning competence before deciding to place a question on its agenda was not, however, upheld by the Assembly.[33]

Certain Charter provisions would seem to imply that action by the Security Council is dependent on a preliminary decision concerning its competence. Article 39, for example, suggests that a preliminary determination of the existence of a threat to the peace, breach of the peace, or act of aggression is required for the Council to exercise its powers under Chapter VII of the Charter. Similarly, it may be argued that action by the Council under Articles 33, 36, or 37 is dependent on a finding that the continuance of a dispute or situation is likely to endanger the maintenance of international peace and security. As will be noted later in this study, the Council has made such findings in only a very few cases. Furthermore, the Council has seldom made any attempt to accord priority or special treatment to the elucidation of these "preliminary" issues.

In contrast, under the Rules of the International Court of Justice, before the hearings on a case begin, a party may file a preliminary objection to the jurisdiction of the Court. In such cases, the proceedings on the merits of the case are suspended until this preliminary point is resolved.[34] Preliminary objections have been raised in a number of cases.[35] In the Anglo-Iranian case, the Court decided in favor of the Iranian claim that the Anglo-Iranian Oil Company case was outside its jurisdiction.[36]

Requests for Advisory Opinions

The most extensive discussions on procedures for handling the issue of competence of the Security Council or the General Assembly have taken place in connection with proposals to refer the matter to the International Court of Justice for an advisory opinion. The

[32] Rules 80 and 120.

[33] See above, Chap. V, p. 105.

[34] See Art. 62 of the Rules.

[35] See, for example, objections by Albania in the Corfu Channel case, *I.C.J. Reports 1947-48*, pp. 15 and 53; objections by the United Kingdom in the Ambatielos case, *I.C.J. Reports 1952*, p. 28; and objections by Guatemala in the Nottebohm case, *Ibid.*, p. 7.

[36] *Ibid.*, p. 93.

Council of the League of Nations quite frequently requested such opinions.

At San Francisco an attempt was made to provide for the reference to the Court of questions on interpretation of the Charter. This effort was unsuccessful although it was agreed that "it would always be open to the General Assembly or to the Security Council, in appropriate circumstances, to ask the International Court of Justice for an advisory opinion concerning the meaning of a provision of the Charter."[37] Furthermore, the Assembly in its resolution encouraging greater use of the Court specifically recommended that the organs of the United Nations refer "points of law relating to the interpretation of the Charter" to the Court for advisory opinions. In general, however, the view has prevailed that the organs of the United Nations should themselves decide any issues concerning their competence.

Neither the Council nor the Assembly has ever adopted any proposal that the Court be requested to give an opinion concerning the competence of either organ to deal with a particular dispute or situation. The first of these proposals was introduced during the consideration of the question of the treatment of Indians in South Africa in the second part of the first session of the Assembly. There were several suggestions regarding the question or questions that might be put to the Court. Most of them dealt with the specific complaint.[38] But one, which was general in nature, asked for an opinion by the Court on (1) the obligations of Members to amend or refrain from enacting legislation embodying racial discrimination and (2) the powers of the General Assembly to make recommendations concerning such legislation. Only one proposal was put to a vote —the request of the Union of South Africa for an advisory opinion on the question whether the matters referred to in the Indian complaint were, under Article 2(7), essentially within the domestic jurisdiction of South Africa. This proposal was rejected.[39] The issue

[37] U.N. Information Organizations and U.S. Library of Congress, *Documents of the United Nations Conference on International Organization*, Vol. 13 (1945), p. 709. For a more extensive discussion of the problem of interpreting the Charter see the volume in this Brookings series, *The Organization and Procedures of the United Nations*.

[38] U.N. General Assembly, First Session, Second Part, Joint First and Sixth Committee, *Official Records*, 3rd Meeting (Nov. 26, 1946), pp. 21 ff.

[39] U.N. General Assembly, First Session, Second Part, Plenary, *Official Records*, 52nd Meeting (Dec. 8, 1946), p. 1061.

of competence was repeatedly raised at subsequent sessions. Although various Members continued to express the view that a request for an advisory opinion was the proper method for handling the question, no other formal proposals to this effect were introduced.

During the debate on the Palestine question, in both the Assembly and in the Council, various proposals were introduced for requesting an advisory opinion by the Court. In each instance the proposal was defeated by a close vote. During the second session of the Assembly, the *Ad Hoc* Committee on the Palestinian Question rejected by a single vote a proposal that a series of eight questions be put to the Court. The last two of these were especially significant. They were:

(vii) Whether the United Nations is competent to recommend either of the two plans and recommendations of the majority or minority of the United Nations Special Committee on Palestine, or any other solution involving partition of the territory of Palestine, or a permanent trusteeship over any city or part of Palestine, without the consent of the majority of the people of Palestine.

(viii) Whether the United Nations, or any of its Member States, is competent to enforce or recommend the enforcement of any proposal concerning the constitution and future Government of Palestine, in particular, any plan of partition which is contrary to the wishes, or adopted without the consent of, the inhabitants of Palestine.[40]

Subseqently, Syria proposed that the Security Council ask for an advisory opinion on the "international status of Palestine after the termination of the mandate." This proposal was also rejected by a single vote.[41] At the third session of the Assembly, Syria introduced a similar proposal on this point and also on the powers of the Assembly to partition Palestine. This proposal was rejected in committee by a tie vote.[42]

In one other instance, a proposal to request an advisory opinion on a question of competence has been put to the vote. During the discussions on the Indonesian question, the Council rejected a Belgian proposal that the Court be asked to give an opinion "con-

[40] U.N. Doc. A/AC.14/32 (Nov. 11, 1947), pp. 57-58. For other proposals concerning a request to the Court see U.N. Docs. A/AC.14/21 (Oct. 14, 1947), 24, and 25 (Oct. 16, 1947).

[41] U.N. Security Council, Third Year, *Official Records,* No. 98, 340th Meeting (July 27, 1948), p. 34.

[42] U.N. General Assembly, Third Session, First Part, First Committee, *Official Records,* 228th Meeting (Dec. 4, 1948), p. 933.

cerning the competence of the Security Council to deal with" the question.[43] The issue of competence was repeatedly raised during subsequent discussions, but this was the only formal proposal to refer the matter to the Court.

The handling by the Council of the Anglo-Iranian question has some relevance to this discussion. The dispute was brought to the Council as a complaint concerning the failure of Iran to comply with the provisional measures indicated by the International Court of Justice. Two issues concerning the competence of the Council were raised: first, whether the Council could act under Article 94(2) if one of the parties to a dispute before the Court refused to comply with provisional measures;[44] and second, whether the dispute was "international" or concerned matters essentially within the domestic jurisdiction of Iran. The suggestion by Ecuador that the Council might request an opinion from the Court concerning its powers under Article 94(2) was not translated into a formal proposal.[45] On the second point, the Court itself had not at that time resolved the question of its own jurisdiction. The Council therefore decided to suspend its consideration until the Court had done so.[46] It was not contended that the decision of the Court would *per se* resolve the question of the competence of the Council, but it was recognized that the action of the Court would elucidate this basic issue. The effect of the decision of the Council was much the same as if an opinion had been requested from the Court.

During the discussion of these proposals, some Members have contended that the questions raised were political not legal in nature and that the Court should not be asked for an opinion. Many Members have desired to avoid any action that might bind the Council or the Assembly to a particular interpretation of its powers and unduly limit their future development. At the same time, it has been argued that a request for an opinion would serve no useful purpose because it would be only advisory in character. One further argument against the reference of such issues to the Court has been that it would delay the proceedings of the Council or the Assembly. Once a resolution on the question before the Council or the Assembly has

[43] U.N. Security Council, Second Year, *Official Records*, No. 84, 195th Meeting (Aug. 26, 1947), p. 2224.

[44] See Chap. XII.

[45] U.N. Security Council, Sixth Year, *Official Records*, 562nd Meeting (Oct. 17, 1951), p. 8.

[46] *Ibid.*, 565th Meeting (Oct. 19, 1951), p. 12.

been adopted, Members have been reluctant to support a request for an advisory opinion and have argued that the issue has been decided or that the request would interfere with the implementation of the resolutions already adopted.

During the discussions in the Interim Committee in 1948, the representative of Ecuador proposed a recommendation by the Assembly that, in any dispute where the issue of domestic jurisdiction was raised, the parties to the dispute agree to submit the issue to the Court and, if the parties did not so agree, that the Council or the Assembly should request an advisory opinion from the Court.[47] Objections, similar to those noted above, were raised. Furthermore, many Members objected because such action would extend the field of compulsory jurisdiction beyond that envisaged in Article 36(2) of the Statute of the Court and pointed to the reservations their governments had made in accepting the jurisdiction of the Court. No action was taken on the proposal by Ecuador at that time. In a later report on the practices of the General Assembly, the Interim Committee made the following comment:

The essentially political character of the General Assembly inclines it to decide its competence for itself or more often to assume competence without an express decision. On the other hand, where opinions among Members differ on the interpretation of the Charter and legal doubts as to the Assembly's competence are strongly and sincerely held, the force of a recommendation by the Assembly will be weakened if it is made without an affirmative decision upon the question of competence, preferably with the assistance of the International Court of Justice in cases where it is practicable.[48]

On a few occasions, it has been suggested that the issue of competence be referred to a special committee, more or less along the lines of the committees of jurists that the League of Nations employed from time to time. Although this procedure has never been followed, the establishment of fact-finding committees and commissions may actually serve this purpose. The establishment of a commission to carry out an investigation within the meaning of Article 34, for example, is a procedure for clarifying the competence of the Security Council to take action.[49]

[47] For summary of discussion on the proposal by Ecuador, see U.N. General Assembly, Third Session, *Official Records*, Supplement No. 10, pp. 30-31.

[48] U.N. General Assembly, Fifth Session, *Official Records*, Supplement No. 14, p. 26.

[49] For discussion on this point see pp. 176ff. See also discussion on the Committee of Experts, p. 158.

Direct Vote on the Issue

Although it has been the usual practice of the Security Council and the General Assembly to proceed without taking explicit decisions concerning their competence, occasionally the Assembly and its committees have voted directly on proposals concerning their competence to deal with a question or to adopt a particular resolution. Most of these votes have been on proposals made by the Union of South Africa in connection with the question of the treatment of Indians in South Africa and the *apartheid* question. During the third session, the First Committee rejected a South African proposal declaring the treatment of Indians in South Africa to be a matter essentially within the domestic jurisdiction of South Africa and outside the competence of the Assembly.[50] At the fifth session, the South African representative pressed for a decision that the General Assembly was not competent "to entertain the subject matter" of the item "nor any draft resolution in regard thereto." There was an interesting debate in the committee regarding whether it could take such a decision. It was argued that the Rules of Procedure only provided for a vote on the competence of the committee or of the Assembly to adopt a specific proposal. The question was raised whether the adoption of the South African proposal would not be in violation of Article 10 of the Charter and an infringement on the prerogatives of the Assembly itself. It was subsequently agreed that the committee would vote on its competence with regard to the specific draft resolutions before it. The committee then decided that it was competent to consider and vote upon the proposals that had been submitted to it.[51]

The Union of South Africa has been equally unsuccessful in getting support for its position that the *apartheid* question is outside the jurisdiction of the Assembly. During the discussions in the seventh session, three separate attempts were made. First, during the discussion on the adoption of the agenda, the representative of the Union of South Africa requested that the Assembly decide that, "having regard to Article 2(7) of the Charter," it was not competent to consider the question. This proposal was ruled out of order. In committee, a similar proposal was rejected.[52] When the As-

[50] U.N. General Assembly, Third Session, Second Part, First Committee, *Official Records,* 268th Meeting (May 11, 1949), p. 321.

[51] U.N. General Assembly, Fifth Session, *Ad Hoc* Political Committee, *Official Records,* 46th Meeting (Nov. 18, 1950), p. 291.

[52] U.N. General Assembly, Seventh Session, Plenary, *Official Records,* 381st

sembly in plenary meeting considered the two resolutions that were recommended by the committee, the Union of South Africa asked the Assembly to decide that it was not competent to adopt either of the proposed resolutions. The Assembly also rejected this proposal.[53]

At the eighth session, the Union of South Africa again attempted to obtain a decision that the *apartheid* question was outside the jurisdiction of the Assembly. The South African representative proposed that the *Ad Hoc* Political Committee of the Assembly should note that the matters to which the item related were among those essentially within the domestic jurisdiction of a Member state and should decide that the committee had no competence to intervene. This proposal was rejected and a subsequent proposal along similar lines was voted down by the Assembly in plenary meeting.[54]

The question whether it is appropriate for a committee to vote on the question of competence except in relation to a specific draft resolution has also arisen in connection with various proposals dealing with the subject of death sentences imposed on certain Greek trade union leaders. During the third session of the Assembly, the First Committee adopted a proposal on this subject introduced by the French representative. The committee decided that it was not competent to entertain either a Yugoslav proposal or a Soviet amendment to a French draft resolution.[55] At the next session, several proposals were introduced, and the committee voted separately on its competence with respect to each of them. The committee decided that it was not competent to entertain any of the proposals except the one which it adopted.[56] At a later session, the Soviet Union again introduced a proposal on this subject. The ruling of the chairman that it was irrelevant to the item under consideration and therefore out of order was upheld by the committee.[57] Later in the debate, following a proposal by Uruguay, there was a

---

Meeting (Oct. 17, 1952), p. 67; U.N. General Assembly, Seventh Session, *Ad Hoc* Political Committee, *Official Records*, 21st Meeting (Nov. 20, 1952), p. 22.

[53] U.N. General Assembly, Seventh Session, Plenary, *Official Records*, 401st Meeting (Dec. 5, 1952), p. 332.

[54] U.N. General Assembly, Eighth Session, *Ad Hoc* Political Committee, *Official Records*, 42nd Meeting (Dec. 5, 1953), p. 228; U.N. General Assembly, Eighth Session, Plenary, *Official Records*, 469th Meeting (Dec. 8, 1953), p. 436.

[55] U.N. General Assembly, Third Session, First Part, First Committee, *Official Records*, 186th Meeting (Nov. 6, 1948), p. 449.

[56] U.N. General Assembly, Fourth Session, First Committee, *Official Records*, 297th and 298th Meetings (Oct. 26-27, 1949), pp. 111-15.

[57] U.N. General Assembly, Sixth Session, *Ad Hoc* Political Committee, *Official Records*, 1st Meeting (Nov. 19, 1951), p. 5.

confused discussion whether the ruling of the chair could be considered as being applicable to all proposals on the subject or only to the specific draft submitted by the Soviet Union. It was argued that the committee could not in advance decide that any proposal would be out of order. The ruling of the chairman that the Uruguayan proposal was "unacceptable" was also upheld, but by a much smaller majority.[58]

In one instance there has been a direct vote on the competence of the Assembly in the light of the restrictions imposed by Article 12(1) of the Charter. During the discussion of the Indonesian question, the chairman of the *Ad Hoc* Political Committee asked the committee to decide by vote whether a Ukrainian proposal constituted a recommendation within the meaning of Article 12, in which case the Assembly would be debarred from adopting the resolution. The committee decided that the proposal was a "recommendation," and the draft resolution was not put to a vote. Later in plenary, it was again decided not to vote upon the Ukrainian proposal.[59]

As already indicated, the method of voting on the issue of competence raises certain questions. Whether the vote is taken by the Assembly in plenary meeting or in committee may be of particular importance because a committee adopts proposals by a simple majority, while the Assembly takes decisions on important questions by a two-thirds vote.[60] The question whether the Assembly should vote on a general proposal concerning its competence or only on a proposal regarding its competence to adopt a specific resolution would seem to have been resolved in favor of the latter course, but the Members are by no means in full agreement. The procedure of voting on a ruling by the chair on the issue of competence has many disadvantages and would prove particularly troublesome in the Security Council because of the rules concerning voting in that organ. It should be noted that if either organ is going to vote on a general

[58] *Ibid.*, 5th Meeting (Nov. 23, 1951), p. 27.

[59] U.N. General Assembly, Fourth Session, *Ad Hoc* Political Committee, *Official Records,* 57th Meeting (Dec. 5, 1949), p. 339; U.N. General Assembly, Fourth Session, Plenary, *Official Records,* 272nd Meeting (Dec. 7, 1949), p. 564.

[60] This point has never been raised in connection with a direct vote on competence, but the Assembly did decide by a very close vote that a proposal to request an advisory opinion from the Court on the matter of competence would require a two-thirds majority. U.N. General Assembly, First Session, Second Part, Plenary, *Official Records*, p. 1061.

proposal concerning its competence, the manner in which the proposal is worded has considerable significance.

Implicit Decision on Issue

Ordinarily, both the Security Council and the General Assembly have followed the procedure of voting directly on a draft resolution without voting separately on the issue of competence. Presumably, those who vote in favor of the resolution consider that the matter is within the competence of the Council or the Assembly. Those voting against may or may not do so on grounds of competence. It would be logical to assume that, if a Member considered that the adoption of a proposed resolution was outside the competence of the Council or the Assembly, that Member would vote against the resolution. This has not, however, always been the case. In some instances, Members that have argued that the organ lacked jurisdiction have merely abstained from taking part in the vote.

There have been innumerable statements in the Council and in the Assembly to the effect that the organ has by implication decided the issue of its competence. It has, for example, been argued that the issue has been decided by the mere placing of a matter on the agenda, although this position has not been supported by the majority of Members. It would be difficult to argue, however, that the adoption of a resolution is anything more than an implicit decision that the Council or the Assembly is competent to adopt that particular resolution. A later objection to the competence of the organ to adopt any other proposal would therefore be in order. Since there have been considerable differences of opinion in many cases concerning the kind of resolution that the Council or the Assembly is competent to adopt, it can hardly be maintained, although it often has been argued, that the mere adoption of a resolution implicitly overrules all the objections to the jurisdiction of the organ that have been raised in the preceding debates.

In this connection, it may be noted that in some cases Members have felt that it would be in order for the Council or the Assembly to make a general or humanitarian appeal without making any specific recommendations on a dispute or situation. It has been suggested also that a provision be incorporated in a resolution specifically reserving questions of competence. France, for example, proposed that the Council, in adopting a resolution calling for the cessation of hostilities and the peaceful settlement of the Indonesian question, include in the preamble of its resolution a phrase specifically reserving the entire question of the competence of the Council.[61] Ecuador made a similar suggestion in connection with a proposal for negotiation on the Anglo-Iranian question.[62] Thus it is clear that caution must be displayed in drawing conclusions from voting regarding the attitudes of Members toward the issue of competence.

[61] U.N. Security Council, Second Year, *Official Records*, No. 68, 173rd Meeting (Aug. 1, 1947), p. 1702.

[62] U.N. Doc. S/2380 (Oct. 17, 1951).

CHAPTER VIII

Fact-Finding Committees and Commissions

BEFORE the First World War, commissions of inquiry were established on the basis of agreement of the parties to a dispute for the purpose of clarifying facts in the dispute between them. The Hague conventions provided for international commissions of inquiry to facilitate the solution of disputes "by elucidating the facts by means of an impartial and conscientious investigation."[1] The characteristic feature of this procedure was that it was instituted by the parties themselves. The report of the commission was limited to a finding of facts; thus the parties remained free to reach their own settlement. This procedure of inquiry has found expression in innumerable treaties for the pacific settlement of disputes. It is in this context that the Charter of the United Nations specifically includes "enquiry" as one of the methods of pacific settlement listed in Article 33.

With the establishment of the League of Nations, the device of impartial fact-finding bodies took on a new significance. The emphasis had previously been on commissions established *by* the parties to perform the very limited function of clarifying facts *for* the parties. With the creation of the League, commissions were established for the additional purpose of assisting the Council and the Assembly of the League in the performance of their functions. However, the procedures of inquiry and conciliation were viewed as part of a single process for bringing about a settlement, and commissions were generally created with the express consent of the parties. Only a few of the commissions of the League were primarily concerned with carrying out an investigation for the Council or the Assembly.

In the United Nations, the members of the Security Council and the General Assembly in many cases have found the information at their disposal inadequate and have therefore established commissions to investigate the facts and render reports on the basis of which the organ can decide what further steps, if any, should be taken.[2]

---

[1] See Arts. 9-14 of the Hague Convention of 1899 and Arts. 9-36 of the 1907 Convention.

[2] This chapter deals with commissions whose functions have been primarily

Powers of Investigation

Although the Charter contains no express authorization for investigations by the Security Council or the General Assembly, except for the limited purpose of enabling the Council to determine the seriousness of a dispute or situation brought before it,[3] the powers of the two organs to investigate have been considered as inherent in their powers to discuss and to recommend. As neither the Assembly nor the Council is a suitable body for carrying out a detailed investigation, the task has been delegated to commissions specifically established for this purpose. Both the Council and the Assembly are authorized under the Charter to establish subsidiary organs necessary for the performance of their functions.[4] The issue of the delegation of powers of investigation to subsidiary organs has arisen in both the Council and the Assembly.[5]

The General Assembly

There has been relatively little discussion concerning the authority of the General Assembly to establish commissions of investigation, partly because the issue first arose at the first special session in 1947 on the Palestine question, on which Members were generally agreed that an investigation was desirable. Later in the same year, during the discussions on the establishment of the Interim Committee, however, the Soviet bloc questioned the authority of the Assembly to confer wide powers of investigation on a subsidiary organ. The Soviet arguments were overridden, but it is worth noting that the terms of reference given to the Interim Committee, in so far as they related to investigation, were more limited than those at first proposed. The original United States proposal was that the committee be authorized to "conduct investigations and appoint

---

of this nature. Thus it is concerned with the elucidation of facts as a stage in the process of the handling of disputes and situations by the Council and the Assembly rather than with the procedure of inquiry as a concomitant to the process of conciliation.

[3] Art. 34.

[4] Arts. 22 and 29.

[5] The International Court of Justice is also authorized in Art. 50 of its Statute to entrust to an individual, bureau or commission, or other organization the task of making an inquiry or giving an expert opinion. The Court has exercised this power only in connection with the Corfu Channel case. As the powers of the Court have not been the subject of discussion, it has not been considered necessary to deal with them here.

commissions of inquiry." Under the resolution as adopted, however, such action could only be taken by a two-thirds vote, and any on-the-spot investigation required the consent of the state or states in whose territory it was to take place.[6]

Although members of the Assembly, in particular the members of the Soviet bloc, have on subsequent occasions opposed the establishment of fact-finding commissions, the objections have not been related to the general question of the power of investigation of the Assembly but have been concerned with the more specific issue of the relation of the power of investigation to Article 2(7) of the Charter. Indeed, although the members of the Soviet bloc opposed many of the provisions of the "Uniting for Peace" resolution, they did not oppose the establishment of the Peace Observation Commission under that resolution. This commission, on which the Soviet Union and Czechoslovakia agreed to serve, was established for the purpose of observing and reporting "on the situation in any area where there exists international tension the continuance of which is likely to endanger the maintenance of international peace and security."[7]

The Security Council

Article 34 of the Charter provides that: "The Security Council may investigate any dispute, or any situation which might lead to international friction or give rise to a dispute, in order to determine whether the continuance of the dispute or situation is likely to endanger the maintenance of international peace and security." The importance initially attached to action by the Security Council under this article was well illustrated by the statement at San Francisco concerning voting procedure in the Council. The statement propounded the thesis that beyond the point where the Council decides to consider a question and to hear the parties concerned:

. . . Decisions and actions by the Security Council may well have major political consequences and may even initiate a chain of events which might, in the end, require the Council under its responsibilities to invoke measures of enforcement under Section B, Chapter VIII [Chapter VII of the Charter]. This chain of events begins when the Council decides to make an investiga-

---

[6] Cf. U.N. Doc. A/C.1/196 (Sept. 26, 1947) with Res. 111 (II), Nov. 13, 1947.

[7] Sec. B(3). Under the terms of the resolution, the commission may be utilized by the Council, and in certain circumstances by the Assembly or by the Interim Committee. The dispatch of the commission by the Assembly or the Interim Committee, however, requires the consent of the state into whose territory it is sent.

tion, or determines that the time has come to call upon states to settle their differences, or makes recommendations to the parties. It is to such decisions and actions that unanimity of the permanent members applies, with the important proviso, . . . for abstention from voting by parties to a dispute.

To illustrate: in ordering an investigation, the Council has to consider whether the investigation—which may involve calling for reports, hearing witnesses, dispatching a commission of inquiry, or other means—might not further aggravate the situation. After investigation, the Council must determine whether the continuance of the situation or dispute would be likely to endanger international peace and security. If it so determines, the Council would be under obligation to take further steps. . . .[8]

Clearly under the wording of Article 34, the Council is under no obligation to carry out an investigation. It is for the Council itself to decide whether or not to do so. Although it has been established that the task of investigation can be delegated to a subsidiary body, the "determination" of the nature of the dispute or situation must be made by the Council itself. Numerous statements in the Council have stressed that an investigation under Article 34 is carried out for a specific purpose, that is, in order to determine whether the continuance of a dispute or situation is likely to endanger the maintenance of international peace and security. There have been few instances, however, in which the Council has carried out an investigation within the limited meaning of Article 34.

The original Australian proposal for the establishment of a subcommittee on the Spanish question called for a report on three questions: whether the situation was essentially within the domestic jurisdiction of Spain; whether it was likely to lead to international friction or give rise to a dispute; and, if so, whether the continuance of the situation was likely to endanger the maintenance of international peace and security.[9] Although the questions themselves and the reference to Article 34 did not appear in the final text, the resolution made clear that the purpose of the inquiry was to determine whether the situation was of the character set out in the above questions and, if so, to determine what practical measures the United Nations should take.[10]

The resolution establishing the commission of investigation concerning the question of the Greek frontier incidents contained an

[8] U.N. Information Organizations and U.S. Library of Congress, *Documents of the United Nations Conference on International Organization*, Vol. 11 (1945), p. 711 ff.

[9] U.N. Security Council, First Year, *Official Records*, First Series, No. 2, 35th Meeting (Apr. 18, 1946), p. 198.

[10] *Ibid.*, 39th Meeting (Apr. 29, 1946), p. 245.

express reference to Article 34, but the task of the commission was not confined to investigating whether the dispute was likely to endanger the maintenance of international peace and security. The commission was instructed "to ascertain the facts relating to the alleged border violations" and was authorized to conduct its investigations throughout Greece, Albania, Bulgaria, and Yugoslavia in order to "elucidate the causes and nature" of the border violations and disturbances.[11]

The India-Pakistan commission was orginally given the function of investigating "the facts pursuant to Article 34 of the Charter."[12] In this case, the parties themselves were agreed regarding the seriousness of the matter, and before the commission began to operate, the Council adopted a resolution containing a finding that "the continuation of the dispute" was "likely to endanger international peace and security."[13]

The power of the Council to continue an investigation *after* it has reached a determination that a dispute is likely to endanger international peace and security was discussed at length during the consideration of a resolution proposed by the United States on the question of the Greek frontier incidents. The proposal, based in large measure on the majority recommendations of the Greek frontier commission, which had been previously established, addressed a series of recommendations to the parties. To assist in the implementation of the resolution, a new commission with defined powers of "investigation" would be established.[14] One of the many proposed amendments to this draft would have included a finding that "a dispute exists, the continuance of which is likely to endanger the maintenance of international peace and security."[15] Such a finding was considered necessary as a basis for the recommendations of the Council. The representative of Syria questioned whether the Council could, in view of the terms of Article 34, adopt such a finding and still continue its investigations. He remarked:

. . . The purpose, the object and the justification for these proposals (to establish a further commission) lie in the necessity for determining whether or not the situation is likely to endanger international peace and security. Therefore, I think we would be prejudging the case if we put it as it is in

[11] U.N. Security Council, First Year, *Official Records*, Second Series, No. 28, 87th Meeting (Dec. 19, 1946), p. 700.
[12] U.N. Doc. S/654 (Jan. 20, 1948).
[13] U.N. Doc. S/726 (Apr. 22, 1948).
[14] U.N. Doc. S/391 (June 27, 1947).
[15] U.N. Doc. S/430 (July 22, 1947).

the French preamble. The act of investigation would be over. There would be no necessity for continuing the investigation as long as we accepted or admitted or determined that the prolongation of the present situation might endanger international peace and security.[16]

A number of representatives expressed the view that the Council had the power to continue an investigation as long as it was necessary. Some of these comments specifically dealt with the powers of the Council under Article 34; others stressed the "primary responsibility" of the Council and its general powers under Chapters VI and VII of the Charter. The French representative stated:

... If the Security Council has had the power to initiate an investigation for the purpose of obtaining information, and of ascertaining whether a situation endangering peace exists, it is reasonable to suppose that it can continue this investigation when the situation itself seems likely to continue. . . . It would be rather paradoxical, I think, that an investigation could be continued if it did not find there was a threat to the peace, if it left the matter in doubt, but could not be continued in the most serious situation, that is, one in which a threat to the peace was found to exist.[17]

That the majority of the members of the Council believed the Council had the power to make such a finding and still continue its investigations was made clear at a subsequent meeting when only the Soviet Union and Poland voted against the amended draft resolution.[18]

The thesis that the Council has a general power of investigation has found expression on various other occasions when it has been proposed to vest a subsidiary organ with the function of investigation but not to authorize it explicitly to carry out an investigation within the scope of Article 34 of the Charter. During the discussions in the Council on the proposals to establish subcommittees for the limited purpose of hearing evidence, it has been stressed that in these cases there is no question of an investigation within the meaning of Article 34. The proposed resolution for the establishment of a subcommittee on the Czechoslovak question contained a specific statement in the preamble that the decision was "without prejudice to any decisions which may be taken in accordance with Article 34."[19]

[16] U.N. Security Council, Second Year, *Official Records,* No. 61, 162nd Meeting (July 22, 1947), pp. 1423-24.

[17] *Ibid.,* p. 1426.

[18] *Ibid.,* No. 66, 170th Meeting (July 29, 1947), pp. 1602-12.

[19] U.N. Security Council, Third Year, *Official Records,* No. 63, 288th Meeting (Apr. 29, 1948), p. 19.

In connection with the establishment of these subcommittees, the application of Article 27 of the Charter concerning voting procedure in the Security Council has been discussed at great length. A decision under Article 29 of the Charter to establish a subsidiary organ has been considered procedural. It does not therefore require the "concurring votes" of the five permanent members, nor is a party to a dispute required to abstain from voting. Whether in any particular instance the provisions of Article 27(3) apply depends on the terms of reference given to the subsidiary organ.[20] A decision to authorize an investigation in accordance with Article 34, however, has not been considered procedural. To entrust to a subsidiary organ the task of investigation for other purposes, for example, to ascertain the compliance of parties with provisional measures under Article 40 of the Charter, also has not been considered a procedural decision.

The majority of the members of the Council have argued that the Council may establish by a procedural vote a subcommittee for the limited purpose of receiving and hearing "evidence, statements and testimonies." In support of this position, it has been argued that since the Council itself may by a procedural vote decide to hear other Members of the United Nations and states not Members of the Organization, and may invite "persons" to supply it with information, the Council may also by a procedural vote authorize a subcommittee to perform similar functions in its behalf. This position has not been accepted by the Soviet Union, which has argued that a decision to establish a subcommittee for the elucidation of facts is a decision "about an investigation" and therefore subject to the provisions of Article 27(3).[21] The Soviet Union has exercised its special privilege under Article 27(3) to veto proposals for commissions of investigation, and by a "double" veto also blocked the establishment of the proposed subcommittee for the collection of evidence on the Czechoslovak question.[22]

[20] For a full discussion on the relation between Arts. 34, 29, and 27, see Eduardo Jiménez de Aréchaga, *Voting and the Handling of Disputes in the Security Council* (1950), Chap. I and pp. 76-83.

[21] U.N. Security Council, Second Year, *Official Records*, No. 21, 114th Meeting (Feb. 27, 1947), p. 427.

[22] The Soviet Union vetoed the proposal even though nine of the members of the Council considered that the decision was "procedural." For further discussion of the "double veto" see the volume in this Brookings series, *The Organization and Procedures of the United Nations*.

Obligation of Parties to Accept Investigation

The Members of the United Nations are not under an obligation to submit a matter to inquiry by the United Nations to the same extent as were the Members of the League of Nations.[23] Nevertheless, if a dispute or situation is brought to the attention of the Security Council, it may decide that an investigation into the facts should be carried out. Under Article 25 of the Charter, "the Members of the United Nations agree to accept and carry out the decisions of the Security Council." The issue of the obligation of parties to co-operate with an investigation by the Council was discussed at some length during the consideration of the question of the Greek frontier incidents. During the discussion of the United States proposal for a new commission of investigation and conciliation, the members of the Soviet bloc stressed that any action taken by the Council under Chapter VI of the Charter was in the nature of a "recommendation," and the states concerned were therefore under no "obligation," other than a moral one, to accept such resolutions. The representative of the Soviet Union stated:

> ... The U.S.S.R. delegation cannot share the view of certain representatives that decisions in connexion with the pacific settlement of disputes (under Chapter VI of the Charter) are of a compulsory character. If we take that path, we shall inevitably reach the conclusion that, if a State does not fulfill certain recommendations, some other measures must automatically be applied to it. The question then arises: what other measures? Obviously, compulsory measures. But, in that event, the whole of Chapter VI regarding the pacific settlement of disputes loses its significance and meaning. All that should be left in the Charter, then, is Chapter VII, which provides for taking compulsory decisions. . . .
>
> No one doubts the Security Council's right to decide to conduct an investigation or enquire into the facts connected with a particular dispute or situation. That is a right conferred upon the Security Council by the Charter. However, all decisions taken under Chapter VI, including decisions to conduct an investigation, are in the nature of recommendations, from the point of view of the attitude taken towards these decisions or recommendations by the countries they affect.[24]

The replies to the Soviet argument drew a distinction between a "decision" to investigate under Article 34 and a "recommenda-

---

[23] See Art. 12 of the Covenant of the League of Nations.
[24] U.N. Security Council, Second Year, *Official Records*, No. 64, 167th Meeting (July 25, 1947), pp. 1539, 1541.

tion" under Article 36 or 37 and stressed that it was only with respect to the former that states were under an obligation to collaborate with the proposed commission. In reply to the Soviet query on how the Council could have greater powers under Article 34 than it had under subsequent articles of Chapter VI, the French representative stated:

> Article 34 refers only to an investigation for the sole purpose of providing the Security Council with information. It is an entirely preliminary measure preceding all the measures which the Security Council may later contemplate. It is a simple measure of enquiry, and it is quite natural that here the Security Council should have greater power—even within the province of Chapter VI—and that it should be able to decide, and not merely recommend, that an investigation should be made.[25]

The United States representative argued that the Council must have "certain operating powers" in order to fulfill its "role as a conciliator and also as the guardian of the peace." He contended that Article 34 gave the Council the "right to investigate any dispute regardless of whether or not the State investigated approves or likes it." Although conceding that the Charter does not "confer on the Security Council, operating under Chapter VI, any power of sanction or any power of enforcement," the United States representative made the following comment regarding the "measure and degree of obligation which the Members of the United Nations are under, within the purview of Chapter VI, to co-operate with such an investigation":

> I do not think it can be denied that, under Chapter VI, certain forms of decisions can be taken; and that, under Article 25, it is the duty of the Members of the United Nations to conform to those decisions. . . .
> I am not claiming that any power of sanctions exists under this Article. However, it does lay non-complying States open to serious charges, which may be brought before the Security Council and acted upon, charges of non-compliance with their own obligations under the Charter to co-operate with the Security Council in its decisions.[26]

That a decision by the Council may be binding on states constitutes an important distinction between the powers of the Council and the Assembly. During the discussion of the Assembly on the establishment of the Interim Committee of the Assembly, the representative of the United Kingdom stated that the fact that a dispute

---

[25] *Ibid.*, No. 65, 168th Meeting (July 28, 1947), p. 1553.
[26] *Ibid.*, No. 64, 167th Meeting (July 25, 1947), p. 1541.

or situation could, under Article 35, be brought to either the Council or the Assembly "attracted to the General Assembly the jurisdiction and functions of the Security Council contained in Article 34."[27] In general, however, it has been stressed that the Assembly has only the power of recommendation. It cannot take "decisions" such as the Council is authorized to take. Moreover, the obligation of Members under Article 25 refers only to the Council, not to the Assembly. The only occasion when a decision by the Assembly to conduct an investigation could have been considered in any way "binding" was in connection with the Eritrean question when France, the United Kingdom, the Soviet Union, and the United States had under the terms of the Italian Peace Treaty agreed to accept the recommendation of the General Assembly and to take appropriate measures for giving effect to it.

Initiation of Proposals for Investigation

In a great many cases, a state bringing a matter to the attention of the Security Council or the General Assembly has requested that the organ carry out an investigation. The United Kingdom, for example, requested the convocation of a special session of the Assembly in April 1947 for the express purpose of "constituting and instructing a Special Committee to prepare for the consideration" of the question of Palestine at the second regular session.[28] And in 1951, the United Kingdom, France, and the United States brought to the Assembly a specific request for the appointment of a commission to carry out an investigation to determine whether existing conditions made it possible to hold free elections in Germany.[29]

Often, a state in bringing a dispute or situation to the Security Council has cited Article 34 of the Charter and has requested an investigation. In December 1946, for example, the Greek Government in bringing to the attention of the Council the situation along the northern borders of Greece, stressed the urgent necessity of an on-the-spot investigation.[30] In other cases, it has not always been clear whether an on-the-spot investigation was being requested.

[27] U.N. General Assembly, Second Session, First Committee, *Official Records*, 96th Meeting (Nov. 6, 1947), p. 328.
[28] U.N. Doc. A/286 (Apr. 3, 1947).
[29] U.N. Doc. A/1938 (Nov. 6, 1951).
[30] U.N. Doc. S/203 (Dec. 4, 1946).

On occasion, it has been the accused state instead of the state bringing charges that has proposed the inquiry. It was the United States, for example, that proposed an investigation of the charges that United States planes operating in Korea had bombed Chinese territory.[31] The United States also made numerous unsuccessful attempts both within and outside the United Nations to obtain an investigation of the charges that United States forces in Korea were engaged in bacterial warfare. When these charges were raised by the Soviet Union in the Disarmament Commission, the United States representative explained that in reply to a request of his Government the International Red Cross had offered to carry out an investigation "subject to the agreement of both parties" and with the assurance of "the cooperation of the authorities on both sides."[32] A few months later the United States proposed that the Council request the International Red Cross to investigate the charges.[33] After the Soviet veto of this proposal, the United States took the question to the Assembly, which adopted a United States proposal for a commission of investigation.[34]

Need for an Investigation

The principal argument for an investigation has been that it was necessary and desirable as a preliminary to any decision by the Security Council or the General Assembly regarding the action, if any, to be taken.[35] Opposition generally has been based on the argument (1) that the Council or the Assembly should take no action whatsoever—often accompanied by a contention that the matter was outside the jurisdiction of the Council or the Assembly—or (2) that action of a different and usually more drastic character was required.

In both the Council and the Assembly, it has been recognized that the decision to undertake an investigation is a step of some

[31] U.N. Docs. S/1727 (Aug. 29, 1950) and S/1752 (Sept. 1, 1950).
[32] See U.N. Disarmament Commission, *Official Records,* 2nd Meeting (Mar. 14, 1952), p. 22; 3rd Meeting (Mar. 19, 1952), p. 6; 5th Meeting (Mar. 21, 1952), pp. 13-16.
[33] U.N. Doc. S/2671 (June 20, 1952).
[34] Res. 706 (VII), Apr. 23, 1953.
[35] Normally, a proposal for an investigation has been submitted at the outset of discussion. In the case of Eritrea, however, the commission was established only after the Members had failed at two Assembly sessions to agree on any of the specific proposals concerning the future status of Eritrea.

seriousness. In 1946 in connection with the proposed inquiry into the situation in Indonesia, many members of the Council stressed the desirability "in principle" of an investigation by the Council of the facts of any question, but attention was drawn to the unsubstantiated character of the original charges. The point was made that "an investigation should not be lightly undertaken." The United States representative expressed the view that "in determining whether or not a situation warrants investigation, the Security Council must have reason to believe, from all the circumstances before it, that the continuance of the situation is likely to endanger international peace,"[36] although from the wording of Article 34, it seems clear that this is indeed the very purpose of the investigation.

The opinion that before undertaking an investigation the Security Council should assure itself that there is a sufficient *prima facie* case to warrant such action has been expressed by many Members on the ground that the Council must guard itself against becoming a mere propaganda forum. In connection with a proposed investigation into certain of the Ukrainian charges against Greece, the Australian representative stated:

> . . . Because of the way this complaint has been brought, because of the way the matters of real substance have been mixed up with extraneous matters, and especially because we believe that this Council has the need to protect itself from misuse and to prevent Chapter VI from being distorted, we on principle oppose the proposal for investigation. . . .[37]

A particularly clear statement on this point has been made by the representative of the Netherlands:

> The mere fact that a complaint which to many of us does not seem fully substantiated is lodged with the Security Council regarding this or that State or Government does not seem to me to be sufficient reason to justify the establishment of a commission of inquiry. If we have to establish commissions of inquiry simply because a Member of the United Nations thinks fit to bring a charge against another State or Government, this Organization might well soon become the obnoxious tool of international ill feeling. . . . I therefore believe that before ever the Security Council decides to set up a committee of inquiry or investigation, the Council should satisfy itself that a sufficient *prima facie* case has been made out by the complaining party to warrant the establishment of such a committee.

---

[36] U.N. Security Council, First Year, *Official Records,* First Series, No. 1, 16th Meeting (Feb. 11, 1946), p. 235.
[37] *Ibid.,* Second Series, No. 15, 69th Meeting (Sept. 18, 1946), p. 379.

Thus alone can we hope to discourage the submission to this Council of inadequately substantiated charges.[38]

In some cases it has been considered that the facts were sufficiently clear to make an investigation unnecessary. Australia, for example, one of the staunchest supporters of "fact-finding" as a preliminary to action by the Council or the Assembly, made the following comment at the outset of the consideration of the Indonesian question, which it had brought to the Council as a "breach of the peace":

. . . The application of the principle of investigation should be considered in the light of each case which comes before the Council. The present situation is completely different from any previous case which has arisen. . . . The parties in this dispute have not only admitted the fact that hostilities are in progress but . . . have issued official *communiqués* regarding them. Investigation is not required to establish the crucial fact, and before the Security Council determines further action, it is essential to call a halt to hostilities which are each day taking their toll of human life and destruction of property. . . .[39]

The Soviet Union, and other members of the Soviet bloc, have repeatedly taken the position that, in the light of the known facts, there was no necessity for an investigation. They have argued that clearly the accused party was either "guilty" (when a member of the Soviet bloc has made the charges) or "innocent" (when the accused has been an ally of the Soviet Union). The Soviet representative opposed the establishment of the Spanish subcommittee on the ground that it was already "fully confirmed" that "the existing fascist regime in Spain" constituted a "serious threat to the maintenance of international peace and security."[40] In opposing the establishment of a commission to investigate the bacterial warfare charges, the Soviet Union contended that the facts had already been confirmed by "impartial international commissions,"[41] a reference to "investigations" by a number of Soviet sponsored bodies.

Another ground on which the Soviet Union has repeatedly opposed proposals for investigations is that they are designed to delay

[38] *Ibid.*, First Series, No. 2, 37th Meeting (Apr. 25, 1946), p. 224.
[39] U.N. Security Council, Second Year, *Official Records,* No. 67, 171st Meeting (July 31, 1947), p. 1624.
[40] U.N. Security Council, First Year, *Official Records,* First Series, No. 2, 39th Meeting (Apr. 29, 1946), p. 243.
[41] U.N. General Assembly, Seventh Session, First Committee, *Official Records,* 591st and 592nd Meetings (Mar. 27 and Apr. 7, 1953), pp. 565, 570.

effective action and divert attention from the substance of the claims. When the United States, for example, proposed an investigation of the charges against it that it had been bombing Chinese territory, the Soviet Union claimed that the United States was attempting to "sidetrack" the Council, "to drag out" the question, and "in reality to bury it by referring it to some sort of a commission of inquiry." It further charged that "under cover of the commission" the United States was trying to make a "spying reconnaissance of the situation in China."[42]

The appointment of a commission of investigation may well be a measure for delay, either because agreement on another course of action cannot be reached, as in the Eritrean question, or because it may be hoped that the situation will improve. The use of an inquiry as a device for delay is, of course, not necessarily reprehensible. Indeed, it was considered that one of the merits of the traditional commission of inquiry was that it afforded a "cooling-off" period.

Members have also on occasion professed a reluctance to support resolutions condemning one of the parties in the absence of an investigation of the charges. After the Soviet Union had vetoed a proposal in the Council for an investigation of the bacterial warfare charges, the United States introduced a draft resolution condemning those who had made the charges. The representative of Pakistan abstained from voting on this draft resolution, explaining that his Government found it somewhat difficult to treat a matter that one wanted investigated as though the investigation had taken place and as though the guilt had been proved.[43] In 1949, when Nationalist China brought charges that the Soviet Union had violated the Sino-Soviet treaty of 1945, the Chinese representative proposed a commission of inquiry. The Assembly instead referred the matter for study to the Interim Committee. Although the committee never inquired into the charges, the Assembly in 1950 adopted a resolution finding that the Soviet Union had failed to carry out its obligations under the treaty. Twenty-five Members abstained on this resolution, and although there were a wide variety of reasons for their doing so, one of the few reasons voiced was that the charges had not been substantiated by an investigation.

[42] U.N. Security Council, Fifth Year, *Official Records,* No. 43, 501st Meeting, (Sept. 12, 1950), pp. 16-17.
[43] U.N. Security Council, Seventh Year, *Official Records,* 589th Meeting (July 8, 1952), p. 14.

Attitudes of the Parties Directly Concerned

One factor of considerable influence on the decision to establish a commission has been the attitudes of the parties directly concerned. Seldom have all the parties agreed to an investigation, but there have been some exceptions. The resolution establishing the India-Pakistan commission was adopted with the approval of both parties. All four parties agreed to the establishment of the commission of investigation concerning the Greek frontier incidents, although a similar proposal made earlier had been vetoed by the Soviet Union. The establishment of the subcommittee of the Security Council on the question of the incidents in the Corfu Channel, although viewed with no great enthusiasm by Albania, was not blocked by the Soviet Union. Later Albania also co-operated with the inquiry carried out by technical experts for the International Court of Justice.

In some instances, in view of the opposition of one of the parties, no commission has been set up. In the Council, the Soviet Union has by its veto blocked the investigation of a number of cases involving its allies. It blocked the proposed investigation of the bombing of Chinese territory and the charges of bacterial warfare, and also prevented the establishment of a subcommittee to hear "evidence, statements and testimony" during consideration of the Czechoslovak question.

Members have often questioned whether any useful purpose would be served by establishing a commission over the objections of one of the parties. A proposed inquiry into the situation in Indonesia in 1946 was not supported by either the Netherlands or the United Kingdom. In this instance no commission was established. In like manner in 1949 the majority of the members of the General Assembly decided against a commission to study the treatment of Indians in South Africa and against a commission to study the situation in Bulgaria and Hungary in respect to human rights and fundamental freedoms.

In other cases, the Assembly established commissions even when it has been clear that there was no likelihood the parties concerned would co-operate. In connection with the establishment of the commission on the *apartheid* question, some Members sympathized with the objections of the Union of South Africa and others questioned whether a commission would serve any useful purpose. Only the Union of South Africa voted against the resolution, although twenty-three Members abstained.

In a number of the cases mentioned above, it was contended that the matters proposed for investigation were essentially within the domestic jurisdiction of the state concerned and therefore not appropriate for study by the United Nations. This was the attitude of the Union of South Africa on the two questions concerning its racial policies. The Soviet bloc has often opposed the establishment of an investigating commission on the ground that it would interfere in the internal affairs of a state. In general, however, Members have not considered that the application of Article 2(7) of the Charter precluded an inquiry into any of the matters that have been brought to the attention of either organ.

In considering the influence of the attitudes of the parties, the action taken by the Assembly with regard to the commission to investigate the bacterial warfare charges and the commission on free German elections is worth noting. In the first case the establishment of the commission was made dependent on "an indication from all the governments and authorities concerned of their acceptance of the investigation."[44] In the second case, a commission was established, but its "simultaneous investigation" was made dependent on the conclusion of satisfactory arrangements with all the governments and authorities concerned.[45] This proviso, an amendment to the original draft, resulted from the opposition of the Soviet Union and the authorities in East Germany to the investigation. It was also on the basis of this opposition that Sweden proposed unsuccessfully that the whole matter be referred back to the parties concerned.[46]

Nature and Purpose of the Investigation

Investigations have differed widely in their character, both with respect to the nature of the matters to be investigated and the scope and purpose of the investigation. In some cases, they have been concerned with establishing the facts regarding an alleged past course of conduct: whether United States forces did bomb Chinese territory or did use bacterial weapons in Korea; whether Albania was responsible for the damage by mines to British vessels in the Corfu Chan-

[44] Res. 706 (VII), Apr. 23, 1952.
[45] Res. 510 (VI), Dec. 20, 1951.
[46] U.N. Doc. A/AC.53/L.15 (Dec. 14, 1951).

nel; or the slightly more complex question of the part played by the Soviet Union in the 1948 coup in Czechoslovakia. In other cases, the matter to be investigated has been the nature of conditions existing at the time in particular areas: the situation in Bulgaria and Hungary with respect to human rights and fundamental freedoms; the situation arising from the racial policies of the Union of South Africa; whether conditions obtained throughout Germany for the holding of free elections. An investigation of the type mentioned in Article 34 of the Charter is concerned not only with past events and present conditions but with the evaluation of possible future developments, for the purpose of the investigation is to determine whether the continuance of the dispute or situation is likely to endanger the maintenance of international peace and security.

The most extensive investigations have been those carried out in Palestine and Eritrea where the complex relationship of political, economic, and social factors was studied so that a future policy could be devised. Indeed, the resolution of the General Assembly gave the Special Committee on Palestine "the widest powers . . . to investigate all questions and issues relevant to the problem of Palestine."[47] These broad terms of reference were granted to the committee, however, over the opposition of the Arab states which wished to specify in the instructions to the committee that "independence" was to be the ultimate purpose of any plan for the future of Palestine. The Arab states also insisted the committee should concern itself solely with the situation in Palestine without reference to the position of Jewish refugees outside the area.

In general, the Security Council and the Assembly have not placed narrow restrictions on the scope of an investigation or inquiry, although the terms of reference of commissions have sometimes emphasized particular aspects of the problem to be investigated. The Special Committee on Palestine was instructed to give most careful consideration to the religious interests in Palestine of Islam, Judaism, and Christianity.[48] The Eritrean commission was instructed to take into account: (1) the suggestions already made in the Assembly; (2) the wishes and welfare of the inhabitants of the area and their capacity for self-government; (3) the rights and claims of Ethiopia; and (4) the interests of peace and security in East Africa.[49] The com-

[47] Res. 106 (S-1), May 15, 1947.
[48] *Ibid.*
[49] Res. 289 (IV), Nov. 21, 1949.

mission on the *apartheid* question was to carry out its study "in the light of the Purposes and Principles of the Charter, with due regard to the provision of Article 2, paragraph 7, as well as the provisions of Article 1, paragraphs 2 and 3, Article 13, paragraph 1 b, Article 55 c and Article 56 of the Charter, and the resolutions of the United Nations on racial persecution and discrimination. . ."[50] The commission on free German elections was instructed to investigate: (1) the constitutional provisions in force and "their application as regards the various aspects of individual freedom. . ."; (2) the freedom of political parties to organize and carry out their activities; and (3) the organization and activities of the judiciary, police, and other administrative organs.[51]

Generally, the purpose, or at least the stated purpose, of any investigation has been to collect information for the Council or the Assembly. Commissions making on-the-spot investigations, of course, have been able to collect information not readily available to the two organs. In the case of the subcommittees appointed by the Council, it was clear that their purpose was to facilitate the work of the Council by examining detailed evidence, a task that it was felt could be more appropriately carried out by a smaller and less formal body than the Council. The Corfu Channel subcommittee, for example, was instructed to examine all the available evidence concerning the incidents in the Corfu Channel and to report on the facts of the case as disclosed by the evidence.[52] The proposed subcommittee on the Czechoslovak question was to receive and to hear evidence, statements, and testimonies.[53] In general, however, the primary purpose of an investigation has not been merely to acquire information. In most cases the facts are already well known. The problem of Palestine, for example, had been the subject of innumerable extensive investigations prior to the appointment of the United Nations Special Committee on Palestine. In this case, as in many others, it was considered that a new inquiry by the United Nations was necessary as a preliminary to further action. That the purpose of an investigation has been not only the collection of information but also the evaluation of that information has been made clear from

[50] Res. 616 (VII), Dec. 5, 1952.

[51] Res. 510 (VI), Dec. 20, 1951.

[52] U.N. Security Council, Second Year, *Official Records*, No. 18, 111th Meeting (Feb. 24, 1947), p. 364.

[53] U.N. Security Council, Third Year, *Official Records*, No. 63, 288th Meeting (Apr. 29, 1948), p. 19.

the inclusion in the terms of reference of most commissions of instructions to present not only findings but also conclusions and recommendations.

There have been many cases where the purpose of an investigation or proposed investigation has been to publicize and draw attention to a particular state of affairs with the hope that this might possibly lead to a condemnation by the United Nations of the actions of a particular state. This was clearly the intent of those supporting an inquiry into the racial policies of the Union of South Africa and the situation concerning human rights and fundamental freedoms in Bulgaria and Hungary.

In some cases the purpose of a United Nations inquiry has been quite similar to that served by a traditional commission of inquiry. It was believed that an impartial investigation by a commission of the United Nations into the charges of the bombing of Chinese territory would provide a basis for settlement. The United States representative announced in the Council that if it was "found that an attack did in fact occur," the United States Government was "prepared to make payment . . . of such damages as the commission shall find to be fair and equitable."[54]

The proposed investigation to determine whether conditions throughout Germany made it possible to hold free elections was another case where the purpose was to assist the parties themselves in reaching a settlement. The original request for an investigation had been made by the Federal Republic of Germany as a counter-move to the intensified campaign for unification of Germany being carried out by the authorities in the Soviet zone. The commission was asked to render a report "for the consideration of the four Powers and for the information" of other Members of the United Nations. Although it was contemplated that the United Nations might under certain circumstances offer its assistance in the holding of such elections, it was clear that the primary purpose of the proposed investigation was not to assist the Assembly in reaching any further recommendations on the matter; it was in fact to be an end in itself. In this instance, as in many other cases where a proposal for an investigation has been put forward with the full realization that one of the parties would not co-operate, the purpose of the move

[54] U.N. Security Council, Fifth Year, *Official Records*, No. 35, 493rd Meeting (Aug. 30, 1950), p. 26.

seems to have been to weaken the case of that party by forcing it to go on record in opposition to a United Nations investigation.

The refusal to accept an investigation has in fact been put forward as a basis for the adoption of a resolution of condemnation. After the Soviet Union vetoed the United States proposal in the Council for an investigation of the charges that United States forces were using germ warfare in Korea, the United States submitted a second draft resolution by which the Council would note the refusal of an investigation, would conclude that the charges were false, and would condemn the practice of fabricating and disseminating such false charges. The Soviet Union of course also vetoed this draft resolution.[55]

Commission Membership

In the League of Nations, commissions were usually composed of individuals chosen on the basis of their personal competence. The desired "nationality" of the members was determined to suit the requirements of the case and governments were then approached unofficially and asked to propose two or three persons. An effort was made to balance the group so that it would work smoothly and effectively as a team. The important point was that the persons so chosen served as individual and independent experts and not as representatives of their governments.

The practice of the United Nations has been just the opposite. With few exceptions, commissions of the Security Council and the General Assembly have been composed of Member states whose governments have appointed the individuals to represent them. The Assembly has on occasion appointed commissions composed of individuals to study and report on particular questions, but, with the exception of the commission on the *apartheid* question, these commissions have not been concerned with "political" questions.

The appointment of individuals has, however, often been discussed. When the Security Council first began its operations, the representative of the United States expressed the view that "as a general rule, any fact-finding or investigating commission ordered by the Council should be composed of impartial persons, chosen for their competence, who would represent not individual countries but

[55] U.N. Security Council, Seventh Year, *Official Records,* 590th Meeting (July 9, 1952), p. 7.

the Security Council."[56] Later, in 1946, the United States proposed an investigating commission of "three individuals to be nominated by the Secretary-General, to represent the Security Council on the basis of their competence and impartiality."[57] With the Soviet veto of this proposal, the United States apparently abandoned its advocacy of fact-finding commissions composed of individuals. Toward the end of the year in accordance with a proposal of the United States, the Council established the Greek frontier commission, composed of the members of the Council. A few months later, during the discussions in the Assembly on the composition of the Special Committee on Palestine, the representative of the United States observed that "any sub-ordinate body of the United Nations, it seems to me, must be composed of States and not of individuals."[58]

In 1952, the United States made a further suggestion for an investigation by "experts" with the proposal in the Security Council that the "International Committee of the Red Cross, with the aid of such scientists of international reputation and such other experts as it may select" investigate the charges that United Nations forces had been conducting bacterial warfare in Korea.[59] After the Soviet veto of this proposal, the Assembly adopted a resolution, sponsored by the United States, that provided for a commission composed of representatives of Members of the United Nations.[60]

During the discussions on the composition of the Special Committee on Palestine, there were some interesting comments on the status of persons appointed by Member governments. It was suggested that "they should perform their duties with complete impartiality and freedom of conscience, subject only to the purposes and principles of the United Nations and without seeking or accepting instructions from any Government or authority other than the General Assembly."[61] The French representative observed:

They would have to act according to their conscience, and impartially; I do not think they should receive instructions from their Governments. They should not, however, be described as "experts," so that their Gov-

[56] U.N. Security Council, First Year, *Official Records*, First Series, No. 1, 16th Meeting (Feb. 11, 1946), p. 235.

[57] *Ibid.*, Second Series, No. 16, 70th Meeting (Sept. 20, 1946), p. 412.

[58] U.N. General Assembly, First Special Session, First Committee, *Official Records,* 57th Meeting (May 13, 1947), p. 336.

[59] U.N. Doc. S/2671 (June 20, 1952).

[60] Res. 706 (VII), Apr. 23, 1953.

[61] U.N. General Assembly, First Special Session, First Committee, *Official Records,* 56th Meeting (May 13, 1947), pp. 318-20.

ernments should not feel in any way bound by whatever attitude they may adopt, as that would, in my opinion, detract from the committee's authority.[62]

Except when some special reasons obtain, however, it has been considered that subsidiary organs of the United Nations should reflect the views of the various groups and interests within the Organization. One of the principal criteria used for deciding the membership of commissions, especially in the General Assembly, has been "geographic distribution," a term that has been the subject of divergent interpretations. The Soviet Union has staunchly supported the position that commissions should be composed of all the members of the Security Council. Most of the proposals by the Soviet bloc have provided for such membership. In support of this method, it has been argued that the membership of the Council is in itself an adequate reflection of membership of the United Nations; and that this procedure will provide for the representation and the conciliation of all interests.

A point that has been discussed at some length has been the inclusion of the permanent members of the Council as members of commissions. Those favoring the inclusion of the permanent members have argued that their presence would add to the authority, prestige, and knowledge at the disposal of the commission. They have stressed the special responsibility of the permanent members with regard to the maintenance of international peace and security and contended that their disagreements should be resolved within the commission. The exclusion of the permanent members has been advocated primarily on the ground that their presence would impair the impartiality and objectivity of the commission. Their special interests and the possibility that differences between them might impair the efficiency of the commission have also been stressed. Generally, the permanent members of the Council have not been members of fact-finding commissions. They were specifically excluded from the Special Committee on Palestine, but were members of the Greek frontier commission, a commission composed of all the members of the Council.

The exclusion of the permanent members has been a part of the more general argument that states directly concerned should be excluded from membership on commissions. On the other hand, the inclusion of such states has been supported on the ground that they

[62] *Ibid.*, 57th Meeting (May 13, 1947), p. 335.

have special knowledge that would be of assistance to the commission and that as the implementation of the solution eventually recommended will depend to a large extent upon their co-operation, they should be represented on the commission.

Balanced representation, that is, having one state sympathetic to each party associated with a number of relatively "disinterested" states, has also been used to determine the membership of commissions. The method by which each of the parties selects one member of the commission and the two so chosen select the "third" member, has occasionally been suggested. It is doubtful whether this method is especially appropriate for the selection of members of a fact-finding body, in which emphasis is normally placed on the desirability of "impartiality and objectivity." This was the method the Council approved for the selection of the members for the India-Pakistan commission. This commission was given certain functions of investigation, but it was primarily a conciliation commission. The argument cannot be overlooked, however, that any commission so selected is more apt to have the confidence of the parties directly concerned.

Operation of Commissions of Investigation

Not only have the terms of reference of fact-finding commissions been, in general, broadly phrased, they have also been broadly interpreted by the commissions themselves. Commissions have usually been left free to determine their own procedures, primarily in recognition of the fact that the commission itself is best able to work out the details of its operations and must be left free to adapt its approach to any changes in the situation.

Co-operation of Parties Concerned

A major problem of most commissions has been to obtain the co-operation of the parties directly concerned. Usually the resolution establishing a commission has called upon the parties to facilitate its work. There have been few cases in which an investigation has been welcomed by all the parties, but this has not prevented commissions from carrying out investigations. Although a certain amount of friction developed from time to time during the investigation of the Greek frontier incidents, the commission was able to carry out its task. When the subsidiary group was established to continue the investigation, however, Albania, Bulgaria, and Yugoslavia refused to co-operate, and investigations could be carried out only on the Greek side of the frontier. Again, although the repeated efforts of the Special Committee on Palestine to obtain the co-operation of the Palestinian Arabs were unsuccessful, the committee carried out its investigations in the Arab areas of Palestine, attempted to ascertain the views of the Arabs by informal contacts, and obtained the views of the neighboring Arab states. The Arab boycott made the work of the committee more difficult, but it did not prevent it from carrying out its task. The commission on the *apartheid* question stated that one reason its first report was "imperfect" was the lack of co-operation from the Union of South Africa, the commission having been unable to visit the area or to obtain from South Africa a statement of its policies. This did not, however, prevent the commission from carrying on studies based upon documents and statements of witnesses.

The commission on the charges of bacterial warfare was never actually established because of the opposition of one of the parties, and the commission on free elections in Germany was unable to perform its functions because of the opposition of one of the parties. The resolution establishing this latter commission, in contrast to most resolutions of the Assembly, contained detailed provisions concerning the manner in which the commission was to proceed. To emphasize the necessity for a simultaneous investigation in all areas of Germany, the resolution called for a report from the commission on its efforts "to make the necessary arrangements with all the parties concerned to enable it to undertake its work."[63] The commission could not obtain replies to its communications to the authorities in the Eastern zone of Germany and in East Berlin. It did not therefore carry out any investigations because it interpreted the directions of the Assembly to mean that it could not do so if it were not able to conclude a satisfactory agreement "with any one of the responsible authorities in Germany."[64]

Sources of Information

Generally, fact-finding commissions have had complete freedom to decide from what sources they will seek and receive information. Most information has been supplied by governments primarily

[63] Res. 510 (VI), Dec. 20, 1951.
[64] U.N. Doc. A/2122 (May 5, 1952), p. 13.

concerned, but no commission has been restricted to considering information solely from official sources. The Special Committee on Palestine and the Eritrean commission were authorized to receive and examine written and oral testimony from governments, from representatives of the population in the area, and from such organizations and individuals as they deemed necessary. In addition to hearing the views of governments, both heard representatives of various political and religious organizations and private persons, and received a large amount of written testimony. As these two commissions were concerned with the attitudes of the population as well as of governments, these wide hearings were necessary.

Even in cases that primarily concerned relations between governments, commissions have similarly been given broad authority. The Greek frontier commission was given authority "to call upon the governments, officials and nationals" of the four countries concerned "as well as such other sources as the Commission deemed necessary for information relevant to its investigation." In establishing the commission on free German elections, the Assembly called upon authorities throughout Germany "to allow the Commission freedom of access to such persons, places and relevant documents as it considers necessary" and "to allow it to summon any witnesses whom it wishes to examine." On occasion, some difficulties have arisen concerning who should be heard, but on the whole there has been little controversy on this point. A problem has arisen, however, from time to time concerning the protection to be accorded to witnesses.

In general, commissions have taken a broad view regarding the sources from which they would seek and receive information. This has been true even of the subcommittees that have carried out limited investigations. The primary sources of information of the Spanish subcommittee, for example, were the replies by governments to a request for information concerning the origin, nature, structure, and conduct, past and present, of the Franco regime. Requests for information on specific points were addressed to such bodies as the War Crimes Commission, the chief prosecutors at Nuremberg, and the Allied councils in Japan, Italy, and Germany. The subcommittee also announced that it would welcome "information received from other sources."[65]

---

[65] See U.N. Press Releases SC/31 and SC/34. This presumably included the Franco regime, which did not, however, take advantage of the invitation. The original Australian proposal, in fact, specifically instructed the subcommittee

Other Factors Influencing
Effectiveness of Investigations

The principal factors influencing the effectiveness of the work of commissions of investigation have been the availability of information and the co-operation of the parties, but there are other factors that have had some influence. The extent to which a commission has been able to carry out a full-scale investigation has been in some measure dependent on the size of the commission, and the time at its disposal. In most cases resolutions establishing commissions have called for reports by a certain date. On the whole, however, it does not appear that the imposition of time limits has had an appreciable effect on the work of the commissions. But a factor of first importance in determining the effectiveness of an investigation has been the competence of the investigators and their ability to work together. The report of the Eritrean commission, for example, leaves no doubt that the effectiveness of the investigation was considerably hampered by the inability of the members of the commission even to agree on points of procedure or relatively nonessential facts.

Events within or even outside the area have affected the ability of a commission to fulfill its role. However, the riots in Eritrea, and the conditions of tension in Palestine and Greece do not appear to have interfered to any major extent with the work of the commissions in these areas. One can only speculate on the effect that the enunciation of the "Truman Doctrine" had on the work of the Greek frontier commission. The announcement of the United States program of aid to Greece while the commission was still carrying out an investigation (on the basis of which presumably a solution was to be sought) may indeed have lessened the significance, if not the effectiveness, of the work of the commission.

Nature and Effect of Reports

Reports of commissions usually have contained: (1) an account of the activities of the commission, (2) a presentation of the facts, and (3) conclusions and/or recommendations. Whether the commission has made recommendations has depended in part upon the

to call for evidence from the Franco regime. Evidence was received from the "Autonomous" Basque Government and the Spanish Republican Government-in-exile.

task it has been asked to undertake and the extent to which it has been able to carry out that task. The report of the commission on free German elections, for example, was merely a factual account of the unsuccessful efforts of the commission to make the necessary arrangements for carrying out its investigations.[66]

In some cases, a commission has not been asked to make recommendations. The Corfu Channel subcommittee, for example, was asked only to report on the facts disclosed by the available evidence. On the other hand, the commission on the *apartheid* question was specifically instructed to report its "conclusions." In its report, however, the commission, admitting that it was giving a broad interpretation to its terms of reference, made suggestions regarding the course of action that the United Nations might follow in dealing with the problem.[67] It is seldom that a commission has been able to present a unanimous report. The Spanish subcommittee presented a lengthy report on its "factual findings" that was subscribed to by all the members of the subcommittee. The Polish representative, however, entered reservations to the most important sections of the report concerning the conclusions of the subcommittee regarding the jurisdiction of the Security Council and the recommendations regarding the action that the Council should take.[68] The members of the Special Committee on Palestine reached agreement on the factual chapters of the report and on a number of "basic recommendations," such as the termination of the mandate and the grant of independence in some form. For the future government of Palestine, the majority favored "partition" with economic union, while the minority favored a "federal state."

The Eritrean commission provided the outstanding example of a case in which the members of a commission failed to reach agreement. The members of this commission could not even reach agreement on the facts of the case and a wide variety of recommendations for the solution of the problem were put forward.[69]

The members of the Greek frontier commission agreed, with some reservations, to the chapters of the report containing an account of the work of the commission and a survey of the evidence sub-

---

[66] U.N. Doc. A/2122 (May 5, 1952).

[67] U.N. General Assembly, Eighth Session, *Official Records,* Supplement No. 16 (Oct. 14, 1953).

[68] U.N. Security Council, First Year, *Official Records,* First Series, Special Supplement (June 1946), pp. 11-12.

[69] U.N. General Assembly, Fifth Session, *Official Records,* Supplement No. 8 (June 8, 1950).

mitted to it.[70] Two sets of "conclusions" were, however, presented, one by the Soviet and Polish members and the other by the majority. Moreover, there were some reservations stated concerning the nature of these conclusions. The Belgian and Colombian representatives expressed the view that it was not for the commission "which was set up in the spirit of conciliation of Chapter VI of the Charter to give any decision as to the possible responsibility of the Albanian, Bulgarian, and Yugoslav Governments." The French representative, in explaining why he did not subscribe to the conclusions of the majority, expressed the view that the conditions under which the inquiry was carried out were not "conducive" to establishing "a body of evidence in the juridical sense of the word." He stated that in reaching "conclusions with insufficient legal foundation" the commission "might only aggravate an already critical situation." For these reasons, he favored a report "limited on the one hand to the statement of facts and on the other hand to the proposing of practical measures to ensure pacification in the troubled area." The French representative did, however, join with the majority of the commission in their proposals to the Council concerning the steps that should be taken. These proposals were not supported by the Soviet and Polish representatives, who did not themselves present any proposals.

The chairman or *rapporteur* of the commission usually has made a formal presentation of the report to the Security Council or the General Assembly. On occasion, the representatives who served on the commission have taken an active part in the subsequent discussions of the report. This was true with regard to the consideration in the Assembly of the report of the Special Committee on Palestine.

It has not been the practice of subsidiary organs of the Assembly and the Council to formulate their recommendations in the form of draft resolutions. What has usually happened is that a state represented on the subsidiary organ has presented in the Council or the Assembly a draft resolution based on the report. In the case of the report of the Greek frontier commission, for example, the Soviet representative introduced a draft resolution in the Council based in large measure on the minority conclusions in the report of the commission. The United States introduced a draft by which the

[70] U.N. Security Council, Second Year, *Official Records*, Special Supplement No. 2 (July 28, 1950).

Council would adopt the proposals made by the majority of the members of the commission.

Of all the reports by fact-finding bodies, the one that had the greatest and most direct effect on the action taken by the principal organ was the report of the Special Committee on Palestine. The plan of partition with economic union that the Assembly adopted was essentially the same as the plan supported by the majority of the members in the committee.[71] The report that appears to have had the least effect was that of the Eritrean commission. The Assembly decided in favor of federation of Eritrea with Ethiopia, a solution supported by two of the members of the commission.[72] Whether the investigations of the commission influenced this decision is questionable. It would appear that this course was taken because it had the support of Ethiopia, the United Kingdom, the United States, and a large number of Latin-American Members.

The report of the commission on free German elections did not indicate that there was any possibility that further action by the Assembly would produce any change in the situation and in fact this report was not even considered by the Assembly. The report of the commission on the *apartheid* question was discussed at length, but the Assembly did not follow the suggestions of the commission concerning further action. Instead it asked the commission to continue its studies.

With regard to the reports of the Spanish subcommittee and the Greek frontier commission, the Council was unable to take any further action. In both cases, the Soviet Union vetoed the proposals supported by the majority of members, and the draft resolutions of the Soviet bloc failed to obtain majority support. The work of these two commissions did, however, have an effect on the action taken in the General Assembly. The resolution of the Assembly on the Balkan question, for example, was in many respects similar to the proposed resolution the United States had introduced in the Council, a resolution based largely on the majority recommendations of the Greek frontier commission.[73] The Spanish subcommittee recommended that the Council endorse a condemnation of the Franco regime and recommend to the Assembly that unless the regime was "withdrawn" and certain other conditions obtained in

[71] Res. 181 (II), Nov. 29, 1947.
[72] Res. 390 (V), Dec. 2, 1950.
[73] Res. 109 (II), Oct. 21, 1947.

Spain, the Assembly should recommend that "diplomatic relations with the Franco regime be terminated" by the Members of the United Nations. But the Assembly merely recommended the recall of ambassadors and ministers plenipotentiary from Spain. The resolution cited the unanimous findings of the Spanish subcommittee and included other provisions concerning the relations of Spain with the United Nations.[74]

Although investigations by the United Nations have not resolved points of essential difference, especially differences between parties directly concerned, these investigations have undoubtedly provided a basis for more substantial agreement among the Members of the United Nations. Without the work of the Special Committee on Palestine, it is unlikely that the resolution on partition would have been adopted by the General Assembly. It is also doubtful that the resolutions of the Assembly on Spain and on the Greek question would have received such wide support had it not been for the investigations undertaken by the Council.

Efforts to base the action of the Security Council and the General Assembly on full and impartial investigation of the facts of a dispute or situation have met with only very limited success. Perhaps the procedure would have won greater acceptance if from the beginning there had been emphasis on investigation as the normal procedure for establishing the facts of a case; if the procedure of inquiry had been used for the purpose of clarifying issues rather than publicizing a situation; if reports had been restricted to factual findings with less emphasis on conclusions and recommendations; if, perhaps, greater use had been made of "experts" instead of governmental representatives.

Suggestions to spell out the obligation of Members to accept investigation by the United Nations, including the suggestion to free the decision of the Council to investigate from the use of the veto by the permanent members, are not realistic. In the League of Nations, not only were Members under an obligation to accept an inquiry but also the Covenant specifically provided that the decision to investigate was not subject to the unanimity rule. Yet the League undertook investigations only with the consent of the states concerned. Even in the Assembly of the United Nations, which has from time to time undertaken an inquiry over the opposition of one

[74] Res. 39 (I), Dec. 12, 1946.

of the parties directly concerned, there has been an increasing realization of the futility of embarking on such a course.

In the political atmosphere in which the United Nations has operated, impartial investigation can play only a limited role. A clarification of facts can contribute little if anything to the resolution of issues arising from the cold war or the conflicts of interest over "colonial" questions. For evidence of the impact of the cold war, one need only note the continued opposition of the Soviet Union to allowing international commissions to enter the territory of any of the members of the Soviet bloc and the refusal of the Soviet Union to accept any commission in which its interests are not directly and equally represented. Indeed, as was clearly demonstrated during the discussions over who could be considered "neutral" with regard to the Korean question, the terms "impartiality," "objectivity," and "neutrality" have quite different meanings to the East and the West.

PART THREE

METHODS OF PEACEFUL SETTLEMENT
AND ADJUSTMENT

CHAPTER IX

Recommendation of General Principles of International Political Co-operation

I T IS a commonly accepted view that the development and the wide acceptance of general principles of international conduct and of procedures for the application of these principles to specific cases contribute to the more effective maintenance of international peace and security. The Charter of the United Nations itself formulates such agreed principles and procedures, but recognizes the need for their further development, both in regard to their scope and their detailed application in particular situations. Broadly speaking, the General Assembly is recognized as the organ best suited for the performance of this particular function.

Respective Roles of the Security Council and the General Assembly

Article 11(1) of the Charter gives the General Assembly the power to consider the "general principles of cooperation in the maintenance of international peace and security" and to make recommendations to the Members of the United Nations and to the Security Council. By the terms of Article 13(1) the Assembly "shall initiate studies and make recommendations" for promoting international co-operation in the political field and encouraging the progressive development and codification of international law. In these two fields the role of the Assembly is paramount. The limitations imposed on the Assembly by the Charter in connection with the consideration of disputes and situations, limitations designed to safeguard the primary role of the Council, do not apply when the Assembly is considering these matters of general concern.[1]

In explanation of the authorization given to the Assembly to consider general principles, Dr. Pasvolsky, as representative of the De-

---

[1] *Cf.* the wording of Arts. 11(1) and 13 with Arts. 10, 11(2), 14, and 35 of the Charter.

partment of State, made the following statement in the hearings
before the Senate Committee on Foreign Relations on ratification
of the Charter.

> It was thought that the general principles of cooperation, as they need
> to develop in relation to changing conditions, would have to be considered,
> formulated, and recommended to Members and to the Security Council
> by the General Assembly rather than by the Security Council, because
> that is not a function of a small number of states; that is a function of all
> the states. So the General Assembly is given the function in connection
> with general principles of cooperation, and that includes the principles
> governing eventual disarmament and the regulation of armaments, when
> the Organization comes to that.[2]

The intention of those who drafted the Charter that the General Assembly and not the Security Council should have the primary
role in recommending general principles of co-operation in the
maintenance of international peace and security has been fulfilled
in the operations of the United Nations. Although the Security
Council has given a broad interpretation to its primary responsibility for the maintenance of international peace and security, the
activities of the Council have, on the whole, been restricted to the
consideration of specific disputes and situations. The Council has
from time to time considered the regulation of armaments and the
international control of atomic energy, usually on the basis of
reports from commissions established to deal with these questions.[3]
In 1946, however, the Council refused to consider a proposal by the
Soviet Union that it request from Members information concerning
their forces stationed in territories other than those of former enemy
states on the ground that this was not a situation such as the Charter
envisaged the Council should consider.[4] In 1952, however, the Council did consider a Soviet request for an appeal to states "to accede
to and ratify" the Geneva Protocol of 1925 for the prohibition of

---

[2] *Charter of the United Nations,* Hearings before the Senate Committee on
Foreign Relations, 79 Cong. 1 sess., p. 245.

[3] For the activities of the Council in this connection, see below, Chap. XXI.
For the role of the Council in connection with strategic trusteeships see the
volume in this Brookings series, *The United Nations and Promotion of the
General Welfare.* See also the volume, *The Organization and Procedures of the
United Nations* for discussion of the activities of the Council in connection with
such matters as admission of new members, appointment of the Secretary-General,
election of judges to the International Court of Justice, and representation of
members.

[4] U.N. Security Council, First Year, *Offical Records,* Second Series, Nos. 17 and
18, 71st and 72nd Meetings (Sept. 23-24, 1946), pp. 423 ff.

bacterial warfare. But the Soviet proposal was not adopted, and many members expressed the view that the Disarmament Commission was a more appropriate agency for considering the matter.[5]

The resolutions of the Council concerning disputes and situations have for the most part been confined to specific recommendations to the states concerned, sometimes accompanied by general requests to Members that they do what they can to facilitate the implementation of the recommendations. The Council has not emphasized general principles of conduct to the same extent as has the Assembly. For example, the resolution proposed by the United Kingdom on the question of incidents in the Corfu Channel contained a statement that the laying of mines in peacetime without notification was an "offence against humanity" and a general reminder to all states that it was incumbent upon them "to sweep or permit to be swept all parts of their territorial waters where there is reason to suspect the presence of mines." This provision was deleted after the representative of the United States suggested that it "would be convenient and appropriate for the Council to refrain from expressing any opinion on a legal question of this character which is not necessary for the decision of this case."[6]

Although Article 11 of the Charter is couched in permissive terms, Article 13 provides that the General Assembly "shall initiate studies and make recommendations, . . ." and the Assembly has recognized the obligatory character of the latter article. In a resolution adopted during the second part of the first session, it recognized "the obligation laid upon it by Article 13, paragraph 1, sub-paragraph a, of the Charter to initiate studies and make recommendations for the purpose of encouraging the progressive development of international law and its codification."[7] Subsequently, the Assembly repeatedly manifested its concern with the development and codification of international law both in its own debates and resolutions and in the work of the International Law Commission, which the Assembly established during its second session.[8] The Assembly has also shown its concern with the promotion of international co-operation in the

[5] U.N. Security Council, Seventh Year, *Official Records,* 583rd Meeting (June 26, 1952), p. 2.

[6] U.N. Security Council, Second Year, *Official Records,* Nos. 27 and 28, 120th and 121st Meetings (Mar. 20 and 21, 1947), pp. 567 and 589-90.

[7] Res. 94(I), Dec. 11, 1946.

[8] For comment on the work of the International Law Commission see the volume in this Brookings series, *The Organization and Procedures of the United Nations.*

"economic, social, cultural, educational and health fields," particularly with that section of Article 13 relating to human rights and fundamental freedoms.[9]

The Assembly has done very little, however, with regard to the promotion of "international cooperation in the political field." The Interim Committee, which the Assembly established during its second session, was assigned the task of considering general principles of co-operation in the maintenance of international peace and security and the promotion of international co-operation in the political field.[10] The committee considered a number of proposals and made a number of studies, primarily in relation to possible improvements in methods for the pacific settlement of disputes and the adjustment of situations.[11] But it never assumed a role of any significance, in large measure because it was boycotted by the Soviet bloc. Although technically the committee is still in existence, actually it ceased to function after the submission of its report to the Assembly in 1950.

Recommendations of General Principles with Respect to Specific Disputes and Situations

To a much greater extent than was foreseen by those who drafted the Charter, the General Assembly has been concerned with specific disputes and situations. In the handling of these matters, the Assembly, in its resolutions, has shown a tendency to emphasize the general principles that should govern the conduct of states in their relations with one another, and its resolutions are replete with references to the purposes and principles of the United Nations, with constant use of the phraseology of the Preamble and Articles 1 and 2 of the Charter. For example, when Nationalist China charged that the peace of the Far East and the political independence and territorial integrity of China were threatened by Soviet violations of the Charter and of the Sino-Soviet Treaty of 1945, the As-

[9] See the volume in this Brookings series, *The United Nations and Promotion of the General Welfare.*

[10] See Res. 111(II), Nov. 13, 1947, Res. 196(III), Dec. 3, 1948, and Res. 295(IV), Nov. 21, 1949.

[11] For the reports of the committee, see U.N. General Assembly, Third Session, *Official Records,* Supplement No. 10; U. N. General Assembly, Fourth Session, *Official Records,* Supplement No. 11; and U. N. General Assembly, Fifth Session, *Official Records,* Supplement No. 14.

sembly approved a resolution entitled "Promotion of the stability of international relations in the Far East," in which it recommended that Members follow general principles such as those laid down in the Charter. The resolution repeated sections of the Preamble, and Articles 1(2), 2(1), and 2(4) of the Charter and called upon states: (1) to respect the political independence of China and be guided by the principles of the United Nations in their relations with China, (2) to respect the right of the Chinese people to choose freely their own government, (3) to respect existing treaties relating to China, and (4) to refrain from seeking to acquire spheres of influence or special rights or privileges.[12]

Another type of general recommendation, which has been employed by the Assembly, has dealt with charges concerning the conduct of a specific state under the guise of a recommendation to all Members. This approach has been used especially in situations where there has been opposition to any action by the Assembly on the ground that the matter under consideration was outside its jurisdiction. For example, a group of Arab-Asian states brought to the attention of the Assembly the *apartheid* question with a request that the Assembly condemn the racial policies of the Union of South Africa. Some Members supported the South African position that this matter was outside the jurisdiction of the Assembly. Others questioned whether it was desirable for the Assembly to adopt such a course of action. In these circumstances, the Scandinavian states introduced a proposal, which was subsequently adopted, calling upon all Members to bring their policies into conformity with their obligations under the Charter to promote the observance of human rights and fundamental freedoms.[13]

The Assembly has also used the device of avoiding an outright condemnation of a particular state by a general condemnation of acts of the kind the state has allegedly committed. This was illustrated by the resolution the Assembly adopted on the "question of atrocities committed by the North Korean and Chinese Communist forces against United Nations prisoners of war in Korea." This resolution referred to various conventions concerning the treatment of prisoners of war and civilians in time of war and stated that these provisions "to the extent they have not become binding as treaty law, have been accorded most general support by the inter-

[12] Res. 291(IV), Dec. 8, 1949.
[13] Res. 616B(VII), Dec. 5, 1952.

national community." The Assembly then expressed its "grave concern at reports and information" concerning the actions of the North Korean and Chinese Communist forces and ended by condemning "the commission by any governments or authorities of murder, mutilation, torture, and other atrocious acts . . . as a violation of rules of international law and basic standards of conduct and morality. . . ."[14]

Recommendations of General Principles by the Assembly

The most important recommendations made by the General Assembly on general principles of co-operation in the maintenance of international peace and security have concerned the regulation of armaments and the international control of atomic energy, which are dealt with later in this volume.[15] Other recommendations of a general nature made by the Assembly that have concerned matters in the political field fall within three principal categories: (1) the general proposals made by the members of the Soviet bloc "to avert the threat of a new world war and to strengthen peace and friendship among nations"; (2) other proposals for strengthening the United Nations system for the maintenance of international peace and security; and (3) proposals reflecting the special concern of the Assembly with regard to the relations among the great powers.

The Soviet "Peace Offensive"

During the second part of the first session of the General Assembly in 1946, the Soviet Union asked the Assembly to consider two items: (1) the presence of troops of Members of the United Nations in territories other than those of former enemy states and (2) the general reduction of armaments.[16] This was the first indication that the Soviet Union intended to use the Assembly as a forum for the consideration of broad questions relating to the maintenance of international peace and security, or more precisely that the members of the Soviet bloc intended to use the meetings of the Assembly for the purpose of firing broadsides against the United States and its

[14] Res. 804(VIII), Dec. 3, 1953.
[15] See below, Chap. XXI.
[16] For a detailed discussion of these items and the decisions the Assembly finally reached see below, Chap. XXI.

allies. At each subsequent session of the Assembly, the Soviet Union or one of the members of the Soviet bloc has asked the Assembly to consider proposals allegedly designed to reduce the threat of war and promote friendly relations among nations. These proposals have been primarily concerned with outlawing atomic weapons and reducing the level of armaments, but they have also touched on other issues.

At the second session of the Assembly in 1947, the Soviet Union asked it to consider "measures to be taken against propaganda and the inciters of a new war." Specifically, the Soviet Union proposed that the Assembly condemn "the criminal propaganda for a new war," citing in particular the activities of "reactionary circles" in the United States, Turkey, and Greece.[17] The Soviet proposal further called upon governments "to prohibit, on pain of criminal penalties, the carrying on of war propaganda in any form, and to take measures with a view to the prevention and suppression of war propaganda. . . ." When the discussion of this proposal began in the First Committee of the Assembly, the United States representative urged the committee to reject the Soviet charges and get on with its work.[18] He also expressed the view that the matter could be more appropriately discussed at the forthcoming Conference on Freedom of Information, and although this latter position was supported by many members of the committee, others did not consider that the committee should take a "merely negative attitude" toward the Soviet proposal. A similar uneasiness on the part of Members when subsequently confronted by Soviet proposals has commonly manifested itself in the Assembly. On the one hand, there has been a reluctance to dismiss such of the proposals as on the surface do not seem completely unreasonable. On the other hand, there has been an increasing realization that more frequently than not the proposals are part of a campaign to convince world public opinion of the peaceful intentions of the Soviet Union and the aggressive designs of the United States and the other Western powers.

In response to the Soviet proposal the Assembly, at its second session, adopted unanimously a resolution condemning "all forms of propaganda . . . designed or likely to provoke or encourage any threat to the peace, breach of the peace, or act of aggression." Each govern-

[17] U.N. Doc. A/Bur. 86 (Sept. 18, 1947).
[18] U.N. General Assembly, Second Session, First Committee, *Official Records,* 80th Meeting (Oct. 23, 1947), pp. 192-95.

ment was requested "to take appropriate steps within its constitutional limits":

(a) to promote by all means of publicity and propaganda available to them, friendly relations among nations based upon the Purposes and Principles of the Charter;
(b) to encourage the dissemination of all information designed to give expression to the undoubted desire of all peoples for peace. . . .[19]

At the third session, in 1948, the Soviet Union limited its proposals to "the prohibition of the atomic weapon and reduction by one-third of the armaments and armed forces of the permanent members of the Security Council." The only part of the original Soviet draft that survived the committee debate was its title.[20] During 1949, the Soviet peace campaign took on more of the character of an organized movement. In April, the month the North Atlantic Treaty was signed, the communist-inspired "Partisans of Peace" movement was launched, and a series of international peace congresses were initiated. At the 1949 session of the Assembly, the Soviet Union called for a condemnation by the Assembly of "the preparations for a new war," citing in particular the United States and the United Kingdom. The Soviet proposal further called for the conclusion among the five permanent members of a "Pact for the Strengthening of Peace."[21] A number of Members questioned the usefulness of these repeated discussions and expressed their lack of enthusiasm regarding them. The representative of New Zealand was reported in the summary record of the committee meeting to have stated:

. . . The Soviet Union draft resolution . . . was the latest in a long series of draft resolutions which that delegation was wont to submit at every session of the General Assembly not with the expectation that they would be acted upon but purely for propaganda purposes. One wondered whether it was useful to discuss them seriously since, quite obviously, anyone who was deceived by them was beyond the reach of logical argument. However, in view of the existing world situation, it did not seem possible to dismiss the Soviet Union proposal without comment.[22]

In the end, this Soviet proposal was overwhelmingly rejected, and the Assembly adopted a resolution sponsored by the United

[19] Res. 110(II), Nov. 3, 1947.
[20] Res. 192(III), Nov. 19, 1948.
[21] U.N. Doc. A/996 (Sept. 24, 1949).
[22] U.N. General Assembly, Fourth Session, First Committee, *Official Records,* 328th Meeting (Nov. 15, 1949), p. 279.

States and the United Kingdom entitled "Essentials of Peace." This resolution declared "that the Charter of the United Nations, the most solemn pact of peace in history, lays down basic principles necessary for an enduring peace," no five-power pact therefore being necessary, and that disregard of these Charter principles "is primarily responsible for the continuance of international tension." The resolution called upon every state to conform to certain basic Charter principles. In particular, states were asked: (1) to refrain from any acts or threats aimed at impairing the freedom, independence, or integrity of any state or at fomenting civil strife; (2) to settle their disputes by peaceful means and co-operate with United Nations efforts to resolve outstanding problems, particularly by participating in the work of United Nations organs and according to them full co-operation; (3) to promote efforts to achieve higher living standards, the free exchange of ideas, and other fundamental rights and freedoms; and (4) to co-operate in attaining international regulation of armaments and control of atomic energy.[23]

The resolution proposed by the Soviet Union during the fifth session of the Assembly contained all the familiar points, and, in addition, made reference to some more recent developments in the cold war.[24] There was, for example, a reference to the Stockholm Peace Appeal, and in line with this appeal the Soviet resolution proposed that the Assembly declare that the first government to use the atomic weapon "will therefore commit a crime against humanity and be regarded as a war criminal." The Soviet draft contained no specific proposals relating to the situation in Korea, but the preamble noted that events in Korea and the Pacific emphasized with added force the extreme importance and urgency from the point of view of international peace and security of unifying the efforts of the five great powers. Of the two resolutions adopted by the Assembly, one concerned the "condemnation of propaganda against peace" and included a specific reference to "measures tending to isolate the peoples from contact with the outside world." The other resolution entitled "Peace through Deeds" reiterated many of the provisions of previous resolutions concerning the control of atomic energy and disarmament, condemned intervention in the internal affairs of a state "for the purpose of changing its legally established government by the threat or use of force," and "solemnly reaffirmed"

[23] Res. 290(IV), Dec. 1, 1949.
[24] U.N. Doc. A/C.1/595 (Oct. 23, 1950).

that "any aggression" was the "gravest of all crimes against peace and security throughout the world."[25]

The "measures to combat the threat of a new world war and to strengthen peace and friendship among nations" that the Soviet Union asked the Assembly to endorse at its sixth session did not depart substantially from previous proposals.[26] The Soviet proposal contained a recommendation for a world disarmament conference and a call for the cessation of military operations in Korea and the withdrawal of foreign troops. The principal innovation was the proposed declaration by the Assembly that "participation in the aggressive Atlantic bloc and the creation . . . primarily by the United States of military, naval and air bases in foreign territories" were "incompatible with membership in the United Nations." The other Members, however, had apparently lost their enthusiasm for adopting further resolutions paraphrasing the various provisions of the Charter. Consequently, at the end of the debate, which was considerably shorter than at previous sessions, the Assembly merely rejected some of the main points of the Soviet proposal and referred the others to the Disarmament Commission.[27]

At the seventh session, the Assembly, at the request of Poland, again placed on its agenda the item "measures to avert the threat of a new world war and to strengthen peace and friendship among nations," and the debate on this item is illustrative of the various turns such generalized discussions can take. The Polish resolution covered such issues as the Korean situation, disarmament, outlawing atomic weapons, bacterial warfare, the North Atlantic Treaty, and the conclusion of a five-power pact.[28] Although the proposal was submitted in October 1952, the discussion did not take place until the following April. In the interim a number of developments had occurred. In particular there was, following the death of Stalin, a change in the approach of the Kremlin, in the direction of more conciliatory gestures. Thus, although the usual arguments were advanced during the discussion of the Polish item, the remarks were considerably less vitriolic than formerly. With the resumption of negotiations in Korea, moreover, the Polish representative stated that he would not press for a vote on his proposal. The Assembly

[25] Res. 380(V) and Res. 381(V), Nov. 17, 1950.
[26] U.N. Doc. A/C.1/698 (Jan. 12, 1952).
[27] Res. 504(VI), Jan. 19, 1952.
[28] U.N. Doc. A/2229 (Oct. 18, 1952).

then proceeded by a unanimous vote to adopt a resolution on the Korean negotiations.

At the eighth session, the Assembly rejected a Soviet proposal for "measures to avert the threat of a new world war and to reduce tension in international relations."[29] This proposal noted that the cessation of hostilities in Korea was "an important contribution to the reduction of tension in international relations" and had "created more favorable conditions for further action to avert the threat of a new world war." The Soviet Union again proposed that the Assembly: (1) declare itself in favor of the unconditional prohibition of atomic, hydrogen, and other weapons of mass destruction; (2) call for the reduction of armaments and the holding of a world disarmament conference; (3) condemn the propaganda being conducted in a number of countries with the aim of inciting enmity and hatred among nations and preparing for a new war; and (4) recommend that the Security Council take steps to ensure the elimination of military bases in the territories of other states on the ground that such bases increased the threat of a new war and operated to undermine the national sovereignty and independence of states.

The speeches made by the representatives of the United States and the United Kingdom during the debate on this item are indicative of the two-fold attitude the Western powers have developed toward these Soviet proposals. The representative of the United States remarked: "It is purely a propaganda proposition, not introduced with a serious purpose of serious action, but solely as a peg on which to hang a number of speeches with a view to getting them into the Press of the world. . . . The main purpose of this exercise is to utter more or less elaborate untruths about the United States."[30] The representative of the United Kingdom stated that: "Experience had shown that there was no simple solution to the problem facing the world. Hope must lie not in the adoption of high-sounding resolutions, but in painstaking and persevering work aimed at solving problems one by one and at courageously seeking new formulas, undaunted by failure or disappointments."[31]

[29] U.N. Doc. A/2485 (Sept. 21, 1953).

[30] U.N. General Assembly, Eighth Session, Plenary, *Official Records*, 461st Meeting (Nov. 30, 1953), p. 335.

[31] U.N. General Assembly, Eighth Session, First Committee, *Official Records*, 673rd Meeting (Nov. 23, 1953), p. 252.

Strengthening the United Nations System

In addition to the specific powers granted under Articles 11(2) and 13 of the Charter, the Assembly is also authorized to discuss "any questions or any matters within the scope of the present Charter or relating to the powers and functions of any organs provided for in the present Charter" and make recommendations thereon to the Members, to the Security Council, or to both.[32] The Assembly has addressed a great number of recommendations to the Security Council, especially with regard to matters, such as the regulation of armaments and the admission of new Members, concerning which the Assembly and the Council share a responsibility under the Charter. The Assembly has also exercised its powers under Article 10 to make recommendations to the Council regarding the manner in which the Council conducts its operations. During the first few years, the question of voting procedure in the Security Council was a favorite topic for discussion in the Assembly, and many recommendations were made to the Council on this subject.[33] Other aspects of the work of the Council with which the Assembly has shown a special concern are: (1) the implementation of Article 43 of the Charter, and (2) the possibility of holding periodic meetings of the Council in accordance with Article 28 of the Charter.

Of considerably more importance are efforts that the Assembly has made to strengthen the United Nations system for the maintenance of international peace and security by compensating for the failure of the Security Council to discharge effectively its primary responsibility under the Charter. The first of these efforts has already been mentioned—the establishment of the Interim Committee of the General Assembly in 1947. The primary purpose of the committee was to assist the Assembly in handling the increased number of disputes and situations that were being brought to the Assembly as a result of the deadlock in the Council. The committee, however, was of little assistance, although it did devote some time to the study of possible ways of improving methods for the pacific settlement of disputes both within and outside the United Nations.[34] On the basis of the report of the committee, the Assembly (1) addressed a

---

[32] Art. 10.

[33] See the volume in this Brookings series, *The Organization and Procedures of the United Nations*.

[34] For additional comment on the role of the committee in connection with the holding of elections in Korea, see below, Chap. X, p. 253.

recommendation to the Council concerning the possible use of the *rapporteur* system,[35] (2) decided to restore the "efficacy" of the General Act of September 26, 1928, a convention concerning the pacific settlement of disputes to which a limited number of Members of the United Nations had been parties, and (3) established a panel for inquiry and conciliation.[36]

Another effort to revitalize the United Nations was the initiative taken by the Secretary-General in the spring of 1950 when the fortunes of the Organization were at low ebb. First, the Secretary-General circulated his views on the issue of Chinese representation in the United Nations, over which the Soviet Union had walked out of the Security Council. He then drew up a ten-point, twenty-year program for achieving peace through the United Nations. The program did not envisage any changes in the structure of the Organization. It merely set out certain subjects, such as control of atomic energy and membership, on which, in the Secretary-General's opinion, a new effort should be made to obtain agreement, and other matters such as technical assistance, the advancement of dependent peoples, and the development of international law, which he felt should be considered with a view to the further development of United Nations activities.

The Secretary-General presented his program personally to top officials in Paris, London, Moscow, and Washington.[37] At the conclusion of his tour, the Secretary-General circulated the program to all Members, but by the time it could be considered, the world situation had changed for the worse as a result of the outbreak of hostilities in Korea. The program was discussed briefly at the fifth session of the Assembly. The Secretary-General was commended for his initiative, and the organs of the United Nations were requested to consider the relevant portions of the program.

Although the first innovation in the structure of the United Nations, the establishment of the Interim Committee, was designed to assist the Assembly in discharging its responsibilities for the pacific settlement of disputes and the adjustment of situations, the second such innovation, the adoption of the "Uniting for Peace" resolution, was directed toward enabling the Assembly to deal more effectively with threats to the peace, breaches of the peace, and acts

[35] See above, Chap. VII, pp. 149-50.
[36] Res. 268(III), Apr. 28, 1949.
[37] See Trygve Lie, *In the Cause of Peace* (1954), Chaps. XVI and XVII.

of aggression. To this end, the United States presented to the Assembly during its fifth session a series of proposals based in large part on the Korean experience. Briefly, it was proposed that the Assembly: (1) take measures to ensure that it would be able to deal immediately with any threat to the peace, breach of the peace, or act of aggression if the Security Council, because of lack of unanimity of the permanent members, failed to exercise its primary responsibility for dealing with such matters; (2) establish a Peace Observation Commission, which would be available to observe and report on developments in any area where international peace might be endangered; (3) recommend that each Member maintain units within its armed forces that could promptly be made available for service on the recommendation of the Council or the Assembly; and (4) establish a Collective Measures Committee to study and report on the measures that might be used to maintain and strengthen international peace and security in accordance with the purposes and principles of the Charter.[38]

Members of the United Nations outside of the Soviet bloc were willing to support this effort of the United States to build up the role of the Assembly, but there were some expressions of concern over the emphasis on coercive measures. Most of the various amendments to the draft resolution were designed to soften its tone.[39] One that was adopted deserves mention. A section added, on the initiative of Chile, recognized that "enduring peace will not be secured solely by collective security arrangements" but that a "genuine and lasting peace" depends on the observance of the purposes and principles of the Charter and the implementation of United Nations resolutions. Members were urged to act jointly to develop human rights and fundamental freedoms and to achieve conditions of economic stability and social progress, especially through the development of underdeveloped countries and areas.

Relations Among the Great Powers

Many of the changes made in the Dumbarton Oaks Proposals during the San Francisco Conference resulted from the dissatisfaction,

[38] For discussion of action taken under the "Uniting for Peace" resolution, see below, Chap. XVI.

[39] Cf. the original draft A/C.1/576 (Oct. 7, 1950), with Res. 477(V), Nov. 3, 1950.

especially of the "small" and "middle" powers, with the predominant role of the Security Council, and, with the special position
of the permanent members of the Council. This concern was based
in part on an apprehension that the great powers might proceed
to deal with questions relating to international peace and security
without paying sufficient attention to the interests of the smaller
states. But by the time the General Assembly met for the second
part of its first session in the fall of 1946, there was already ample
evidence that the ability of the Council to discharge its functions
was being seriously affected by the failure of the permanent members
to agree. It was in these circumstances that the Assembly addressed
the first of its many recommendations and appeals to the great
powers. In the succeeding years there has been from time to time
some feeling that the United Nations was being or might be "by-
passed" by the great powers, but the Members of the Organization
have been concerned more with the deterioration of the relations
among the great powers, especially with the effect this has had on
the Organization itself.

The Assembly has addressed a number of specific requests to the
great powers to consult and attempt to reach agreement on various
questions of general interest to the Organization, such as the voting
procedure in the Security Council, the regulation of armaments,
control of atomic energy, and the admission of new Members.
During its third session, the Assembly discussed the relations of
the great powers as a separate and distinct question. It will be recalled that this session of the Assembly, which opened in the fall of
1948, was held in an atmosphere of great tension. The tightening
of Soviet control over Eastern Europe had been countered by an
intensification of efforts to consolidate the Western bloc. There
seemed little possibility that any of the issues on which the powers
were deadlocked could be settled by negotiation, with the crisis over
Berlin dramatically demonstrating the gravity of the impasse. In
these circumstances, Mexico proposed that the Assembly appeal to
the great powers "to renew their efforts to compose their differences
and establish a lasting peace." Other business was set aside in order
to give priority to this item. As the first important decision of this
session, the Assembly unanimously adopted a resolution that endorsed "the declaration made at Yalta on February 11, 1945, by
Churchill, Roosevelt and Stalin" reaffirming their faith in the principles of the Atlantic Charter and in the Declaration by United

Nations of January 1, 1942, and their determination to build in co-operation with other peace-loving nations "a world order under law, dedicated to peace, security, freedom and the general well-being of mankind." The resolution recommended that the great powers "redouble their efforts, in a spirit of solidarity and mutual understanding, to secure in the briefest possible time the final settlement of the war and the conclusion of all the peace settlements."[40]

The relations among the great powers continued to deteriorate, however, and it would be difficult to contend that this expression of concern by the General Assembly even appreciably decelerated the process. Equally unsuccessful were subsequent efforts, such as: the action of the Secretary-General in the spring of 1950 in circulating his twenty-year peace program, an initiative that was prompted by the effect that the deterioration of great power relations was having on the activities of the United Nations; and a specific recommendation of consultation incorporated in the "Uniting for Peace" resolution. By the latter, the Assembly recommended that the permanent members of the Council "meet and discuss, collectively and otherwise, and, if necessary, with other States concerned, all problems which are likely to threaten international peace and hamper the activities of the United Nations with a view to their resolving fundamental differences and reaching agreement in accordance with the spirit and letter of the Charter."[41]

At the sixth session during the discussion, which was based on the report of the Collective Measures Committee, of "methods which might be used to maintain and strengthen international peace and security in accordance with the Purposes and Principles of the Charter," the Soviet Union proposed that the Assembly recommend that the Security Council should "without delay" call a periodic meeting under Article 28 of the Charter to consider measures to remove the present international tension.[42] Although such meetings had been provided for by the Charter, on the assumption that periodic meetings at which members would be represented by foreign ministers or other high government officials with special authority would facilitate agreement on important issues, none had been held. The Soviet suggestion for this kind of a special Council meeting was adopted by the Assembly, but in an amended

[40] Res. 190(III), Nov. 3, 1948.
[41] Pt. C(a). See App. F.
[42] U.N. Doc. A/C.1/688 (Jan. 3, 1952).

form, which recommended that such a meeting be convened whenever it "would usefully serve" to remove "the tension at present
existing in international relations" and to establish "friendly
relations between countries" in furtherance of the purposes and
principles of the Charter.[43] Although the Soviet Union has objected
to many of the measures that the Assembly has adopted on the
grounds that they are designed to undermine the primary responsibility of the Council and are attacks on the principle of the
unanimity of the permanent members, and although it has also objected to the consideration of a number of questions by the United
Nations on the ground that they should be handled by the great
powers themselves, the Soviet Union itself has brought the issue
of great power relations to the Assembly by its proposal that the
Assembly address specific recommendations to the great powers on
such subjects as the reduction of armaments and the conclusion of
a five-power pact for strengthening peace.

In performing the task of formulating general principles of co-
operation, the General Assembly has been increasingly subject to
pressures and demands of the cold war, with the result that its
recommendations have to a large extent assumed the character of
majority proposals unacceptable to a minority. Furthermore, the
discussions, in the course of which these principles have been formulated, have often taken on the character of debates for the purpose
of gaining some propaganda advantage, not for the purpose of
clarifying issues and establishing a basis of general agreement.

On the assumption that one of the major functions of the United
Nations in present conditions of conflict is to serve the interests
of major groups in the struggle for the minds of men and the
support of governments, the use of the Assembly as a propaganda
instrument is understandable. Eight years of experience seems to
indicate that great importance is attached to its use for this purpose
by all Members. Some would say, however, that the Assembly has
been misused, that it has been diverted from its proper function
under the Charter of serving as a center for clarifying issues and
promoting agreement; but there seems to be no practical way of
avoiding this diversion. If the Members of the Assembly refuse to
consider proposals of an obviously propaganda nature, such as
some of those submitted by the Soviet Union, they would in all

[43] Res. 503B(VI), Jan. 12, 1952.

likelihood be brought up in some other way. The very character of the United Nations makes all but impossible any rigid control of discussions in it.

If the assumption is made that the major concern of the United Nations should be to enlarge the area of agreement among nations and to contribute to the solution of common problems by agreement, it is not clear that the discussion of and resolutions on general principles by the Assembly have made any important contribution. In most instances, resolutions have been adopted despite the open opposition of members of the Soviet bloc, with a varying number of other Members joining in the opposition or abstaining. There is little evidence that the moral pressure exercised by such resolutions on the dissenting Members has been very great, or has influenced them to take more conciliatory attitudes in subsequent discussions on concrete problems. Even when resolutions dealing with general principles have been adopted by unanimous vote, it has not been found easy to translate this unanimity into agreement on specific issues. For example, the resolution of the Assembly of December 14, 1946 on the general principles governing the reduction and regulation of national armaments was unanimously adopted, but the permanent members of the Council were unable to agree subsequently on the details of a plan for the reduction and regulation of armaments. This may have been due in part to the fact that the resolution of the Assembly had to be stated in such general terms to achieve agreement that it contributed little to the solution of specific issues.

In dealing with questions that are of particular concern to the free world, and with respect to which effective action can be taken without the agreement of the Soviet Union and its associates, the Assembly has been able to perform with some success the function that the Charter envisaged. But experience with the implementation of the "Uniting for Peace" resolution demonstrates that states, like legislators, are often more willing formally to subscribe to general principles than to take the necessary specific measures to implement them.

CHAPTER X

Recommendations for the Adjustment
of Situations

THE Charter emphasizes the importance of bringing
about the peaceful adjustment of situations that arise before they
develop into actual disputes between states or assume the form of
immediate threats to international peace. For purposes of analysis,
these situations can be considered as falling into two categories defined by the language of the Charter itself. In the first place, there
are those situations referred to in Article 34 of the Charter the
continuance of which "is likely to endanger the maintenance of
international peace and security." These situations under the terms
of the Charter are primarily the concern of the Security Council.
The approach of the Charter to the adjustment of such situations is
in most respects similar to the approach to the pacific settlement
of disputes. In so far as the Charter draws a distinction between the
handling of disputes and situations of this nature, in the case of
disputes there is a greater emphasis in the Charter on the responsibilities of the parties directly concerned.[1]

The second category of situations with which the Charter is
concerned consists of those likely to impair the general welfare or
friendly relations among nations. The adjustment of these situations
falls within the scope of the authority of the General Assembly and
may be considered as a specific application of the more general
function of the Assembly in promoting international co-operation.
In the Dumbarton Oaks Proposals, the two functions were dealt with
in the same article, and together they have been described as "creating conditions in which the maintenance of peace and security
would be possible and in which humanity can progress by joint
effort and action."[2]

The emphasis in the Charter on the adjustment of situations
resulted largely from changes made during the San Francisco Con-

[1] See in particular, Arts. 33 and 37(1) of the Charter.
[2] *The Charter of the United Nations,* Hearings before the Senate Committee
on Foreign Relations, 79 Cong. 1 sess., p. 249.

ference in the original Dumbarton Oaks Proposals.[3] This action may be considered as an effort on the part of the Conference to broaden the authority and the responsibility of the United Nations to deal with questions before they reach a critical stage.

In considering the adjustment of situations, it is important to keep in mind that the term "situation" has been used quite loosely during discussions in the United Nations to refer to a variety of types of questions. Indeed, the Charter itself uses the term "situation" in different contexts, and the language of the Charter suggests varying degrees of seriousness in relation to the primary purpose of the United Nations—to maintain international peace and security. Article 14 speaks of situations "likely to impair the general welfare or friendly relations among nations." Article 34, as noted above, concerns those situations that may lead to international friction or give rise to disputes and situations the continuance of which "is likely to endanger the maintenance of international peace and security." Article 1 of the Charter gives as one of the purposes of the United Nations, the peaceful adjustment of situations that "might lead to a breach of the peace." Finally, the term "situation" is used in Article 40 of the Charter to refer to a state of affairs that is, or is likely to be, of the nature described by Article 39, that is, "any threat to the peace, breach of the peace, or act of aggression."

The Security Council and the General Assembly have tended to deal with the questions brought to their attention in the light of the particular circumstances of each case and have not attempted, and in fact have avoided, basing their action on the specific provisions of the Charter. It would be impossible, and not particularly useful, to deal here with all questions that have been characterized as "situations" by members of the Council and the Assembly. Therefore, attention will first be given to the powers of the Assembly under the Charter in the adjustment of situations, and how these powers have been applied, and then to the powers of the Council and their application. The manner in which certain specific situations have been handled will then be considered. A highly flexible view will be taken of the meaning of the term "situations," the attitudes of the Council and the Assembly, as well as the inherent nature of the matters in question, being considered significant.

[3] At the Conference, what are now Arts. 11(3), 14, and 40 and the references to the adjustment of situations in Arts. 1(1) and 36 of the Charter were added to the original Proposals.

Powers of the General Assembly

The Charter makes no distinction between the authority of the General Assembly to make recommendations for the adjustment of situations and its authority to make recommendations on other questions. Nor does the Charter indicate that the Assembly should follow any special procedures in dealing with situations. Its powers with respect to situations are subject to the limitations that are generally imposed on it. It must act "in pursuit of the purposes" of the United Nations as stated in Article 1 of the Charter and in accordance with the principles of the United Nations as stated in Article 2. The Assembly must also recognize the primary responsibility of the Security Council for the maintenance of international peace and security. It may not make recommendations, unless requested to do so, on any situation that is being handled by the Council, and it must refer to the Council any question on which "action" is necessary.

The Assembly may make recommendations under Articles 10, 11, and 14 of the Charter. Under Article 10, it may make recommendations to Members or to the Council on "any questions or any matters within the scope of the . . . Charter." Articles 11 and 14 set forth specific applications of this broad authority. Under Article 11(2), the Assembly may make recommendations to the Council and to the "state or states concerned" on any questions relating to the maintenance of international peace and security. The authority of the Assembly under Article 14 calls for special comment. This article provides that the Assembly may "recommend measures for the peaceful adjustment of any situation, regardless of origin, which it deems likely to impair the general welfare or friendly relations among nations, including situations resulting from a violation of the provisions of the present Charter setting forth the Purposes and Principles of the United Nations." The early drafts of Article 14 explicitly authorized the Assembly to consider and make recommendations concerning the revision of treaties.[4] It will be recalled that the Assembly of the League of Nations was authorized to "advise the reconsideration . . . of treaties which have become inapplicable, and the consideration of international conditions whose continuance might endanger the peace of the world."[5]

[4] See the volume in this Brookings series, *A History of the United Nations Charter*.

[5] See Art. 19 of the Covenant of the League of Nations.

Support for the inclusion of such a provision in the Charter was based on the realistic view that an organization established for the purpose of maintaining international peace and security should not be one exclusively devoted to the maintenance of the *status quo*. It was thought that the United Nations should by its efforts assist in bringing about by peaceful means such changes in the existing order as would contribute to the fuller implementation of the basic purposes and principles of the Charter. There was, however, considerable opposition to the inclusion in the Charter of any specific provisions concerning the revision of treaties on the ground that this might be construed as an invitation to widespread revision, particularly of the peace treaties, and that the whole structure of international contractual obligations might thus be weakened. Furthermore, it was recognized that revision of treaties was only one aspect of the problem. Consequently, it was decided to phrase the article broadly, and the Assembly was therefore authorized to make recommendations for the adjustment of "any situation, regardless of origin," it being understood that this covered the possibility of recommendations for the revision of treaties.

In the discharge of its functions under these provisions of the Charter, the Assembly has taken a broad view regarding the type of question it will consider and the type of recommendation it will make. It has, in general, avoided basing its actions on specific provisions of the Charter. It is interesting to note, for example, that the subcommittee established by the Security Council while it was considering the Spanish question concluded that the situation was likely to endanger the maintenance of international peace and security and that the Assembly had the authority under Articles 10 and 14 to recommend to Members the severance of diplomatic relations with Franco Spain.[6] Presumably the reason the subcommittee did not cite the authority of the Assembly under Article 11 was that this article specifies that the Assembly may make recommendations to the "state or states concerned," while Article 14 does not indicate to whom the recommendations are to be addressed. The Assembly, however, in its resolution on the "situation" in Spain made no reference to either Article 11 or Article 14.

One of the few instances in which the Assembly in a resolution

[6] U.N. Security Council, First Year, *Official Records,* First Series, Special Supplement, pp. 10-11.

has actually cited Article 14 was in connection with the *apartheid* question. The Assembly requested its commission to study the situation "in relation to the provisions of the Charter and, in particular, to Article 14" and to suggest measures that would help to alleviate the situation and promote a peaceful settlement.[7] The Assembly has, however, employed the phraseology of Article 14 in many of its resolutions. In adopting its resolution for the partition of Palestine, for example, the Assembly stated that it considered that "the present situation in Palestine is one which is likely to impair the general welfare and friendly relations among nations."[8]

The Assembly in its resolutions has also tended to avoid using the rather precise term "dispute" in favor of the more general term "situation," probably because the distinctions the Charter draws between the handling of disputes and situations are not applicable to the Assembly. Even in cases where the Assembly has approached a question as though it were a dispute, for example in dealing with the Balkan question, it has usually avoided using the term in its resolutions and has referred to the question as a "situation."

Powers of the Security Council

A comparison of the authority granted to the General Assembly to recommend the peaceful adjustment of situations with the authority of the Security Council to deal with situations under Chapter VI of the Charter, reveals certain similarities and certain differences. The Council, like the Assembly, must act in conformity with Articles 1 and 2 of the Charter. This point is emphasized in Article 24(2), which states that the Council in the discharge of its duties "shall act in accordance with the Purposes and Principles of the United Nations." The Council, like the Assembly, is restricted to making "recommendations" for adjusting situations; but the explicit authority that is conferred on the Council is further restricted to recommending "appropriate procedures or methods of adjustment,"[9] whereas the Charter contains no indication regarding the type of recommendation the Assembly is to make. The Council has, however, interpreted with great liberality its powers to deal with

[7] Res. 721(VIII), Dec. 8, 1953.
[8] Res. 181(II), Nov. 29, 1947.
[9] Art. 36.

situations of the kind described in Chapter VI. Should a situation develop to the point where the Council finds that a threat to the peace exists, it may of course, and in fact is expected to, adopt the measures set forth in Chapter VII of the Charter.

The provisions of Chapter VI of the Charter draw a distinction between the powers of the Council to deal with situations on the one hand and disputes on the other. The articles concerning the handling of situations by the Council are phrased in permissive terms, *i.e.* the Council "may investigate" and "may recommend."[10] This is in contrast to the phraseology of the articles dealing with disputes, such as Articles 33 and 37, which impose a duty on the Council. Furthermore, the authority of the Council under Article 37 to recommend "terms of settlement" and under Article 38 to make recommendations at the request of the parties, is restricted to disputes. A great many other articles also contain provisions that are specifically applicable only in the case of a "dispute."[11] In practice, however, it has proved difficult to maintain any sharp distinction between a dispute and a situation, and in fact the Council has seldom attempted to do so.

The major questions raised by the provisions relating to the handling of situations by the Council are: (1) whether the question before the Council is a "dispute" or a "situation"; (2) if it is a "situation," whether it "might lead to international friction or give rise to a dispute," and, if so, whether the continuance of the situation "is likely to endanger the maintenance of international peace and security"; and (3) what may be considered "appropriate procedures or methods of adjustment."

Distinction between a Dispute and a Situation

Under certain provisions of the Charter, the distinction between a dispute and a situation appears to be a matter of considerable importance to the Security Council. In practice, the distinction has had less significance. The Charter contains no precise indication regarding what constitutes a "situation." It may be presumed that the term is used to describe a set of conditions slightly broader in implication than a "dispute," which may be considered as a controversy in which the parties and the issues are capable of fairly definite

---

[10] Arts. 34 and 36.
[11] See Arts. 2(3), 27(3), 32, 33(1), 35(2), 36(2), 36(3), and 37(1).

determination.[12] Every dispute arises from some situation, and any dispute may in turn give rise to new situations. A situation may or may not give rise to a dispute; it may, moreover, develop directly into a threat to the peace.

During the first few years of its operations, when the Council from time to time attempted to relate its action to particular provisions of the Charter, there was considerable discussion concerning the distinction between a dispute and a situation. The discussion did not concern so much the criteria for deciding this point as the procedure for making the decision. The two issues most fully debated were (1) whether the Council should independently decide this point or follow the indications of the state submitting the question, and (2) whether the decision was subject to the veto.[13] No agreement has been reached on this second point. The point may be considered established that it is for the Council itself to decide whether a question is a dispute or a situation if the determination is to be made. Many of the cases brought to the Council as "situations," such as the India-Pakistan question and the question of the Greek frontier incidents, have been, in fact, handled as disputes.

The distinction made between a dispute and a situation in the application of Articles 32 and 35 of the Charter has been discussed earlier in this volume in connection with the submission of questions and the participation of states in the discussions of the Security Council.[14] One point that deserves further attention is the significance of this distinction in the application of the provisions of Article 27(3) of the Charter. This article, as has been explained, requires that whenever a member of the Council is a party to a dispute that is being considered by the Council, that member must abstain from voting on nonprocedural decisions under Chapter VI of the Charter or under Article 52(3). The Council has not found it necessary to take any decisions concerning the application of this provision, partly because its members have abstained voluntarily in most instances where the provisions seemed to apply. But the

---

[12] For comment on the definition of the dispute, see the reports of the Interim Committee, U.N. General Assembly, Third Session, *Official Records,* Supplement No. 10, pp. 7-8 and U.N. General Assembly, Fifth Session, *Official Records,* Supplement No. 14, pp. 6-7.

[13] See in particular the discussion on the Syrian-Lebanese question, U.N. Security Council, First Year, *Official Records,* First Series, No. 1, 19th Meeting (Feb. 14, 1946), pp. 272 ff.

[14] See above, Chap. IV, pp. 71, 73-75 and Chap. VI, pp. 132-34.

abstention provision becomes of real importance in a particular case only if (1) a permanent member of the Council is involved and might veto a resolution, or (2) there is some question whether the necessary majority of seven can be mustered in support of a resolution.[15]

It appears that Member states have seldom in their own actions considered the distinction between a dispute and a situation to be of significance. For example, there have been innumerable instances in which a Member has submitted a question to the Council as a "situation," and has at the same time described the measures it has taken to comply with the obligation imposed by Article 33 of the Charter, which applies only to disputes. France, the United Kingdom, and the United States when bringing the Berlin question to the Council referred to the matter as a "situation" and alleged that a "threat to the peace" existed. In their communications and statements on this question, the three parties made repeated references to their compliance with the obligations imposed not only by Article 33 but also by Article 37.[16]

Seriousness of the Situation

During the initial discussion of a question, members of the Security Council have many times expressed the view that the situation confronting the Council was not of such a serious character as to justify any action by it. The only time the Council discussed at length whether a question brought to its attention was a situation that might "lead to international friction or give rise to a dispute" was in connection with a Soviet proposal that the Council request information from Members concerning their forces stationed in territories other than those of the former enemy states. The discussion on the inclusion of this item in the agenda of the Council revealed the attitudes of some members regarding the type of situation considered as likely to lead to international friction or to give rise to a dispute within the meaning of Chapter VI of the Charter. The representative of Australia was of the opinion that "there must

[15] This latter situation might arise from a failure of members to agree or if five or more members were called upon to abstain as parties to a dispute. For detailed discussion of application of Art. 27, see the volume in this Brooking series, *The Organization and Procedures of the United Nations.*

[16] U.N. Doc. S/1020 (Sept. 29, 1948), and U.N. Security Council, Third Year, *Official Records*, No. 115, 363rd-64th Meetings (Oct. 6, 1948), pp. 3-4 and 33-36, and No. 118, 368th Meeting (Oct. 19, 1948), pp. 54-55.

be some indication of where and between whom the friction is likely to arise and where and between whom the possible dispute may be occasioned." He also stated that a "situation of the kind described in Article 34 seems to us to be a particular situation, not a general world situation. . . ."[17] The French representative, however, stated that he did not think that Article 34 "ought to be understood only in the sense of a very definite and specific situation concerning a given country." He stated that "an excessively narrow interpretation of the Charter in regard to this matter would involve a dangerous limitation of the powers of the Security Council and would not in reality correspond to the duties incumbent upon us according to the terms of the Charter."[18] In this case the Council refused to place the matter on its agenda, but, in general, it has taken a broad view of its authority to deal with situations.

The determination whether the continuance of a situation is "likely to endanger the maintenance of international peace and security" is important because the authority of the Council to make recommendations under Articles 33 to 37 of the Charter is presumably contingent on the situation being of such a serious character. The Council has addressed itself to this point on relatively few occasions, however, with the most important discussion taking place in connection with the Spanish question. The action of the Council in establishing a fact-finding subcommittee in this case and the results of the investigation by the subcommittee have been dealt with earlier in this volume where it was noted that the subcommittee concluded that the situation was likely to endanger the maintenance of international peace and security and that the Council had the authority to make recommendations.[19] This conclusion was a compromise between two extreme views in the Council. On the one hand, some members questioned whether the nature and activities of the Franco regime were not matters of domestic jurisdiction. On the other hand, it was argued that these activities created a threat to the peace. Although the majority of the members of the Council supported the conclusion of the subcommittee, the Soviet Union vetoed a proposed resolution that would have given effect to the conclusion.

[17] U.N. Security Council, First Year, *Official Records*, Second Series, Nos. 17-18, 71st-72nd Meetings (Sept. 23-24, 1946), pp. 425, 454.

[18] *Ibid.*, No. 26, 72nd Meeting (Sept. 24, 1946), p. 445.

[19] See above, Chap. VIII.

The handling of the Spanish question demonstrated the difficulty of establishing criteria for deciding whether a situation is likely to endanger the maintenance of international peace and security. The discussion at that time also raised the problem, which has come up in other cases, of the distinction between a situation of this nature and a threat to the peace. It may be considered that the distinction is primarily a matter of the immediacy and seriousness of the danger to peace. However, there have been statements by Members to the effect that matters dealt with under Chapter VII of the Charter may be of quite a different character from those covered in Chapter VI. It is clearly the intent of the Charter that all possible steps should be taken to prevent a situation from developing into a threat to the peace. The question can be raised, however, whether a threat to the peace may develop from a situation over which the Council has no jurisdiction and whether, therefore, in such a case the competence of the Council to deal with the matter is dependent on the development of the situation into a really serious danger to the peace. Some statements, especially in the course of the consideration by the Council of the Tunisian and Moroccan questions, suggest the rather disturbing thesis that the United Nations has no authority to deal with certain questions unless and until peace is directly and immediately threatened, when it may be too late to take effective preventive measures.

Appropriate Procedures and
Methods of Adjustment

In the few cases where the Security Council has reached the point of considering what recommendations it should make for the adjustment of situations, Members have taken a broad view of the kind of recommendations the Council can make. The Spanish subcommittee, for example, considered that under Article 36 the Council could recommend that the General Assembly make recommendations on the Spanish question. The opposing position was that the Council should itself act, and that it could not ask the Assembly to recommend the severance of diplomatic relations with Franco Spain because this was a measure reserved to the Council under Article 41 of the Charter. The majority of the Members, however, supported the view of the subcommittee that a recommendation to the Assembly fell within the terms of Article 36.

The broad view that the Council has adopted with regard to the measures it may take in dealing with a situation is also illustrated by the initial approach of the Council to the Palestine question. During the spring of 1948, prior to its determination that the situation in Palestine constituted a threat to the peace, the Council adopted a series of resolutions calling for measures similar to the provisional measures that it can call for under Article 40 of the Charter.[20] Throughout the discussions, there were repeated statements that the Council should continue to handle the situation under Chapter VI of the Charter rather than under Chapter VII. None of the representatives, however, expressly stated that the Council was adopting these resolutions under Article 36.[21]

Adjustment of Particular Situations

The questions that have been singled out for special treatment here are of significance in that they represent an active effort by the United Nations to bring about by peaceful means extensive changes in an existing situation. Attention will be given to the Spanish question, the Palestine question in its initial phases, the problem of the independence of Korea prior to the outbreak of aggression in 1950, and the question of the disposal of the former Italian colonies. Certain other questions of less significance, Formosa, Trieste, and the holding of elections in Germany, will also be considered.

These questions have certain characteristics in common. Most of them have been brought to the United Nations only after the parties directly concerned have failed to reach agreement among themselves. Although they have been viewed as matters of real concern to the international community, they have not usually been considered at the time of their submission as representing direct or immediate threats to the maintenance of international peace and security. Most of these situations have also been characterized by a multiplicity of conflicting interests involved, interests not only of Members of the United Nations but also of authorities and organized groups, some of which have enjoyed a quasi-governmental status. Another common characteristic of these situations has been the

[20] See below, Chap. XV.

[21] The Secretary-General, however, at one point stated that "presumably" the Council was exercising its authority under that article. U.N. Security Council, Third Year, *Official Records*, 331st Meeting (July 7, 1948), p. 34.

existence of a broad agreement among the Members of the United Nations that a revision of the existing legal order was desirable, although considerably less agreement has existed regarding the steps that should be taken to bring about such a change. These situations do not, however, by any means constitute all of the instances in which the assistance of the United Nations has been enlisted for the purpose of bringing about a change in the existing order. But in many of the other cases, such as those of Indonesia, Tunis, and Morocco, the United Nations has adopted a different approach. It has played a less direct role and has concentrated its efforts on obtaining an agreement between those most directly concerned. The activities of the United Nations in this connection have been reserved for treatment later in this volume.[22]

For the most part the situations that will be considered have been primarily the concern of the General Assembly and have fallen within the scope of its authority by reason of Article 14 of the Charter. The resolutions adopted in these situations have differed in character from resolutions of United Nations organs on other questions, for they have to a considerable extent represented pronouncements by the international community concerning the nature of solutions considered most desirable. As such, they have dealt in considerable detail with the substantive issues involved in the situations. In so far as the resolutions have been concerned with "procedures," they have been concerned not with the procedures for working out a solution, but with procedures for implementing the solutions the Assembly has endorsed. The inclusion of detailed provisions in these resolutions has been the result of a number of factors. The fact that many interests must be accommodated before sufficient support can be obtained for any course of action usually has made necessary the inclusion of specific provisions to meet the demands of interested Members. Furthermore, the Assembly by reason of its size, organization, and procedures is not in a good position to exercise a continuing control over developments. Thus it has tended to set forth in rather specific terms the measures to be taken, and this is especially apparent in the instructions that it has given to the special organs it has established to assist in the implementation of resolutions.

Despite the characteristics these matters have had in common, each has been in important respects quite unique. It may therefore

[22] See below, Chaps. XI and XII.

be useful, before attempting to draw further conclusions from this experience, to summarize briefly what the United Nations was asked to do in each case and what solution the United Nations endorsed.

Spanish Question

Even before the United Nations held its first meetings, the policy of the Organization with regard to Franco Spain had been formulated. During the San Francisco Conference, it was agreed that the provisions of the Charter regarding the admission of new Members could not be applied to states whose regimes had been established with the help of the military forces of the Axis,[23] and during the Potsdam Conference, the United States, the United Kingdom, and the Soviet Union stated that they would not support a membership application by the Franco regime. The General Assembly in the resolution adopted in February 1946 recommended that Members, in the conduct of their future relations with Spain "act in accordance with the letter and spirit" of these two understandings.[24]

Two months later Poland brought the Spanish question to the Security Council and requested the Council to declare that the existence of the Franco regime constituted a threat to the peace and to call upon Members to sever diplomatic relations with Spain. But the majority of the members of the Council refused to support this move. Furthermore, because of a Soviet veto, the Council was unable to adopt a weaker resolution requesting the Assembly to make recommendations on the Spanish question. Several Members then asked the Assembly to take up the question, and during the second part of its first session, the Assembly adopted a resolution citing the findings of the fact-finding subcommittee established by the Security Council and recommending that all Members immediately recall their ambassadors and ministers from Madrid. The resolution also contained a recommendation that Franco Spain be barred from membership in international agencies established by or brought into relationship with the United Nations and from participation in conferences held under the auspices of the United Nations. Finally, the Assembly recommended that "if within a reasonable time" a satisfactory government was not established in

[23] U.N. Information Organizations and U.S. Library of Congress, *Documents of the United Nations Conference on International Organization,* Vol. I (1945), pp. 615-16.

[24] Res. 32(I), Feb. 9, 1946.

Spain "the Security Council consider the adequate measures to be taken in order to remedy the situation."[25]

Palestine Question

The Palestine question was brought to the General Assembly by the United Kingdom, which under a mandate of the League of Nations exercised authority over the area. Initially, the British merely requested the dispatch of a United Nations investigating committee, a suggestion to which the Assembly acceded, but it was clear that the United Kingdom had brought the question to the Assembly ultimately for its recommendations. It was less clear, however, what kind of a recommendation the United Kingdom desired. For example, before the question was brought to the Assembly, the British Foreign Secretary stated that the United Nations would be asked "to recommend a settlement of the problem" but that the United Kingdom itself did not intend to "recommend any particular solution." Later, however, the Colonial Secretary, stated that the United Kingdom "was not going to the United Nations to surrender the Mandate" but for "advice" on how it could be administered.[26]

Nevertheless the United Kingdom accepted the unanimous recommendation of the United Nations Special Committee that the mandate be terminated. The broad agreement that was reached in the United Nations for the termination of the mandate was not, however, accompanied by agreement regarding the form of government that should replace it. It was only after a lengthy debate, that the Assembly on November 29, 1947, adopted a plan for the partition of Palestine, which was based for the most part on the recommendations of the majority of the Special Committee. The plan provided for: (1) separate Jewish and Arab states with economic union; (2) a special international regime for Jerusalem; and (3) the structure of the new governments and the procedures by which they were to be established. The United Nations Palestine Commission was established to assume certain responsibilities during the transitional period and to assist and supervise the transfer of authority to the new states, and the Security Council was requested to take certain measures for implementing the plan if they should be required.[27]

[25] Res. 39(I), Dec. 12, 1946.

[26] Quoted in L. Larry Leonard, "The United Nations and Palestine," *International Conciliation,* No. 454 (Oct. 1949), p. 614.

[27] Res. 181(II), Nov. 29, 1947.

Question of Korean Independence

Although the major powers engaged in the war with Japan had agreed that Korea should become "free and independent," it proved impossible for them to agree on the manner of achieving this objective. Negotiations between the two occupying powers—the United States in the south and the Soviet Union in the north—led to repeated deadlocks. In 1947, the United States brought the problem of Korean independence to the General Assembly. In doing so, the United States announced that the problem was one that required "the impartial judgment of the other Members," but at the same time, the United States declared it was "prepared to submit suggestions as to how the early attainment of Korean independence might be effected."[28]

The proposals made by the United States were adopted by the Assembly with only a few modifications. The essence of the resolution approved by the Assembly on November 14, 1947, was that elections be held in Korea for the purpose of constituting a National Assembly. The National Assembly would in turn establish "a National Government of Korea," which would take over the functions of government from the occupying authorities, constitute its own national security forces, and arrange for the withdrawal of the occupying forces. To facilitate and expedite the fulfillment of this plan, the United Nations Temporary Commission on Korea was established, its principal function being to "observe" that the Korean representatives were "in fact duly elected by the Korean people and not mere appointees by military authorities in Korea."[29]

Disposal of the
Former Italian Colonies

The question of the disposal of the former Italian colonies of Libya, Eritrea, and Italian Somaliland was brought to the General Assembly in September 1948 as the result of a previous agreement between the United States, the United Kingdom, France, and the Soviet Union. That agreement had provided that if they were unable to reach a solution within a specified time, the question would be submitted to the Assembly for its recommendation. Furthermore,

[28] U.N. General Assembly, Second Session, Plenary, *Official Records,* 82nd Meeting (Sept. 17, 1947), p. 22.
[29] Res. 112(II), Nov. 14, 1947.

the four powers had agreed to accept this recommendation and "to take appropriate measures for giving effect to it."[30]

The question was debated at length in the spring of 1949, during the second part of the third session of the Assembly, but it was impossible to reconcile the conflicting interests, and no recommendations were made. During the fourth session, however, agreement was reached with regard to the disposition of two of the colonies—Libya and Italian Somaliland. The Assembly recommended that the latter become independent in ten years, and that during this period it should be placed under trusteeship, with Italy as the administering authority. The Assembly also recommended that the negotiation of the trusteeship agreement should be in accordance with a set of principles laid down by it, and that a special council be established to aid and advise Italy in administering the territory. In regard to Libya, the Assembly recommended that it become independent "as soon as possible," and to assist in the formulation of a constitution and the establishment of a government, a United Nations Commissioner with an Advisory Council was established.[31] During the fifth session, the Assembly recommended that Eritrea be constituted as an autonomous unit federated with Ethiopia. In its resolution the Assembly also made a number of detailed provisions concerning the status and rights of the Eritreans and established a United Nations Commissioner to assist in the implementation of the resolution.[32]

Other Questions

There are three other questions that deserve brief mention in any consideration of the efforts of the United Nations to bring about a change in the existing order: Formosa, the holding of free elections in Germany, and Trieste.

With respect to the question of Formosa, no resolutions were ever adopted. At the time the United States sent armed forces to assist in repelling the aggression against the Republic of Korea, it took steps to "neutralize" Formosa, and later the People's Republic of China brought to the Security Council a complaint that the action of the United States constituted aggression against China, a charge that

[30] See "Treaty of Peace with Italy," Art. 23 and Annex XI, *United Nations Treaty Series* (1950), Vol. 49, pp. 139, 214-15.
[31] Res. 289(IV), Nov. 21, 1949.
[32] Res. 390(V), Dec. 2, 1950.

was also brought before the session of the General Assembly in 1950. In both organs, however, proposed resolutions condemning the action of the United States were voted down. Also, at the session of the Assembly in 1950, the United States asked that the question of Formosa be considered. The United States declared that it sought no special position or privilege in Formosa, stressed the desirability of settling the future of the island by peaceful means, and suggested that the Assembly should study the situation with a view to formulating appropriate recommendations.[33] What kind of recommendations the United States considered appropriate was never made clear, for, by the time the question came up for discussion, the situation in the Far East had changed drastically as the result of the military intervention in Korea of the People's Republic of China. Thus consideration of the question of Formosa was "postponed" and not again taken up.

The question of free elections in Germany was not brought to the United Nations primarily to obtain a recommendation on the problem of a divided Germany. Instead, the General Assembly at its sixth session was confronted by the specific request that it appoint a commission to investigate whether conditions obtained throughout Germany for the holding of free elections. The Assembly complied with this request, but it was envisaged that the commission might, as a result of its investigations, recommend "further steps which might be taken in order to bring about conditions in Germany necessary for the holding of free elections."[34] The commission was unable to carry out its task, but had this effort been successful, it might have represented a considerable contribution by the United Nations toward the solution of a most important question.[35]

The Trieste question was not brought to the Security Council for its recommendations. Instead, the question was presented in the form of a specific request by the United States, the United Kingdom, the Soviet Union, and France that the Council accept certain responsibilities in connection with a settlement on which the four powers themselves had agreed. In accordance with this request, the Council in January 1947 approved (1) the Instrument for the Provisional Regime of the Free Territory of Trieste; (2) the Permanent Statute for the Free Territory of Trieste; and (3) the Instru-

---

[33] U.N. Docs. A/1373 (Sept. 20, 1950) and A/1381 (Sept. 21, 1950).
[34] Res. 510(VI), Dec. 20, 1951.
[35] See above, Chap. VIII.

ment for the Free Port of Trieste.[36] In taking this action, the Council also recorded its acceptance of the responsibilities devolving upon it under these instruments. The most important of these responsibilities was that of ensuring the "integrity and independence" of the Territory, which meant ensuring the observance of the Statute, the protection of the rights of the inhabitants, and the maintenance of public order and security.

The Trieste question had been a source of international friction for decades, but it was clearly not a "situation" such as Chapter VI of the Charter authorized the Council to consider. With one exception, however, Members considered the performance of the duties requested by the four powers to be a legitimate discharge by the Council of its primary responsibility for the maintenance of international peace and security. The handling of the Trieste question, like that of the disposition of the former Italian colonies, has special significance in that it illustrates how, by agreement of the states responsible for the settlement of a particular situation, the functions and powers of an organ of the United Nations with respect to that particular matter may be enlarged beyond normal limits.

Considerations Influencing the Nature of Recommendations

A major task of the United Nations organ that is called upon to deal with a particular situation is that of devising a plan that will not only be agreeable to the parties most directly concerned, but also will command sufficient support among the other Members of the Organization to ensure its adoption. For example, in dealing with the Spanish question, the Palestine question, and the question of the disposal of the former Italian colonies, it was extremely difficult to find a solution that would receive the necessary two-thirds vote in the General Assembly. None of these questions was viewed as a direct conflict of interest between the Soviet Union and the Western powers, and consequently, many Members, especially the Latin American states, which with almost complete regularity have supported the United States in any controversy with the Soviet Union, felt free to press for the adoption of their own proposals.

The Korean question, on the other hand, was viewed from the

[36] U.N. Security Council, Second Year, *Official Records*, No. 3, 91st Meeting (Jan. 10, 1947), p. 61.

outset as a matter involving directly the interests of the two major protagonists in the cold war. In this case there was no serious difficulty in obtaining sufficient support in the Assembly for the adoption of recommendations, because, prior to the outbreak of hostilities, very few of the Members had any direct interest in the area or held strong views on the most desirable course of action, and the great majority were prepared to follow the leadership of the United States.

In every case the political preoccupations of the Members of the Organization have had a decisive influence on the nature of the resolution adopted. The efforts of the General Assembly to find a solution for the question of the disposition of the former Italian colonies were especially illustrative of the difficulties that may be encountered in reconciling a wide variety of conflicting interests.[37]

During the period from 1945 to 1948 when the United States, the United Kingdom, France, and the Soviet Union attempted without success to reach agreement with regard to the disposition of the former Italian colonies, there were many changes in the attitudes of the four powers toward the solution that they would support. But their basic positions remained much the same. France was especially concerned with the effect that any decision, especially with regard to Libya, might have on the territories under its control in North Africa. The interests of the United States and the United Kingdom were primarily strategic. The British were also especially concerned over the future of the eastern section of Libya as the result of British wartime promises to the inhabitants of the area that they would not again be placed under Italian rule. The Soviet Union was at first desirous of obtaining a direct voice in the affairs of the territories and for this reason supported proposals for placing the colonies under trusteeship. The primary interest of the Soviet Union, however, was to reduce as much as possible the influence of the United Kingdom and the United States in the area. The desire of Italy to regain its position in the colonies acquired special importance because of the solid support it received from the Latin American states. Ethiopian claims in Eritrea and the support of most of the Arab and Asian states for the granting of independence to the territories were also significant. The interests of these various blocs were primarily political and strategic, because the colonies were of no special economic importance.

[37] For a valuable discussion of the handling of this question see Benjamin Rivlin, *United Nations and the Italian Colonies* (1950).

The various interests of the Members of the United Nations were reflected in the many proposals introduced during the initial discussion of the question in the third session of the Assembly. Eventually, a set of proposals, based in large part on agreement between Italy and the United Kingdom, obtained the support of the majority of the Members. The proposals were unacceptable to the Soviet bloc, and the Arab and Asian Members refused to support the provisions for Italian trusteeship over a part of Libya and all of Italian Somaliland. Thus the proposed resolution failed to obtain the necessary two-thirds vote, and the entire question was postponed for further action at the next session. It was clear that any hope for a solution depended on the formulation of proposals acceptable to the Arab-Asian bloc. When the United States, the United Kingdom, and Italy came out in support of independence for Libya, it seemed probable that a solution could be reached. After a lengthy debate over the details of the plan, a recommendation of an independent Libya and Italian trusteeship over Somaliland was finally adopted by the Assembly with only one Member, Ethiopia, voting against the resolution.

Despite the many difficulties the Assembly faced in working out a solution for this question, its task was considerably facilitated by the fact that it could be reasonably assured that whatever solution it recommended would be put into effect. The two powers in control of the areas, the United Kingdom and France, had pledged themselves in advance to carry out the recommendations of the Assembly. Thus, although the views of these two powers were to be given considerable weight, the Assembly was under no compulsion to find a solution completely acceptable to them. In fact, France was one of the few states that did not support the recommendations, but after their adoption the French representative stated in the Assembly that France would "accept the verdict of the United Nations" and "would give all the assistance required" for its implementation.[38] It was also obviously desirable that the recommendation of the Assembly should be acceptable to the inhabitants of the territories. There were numerous organized groups within the territories that were inclined to be obstructive, but they did not enjoy sufficient support from states outside the area nor did they possess the means themselves to prevent the carrying out of a United Nations

[38] U.N. General Assembly, Fourth Session, Plenary, *Official Records*, 249th Meeting (Nov. 21, 1949), pp. 296-97.

program. The Assembly therefore had no reason to feel that the opposition of such groups would block a settlement.

The situation confronting the Assembly in dealing with the Palestine question was quite the reverse. The Jewish community was well organized with quasi-governmental institutions, including an armed force in the territory, and with influential backing from abroad. The Arab community was less well organized, but it had the support of the surrounding Arab states. Whether the United Nations followed the wisest approach in adopting the partition plan in the face of the Arab opposition and whether a greater effort should not have been made to find a solution acceptable to both the Jews and the Arabs may be questioned. The reluctance of many Members to support the partition plan arose not only from recognition of the extent of Arab opposition but also from a feeling that further attempts should be made to find an agreement. In view of the fact that the United Kingdom, over a period of decades, had been unable to work out an agreement between the two communities, it is not likely that the United Nations would have been any more successful, but it has been argued that the attempt nevertheless should have been made.

The necessity of finding a plan acceptable to both the Jews and the Arabs assumed an even greater importance in view of the attitude of the United Kingdom. Inasmuch as the United Kingdom was in control of the area, it was obvious that the success of any plan was dependent primarily on British co-operation. As early as the first special session, the representative of the United Kingdom had made the position of his Government clear: "If the United Nations can find a just solution which will be accepted by both parties, it could hardly be expected that we should not welcome such a solution. . . . We should not have the sole responsibility for enforcing a solution which is not accepted by both parties and which we cannot reconcile with our conscience."[39] Later during the discussions at the second session, the representative of the United Kingdom stated that his country would not play a "major" role in the implementation of a "scheme which was not acceptable to both the Arabs and the Jews."[40] He therefore opposed the plan

[39] U.N. General Assembly, First Special Session, First Committee, *Official Records*, 52nd Meeting (May 9, 1947), pp. 183-84.

[40] U.N. General Assembly, Second Session, *Ad Hoc* Committee on the Palestinian Question, *Official Records*, 15th Meeting (Oct. 16, 1947), pp. 96 ff., and *Ibid.*, 25th Meeting (Nov. 20, 1947), pp. 153 ff.

supported by the Arabs for a unitary state and announced that his Government would insist on undivided control over Palestine for as long as it continued to hold the mandate, and was not therefore prepared to transfer authority to the councils of government as proposed in the partition plan.

The proposal to partition Palestine enjoyed a slight margin of support among the Members of the Organization. The possibility that the United Kingdom would not co-operate in executing the plan was therefore of great significance inasmuch as many Members, especially the Western European states, were reluctant to support the plan unless some means of implementation were available. For this reason, the plan was subjected to reconsideration before final approval, and the provisions enlisting the support of the Security Council were added. The proposal for partition was adopted by the committee, but by a majority insufficient to ensure its adoption in plenary. As the result of the exercise of considerable pressure and a number of changes in votes, the plan was adopted despite Arab opposition and in light of the probability that the steps required for its implementation would not be taken by the United Kingdom.

In considering the problem of the independence of Korea, the Assembly faced a somewhat similar situation. In this case, however, the Members were considerably less concerned with trying to find a solution acceptable to the parties or one that at least had some hope of implementation. The Soviet bloc at first opposed any action by the Assembly and later introduced proposals unacceptable to the United States. Initially, the Members of the Organization seemed to be little concerned over the effects that the adoption of the plan sponsored by the United States might have. It was only at later stages, when difficulties arose over the implementation of the plan, that apprehension was expressed whether the Assembly was following the wisest course of action. Even then there was little real support for any move to explore other possible lines of approach.

It is interesting to contrast the action the Assembly took on this question with its approach to the question of free German elections four years later. In the latter case, the suggestion was made that the United Nations should take no action beyond referring the question back to the major powers with an appeal that they seek a solution of the problem of German unification. The suggestion was not followed, but the Assembly was most careful to ensure that its action would not, as it had in Korea, further solidify the division of the country. Of course, with regard to Germany there was not the same desire as there was in the Korean situation for the withdrawal of occupation forces nor did the Members view the German problem with the same lack of interest that they showed when the Korean question was first brought to the Assembly.

It is obvious that many considerations have influenced the course of action that the United Nations has endorsed. Any listing of them should include the following: the obvious attractiveness to the Soviet bloc of the possibility that it might do some "good fishing" in troubled waters; its desire to reduce the influence of the Western allies in the Middle East and the Mediterranean region, as in the Palestine question and the question of the former Italian colonies; its desire to exploit any possible division among the Western allies as in the Spanish question; the lack of adequate knowledge of the actual conditions in certain areas; the political, religious, and cultural ties of Members, which have been of particular importance in the handling of the questions of Spain, Palestine, and the former Italian colonies; and the desire of many Members, especially during the early sessions, that the General Assembly adopt some resolution even if a matter was not especially urgent.

It is significant that the debates on the type of measures the Assembly should adopt for the adjustment of situations have been largely concerned with the desirability or feasibility of particular courses of action. They have been much less concerned with the competence of the organs involved to adopt a particular course of action. The arguments of the Soviet bloc that Article 107 precluded any action by the Assembly on the Korean question and on the question of free German elections and their contention that the actions of the Assembly violated the "rights" of the German and Korean peoples received no support from the other Members of the Organization. Australia was alone in its contention that the Security Council had no authority under the Charter to accept the responsibilities set forth in the Statute for Trieste. The Arab states received little support for their position that the Assembly had no power to recommend the partition of Palestine, and that furthermore the partition resolution violated the principle of "self-determination" as set forth in Article 1(2) of the Charter. In this case, however, the issue of the power of the Council to take steps in implementation of the resolution and that of the power of the Assembly to call on the Council to do so received considerable attention. In the Spanish case, also, the attitudes of Members toward the powers of the United Nations under the Charter, especially the application of Article 2(7), and the division of functions between the Council and the Assembly had a significant influence on the nature of the resolutions adopted.

Authority of Assembly Resolutions

The General Assembly has the power of final decision on certain matters such as the admission of new Members, the expulsion of Members, and the approval of the budget of the Organization. However, in so far as the Charter authorizes the Assembly to deal with "situations," it is clear that the Assembly is restricted to making recommendations and that the Members are free to decide for themselves whether they will comply with them. For example, when the Assembly set out the steps that the United Kingdom "shall" take in implementation of the Palestine partition resolution, it was in effect only making recommendations. The resolution itself made this clear, for, in the opening paragraphs, the Assembly "recommends" the adoption and implementation of the plan.[41] Thus when Members, as they constantly have, assert that states, or the Organization itself, are "bound" to act in accordance with a resolution, they have been referring to a moral rather than a legal obligation. On the other hand, the Members are "bound" to act in accordance with their obligations under the Charter, and in particular to refrain from the threat or use of force in any manner inconsistent with the purposes of the United Nations. Also, by special agreement states may decide to accept a recommendation as "binding." The question of the disposal of the former Italian colonies is a case in point, for in this instance the United States, the United Kingdom, France, and the Soviet Union had agreed in advance to accept and carry out the recommendations of the Assembly.[42]

It has been repeatedly stated that regardless whether a resolution of the Assembly has any legal binding effect, it carries great "moral"

[41] Res. 181(II), Nov. 29, 1947.
[42] Even in this case not all of the recommendations were carried out. The Assembly recommended the admission of Libya to the United Nations, but the Soviet Union vetoed the application of Libya in the Security Council.

weight. The effect of moral weight in the light of existing political relationships, however, may be seriously questioned. Argentina, for example, was one of the few states that did not comply with the recommendations of the Assembly for the withdrawal of ambassadors from Spain. No opprobrium followed this refusal to accept the recommendations of the Assembly. On the contrary, Argentina was accorded the "honor" of election to the Security Council and even obtained the presidency of the General Assembly. It is, however, true that, in general, an Assembly resolution backed by the great majority of the Members will not be lightly ignored; but, so long as there are influential Members of the Organization that do not support a recommendation, each state enjoys considerable freedom of action in determining whether or not it will accept and carry out a recommendation.

Despite the fact that the power of the Assembly is restricted by its limited ability to bring pressure to bear upon states, it may elicit the support of the Security Council in its efforts to obtain the implementation of its recommendations. The Assembly is not only authorized to bring a matter to the attention of the Council but also to make recommendations to it. In two cases, the Assembly has attempted to back up its recommendations by a threat of possible action by the Council. In the Spanish case, the Assembly recommended that if certain changes in Spain did not occur, the Council should consider adequate measures for remedying the situation; and in a later resolution, the Assembly expressed its confidence that the Council would "exercise its responsibilities under the Charter" should the situation so require.[43]

In view of the fact that the Council had reached a deadlock over the handling of the Spanish question even before these resolutions were adopted, it can be doubted that the Members seriously considered the Council would take any action, and these resolutions were never even discussed in the Council. In the Palestine case, however, there was some reason to believe that the Council would take effective measures if they proved necessary, inasmuch as both the United States and the Soviet Union had supported the partition resolution. The Assembly does not, however, have the authority to commit the Security Council to a particular course of action. This was made clear during consideration of the Palestine question when the Council took the position that it had to decide on the

[43] Res. 39(I), Dec. 12, 1946, and Res. 114(II), Nov. 17, 1947.

basis of its own evaluation of the situation what, if any, measures it would take.

Although a recommendation of the Assembly is not legally binding, and although the Charter provides no basis for making the Council an enforcement agency for the resolutions of the Assembly, the framers of the Charter expected that the effective discharge by the Council of its responsibility for the maintenance of international peace and security would strengthen the practical force of the recommendations of the Assembly. Confronted by the prospect of effective action by the Council in case of threat or use of force in disregard of a recommendation by the Assembly for peaceful adjustment, interested states might be strongly moved to accept the recommendation of a body representing the full membership of the organized community of nations. With the Council powerless or unwilling to act, however, states might be inclined to believe, as indeed they did in the Palestine case, that they could gain their ends to a greater degree by refusing to accept the recommendations of the Assembly and thus prolong or even intensify the crisis.

Implementation of Resolutions

The General Assembly, in its efforts to bring about the adjustment of situations, has tried by various means to obtain the implementation of its resolutions. First of all, it has recommended the action that Members themselves should take. In the Spanish question, the recommendation was addressed to all Members. In the cases of Palestine, Korea, and the Italian colonies, the Assembly set forth in some detail specific measures that those in authority were to take. The Assembly has also made general appeals for support in the implementation of its resolutions. The initial resolution on the Korean question, for example, called upon all Members "to refrain from interfering in the affairs of the Korean people during the interim period preparatory to the establishment of Korean independence" and "to refrain completely from any and all acts derogatory to the independence and sovereignty of Korea."[44] The resolution on the partition of Palestine contained a somewhat similar appeal.[45]

The Assembly has also enlisted the support of other organs and agencies of the United Nations, such as the Economic and Social

[44] Res. 112(II), Nov. 14, 1947. See also Res. 195(III), Dec. 12, 1948.
[45] Res. 181(II), Nov. 29, 1947.

Council, the Trusteeship Council and, as already mentioned, the Security Council. Implementation of the resolution of the Assembly on the Spanish question, for example, required action by various agencies associated with the United Nations. Whether effective steps will be taken by these other agencies in support of such resolutions will be dependent on the action taken by Members of the Organization through the agencies. In setting out the steps that the other organs and agencies should take, the Assembly is in effect making recommendations to Members on the policies they should follow in such organs and agencies.

The Assembly also has on many occasions established special machinery to perform specific functions in implementation of its resolutions. In some cases the Assembly has established commissions composed of representatives of Members; in others it has appointed individuals. In Eritrea and Libya, for example, United Nations commissioners were appointed in their individual capacities. In view of the fact that these jobs were highly technical, an individual with a competent staff was considered suitable. In Libya, however, where political considerations were of greater importance, an advisory council composed largely of representatives of interested governments was also appointed. That this council was of much assistance to the commissioner is doubtful.[46] However, some such device for allowing the states primarily concerned to voice their views was probably necessary if only to obtain the required support for the adoption of the resolution.

It is understandable that the Temporary Commission on Korea was composed of representatives of Members. The commission was obviously not expected to carry out a minute supervision of an actual election but instead to give an evaluation of the conditions in which the elections were held and the results obtained. In view of the fact that the primary purpose was to associate the United Nations with the establishment of a government in Korea, a commission of experts was not likely to be as effective as a body composed of representatives of governments.

The implementation of the recommendations of the Assembly for the disposal of the former Italian colonies represents its outstanding success. A trusteeship agreement for Italian Somaliland,

[46] One may speculate whether in the light of the experience in Libya, the General Assembly deliberately refrained from saddling the commissioner in Eritrea with an advisory council.

with special provisions along the lines of the recommendations of the Assembly, was concluded, and the administration of the territory has become an integral part of the United Nations trusteeship system.[47] The implementation of the resolution of the Assembly on Eritrea was a lengthy process, which was carried out, however, without any further intervention by the Assembly. An Eritrean Constitution and the Act of Federation were finally adopted and during its seventh session, the Assembly formally and unanimously "welcomed" the federation of Eritrea with Ethopia.[48]

The implementation of the recommendation on Libya was a more complicated problem, but, despite delays, disagreements, and occasional friction, especially between the United Nations Commissioner and his Advisory Council, it proceeded without serious difficulties. The question was considered by the Assembly at various times with some criticism voiced by Egypt and unsuccessful efforts by the Soviet bloc to get the Assembly to endorse immediate independence and the withdrawal of foreign troops and bases. During its session in 1950, the Assembly set up a time table, which was eventually met.[49] Finally, on December 24, 1952, the United Kingdom of Libya was proclaimed and the French and British administrations were terminated.[50]

The Assembly was successful in this instance because of the advance agreement among the major powers to accept its recommendation and also because it was able to devise a plan that was not opposed by any groups within the Organization. But in the only other case, the Trieste question, when there was a similar unanimity at the outset, the efforts of the United Nations were unsuccessful. Although all the members of the Security Council, with the exception of Australia, supported the assumption by the Council of the responsibilities given it under the arrangement that the four major powers had worked out, the Council was unable to discharge these responsibilities in practice. Despite repeated attempts, the Council was unable to reach agreement on the initial step, the appointment of a governor for the Free Territory of Trieste. In the other cases in which the Assembly has been confronted by a split

[47] For further discussion see the volume in this Brookings series, *The United Nations and Promotion of the General Welfare.*

[48] Res. 617(VII), Dec. 17, 1952.

[49] Res. 387(V), Nov. 17, 1950.

[50] Shortly thereafter, the Assembly took note of these developments and extended its congratulations, Res. 515(VI), Feb. 1, 1952.

between the Soviet bloc and the Western allies, it has been impossible to carry out as planned the resolutions of the Assembly. The commission on free German elections was unable to obtain any co-operation from the authorities in East Germany and consequently abandoned its efforts.

The plan of the Assembly for supervision by the United Nations of elections throughout Korea, with a view to the establishment of a free and independent Korea, also proved to be incapable of implementation. In view of the opposition of the Soviet bloc to the original resolution of the Assembly, it was understandable that the United Nations Temporary Commission received no co-operation from the authorities in North Korea. When it became apparent that elections could not be held throughout Korea, the question arose whether the commission should observe elections in the southern zone only. The commission decided to consult the Interim Committee of the General Assembly on this point, and the committee adopted a resolution sponsored by the United States endorsing the observation of elections "in such parts of Korea as are accessible to the Commission."[51] The commission proceeded to observe these elections and later concluded that they were a "valid expression of the free will of the electorate in those parts of Korea which were accessible" to it.[52]

After considering the report of the Temporary Commission at its third session, the Assembly adopted a resolution declaring that there had been established "a lawful government (the Government of the Republic of Korea) having effective control and jurisdiction over that part of Korea" where the commission had been able to operate; that this government was based on elections that were a valid expression of the free will of the electorate in that area; and that this was "the only such Government in Korea." The Assembly also recommended that occupation forces be withdrawn "as early as practicable." The United Nations Commission on Korea was established to observe the withdrawal of forces and was also to be available to assist in bringing about the desired goal of unification of Korea and the development of representative government in Korea.[53]

[51] U.N. General Assembly, Third Session, *Official Records,* Supplement No. 10, p. 21.
[52] *Ibid.,* Supplement No. 9, p. 47.
[53] Res. 195(III), Dec. 12, 1948.

The question was again considered at the fourth session of the Assembly, and the commission was given the further task of observing and reporting on "any developments which might lead to or otherwise involve military conflict in Korea."[54] This authorization proved to be of considerable importance when in June 1950 North Korean military forces invaded the Republic of Korea. The commission had barely established machinery for observing developments along the northern frontier, but it was able to make a report that greatly expedited the action taken by the Security Council. This action and that taken by the Assembly in dealing with the situation created by Chinese Communist military intervention will be dealt with in later chapters of this study.[55]

The resolution of the Assembly recommending the partition of Palestine, like its resolutions on the problem of Korean independence, was adopted over the opposition of one of the parties and with the realization that the possibilities of implementing the plan were limited. The Jewish authorities in Palestine, having accepted the resolution, proceeded to prepare for the establishment and defense of a Jewish state. The Arab authorities and the neighboring Arab states continued to oppose the plan and refused to cooperate in any way. The United Kingdom, shortly after the adoption of the partition resolution, announced that the mandate would be terminated on May 15, 1948, a date well in advance of that recommended by the Assembly. The United Kingdom refused to take the steps set out in the resolution and, in particular, refused to transfer any authority to the United Nations Palestine Commission or to allow the commission to proceed to Palestine. It was in these circumstances that, in February 1948, the Palestine Commission reported to the Security Council on the difficulties it was encountering in carrying out its tasks and called attention to the rapidly deteriorating situation in Palestine.[56]

The Council discussed at some length the measures that it could take to implement the partition plan and to maintain peace and security in the area. It was clear that members of the Council were not willing to take effective measures to enforce partition. With their failure to agree on any effective action, and confronted by the further deterioration of the situation and the imminent possibility

---

[54] Res. 293(IV), Oct. 21, 1949.
[55] See below, Part Four.
[56] U.N. Docs. S/663 (Feb. 29, 1948), and S/676 (Feb. 16, 1948).

that widespread hostilities might break out, the United States suggested that a special session of the Assembly be called to consider the establishment of a temporary trusteeship for Palestine. This position was not supported by the other members of the Council, which decided to convoke a special session of the Assembly to consider further the question of the future government of Palestine.[57] While the Council continued its efforts to bring the situation under control, the Assembly debated the question and on May 14, 1948, decided to establish a United Nations Mediator.[58] The subsequent efforts of the Council and the Assembly, which were directed toward obtaining agreements between Israel and the neighboring Arab states for the cessation of hostilities and the settlement of their differences, are described later in this study.[59]

The Spanish question presents an interesting example of a case in which a recommendation of the Assembly was for the most part "implemented" but had little, if any, effect on the situation. Most of the Members complied with the recommendation for the withdrawal of ambassadors, although it should be noted that few were affected, because several had no diplomatic relations with Spain, and others did not have ambassadors or ministers in Madrid. In accordance with the terms of the resolution, various actions were also taken in the specialized agencies and in the special conferences held under the auspices of the United Nations.[60]

The resolution of the Assembly on the Spanish question had not enjoyed solid support in the Assembly and had been attacked on two lines. First of all, some Members, primarily the Soviet bloc, had pressed for more drastic action, and this they continued to do at subsequent sessions during which the question was discussed. It is doubtful whether even the measures that they supported would have had any real effect, and it was clear that the Soviet bloc was primarily concerned with exploiting the differences among the Western allies over the treatment of Franco Spain. The other general line of attack on the original resolution, which was taken, for example, by the United Kingdom, was that the recommended action would serve no useful purpose, that it might indeed have an effect directly

---

[57] U.N. Doc. S/705 (Mar. 30, 1948).

[58] Res. 186(S-2), May 14, 1948.

[59] See below, Chaps. XII and XV.

[60] For a report on the action taken, see U.N. General Assembly, Second Session, *Official Records*, Supplement No. 1, pp. 2-4.

opposite to that intended by isolating and consolidating the Franco regime, and that, considering the nature of the functions of the specialized agencies and the special organizations and groups operating under the auspices of the United Nations, the United Nations might be doing itself harm by excluding Spain, and at the same time this would have little beneficial effect on the situation in that country.

The ineffectiveness of the initial action taken may have had some influence on the subsequent action of the Assembly, but it is clear that the primary reasons for the change in policy were a change in the attitudes of many Members toward Franco Spain and an increasing preoccupation on the part of certain Members with the strategic position of Spain in relation to the defense of Europe against Communist aggression. As has been pointed out, no consideration was given to the Spanish question by the Security Council subsequent to the recommendation of the Assembly. In the Assembly, a less unfriendly attitude toward Spain was already evident at the second session in 1947, when a proposal to reaffirm the previous resolution of the Assembly in 1946 was defeated by a very close vote.[61] During the third session, a draft resolution leaving Members "full freedom of action as regards their diplomatic relations with Spain" was adopted in committee but failed to obtain the necessary two-thirds vote in plenary.[62] Finally, during the session of 1950, the Assembly revoked its recommendations for the withdrawal of ambassadors and for debarring Spain from United Nations agencies.[63]

This is the only instance in which the Assembly has formally revoked a resolution, although in many cases recommendations have been tacitly abandoned. In some instances, as in the cases of Trieste and free elections in Germany, efforts have been made to bring about a settlement outside of the United Nations. With respect to Germany, the United States, the United Kingdom, and France, while stating their support for the United Nations Commission, accepted an invitation from the Soviet Union to consider other means for bringing about a unified Germany, but no solution was reached. In the Trieste case, the three Western powers abandoned at an early stage the original plan for a Free Territory, and pressed for a nego-

[61] U.N. General Assembly, Second Session, Plenary, *Official Records,* 118th Meeting (Nov. 17, 1947), p. 1095.

[62] U.N. General Assembly, Third Session, Plenary, *Official Records,* 214th Meeting (May 16, 1949), p. 501.

[63] Res. 386(V), Nov. 4, 1950.

tiated settlement between Italy and Yugoslavia. At one point in the fall of 1953, when the crisis over a Trieste settlement became especially acute, the Soviet Union asked that the Council again make an effort to discharge its responsibilities under the Statute, but the Western powers blocked the Soviet attempt to have a discussion of the question in the Council.

Effectiveness of United Nations Action

The efforts of the United Nations to bring about the adjustment of situations must, on the one hand, be judged against the background of the general purposes of the Organization to maintain international peace and security and to promote the general welfare and friendly relations among nations, and, on the other hand, be considered in the light of the specific objectives that the United Nations seeks to attain in the circumstances of a particular case.

The action of the General Assembly on the disposal of the former Italian colonies represented a very real achievement by the United Nations in that it was able to take up a problem, on which no agreement could be reached outside the United Nations, work out a plan, and obtain the full implementation of that plan. Whether the United Nations chose the wisest course and what the full consequences of the course it adopted will be, remain to be seen. It is too early to predict what will be the fate of an independent Libya and of an eventually independent Somaliland. Yet the action of the United Nations did at least remove this question from those likely to endanger peace or the friendly relations among nations. The efforts of the United Nations with respect to free German elections and Trieste had no appreciable effect on international relations in these two areas. The United Nations was also unable to achieve its objective in the Spanish case, *i.e.* the replacement of the Franco regime, and it may be questioned whether there were any means by which this objective could have been attained short of the use of armed force.

In the Palestine case the United Nations was unable to bring about the implementation of its original partition plan. A state of Israel was, however, established, although it was created and maintained by force of arms. No Arab state was set up, nor was the Assembly successful in creating a special regime for Jerusalem. The failure of the United Nations, however, was not that the solution it endorsed was not carried out, but that the Organization failed to bring about the adjustment of the situation by "peaceful means." The questions may be asked whether the United Nations should have taken a different line, whether it should not have taken more effective measures to ensure the implementation of the partition plan, and whether it should not have abandoned the plan in the light of the opposition to it. Although one of the basic objectives of the United Nations, the peaceful termination of the mandate, was not achieved, the United Nations did play a significant role in stopping the fighting that ensued. Despite the fact that no final settlement has been reached, through the armistice agreements, the situation has been brought under a rather tenuous control.

It is primarily in connection with the handling of the problem of the independence of Korea that it may be seriously questioned whether the course the United Nations followed did in fact contribute to the achievement of the purposes of the Organization. Foreign troops were withdrawn from Korea, and that was one stated objective of the United Nations resolutions and one of the reasons the matter was brought to the United Nations. It would be difficult to contend, however, that this action contributed to the maintenance of international peace and security. Furthermore, the objective of a free, unified, and democratic Korea was not achieved. Instead the Republic of Korea was established in the southern zone and the People's Democratic Republic of Korea proclaimed in the north.

As early as 1948, the United Nations Temporary Commission had warned against the danger of a divided Korea and had stressed the desirability of instituting some procedure for seeking a pacific settlement of the issue.[64] In 1949, the United Nations Commission reported that the situation was "no better than it was at the beginning" and that the commission had been unable to "facilitate the achievement" of the objectives of the Assembly. The commission stressed that the prospect of unification was more and more remote and that without a "new effort" by the United States and the Soviet Union to reach agreement "no substantial progress toward the achievement of unification on the basis of the principles approved by the General Assembly" could be made.[65] The question may be

[64] U.N. General Assembly, Third Session, *Official Records,* Supplement No. 9. Second Part of the Report, I, pp. 13-14.

[65] U.N. General Assembly, Fourth Session, *Official Records,* Supplement No. 9, I, p. 34.

raised whether in the light of these warnings, and indeed in the light of the opposition of the Soviet bloc to the original resolution of the Assembly, the United Nations should not have continued to explore the possibility of working out an agreement between the United States and the Soviet Union, despite the deadlocks that had developed before the question was brought to the General Assembly, and despite the progressive deterioration of the relations between the two powers.

Although the United Nations was unable to bring about the solution that it considered best for achieving the independence of Korea, the action taken by the United Nations was not without "effect." It is necessary only to compare the reaction of the Organization, and the Members themselves, to the invasion of the Republic of Korea in 1950 with the subsequent reaction to the situation that arose in Indochina a few years later. There can be little doubt that the support given by most Members to the Republic of Korea was in large measure due to the part the United Nations had had in the creation of the Republic. Had the states of Laos, Cambodia, and Viet Nam enjoyed a similar relationship to the United Nations, the situation in Indochina would probably have been handled quite differently, although only a conjecture can be made on what the consequences would have been.

CHAPTER XI
Negotiations Between the Parties

A PRIMARY reason for establishing an international organization to maintain international peace and security is to provide means by which disputes between nations can be peacefully settled. The lack of permanent machinery to assist disputants in reaching such settlements or to decide disputes for them was one of the basic considerations leading to the establishment after the First World War of the League of Nations and the Permanent Court of International Justice. The theory that there should be some forum available for the consideration of all types of disputes likely to disturb peaceful relations among nations was reflected in the provisions of the Covenant of the League under which the Members of the League agreed to submit "any dispute likely to lead to a rupture" to arbitration, judicial settlement, or to inquiry by the Council of the League.[1]

The provisions of the Charter of the United Nations show less concern than did the Covenant of the League with the settlement of disputes *per se*. The Charter imposes no general obligation on Members to settle their disputes, but it does require them to settle them by peaceful means, instead of by methods that would endanger international peace and security. The Charter is primarily concerned with preventing any dispute from resulting in a threat to, or a breach of, international peace and security. In accordance with this basic concept, Article 1(1) of the Charter declares one of the purposes of the United Nations to be "to bring about by peaceful means, and in conformity with the principles of justice and international law, adjustment or settlement of international disputes or situations which might lead to a breach of the peace." To achieve this aim, the Charter imposes certain obligations on Members of the Organization and authorizes the Security Council and the General Assembly to consider international disputes and under certain conditions to make recommendations regarding them.

[1] Art. 12(1).

The Charter System for the Pacific Settlement of Disputes

The basic approach of the United Nations Charter to the pacific settlement of disputes is that the parties themselves should seek a settlement by means of their own choice and that they should be given every opportunity to do so. The Charter envisages that the United Nations normally will not intervene unless the failure of the parties to settle their dispute results in a possible danger to peace and that in the first instance, the efforts of the Organization will be directed toward urging the parties to reach a settlement or recommending the "appropriate procedures" that they should follow.

The Members of the United Nations have agreed to act in accordance with the principles set down in Article 2 of the Charter, one of which is that: "All Members shall settle their international disputes by peaceful means in such a manner that international peace and security, and justice, are not endangered."[2] This general obligation is reinforced by the specific obligation laid down in Article 33 that the parties to a dispute the continuance of which is likely to endanger the maintenance of international peace and security shall "first of all" seek a solution by the peaceful means listed in that article. The principal intent of Article 33 obviously is to ensure that the Security Council, the organ primarily responsible for handling disputes of such a serious nature, will not be called upon to deal with disputes until the parties themselves have made a real effort to reach a solution. In fact the parties to a dispute are under an obligation to submit it to the Council only if it is of a serious character and if their efforts to reach a settlement have failed.[3]

Role of the Security Council

The Charter sets forth with some precision the type of disputes the Security Council is to handle and the manner in which the Council is to deal with disputes brought to its attention. As already noted, any dispute may be brought to the attention of the Council, and the Council may investigate it in order to determine whether its continuance is likely to endanger the maintenance of interna-

[2] Art. 2(3).
[3] Art. 37(1).

tional peace and security. If the dispute is of such a serious character, the Charter states that the Council may take the following
courses of action: (1) it may call upon the parties to settle the dispute
by the peaceful means listed in Article 33; (2) it may under Article
36 recommend "appropriate procedures or methods of adjustment";
and (3) it may in the circumstances set forth in Article 37 recommend "terms of settlement."

The distinctions that the Charter seeks to make among these
possible courses of action are not, however, clear. Presumably, for
the Council to adopt any one of the three requires that the dispute
be one the continuance of which is likely to endanger the maintenance of international peace and security, although it has occasionally been maintained that the Council may appeal to the parties
to seek a solution by the means listed in Article 33 of the Charter
without, or even before, determining whether the dispute is of the
serious character mentioned in that article.[4] The main difference
between an appeal by the Council under Article 33 and a recommendation under Article 36 appears to be that in the former case
the resolution of the Council is to be couched in general terms
urging the parties to comply with their obligations under Article
33(1), and, in acting under Article 36 of the Charter, the Council
may single out the particular procedure that it considers appropriate. In practice, however, this distinction has not been maintained. Many Members have expressed the view that the Council
can under Article 33 "recommend" a particular procedure.

Although the Council is given discretion regarding the type of
recommendation it may make, it is expected under Article 36(2)
to take account of "any procedures for the settlement of the dispute
which have already been adopted by the parties." This injunction
applies to whatever agreements the parties have reached for the
handling of the dispute prior to its consideration by the Council, and
also to any agreements they may have entered into concerning the
manner in which disputes that may arise between them are to be
handled. Furthermore, under Article 36(3), the Council is enjoined
to "take into consideration that legal disputes should as a general

[4] During the consideration of the Anglo-Iranian question, for example, the
Brazilian representative stated that the Council had "the power to call upon
the parties to seek, of their own accord, a peaceful settlement of their dispute"
even before the question of the competence of the Council was decided. U.N.
Security Council, Sixth Year, *Official Records*, 562nd Meeting (Oct. 17, 1951), p. 2.
See also above, Chap. VII, p. 163.

rule be referred by the parties to the International Court of Justice."[5]

The authority of the Council to recommend appropriate procedures or methods of adjustment under Article 36 and its authority to recommend "terms of settlement" under Article 37 raise several questions. Presumably, in the first case, the Council is merely recommending to the parties the way in which they should seek a solution to their dispute, and, in the second case, the Council is expressing its views on the nature of the settlement itself. Taking a narrow view, it could be argued that, in recommending procedures, the Council can do no more under Article 36 than single out which of the means listed in Article 33 it considers the most appropriate, but such a view seems unnecessarily restrictive. The handling of the India-Pakistan question by the Council is a good illustration of the difficulty in trying to draw a line between "procedures" and "terms" of settlement. In this case, the Council recommended that the central issue in dispute, the accession of the State of Jammu and Kashmir to either India or Pakistan, should be decided by a plebiscite.[6] Was the Council in this case recommending "terms of settlement" or recommending a plebiscite as the appropriate procedure for settling the dispute?

Concerning the circumstances in which the Council may exercise its authority under Article 37, many students of the subject have held that the Council may recommend terms of settlement only when a dispute is referred to it in accordance with Article 37(1). Under this provision, the parties to any dispute the continuance of which is likely to endanger the maintenance of international peace and security are under an obligation to refer the dispute to the Council if they fail to settle it by the peaceful means listed in Article 33. It is not contended that both parties must agree to refer the dispute to the Council, but that at least one of the parties must take this step in order that the Council may recommend terms of settlement.

Although the Charter itself provides support for this interpretation, it would seem somewhat inconsistent with the general theory of the Charter regarding the responsibility of the Security Council. For example, a dispute might be brought to the Council, as in the Indonesian case, by a Member not a party thereto when circum-

[5] For further discussion of these two provisions see below, Chap. XIII.
[6] U.N. Doc. S/726 (Apr. 22, 1948).

stances have made it clear that the parties are unable to settle the dispute by means of their own choice, and its continuance constitutes a danger to international peace. It would scarcely be consistent with the concept of the Charter to contend that, in such circumstances, the Council is precluded from recommending terms of settlement merely because its consideration of the question has not resulted from the initiative of one of the parties.

Although the Charter is primarily concerned with the action of the Council in handling disputes the continuance of which is likely to endanger the maintenance of international peace and security, the authority of the Council to make recommendations is not entirely restricted to such disputes. Under Article 38 the Council may, if all parties so request, make recommendations with a view to a pacific settlement of any dispute. Furthermore, it should be noted that recommendations by the Council under Article 39 of the Charter with respect to a threat to the peace, breach of the peace, or act of aggression may be similar to those it is authorized to make under Chapter VI of the Charter.

The provisions of the Charter concerning the action of the Security Council are spelled out in considerable detail. There are various explanations for this. On the one hand, in conferring such extensive powers on the Council, Members were naturally apprehensive regarding the manner in which those powers would be exercised and were therefore desirous of specifying how the Council should act. On the other hand, the desirability of ensuring that the Council discharged its primary responsibility for the maintenance of international peace and security led the drafters of the Charter not only to confer certain powers on the Council but also to impose certain duties on it. Thus Articles 33 and 37, like Chapter VII of the Charter, state what the Council "shall" do in certain stated circumstances. In fact, however, the Council is given considerable leeway on when and how it shall discharge its duties. Article 33 provides that the Council "shall, when it deems necessary, call upon the parties to settle their dispute" by peaceful means. Article 36 authorizes the Council to recommend appropriate procedures "at any stage." Article 37, although authorizing the Council to recommend terms of settlement, leaves it free to decide whether it will do so or whether it will merely recommend appropriate procedures. Even in the case of the duties imposed under Chapter VII of the

Charter, the Council is given discretion regarding the manner in which it will proceed.[7]

Role of the General Assembly

The Charter contains little indication of the role of the General Assembly in the pacific settlement of disputes. Under Article 35 a dispute may be brought to either the Security Council or the General Assembly. The Assembly, like the Council, may consider and make recommendations with regard to disputes the continuance of which is likely to endanger the maintenance of international peace and security.[8] But it seems clear that the framers of the Charter envisaged that such serious disputes would generally be handled by the Security Council. Although the Charter in Chapter VI contains very specific provisions on how the Council shall proceed in dealing with such disputes, it does not give any similar indication on how the Assembly should act. In contrast to the provisions of Articles 36 and 37 relating to action by the Council, the Charter makes no distinction, in regard to the Assembly, between the circumstances in which it is to recommend "terms" and those in which it recommends procedures of settlement. The Covenant of the League, on the other hand, specifically provided that the Assembly and the Council of the League should follow the same pattern in dealing with disputes under Article 15. The Charter of the United Nations and the Covenant of the League of Nations also differ in another respect regarding the division of functions between the Council and the Assembly. Under the Covenant of the League, the Council was obliged to transfer a dispute to the Assembly if one of the parties so requested. The Charter contains no such provision, and, in fact, precludes the Assembly from making recommendations with respect to a dispute that the Security Council is handling unless so requested by the Council.[9]

Although the Security Council, in general, is limited to making recommendations for the settlement of disputes the continuance of which is likely to endanger international peace and security, the Charter places no such limitation on the General Assembly. The

---

[7] See below, Chap. XIV.

[8] Arts. 11(2) and 35.

[9] *Cf.* Art. 15 of the Covenant of the League of Nations and Art. 12 of the Charter of the United Nations.

powers of the Assembly to discuss and to make recommendations on any matters under Article 10 and to make recommendations on any situation likely to impair the general welfare or the friendly relations among nations under Article 14 give to the Assembly a much broader range of activity than that conferred on the Council. Under these provisions the Assembly may deal with disputes of a much less serious character than those specifically mentioned in Chapter VI of the Charter.

The power of the Assembly to make recommendations for the pacific settlement of disputes is subject to the same limitations that apply generally with regard to the authority of the Assembly.[10] The Assembly may only make recommendations, and in doing so it must act in conformity with the purposes and principles of the Organization and respect the primary responsibility of the Security Council for the maintenance of international peace and security.

Circumstances of Appeals to Parties for Settlement by Means of Their Own Choice

Among the procedures listed in Article 33 of the Charter, by which the parties to a dispute should seek a solution of it, are negotiation or other peaceful means of their own choice.[11] Both the Security Council and the General Assembly have urged the parties to a dispute to seek a solution by these procedures. The Assembly and the Council have considered it appropriate to adopt resolutions urging the parties to negotiate or calling upon them to settle their disputes by peaceful means in various circumstances. Such resolutions frequently have been adopted during the initial stages of the consideration of questions in line with the general theory that if there is a possibility the parties can themselves settle the dispute, the Council and the Assembly should not intervene beyond urging them to do so. The initial resolution on the Iranian complaint against the Soviet Union, the Indonesian question, and the Tunisian and Moroccan questions are illustrations of this approach. Similar resolutions have also been adopted during the later stages of the han-

[10] See above, Chap. X.

[11] The efforts of the Security Council and the General Assembly to bring about the settlement of disputes through procedures of mediation and conciliation and the use of the procedures of arbitration and judicial settlement will be dealt with below in Chaps. XII and XIII, respectively.

dling of questions, in order to emphasize the continuing responsibility of the parties to reach a settlement. The repeated resolutions of both the Council and the Assembly urging negotiations on various issues in connection with the Palestine question, and the series of resolutions of the Assembly on the Balkan question are examples.

These resolutions have usually been in the nature of compromises between the positions taken by the parties, of which one has in most cases objected to the adoption of any resolution by either the Council or the Assembly. Although a state may bring a dispute to the Council or the Assembly in order to put pressure on the other party to enter into negotiations, for the most part the state submitting the question has desired that the organ do more than merely indicate the procedure to be followed. The Council and the Assembly have usually been asked to support the position of the submitting state, pass judgment on the legitimacy of its claims, and call for the taking of appropriate measures by the other party. This the Council and the Assembly have usually been reluctant to do, especially during the initial stages of the handling of a dispute, and the two organs have therefore in most instances directed their efforts toward stimulating a settlement by the parties themselves.

The principal argument against a recommendation or appeal by the Council or the Assembly to the parties to settle their dispute by negotiation or other peaceful means of their own choice has been that the organ has no authority to adopt such a resolution or that it would serve no useful purpose. More specifically, it has been contended that no dispute existed or that the matter should be left to the parties themselves to settle without any expression of opinion by the Council or the Assembly. It has also been argued that the circumstances of the case, *i.e.* the serious nature of the dispute or the failure of previous efforts to reach a settlement through negotiations, required the Council or the Assembly to do more than merely recommend or urge negotiations, that the organ should call upon one or both of the parties to comply with certain measures, or that the organ should itself state how the dispute should be settled.

Another argument of relatively less significance, has been that a resolution calling for direct negotiations is not in order because some other procedure has already been agreed upon. For example, in view of the previous agreement between the Netherlands and the Republic of Indonesia to settle their disputes by arbitration, many members of the Security Council considered that the Council should in its resolution endorse this particular procedure for the settlement of the dispute before it. Somewhat similar in character have been the arguments raised from time to time against proposals for "direct negotiations" in the Palestine and Indonesian cases. In these cases, the Council and the Assembly had indicated the lines along which a settlement should be sought, and special subsidiary organs had been established to assist in bringing about a solution in accordance therewith. In neither case did either the Council or the Assembly insist that the exact provisions of its resolutions be followed, but there was an effort to ensure that the principles of these resolutions would be observed and that the position of the special organs would not be weakened.

In obtaining acceptance by the parties of a procedure of negotiation, the Council and the Assembly frequently have been confronted by the refusal of one of the parties to enter into negotiations until certain prior conditions had been met. The Arab states, for example, have refused to enter into general negotiations with Israel with a view to a political settlement until a satisfactory solution of the refugee question has been obtained. Also during the consideration of the Berlin question by the Council, the United States, France, and the United Kingdom expressed their unwillingness to enter into negotiations until the Soviet Union had lifted the Berlin blockade. In line with this position, the proposal supported by the majority of the members of the Council specified that certain measures were to be taken before negotiations on the German question were initiated.[12] On the question of the treatment of Indians in South Africa, India refused to go on with the round table conference because the Union of South Africa refused to suspend its racial segregation legislation. India was successful in obtaining support for this position when the Assembly, during its fifth session, called upon the governments concerned "to refrain from taking any steps which would prejudice the success of their negotiation and in particular, the implementation or enforcement of the provisions of 'the Group Areas Act.' "[13] This issue of prior conditions was of particular significance to the Security Council during the first few years of its operations when it was confronted by a number of disputes that arose from the presence of foreign troops on the territory of Member states.

[12] U.N. Doc. S/1048 (Oct. 22, 1948).
[13] Res. 395(V), Dec. 2, 1952.

This was a central issue in the dispute between Iran and the Soviet Union, between Egypt and the United Kingdom, and between France and the United Kingdom on the one hand and Syria and Lebanon on the other. In each of these cases, one of the parties contended that the subject of the withdrawal of troops was not a matter for negotiation, and that the Council should call for such withdrawal. This position received considerable support from other members of the Council.

Considerations Influencing Decisions to Appeal

In the discussions on whether the Security Council or the General Assembly should make a recommendation or an appeal to the parties to settle their dispute by negotiations or peaceful means of their own choice, two considerations have been of special importance: (1) the nature of the question before the Council or the Assembly, and (2) interpretations of the obligations set forth in Article 33.

Nature of Questions

Seldom has there been majority support for the view that, by reason of the nature of the question before it, either the Security Council or the General Assembly was precluded from expressing an opinion that the parties directly concerned should seek a settlement. As pointed out earlier in this study,[14] the argument has been frequently made that neither the Council nor the Assembly could adopt any resolution on a question because of the provisions of Article 2(7) of the Charter concerning domestic jurisdiction. Although the attitudes of Member states toward the application of this article have had considerable influence on the nature of the resolutions adopted, there have been few cases in which the majority have felt that the article precluded an appeal to the parties for the settlement of the dispute. The contentions of the Netherlands in the Indonesian case, of France in the Tunisian and Moroccan cases, and of the Union of South Africa in the matter of the treatment of Indians in South Africa have all been overriden. In each of these instances an appeal for a settlement was made, although in each case proposals for more extreme action by the Council and the Assembly

[14] See above, Chap. VII, pp. 168-72.

were defeated. It would appear that the majority of Members have adopted an attitude more or less along the line expressed by the representative of the United States during one of the discussions on the question of the treatment of Indians in South Africa. It was his contention that Article 2(7) was not intended to prevent "any expression of opinion in the form of a recommendation designed to assist the parties in reaching a settlement."[15]

Another argument that has been put forward in many cases is that the continuance of a dispute is not likely to endanger the maintenance of international peace and security. This argument was used by the Soviet Union in connection with the dispute with Iran, by the United Kingdom and France in their dispute with Syria and Lebanon, by the Soviet bloc in connection with the question of the incidents in the Corfu Channel, by the United Kingdom in the Anglo-Egyptian dispute, and by Iran in the Anglo-Iranian case. In view of the fact that the majority of the members of the Council have felt that the Council could and should adopt resolutions on such questions, it might be contended that the members of the Council have given a broad interpretation to the phrase "the continuance of which is likely to endanger the maintenance of international peace and security." The records of these discussions seem to indicate, however, that Members have preferred to ignore this language of the Charter.

The various discussions in the Council in connection with the pacific settlement of disputes reveal considerable differences of opinion concerning the basis, and the necessity, for a determination that the continuance of a dispute is likely to endanger the maintenance of international peace and security. Both a broad and a narrow construction of the powers of the Council have received support. Generally speaking, whether a state has supported the broad or narrow view has been determined by its concern with the issues in a particular dispute. Almost without exception every state bringing a question to the Council has argued that the dispute is likely to endanger peace and security, and every state against which charges have been brought has denied that any such danger exists. To the United Kingdom, for example, the Anglo-Egyptian dispute presented no such danger but the Anglo-Iranian dispute did. And in each case the position of the United Kingdom was supported by some members of the Council and opposed by others.

[15] U.N. General Assembly, Third Session, Second Part, First Committee, *Official Records*, 266th Meeting (May 10, 1949), p. 294.

Largely because of objections by states to any implication that their actions endangered international peace and security, the Council has not followed the pattern laid down in Chapter VI of the Charter and has not made any finding regarding the serious nature of a dispute that has been brought before it for consideration. Only in connection with the India-Pakistan question has the Council made a finding that the dispute before it was one the continuance of which was likely to endanger the maintenance of international peace and security, and in this case both parties agreed on the seriousness of the question.[16] The Council was prevented by a Soviet veto from adopting a similar finding on the question of the Greek frontier incidents. These two cases have been the only ones in which the Council has been confronted by a formal proposal that it declare that the continuance of a particular dispute was likely to endanger the maintenance of international peace and security, although almost every member of the Council has at one time or another contended that the authority of the Council to make a recommendation necessitated such a finding.

Generally, the majority of the members of the Council have considered that the Council should urge the parties to seek a settlement but should avoid any implication concerning the nature of the dispute, especially because in many cases both parties have seemed willing to accept an appeal for a settlement. On the whole, Members have considered that any effort that might bring about a settlement of a dispute should be made. They have been reluctant to dismiss a dispute even when the danger to peace, or indeed the international character of the question, has seemed highly doubtful.

Such an approach to the role of the Security Council in the field of pacific settlement has, however, been considered by some to be inappropriate and at variance with the concept of the role of the Council as laid down in the Charter. They argue that those who drafted the Charter attempted to limit the action of the Council to serious disputes because they conceived of the Council not primarily as an instrumentality for the settlement of disputes but rather as a means for preserving peace and security. For the Council to take a broad view of its functions and to attempt to bring about the peaceful settlement of each and every dispute arising between states, would vitiate much of the force of the original concept of the Charter. It would weaken the emphasis on the responsibilities of the parties themselves to reach a settlement and would transform

[16] U.N. Doc. S/726 (Apr. 22, 1948).

the recommendations of the Council from an expression of the considered concern of the international community with the necessity of preventing any threat to international peace into an expression of opinion on the manner in which difficulties between states might possibly be resolved. Thus a broad view of the role of the Council would make that organ merely another instrumentality for adjusting the relations among nations, and this would deny to it the special role envisaged for it under the Charter.

One of the most articulate exponents of the thesis that the Council should restrict its activities to disputes of a truly serious nature has been the representative of Brazil who has made two lengthy statements concerning the proper role of the Council. During the discussion on the question of the incidents in the Corfu Channel, he made the following observation:

> Whatever the nature of the dispute, it can become the object of the Council's consideration only if its continuance is likely to endanger the maintenance of international peace and security. . . . Our function is political, not judicial. Our consideration of a dispute or situation should limit itself to that part of the one or the other which may endanger the maintenance of international peace and security . . . it is not our function to conciliate parties, to harmonize differences, to negotiate understandings, to arbitrate disputes, to pronounce sentence. We act principally to protect and ensure international peace and security, whenever these are threatened. . . . Our decisions are based exclusively on the interests of international peace and security and not on other considerations. . . .[17]

In the course of the consideration of the Anglo-Egyptian dispute, he said:

> Considering the complexity of present international relations and the ever-growing interdependence among States, as well as the frequent divergencies ensuing from this interdependence, one may legitimately doubt the existence of a single dispute the continuance of which might not eventually be capable of affecting international peace and security. Such a broad interpretation of the language of the Charter, which, be it said, is vague and imprecise, would furthermore lead the Council to convert into a rule that which should constitute an exception, namely, its intervention in the relations between states to adjust matters which would be handled with better results through direct negotiations or other means afforded by diplomacy. In our opinion, such intervention by the interna-

[17] U.N. Security Council, Second Year, *Official Records*, No. 32, 125th Meeting (Apr. 3, 1947), pp. 686-88.

tional agency should take place only when the parties have shown themselves incapable of arriving at a satisfactory settlement or have exhausted the ways of diplomacy, *i.e.* when the dispute, in the light of the particular circumstances of each case, may be deemed grave enough to constitute an unequivocal menace to international peace and security.

Recourse to an international agency has its disadvantages as well as its advantages. Among the former, we might mention the tendency it has to accentuate divergencies. That is why it should not be allowed as a form of pressure or threat to bring about or to influence negotiations. Its use should be restricted to questions presenting a character of immediateness and urgency, which do not permit sufficient time for more extended treatment, but which must be handled at once to avoid the materialization of a threat to the peace. The intervention of the Security Council should be considered in that respect as an *ultima ratio* or heroic remedy, to be resorted to only after others have been tried and found inadequate. To seek redress in the Security Council before the traditional means of settlement have been exhausted would amount to transferring to that body all the diplomatic difficulties emerging from the relations between States.[18]

Such a restricted view has not generally been favored by other members of the Council. For example, in reply to the statement by the Brazilian representative, the representative of Poland stated that the competence of the Council could not be confined to cases that constituted "only an unequivocal menace to the peace." He considered that the Council could not wait until a dispute became so serious; that it was the "primary duty of the Council to act in an early stage of a dispute"; and that the Council could not wait until hostilities began or until the situation was out of control.[19]

An excessively narrow view of the role of the Council in connection with the pacific settlement of disputes presents grave disadvantages. The adoption of the Brazilian thesis would exclude a wide range of matters, which admittedly cause serious friction among states, from consideration by the Council. Moreover, it would defer consideration of potentially dangerous situations until there was an imminent threat to or breach of the peace. Such a narrow view concerning the basis on which the Council should act also might encourage those parties that felt they had much to gain by enlisting the support of the United Nations to adopt a policy that would make of any dispute such a serious matter that the Council could not ignore it.

[18] *Ibid.*, No. 80, 189th Meeting (Aug. 20, 1947), pp. 2105 ff.
[19] *Ibid.*, No. 84, 196th Meeting (Aug. 26, 1947), p. 2249.

Interpretations of Article 33 of the Charter

As has already been noted, Article 33 of the Charter was designed to ensure that the parties to a dispute would make an effort to settle the dispute before referring it to the Security Council. They are not required to attempt a solution by all the means listed in Article 33, and indeed many of the procedures are overlapping when actually applied. It was, however, expected that a real effort would be made before the Council would be requested to intervene. Members have frequently expressed the view that, in the light of the possibility that the parties would settle their disputes by their own efforts, the Security Council or the General Assembly should take no action or should merely urge the parties to seek a solution. For example, in the Anglo-Egyptian dispute one draft resolution submitted to the Council contained a finding to the effect "that the methods of adjustment provided for by Article 33 of the Charter have not been exhausted, and . . . that the settlement of the dispute may best be attained, under present circumstances, through recourse to those methods."[20] A somewhat similar proposal was presented during consideration of the question of incidents in the Corfu Channel. In the latter case, the resolution proposed by the Polish representative stated that the parties had not exhausted "the means of peaceful settlement before bringing their case to the Security Council." It was therefore proposed that the Council should, "pursuant to Article 33 of the Charter," call upon the United Kingdom and Albania to settle the dispute by the means provided for in that article "subject to their own agreed choice."[21]

The majority of the members supported a recommendation by the Council for direct negotiations in the Anglo-Egyptian case, but in the Corfu Channel case the majority supported the view of the United Kingdom that the circumstances required the Council to do more than merely urge the parties to reach a settlement. In this latter instance, the representative of the United Kingdom contended that the question had been brought to the Council precisely because of the failure of efforts to reach a negotiated settlement with Albania. He felt that a request by the Council that a further effort be made would not be particularly useful and stated that, in the opinion of the United Kingdom, further negotiations "might have

[20] *Ibid.*, No. 80, 189th Meeting (Aug. 20, 1947), p. 2109.
[21] *Ibid.*, No. 29, 122nd Meeting (Mar. 25, 1947), p. 600.

some prospect of success" if the Council would assist by making a "finding of fact" on the basis of which such negotiations might proceed. He proposed that the Council recommend that the parties settle their dispute on the basis of a finding by the Council of the responsibility of Albania for the damage that had been suffered by the British ships in the Corfu Channel.[22] This proposal was vetoed by the Soviet Union, however, and in the end the Council recommended that the parties refer the dispute to the International Court of Justice.

Although the original intent of Article 33 to establish an obligation to be met prior to the intervention by the Council has not been lost sight of, Article 33 has also been used as a basis for emphasizing (1) the primary responsibility of the parties to seek a settlement even after a dispute has been taken up by the Council or the Assembly, and (2) the continued necessity for the two organs to refrain from any action that might interfere with the efforts of the parties themselves. On this last point, for example, during the consideration of the India-Pakistan question in December 1949, almost two years after the question had been brought to the Council, the representative of the United States remarked that "no suggestion should be made which would put obstacles in the way of the selection by the parties of those means, under Article 33 of the Charter, which seem to them most effective and most suitable to settle this dispute by peaceful methods."[23]

The handling of the Palestine question provides an illustration of emphasis on the continuing responsibilities of the parties themselves. Since 1948, the Assembly has called upon the parties to negotiate a settlement of their disputes. During the sixth session, the Assembly adopted a resolution stressing that "the Governments concerned have the primary responsibility for reaching a settlement of their outstanding differences."[24] During the seventh session a majority of Members supported a resolution urging the governments to enter into direct negotiations and stressing that "it is the primary duty of all Members of the United Nations, when involved in an international dispute, to seek the settlement of such a dispute by

[22] *Ibid.*, No. 27, 120th Meeting (Mar. 20, 1947), p. 568, and *Ibid.*, No. 32, 125th Meeting (Apr. 3, 1947), p. 685.
[23] U.N. Security Council, Fourth Year, *Official Records*, No. 54, 458th Meeting (Dec. 29, 1949), p. 20.
[24] Res. 512(VI), Jan. 26, 1952.

peaceful means, in accordance with Article 33 of the Charter."[25] This draft resolution was not, however, adopted in plenary.

Nature of Resolutions Urging Negotiations

The resolutions that the Security Council and the General Assembly have adopted have varied considerably in content. In some cases, the organ has made a general appeal for a settlement without any indication of the methods to be followed. On the Yugoslav complaint concerning the activities of the Soviet bloc, for example, the Assembly recommended that the governments concerned "conduct their relations and settle their disputes in accordance with the spirit of the United Nations Charter."[26] In other cases, a particular procedure has been singled out for emphasis. For example, on the question of the treatment of Indians in South Africa, the Assembly recommended a round table conference, and on the Indonesian question, the initial resolution of the Council, while leaving the choice of procedures to the parties themselves, especially stressed the procedure of arbitration.

Resolutions have also differed in the extent to which they have dealt with the specific issues in dispute. In some cases, general appeals have been made. On the Palestine question, for example, both the Assembly and the Council have urged the parties to negotiate with a view to the final settlement of all questions outstanding between them.[27] Other resolutions have been more specific, but, as will be noted later, there has been considerable controversy in both the Council and the Assembly over their attempts to deal with the substantive issues of disputes.

It is interesting to note that, although the Charter speaks of "recommendations" by the Council and the Assembly, it is seldom that resolutions have been in the form of recommendations. In its resolution on the dispute between the Soviet Union and Iran, for example, the Council merely noted the "readiness" of the parties to negotiate. The Assembly "invited" India, Pakistan, and the Union of South Africa to enter into discussions at a round table conference.

---

[25] See U.N. Doc. A/2310 (Dec. 15, 1952).

[26] Res. 509(VI), Dec. 14, 1951.

[27] See, for example, U.N. Security Council, Fourth Year, *Official Records*, No. 38, 437th Meeting (Aug. 11, 1949), p. 12; and General Assembly Res. 194(III), Dec. 11, 1948.

The Assembly "appealed" for a new effort to reach agreement on an Austrian treaty. The Assembly "called upon" the parties to negotiate on the Palestine and Balkan questions.

By not using the term "recommends" in its resolutions, the Council has attempted to avoid any implication that the question before it comes within the scope of its authority under a specific provision of the Charter. It has been argued that when the Council "recommends" to the parties the course they should follow, it is implicitly determining that the dispute is one the continuance of which is likely to endanger the maintenance of international peace and security.[28] Precisely on this ground, for example, it was proposed that the Council should not "recommend" negotiations on the Anglo-Iranian dispute but should merely "advise" the parties to enter into negotiations.[29]

A recommendation by the Assembly does not, of course, carry the same implication. As has been frequently stated, however, the Assembly has also tended to avoid indicating in its resolutions the provisions of the Charter under which it acts. The resolution adopted on the Tunisian question well illustrates this point. The Arab-Asian states contended that the Assembly had competence to act under Article 11 of the Charter. The resolutions urging negotiations, however, contained no intimation that this was a question relating to the maintenance of international peace and security. Indeed the Assembly did not, as is its more usual course, employ the terminology of Article 14 in characterizing the matter as one likely to impair the general welfare or friendly relations among nations. The preamble to the resolution[30] stated that the Assembly was "mindful of the necessity of developing friendly relations among nations based on respect for the principle of equal rights and self-determination of peoples" (the phraseology of Article 1(2) of the Charter), and that the United Nations, "as a centre for harmonizing the actions of nations in the attainment of their common ends under the Charter, should strive towards removing any causes or factors of misunderstanding among Member States, thus reasserting the gen-

[28] See, in particular, the discussion on the Anglo-Egyptian dispute, U.N. Security Council, Second Year, *Official Records*, No. 84, 196th Meeting (Aug. 26, 1947), p. 2245 and *Ibid.*, No. 86, 198th Meeting (Aug. 28, 1947), p. 2294.

[29] U.N. Security Council, Sixth Year, *Official Records*, 561st Meeting (Oct. 16, 1951), pp. 20-21, and *Ibid.*, 562nd Meeting (Oct. 17, 1951), pp. 8 ff.

[30] The Assembly, like the Council, often includes statements of purpose in the preambles of its resolutions that are in the language of the Charter.

eral principles of co-operation in the maintenance of international peace and security."[31]

In addition to its powers of recommendation, the Council is authorized under the Charter to "call upon" parties to take certain steps under either Article 33 or Article 40.[32] The Council has done so in a number of cases, such as the Palestine and Indonesian questions, often without indicating whether it was acting under either of these articles. The original resolution on the Indonesian question, for example, contained no such indication but merely called upon the Netherlands and Indonesia to cease hostilities and to settle their disputes by arbitration or by other peaceful means.[33] On the other hand, the proposed resolution on the Berlin question, which was supported by the majority of the Council and which called upon the four powers to take certain steps including the re-opening of negotiations on the German problem, contained a specific reference to Article 40 of the Charter.[34] One of the proposals made by the United States on the question of the Greek frontier incidents also would clearly have established that the Council was, in accordance with Article 40, calling upon the parties to settle their disputes. A similar proposal by Australia would have "directed" the parties to enter into direct negotiations.[35]

Concern of Resolutions with Substantive Issues

In many cases where there has been general agreement that the Security Council or the General Assembly might best urge the parties to settle their disputes themselves, considerable difference of opinion has existed whether the organ should at the same time indicate how, between whom, and on what subjects the negotiations should be conducted, and what the basis for a settlement should be. Indeed, there have been differing opinions whether either the Council or the Assembly should in any way express its opinion on the substantive issues of the dispute and the merits of the positions

---

[31] Res. 611(VII), Dec. 17, 1952. See similar provisions in the resolution on Morocco, Res. 612(VII), Dec. 19, 1952.

[32] See below, Chap. XV.

[33] U.N. Doc. S/459 (Aug. 1, 1947).

[34] U.N. Doc. S/1048 (Oct. 22, 1948).

[35] U.N. Docs. S/471 (Aug. 6, 1947) and S/486 (Aug. 12, 1947).

of the parties. Here, again, the discussions have been on two distinct issues: first, whether the Council or the Assembly "should" in the light of the circumstances of the case follow a particular course, and second, whether the authority of the organ under the Charter permits it to do so.

In the Assembly, the basic issue has frequently been whether it had authority to adopt any resolution on a question. Generally speaking, when Members have considered the adoption of a resolution to be in order, their arguments on the terms of the resolution have been based on practical considerations and not on arguments concerning the competence of the Assembly. In the Council, the situation has often been the reverse in that there have been numerous occasions when Members have believed that the Council should adopt a resolution but have considered that the terms of a particular proposal went beyond the authority of the Council.

The efforts of the Council to recommend the basis on which the question of the incidents in the Corfu Channel should have been settled have already been mentioned. A number of other cases have raised a similar problem—whether the Council should attempt to delimit the scope of the recommended negotiations. The discussions on the Syrian-Lebanese question provide a good illustration of the difficulties the Council has faced in this connection. Syria and Lebanon brought the question to the Council with a request that it call for the evacuation of British and French troops from their territories. Although the Syrian-Lebanese position—that this action should be taken unilaterally and that there was no need for "negotiations"—was supported by some of the members of the Council, most of them considered that the Council should urge the parties to enter into negotiations on the matter. The representatives of the United Kingdom and France were willing to accept a resolution calling for the re-opening of negotiations but objected to any action by the Council that might be construed as precluding negotiations on other issues. Syria and Lebanon, on the other hand, were unwilling to enter into negotiations on other issues until the question of withdrawal of troops had been settled. After a number of proposals had been put forward, there was the necessary number of votes in support of a proposed resolution that expressed confidence that the foreign troops in Syria and Lebanon would be withdrawn "as soon as practicable, and that negotiations to that end," would be undertaken by the parties without delay. This resolution was vetoed by the

Soviet Union because it did not, in the Soviet view, go far enough in supporting the Syrian-Lebanese positions.[36]

The handling of the Anglo-Egyptian dispute is a further example of an impasse resulting from differing opinions concerning the extent to which the Council, when urging the parties to negotiate, should express its views concerning the issues in dispute. In this case three draft resolutions were presented, all of which aimed at a settlement of the dispute through direct negotiations between the parties.[37] The first proposal, introduced by Brazil, recommended that the parties resume negotiations and, if such negotiations failed, seek a solution by other peaceful means of their own choice. To this proposal, various amendments were submitted, including one by China emphasizing the issue of troop withdrawal, and a second by Belgium specifically mentioning the submission to the International Court of Justice, as a peaceful means that the parties might use, of the dispute over the validity of the Anglo-Egyptian Treaty of 1936. These two amendments, it will be noted, supported the positions of Egypt and the United Kingdom respectively. The second proposal, made by Colombia, dealt in more detail with the issues of the dispute in that it called for the resumption of negotiations with a view to (1) the termination of the joint administration of the Sudan and (2) the evacuation of British forces with special provision for the protection of the Suez Canal. The third proposal, submitted by China, merely recommended the resumption of negotiations without indicating their subject matter, but it also contained in its preamble a number of statements concerning the issue of troop evacuation. In the end, no resolution was adopted because the members could not agree whether the Council should express an opinion on the issues in dispute, and if so, what issues should be singled out for emphasis.

The Anglo-Egyptian dispute is also one of the few cases considered by the Council in which the question of the application of Article 37 of the Charter has been discussed. Egypt, in submitting the question to the Council, had referred to Article 37. It had contended that efforts to settle the dispute had failed, and had requested that the

---

[36] U.N. Security Council, First Year, *Official Records,* First Series, No. 1, 21st-23rd Meetings (Feb. 15-16, 1946), pp. 296-368.

[37] For the text of the three proposals, see U.N. Security Council, Second Year, *Official Records,* No. 80, 189th Meeting (Aug. 20, 1947), pp. 2108-09; *Ibid.,* No. 86, 198th Meeting (Aug. 28, 1947), p. 2305; and *Ibid.,* No. 88, 201st Meeting (Sept. 10, 1947), p. 2344.

Council call upon the United Kingdom to take certain steps. The United Kingdom argued that the continuance of the dispute did not endanger the maintenance of international peace and security, and that, therefore, Article 37 did not apply. The United Kingdom further maintained that it was willing to enter into negotiations with Egypt, but was under no obligation to do so. Throughout the discussion, the United Kingdom objected to any expression of opinion by the Council on the issues in dispute because it claimed that the Council in adopting a resolution with such provisions would be implying that it had competence to act under Articles 36 and 37 and would thus be denying the British contentions. The majority of the members of the Council, while desiring to contribute if possible to the settlement of the dispute by encouraging the parties to reach an agreement, were generally reluctant to support the positions of either party and wanted to find a formula that would represent a middle ground. This they were unable to do.

The handling of the Anglo-Egyptian dispute and later the dispute between the United Kingdom and Iran presents a number of interesting contrasts and comparisons. Both disputes involved the basic issue of efforts by the United Kingdom to maintain special privileges that it had previously obtained. The Anglo-Iranian question was brought to the Security Council by the United Kingdom in an effort to enlist support for the maintenance of its position. In contrast, the Anglo-Egyptian dispute was brought to the Council by Egypt in an effort to obtain a change in the existing relationship. In both cases, the majority of the members of the Council endorsed an effort to reach a settlement by negotiations between the parties, but in each case it was found impossible to reach agreement on a resolution.

The Anglo-Iranian case was brought to the Council by the United Kingdom with a request that the Council call upon Iran to comply with the provisional measures indicated by the International Court of Justice which, at the request of the United Kingdom, had set forth the steps that the parties should take in order not to prejudice the consideration by the Court of the merits of the dispute. Shortly after the submission of the dispute, the United Kingdom proposed that the Council call for an early resumption of negotiations between the parties "in order to make further efforts to resolve" their differences "in accordance with the principles of the provisional measures" indicated by the Court, unless "mutually agreeable arrangements" were made "consistent with the purposes and principles of the United Nations Charter."[38] There were serious differences of opinion within the Council concerning its competence in this case: whether the matter was essentially within the domestic jurisdiction of Iran; whether any possible danger to international peace and security existed; whether the special provisions of Article 94 of the Charter applied.[39] At the suggestion of India and Yugoslavia, the United Kingdom agreed to delete from the proposed resolution any reference to the measures indicated by the Court, thus changing the proposal into a mere recommendation for negotiations. It became apparent, however, that the proposal, even in this form, would not obtain the necessary seven votes in the Council. When the United Kingdom recognized that any resolution the majority of the members were willing to support would be devoid of substance, it did not press for a vote, and the Council adjourned its discussion.

As the handling of these questions demonstrates, the inability of the Council to act has not always been the result of a split between the Soviet Union and the Western powers, although admittedly in these cases the positions of the two blocs have not been identical. The cases illustrate the tendency of the Council to try to bring about a settlement of a dispute even when it is questionable whether the dispute comes within the limits of the competence of the Council as set down in the Charter. They show how difficult it is to obtain sufficient support for any expression of an opinion by the Council on the issues of a dispute.

In the discussions in the General Assembly, less attention has been devoted to the serious character of a dispute or to the competence of the Assembly to recommend "terms" as distinct from procedures of settlement. In the Assembly, however, there have been the same differences of opinion as in the Council concerning the extent to which the Assembly, in encouraging the parties to reach a settlement, should pass judgment on the merits of the positions of the parties. As in the Council, many of these questions have involved controversies between an Arab or Asian state and one of the Western powers, with the Arab and Asian states generally having the support of the Soviet bloc. Generally, the Arab and Asian states have found that even a qualified endorsement of their positions has been de-

[38] U. N. Doc. S/2358, Rev. 1 (Oct. 12, 1951).
[39] See below, Chap. XIII, pp. 338 ff.

pendent on support by the United States and the Latin American Members of the United Nations.

Three questions handled by the Assembly are of interest in this connection: the treatment of Indians in South Africa, and the Tunisian and Moroccan questions. In all three cases the central point at issue was whether the Assembly could or should adopt any resolutions, but in each case there was also considerable discussion concerning the form of resolution to be adopted and, in particular, whether the Assembly should go beyond merely appealing to the parties to make an effort to reach a settlement.

The original resolution of the Assembly on the first of these questions only expressed the opinion that the treatment of Indians in South Africa "should be in conformity with the international obligations under the agreements concluded between the two Governments and the relevant provisions of the Charter."[40] During the second session of the Assembly, a number of proposals were introduced concerning the procedures by which a settlement should be sought, but none was adopted. During the third session, a resolution proposed by India, which contained an expression of opinion by the Assembly that the treatment of persons in South Africa of Indian and Pakistan origin was not "in conformity with the relevant provisions of the Charter, the resolutions of the Assembly and the international obligations under the agreements concluded" between India and South Africa, received sufficient support to be adopted in committee but failed of adoption in plenary. The Assembly therefore merely invited the three governments to enter into a round table conference "taking into consideration the purposes and principles of the Charter of the United Nations and the Declaration of Human Rights."[41]

With the failure of this conference, the question was again considered during the fifth session of the Assembly. The Assembly again recommended a conference, drew attention to various of its previous resolutions on this question and on the general question of racial persecution and discrimination, and called upon the parties to refrain from taking certain steps, especially the implementation or enforcement of South African racial segregation legislation.[42] All of the discussions leading to the adoption of this and prior resolutions on this question followed more or less the same

[40] Res. 44(I), Dec. 8, 1946.
[41] Res. 265(III), May 14, 1949.
[42] Res. 395(V), Dec. 2, 1950.

pattern: first, the contention of South Africa that the Assembly lacked jurisdiction to adopt any resolution; second, the efforts of India to obtain endorsement of its position; third, efforts by various Members, especially the Latin American states, to work out proposals that would express the concern of the Assembly without at the same time supporting the Indian position in its entirety; fourth, expressions of opinion by many Members that although the Assembly might urge a settlement of the question, it had no authority to deal with the substance of the issues in dispute.

On the Tunisian question, the Arab-Asian states, which had taken the initiative in bringing the question to the seventh session of the Assembly, were unable to obtain sufficient support for their own proposals, but they did manage to obtain the adoption of a resolution expressing the hope that the parties would continue negotiations on an urgent basis "with a view to bringing about self-government for Tunisians in the light of the relevant provisions of the Charter."[43] A similar proposal on the Moroccan question was adopted by a committee of the Assembly, but in the plenary meeting the reference to "self-government" was deleted. The final resolution merely referred to negotiations "toward developing the free political institutions of the people of Morocco, with due regard to legitimate rights and interests under the established norms and practices of the law of nations."[44] The Arab-Asian states were not successful in obtaining the deletion from these two resolutions of an expression of confidence that France "in pursuance of its proclaimed policies" would endeavor to further the effective development of the free institutions of the Tunisian people and the fundamental liberties of the people of Morocco, in conformity with the purposes and principles of the Charter.

When the two questions were again considered during the eighth session, the Arab-Asian states were even less successful. Their proposal that the Assembly call for the termination of martial law and the restoration of public liberties in Morocco, the establishment of democratic representative institutions through free elections, and steps to ensure within five years the realization by the people of their rights to full sovereignty and independence was not supported by the majority of members. A proposed resolution, approved in committee, that appealed for the reduction of tensions in Morocco

[43] Res. 611(VII), Dec. 17, 1952.
[44] Res. 612(VII), Dec. 19, 1952.

and urged that the right of the people to free democratic political institutions be ensured, was not adopted by the Assembly.[45] On the Tunisian question, the First Committee of the Assembly endorsed a resolution recommending that all necessary steps be taken to ensure the realization of the right of the Tunisians to full sovereignty and independence. This proposed resolution was much less far-reaching than the proposal introduced by the Arab-Asian bloc.[46] In the light of the defeat in plenary of the proposal on Morocco, a series of amendments to the proposed resolution on Tunisia were introduced in the hope that they would make the proposal more palatable, but even in its watered down version, the proposal failed to obtain the necessary two-thirds support.[47] Thus in the end the Assembly did not adopt a resolution on either of these questions.

Implementation of Resolutions

To ensure that negotiations take place, the Security Council and the General Assembly have resorted to various devices. They have requested reports from the parties on the progress or the results of their negotiations; they have indicated their intention to consider a question further after the parties have had an opportunity to attempt to reach an agreement; and sometimes they have made clear that if no settlement was reached, other measures might be taken. All of these devices have been designed to put additional pressure on the parties to make an effort to reach an agreement.

The action of the Security Council in the dispute between Iran and the Soviet Union is the outstanding example of resort to measures of this type, and a case in which such measures apparently had much influence on the settlement of the dispute. The resolution originally proposed for action by the Council in January 1946 noted that "both parties" had affirmed their readiness to seek a solution by negotiations and that such negotiations would "be resumed in the near future," but it also requested "the parties to inform the Council of any results achieved in such negotiations." Iran had stated, during the discussions in the Council, that it was willing to negotiate with the Soviet Union under the aegis of the Council, and,

---

[45] U.N. Doc. A/2526 (Oct. 22, 1953).

[46] U.N. Doc. A/2530 (Oct. 28, 1953).

[47] U.N. General Assembly, Eighth Session, Plenary, *Official Records*, 457th Meeting (Nov. 11, 1953), p. 289.

in support of this position, it was proposed that the question be retained on the agenda of the Council. The representative of the
Soviet Union objected to this step because in his opinion it would
imply that the Council had the authority to deal with the question
under Articles 36 and 37 of the Charter. In the end a compromise
was reached. A provision was included in the resolution as finally
approved by the Council that reaffirmed the "right" of the Council
"at any time to request information on the progress of the negotiations."[48]

When the question was considered two months later at the request
of Iran, and over the vehement protest of the Soviet Union, the
Council requested the Secretary-General to ascertain from the
parties the status of the negotiations and in particular whether the
withdrawal of Soviet troops was "conditioned upon the conclusion
of agreement . . . on other subjects."[49] Subsequently, after considering the replies received from the parties, the Council decided to
defer its proceedings for a month and asked the parties to report
whether the troop withdrawal had been completed. When Iran later
stated that it had not been possible to verify the evacuation in certain areas, the Council adopted a resolution requesting another
report within the next few weeks. When the Council considered the
question again, it merely decided to retain the question on the
agenda and, subsequently, Iran informed the Council that the
evacuation had been completed.

Although there was considerable confusion at various stages over
the situation in northern Iran and over the exact status of the negotiations between the parties, these repeated requests by the Council for reports were not designed for the sole purpose of obtaining
information. The device was also used to express the continuing and
active concern of the Council, to support the position of Iran during
the negotiations with the Soviet Union, and to put pressure on the
Soviet Union for an early evacuation of Soviet troops. There can
be little doubt that the relatively early and satisfactory settlement
of the dispute was to a considerable extent a result of the action
that the Council took.

As will be noted later,[50] another step the Council and the Assem-

[48] U.N. Security Council, First Year, *Official Records,* First Series, No. 1, 5th
Meeting (Jan. 30, 1946), p. 70.

[49] For subsequent actions taken by the Council see *Ibid.,* No. 2, 28th Meeting
(Mar. 29, 1946), pp. 75 ff.; and *Ibid.,* 40th Meeting (May 8, 1946), pp. 248-52.

[50] See below, Chap. XII.

bly have taken when their initial appeals and recommendations to the parties have been ineffective has been to establish special subsidiary organs to assist the parties in reaching a settlement, a step that has also at times been taken concurrently with a recommendation or appeal to the parties to reach a settlement themselves.

In considering the means available to obtain the implementation of resolutions by the Council or the Assembly calling for the pacific settlement of disputes by the parties, mention must be made of the powers of the Council under Chapter VII of the Charter. Although the Charter contains no provision authorizing the Council to enforce the terms of a political settlement that it recommends, the threat of possible action by the Council under Chapter VII in case of a threat to or breach of the peace may have a direct influence on the willingness of parties to accept such recommendations.[51] The possibility that the Council might take the forceful measures open to it under Chapter VII was of some consequence during the first few years of the operations of the Council. Thus, for example, at one point during the discussion of the question of the Greek frontier incidents, the representative of Brazil stated that once the Council had decided a dispute was likely to endanger the peace, the parties were obliged to settle the dispute "under penalty of having the situation become a threat to the peace, in which case Chapter VII would apply." He later went so far as to state that the failure of the parties to settle the dispute "compels the Security Council to go still further and apply Chapter VII."[52]

The Charter does not, however, establish any direct link between the failure of parties to comply with recommendations for the pacific settlement of disputes and the powers of the Council to take action under Chapter VII of the Charter. The link between these two kinds of action was indeed closer in the provisions of the Dumbarton Oaks Proposals, in which the powers of the Council under what eventually became Chapters VI and VII of the Charter were treated as a whole. The provisions concerning the action of the Security Council with respect to threats to the peace or acts of aggression

---

[51] See discussion below, Chap. XIX, pp. 490-92.

[52] U.N. Security Council, Second Year, *Official Records*, No. 61, 162nd Meeting (July 22, 1947), p. 1422, and *Ibid.*, No. 64, 167th Meeting (July 25, 1947), p. 1530. This whole discussion on the question of the Greek frontier incidents is especially interesting in so far as it reflects the views of Members concerning the force of a resolution by the Security Council under Chapter VI of the Charter. See above, Chap. VIII, pp. 180-82.

provided that should the Council deem that a threat to the peace had resulted from the failure of the parties to settle their dispute by peaceful means of their own choice or to settle their dispute in accordance with the appropriate procedures that the Council had recommended, the Council "should take any measures necessary for the maintenance of international peace and security."[53] Under the Charter as adopted, however, the relationship between Chapters VI and VII is less clear.

Effect of Resolutions

In considering both the extent of compliance with the recommendations and appeals of the Security Council and the General Assembly that the parties seek a solution of their disputes by negotiations or other peaceful means, and the extent to which such resolutions have been effective, it is necessary to keep in mind that the intervention of the Council and the Assembly in such cases has been strictly limited. These resolutions have represented expressions of opinion by the Organization that a dispute existed that might disturb the friendly relations among nations. For the most part, they have been in the nature of opinions that the issues in controversy should be settled, but they have not represented judgments by the Organization that the settlement of these disputes was essential to the maintenance of international peace and security. The actions of the Assembly and the Council therefore must be judged not on the narrow ground of whether the provisions of the particular resolutions have been implemented but on the broad basis of the extent to which the consideration of the disputes by the United Nations has had an influence on the policies that the states concerned have pursued.

In those disputes that have involved the members of the Soviet bloc, the efforts of the Council and the Assembly, although they may have exerted some restraining influence, have had little direct effect. The outstanding exception was the dispute between the Soviet Union and Iran, when the action of the Council had a real influence on the settlement of the question.[54] But the various resolutions

[53] See Chap. VIII, Sec. B(1), of the Dumbarton Oaks Proposals, U. S. Department of State, *Dumbarton Oaks Documents on International Organization* (1944), p. 16.

[54] Concerning the results of the recommendation of the Council on the question of the incidents in the Corfu Channel, see below, Chap. XIII.

of the Assembly calling for the settlement of the differences between Greece and its northern neighbors did not induce the interested parties to settle their differences, and the recommendations on the Yugoslav complaint against the members of the Soviet bloc were of no measurable effect in reducing tension. In both cases, however, it could be argued that the consideration of the questions and the adoption of the resolutions served the purpose of consolidating support for one of the parties.

On those questions involving direct controversies between the major powers, the Council and the Assembly have been able to do very little. Following the appeal for a new effort for the conclusion of an Austrian Treaty, negotiations were re-opened but were again unsuccessful. On the Berlin question, the Council was prevented by a Soviet veto from adopting any resolution, and the central issue, the Berlin blockade, was subsequently settled directly by the occupying powers themselves. The discussions in the Council and the subsequent efforts of the informal committee established under the auspices of the president of the Council did, however, make a contribution to clarifying the issues. Furthermore, the discussions in the Council, the later appeal by the President of the Assembly and the Secretary-General, and the appeal by the Assembly itself may indeed have contributed to the resumption of direct negotiations, inasmuch as these various initiatives reflected the considerable concern of the other Members of the United Nations over the gravity of the impasse that had developed.

Similarly, the Council and the Assembly have had only limited success in their efforts to bring about the settlement of controversies not directly related to the split between the Soviet bloc and the Western powers. The various resolutions of the Assembly on the treatment of Indians in South Africa have brought no improvement in the situation, and it seems unlikely that the United Nations can do anything to bring about a modification of the racial policies of South Africa. Although the discussions in the Assembly on the Tunisian and Moroccan questions may have served a useful purpose in providing an outlet for Arab complaints and a means of clarifying the issues, there is no clear evidence regarding the influence of the discussions and resolutions of the Assembly on French policy. It must be noted, however, that in none of these cases has the Assembly adopted a very strong position, nor have its resolutions enjoyed very solid support.

The Council has been slightly more successful than the Assembly in handling disputes between the Western powers and the Arab-Asian states. In the Indonesian case, the original resolution of the Council calling upon the parties to settle their dispute proved to be inadequate, but the subsequent efforts of the Council were successful and a settlement was eventually achieved.[55] With respect to the dispute between Syria and Lebanon on the one hand and France and the United Kingdom on the other, the Council was unable to adopt a resolution because of the Soviet veto. However, France and the United Kingdom announced that they would follow the course of action supported by the majority of the members of the Council and eventually a settlement was reached. In all likelihood this dispute would have been settled in any case, but the discussion of the question in the Council undoubtedly did speed up the settlement and possibly had an influence on the terms eventually reached.

In the other two disputes in which the Council was unable to adopt a recommendation for negotiations between the parties, *i.e.* the Anglo-Egyptian and Anglo-Iranian cases, through subsequent negotiations acceptable agreements seem to have been reached. The Council can claim no direct credit for the developments in these two cases, although in both instances the discussions in the Council at least indicated to the parties the amount of support they were likely to obtain for their respective positions.

[55] See below, Chap. XII.

CHAPTER XII
Mediation and Conciliation

ALTHOUGH the procedure most commonly used for the pacific settlement of disputes is direct negotiation, by which the parties to a dispute seek a settlement between themselves, there are other procedures of peaceful settlement that have also been employed with some frequency. A distinction can be made among these other procedures according to the degree to which third parties participate, and the extent to which the parties to the dispute are obligated to accept the results of the procedures. Certain of these procedures, such as arbitration and judicial settlement, which involve important legal commitments for the parties to a dispute, will be considered later in this study.[1] Consideration will be given here to the use by the United Nations of procedures of good offices, mediation, and conciliation, which, although involving the participation of third parties, are essentially voluntary in character and depend at each stage in the process on the co-operation of the parties to the dispute. Attention will be especially focused on the use that has been made of special subsidiary organs by the United Nations to perform the functions of good offices, mediation, or conciliation in order to assist the parties in reaching a settlement.

Nature of Good Offices, Mediation, and Conciliation

Writers on international law and organization have sought to make sharp distinctions among the procedures of good offices, mediation, and conciliation. The procedure of good offices is considered to be the least formal and to have the limited function of simply bringing the parties together; mediation implies an effort by an outside party to assist the disputants in reaching a solution; and conciliation is generally defined as a process instituted by the parties themselves, who agree to submit their dispute to a specially con-

[1] See below, Chap XIII.

stituted organ for investigation and efforts to effect a settlement. In practice, however, these terms have been used with considerable looseness and flexibility.

The use of these procedures has a long history; they have been successfully employed and have been the subject of many bilateral and multilateral treaties. With the establishment of the League of Nations, however, permanent agencies were provided to perform functions of good offices, mediation, and conciliation. Thus the League was authorized to "take any action that may be deemed wise and effectual to safeguard the peace of nations," and, under certain conditions, disputes were to be submitted by the parties to the Council or the Assembly, each acting as an organ of conciliation. Much of the activity of the League in the political field was directed toward settling disputes by these procedures.

The Charter of the United Nations lists mediation and conciliation as methods of peaceful settlement available to the parties to a dispute, but it does not specify the procedures that may be used or recommended by the Security Council or the General Assembly. The Council may at any stage of a dispute the continuance of which is likely to endanger international peace and security "recommend appropriate procedures or methods of adjustment" and under certain circumstances may recommend "such terms of settlement as it may consider appropriate" as well.[2] Both the Council and the Assembly have felt free to adopt whatever procedures and make whatever recommendations seem best suited to bring about the satisfactory settlement of disputes. But they have not been especially consistent in the use of terms to describe the methods they have employed.

These procedures have not been used only by the United Nations in recent years. Since the establishment of the Organization, there have been a number of instances in which states themselves have offered their good offices or attempted in other ways to assist the parties to disputes to work out settlements. The dispute between France and Thailand, for example, was submitted to the United Nations, but before it was discussed there, the dispute was settled by agreement of the parties, largely through the "good offices" of the United States.[3] The United States also made repeated efforts to bring about the settlement of the Anglo-Iranian Oil Company dis-

---

[2] Arts. 36 and 37.
[3] See U.N. Doc. S/199 (Nov. 28, 1946).

pute, and it has used its influence to achieve a settlement of the dispute over the presence of Chinese Nationalist troops on the northern borders of Burma.

In a few cases, in view of the possibility that a dispute might be settled by other means, the United Nations has not itself intervened. An argument advanced in the Security Council against sending a commission to Indonesia in the spring of 1946 was that this step might interfere with the mediation efforts being carried on independently. When the Indonesian case was considered in 1947, however, the Council itself decided to deal with the question, although there was considerable pressure for seeking a solution of the dispute outside the framework of the United Nations. The establishment, subsequently, of the Committee of Good Offices to deal with the Indonesian question was the first of many efforts by the United Nations to achieve the settlement of disputes by referring them to commissions of conciliation.[4] This approach to the pacific settlement of disputes has found increasing favor in the United Nations primarily because it offers the only feasible way of circumventing the increasing difficulties confronting the Council in the light of differences among the permanent members on the terms of substantive recommendations.

The increased emphasis on the use of organs of conciliation has not been confined to the application of these procedures to specific cases. In 1949, the Assembly, for example, established a Panel for Inquiry and Conciliation, which comprised a list of persons available to assist the parties at their request, and also decided that the General Act for the Pacific Settlement of International Disputes of September 26, 1928, should be revised and open to accession by states.[5] These steps were directed toward encouraging wider use of conciliation in the settlement of disputes. Other suggestions that have been considered include a Lebanese proposal for a "permanent committee of conciliation," a joint proposal by the United States and China for a multilateral convention or a resolution by the Assembly elaborating procedures for pacific settlement,[6] and a Yugo-

---

[4] In this chapter the general term "conciliation organ" will be used to cover all subsidiary organs, whether individuals, committees, or commissions that have been established to assist the parties in reaching a settlement regardless whether they have been vested with functions of good offices, mediation, or conciliation in the technical sense of those terms.

[5] Res. 268 (III), D, Apr. 28, 1949.

[6] See U.N. General Assembly, Third Session, *Official Records,* Supplement No. 10, pp. 22 ff.

slav proposal for the establishment of a permanent commission of good offices.[7]

Although the availability of machinery is of some importance, as the existence of the United Nations itself bears witness, the history of the handling of international disputes indicates that the proliferation of machinery and agreements for pacific settlement has produced a disappointingly small impact on the practice of states in the settlement of international disputes. The vast number of treaties of pacific settlement may have had a salutary effect on the relations between states, but they have seldom been successfully invoked when disputes have actually arisen. These commitments, made in advance to settle disputes peacefully, can perhaps more accurately be viewed as barometers indicating the state of relations between particular states, rather than as dependable prophesies of future state action with respect to specific disputes.

Establishment of Conciliation Organs

The general attitude of the Security Council and the General Assembly toward the institution of procedures of mediation and conciliation has been that the parties should be given every opportunity to work out an acceptable settlement themselves. A conciliation organ has usually been established only after it has been demonstrated that the parties themselves are not likely through their own efforts to reach a satisfactory solution. To illustrate, the establishment of the Committee of Good Offices in the Indonesian case followed the lack of response to the initial resolution of the Council of August 1, 1947, calling on the parties themselves to settle their dispute; and the recommendation for the establishment of a commission in connection with the question of the treatment of Indians in South Africa was preceded by recommendations of the Assembly that the parties seek a solution through a round table conference.

In some cases, it has been clear from the outset that the parties have exhausted the possibilities of reaching a settlement through their own efforts. In the India-Pakistan case, for example, both parties agreed on the serious nature of the dispute, and the establishment by the Council of a commission was accepted by both parties and indeed resulted from a series of informal conversations

[7] U.N. Doc. A/1401 (Sept. 27, 1950).

between the parties under the auspices of the President of the Council.[8]

The decision of the Assembly that a solution to the Palestine question should be sought through a United Nations mediator was taken only after it became apparent that the original recommendation by the Assembly for partition would not be implemented. Conferring of the functions of good offices on the United Nations Commission on Korea likewise followed the failure of the original action of the Assembly to achieve the solution desired.

A major argument in favor of establishing special conciliation organs has been that the parties have not been able to work out a settlement. Opposition to the setting up of such organs has been based on the contention that the failure to work out a settlement has not been demonstrated and that the parties should be allowed to deal with the controversy themselves without outside interference. This was one argument used by those opposed to establishing a committee of good offices on the Tunisian question, and by the Soviet bloc in opposing the establishment of a commission to assist Greece, Albania, Bulgaria, and Yugoslavia in working out a settlement of their differences. Experience would seem to show, however, that the success of a conciliation effort is in part dependent on instituting the procedure before the parties have reached a complete deadlock. The opinion has also been expressed that the existence of a United Nations conciliation organ has the undesirable effect of shifting responsibility from the parties to the organ. This was the basis of the position of Israel that the Assembly should urge direct negotiations on the Palestine question rather than continue to seek a settlement through the Palestine Conciliation Commission. In this connection, the report of Sir Owen Dixon, the United Nations Representative, appointed to seek an agreement between India and Pakistan, contains some very interesting observations:

. . . For myself I doubt whether it may not be better to leave the parties to themselves in negotiating terms for the settlement of the problem how to dispose of Jammu and Kashmir between them. So far the attitude of the parties has been to throw the whole responsibility upon the Security Council or its representatives of settling the dispute, notwithstanding that, except by agreement between them, there was no means of settling it.

When actual fighting was going on between them it was natural, if not necessary, that the Security Council and the Commission as its delegate

[8] See above, Chap. VII, pp. 149-51.

should intervene between them and propose terms to stop the hostilities. But when this was done to the extent of stopping open hostilities and the question came to be how to settle the rival claims to Kashmir, the initiative was still left with the Security Council and the Commission. The whole question has now been thoroughly discussed by the parties with the Security Council, the Commission and myself and the possible methods of settlement have been exhaustively investigated. It is perhaps best that the initiative should now pass back to the parties. At all events I am not myself prepared to recommend any further course of action on the part of the Security Council for the purpose of assisting the parties to settle between them how the State of Jammu and Kashmir is to be disposed of.[9]

In many cases the competence of the Council or the Assembly to establish conciliation organs has been questioned. On the Tunisian question, an argument against a committee of good offices was that the matter fell within the domestic jurisdiction of France. And on the Indonesian question and the question of the treatment of Indians in South Africa, the Netherlands and the Union of South Africa respectively maintained that the United Nations had no competence to "intervene." Although both states were willing to negotiate on these questions outside the framework of the United Nations, they opposed any action by the United Nations. The Netherlands, however, finally accepted the Committee of Good Offices of the Security Council.

The establishment of this committee, as in a number of other cases, was in the nature of a compromise between the extreme positions of the parties. It was an attempt to reconcile the position of the Netherlands and those members that endorsed efforts to seek a solution outside the framework of the United Nations, with the position of the Republic of Indonesia and other members who believed that the controversy should be submitted to arbitration. The latter, it was pointed out, was the procedure to which the parties had agreed under the terms of the Linggadjati Agreement, which they had signed a few months previously.

Terms of Reference

The resolutions of the Security Council and the General Assembly establishing conciliation organs have differed with regard to both the terms of reference given to the organs and indications of the lines along which a settlement should be sought. It should

[9] U.N. Security Council, Fifth Year, *Official Records,* Supplement for September-December 1950, p. 46.

be noted that these organs have served a dual purpose. Their primary task, of course, has been to assist the parties themselves in reaching an agreement, but as agents of the United Nations, they have also been called upon to perform other tasks. Through these organs, the Council or the Assembly has been kept informed of developments in the situation and has attempted to keep the situation under control.

Many of the resolutions of the Council and of the Assembly have conferred on the conciliation organ the express authority to use good offices. As already noted, the term "good offices" has been used quite loosely in the practice of the United Nations, and, on the whole, the organs involved have interpreted their powers very broadly. For example, the Committee of Good Offices in its actual conduct in the Indonesian case clearly went beyond the technical limits of good offices as generally understood. In fact, of all the conciliation organs, this committee functioned with the least direction from the parent organ. By its resolution of August 25, 1947, the Security Council resolved: "to tender its good offices to the parties in order to assist in the pacific settlement of their dispute, in accordance with paragraph (b) of the resolution of the Council of August 1, 1947." The Council expressed its readiness, if the parties so requested, "to assist in the settlement through a committee of the Council."[10] Although various suggestions for changes in the terms of reference of the committee were made from time to time in the Council, the committee continued to operate under this original mandate until the end of 1948.[11] At that time, negotiations under the auspices of the committee had broken down, and in December the Netherlands launched a second "police action." The Council, on January 28, 1949 after lengthy consideration, reconstituted the Committee of Good Offices as the United Nations Commission for Indonesia and at the same time recommended the basis on which a settlement should be sought.[12] The terms of the resolution made clear that the commission was the "agent" of the Council and stressed the authority of the commission to make recommendations to the parties and to the Council. The Indonesian practice thus illustrates the two extremes: a committee of good offices operat-

[10] U.N. Security Council, Second Year, *Official Records*, No. 83, 194th Meeting (Aug. 25, 1947), p. 2209.

[11] For the role of the committee in connection with the negotiation of a cease-fire agreement, see below, Chap. XV.

[12] U.N. Doc. S/1234 (Jan. 28, 1949).

ing under the vaguest of mandates, and a commission operating under specific instructions regarding both the methods to be followed and the results to be achieved.

The approach of the General Assembly to the question of the treatment of Indians in South Africa presents some similarities to the handling by the Security Council of the Indonesian question. In both cases one of the parties denied the competence of the United Nations to deal with the question, and an initial effort was made to induce the parties to settle the question directly. The resolution of the Assembly in 1950, suggesting a commission of good offices on the question of the treatment of Indians in South Africa, like the resolution of the Council providing for a similar organ on the Indonesian question, made the establishment of the committee dependent on the initiative of the parties. In contrast to the action by the Council, however, it should be noted that the Assembly adopted the good offices approach only after years of discussion and after the members and the Assembly had taken positions regarding the issues in controversy. South Africa did not comply with the recommendation to the parties that they establish a commission to assist them "in carrying through appropriate negotiations."[13] During the seventh session, the Assembly itself established a Good Offices Commission "with a view to arranging and assisting in negotiations" between the parties "in order that a satisfactory solution of the question in accordance with the Purposes and Principles of the Charter and the Universal Declaration of Human Rights may be achieved."[14] South Africa has, however, refused to co-operate with the commission.

In the India-Pakistan dispute, the Council established a commission "to exercise . . . any mediatory influence likely to smooth away difficulties."[15] Later, as a result of further informal conversations with the parties under the auspices of the President of the Council, the commission was given more precise terms of reference. By its resolution of April 22, 1948, the Council addressed a series of recommendations to the parties that it considered "appropriate to bring about a cessation of fighting and to create proper conditions for a free and impartial plebiscite." The commission was instructed

[13] Res. 395 (V), Dec. 2, 1950. The second effort of the Assembly met a similar fate. Res. 511 (VI), Jan. 12, 1952.
[14] Res. 615 (VII), Dec. 5, 1952.
[15] U.N. Doc. S/654 (Jan. 20, 1948).

to "place its good offices and mediation at the disposal of the Governments of India and Pakistan with a view to facilitating the taking of the necessary measures, both with respect to the restoration of peace and order and to the holding of a plebiscite."[16] The commission operated under this resolution until it was relieved of its functions in the spring of 1950. At that time, the Council appointed the United Nations representative for India and Pakistan, who was "to exercise all the powers and responsibilities" devolving on the commission by reason of previous resolutions by the Council and existing agreements between the parties. He was specifically authorized "to place before" the parties or the Security Council "any suggestions which, in his opinion, were likely to contribute to the expeditious and enduring solution of the dispute which has arisen between the two Governments in regard to the State of Jammu and Kashmir."[17] The primary function of the representative was to assist in the preparation of a plan of demilitarization, to supervise its implementation, and to interpret the agreements reached between the parties. A year later the Council appointed a second representative who continued, under a succession of resolutions by the Council, to negotiate with the parties, in an effort to obtain an agreement on the issue of demilitarization.[18]

In regard to the Palestine question, although the Security Council and the General Assembly have created a great many subsidiary organs to deal with various aspects of it, only two of these organs were directly concerned with assisting the parties in reaching an over-all political settlement. The United Nations Mediator for Palestine, established by the Assembly in May 1948, was instructed "to use his good offices with the local and community authorities in Palestine to . . . promote a peaceful adjustment of the future situation of Palestine."[19] The mediator took a broad view of his functions. His principal task was to work out a cease-fire agreement between the parties, a role undertaken in accordance with various resolutions of the Security Council. However, he also put forward suggestions of a basis for settlement of the whole problem. In December 1948, the Assembly established the Palestine Conciliation

[16] U.N. Doc. S/726, (Apr. 22, 1948).

[17] U.N. Doc. S/1461 (Feb. 24, 1950).

[18] U.N. Docs. S/2017/Rev. 1 (Mar. 30, 1951), S/2392 (Nov. 10, 1951), and S/2883 (Dec. 24, 1952). See also statement by the President, U.N. Security Council, Seventh Year, *Official Records,* 572nd Meeting (Jan. 31, 1952), p. 8.

[19] Res. 186 (S-2), May 14, 1948.

Commission, which was to assume whatever functions of the mediator it considered necessary. It was instructed "to take steps to assist the Governments and authorities concerned to achieve a final settlement of all questions outstanding between them."[20] Under this and subsequent resolutions of the Assembly, the commission was given additional tasks to assist in the implementation of various resolutions, but no basic change was made in its terms of reference.[21]

The United Nations Special Committee on the Balkans and the United Nations Commission on Korea were also vested with the function of "good offices." This was not, however, the principal role of either commission, as each was established primarily in order that the United Nations might have an agency in the area to observe and report on developments. Because of the opposition of the Soviet Union and its satellites, neither commission had an opportunity to carry out its function of good offices.

The United Nations Special Committee on the Balkans, established at the 1947 session of the Assembly, was to be available "to assist" Yugoslavia, Albania, Greece, and Bulgaria in the implementation of recommendations the Assembly addressed to those states.[22] These recommendations called for the establishment of normal relations between the countries, the conclusion of frontier conventions, and the settlement of refugee and minority problems. At its session in 1948, the Assembly specifically authorized the committee to use the good offices of one or more persons to assist in the implementation of its recommendations to the parties.[23] The inclusion of this provision was for the most part the result of an initiative by the Australian delegation, which felt strongly that the committee should be primarily an organ of mediation and conciliation with secondary functions of observation.[24] No changes were made in the terms of reference of the committee during subsequent sessions of the Assembly. In December 1951, the Assembly decided to discontinue the committee and to vest its functions of observation in a Balkan subcommission of the Peace Observation Commission.[25]

[20] Res. 194 (III), Dec. 11, 1948.
[21] See, in particular, Res. 394 (V), Dec. 14, 1950 and Res. 512 (VI), Jan. 26, 1952.
[22] Res. 109 (II), Oct. 21, 1947.
[23] Res. 193 (III), Nov. 27, 1948.
[24] For the position of Australia, see reservations to the Report of the Committee, U.N. General Assembly, Third Session, *Official Records*, Supplement No. 8, pp. 35 ff.; *Ibid.*, Supplement No. 8A, p. 11.
[25] Res. 508 (VI), Dec. 7, 1951.

When the United Nations Commission on Korea replaced the United Nations Temporary Commission in December 1948, it was clear that the new commission would receive no more co-operation from the Soviet Union and the North Koreans than its predecessor. Nevertheless, under its terms of reference, the commission was to "lend its good offices to bring about the unification of Korea and the integration of all Korean security forces in accordance with principles laid down by the General Assembly" in its resolution of 1947 and to "seek to facilitate the removal of barriers to economic, social and other friendly intercourse caused by the division of Korea."[26] After the outbreak of aggression in Korea, a different approach was adopted toward the solution of the Korean problem. In October 1950, the commission was replaced by the United Nations Commission for the Unification and Rehabilitation of Korea,[27] which was to assist in carrying out the program set forth in the resolution of the General Assembly of October 7, 1950.

Composition of Conciliation Organs

The considerations influencing decisions concerning the composition of conciliation organs have differed in many respects from those that have obtained in connection with other subsidiary organs. Conciliation organs have usually had a small membership. In contrast to commissions of investigation, there has been less emphasis on "geographic distribution" and more on acceptability to the parties.

Various methods have been used for selecting the members of these organs, but the only one that calls for comment is the method whereby each of the parties is given the opportunity to designate one of the members. This was the method used in establishing the Committee of Good Offices on the Indonesian question, when the Republic of Indonesia and the Netherlands selected Australia and Belgium, respectively, and the latter two states selected the United States as the "third" member. Provided both parties are willing to co-operate, this method has considerable merit. The parties are likely to have greater confidence in the organ, and the work may even be facilitated if one of the members has ready access to each of the parties.

[26] Res. 195 (III), Dec. 12, 1948.
[27] See below, Chap. XVIII, pp. 479-80.

This method may, however, result in the "third" member having the additional task of conciliating his co-members as well as the parties. A further difficulty is that the two states selected by the parties may not be able to agree on a third member. In the case of the India-Pakistan commission, for example, India chose Czechoslovakia, and Pakistan selected Argentina; but these two states failed to agree on a third member. The Security Council itself decided to add two additional members—Belgium and Colombia—and the President of the Council designated the United States as the final member of the commission. In order to avoid the possibility of a similar stalemate in the establishment of the commission on the question of the treatment of Indians in South Africa, the General Assembly empowered the Secretary-General to appoint the third member if the two states selected by the parties failed to agree. In this case, the Union of South Africa refused to make any nomination, and consequently no commission was established. At its next session the General Assembly established a United Nations Good Offices Commission consisting of three Members nominated by the President.

Another question that has received attention is whether a conciliation organ should be composed of representatives of governments or individuals operating without instructions from their governments. Both methods have been followed by the United Nations. The latter method was followed in the India-Pakistan case, when the Security Council appointed as United Nations representative, first Sir Owen Dixon, and later Dr. Frank P. Graham. Similarly, in the Palestine case, the Assembly appointed Count Bernadotte to act as mediator, and after his assassination, his functions were taken over by Dr. Ralph Bunche as acting mediator. In the former case the commission of the Council itself recommended that it be replaced by a single individual. In the latter case, the situation was reversed. The acting mediator endorsed the appointment of a commission. The Palestine Conciliation Commission, which the Assembly then established, was composed of representatives of France, Turkey, and the United States.

A commission composed of government representatives has certain undoubted advantages. Its representative character ensures continuity in the handling of a question, and the actions of such commissions are likely to carry a degree of authority that cannot normally be expected from a private individual or group of individuals. It is unlikely that any group of individuals, for example, would have been able to wield the same influence in Indonesia as did the governmental representatives on the Committee of Good Offices. On the other hand, a private individual or group of individuals may be able to achieve better results in a given situation through greater independence, objectivity, disinterestedness, and freedom of maneuver, as witness the success of Dr. Bunche in the negotiation of the Palestine armistice agreements.

Attitudes of the Parties toward Conciliation Organs

In view of the fact that the procedures of mediation and conciliation depend for their success on the co-operation of the parties themselves, the attitudes of the parties toward the establishment and functioning of a conciliation organ are naturally of great importance. In only three cases, India-Pakistan, Indonesia, and Palestine, have United Nations conciliation organs been accepted by the parties. The establishment of the Special Committee on the Balkans was opposed from the outset by Yugoslavia, Bulgaria, and Albania. They refused to co-operate with the committee in any way. The Korean commission found itself in a similar position. It was opposed by the Soviet bloc and was unable to negotiate with the authorities in North Korea. And on the question of the treatment of Indians in South Africa the Good Offices Commission has been unable to obtain any co-operation from the Union of South Africa.

With regard to the India-Pakistan question, the resolution establishing the commission resulted from the agreement of the parties. The parties, however, did not accept in its entirety the comprehensive resolution that the Council later adopted. Both parties accepted the appointment of the United Nations representatives. In the main, the parties have been continuously willing to enter into negotiations with the commission and with the representatives even though their suggestions for the settlement of the dispute have not found full acceptance.

On the Indonesian question, the Netherlands originally objected to any action by the United Nations. It co-operated with the Committee of Good Offices, however, although from time to time it questioned whether the committee in making suggestions was acting within its terms of reference. The Netherlands also opposed many provisions of the resolution reconstituting the committee as the United Nations Commission, but finally accepted the commission and agreed that it should take part in the Hague Conference.

In regard to Palestine, the Arab states abstained from voting on the resolution of the Assembly appointing the United Nations Mediator and voted against the resolution establishing the Palestine Conciliation Commission. However, like Israel, they were willing to negotiate with the mediator and with the commission. There has, however, been disagreement between the parties over the proper role of the commission. Israel has questioned whether the formulation of specific proposals comes within the terms of reference of the commission and at one time pressed for the replacement of the commission with a committee of good offices, which would function only at the request of the parties. In the beginning, the Arab States criticized the commission for confining itself to transmitting the views of one party to the other and urged the commission to offer its own proposals. When the commission did so, however, the Arabs objected that it was exceeding its terms of reference by departing from previous resolutions of the Assembly. They also criticized the commission for suspending its efforts after a deadlock had been reached.

Relation of Conciliation Organs to the Security Council and the General Assembly

It has been recognized that a subsidiary organ on the spot is better able to judge the situation than the parent organ, and for this reason conciliation organs have generally been given broad terms of reference. Although the Security Council and the General Assembly may indicate in their resolutions the approach that the conciliation organ should follow, the organs have usually been left free to decide for themselves how they will operate. The relation of an organ to the Council has been the subject of extended discussion only in regard to the Committee of Good Offices on the Indonesian question. In that case, the Council originally had made no provision for the submission of reports by the committee to the Council. Later, because of the objections that the committee was not keeping the Council adequately informed of its activities, the Council adopted a resolution requesting the committee to keep it "directly informed about the progress of the political settlement in Indonesia."[28] In June and July 1948, when negotiations under the committee had broken down, the Council discussed at length whether it should request a report and, in particular, whether the Council should ask that there be made available to it the text of a proposal made to the parties by Australia and the United States. The proposed request failed of adoption by a single vote. It is interesting to note that Australia, one of the members of the committee, favored the request, while the other two members of the committee argued that the Council should not interfere with the work of the committee.

After the outbreak of hostilities in December 1948, the role of the committee was again discussed at length. The particular issue was whether it would be proper for the committee (1) to report to the Council assessing the responsibility for the outbreak of hostilities or (2) to recommend what steps the Council should take. Proposals that it be asked to undertake these tasks were defeated in the Council by a narrow vote. When the Council reconstituted the committee as the United Nations Commission for Indonesia, one point specifically stressed was the authority of the commission to make recommendations to the Council.[29]

In general, the Council and the Assembly have discussed questions on the basis of the reports of conciliation organs. The reports have not only provided the Council and the Assembly with the information they need to decide what, if any, further action should be taken, but they have also contained suggestions for further action by the conciliation organs themselves. These recommendations have not always been followed. A suggestion by the Indonesian commission, for example, that the Council reinforce its authority by calling upon Indonesia to utilize the services of the commission in connection with a revolt in the South Moluccas was never even discussed by the Council.[30]

The difficulty in obtaining the adoption of a resolution by the Assembly, and especially by the Council with the ever-present possibility of a veto, provides a strong argument in favor of giving a conciliation organ a broad mandate. Such an organ can count on its

[28] U.N. Doc. S/678 (Feb. 18, 1948).

[29] U.N. Doc. S/1234 (Jan. 28, 1949).

[30] See U.N. Security Council, Fifth Year, *Official Records*, Supplement for September-December 1950, pp. 78 and 96.

report being "noted." It may get an expression of "appreciation" and be asked to continue its efforts. Any concrete suggestions it makes, however, are apt to emerge in diluted form from discussion in the Council or the Assembly. It is perhaps in recognition of this that conciliation organs have been modest in their requests to the Council or the Assembly either for instructions or for further action.

Working Out the Terms of Settlement

Establishing a basis of settlement is a three-way proposition. First of all, there are the recommendations and injunctions that the Security Council or the General Assembly addresses to the parties, the instructions given to conciliation organs, and opinions expressed by the Council or the Assembly regarding the basis of settlement. Second, there are the suggestions by the conciliation organs to the parties and to the Council or the Assembly. And third, there are the suggestions that the parties themselves make to the organs and in the Council or the Assembly.

Recommendations by the Security Council and the General Assembly

In deciding whether to recommend the lines along which a settlement should be reached, the Security Council and the General Assembly have often found themselves in a dilemma. On the one hand, it has been recognized that the parties to a dispute should be encouraged to reach a solution themselves, and that the conciliation organ should be left free to pursue the course that seems to it most likely to promote a solution. On the other hand, when a deadlock has been reached, it has seemed desirable that the Council or the Assembly should express an opinion on the issues involved. The conciliation organs themselves have occasionally pressed for action by the Council and the Assembly, and, of course, the parties have always been anxious that their positions should be supported by the resolutions of the United Nations. When the Council and the Assembly have recommended the basis for a settlement, their recommendations have usually been of a compromise character. Seldom has the position of either of the parties been fully supported.

In making recommendations, the Council and the Assembly have been confronted not only by the difficulties of reconciling the attitudes of the parties but also by the problem of devising recommendations acceptable to the members themselves. And in some cases the political preoccupations of members have had a considerable influence on the nature of the recommendations that have been made.

In the Indonesian case, the Council, despite pressure from some quarters, initially refrained from expressing any opinion with respect to the basis for a political settlement. The Council did, however, adopt a number of resolutions on one aspect of the question, the basis for a cease-fire. It was only after the negotiations had reached a complete deadlock and the Netherlands, in violation of the truce agreement, launched its second "police action" that the Council proceeded to deal with the substance of a political settlement. The principal reason the Council was able to adopt its comprehensive resolution of January 28, 1949 was that on this occasion the United States and the Soviet Union did not hold diametrically opposed views. The resolution that the Council adopted called upon the parties to take specific steps and recommended precise terms of settlement.[31]

On the India-Pakistan question, the Council encountered little difficulty in agreeing on its comprehensive resolution of April 22, 1948.[32] The resolution was not in fact discussed at great length in the Council primarily because many of the members had taken part in the informal discussions from which the resolution emerged. The resolution was an attempt to work out a compromise between the positions of the two parties and, like many compromises, was acceptable to neither. At a later stage the opposition of the parties resulted in the defeat of an attempt to indicate the lines along which a settlement should be sought. The United States and the United Kingdom sought unsuccessfully to include, in the resolution appointing the second United Nations representative, a directive that the representative "take into account" the suggestions of the first representative and certain other suggestions that apparently arose from the Commonwealth Prime Ministers' Conference and Anglo-American discussions.[33]

The handling of the Palestine question illustrated the difficulties that arise in connection with efforts of United Nations organs to

[31] U.N. Doc. S/1234 (Jan. 28, 1949).

[32] U.N. Doc. S/726 (Apr. 22, 1948).

[33] *Cf.* U.N. Doc. S/2017 (Feb. 21, 1951), with U.N. Doc. S/2017/Rev. 1 (Mar. 21, 1951).

establish a basis for settlement. The political settlement of the question, as distinct from the truce effort and the maintenance of the armistice agreement, has been primarily the concern of the General Assembly. As a result, it has been necessary to reconcile the conflicting interests of many Member states. Furthermore, the mediation and conciliation effort in this case was begun only after the Assembly had adopted the partition resolution; and although it proved impossible to implement that resolution, there was continuing support for some of its provisions, especially those regarding the internationalization of Jerusalem, an issue of considerable concern to the Latin American and some other Member states. The resolution of the Assembly appointing the mediator did not contain any reference to the lines along which a settlement should be attempted. When the Assembly was considering the terms of reference that should be given to the Palestine Conciliation Commission—the successor to the mediator—there were two distinct points of view concerning the basis on which a settlement should be sought. Some Members—the United Kingdom in particular—supported an endorsement of the suggestions made by the mediator for a settlement, and the inclusion in the terms of reference of the commission of various references to the report of the mediator. Other members pressed for the incorporation of provisions envisaging a settlement on the basis of the partition resolution. Neither group was successful; the resolution as adopted contained no reference to either the report of the mediator or the partition resolution.[34] This and subsequent resolutions did, however, include provisions concerning the basis for settling the refugee question and specific instructions concerning the status of Jerusalem.

In no case have such comprehensive resolutions been implemented in detail. A settlement of the Indonesian question was reached in harmony with the substantive recommendation of the Council, but the procedure laid down by the Council was not followed. The detailed provisions of the resolution of the Council in 1948 on the India-Pakistan question, particularly those concerning the holding of a plebiscite, were not implemented and in the light of subsequent developments have lost much of their relevance. The recommendations of the Assembly on the Palestine question

[34] *Cf.* original proposals by the United Kingdom, U.N. Doc. A/C.1/394 (Nov. 18, 1948), and Australia, U.N. Doc. A/C.1/396 (Nov. 23, 1948) with Res. 194 (III), Dec. 11, 1948.

illustrate two difficulties that arise from efforts to deal with the substance of any problem: (1) the impossibility of implementing a resolution opposed by the parties; and (2) the propensity of the parties to seize on specific provisions in resolutions to support their positions and to ignore other provisions. The insistence of the Assembly on the internationalization of Jerusalem has been of no avail because of the opposition of both Israel and Jordan. But this issue has continued to be of importance because the continued support of many Members for internationalization has resulted in pressure for the reaffirmation of previous resolutions of the Assembly, a point that the Arabs for their own reasons have insisted on, while Israel has pressed for a "new approach" to the Palestine question.

The position of the Arab states is largely a result of the support that they have received from the resolutions of the Assembly on the refugee issue. In its resolution of 1948, the Assembly stated that the refugees should be allowed to return to their homes and that they were entitled to compensation for their losses.[35] In its resolution of 1950, the Assembly recognized that the refugee question should be dealt with as a "matter of urgency."[36] The Arab states have maintained that negotiations with Israel be conditioned on prior agreement on the refugee question and, in particular, on acceptance by Israel of the "principles" of repatriation and compensation. Israel has contended that negotiations cannot be made dependent on the acceptance of prior conditions, that Israel is not responsible for the flight of the refugees, and that their repatriation is impossible for reasons of security and because of the vast number of Jewish refugees who have been received in Israel. Israel has also insisted that the Arab states enter into direct negotiations with it, which they have refused to do, and Israel, in support of its position, has stressed the repeated recommendations by the Assembly that the parties enter into negotiations for an over-all settlement.

Suggestions by Conciliation Organs

The initial efforts of conciliation organs have generally been directed toward instituting negotiations between the parties. In doing so, they have been confronted by a number of problems: where the negotiations are to take place, between whom, and how they

[35] Res. 194 (III), Dec. 11, 1948.
[36] Res. 394 (V), Dec. 14, 1950.

are to be carried on. These issues have been of importance. For example, the major problem of the Palestine Conciliation Commission has been to obtain an agreement between the parties regarding procedures for negotiations. During the meetings at Lausanne in 1949, the commission was unable to effect an agreement on procedures and was forced to carry on separate discussions with each of the parties. During the meetings in Geneva in the spring of 1950, the commission proposed a new procedure of "triangular negotiations," but this suggestion for the establishment of "mixed committees" was not accepted.

One part of the work of conciliation organs has been to transmit the suggestions of one party to the other. Although some progress toward a settlement may be made in this way, it is seldom that such a limited contribution will greatly improve the situation. If the parties themselves cannot reach an agreement, organs have usually found that they must make their own suggestions to the parties. The extent to which they will intervene by making suggestions has in large measure depended on their terms of reference and the indications given by the Council and the Assembly regarding the basis on which a settlement should be sought.

In the beginning, the Committee of Good Offices on the Indonesian question stated that it was ready to make suggestions "if and when" it was requested to do so by the parties. Although the Republic of Indonesia suggested that the committee propose a basis for discussion, the Netherlands was willing to consider only suggestions concerning procedure. Later when negotiations were not progressing, the committee decided on its own initiative to send to the parties suggestions for a truce and a statement of political principles to serve as a basis for further discussions. The committee stressed that the whole procedure was "informal within the limits of good offices," and on the basis of these suggestions, an agreement was reached.[37] During the discussion in the Council of the report of the committee on this agreement, several statements were made concerning the right of the committee to initiate and publish its suggestions. It was decided that it was unnecessary for the Council to adopt any resolution on this point in the light of various statements upholding the right of the committee to decide on its own procedures. Subsequently, while the committee was continuing its negotiations with a view to translating the agreements on principles into an actual settlement, further deadlocks developed. At one point,

[37] See U.N. Doc. S/649 (Feb. 17, 1948).

the Australian and United States members, without the support of the Belgian member, presented to the parties a concrete proposal for a settlement. No agreement was reached between the parties, but the substance of a later Australian-United States plan was in large part incorporated in the resolution adopted by the Security Council after the outbreak of the second Netherlands "police action."

The United Nations Commission for Indonesia, the successor to the Committee of Good Offices, played a much more active role. This was not only because of its expanded terms of reference but also because of the clearly indicated changes in the temper of the Council itself. The commission, acting under a directive of the Council, made a number of suggestions during the period preliminary to the holding of the round-table conference at The Hague. The commission also played an important role during the conference.

Neither the United Nations Commission for India and Pakistan nor the two United Nations representatives were at all hesitant in presenting proposals to the parties for the settlement of the Kashmir dispute. The commission was primarily concerned initially with obtaining a cessation of hostilities. It was successful in obtaining an agreement on this point and on principles concerning the demilitarization of the area and the holding of a plebiscite, but it was unable to obtain from the parties acceptance of a concrete plan for demilitarization. The first United Nations representative, acting under the broad authorization given him by the Security Council, suggested a new approach to the Kashmir issue. His suggestions entailed modifications in the original plan, which had been accepted by the parties and endorsed by the Council for a plebiscite for the whole area. The proposals of the representative for a limited plebiscite were not, however, acceptable, especially to India. The second representative has concentrated on the issue of demilitarization and, acting under increasingly specific resolutions by the Council, has had some success in narrowing the area of disagreement. India, however, remains adamant on a number of points, basing its position in large part on allegations that Pakistan was the aggressor in Kashmir and should be treated as such.

Although the United Nations Mediator for Palestine was primarily concerned with obtaining and maintaining a truce in Palestine, at an early stage in his negotiations, he put forward a series of suggestions that he hoped might serve as a basis for discussions on a political settlement. They were not accepted by the parties, and these mediation efforts were interrupted by a further outbreak of hostilities. Later, even with the backing of a resolution by the Council,[38] the mediator was unable to institute negotiations for a pacific settlement. He made no further suggestions to the parties, but he did submit suggestions to the General Assembly.

The resolution establishing the office of the mediator contained no provisions for recommendations by him to the Assembly. In his report to the Assembly he recognized this fact and stated that it was not within his province to recommend to the Members a proposed course of action on the Palestine question. At that same time, he considered that the "conclusions" drawn from his experience might be of "assistance to Members in charting the future course of United Nations action on Palestine."[39] His specific proposals for a settlement were not accepted by the parties nor were they endorsed by the Assembly. They were in fact criticized for departing from the partition resolution, which they most certainly did, although his terms of reference would appear to have justified such departures. In his report the mediator urged the Assembly to take a firm position on the political aspects of the Palestine problem, stating that the parties might well acquiesce in any reasonable settlement that the United Nations approved. But the resolution adopted by the Assembly establishing the Conciliation Commission could hardly be considered as a firm stand.

With a few exceptions, the Palestine Conciliation Commission has been unable to gain acceptance of its suggestions, including its suggestions concerning procedures to be followed. During its initial negotiations, it was successful in getting the parties to sign the Lausanne Protocol of May 12, 1949, which was to be a basis for further negotiations, but it was unsuccessful in its efforts to initiate the negotiations themselves. It was not until after the repeated rejection of its proposals on procedure that the commission decided to submit concrete suggestions to the parties concerning the basis for a settlement. In September 1951, the commission convoked a conference in Paris and presented a five-point plan covering various subjects such as war damages, refugees, blocked accounts, and possible revision or amendments to the armistice agreements. After considering the comments of the parties, the commission de-

[38] U.N. Doc. S/902 (July 15, 1948).

[39] U.N. General Assembly, Third Session, *Official Records*, Supplement No. 11, p. 17.

cided to terminate the conference on the grounds that neither party had indicated a willingness to recede from its original position and "to seek a solution through mediation along the lines set forth in the comprehensive pattern of proposals."[40] Since the Paris conference, no full-scale negotiations have been held.[41] But the commission has remained available to the parties and has expressed the view that its comprehensive proposals continue to offer a useful basis for further efforts at settlement.[42]

Special Problems Arising from Hostilities

In the cases of Indonesia, Palestine, and India-Pakistan, a major difficulty confronting the commissions was that, when they began to work, a state of hostilities existed between the parties. The India-Pakistan commission dealt with this problem without any intervention by the Security Council and eventually obtained the agreement of the parties on a cease-fire. In the Palestine and Indonesian cases, the Council made initial efforts to obtain a cease-fire before either the mediator or the Committee of Good Offices began to function. The Council requested the mediator and the committee to take over the function of negotiating a cease-fire, and with the backing of resolutions by the Council a cessation of hostilities was arranged in each case.

The measures taken to obtain a cessation of hostilities are dealt with later in this study,[43] but a few of the problems are touched on at this point because they have been so closely related to the mediation and concilation effort. First, is the problem whether an attempt to achieve an over-all settlement of a dispute should be postponed until hostilities have been brought to an end. This is a general problem and one that has confronted the United Nations in a number of cases, most notably in connection with the hostilities in Korea.

In the Kashmir and Indonesian cases, on the insistence of one of the parties, the original agreements for the cessation of hostilities were coupled with agreements on political principles to govern a

[40] U.N. General Assembly, Sixth Session, *Official Records*, Supplement No. 18, p. 10.
[41] Negotiations have continued, however, on the very specific issue of blocked accounts and some progress has been made.
[42] U.N. General Assembly, Seventh Session, *Official Records*, Supplement No. 17.
[43] See below, Chap. XV.

final settlement. The cessation of hostilities in Kashmir was achieved only after the United Nations commission had obtained acceptance by the parties of a set of principles governing the holding of a plebiscite.[44] The signing of the Truce Agreement between the Netherlands and the Republic of Indonesia on January 17, 1948, following negotiations assisted by the Committee of Good Offices of the Security Council, was accompanied by agreement on "principles," which formed an agreed basis for subsequent political discussions.[45]

The practice in the Palestine case differed from that in the cases of Kashmir and Indonesia, but this was not because of an insistence in principle that a cease-fire must be achieved before discussion of a political settlement was initiated. In fact, the suggestions of the United Nations Mediator concerning the basis of a political settlement were rejected by the parties. Nevertheless the mediator, acting under and aided by explicit and forceful resolutions of the Security Council, was able to obtain a truce between Israel and the Arab states, and later the conclusion of armistice agreements. No progress, however, has yet been made toward settlement of outstanding economic and political issues.

On the relation between a truce agreement and political negotiations, the action of the Council in dealing with the second Netherlands "police action" in Indonesia is especially interesting. In its resolution of January 28, 1949, the Council made the initiation of political discussions conditional on the restoration of peace and order and the establishment of conditions in which the Republic of Indonesia would enjoy freedom of action in negotiations.[46] Later, when the United Nations Commission for Indonesia requested instructions from the Council concerning a Netherlands proposal for a round-table conference at The Hague, the Council issued a directive that the participation of the commission in such a conference would be consistent with the purposes and objectives of the resolution of the Council *if* an agreement were reached between the parties concerning the cessation of military operations and restoration of the Republican Government.[47]

The Security Council and the General Assembly have generally

[41] U.N. Doc. S/1196 (Jan. 10, 1949).
[45] See U.N. Doc. S/649 (Feb. 10, 1948).
[46] U.N. Doc. S/1234 (Jan. 28, 1949).
[47] U.N. Security Council, Fourth Year, *Official Records*, No. 24, 421st Meeting (Mar. 23, 1949), p. 25.

proceeded on the assumption, which appears to underlie the Charter provisions, that it is desirable to achieve a situation in which force is not being used or threatened before efforts are made to achieve a final settlement. This reduces the likelihood of improper influence being used and increases the chances of a freely negotiated settlement. On the other hand, as a practical matter, in situations in which there are no adequate means at the disposal of the Council or the Assembly for enforcing a cease-fire order, and in which the parties to hostilities are not convinced that further political advantages cannot be gained by the use of force, it may be necessary, in order to achieve a cease-fire, to explore the possible basis of a political settlement.

Another problem, which also frequently occurs, is whether the subsidiary organ charged with working out a political settlement should be vested with responsibilities in connection with the negotiation and maintenance of a truce. There are obvious advantages in having responsibility centered in one subsidiary organ, and, indeed, some confusion has arisen at various times over the respective roles of the subsidiary organs operating in Indonesia and Palestine. Although there may be advantages in vesting responsibility for negotiations on all aspects of a problem in one subsidiary organ, there would seem to be definite disadvantages in making a subsidiary organ whose primary purpose is the negotiation of a political settlement responsible for supervising or enforcing any cease-fire agreements that may be reached.

This problem evidently did not arise in connection with the handling of the Indonesian question. It did, however, in Palestine. It was the experience of the acting mediator: "that having held discussions with the parties, and having created a situation in which we thought we could make progress toward settlement, some problem of truce violation would arise at an inopportune moment and would create a situation in which we would have to divert our attention from mediation to truce enforcement."[48] He therefore recommended that the Palestine Conciliation Commission should concentrate on the problem of peaceful settlement, leaving to the Truce Supervision Organization responsibility for the maintenance of the truce agreements. This division of functions was accepted by the Council.

[48] Ibid., No. 36, 434th Meeting (Aug. 4, 1949), pp. 27-28.

Results of United Nations Efforts

In considering the success or failure of the efforts made by the United Nations in the mediation and conciliation of disputes, it is necessary to bear in mind that such efforts cannot be judged solely on the basis of whether a settlement has actually been reached. A settlement may be reached for reasons extraneous to the effort made by the United Nations. Moreover, it is not the primary purpose of the United Nations to settle disputes *per se* but to maintain international peace and security. It would, for example, be difficult to maintain that the failure of the United Nations to bring about a settlement of the question of the treatment of Indians in South Africa has been a failure to maintain peace and security, and in any case one may legitimately question whether this matter was suitable for action by the United Nations.

The contribution of the United Nations to a settlement of the Balkan question was not of major significance. Through discussion and investigations, the United Nations did focus attention on the situation and established and publicized the facts. The recommendations of the Assembly for a political settlement, however, were of no effect and the conciliation efforts made during the 1948 and 1949 sessions of the Assembly were unsuccessful. The Special Committee of the Assembly was unable in the discharge of its function of "good offices" to achieve a settlement, although its continued observation in the area may have been of some importance. This case does, however, represent an example of a situation in which the dangers of an open conflict have been lessened although no "settlement" between the parties has been reached. The threat to Greece was removed by the success of the Greek forces, with United States aid, in bringing an end to the civil war and by the defection of Yugoslavia from the Soviet bloc. Friendly relations have been established between Greece and Yugoslavia, and there is even some indication that by direct negotiations some of the problems existing between Greece on the one hand and Albania and Bulgaria on the other may be solved.

The Palestine question and the dispute over Kashmir remain unresolved, but the United Nations can point with satisfaction to the contribution it has made to alleviating the dangers inherent in these two disputes.

A cease-fire has been effected and maintained in Kashmir, and the area of disagreement has been reduced. But it seems unlikely that the original program endorsed by the Council for a plebiscite under United Nations supervision will ever be carried out, or that a satisfactory settlement along other lines is imminent. The Council and its agents have been unable to obtain an agreement between the parties, and efforts of individual Members and of the Conference of Commonwealth Prime Ministers have also been unsuccessful. It is unlikely, however, that any settlement by resort to force will be attempted or, if attempted, will succeed, for although neither the Council nor individual Member states have been willing to bring substantial pressure to bear on the parties, either or both would be quite likely to do so if the situation were to deteriorate to the point at which a breach of the peace seemed imminent.

The initial efforts to bring about a peaceful solution of the Palestine question were unsuccessful. The plan originally endorsed by the Assembly was not implemented, but through the machinery of the United Nations, the parties reached agreement for the cessation of military operations. Thus an open conflict was converted to a shaky armistice. When the armistice agreements were signed, it was hoped that they would be a step toward the conclusion of a settlement of the outstanding issues in the dispute between Israel and the Arab states. The efforts of the Assembly and the Palestine Conciliation Commission to obtain a settlement have been so fruitless that probably no further effort will be made until there are definite indications of changes in the attitudes of the parties. It is, of course, always possible that certain minor issues will be resolved either directly or through the agencies of the United Nations. The United Nations is likely to continue through the provision of machinery and funds to do what it can to alleviate the plight of the refugees. But as on other issues, any real settlement is dependent on the parties themselves.

There is only one case, the Indonesian question, in which the effort made by the United Nations can be considered an unqualified success. The role of the Security Council, and especially of its subsidiary organs, was unquestionably of great significance, for although a settlement might have been reached even without intervention by the Council, the action of the Council decreased the bloodshed and increased the speed with which an independent Indonesia was established. It must also be recognized that certain Members, for example, the United States, India, and Australia, by independent action in support of resolutions of the Council, made an important contribution to the success of the United Nations in this case. It seems clear, however, that discussion in the Council and the action taken by that organ influenced not only the parties concerned but also the action of other states in the course of their relations with the parties.

The procedures of mediation and conciliation by their very nature are subject to important limitations. They cannot be successful, or even be undertaken, without the co-operation of the parties. One of the greatest difficulties confronting the United Nations is that of getting the parties to accept its efforts, let alone its suggestions for a settlement, especially as both parties are seldom equally anxious to reach an agreed settlement. In this connection, it should be noted that the success the United Nations has had has been based in large measure on the fact that the parties are willing to accept the procedures of mediation and conciliation in order to avoid more drastic action by the United Nations and by the Members themselves. It would seem that any attempt by the United Nations to bring about a settlement through mediation and conciliation is most likely to be successful if it has the strong backing of the United Nations, and if Members both through the United Nations machinery and their own independent initiatives are willing to give their support to the efforts of the Organization.

CHAPTER XIII
Arbitration and Judicial Settlement

THE Charter of the United Nations explicitly includes arbitration and judicial settlement among the means of peaceful settlement that Members are encouraged to use in seeking a solution of their international disputes.[1] The Security Council in recommending to the parties procedures for peaceful settlement is expected to take into account the procedures that the parties have already agreed to use.[2] More particularly, the Charter states for the special guidance of the Security Council, "that legal disputes should as a general rule be referred by the parties to the International Court of Justice."[3] The International Court of Justice is declared to be "the principal judicial organ of the United Nations" and its Statute is "an integral part" of the Charter.[4] The provisions of the Charter and the experience of the United Nations with the use of the procedures of arbitration and judicial settlement must be viewed, however, against the historical background of the developing use of these procedures during the past century.

Role in Peaceful Settlement

During the nineteenth and the early part of the twentieth centuries down to the First World War, arbitration was used with increasing frequency in the settlement of international disputes. In the practice of this period, arbitration was a method by which the parties to a dispute agreed to submit their differences to a third party, or to a tribunal especially constituted for the purpose, for decision on the basis of such rules as the parties might specify, usually the principles of international law and justice. It was understood that the decision would be accepted by the parties as a final settlement of the controversy. Arbitration was widely accepted as a

[1] Art. 33.
[2] Art. 36(2).
[3] Art. 36(3).
[4] Art. 92.

suitable method for the settlement of disputes resulting from conflicting legal claims, such as disputes over boundaries, fishing rights,
and injuries to foreign nationals or their property. Disputes resulting
from claims based wholly or in part on non-legal grounds were generally not considered suitable for arbitration and efforts to induce
states to submit such differences to arbitration were usually without
success.

To facilitate and encourage the use of arbitration, states entered
into bilateral or multilateral treaties, by which they agreed to submit to arbitration disputes of a defined character, usually of a legal
nature, subject to specific reservations on categories of disputes excluded from the treaty obligation. Furthermore, at the Hague Conferences of 1899 and 1907, broad agreement was reached concerning
the method of constituting arbitral tribunals and the procedures
to be followed in the hearing and deciding of cases.

Widespread recognition of certain serious deficiencies in arbitration as a procedure for the peaceful settlement of disputes led to a
movement for the establishment of a permanent international court
with jurisdiction and procedures similar to those of national courts.
At the two Hague Conferences, serious efforts were made to establish
such a permanent tribunal. At the 1907 Conference, considerable
progress was made in the drafting of the constitution of such a court,
but the participants were unable to agree on the method of constituting it. The method of judicial settlement, that is the submission of
international disputes to a permanent tribunal for decision on the
basis of international law and justice, continued to be strongly advocated, especially in the United States, down to the outbreak of
the First World War. The United States Government had in fact
taken a leading role at the Hague Conferences in favoring the establishment of a world court.

The establishment of the League of Nations marked an important
advance in the development of the role of arbitration and judicial
settlement in the adjustment of international disputes. With the
establishment of the Permanent Court of International Justice under
the provisions of Article 14 of the Covenant, and the subsequent
amendment of Articles 12 and 13 of the Covenant to provide for
judicial settlement by the Court, Members of the League were
bound to submit "to arbitration or judicial settlement" all disputes
that they recognized "to be suitable for submission" and that they
had not been able to settle by diplomacy. Furthermore, Members

recognized as "generally suitable for submission to arbitration or judicial settlement" disputes "as to the interpretation of a treaty, as to any question of international law, as to the existence of any fact which, if established, would constitute a breach of any international obligation, or as to the extent and nature of the reparation to be made for any such breach."[5] Subject to the conditions set forth in their declarations, those states that accepted the compulsory jurisdiction of the Court by adherence to the optional clause under Article 36 of the Statute of the Court relinquished the right to determine for themselves whether disputes fell within these categories. They thereby agreed to accept the decision of the Court whether it had jurisdiction over a dispute that one party alone might submit to it. Although the Permanent Court was not technically an organ of the League of Nations, and there was no complete identity of membership, membership in the two bodies was substantially the same. By March 1938, forty states, including the greater part of the Members of the League, had accepted the compulsory jurisdiction of the Court.

During the period of the active existence of the League, a great deal of attention and energy was devoted by governments to the development of procedures especially suitable for the settlement of legal disputes. In addition, efforts were made, but without notable success, to extend the use of arbitration to disputes not strictly legal in nature.[6] The organs of the League, especially the Assembly, took an active part in this development. The Geneva Protocol of 1924 was an ambitious but unsuccessful attempt to obtain wider acceptance of the compulsory jurisdiction of the Court and to extend the use of arbitration in the settlement of all international disputes. The General Act of 1928 was another attempt, largely unsuccessful, to extend the use of arbitration in the settlement of all disputes whatever their nature.

Progress in the development of a network of treaty obligations providing for arbitration and judicial settlement was not accompanied, however, by a corresponding advance in their actual use. As a matter of fact, although no satisfactory method is available for comparing the practice before and after the First World War,

---

[5] Art. 13 of the Covenant.
[6] For texts and analysis of treaties concluded down to 1931 providing for the use of arbitration and judicial settlement, see Max Habicht, *Post-War Treaties for the Pacific Settlement of International Disputes* (1931).
for the Pacific Settlement of International Disputes (1931).

there is reason to believe that if the cases of arbitration and resort to the Court are taken together, and account is taken of the great increase in international disputes after the First World War because of the dislocations and uncertainties resulting from it, there was no marked increase, if indeed there was any, in the use of these procedures during the interwar period as against the preceding decades. The important development was the frequent substitution of resort to the Permanent Court for the more cumbersome procedure of arbitration. A large number of cases that earlier would undoubtedly have been submitted to arbitration were instead submitted to the Court, and the submission of disputes to arbitration, with the possible exception of private claims, markedly decreased. In addition, a number of legal questions arising in connection with disputes brought to the Council of the League were referred to the Court for advisory opinions, with the Council and the parties reserving the right to attach such weight to the opinions as they might choose. These opinions were generally accepted, however, and, consequently, the scope of the contribution of the Court to the settlement of disputes was correspondingly increased. During the period 1920 to 1942, the Court handed down 37 judgments and 27 advisory opinions, but many of the latter were on questions not connected with actual disputes.

Generally speaking, states, especially the more powerful ones, were unwilling to submit to arbitration or judicial settlement their more serious differences. No attempt was made to use the Court to resolve differences that led to armed conflicts or unilateral uses of force such as the bombardment of Corfu in 1923, the Japanese military occupation of Manchuria in 1931, the Chaco War between Bolivia and Paraguay, and the war between Italy and Ethiopia in 1935-36. Nor was the structure of international commitments covering the use of procedures of arbitration and judicial settlement effective in preventing the Second World War. Consequently, in the plans that were made during the war for establishing a new international organization to maintain peace and security, there was a reaction against placing as much emphasis on the use of these methods for the settlement of disputes as had been placed on them in previous decades. Little attention was given in the Dumbarton Oaks Proposals to the role of law and the judicial process in the settlement of disputes. Although it was agreed in principle that there should be an international court, the exact character of the court, its competence and jurisdiction, were left to be decided at a later time.

In the final drafting and negotiation of the Charter at the San Francisco Conference, international law was viewed with less confidence than formerly as offering a satisfactory guide for the settlement of international disputes. Rather the emphasis was on the incomplete and ill defined nature of international law and the need for its further development and codification. Arbitration was mentioned only once in the Charter, and then as only one of the means of their own choice by which parties should seek to settle disputes. The International Court of Justice was made a principal organ of the United Nations and its Statute an integral part of the Charter, but the method of choosing judges and their qualifications remained the same as under the Statute of the Permanent Court, and the contentious jurisdiction of the International Court remained optional except for states accepting compulsory jurisdiction by special declaration. From the discussions at San Francisco, as well as the explicit provisions of the Charter, it seemed that the International Court was not intended to have a role of greater importance than the Permanent Court had enjoyed. Indeed, it would appear that certain of the major states envisaged for it a role of less importance.

Since the Second World War, acceptance of the principle and use of the procedures of arbitration have been less frequent than during the interwar period, when—in contrast to the decades preceding the First World War—there had already been a relative decline in its use, even though states had continued to be willing to enter into treaties embodying the principle. Nor has judicial settlement enjoyed the prestige since the Second World War that it did in the interwar period, although it has received more attention than arbitration as a procedure of peaceful settlement and has been used in a considerable number of cases.

There are many considerations that help to explain these trends. First, the emphasis in postwar international relations on the organizing and adjusting of political and economic relations after the violent dislocations of the Second World War has served to focus attention on methods other than arbitration and judicial settlement for the settlement or adjustment of differences. Second, the cold war, by reducing relations between two important groups of nations to essentially a power struggle with all differences assuming political importance and with few generally accepted rules of conduct, has made arbitration and judicial settlement unacceptable procedures for the settlement of differences between members of the two opposing blocs. Then, too, many of the issues that have arisen between the more advanced Western powers and the underdeveloped countries, some of which have only recently acquired their independence, have not been of such a nature as to lend themselves to settlement by procedures involving the application of rules of law and generally accepted principles of justice. Before and even to some extent after the First World War, disputes between the more powerful of the economically advanced nations and the backward countries over the treatment by the latter of the nationals of the former were submitted to arbitration and decided on the basis of principles, which if not imposed by, were at least highly acceptable to, the more powerful nations. Since the Second World War, however, the underdeveloped countries, partly because of their strategic importance in the cold war, have been more successful in maintaining their right to determine the treatment to be accorded to foreign nationals and the property of such nationals, and have resisted attempts through international law and legal procedures to curb their efforts, often by confiscatory policies, to carry out programs of economic and social reform.

The fact that arbitration has experienced a relatively greater decline than judicial settlement is to be explained largely in terms of the advantages of using the International Court of Justice in those cases where a settlement is desired on the basis of law and justice. The considerations that during the interwar period resulted in the use of the Permanent Court in preference to specially constituted arbitral tribunals have continued to be operative. Only in very special circumstances has arbitration seemed a preferable procedure. For example, the Members of the Soviet bloc and the Western powers did agree in the peace treaties concluded with Italy, Bulgaria, Hungary, and Rumania to the use of arbitration for the settlement of certain differences, but in the one instance in which these provisions have been invoked before organs of the United Nations—the alleged violations of human rights by Bulgaria, Hungary, and Rumania—the Communist states refused to arbitrate.

Arbitration under the Charter

The Charter does not place Members under any specific obligation to use arbitration. By implication it recognizes the validity of
special agreements between Members calling for the use of arbitration in the settling of disputes between them by requiring them
"first of all" to seek the peaceful settlement of their disputes by
methods of their own choice. This applies to those agreements to
use arbitration that were concluded before the Charter entered into
force as well as to those concluded subsequently, and the Security
Council in recommending "appropriate" procedures to the parties
to a dispute under Article 36 is supposed to take account of these
agreements.

Some efforts have been made by the organs of the United Nations
to encourage the use of arbitration by Member states. The General
Assembly gave its support to arbitration as a procedure for settling
all disputes, when, during its third session, on the basis of a recommendation of its Interim Committee, it adopted and submitted to
Members a proposal for restoring to its original efficacy the General Act of September 26, 1928.[7] The United Nations has also made
an effort to bring about improvements in the procedures for
arbitration. The International Law Commission has drawn up a
"Draft on Arbitral Procedure," which sought on the one hand to
codify existing practices and on the other hand to introduce new
methods for resolving some of the difficulties that have arisen in
connection with the use of arbitration.[8] It was submitted to the
Assembly, which, in turn, transmitted it to the Members for their
comments.[9]

The International Court of Justice performed useful functions in
connection with the arbitration of several disputes. For example,
at the request of France, the United States, and the United Kingdom, the President of the International Court designated an emi-
nent and impartial jurist to give an "arbitral advice" on the claims
of Albania and Italy to a certain quantity of gold that had been re-

[7] Res. 268 (III), Apr. 28, 1949. During the decade 1928-38 over twenty states had
adhered to all or part of the provisions of the General Act, subject to stated reservations or conditions.

[8] U.N. General Assembly, Eighth Session, *Official Records,* Supplement No. 9,
pp. 9 ff.

[9] Res. 797 (VIII), Dec. 7, 1953.

moved from Italy by Germany during the war. In deciding disputes over the interpretation of treaties, the Court has also had some influence on the submission of disputes to arbitration. In its judgment of May 19, 1953, the Court held that the United Kingdom was under an obligation to submit to arbitration the differences with Greece on the validity of the Ambatielos claim.[10] Furthermore, the "Draft on Arbitral Procedure" contained provisions authorizing the International Court to perform important functions in connection with the interpretation of the obligation to arbitrate, the constituting of the arbitral tribunal, and the revision or amending of the award.

In dealing with specific disputes, both the General Assembly and the Security Council have on occasion recommended the use of arbitration. In some cases, the recommendation has been based on a previous undertaking of the parties; in others it has been advanced on its merits. The original resolution adopted by the Council on August 1, 1947, in the Indonesian case, for example, called upon the parties to cease hostilities and settle their disputes "by arbitration or by other peaceful means."[11] In this case the parties to the dispute—the Netherlands and the Republic of Indonesia— had agreed some months previously under the terms of the Linggadjati Agreement to submit to arbitration any differences that might arise regarding the interpretation and application of the Agreement. The resolution initially submitted by Australia provided that the Security Council would call on the parties to settle their dispute in accordance with this Agreement. However, while the Republic of Indonesia supported the submission of the dispute to arbitration, the Netherlands did not consider this course of action acceptable. As the Council did not have the power to impose a particular procedure on the parties, it rejected proposals to establish a commission of arbitration in favor of a committee of good offices. At later stages in the consideration of the question, when suggestions were made for enlarging the powers of this committee, similar arguments were raised regarding the appropriateness of the procedure and its acceptability to the parties concerned.

When, during its third session, the General Assembly considered the matter of the observance of human rights and fundamental freedoms in Bulgaria and Hungary, it concluded that the appropriate method for seeking a satisfactory solution was through the

---

[10] *I.C.J. Reports 1953*, p. 23.
[11] U.N. Security Council, Second Year, *Official Records*, No. 68, 173rd Meeting, (Aug. 1, 1947), p. 1703.

procedures laid down in the peace treaties with those states. As previously noted, sections of these treaties concerned respect for human rights and fundamental freedoms and also provided for settling disputes regarding their interpretation through the appointment of commissions. In its first resolution on this question, the Assembly merely noted "with satisfaction" the steps taken by some of the signatories, expressed the hope that measures would be "diligently" applied in accordance with the treaties to ensure respect for human rights and fundamental freedoms, and drew the attention of Bulgaria and Hungary to their obligations under the treaties.[12] At its fourth session, the Assembly voted to deal with an Australian complaint against Rumania and the other complaints against Bulgaria and Hungary as one item. The Assembly noted the reports by several signatories that Bulgaria and Hungary had rejected the charges brought against them, had refused to appoint representatives to the commissions, and had denied that they were under any obligation to do so.[13] The Assembly also requested an advisory opinion from the Court on the interpretation of those provisions of the peace treaties that pertained to the appointment of the commissions.[14] Bulgaria, Hungary, and Rumania refused to modify their position, despite the advisory opinion of the Court that they were under obligation to appoint representatives. As the Court also expressed the opinion that the commissions could not be legally constituted without the participation of these countries, the Assembly abandoned its efforts to obtain a settlement.

In the course of considering the India-Pakistan question, the Security Council and its subsidiary organ, the United Nations Commission, had occasion to recommend the use of arbitration, and this particular experience also throws considerable light on the conditions under which a recommendation of arbitration is not likely to be acceptable to the parties as a means of settlement. In this case, there was agreement that a plebiscite should be used to decide the central issue whether Jammu and Kashmir should accede to India or Pakistan. The subsequent efforts made by the Council and its commission to work out a detailed plan for a plebiscite that would be acceptable to the parties were, however, unsuccessful.

The major point of disagreement concerned the demilitarization of the area prior to the holding of the plebiscite. Because of re-

[12] Res. 272 (III), Apr. 30, 1949.
[13] See Res. 294 (IV), Oct. 22, 1949.
[14] For the questions put to the Court, see above, Chap. VII, p. 159.

peated deadlocks on this issue, and in order to avoid the necessity of returning to the Council for the settlement of differences that continued to exist, the suggestion was made that the differences with respect to the demilitarization of the area should be submitted to arbitration. Both parties viewed the terms of demilitarization as of vital importance because of their possible influence on the results of the plebiscite. Full agreement on the principles that were to govern demilitarization was lacking. The arbitral body would have had to decide on the basis of what it considered fair and equitable, with an inevitable inclination to give something to both sides.

As the Indian forces were in military occupation of the greater part of the territory in dispute, the bargaining position of India was considerably stronger than that of Pakistan, and Pakistan stood to gain more from submission of the issues in dispute to arbitration. When the United Nations Commission, and later the Security Council, proposed that the parties submit to arbitration outstanding points of difference,[15] Pakistan accepted, but India refused. Subsequently, however, the United Nations representative was able to obtain the acceptance by India as well as Pakistan of a proposal that any differences regarding the implementation of a program of demilitarization would be referred to the United Nations representative "whose decisions would be final."[16] But, no agreement was reached on the program itself.

In regard to disputes that might arise over the boundaries of the former Italian colonies, the resolution of the Assembly concerning procedures for settlement recommended the submission of such disputes to arbitration if the parties failed to reach an agreement by direct negotiation or by a procedure of mediation.[17]

It has been suggested that the principal organs of the United Nations might arbitrate a dispute at the request of the parties themselves. During the discussions in the Interim Committee of the General Assembly, Belgium suggested that the parties to a dispute might authorize the Security Council to arbitrate or might undertake in advance to abide by an advisory opinion requested by the Council from the International Court of Justice. Attention was drawn to the authorization of the Council under Article 38 of the Charter to make

[15] U.N. Security Council, Fourth Year, *Official Records*, Special Supplement No. 7, and Resolution of the Security Council S/2017/Rev. 1 (Mar. 21, 1951).

[16] U.N. Doc. S/2448 (Dec. 19, 1951).

[17] Res. 392 (V), Dec. 15, 1950.

recommendations at the request of the parties and also to the freedom of the parties under Article 33 to seek a settlement by peaceful means of their own choice.[18] The acceptance by the Security Council of special responsibilities with respect to Trieste under the terms of the Italian peace treaty suggests that such use of the Security Council would be fully consistent with the Charter.

Use of the International Court

The International Court of Justice is "the principal judicial organ of the United Nations" and, as such, is the chosen instrument for judicial settlement.[19] Only states can be parties in cases before the Court, and, consequently, only disputes between states can be submitted directly to the Court for decision.[20] Other questions can come before the Court only through the use of the advisory opinion procedure.

Extent of Jurisdiction

All Members of the United Nations are *ipso facto* parties to the Statute of the International Court.[21] A state not a Member of the Organization can become a party to the Statute on conditions determined by the General Assembly on the recommendation of the Security Council. In 1946, during the second part of its first session, the General Assembly, on recommendation of the Council, adopted a resolution defining the conditions under which Switzerland, not a Member of the United Nations, might become a party. These conditions were as follows:

(a) Acceptance of the provisions of the Statute of the International Court of Justice;
(b) Acceptance of all the obligations of a Member of the United Nations under Article 94 of the Charter;
(c) An undertaking to contribute to the expenses of the Court such

[18] See U.N. General Assembly, Third Session, *Official Records,* Supplement No. 10, p. 29.
[19] For detailed discussion of the organization, competence, and procedures of the Court see the volume in this Brookings series, *The Organization and Procedures of the United Nations.*
[20] Art. 34 of the Statute of the International Court of Justice.
[21] Art. 93 of the Charter.

equitable amount as the General Assembly shall assess from time to time after consultation with the Swiss Government.[22]

In addition to Switzerland, Liechtenstein, Japan, and San Marino have become parties to the Statute under these same conditions.[23]

The Court is open to all states parties to the Statute on the terms laid down in the Charter, the Statute, and the Rules of the Court. The conditions under which the Court is open to other states, subject to the special provisions of treaties in force, are laid down by the Security Council, but Article 35 of the Statute specifies that "in no case shall such conditions place the parties in a position of inequality before the Court." By resolution adopted on October 15, 1946, the Council defined these conditions as follows: Each such state must deposit with the Registrar of the Court a declaration by which it accepts the jurisdiction of the Court, undertakes to comply with its decisions, and "accepts all the obligations of a Member under Article 94 of the Charter." The declaration of acceptance may be particular or general.

In accordance with these provisions and the provisions of the Treaty of Peace with Japan, a number of states not parties to the Statute—Ceylon, Cambodia, Laos, and Viet Nam—filed declarations accepting the jurisdiction of the Court over disputes that might arise in relation to the interpretation or execution of the treaty.[24] Finland has filed declarations accepting the jurisdiction of the Court over disputes relating to the interpretation of agreements with Sweden, Norway, and Denmark. Italy filed a specific declaration accepting the jurisdiction of the Court in connection with the Monetary Gold case as did Albania with respect to the Corfu Channel dispute with the United Kingdom.[25]

The Charter emphasizes to a greater extent than did the Covenant the special appropriateness of the use of the Court in the settlement of legal differences. Nevertheless, it does not impose on Members the obligation to submit any disputes to the Court, even legal disputes. Articles 36(3) of the Charter does, however, provide that the Security Council in making recommendations "should also take into consideration that legal disputes should, as a general rule,

---

[22] Res. 91 (I), Dec 11, 1946.

[23] Instruments accepting these conditions were deposited as follows: Switzerland, July 28, 1948; Liechtenstein, Mar. 29, 1950; San Marino, Feb. 18, 1954; and Japan, Apr. 2, 1954.

[24] International Court of Justice, *Yearbook 1953-54*, pp. 36-37.

[25] *Ibid.*, p. 37.

be referred by the parties to the International Court of Justice." Under the terms of Article 36(2) of the Statute of the Court, states parties thereto may at any time declare that:

> . . . they recognize as compulsory *ipso facto* and without special agreement, in relation to any other state accepting the same obligation, the jurisdiction of the Court in all legal disputes concerning:
> a. the interpretation of a treaty;
> b. any question of international law;
> c. the existence of any fact which, if established, would constitute a breach of an international obligation;
> d. the nature or extent of the reparation to be made for the breach of an international obligation.

Furthermore, it is provided that declarations made under Article 36 of the Statute of the Permanent Court of International Justice still in force at the time the United Nations Charter entered into effect shall be deemed, as between parties to the new Statute, acceptance of the compulsory jurisdiction of the Court. Under the resolution of the Security Council of October 15, 1946, a state not a party to the Statute may in its general declaration of acceptance of the conditions of access to the Court, accept the compulsory jurisdiction of the Court subject to certain conditions. At the end of 1953, thirty-two states, including two states not Members of the United Nations but parties to the Statute, had accepted the compulsory jurisdiction of the Court under Article 36.[26]

These acceptances, however, have been subject to various conditions, some of which have gone far to deny the very result that compulsory jurisdiction is intended to achieve. For instance, the declaration by the United States of its acceptance of compulsory jurisdiction, deposited with the Court on August 26, 1946, excluded "disputes with regard to matters which are essentially within the domestic jurisdiction of the United States of America as determined by the United States of America."[27] Similar conditions have been attached by France, Mexico, and Pakistan, but for the most part the conditions attached to acceptance have gone little beyond reaffirming or clarifying the provisions of the Statute and the Charter. Members of the Commonwealth of Nations, for example, have excluded matters of domestic jurisdiction according to international law—a result already achieved in the opinion of most jurists by

[26] *Ibid.*, pp. 213-24.
[27] *United Nations Treaty Series,* Vol. 1 (1946-47), pp. 9-13.

Article 2(7) of the Charter—without, however, denying to the Court the power to decide whether a particular matter comes within the sphere of domestic jurisdiction. Reciprocity is generally made a condition of acceptance, and acceptance is commonly made operative for a term of years, with the possibility of renewal.

Special categories of disputes other than those arising from matters within domestic jurisdiction are sometimes excluded from compulsory jurisdiction, and the acceptance of compulsory jurisdiction in some cases is limited to future disputes or disputes arising with regard to situations or facts subsequent to the date of acceptance of the optional clause. The members of the Commonwealth exclude disputes among themselves, and the Guatemalan declaration of February 27, 1947, not renewed five years later, contained a specific reservation concerning its dispute with the United Kingdom over the territory of Belize.[28]

In a resolution adopted on November 14, 1947, during its second session, the General Assembly drew the attention of states that had not accepted the compulsory jurisdiction of the Court by declaration under Article 36 of the Statute "to the desirability of the greatest possible number of States accepting this jurisdiction with as few reservations as possible."[29] In addition to declarations under Article 36 of the Statute of the Court, however, states may by agreement among themselves accept the compulsory jurisdiction of the Court in specified categories of disputes and under defined conditions. Such agreements may be bilateral or multilateral in character. All of the bilateral economic co-operation agreements entered into by the United States, for example, contain a clause whereby the parties agree to submit to the Court private claims that might arise from governmental measures taken after the date of the signing of the agreements. In fact, it is common practice for a treaty to include a specific provision that any dispute regarding its interpretation or application will be referred to the Court. Such provisions are to be found in the Japanese Peace Treaty, in numerous conventions concluded under the auspices of the United Nations, and in a number of bilateral treaties such as the Treaty of Friendship, Commerce, and Navigation between the United States and Italy

---

[28] For a summary of the reservations attached to the declarations accepting the jurisdiction of the Court, see International Court of Justice, *Yearbook, 1952-53*, pp. 171 ff.

[29] Res. 171 (II), Nov. 14, 1947.

and the treaty between the United Kingdom and Burma recognizing Burmese independence.[30]

Except in those cases in which states have agreed in advance to accept the jurisdiction of the Court, Members of the United Nations are under no obligation to accept such jurisdiction over a particular dispute without specific consent being registered. This consent may be expressed by the conclusion and submission of a special agreement under which the parties to the dispute agree to submit it to the Court for final decision in accordance with the Statute and Rules of the Court. Consent can also be expressed by separate communications in which the parties inform the Court of their willingness to accept its jurisdiction, as was done in the Corfu Channel case. The British Government argued in this case that the Security Council could, by recommending the reference of a dispute to the Court under certain circumstances, give the Court jurisdiction, but there is no support for this view either in decisions of the Court or in the language of the Charter. Although the Court itself found it unnecessary to pass on the British contention, seven of the judges in a separate opinion stated that they found it impossible to accept the British view.[31]

Disputes Submitted to the Court

Considering the unsettled state of world affairs since the Second World War and the number of disputes that have arisen between states, relatively little use has been made of the facilities the Court provides.[32] Down to the end of 1953, eleven disputes had been submitted to the Court. Of the seven requests for advisory opinions during this period, only one related to an actual dispute between states.[33]

Those disputes that have thus far been submitted to the Court fall in the category of legal disputes. They have arisen from conflicting claims by the parties regarding the interpretation and application of international law, whether taking the form of international agreements, international custom, or general principles of

[30] For a listing of these various instruments providing for the jurisdiction of the Court, see I. C. J. *Yearbook, 1953-54,* pp. 226-47.

[31] See Order of Dec. 17, 1948, *I.C.J. Reports 1947-1948,* pp. 31-32.

[32] See above, Chap. IV, for further discussion.

[33] International Court of Justice, *Yearbook, 1953-54,* pp. 54-74.

law. Furthermore, most of these disputes have been characterized by a relatively low degree of political importance. They may involve contested titles to territory, claims to jurisdiction, or responsibility for injuries done to persons or property, but the terms of their settlement have not in the majority of cases affected any vital interests of the parties. There have, however, been exceptions to this generalization. The Corfu Channel case, for example, involved security interests. The dispute between Colombia and Peru over the right of asylum raised an issue of great importance to the Latin American republics, plagued as they have been by political revolutions. In the Anglo-Iranian oil case, important economic and security interests were at stake.

Disputes between states on opposite sides of the Iron Curtain have generally not been submitted to the Court. In the one instance where such a dispute was submitted, the Corfu Channel case, Albania refused to execute the judgment of the Court on the amount of compensation due to the United Kingdom. Nor have disputes resulting from the efforts of states to achieve full independence in the management of their own affairs generally lent themselves to settlement by submission to the Court. Three cases of this type have, however, been submitted. In 1948, France submitted claims concerning the treatment of French nationals and protected persons by Egypt, but the dispute was settled before the Court began its consideration of the case. France also submitted to the Court the *Electricité de Beyrouth Companie* case, involving charges of noncompliance by Lebanon with the Franco-Lebanese Agreement of January 24, 1948. In the third case, the Anglo-Iranian Oil Company case, brought to the Court by the United Kingdom following the nationalization of British-owned oil properties by Iran, the latter contested the jurisdiction of the Court, and the Court upheld the Iranian contention.

It is significant that the bulk of the disputes that have been submitted to the Court have involved states with similar legal traditions, with common attachment to Western social and political ideals, and whose relations have been characterized by mutual respect for the independence of one another. Of the cases considered by the Court, for example, one involved the United Kingdom and Greece (the Ambatielos case); one, the United Kingdom and Norway (the fisheries case); one, the United Kingdom and France (the Minquiers and Ecrehos case); one, France and the United States (the case concerning the rights of United States nationals in Morocco); and one, Italy, France, the United Kingdom, and the United States (the case of monetary gold removed from Rome). In addition, the asylum case involved two Latin American states, Colombia and Peru, and the Nottebohm case involved a European and a Latin American state (Liechtenstein and Guatemala). In some of these instances, as in the case of the dispute between France and the United Kingdom over the title to the two Channel islands (the Minquiers and Ecrehos case), the Court has provided a convenient means of getting rid of a sticky but relatively unimportant dispute of long standing. But even states with common cultural backgrounds have not, in general, been willing to submit to the Court disputes of political importance involving in a serious way their national security or the welfare of their people.

The records of the Security Council and the General Assembly contain many statements by Member states, other than those from the Soviet bloc, extolling the virtues of judicial settlement. It is seldom, however, that this procedure is advocated for the settlement of actual disputes that the Council or the Assembly is called upon to handle. During the initial discussions on certain questions, especially those involving the alleged violations of treaties, the question has been raised whether the charges might not more properly be considered by the Court. In only one case, however, has there been a recommendation by the Council or the Assembly that a dispute be submitted by the parties to the Court, in accordance with Article 36(3) of the Charter. In dealing with the dispute between the United Kingdom and Albania over incidents in the Corfu Channel, the Council recommended that the parties immediately refer the matter to the Court in accordance with the provisions of the Statute,[34] and this was done only after the Soviet Union had vetoed a proposal that the Council itself make a finding. In two other cases where some members advocated reference by the parties of issues in dispute to the Court, the proposal failed to obtain the support necessary for adoption. Only six members voted in support of such a recommendation on the Anglo-Egyptian dispute, and less than the necessary majority voted in favor of such a course in the Assembly during consideration of the question of the treatment of Indians in the Union of South Africa.

[34] U.N. Security Council, Second Year, *Official Records*, No. 34, 127th Meeting (Apr. 9, 1947), p. 727.

Although states have not shown a willingness to submit political differences or disputes of political importance to the Court, the Charter, including the Statute, does provide a way by which legal questions that arise in connection with the consideration of political disputes, or legal aspects of disputes predominantly political in character, can receive judicial consideration. By the use of the advisory opinion procedure, either the Security Council or the General Assembly can make use of the Court in the resolution of legal questions that arise in the course of the consideration of disputes before them, a procedure frequently used by the Council of the League of Nations. Except in the case of the alleged violation by Bulgaria, Rumania, and Hungary of the provisions of the peace treaties relating to human rights and fundamental freedoms, no comparable use of this procedure has been made by the Assembly and the Council. Nor is there likely to be any change in practice so long as the parties are unwilling to submit their serious disputes to the Court. For, although opinions of the Court are in principle advisory only, once an opinion on a question has been given, that opinion is bound to have a considerable authority, and a state that chooses to disregard it will suffer a serious loss of prestige, even though enforcement may not be possible.

The Implementation of Judgments

The record of implementation of international arbitral awards and court judgments has on the whole been a good one. Quite clearly, the main difficulty in the past has been not that states have accepted arbitration or judicial settlement but failed to carry out awards and judgments, but that they have refused to submit their differences in the first place. All of the judgments of the Court except that on compensation to be paid by Albania in the Corfu Channel case have been accepted, and the states concerned have taken measures to comply with them.

A judgment of the Court may not by itself, however, bring about a final settlement of the dispute between the parties. This was illustrated in the dispute previously referred to between Colombia and Peru over the asylum granted by Colombia to the Peruvian leader, Haya de la Torre. In its judgment of November 20, 1950, the Court defined the legal relations between Colombia and Peru in regard to the matter. A request by Colombia for an interpretation of this judgment was held inadmissible by the Court because the request did not meet the conditions laid down in Article 60 of the Statute. When Peru requested Colombia to execute the judgment of the Court and surrender Haya de la Torre to its custody, Colombia denied that it was under any obligation to do so. Colombia then instituted new proceedings before the Court. The Court stated that it was clear that the parties desired the Court to make a choice among the various courses by which the asylum might be terminated. This the Court refused to do. In its judgment of June 13, 1951, the Court made the following statement on this point:

> It [the Court] is unable to give any practical advice as to the various courses which might be followed with a view to terminating the asylum, since, by doing so, it would depart from its judicial function. But it can be assumed that the Parties, now that their mutual legal relations have been made clear, will be able to find a practical and satisfactory solution by seeking guidance from those considerations of courtesy and good-neighbourliness which, in matters of asylum, have always held a prominent place in the relations between the Latin-American republics.[35]

Thus it remained for the parties themselves, with the assistance of certain members of the Organization of American States, to work out a settlement.

In only one case has a party refused to carry out a judgment by the Court. As noted earlier, the Court found in favor of a claim by the United Kingdom against Albania for compensation arising from the damage to British warships in the Corfu Channel and fixed the amount, but Albania refused to pay.[36] Consequently, the United Kingdom has attempted to recover the sum by other means, which subsequently became a central issue in the Monetary Gold case, brought to the International Court by Italy in May 1953. This case had its origin in the conflicting claims to a certain amount of monetary gold that had been removed from Rome by Germany during the Second World War. In order to resolve the issue, the United States, the United Kingdom, and France agreed to submit to arbitration the question whether the gold belonged to Italy or Albania. The arbitrator subsequently upheld the Albanian claim, but the three powers had also previously agreed that if the Albanian claim were to be upheld, the gold would be given not to

---

[35] Judgment of Dec. 15, 1949, *I.C.J. Reports 1951*, p. 83.
[36] *I.C.J. Reports 1949*, p. 250.

Albania itself but to the United Kingdom in partial satisfaction of the claims arising from the Corfu Channel case. At the same time, however, it was left open to Italy to apply to the International Court of Justice for a determination whether by reason of certain Italian claims against Albania the gold should go to Italy and whether the Italian or British claim should receive priority. It was this issue that Italy brought to the Court.[37]

In another case, the Court was confronted by the prospect that a party would refuse to carry out its judgment. In the Anglo-Iranian Oil case, the Iranian Government refused to carry out the provisional measures that the Court, acting under Article 41 of the Statute, had indicated should be taken "to preserve the respective rights" of the parties. As the Court finally decided, however, that it had no jurisdiction in the case, the Iranian Government was not required to take a position with respect to a judgment on the merits of the case.

It should be noted that these two cases, the Corfu Channel case and the Anglo-Iranian Oil Company case, came within the category of disputes that were not generally submitted to the Court. In one case, the parties were on opposite sides of the Iron Curtain, and in the other, one party was an underdeveloped state, asserting its independence of outside interference and its right to legislate with respect to the property rights of foreigners. In both cases the parties were not in agreement on the nature of the jurisdiction of the Court or on the authority of the Court, under the circumstances, to decide that jurisdiction.

Reliance in the past has been placed on good faith and self-interest to obtain respect for arbitral awards and court judgments. The Covenant gave the Council of the League of Nations the power to propose what steps should be taken to give effect to an award or judgment in the event of failure to carry it out, but no use was made of this power. The Charter of the United Nations provides that the Security Council "may, if it deems necessary, make recommendations or decide upon measures to be taken to give effect" to a judgment of the International Court of Justice.[38] In testifying as the Department of State expert before the Senate Committee

---

[37] The Court decided on June 15, 1954 that it could not adjudicate the Italian claim in the absence of Albanian consent; and that it could not adjudicate the question of priority until it was decided whether the gold belonged to Albania or to Italy.

[38] Art. 94(2).

on Foreign Relations during the hearings on ratification of the Charter, Dr. Pasvolsky interpreted this provision as follows:

Article 94 would have to be governed by the powers conferred upon the Council in other parts of the Charter; that is, the language there would have to be governed by the powers which the Security Council possesses. If the Security Council possessed powers of imposing settlements, then this paragraph would be read in terms of enforcement action. But since it does not possess those powers, I think this paragraph must be read in terms of such powers as it does possess.[39]

According to this interpretation, the Council could deal with the matter under Chapter VI of the Charter, but only if the situation developed to the point where there was a threat to or a breach of the peace could it take action under Chapter VII, and then only for the purpose of maintaining or restoring international peace and security.

Such a restricted interpretation of the powers of the Council does not appear to be required by the phraseology of the article. Nonetheless, the Council appears in substance to have adopted this view in the Anglo-Iranian Oil Company dispute. The United Kingdom had obtained an order from the Court indicating provisional measures that the Iranian Government should take.[40] When Iran refused to respect the order of the Court, the United Kingdom brought the matter of the noncompliance of Iran to the attention of the Council and invoked the competence of the Council under Article 94 of the Charter by proposing a resolution under which the Council would call upon Iran to act in conformity with the provisional measures and inform the Council of the steps it had taken.[41] The extent of the competence of the Council to take measures to enforce the order of the Court was not the primary issue. Not only was the jurisdiction of the Court in doubt but also there was disagreement whether the order under Article 41 of the Statute was a judgment within the meaning of Article 94 of the Charter. Nevertheless, the handling of the question by the Council suggested that its approach was essentially political and that it would not be inclined to deal with a clear case of failure to comply with a judgment of the Court as a strict matter of law

[39] *The Charter of the United Nations,* Hearings before the Senate Committee on Foreign Relations, 79 Cong. 1 sess., p. 286.

[40] Order of July 5, 1951, *I.C.J. Reports 1951,* pp. 89 ff.

[41] U.N. Doc. S/2358 (Sept. 29, 1951).

enforcement. Rather it would treat such a case as a dispute or situation with respect to which it would exercise its powers in accordance with the provisions of Chapters VI and VII of the Charter.

The use that has been made of arbitration and judicial settlement since the United Nations was established and the attitude of Member states toward their use do not suggest that up to now these procedures have succeeded in establishing themselves as highly important parts of the United Nations system for the maintenance of international peace and security. The decline, which began in the interwar period, in the practical importance of arbitration because of its numerous defects in comparison with judicial settlement has, if anything, been accelerated. Judicial settlement has gradually become the accepted procedure for settling legal disputes by third party decision on the basis of law and justice. But the role of judicial settlement has seemed relatively unimportant in settling disputes in the postwar world where issues with political implications are hotly debated, whether for the purpose of hammering out a political settlement or to obtain some political or psychological advantage in a continuing struggle for power. So long as deep chasms of opposing purposes and conflicting interests continue to exist, it is highly problematic whether judicial settlement can in the near future acquire the general recognition and established place in an international order of peace and security that it deserves. Nevertheless, there is reason to hope that among those Members of the United Nations enjoying common cultural backgrounds and possessing similar political and legal systems and ideas, judicial settlement will be increasingly accepted as an important procedure for settling international legal disputes and for developing a body of international law more adequate in scope and definiteness to the needs of international peace and justice.

PART FOUR

ACTION WITH RESPECT TO THREATS TO THE
PEACE, BREACHES OF THE PEACE, AND
ACTS OF AGGRESSION

CHAPTER XIV

Determination of a Threat to the Peace, Breach of the Peace, Or Act of Aggression

ARTICLE 1 of the Charter of the United Nations emphasizes two principal ways of dealing with specific disputes and situations with a view to the maintenance of international peace and security. One is that of seeking the peaceful settlement or adjustment of disputes and situations by the methods for which the Charter provides.[1] The other is that of taking collective measures of a coercive nature for the prevention and removal of threats to the peace and for the suppression of acts of aggression and other breaches of the peace.

These two ways represent different approaches, historically, to the problem of maintaining international peace. Before the establishment of the League of Nations, various methods of peaceful settlement, such as diplomacy, mediation, conciliation, and arbitration, were used in order to achieve the peaceful settlement or adjustment of international disputes and situations of a serious nature. At the same time, states entered into alliances and agreements under the terms of which they were to come to the assistance of one another in case of attack, or, in some instances, they agreed to take common action to remove a specific threat to the peace. Occasionally, the major powers concerted together to achieve the adjustment of a specific situation, putting their combined power behind a proposed solution.

Not until the establishment of the League of Nations after the First World War was an organized effort made on a large scale to combine these two approaches in such a way that methods of adjustment and collective coercion were joined together and used for the achievement of a common purpose. The League system proved, in practice, to have serious defects. The Covenant of the League did not sufficiently recognize the importance of taking effective preventive measures in advance of an actual breach of the peace. Further-

[1] The use of these methods is analyzed in Part Three of this study.

more, by placing on Members the obligation to apply sanctions against a state resorting to war, and by according to each Member the independent right of deciding when and to what extent it should apply sanctions, the Covenant failed to make adequate provision for the co-ordination of efforts of the League to achieve an acceptable settlement and the use by Members of collective measures of a coercive nature to suppress the unauthorized use of force. Although efforts were made to strengthen the League system, they met with little success, in large measure because of the lack of co-operation of the major powers.

In writing the Charter of the United Nations, a serious effort was made to remedy these defects. The importance of the full co-operation of the major powers was recognized. Not only was it considered essential to the success of the United Nations for the major wartime allies to be Members, but action by the Security Council in dealing with threats to the peace and breaches of the peace was made dependent on the agreement of those states that were considered best able to take effective measures of coercion and most inclined on the basis of interest to do so. Furthermore, the Security Council, when dealing with any alleged threat to the peace or breach of the peace, was given broad powers to do what, under the circumstances, seemed most advisable to maintain or restore international peace and security. It might concentrate on seeking a peaceful settlement or adjustment; it might first attempt, by the use of provisional measures, to prevent the further deterioration of the situation or to create conditions favorable to peaceful settlement; or it might initially use coercive measures to suppress any act of aggression, and postpone until this task had been completed its efforts to achieve a peaceful settlement. Thus the Charter emphasized (1) the essential unity of the task of dealing with disputes and situations in such a way as to preserve or restore international peace and security, and (2) the importance of enabling the responsible organs to use whatever methods in whatever order or combination seemed most likely under the circumstances to achieve the desired end.

A system of collective measures to prevent or suppress threats to or breaches of the peace must make provision for determining the occasion for such action as well as the measures to be taken. The Covenant of the League of Nations defined the occasion for the application of collective measures under Article 16 as the action of any Member in resorting to war "in disregard of its covenants under Articles 12, 13 or 15"; it was left to each Member to determine when that occurred. Under Article 10, the Members undertook to "preserve as against external aggression the territorial integrity and existing political independence" of all Members; here, also, each Member was left free to determine when the occasion for collective action had arisen.

During the period of the League of Nations, a number of efforts were made to define the occasion for the application of sanctions in a more satisfactory manner. The Geneva Protocol of 1924, for example, established the assumption that a state was the aggressor if it engaged in hostilities without submitting to the prescribed procedures of peaceful settlement or violated the provisional measures prescribed by the Council. For the most part, however, these efforts were without success.

The authors of the Charter of the United Nations sought to find another, and what they thought would be a more satisfactory solution of this problem. Under the terms of the Charter, Members undertook to "refrain in their international relations from the threat or use of force against the territorial integrity or political independence of any state, or in any other manner inconsistent with the Purposes of the United Nations."[2] The Security Council is directed to "determine the existence of any threat to the peace, breach of the peace, or act of aggression," and to decide whether measures of a coercive nature are to be taken by Members of the United Nations in order to maintain or restore international peace and security, and if so, what these measures are to be.[3] The General Assembly, however, is not prevented from sharing in this function, because the definition in the Charter of the responsibility of the Council as "primary" and not exclusive, admits the possibility that a serious dispute or situation may come before the General Assembly for discussion and preliminary consideration, and does not expressly deny the possibility of a residual responsibility being assumed if the Council is unable to function. In fact, by the "Uniting for Peace" resolution of November 3, 1950, the Assembly asserted its right to exercise a residual responsibility. The resolution provides that the Assembly shall, in case of deadlock in the Council, consider immediately any alleged threat to the peace, breach of the peace, or act of aggression and recommend collective measures deemed necessary to the restora-

[2] Art. 2(4).
[3] Art. 39.

tion of international peace and security. The clear implication is that the Assembly shall make a preliminary determination regarding whether the conditions exist for the exercise of these powers.

Significance of a Formal Determination

The determination of the existence of a threat to the peace, breach of the peace, or act of aggression is a decision of great significance because it is a condition to the exercise by the Security Council of powers of an exceptional nature under Articles 41 and 42 of the Charter. Even Article 40 is open to the interpretation that action under it must follow such a determination. In the practice of the United Nations, partly because of the failure to conclude the special agreements under Article 43, and partly because of the flexibility with which the powers of the General Assembly and the Council have been interpreted and applied, the importance of this decision has been greatly reduced. The Council has adopted measures of the kind expressly authorized by Article 40 without any previous determination under Article 39.[4] The fact that the Council has not had armed forces and facilities at its disposal has greatly weakened its authority, and, like the Assembly, it has had to rely more on its power to recommend and to exhort than on its power to order. This has tended to reduce the importance of the distinction between measures taken under Chapter VI and action under Chapter VII of the Charter.

Nevertheless the making of such a determination in the practice of the United Nations has been treated as an act of considerable significance. Even if not regarded as necessarily a prelude to enforcement action, it has been viewed as an expression of moral condemnation, which, irrespective of its material effects, is not to be treated lightly and as of no consequence. For example, the threat of the Council, expressed in its resolution of May 29, 1948, to consider the situation in Palestine with a view to action under Chapter VII of the Charter if the governments and authorities concerned did not order a cessation of hostilities was an important factor in causing the parties to agree to a cease-fire.[5] Later, the decision of the Council that a threat to the peace did exist, recorded in its resolution of

[4] See below, Chap. XV.
[5] U.N. Security Council, Third Year, *Official Records*, Supplement (May 1948), pp. 103-04.

July 15, 1948, and its announcement that failure of the parties to desist from military action would demonstrate the existence of a breach of the peace and require the consideration of further action under Chapter VII were of great influence in bringing the parties to accept a permanent cease-fire.[6] In the case of the North Korean attack on the Republic of Korea, the United States immediately requested a meeting of the Council and proposed a draft resolution declaring that the action constituted "a breach of the peace." This determination, however, even when accompanied by a call for provisional measures under Article 40, was insufficient to produce the desired result and had to be followed up immediately by military measures. But the determination was considered necessary to provide a basis under the Charter for the military assistance rendered, first by the United States and subsequently by other Members.

In the course of the consideration by the Assembly of Chinese Communist intervention in Korea, considerable attention was given to the significance of a formal determination of aggression by the Assembly. Supporters of the proposed resolution introduced by the United States,[7] which would have declared Communist China guilty of aggression, argued that such action was desirable as a moral judgment that the Organization was committed to make, that it would provide the basis for additional collective measures, and that it would have effect by itself as a restraining influence on the Peiping Government.[8] In its first report to the General Assembly, the Collective Measures Committee characterized such a determination as a collective measure of a political character, saying: "Such determination and denunciation, either by the Security Council or the General Assembly, even if not followed immediately by other collective measures, clearly constitute a strong warning signal, not only for the party or parties concerned but for all other nations."[9]

Responsibility for Making Determination

The authority and primary responsibility of the Security Council have been constantly asserted. In the discussion of the Spanish ques-

[6] *Ibid.*, Supplement (July 1948), pp. 76-77.
[7] U.N. Doc. A/C.1/654 (Jan. 20, 1951).
[8] For discussion, see U.N. General Assembly, Fifth Session, First Committee, *Official Records*, 428-38th Meetings (Jan. 20-30, 1951), pp. 517-603.
[9] U.N. General Assembly, Sixth Session, *Official Records*, Supplement No. 13, p. 5.

tion in the Council, for example, the Netherlands representative argued that any action taken should be that of the Council as it was primarily responsible. When the Greek question was before the Security Council in 1947, following the report of its Commission of Investigation, the Soviet Union argued that the responsibility of determination was solely that of the Council, that no commission could receive authority to make the finding or to bind the Council, and that the determination had to be made with respect to an actual situation. This view was generally accepted in principle.

When violence broke out in Palestine, the United States asserted that, under Article 39 of the Charter, the Council was under a mandate to determine the existence of any threat to the peace, breach of the peace, or act of aggression and that it was for the Council alone to determine whether the facts justified such a determination.[10] The question was considered whether an attempt to alter by force the plan of partition recommended by the General Assembly in its resolution of November 29, 1947 should be determined by the Council to be a "threat to the peace, breach of the peace, or act of aggression," as the Assembly had requested. The Palestine Commission reported to the Council that the implementation of the recommendations of the Assembly was possible only if the Council took measures, including the use of force if necessary, to maintain order and security in the area. The representative of the United States argued that the Council did not have sufficient evidence before it to justify a determination that a threat to the peace existed. He further contended that it had no authority under the Charter to enforce a political settlement. It would seem, however, that the Council clearly had the authority to prevent the use of force to obstruct the carrying out of the settlement. The Council did not make the finding that the Assembly requested and asserted its right to make its own independent determination.

The primary responsibility of the Council for making the determination under Article 39 was fully recognized following the North Korean attack on the Republic of Korea on June 25, 1950. There is reason to believe that had it not been for the special circumstances that permitted the Council to take a decision, the Assembly would have been requested by the United States to consider the matter.

In the early years of activity of the United Nations, there was no

[10] U.N. Security Council, Third Year, *Official Records*, Nos. 16-35, 360th Meeting (Mar. 2, 1948), pp. 400-01.

consideration given to the possibility of a formal determination by the Assembly. In the case of the Greek frontier incidents, after it became clear that the Council, following the report of its Commission of Investigation, would not be able to adopt any resolution because of Soviet opposition, the United States requested action under Chapter VII. It argued that a clear case could then be presented to the Assembly, even if the veto were used by the Soviet Union. After considering the situation during its second session in 1947, the Assembly called upon the neighbors of Greece to cease assistance to the Greek guerrillas, called upon all of the parties to co-operate in settling their disputes, and set up a special committee.[11] No determination of a threat to or breach of the peace was made. The next year, however, the Assembly noted the conclusion of its Special Committee that a continuation of the current situation constituted a threat to the political independence and territorial integrity of Greece and to peace in the Balkans. It considered that the continued aid given to the guerrillas by Albania, Bulgaria, and Yugoslavia "endangers peace in the Balkans, and is inconsistent with the purposes and principles of the Charter of the United Nations."[12]

The fact of its being unlikely that the circumstances that permitted the Council to act following the North Korean attack of June 25, 1950, would be repeated led the United States to propose in the Assembly that, if the Council failed to discharge its primary responsibility in any situation of the kind mentioned in Article 39, the Assembly should consider the matter immediately with a view to making appropriate recommendations. In the course of the debate on the proposed joint resolution embodying these proposals, the United States delegate argued that Articles 10, 11, and 14 gave the Assembly the right to recommend in all matters except where the Council was acting under Article 12, and, although a recommendation by the Assembly would not have the force of a decision of the Council, the Korean incident demonstrated that a voluntary response might be more favorable than the response to an order.[13] Most Members agreed, although doubts were expressed by some regarding the consistency of this position with Article 11(2). The position of the Soviet bloc was that the Council alone could take

[11] Res. 109 (II), Oct. 21, 1947.
[12] Res. 193 (III), Nov. 27, 1948.
[13] U.N. General Assembly, Fifth Session, First Committee, *Official Records*, 354th Meeting (Oct. 9, 1950), p. 64.

coercive measures and that consequently the proposal that the Assembly might under certain conditions recommend such measures was a violation of the Charter.

The view of the majority appears to have been that, although the Assembly must refer to the Council "any question on which action is necessary" if that question is first brought before the Assembly, once the question has been referred to the Council and the Council has failed to take action, nothing in the Charter prevents the Assembly in the exercise of its powers under Article 10 from recommending measures of the kind described in Articles 41 and 42. Furthermore, it was pointed out that, according to the last sentence of Article 11(2), the Assembly must decide whether "action is necessary" before it is required to refer the matter to the Council. That decision would not be binding on the Council, but it would be in the nature of a determination similar to that which the Council is required to make under Article 39. Although the Soviet Union contested the legality of the provision of the "Uniting for Peace" resolution under which the General Assembly might make a determination that a threat to or breach of the peace existed, it has in specific cases itself proposed that the Assembly address a request for action to the Council, containing a finding that a condition existed that justified the action requested. Thus the Soviet Union supported the request of the Central People's Government of China of September 30, 1950, that the Assembly immediately recommend to the Security Council that it take effective measures to condemn flights over and bombings of Chinese territory by United States aircraft as aggressive crimes and bring about the prompt withdrawal of United States military forces from Korea, and it requested that this item be included in the agenda of the Assembly.[14] Later, when the complaint of armed invasion of Formosa by the United States was being considered, the Soviet Union introduced a resolution[15] proposing that the Assembly "request the Security Council to take the necessary steps to insure the immediate cessation of aggression against China by the United States." If this proposal had been approved by the Assembly, it would have amounted to a finding that the acts performed by the United States in connection with the "neutralization" of Formosa constituted aggression against China.

[14] U.N. Docs. A/1415 (Sept. 30, 1950); A/1416 (Sept. 30, 1950); and A/1419 (Oct. 2, 1950).
[15] U.N. Doc. A/C.1/637 (Nov. 27, 1950).

Procedure of Formal Determination

The procedure by which a formal determination is made that a threat to the peace, breach of the peace, or act of aggression exists has not differed in essence from that by which any question is considered by the Security Council or the General Assembly and a decision is taken. Neither the Council nor the Assembly has considered itself limited by the terms of submission in making its own independent judgment regarding whether in a particular dispute or situation before it, a determination is justified. The determination has taken the form of a resolution based on a draft submitted by one or more members.

As such a determination rests on a factual finding, as well as on an interpretation of Charter provisions and a weighing of political considerations, procedures for clarifying the facts have assumed special importance. Both the Council and the Assembly have established subsidiary organs to keep them informed regarding developments in disputes and situations that have been brought to their attention.[16] These subsidiary organs have been of great value in providing the parent organ with the facts needed for determining whether a particular dispute or situation has deteriorated to the point where a determination of the existence of a threat to or breach of the peace is justified, and if so, what action is required under the circumstances. The North Korean attack of June 25, 1950, emphasized the need of a special procedure for dealing with surprise situations. It was only by coincidence that the Council had the benefit of detailed reports from the United Nations Commission on Korea, since it was only in the preceding October that the Assembly had authorized the commission to employ military observers to watch and report on developments along the thirty-eighth parallel.

To meet this kind of a situation in the future, the Assembly, by the "Uniting for Peace" resolution, established the Peace Observation Commission, which could be utilized by the Council, by the Assembly, or by its Interim Committee on the invitation or with the consent of the state into whose territory it would go.[17] Its purpose would be to "observe and report on the situation in any area where there exists international tension the continuance of which is likely

---

[16] See above, Chap. VIII, for discussion of the use of fact-finding commissions.
[17] Pt. A, Sec. B(3). See App. F.

to endanger the maintenance of international peace and security."
The commission was authorized to appoint subcommittees and to
utilize the services of observers. The Secretary-General was requested
to provide the necessary staff and facilities, utilizing, when directed
by the commission, the United Nations Panel of Field Observers, for
which provision had been made the previous year.[18]

Although it still remained necessary for the Council, the Assembly,
or the Interim Committee to take the initial decision to use the
Peace Observation Commission, there was clearly an advantage in
having a body available, provided with necessary staff and facilities,
that might be used to observe and report in any critical situation
that might arise. In 1951, the commission was requested by the
Assembly to appoint a Balkan subcommission to observe and report
on "the situation in the Balkans."[19]

Discretion in Making Determination

An important question in connection with the interpretation and
application of the Charter provisions regarding enforcement action
is whether the Security Council or the General Assembly is required
by the Charter to make a determination or has the discretionary
power to postpone such determination for reasons deemed justifiable. It must of course be admitted that a measure of discretion
is always involved in the evaluation of any factual situation. When
the Charter was being written, emphasis was placed on the desirability of vesting wide discretion in the Security Council to avoid, on
the one hand, the possibility that the aggressor might turn any detailed definition to his advantage, and on the other, the danger of
premature action.[20] It was stressed by the technical committee dealing
with the matter at San Francisco, however, that "in the case of
flagrant aggression imperilling the existence of a member of the

[18] Res. 297B (IV), Nov. 22, 1949.

[19] Res. 508B (VI), Dec. 7, 1951. On June 3, 1954, Thailand made a request that
the Security Council send a mission of the Peace Observation Commission to
observe and report on the situation along the frontier between Thailand and
Indochina. Following a Soviet veto, Thailand made a similar request to the
General Assembly.

[20] U.S. Department of State, *Charter of the United Nations, Report to the
President* . . ., Publication 2349 (1945), pp. 91-92.

Organization, enforcement measures should be taken without delay, and to the full extent required by circumstances."[21]

This question received extensive consideration when the Palestine situation was before the Council. Two opposing points of view were expressed. The French representative took the position that the Council "cannot, under Article 39, refuse to note the existence of a threat to the peace when such a threat exists."[22] A similar position was taken by the United States representative who argued that "the Security Council has a duty that is laid down in Chapter VII, and which we claim it cannot evade or avoid. The facts being perfectly clear, graphically described as a condition of warfare, how can the Security Council avoid this duty prescribed by Article 39 of the Charter?"[23] On the other hand, the Belgian representative argued that the making of the determination should not be considered apart from its consequences. He said:

> The determination of the existence of a breach of the peace in accordance with Article 39 has no meaning unless it is connected with the whole series of enforcement measures provided for in Chapter VII. As soon as that finding is reached, the Council must be prepared to apply those enforcement measures, including armed force if necessary. We have no objection to that in principle, but we doubt whether the application of such measures would be possible or effective in the present state of international relations.[24]

The representative of the United Kingdom took the same position, arguing that Members should not invoke Article 39 unless they were prepared eventually to use force if necessary.

A similar discussion and divergence of views occurred when the matter of Chinese Communist intervention in Korea was before the General Assembly. Initially, the United States was willing that the Assembly explore the possibilities of peaceful settlement. Following the rejection by the Peiping Government of the so-called "Five Principles,"[25] the United States demanded prompt determination by the Assembly that Communist China was the aggressor and the

[21] U.N. Information Organizations and U.S. Library of Congress, *Documents of the United Nations Conference on International Organization*, Vol. 12 (1945), p. 507.

[22] U.N. Security Council, Third Year, *Official Records*, No. 70, 298th Meeting (May 20, 1948), p. 18.

[23] *Ibid.*, No. 69, 296th Meeting (May 19, 1948), p. 6.

[24] *Ibid.*, No. 77, 309th Meeting (May 29, 1948), p. 13.

[25] See below, Chap. XIX, pp. 500-01.

recommendation by the Assembly of additional measures. Although there was no explicit provision in the Charter that could be interpreted as requiring the General Assembly to act promptly once the act of aggression occurred, the United States delegate argued that such action was necessary if collective security under the Charter was to be a reality.[26] Other delegations argued that the registering of a moral judgment was necessary even if further measures might be postponed. On the other hand, some delegations, including those of the United Kingdom and Canada, repeated in essence the argument advanced in the Palestine case: that a formal determination should not be made unless Members were prepared to take necessary measures to support it. The Assembly finally made the determination that the Chinese Communists had committed aggression, but only after repeated efforts to achieve a cease-fire by agreement had failed and three months after the original military intervention was reported.

Meaning of Terms

In the discussions of the Security Council and the General Assembly, as well as in some of the complaints presented, the terms "threat to the peace," "breach of the peace," and "act of aggression" have been used loosely and often exaggeratedly. Nevertheless, there have been some serious and thoughtful efforts to define the meaning of these terms so as to provide useful guidance to action. However, as the decisions of the Council and the Assembly with respect to formal determinations have been decisively influenced by various considerations, it is not easy to find in the practice of these two organs any clearly defined and generally accepted view regarding the meaning of these terms.

"Threat to the Peace"

In the Spanish case, the subcommittee of the Security Council took the view that the existence of the Franco regime in Spain and its potential threat to peace did not justify a finding by the Council of an existing "threat to the peace."[27] The Polish representative took

[26] U.S. Department of State *Bulletin*, Vol. 24 (Jan. 29, 1951), p. 169.
[27] U.N. Security Council, First Year, *Official Records*, Second Series, Special Supplement (June 1946), Rev. ed., p. 10.

issue with the conclusion, arguing that "any threat to the peace is potential by nature. It may mature tomorrow, after tomorrow, or in five years. It is a question of time. If the threat to the peace is no longer potential, then we have to do with actual aggression."[28] This view was shared by the Soviet representative. The French representative, in defending the report of the subcommittee, took the position that "threat to the peace" clearly implied a state of affairs in which there was a situation of potential danger. Nevertheless, he asserted, the steps to be taken by the Council, whether under Article 39 or Article 34, might depend on whether the threat to the peace was immediate or remote.[29]

The majority of the members of the commission, appointed by the Security Council to investigate and to report on the Greek complaint of December 1946, were of the opinion that support of armed bands, formed in the territory of one state and crossing into the territory of another, or the refusal of a government, in spite of the demands of the state concerned, to take all possible measures in its own territory to deprive such bands of any aid or protection should be considered by the Council as a threat to the peace within the meaning of the Charter. All members of the Council except Poland and the Soviet Union were prepared to accept this view. A draft resolution introduced by the United States on August 12, 1947, and defeated by the negative vote of the Soviet Union, declared that assistance and support given to the guerrillas fighting against the Greek Government by Albania, Bulgaria, and Yugoslavia constituted "a threat to the peace within the meaning of Chapter VII."[30] The Assembly, by its resolution of November 27, 1948, found that the continued aid "endangers peace in the Balkans."

When the Palestine question first came before the Council, the United States representative expressed the view that armed incursions or internal disorder could constitute a threat to the peace. The United Kingdom representative argued, however, that "any threat to the peace" must be a threat to international peace and supported this view by reference to the concluding words of Article 39, "international peace and security." The United States representative took issue with the United Kingdom representative and called attention to the fact that the significant word "any" was used. The

[28] *Ibid.*, First Series, No. 2, 47th Meeting (June 18, 1946), p. 370.
[29] *Ibid.*, 44th Meeting (June 6, 1946), p. 322.
[30] U.N. Doc. S/486 (Aug. 12, 1947).

Syrian representative thought the word "any" qualified "threat," not "peace." The French representative was of the opinion that, once the regular forces of several countries crossed a frontier, it was a question of international peace being threatened or breached, although this might not be the case if the struggle were between two parts of a population or if armed bands invaded a country.[31] By its resolution of July 15, 1948, however, the Security Council determined that continued fighting between Arab and Israeli forces in Palestine "constitutes a threat to peace within the meaning of Article 39 of the Charter."

Later, in 1950, in response to the Soviet argument that the Korean conflict was solely a civil war, the United Kingdom representative argued that "a civil war in certain circumstances might well, under Article 39 of the Charter, constitute a 'threat to the peace,' or even a 'breach of the peace,' and if the Security Council so decided, there would be nothing whatever to prevent its taking any action it liked in order to put an end to the incident, even if it should involve two or more portions of the same international entity."[32]

When the Berlin situation was being discussed in the Council, the United States representative defined "threat to the peace" in the following words:

> What constitutes a "threat to the peace" as that term is used in Article 39 of the Charter? A threat to the peace is created when a State uses force or the threat of force to secure compliance with its demands. The acts of the Government of the USSR in illegally obstructing by threat of force the access of the three Western Powers to Berlin creates a threat to the peace. . . .[33]

"Breach of the Peace"

During the consideration of the Indonesian question by the Security Council, Australia suggested that, although no precedents existed for determining the meaning of "breach of the peace," it signified a situation "where hostilities are occurring, but where it is not alleged that one particular party is the aggressor or has

[31] For discussion see U.N. Security Council, Third Year, *Official Records*, Nos. 69-70, 296th and 298th Meetings (May 19-20, 1948).

[32] U.N. Security Council, Fifth Year, *Official Records*, No. 28, 486th Meeting (Aug. 11, 1950), p. 6. Some members of the Security Council appear to have taken this position in discussions on the Indonesian question in 1947 and 1948.

[33] U.N. Security Council, Third Year, *Official Records*, No. 115, 363rd Meeting (Oct. 6, 1948), p. 4.

committed an act of aggression."[34] The Soviet representative expressed the opinion that "if military operations by one country against another cannot be called a breach of international peace, then I am at a loss to know what could be called a breach of the peace."[35]

By its resolution of July 15, 1948, the Council declared that failure of the parties to comply with its cease-fire order in Palestine would "demonstrate the existence of a breach of the peace within the meaning of Article 39."[36] From the discussion leading up to the adoption of this resolution, it appeared that the majority of the Council thought a determination of a breach of the peace more serious in its implications of future action than a determination of the existence of a threat to the peace, but less serious in its implications of individual responsibility and consequences for a particular state than a finding of aggression.

Presumably the North Korean attack on the Republic of Korea was declared by the Security Council to be "a breach of the peace" instead of an act of aggression because it was not considered wise, in view of the risk of considerable delay that might be involved, to press for the more serious determination with all its special connotations. The Council never made a formal determination that the North Korean action constituted aggression, although this inference could be clearly drawn from its resolution of June 27.

"Act of Aggression"

What constitutes an act of aggression has been considered on numerous occasions by the Security Council and the General Assembly. During the consideration of the Palestine question by the Council, the United Kingdom representative called attention to the difficulty of fixing responsibility in a situation where contending forces were intermingled and there was no agreement on the actual facts. The representative of the Jewish Agency, although recognizing the difficulty of determining the aggressor, thought there was "only one criterion of aggression, and that is the criterion of initiative:

---

[34] U.N. Security Council, Second Year, *Official Records*, No. 67, 171st Meeting (July 31, 1947), p. 1623.

[35] *Ibid.*, No. 68, 173rd Meeting (Aug. 1, 1947), p. 1692.

[36] U.N. Security Council, Third Year, *Official Records*, Supplement (July 1948), pp. 76-77.

Who started the fighting?"[37] On the question whether the existence or nonexistence of the state of Israel had relevance, the representative of Israel observed: "The theory that the Charter forbids acts of aggression only against States is utterly without foundation. . . . There is no provision whatever that the attacked party must be universally recognized as a State before an armed attack upon it can be determined as an act of aggression."[38]

The North Korean attack on the Republic of Korea on June 25, 1950, as already noted, was declared to constitute "a breach of the peace," not an "act of aggression," although the attack was later referred to in discussions of the Council and the Assembly as an act of aggression. Furthermore, the Assembly, by its resolution of February 1, 1951, found that the People's Republic of China, "by giving direct aid and assistance to those who were already committing aggression in Korea and by engaging in hostilities against United Nations forces there, has itself engaged in aggression in Korea."[39]

In the discussion in the Assembly that preceded the adoption of this resolution, most Members, including many of those that were skeptical about the wisdom of a formal determination of aggression, were in agreement that the attack by Communist Chinese forces on the forces of the United Nations constituted an independent act of aggression. The claim of the Peiping Government that only individual volunteers were involved received little credence. Sir Benegal Rau of India, however, was unable to see how an unrecognized government—a "private political organization"—could be declared an aggressor.[40] He also expressed the view, shared by a number of other delegations, that the Chinese Communists may well have acted from fear for their own security and territorial integrity, and therefore in the exercise of what they, with some justification, regarded as their right of self-defense. The members of the Soviet bloc argued that the United States was the initial aggressor as the result of its "neutralization" of Formosa, its violations of Chinese territory, and its initial illegal use of armed force in Korea.

During the fifth session of the General Assembly, the Soviet Union

[37] *Ibid.*, No. 69, 296th Meeting (May 18, 1948), p. 18.
[38] *Ibid.*, No. 98, 340th Meeting (July 27, 1948), p. 29.
[39] Res. 498 (V), Feb. 1, 1951.
[40] The great majority of the Members of the United Nations recognized the National Government in Formosa as the government of China and had given neither *de facto* nor *de jure* recognition to the Peiping regime.

proposed a definition of aggression. It argued that in an international conflict the aggressor was the state first committing one of the following acts: declaring war; invading the territory of the other with armed forces; bombarding the territory of the other; deliberately attacking the ships or aircraft of the other state; landing or leading armed forces inside the boundaries of the other state without permission; or using a naval blockade.[41] It was pointed out in the course of the discussion that failure to prevent assistance being given to armed bands that were invading another country was included in a definition of aggression contained in a convention signed by the Soviet Union at London in 1933.[42] The United States representative had claimed in the course of consideration by the Council of the question of the Greek frontier incidents that invasion by organized armies was not the only means of delivering an attack against the independence of a country. "Force," he argued, "is effectively used today through devious methods of infiltration, intimidation and subterfuge."[43]

The Soviet proposal for the definition of aggression was referred to the International Law Commission, which decided to deal with the matter by inserting in Article 2 of the proposed Code of Offenses against the Peace and Security of Mankind the following definition of such an offense: "(1) Any act of aggression, including the employment by the authorities of a State of armed force against another State for any purpose other than national or collective self-defence or in pursuance of a decision or recommendation by a competent organ of the United Nations."[44] When the question of defining aggression was again considered by the Assembly in its sixth session, the Sixth Committee, to which the item was referred, had before it a number of draft resolutions and amendments including a revised Soviet resolution, which included among the acts constituting aggression "support of armed bands organized in its own territory which invade the territory of another state, or refusal on being requested by the invading State, to take in its own territory any action within its power to deny such bands any aid or

[41] U.N. Doc. A/C.1/608 (Nov. 4, 1950).

[42] For text see League of Nations, *Treaty Series*, Vol. 147, pp. 67 ff.

[43] U.N. Security Council, Second Year, *Official Records*, No. 51, 147th Meeting (June 27, 1947), p. 1120.

[44] U.N. General Assembly, Sixth Session, *Official Records*, Supplement No. 9, p. 11.

protection."[45] In the discussion that took place on these proposals, opposing views were expressed both with respect to the desirability of attempting a definition of aggression and with respect to the substance of any such definition. Some thought a definition desirable for the guidance it would give both to Members and to organs of the United Nations. They would define the term by enumerating the specific acts that constituted aggression. In answer to the argument that no such enumeration could possibly anticipate all cases, it was suggested that there should also be a general formula that would cover cases not included in the detailed enumeration and that would leave some discretion to the responsible organ in dealing with unforeseen situations. Other members argued that no attempt should be made to define aggression in advance and that full discretion should be left to the responsible organs of the United Nations.

The resolution, which the General Assembly finally adopted, postponed further discussions to the seventh session.[46] It recognized, in its preamble, the possibility and desirability of defining aggression "by reference to the elements which constitute it," and of the advantage that could result "if directives were formulated for the future guidance of such international bodies as may be called upon to determine the aggressor." These two paragraphs were adopted, however, by close votes. The Assembly in its seventh session established a special committee to make a further study of the definition of aggression and report to the ninth session.[47] This committee met in August 1953. After an extended discussion, which covered the desirability of a definition or possible definitions, the concept of indirect aggression as distinguished from direct, and the effect of adopting a definition on the functioning of United Nations organs, the committee decided not to put various proposed definitions of aggression to a vote but instead to transmit them to Members and to the Assembly.

Consequences of Determination

A determination under Article 39 of the Charter that a threat to the peace, breach of the peace, or act of aggression exists, is a

---

[45] U.N. Doc. A/C.6/1. 208.
[46] Res. 599 (VI), Jan. 31, 1952.
[47] Res. 688 (VII), Dec. 20, 1952.

necessary condition to coercive action by the Security Council of the kind described in Articles 41 and 42. Early in the history of the Council, the Australian representative said:

. . . Once it is determined that a threat to the peace exists under Article 39, the Security Council is entitled to proceed towards any measures mentioned in Articles 41 or 42 in order to prevent a breach of the peace or to maintain international peace and security.

I have mentioned these matters only in order to indicate the seriousness and solemnity of determining under Article 39 that there has been a threat to the peace. It is only in such a case that this Council can take direct executive action; it is only in such a case that we can act on behalf of all the nations. If the Security Council calls for action in such a case, the other nations are bound under the Charter to act in accordance with the directive of this body.[48]

Early in the course of the consideration by the Council of the Palestine question, the representative of the United States stated that:

A finding by the Security Council that a danger to peace exists places all Members of the United Nations, regardless of their views, under obligation to assist the Security Council in maintaining peace. If the Security Council should decide that it is necessary to use armed force to maintain international peace in connexion with Palestine, the United States would be ready to consult under the Charter with a view to such action as may be necessary to maintain international peace and security.[49]

Presumably, the statement referred to the obligation of Members to co-operate in accordance with and for the promotion of the Purposes and Principles of the Charter, and to the special duty that Article 106 places on the permanent members to take joint action in the maintenance of international peace and security, so long as the Council is unable to discharge its responsibilities under Article 42.

In the Korean conflict, the Council combined the formal determination with a call for a cessation of hostilities and withdrawal of forces, and a request to Members to render assistance to the United Nations and to refrain from aiding the North Koreans. On June 27, 1950, two days after the adoption of its first resolution, the Council noted the previous determination and the failure of the North Koreans to comply and recommended that Members furnish assistance to repel the attack.

[48] U.N. Security Council, First Year, *Official Records*, First Series, No. 2, 47th Meeting (June 18, 1946), p. 375.

[49] U.N. Security Council, Third Year, *Official Records*, Nos. 16-35, 253rd Meeting (Feb. 24, 1948), p. 267.

During the consideration by the General Assembly of the intervention in Korea by the Chinese Communists, it was stressed that a determination of aggression gave the legal and moral basis for further coercive measures by the United Nations, but that it was not essential that any specific measures be taken immediately following the finding. On the other hand, it was stated that a determination of aggression "would imply certain responsibilities and produce certain consequences." The Canadian representative said that: "no Member had any right to feel that it would be automatically discharging its duty by expressing moral condemnation. . . . The League of Nations actually had called Italy an aggressor; but the reason for the League's failure was precisely that it had expressed moral condemnation without following up that condemnation with effective measures."[50] Although the resolution of the Assembly of February 1, 1951 provided for the establishment of a committee to study and recommend additional measures, such measures were not actually recommended until May 18, 1951, two and a half months after the determination of aggression.

Considerations Governing the Making
of a Determination

A variety of considerations, legal and political, psychological and material, have influenced the Security Council or the General Assembly in making a formal determination of the existence of a threat to the peace, breach of the peace, or act of aggression. No one consideration can be regarded as decisive in all cases. It can be said, however, that the approach of both the Council and the Assembly has been an eminently practical one. Each has been concerned with the extent to which such a formal determination will contribute to the maintenance or restoration of international peace and security. Individual members have of course been influenced in determining their positions by considerations of national interest.

It has not been considered essential to the making of a determination that a formal request should have been made by a state directly concerned. Nor has such a request, with supporting data, been given more than evidential value. When the Council was consider-

[50] U.N. General Assembly, Fifth Session, First Committee, *Official Records*, 432nd Meeting (Jan. 26, 1951), Vol. 2, p. 555.

ing the report of its Commission of Investigation on the Greek Frontier Incidents, the Greek representative addressed a letter to the President of the Council in which he stated that the state of affairs originally described as one "likely to endanger the peace" was under the circumstances then prevailing "a definite and existing threat to the peace, breach of the peace or act of aggression." He continued: "If it becomes the view of the Council that to make the necessary determination there has to be a charge by one of the [parties] concerned that such a threat, breach of the peace or act of aggression exists, it is requested that this statement be accepted as such a charge."[51] The fact that the Council continued for another month to consider the matter under Chapter VI of the Charter strongly suggests that the Council was not greatly influenced by this request. Nor is there any evidence that the action of the Council, in considering the matter under Chapter VII in August, was the result of the later request by the Government of Greece (on July 31) that a determination be made under Article 39. In the Palestine case, although the Jewish agency had requested a formal determination as early as April, the Council waited until July 15 before making one. In the meantime it had tried less drastic measures that had failed of their purpose.

An important consideration always is whether the facts justify a finding that a threat to the peace, breach of the peace, or act of aggression exists. If this were accepted as the decisive consideration, and if there were agreement that the concepts employed in Article 39 were legal in nature, then it might be possible to treat the problem of determination as basically a legal one. The fact that there has been little inclination to do so, or to envisage any use of the International Court of Justice by the Council or the Assembly in the making of this determination, demonstrates that adequacy of factual basis is only one consideration entering into the making of a determination. Although the General Assembly and the Security Council have insisted on a factual situation that would justify a determination, the existence of such a situation has not necessarily meant that a determination would be made—at least promptly.

Both the Council and the Assembly in making a determination have been influenced by the desire to see a peaceful settlement of the dispute and to avoid any unnecessary difficulties in reaching that result. In the Palestine case, the Council refrained from making a

[51] U.N. Doc. S/389 (June 26, 1947).

determination under Article 39 until after efforts had failed to obtain agreement of the parties to a cease-fire and a peaceful settlement. In dealing with the Indonesian question, the Council deliberately refrained from taking formal action under Chapter VII in order to avoid the necessity of having to decide difficult questions of competence and of offending one of the parties. In the Kashmir case, by agreement of the parties, the Council, or more accurately its commission, concentrated its efforts on obtaining an agreed cease-fire and political settlement. The promptness of the action of the Council following the North Korean attack—although in this case it is significant that the Council did not make a finding of aggression—was largely due to the conviction of most members that there was no possibility of getting the North Korean regime to accept satisfactory cease-fire terms. When the matter of Chinese Communist intervention in Korea was brought before the Assembly, the Assembly concentrated its efforts for a month and a half on trying to find the basis for agreement on a cease-fire and political settlement before finding that the Central People's Government of China had engaged in aggression. An argument that had considerable influence was that once Communist China had been declared an aggressor, the chances of peaceful settlement would be greatly reduced, if not destroyed.

An extremely important practical consideration has been whether a determination that a threat to the peace, breach of the peace, or act of aggression existed would be followed by effective supporting action. Some Members have contended that a finding of aggression should be made if the facts warrant it, irrespective of the possibility of effective supporting action, in order to make the moral position of the United Nations clear and to bring to bear upon the guilty party the full moral force of the Organization. Others have argued, however, that no determination should be made unless the Members of the United Nations, and especially the major powers, are prepared and able to take effective supporting action. In the Palestine case, this was one important reason for postponing any action by the Council under Article 39. This position was clearly stated by the Canadian representative in the Council in the following words:

> I therefore submit that, before the Security Council embarks upon a course of action under Chapter VII, it is imperative that consultation should take place between the permanent members of the Security Council, with a view to establishing a basis of agreement, which at present is ap-

parently nonexistent, as to what consecutive steps might follow, in the way of diplomatic, economic or even military pressure, if an order of the Security Council to cease military action in Palestine were not obeyed.[52]

A similar consideration played a decisive role in delaying the determination by the Assembly that Communist China had committed aggression in Korea. In this case, the argument was that such action seriously risked expanding the police action into a general war, which the Members of the United Nations, including the major powers, were anxious to avoid. Certain Members especially objected to risking expansion of the war because of the disadvantages of fighting in the Far East. Furthermore, it was suggested in the course of the debate in the Assembly that it was not feasible to apply collective measures against a major power because of the small chances of success. On the other hand, a prompt determination was made following the North Korean attack largely because of the willingness of the United States to take the initiative. That the United States had armed forces readily available in Japan, that it was willing to use these forces, and that neither Soviet nor Chinese Communist forces were directly engaged were important considerations in influencing members of the Security Council to support a finding that a breach of the peace existed and the subsequent recommendation that direct aid be given to the Republic of Korea.

An important factor has been the world political situation, and, in particular, the relations between the Soviet Union and the Western powers. The existence of conflicting interests, tensions, and distrust among the major powers has resulted in the frequent use of the veto, and has prevented the Security Council from making full use of its powers under Articles 39 and 40. In some cases, as in Palestine and Indonesia, the Western powers have resisted certain proposals to take collective military measures because of their unwillingness to have Soviet forces brought into strategic areas. On the other hand, it would appear that the quick reaction to the North Korean attack was due in large part to the cold war, in particular, to United States "containment" policy as stated by President Truman on March 12, 1947. Cold war strategy appears to have been a major consideration influencing the attitudes of Members of the United Nations, especially the major powers, regarding whether they should support the initiation of coercive measures by the Council or the As-

[52] U.N. Security Council, Third Year, *Official Records,* No. 70, 298th Meeting (May 20, 1948), p. 14.

sembly to remove or suppress threats to the peace, breaches of the peace, or acts of aggression.

The determination of the existence of a threat to the peace, a breach of the peace, or an act of aggression by the Security Council or the General Assembly has, in the practice of the United Nations, been a political act. Such determination has been a method of collective coercion as well as a preliminary to collective measures of coercion. Responsibility for making this determination has been assumed by the Assembly in cases in which disagreement among the permanent members of the Council prevents that organ from acting. Although a determination by the Assembly does not have the binding force of a determination by the Council under Article 39, it may have extensive moral authority, and may receive wide support from Members. A determination by the Council has lost much of the authority that it was initially expected to have as the result of the failure of the Council to conclude agreements with Members by which armed forces and facilities would be placed at its disposal, and the inability of the permanent members to agree among themselves on joint action under Article 106.

CHAPTER XV

Provisional Measures to Avert
or End Hostilities[1]

A PROCEDURE of established value in dealing with international disputes and threatening situations is to get the interested parties to take measures that will prevent the further aggravation of the situation and that will safeguard the rights of parties. The method was used by the Council and the Assembly of the League of Nations, especially the former, and by the Permanent Court of International Justice under explicit provisions of the Statute of the Court. Under the Charter of the United Nations, the Security Council is expressly authorized in Article 40, to utilize provisional measures in dealing with a threat to the peace, breach of the peace, or act of aggression. The general powers of both the Security Council and the General Assembly appear to be adequate to cover the use of such methods by either organ in dealing with any dispute or situation. The International Court of Justice is also authorized by Article 41 of its Statute to make use of provisional measures to protect the rights of parties.[2]

Provisions of the Charter

When the Security Council or the General Assembly is dealing with a dispute or situation in which there is a threat to the peace or an actual breach of the peace, the practical question arises regarding the manner in which the organ may and can best proceed to achieve the objective of the United Nations—the restoration or maintenance of international peace and security. The Charter is quite explicit regarding what the Council shall and may do. Article 39 provides that it "shall determine the existence of any threat to the peace, breach of the peace, or act of aggression and shall make recommendations, or decide what measures shall be taken in ac-

[1] For an excellent analysis of measures taken by the United Nations to avert or end hostilities during the period down to 1950, see Eduardo Jiménez de Aréchaga, *Voting and Handling of Disputes in the Security Council* (1950), pp. 117-58.

[2] See above, Chap. XIII.

cordance with Articles 41 and 42, to maintain or restore international peace and security." Article 40 then states that "in order to prevent an aggravation of the situation"—presumably referring to any situation of the kind described in Article 39—the Security Council may, before making recommendations or deciding upon measures to be taken to maintain or restore international peace and security, "call upon the parties concerned to comply with such provisional measures as it deems necessary or desirable. Such provisional measures shall be without prejudice to the rights, claims, or position of the parties concerned. The Security Council shall duly take account of failure to comply with such provisional measures."

Article 40 had its origin at the San Francisco Conference in a proposal by the sponsoring governments designed to prevent a threat to the peace from developing into an actual breach of the peace. This proposal was incorporated in a substantial revision of that part of the Dumbarton Oaks Proposals dealing with the powers of the Security Council to act in case of a threat to the peace, a breach of the peace, or an act of aggression. The revision included the dropping of a paragraph, which the sponsoring governments initially had proposed, under which the Security Council, if it found that a failure to settle a dispute constituted a threat to international peace and security, could take necessary measures, in accordance with the purposes and principles of the Charter, to maintain international peace and security. The text of what subsequently became Article 40 was approved by Committee III/3 of the Conference and by the Conference in plenary meeting. This approval was given in the light of certain observations, made by the Belgian delegate, that included the following:

It is the Committee's view that the power given to the Council under paragraphs 1 and 2 [Articles 39 and 40 of the Charter] not to resort to the measures contemplated in paragraphs 3 and 4 [Articles 41 and 42 of the Charter], or to resort to them only after having sought to maintain or restore peace by inviting the parties to consent to certain conservatory measures, refers above all to the presumption of a threat of war. The Committee is unanimous in the belief that, on the contrary, in the case of flagrant aggression imperiling the existence of a member of the Organization, enforcement measures should be taken without delay, and to the full extent required by circumstances, except that the Council should at the same time endeavor to persuade the aggressor to abandon its venture, by the means contemplated in Section A [Chapter VI of the Charter] and by prescribing conservatory measures.[3]

[3] U.N. Information Organizations and U.S. Library of Congress, *Documents of the United Nations Conference on International Organization*, Vol. 12 (1945), p. 507.

The Charter contains no specific provisions regarding the power of the Assembly to take provisional measures to avert or end hostilities. This absence of specific provisions is consistent with the general terms in which the powers of the Assembly in the political field are defined and the explicit instruction to the Assembly, contained in Article 11(2), to refer to the Council all questions on which action is necessary.

Relation to Formal Determination under Article 39

The practice of the United Nations regarding the manner in which provisional measures have been related to a formal determination of a threat to or a breach of the peace, has not been consistent. In the case of the General Assembly, the Charter contains no detailed provisions regarding the course to be followed. In the case of the Security Council, however, Article 40 of the Charter, which makes explicit provision for provisional measures, follows on Article 39, and therefore is open to the interpretation that the measures for which it provides are to be taken after a determination by the Council of the existence of a threat to the peace, breach of the peace, or act of aggression. In practice, the Council has shown a preference for great flexibility in the manner in which it exercises its functions. This is in line with the discussion at San Francisco to the effect that the Council was not to be considered bound to follow any set progression in the actions it was authorized to undertake. The Council has called upon the parties to apply measures of a provisional nature without any preliminary determination under Article 39 or any explicit reference to Article 40, and concurrently with making a determination or after having made one. It has called upon the parties to take such measures while performing its functions under Chapter VI of the Charter.

In the Greek case, after the Commission of Investigation of the Council had made its report, the Soviet Union and the United States introduced draft resolutions calling for the adoption of measures of a provisional nature. After these two proposals had been defeated, the representatives of Australia and the United States introduced draft resolutions by which the Council would have explicitly linked a determination under Article 39 with provisional measures under Article 40.

In bringing the Indonesian question to the attention of the Council, Australia invoked Article 39. In the draft resolution that the

Australian representative introduced, provisional measures under
Article 40 were explicitly related to a determination that the fighting in progress constituted a breach of the peace under Article 39.
In order to avoid complex legal discussions and without prejudice to
the rights of parties or the views of Members on questions of competence, the Council adopted this proposal in a revised form, which
omitted any explicit reference to a determination under Article 39
or to Article 40.[4] This continued to be the basis of action by the
Council down to the time of the second Netherlands "police action"
in December 1948. When this was brought to the attention of the
Council, the Soviet Union introduced a proposal condemning Netherlands aggression and ordering provisional measures. The resolution finally adopted followed the pattern of the earlier resolution.[5]
The resolution of January 28, 1949, which provided the basis for a
final settlement, followed the same general pattern of avoiding any
explicit reference to Articles 39 and 40.[6] During the discussions in
the Council, several members expressed the view that action was in
fact being taken under Articles 39 and 40, and that the measures
adopted implied recognition of the existence of "a threat to the
peace."

In dealing with the peace and security aspects of the Palestine
question, the Council adopted a series of resolutions beginning in
March 1948 in which with increasing insistence it requested that
measures be taken to put an end to violence. On May 29, it called
upon "Governments and authorities" to adopt a number of specific
measures, including a four-week truce, and decided that if these proposals were rejected by either party or by both, or, if accepted, were
subsequently repudiated or violated, the situation would be "reconsidered with a view to action under Chapter VII of the Charter."[7]
The implication certainly was that the Council had not up to this
time considered itself as acting under Article 40, yet the measures
that the Council had previously asked the parties to adopt were
clearly of the kind described in Article 40. After the expiration of
the four-week truce, there was a renewal of hostilities, and the
Council, by its resolution of July 15, 1948, explicity determined that
a threat to the peace existed under Article 39 and ordered that provisional measures be adopted under Article 40. Later resolutions of

[4] U.N. Doc. S/459 (Aug. 1, 1947).
[5] U.N. Doc. S/1150 (Dec. 24, 1948).
[6] U.N. Doc. S/1234 (Jan. 28, 1949).
[7] U.N. Security Council, Third Year, *Official Records*, Supplement (May 1948),
pp. 103-04.

the Council were related to this finding. Thus the resolution of November 16, *"calls upon* the parties directly involved in the conflict in Palestine, as a further provisional measure under Article 40 of the Charter, to seek agreement forthwith" with a view to the immediate establishment of an armistice.[8] The resolutions adopted in late 1948 to put an end to renewed fighting in the Negeb area also adopted the language of provisional measures without explicitly mentioning Article 40.

The Indian complaint against Pakistan in January 1948, claimed that support was being given to Pakistani nationals and tribesmen forcibly entering the territory of Jammu and Kashmir. The Indian Government had brought the question to the Council under Article 35, and the Council in its resolution limited itself to calling upon the parties to take measures calculated to improve the situation and to refrain from acts likely to aggravate it. After establishing a commission to perform investigating and mediatory functions, the Council adopted a resolution in April by which it recommended to the two governments certain enumerated measures considered to be appropriate to bring about a cessation of fighting and to create conditions under which a plebiscite might be held. No reference was made to Articles 39 and 40 in the discussions of the Council, and action was presumably taken under Chapter VI of the Charter.

When the Berlin question was being considered by the Council in the fall of 1948, a draft resolution was submitted by a group of members, excluding the parties to the dispute. It proposed action under Article 40 without any reference to the existence of a threat to the peace. The proposal was defeated in the Council by a Soviet veto.

In dealing with the complaint of North Korean aggression on the Republic of Korea, the Council combined in one resolution a determination that a breach of the peace existed and a request that provisional measures be adopted. While the matter of Chinese Communist intervention was being considered in the Council in November, a six-power draft resolution, later vetoed by the Soviet Union, was introduced, calling for measures to prevent "the spread of the Korean conflict"; but it contained no determination under Article 39.[9]

Subsequently, the matter of the Korean conflict was brought to the attention of the Assembly, which first centered its efforts on obtain-

[8] *Ibid.,* Supplement (November 1948), pp. 13-14.
[9] U.N. Doc. S/1894 (Nov. 10, 1950).

ing agreement to a cease-fire. The resolution that the Assembly adopted on February 1, 1951, contained a finding of aggression and called upon the People's Republic of China "to cause its forces and nationals in Korea to cease hostilities . . . and to withdraw from Korea."[10]

Nature of Measures Adopted

The Charter does not specify in detail the nature of the provisional measures that the parties may be called upon to adopt. Under Article 40, the Security Council has complete freedom to determine such measures in the light of what "it deems necessary or desirable." The measures are to be taken, however, "without prejudice to the rights, claims, or position of the parties concerned." Presumably, they can only be measures of such a nature as are considered "necessary or desirable . . . in order to prevent an aggravation of the situation." That is, they must be directed toward creating conditions more favorable to the maintenance or restoration of international peace and security. The use of the term "call upon" in Article 40, however, leaves undefined the exact force of any action that the Council may take. Furthermore, the range of the discretion of the Council in determining the nature of provisional measures is emphasized by the fact that, instead of taking action under Article 40, it may act under its primary responsibility for maintaining international peace and security or under the special powers conferred on it under Chapter VI of the Charter inasmuch as "procedures or methods of adjustment" can be interpreted to cover measures of a preliminary nature necessary to a peaceful adjustment.

The wide scope of the discretion vested in the General Assembly is obvious as there is no Charter provision explicitly authorizing it to adopt provisional measures. Subject to the provisions of the Charter governing its competence, and more especially, the limitations of Article 11(2) and Article 12(1), it can make recommendations with respect to any matter that comes before it. Although it may not have the range of authority of the Council, *i.e.* power to order as well as recommend, the variety of the possible measures it can recommend is as wide as that of the Council.

Under the League of Nations, it was established procedure for the

[10] Res. 498 (V), Feb. 1, 1951.

President of the Council to make an appeal to the parties to cease hostilities in advance of the meeting of the Council to consider the situation.[11] Neither the Charter itself nor the rules of procedure of either the Security Council or the General Assembly make any explicit provision for such advance action. Only in the dispute between India and Pakistan has the United Nations followed a procedure similar to that of the League of Nations. In this case, the original Indian communication, addressed to the President of the Security Council on January 1, 1948, stated that a situation coming under Article 35 existed and called attention to aid that invaders of Jammu and Kashmir were receiving from Pakistan. Before the Security Council considered the complaint, the President sent identical appeals to the two governments informing them that the Council was about to consider the Indian complaint and appealing to each, "without prejudice to any decision on the part of the Council, . . . to refrain from any step incompatible with the Charter and liable to result in an aggravation of the situation, thereby rendering more difficult any action by the Security Council."[12] In their replies the two governments gave assurances that they would refrain from any such action.

When a situation has not developed to the point where actual hostilities are in progress, or when the two parties indicate a willingness to seek a settlement by direct negotiations, a general appeal to take measures calculated to improve the situation and not to take measures likely to aggravate it may seem most appropriate. In the India-Pakistan dispute, the Security Council by its resolution in January 1948, called upon the two governments "to take immediately all measures within their power (including public appeals to their people) calculated to improve the situation and to refrain from making any statement or from doing or causing to be done or permitting any acts which might aggravate the situation."[13] Similarly, when setting up its Special Committee to investigate and report on the Palestine question, the Assembly called upon "all Governments and peoples, and particularly upon the inhabitants of Palestine, to refrain, pending action by the General Assembly on the report of the Special Committee on Palestine, from the threat or use of force

[11] See T. P. Conwell-Evans, *The League Council in Action* (London 1929), pp. 35-46.
[12] U.N. Doc. S/636 (Jan. 6, 1948).
[13] U.N. Doc. S/651 (Jan. 17, 1948).

or any other action which might create an atmosphere prejudicial to an early settlement of the question of Palestine."[14]

When hostilities have already broken out, or when disorder characterized by the widespread use of armed force already exists, provisional measures of a more specific and compelling nature may be called for, ranging from an appeal that steps be taken to end the disorder to an order that hostilities cease. In the Palestine case, after the existence of disorder in Palestine had been brought to its attention by the first special report of the Palestine Commission, the Council adopted a resolution appealing "to all Governments and peoples, particularly in and around Palestine, to take all possible action to prevent or reduce such disorders as are now occurring in Palestine."[15] After this appeal failed, the Council called upon Arab and Jewish armed groups in Palestine "to cease acts of violence immediately."[16] On April 17, the Council also called upon all persons and organizations in Palestine to "cease all activities of a military or para-military nature," to refrain from bringing and assisting the entry into Palestine of armed bands and fighting personnel, to refrain from importing and assisting in the importation of weapons and war materials, to refrain from prejudicial political activity, to co-operate with the mandatory authorities in the maintenance of law and order and essential services, and to refrain from any action that might endanger or interfere with access to the Holy Places.[17] But this appeal also failed, and fighting broke out between organized Arab and Jewish forces following the termination of the mandate on May 15, 1948 and the declaration of independence of Israel.

A week later, the Council called upon all "Governments and authorities . . . to abstain from any hostile military action in Palestine and to that end to issue a cease-fire order to their military and para-military forces to become effective within thirty-six hours after midnight New York Standard Time, 22 May 1948."[18] When the parties failed to heed this appeal, the Council, on May 29, called upon "all Governments and authorities . . . to order a cessation of all acts of armed force for a period of four weeks," called upon them to

[14] Res. 107 (S-1) , May 15, 1947.

[15] U.N. Doc. S/691 (Mar. 5, 1948) .

[16] U.N. Security Council, Third Year, *Official Records,* Supplement (April 1948), pp. 4-5.

[17] *Ibid.,* pp. 7-8.

[18] *Ibid.,* Supplement (May 1948), p. 97.

adopt a number of specific measures such as were enumerated in the resolution of April 17, and invited the states members of the Arab League and the Jewish and Arab authorities in Palestine to communicate their acceptance not later than 6:00 P.M. June 1.[19] The Council also decided that if the resolution were rejected by either party or by both, or if accepted, was subsequently repudiated or violated, the situation would "be reconsidered with a view to action under Chapter VII of the Charter." This apparently was an important factor in causing the parties to agree to a cease-fire. However, the parties refused to extend the cease-fire on the expiration of the four-week period. The Council then *ordered* the Governments and authorities concerned, "pursuant to Article 40, . . . to desist from further military action and to this end to issue cease-fire orders to their military and para-military forces" to take effect at a time to be determined by the United Nations Mediator.[20]

When fighting subsequently broke out in the Negeb area in violation of this order, the Council, in its resolution of November 4, called upon the interested Governments "without prejudice to their rights, claims or position with regard to a peaceful adjustment . . . to withdraw those of their forces which have advanced beyond the positions held on 14 October . . . to establish, through negotiations . . . permanent truce lines and such neutral or demilitarized zones as may appear advantageous, in order to ensure henceforth the full observance of the truce in that area."[21] On November 16, on the recommendation of the acting mediator, the Council decided that an armistice should be established "in all sectors," and called upon the parties directly involved in the conflict "as a further provisional measure under Article 40 of the Charter, to seek agreement forthwith, by negotiations conducted either directly or through the Acting Mediator on Palestine, with a view to the immediate establishment of the armistice," including the delineation of permanent demarcation lines limiting the movement of armed forces and the withdrawal and reduction of armed forces.[22]

In other cases brought before the Security Council or General Assembly where there has been armed conflict between organized forces, a variety of measures have been proposed or adopted for

[19] *Ibid.*, pp. 103-04.
[20] *Ibid.*, Supplement (July 1948), pp. 76-77.
[21] *Ibid.*, Supplement (November 1948), p. 7.
[22] *Ibid.*, pp. 13-14.

the purpose of preventing further aggravation of the situation and to create conditions permitting a peaceful settlement. In the Greek case, the resolution proposed by Australia on August 6, 1947, would have called upon the parties involved, namely Greece, Albania, Yugoslavia, and Bulgaria, "to cease all acts of provocation."[23] The resolution proposed by the United States on August 12 was more specific, in that it would have called upon "Albania, Bulgaria and Yugoslavia to cease and desist from rendering any further assistance or support in any form to the guerrillas fighting against the Greek Government."[24] The Assembly, in its resolution of November 27, 1948, called upon the northern neighbors of Greece to cease rendering assistance or support in any form, "including the use of their territories as a base for the preparation or launching of armed action."[25]

In the Indonesian case, the Council first limited itself to calling upon the parties "to cease hostilities forthwith." Following the second Netherlands "police action" in December 1948, it repeated this appeal and in addition called for the release of "the President [of the Republic of Indonesia] and other political prisoners arrested since 18 December."[26] The Council repeated this appeal in greater detail in its resolution of January 28, 1949, after it had turned down a Soviet proposal that the Council request the Netherlands to withdraw its forces immediately to the positions provided for in the Renville Agreement concluded between the parties during the previous year.

In the Korean situation, after the North Korean attack on the Republic of Korea, the Council adopted a resolution on June 25, 1950, in which it called for "the immediate cessation of hostilities" and called upon "the authorities of North Korea to withdraw forthwith their armed forces to the thirty-eighth parallel."[27] Following the submission to the Council of the Special Report of the United Nations Command on the intervention of Chinese Communist forces in Korea on November 6, a six-power draft resolution was introduced under the terms of which the Council would call upon "all States and Authorities, and in particular those responsible for the action noted above, to refrain from assisting or encouraging the North Korean authorities, to prevent their nationals or individuals

[23] U.N. Doc. S/471 (Aug. 6, 1947).
[24] U.N. Doc. S/486 (Aug. 12, 1947).
[25] Res. 193 (III).
[26] U.N. Doc. S/1150 (Dec. 24, 1948).
[27] U.N. Doc. S/1501 (June 25, 1950).

or units of their armed forces from giving assistance to North Korean forces and to cause the immediate withdrawal of any such nationals, individuals, or units which may presently be in Korea."[28] This proposal was subsequently introduced without substantial modification in the Assembly, which in its resolution of February 1, 1951, found that Communist China had engaged in aggression, called upon "the Central People's Government of the People's Republic of China to cause its forces and nationals in Korea to cease hostilities against the United Nations forces and to withdraw from Korea."[29]

The meaning of the terms used has been the subject of some disagreement. In the Indonesian case, where the Security Council first called for a cessation of hostilities, the United States representative in the course of subsequent Council discussion stated that this meant that neither party, by the use of military measures, was to be permitted to alter the territory under its control when hostilities ceased. The Consular Commission of the Council reported that each party interpreted the terms differently. Although military practice makes a distinction between a cessation of hostilities, which entails a cessation of all warlike operations (including movement of troops, reconnaissance by air, blockade, etc.), and a cease-fire, which entails only the cessation of military advances and actual firing, it is usually difficult to tell from the terms used the nature of the intended action because the Council, the Assembly, and subsidiary organs have used such terms as "cease-fire," "standstill," "cease hostilities," "cessation of all acts of armed force," "discontinuance of military operations," "truce," and "armistice" with little discrimination and little effort at definition. Some experts argue for a standard progression from cease-fire (a freezing of the military situation, an end of firing, and a standstill), through a truce (which includes the fulfillment of conditions), to an armistice (which includes a positive commitment to a peaceful settlement).[30]

Conditions Influencing Nature and Timing

In determining the nature and timing of provisional measures, members of the Security Council and the General Assembly have been influenced by a variety of considerations, not all of which are set forth in the words of the Charter itself. A constant concern of

[28] U.N. Doc. S/1894 (Nov. 10, 1950).

[29] Res. 498 (V), Feb. 1, 1951.

[30] See Paul Mohn, "Problems of Truce Supervision," *International Conciliation*, No. 478 (February 1952), pp. 52-53.

most Members is to obtain an improvement of the situation that will facilitate a political settlement. Closely related is the desire to find a basis of agreement among the parties themselves, and to take advantage of any momentary development that appears favorable to that result. Members have tended to regard the achievement of the objectives of provisional measures as more important than strict conformity to a legalistic interpretation of Charter prescriptions. Members have not been unmindful of their national interests, and their attitudes toward particular measures have generally been strongly influenced by the manner in which these are likely to affect important national interests.

When the Indonesian question was brought to the attention of the Council in the summer of 1947, detailed information was lacking regarding the conditions of fighting, and consequently the request of the Council to the parties had to be couched in general terms. After the second Netherlands "police action," the Council had the benefit of a detailed report from its Committee of Good Offices, which enabled it to be more specific in its resolution. Similarly, in the Palestine case, the Council was kept informed by the Palestine Commission, the Truce Commission, the mediator, and the acting mediator, and although its members, for different reasons, were unwilling to support strong measures to restore order, the resolutions adopted were specific. Also in the Korean case, the Council had the benefit of up-to-date factual reports from the Commission on Korea. Consequently, an attempt was made in the "Uniting for Peace" resolution to meet the need for complete factual information by providing permanent machinery that would be readily available to inform the Council or Assembly regarding the facts of the situation and thus to enable it to act promptly and concretely in specifying provisional measures to be taken.

Generally speaking, both the Council and the Assembly in principle have recognized the desirability of restoring the situation that existed before armed force was used in order that no party would be in the position where it might profit from the use of force. But for a variety of reasons, the resolutions adopted have not always been fully consistent with this general principle. In the Palestine case, for example, the situation had changed so completely that there was no possibility of restoring the conditions that existed before fighting began. Even though the territorial provisions of the resolution of the Assembly for the partition of Palestine provided a possible basis for the cessation of hostilities, this resolution was technically only a recommendation. To bring an end to fighting in the Negeb, after the parties had agreed to abide by the cease-fire order of the Council of July 15, 1948, the Council called upon the interested parties to withdraw their forces to positions held before the outbreak of fighting.

In the Indonesian case, following the first Netherlands "police action," extensive consideration was given by the Security Council to the question whether the parties should be called upon to withdraw their forces to *ante bellum* positions. After the adoption by the Council of its resolution of August 1, 1947, the Netherlands military forces made substantial territorial advances. In the debate preceding the adoption of the resolution, the Soviet representative had proposed that "the troops of both sides . . . should be immediately withdrawn to the previous positions which they occupied before the beginning of military operations."[31] But this was opposed by the United States because of "the chaos and disorder which would result by having a precipitate withdrawal of the civil administration from the areas in which it is now located."[32] Subsequently, the Brazilian representative objected to a similar proposal on the ground that, without the presence of a neutral military body, "the withdrawal of the forces might become a disorderly operation and give rise to new protests and complaints and, perhaps, to new violence."[33] In the resolution adopted on November 1, 1947, however, the Council advised the parties that its earlier resolution of August 1 was not to be interpreted as permitting either party to extend its control by hostile action over territory not occupied on August 4. It invited the parties to consult with one another, either directly or through the Committee of Good Offices, regarding the means to be employed in order to give effect to that resolution. This resolution was weaker than proposals made by the Soviet Union and Australia, which had not received the necessary support. It reflected a desire on the part of the majority to find a formula that, without sacrificing principle, would be acceptable to the Netherlands.

Subsequent to the second Netherlands "police action," there was

---

[31] U.N. Security Council, Second Year, *Official Records*, No. 68, 172nd Meeting (Aug. 1, 1947), p. 1665.

[32] *Ibid.*, p. 1704.

[33] *Ibid.*, No. 96, 210th Meeting (Oct. 11, 1947), p. 2548.

substantial support in the Council for requesting the parties to withdraw their armed forces "to their respective sides of the demilitarized zone established under the truce agreement of 17 January 1948."[34] It was finally decided, however, by resolution of January 28, 1949, to call upon the parties to cease hostilities, leaving to the United Nations Commission for Indonesia the responsibility of assisting the parties in working out concrete arrangements. The commission was authorized after consultation with the parties to recommend "the extent to which, consistent with reasonable requirements of public security and the protection of life and property, areas controlled by the Republic under the Renville Agreement (outside of the Jogjakarta area) should be progressively returned to the administration of the Government of the Republic of Indonesia, and shall supervise such transfers." It was also to recommend, after consultation with the parties, "which if any Netherlands forces shall be retained temporarily in any area . . . in order to assist in the maintenance of law and order."[35] The case for not insisting on withdrawal in the resolution itself was thus stated by the United States representative:

> The problem before us is not whether the troops should be withdrawn; the real problem is the method and timing of withdrawal, worked out in such a way as not to create other and perhaps even greater difficulties. In solving a problem of this nature, we all recognize that there are local conditions which must be taken into account. Practical matters such as the maintenance of order and the supply and delivery of food and other every-day necessities are vital to the success of an operation of this character.[36]

After the North Korean attack, the Council did not hesitate to call upon the North Korean authorities to withdraw their armed forces back of the thirty-eighth parallel, even though no consideration was given to the practical consequences of such withdrawal. The assumption apparently was that the Republic of Korea would be able to re-establish its authority quickly and effectively. Similarly, under the terms of the six-power draft resolution introduced when the report of Chinese Communist intervention was being considered, the Council would have called upon "all States and authori-

---

[34] U.N. Security Council, Third Year, *Official Records,* No. 134, 392nd Meeting (Dec. 24, 1948) , p. 32.

[35] U.N. Security Council, Fourth Year, *Official Records,* Supplement (February 1949), pp. 1-4.

[36] *Ibid.,* No. 6, 402nd Meeting (Jan. 21, 1949) , p. 8.

ties" to withdraw immediately all nationals, individuals or units that were in Korea for the purpose of assisting the North Korean authorities.

Another consideration influencing the nature of provisional measures has been the desire, and in the case of the Council, the explicit obligation under Article 40, to avoid prejudice to the rights, claims, or position of the parties. The absence of a specific obligation in the case of the General Assembly is not too important inasmuch as the Assembly can only recommend in any case. This does not mean that the measures adopted must necessarily avoid any indication of responsibility for the situation with which the United Nations is called upon to deal, although there has been a definite preference expressed by many Members for avoiding an assessment of responsibility at this stage. When the Council was considering the situation created by the first Netherlands "police action" in Indonesia, the United States representative argued that consideration must be given to the question whether the withdrawal of forces might not prejudice the rights, claims, or positions of the parties. He thought the Council should have further evidence on the point before requesting such withdrawal. The Australian representative, however, pointed out that any provisional measure the Council might ask the parties to take, whether involving withdrawal or not, would be without prejudice to the rights of the parties. Subsequently, this qualification has often been incorporated in resolutions adopted by the Council, but it can be argued that provisional measures under certain circumstances will have a practical effect on the negotiating positions of the contending parties and, consequently, on the terms of any settlement that the parties arrive at by a process of negotiation.

Decisions regarding the nature of provisional measures have also been influenced by the purpose that these measures are intended to serve of assisting in the determination of the future course to be followed, whether peaceful settlement or enforcement action, and of preparing the way for whatever course is adopted. Following the Soviet veto, in 1947, of the proposed resolution intended to implement the recommendations by the Commission of Investigation of the Council in the Greek case, the Australian representative introduced a draft resolution declaring the situation a threat to the peace and calling upon all parties to take provisional measures. The United States representative, on the other hand, proposed a resolu-

tion declaring the conduct of Yugoslavia, Albania, and Bulgaria to
be a threat to the peace and calling upon them to cease and desist
from rendering further assistance to the Greek guerrillas. This latter
proposal seemed to be primarily intended to prepare the way for
further assistance to Greece. The dominant purpose of the Australian proposal appeared to be to facilitate acceptance and thus to
exhaust every possibility of peaceful settlement and, at the same
time, to assist the Council in fixing responsibility for a continued
threat to the peace.

Again, in the Indonesian case, the resolution of August 1, 1947,
was directed equally to the parties, and the resolution of December
24, 1948, adopted subsequent to the second "police action," was directed to both parties. By its resolutions of December 28, 1948, and
January 28, 1949, however, the Council called upon the Netherlands
Government to perform certain specific acts, thereby implying
Netherlands responsibility for at least one aspect of the situation. If
the Netherlands Government had not finally yielded, this would
have prepared the way for collective measures intended to force
compliance if the members of the Council had so desired. In the
Korean case, the initial resolution of the Council of June 25, 1950,
appears to have been intended as an initial step toward the possible
use of collective measures, as was evidenced by the reference in the
resolution of June 27 to the failure of the North Korean authorities
to withdraw armed forces to the thirty-eighth parallel as requested in
the earlier resolution.

The Assembly has given consideration to the matter of defining in
advance the obligation of states to adopt provisional measures in the
event of the outbreak of hostilities, largely with a view to assisting
in the determination of responsibility for aggression. Yugoslavia proposed in the fifth session of the Assembly the adoption of a draft
resolution that would require each party to hostilities (1) to pro-
claim within twenty-four hours its readiness to issue a cease-fire
order and withdraw its forces, (2) to put the cease-fire into effect
and to begin withdrawal of forces by midnight of that day, and (3)
to complete withdrawal within forty-eight hours after the cease-fire.[37]
Furthermore, the proposal provided that any state that failed to
act in accordance with these provisions should be considered as an
aggressor.

[37] U.N. Doc. A/1399 (Sept. 27, 1950).

Although Yugoslavia was attempting, by obtaining an endorsement of a set of general principles, to cover a specific situation, which it feared might arise in the near future, the other members of the Assembly were reluctant to commit themselves to a particular line of action in advance. Thus the resolution as adopted by the Assembly was considerably watered down.[38] It was cast in the form of a recommendation that, if a state became engaged in hostilities, it should take "all steps practicable in the circumstances and compatible with the right of self-defense to bring the armed conflict to an end at the earliest possible moment." The idea of a proclamation was retained, but the discontinuance of military operations and the withdrawal of forces were made dependent on an agreement between the parties or an indication of conditions by appropriate organs of the United Nations. States were to communicate their statements to the United Nations and to invite the dispatch of the Peace Observation Commission. In place of the almost automatic determination of aggression, the resolution provided that the conduct of states in regard to the procedure laid down in the resolution would be "taken into account" in any determination of responsibility and in relevant proceedings in the United Nations.

Legal Force of Provisional Measures

In a study of Security Council procedures in the handling of disputes one expert observed that "the legal effect of the precautionary resolutions adopted by the Security Council seems to depend largely upon their wording and the provisions of the Charter under which the decision is adopted."[39] A more realistic conclusion might be that the effect of such provisional or preliminary measures depends on the willingness of the members of the Council, especially of the major powers, to back up a resolution with the serious threat of enforcement action. The expression of that willingness may be in words that convey the intent without necessarily reflecting any consistent interpretation of provisions of the Charter. It is, for example, significant that in dealing with the Palestine question, the Council allowed the term "calls upon"—the language of Article 40—to become so weakened by repeatedly ineffective use that, when

---

[38] Res. 378 (V), Nov. 17, 1950.
[39] Jiménez de Aréchaga, op. cit., p. 149.

it finally decided to take action expressly under Article 40, it was considered necessary to use the word "orders"—which does not appear in Article 40.

Any attempt to analyze the legal effects of provisional measures adopted by the Security Council within the context of the Charter becomes difficult if not impossible as a result of the unwillingness of the members of the Council in their discussions and in the resolutions that they adopt to relate specific measures to specific Charter provisions. The reasons for this vary. In the consideration of the Palestine question by the Council, there were numerous references to Chapter VII and more specifically to Article 40, in the discussions during the period March to May 1948. It was not until May 29 that Chapter VII was specifically referred to in a resolution, and then in connection with a threat that if the measures adopted by the Council were not accepted and carried out by the parties, the situation would be reconsidered "with a view to action under Chapter VII of the Charter." The implication clearly was that, up until this time, the Council had not been acting under Chapter VII, although it was never made clear whether the Council was acting under Chapter VI or under its general authority under Article 24. Similarly, in the Indonesian case, the Australian proposal, introduced on August 1, 1947, at the beginning of the consideration of the question by the Council, contained an explicit reference to Article 40. However, that was omitted from the resolution finally adopted, and it was never made clear in the course of subsequent discussions—even though claims were from time to time made that action was being taken under Article 40—whether the Council was acting under Article 40 or under Chapter VI (Articles 33 or 36) or possibly under Article 24.

If the legal effect of the various provisional measures adopted by the Council is considered from the point of view of the language used by the Council, the interpretation placed on resolutions by members of the Council, the reaction of the parties, or the subsequent action of the Council, it is equally difficult to arrive at any clear conclusion that would satisfy a jurist. For example, in its first resolution on the Palestine question on March 5, 1948, the Council "appeals to all Governments and peoples." In its resolutions of April 1 and 16, it "calls upon." Speaking of the proposal the Council adopted on April 1, the United States representative said it "would impose an obligation under the Charter upon every Member of the

United Nations to carry out the decision made in it."[40] But none of these resolutions was heeded by the parties, and no adverse consequences were suffered by them. The resolution of May 22 "calls upon all governments and authorities." Although this resolution paraphrased the language of Article 40 and asked the Truce Commission to report on compliance, it was not heeded by the parties. The resolution of May 29 likewise "calls upon," substantially in the language of Article 40, but also "decides" that if "the resolution is rejected," "the situation will be considered" with a view to action under Chapter VII. The United States regarded this as "a provisional measure with which we expect the parties will promptly comply in order to prevent an aggravation of the situation."[41] This time the parties yielded.

When the Arab states refused to accede to "an urgent appeal" to prolong the truce, the Council then took its most forceful action. On July 15 it ordered the governments and authorities concerned, "pursuant to Article 40 of the Charter of the United Nations," to desist from further military action and to issue cease-fire instructions. The use of the word "orders" and other provisions of the resolution clearly indicated the intention of the Council that the parties should comply, subject to further action under Chapter VII of the Charter. In dealing with the failure of Egypt and Israel to terminate hostilities in the Negeb, the Council again reverted to the use of "calls upon" and the language of Article 40 without express reference to it. Considerable difficulty was experienced in implementing this resolution. When on November 16 the Council called upon the parties to enter into armistice agreements, this was referred to as "a further provisional measure under Article 40 of the Charter."

In regard to the Indonesian conflict, the resolutions of the Council of August 1 and November 1, 1947, used the words "calls upon" in asking the parties to cease hostilities and conclude negotiations to that effect. The United States representative later argued that the resolutions were adopted under Article 40 and that, in accordance with the terms of the Charter, the Netherlands Government was under obligation to comply with their provisions. The Belgian representative disagreed, arguing that, if the Council had intended

<hr/>

[40] U.N. Security Council, Third Year, *Official Records*, No. 52, 277th Meeting (Apr. 1, 1948), p. 31.

[41] *Ibid.*, No. 72, 302nd Meeting (May 22, 1948), p. 65.

to take such a serious step, it would have said so and justified its action. He pointed out that it was understood when these resolutions were adopted that the question of the competence of the Council to take action was unprejudiced. The Council continued to use the words "calls upon" in its resolution, subsequent to the second Netherlands "police action," that requested the parties to take provisional measures. This was in contrast to the use of the word "recommends" in its proposals for peaceful settlement in its resolution of January 28, 1949. In dealing with both the first and second Netherlands "police actions," the Council was eventually successful in getting the parties to agree to a cessation of hostilities and a political settlement, although the agreement proved to be temporary in the first instance.

It is interesting to note that in its first resolution dealing with the complaint of North Korean aggression, the Council, although willing two days later to recommend collective measures, used the terms "calls for" in making its request for the cessation of hostilities and "calls upon" in requesting the North Korean authorities to withdraw their armed forces to the thirty-eighth parallel. This would seem to have clearly been a situation in which the phraseology of the Palestine resolution of July 15, 1948 could properly have been used if the distinction between "orders" and "calls upon" then suggested was to be consistently maintained. The use of "calls upon" in the Korean resolution can possibly be explained by (1) uncertainty at the time whether the United States would be prepared to send armed forces to the assistance of the Republic of Korea and (2) the desire to avoid any delay that the use of the stronger language might have entailed. Furthermore, the resolution of June 25 contained no reference to Article 40. It did, however, contain a finding that a breach of the peace had been committed. It is to be noted that, in the resolution of June 27, the failure of the North Korean authorities to cease hostilities and withdraw their armed forces is given as a reason for collective measures to restore international peace and security.

It would seem difficult on the basis of the record to draw any clear conclusions regarding the legal effect of provisional measures or the legal significance of particular terms used. It cannot be doubted that the Council has the authority under the Charter to *order* provisional measures, as it did explicitly in the resolution of July 15, 1948, on the Palestine question, that the parties directly concerned are bound to observe such an order, that other Members are obligated to assist in carrying it out, and that the Council can adopt necessary measures to enforce the order, subject to such limitations as the Charter imposes. Nevertheless, it is not at all clear that the Council considers that, in order that these consequences may follow, it must use the word "orders," must explicitly relate its action to Article 40, and must precede it by an explicit determination under Article 39. In practice, the Council seems to have exercised the widest discretion in the choice of words to give expression to its will and in determining the degree of compulsion it wishes to apply. Furthermore, it is authorized, in fact directed, by Article 40 to "duly take account of failure to comply."

It is interesting to note that the Assembly, even though the Charter limits its powers in dealing with disputes and situations to making recommendations, has in fact, when asking the parties to adopt provisional measures, used the words "calls upon" instead of "recommends." Although the intention presumably has been to stress the urgency and desirability of compliance, the parties have been under no clear legal obligation to comply. Nevertheless, the Assembly is free to draw its own conclusions from failure to comply, and in the exercise of the powers that it assumes under the "Uniting for Peace" resolution, may in case of noncompliance recommend measures that may have significant coercive effects. Although the measures recommended by the Assembly are not legally binding, they may have effects on the conduct of the parties not greatly different from those of the Council. This becomes especially apparent when the Council is incapable or unwilling to use its enforcement powers under Chapter VII of the Charter.

Implementation of Provisional Measures

Whether or not the provisional measures that parties to a dispute or situation are called upon or otherwise asked to adopt are legally binding, the method of implementation is a matter of great importance. It will rarely happen that a provisional measure is carried out by the free and independent action of the parties. A party may feel that its interests are not adequately protected under the proposed measure. It may be unwilling to act without assurance that the other party will do likewise. Detailed co-ordination of the various steps that implementation involves may be necessary. The measures that the parties are called upon to take may be of such a nature that additional details must be settled, either by order of an international agency or by agreement between the parties. As in the case of the resolution of the Council of November 15, 1948, in the Palestine case, the provisional measure that the parties are called upon to adopt may be a negotiation to achieve a certain result that may prove impossible if the parties are left to themselves, even though they show complete good faith. Various methods have been adopted, especially by the Council, to implement its resolutions. These have included the threat of enforcement action under Chapter VII of the Charter, a request to Members to support the action taken, and the establishment of subsidiary organs to assist the parties in reaching necessary agreements and to check on compliance. In addition, individual Members or groups of Members have brought pressure to bear on parties to obtain implementation.

In its resolution of May 29, 1948, on the Palestine question, the Council threatened action under Chapter VII if the parties did not accept its terms. The order of the Council of July 15 was accompanied by a declaration that failure to comply "would demonstrate the existence of a breach of the peace" requiring immediate consideration with a view to further action under Chapter VII. In its resolution of November 4 dealing with the situation in the Negeb, the Council appointed a committee to study as a matter of urgency and report to the Council on further measures it would be appropriate to take under Chapter VII if the parties failed to comply with the provisional measures. On the Indonesian question, the Security Council made no such direct threats, but the parties, especially the Netherlands, were subjected to important pressures, by the states participating in the New Delhi Conference, by the Commission for Indonesia, and by individual states, especially the United States, which discontinued aid under the Marshall Plan to the Netherlands in Indonesia.[42]

According to Article 2(5) of the Charter, Members "shall give the United Nations every assistance in any action it takes in accordance with the present Charter." In its resolution of May 29, 1948, dealing with the Palestine question, the Council called upon "all Governments to take all possible steps to assist in the implementation of this resolution." The term "all Governments" was

[42] See J. Foster Collins, "The United Nations and Indonesia," *International Conciliation*, No. 459 (March 1950), pp. 176-83.

said to include states not Members of the Organization which, in accordance with the terms of Article 2(6), would also be subject to the resolution. By declaration of May 25, 1950, the governments of France, the United Kingdom, and the United States declared that should they find that Israel or any of the Arab states was "preparing to violate frontiers or armistice lines," consistent with their obligations as Members of the United Nations, they would "immediately take action, both within and outside the United Nations, to prevent such violation."[43]

In its resolution of June 25, 1950, dealing with the North Korean military attack, the Council called upon "all Members to render every assistance to the United Nations in the execution of this resolution" and even though the resolution only called for the immediate cessation of hostilities and the withdrawal of armed forces by the North Korean authorities, the United States interpreted the provision quoted as justifying the sending of armed assistance to the Republic of Korea and the use of armed force to repel the North Korean military attack.[44]

Both the Council and the Assembly have commonly followed the practice of directing a subsidiary organ to undertake the task of assisting the parties in reaching the detailed agreements necessary to the implementation of provisional measures. This subsidiary organ may be especially created for the purpose, but in most instances, it has been an organ already in existence which was established for other purposes. Thus in the Indonesian case, the Council requested the Committee of Good Offices, which had been originally created to assist in a peaceful settlement, to help the parties reach an agreement that would ensure the observance of the cease-fire resolution. In answer to an objection that this was an improper function for the Good Offices Committee to perform, the Brazilian representative said:

I cannot see why we should not use the means available to us, and the Committee is undoubtedly the best means at our disposal. I have referred here to the experience we have had in these matters in Latin America, in similar cases. We have always had recourse, with great success, to an organ of mediation to which military authorities were attached. For these reasons, and because it represents, in our opinion, the best approach to the solution of this question, we give our full support to the United States draft resolu-

[43] U.S. Department of State *Bulletin*, Vol. 22 (June 5, 1950), p. 886.
[44] See President Truman's statement of June 27, 1950, U. S. Department of State *Bulletin*, Vol. 23 (July 3, 1950), p. 5.

tion, the main purpose of which is to co-ordinate the efforts of the Committee of Good Offices and the consular and military authorities in Batavia for the purpose of establishing contact with the parties, bringing about consultation between them and obtaining complete cessation of hostilities as a prerequisite for the peaceful settlement of the dispute.[45]

Similarly, when the Security Council decided that an armistice should be established in all sectors of Palestine, it made use of the acting mediator to assist the parties in reaching the necessary agreements. The office of United Nations Mediator had been created by the Assembly in May 1948, primarily to promote a peaceful settlement but also to be at the service of the Security Council in performing such functions as it might direct.[46]

Once the parties have accepted provisional measures and concluded such agreements as may be necessary for their detailed implementation, there still remains the problem of ensuring continued compliance, and of dealing effectively with violations that occur or that are claimed to have taken place. To this end, it is essential that the United Nations organ concerned have full and reliable information. One method that is always available is to request the parties to provide information directly, but neither the Council nor the Assembly can remain wholly dependent on information provided by the parties themselves if either is to be in any real sense master of a situation, nor can either rely exclusively on the good faith of the parties to achieve compliance. To assist the organ in obtaining the kind of information it needs and in discharging its responsibility for achieving compliance, the establishment of special machinery has been found necessary. This machinery has in some instances been especially created for the purpose, as in the cases of the Consular Commission set up to report on the observance of cease-fire orders and conditions prevailing in areas of military occupation in Indonesia, and the Truce Commission set up to supervise the implementation of the resolution of the Council on the Palestine question of April 17, 1948. More frequently, use has been made of subsidiary organs already established for other purposes, as, for example, when the Council by its resolutions of May 29 and July 15, 1948, requested the United Nations Mediator to supervise the observance of the truce.

[45] U.N. Security Council, Second Year, *Official Records,* No. 102, 216th meeting (Oct. 31, 1947), pp. 2692-93.

[46] Res. 186 (S-2) , May 14, 1948.

Various considerations have led to the adoption of particular arrangements for checking compliance. An important factor in influencing the decision to call on career consuls in Indonesia was the need for quick action, but another was the desire of certain Members to exclude the Soviet Union from participating. The use of the mediator in Palestine appeared to have many advantages: it assured prompt action; it centered responsibility for dealing with the numerous facets of a very complicated situation; it recognized the necessity of full compliance as a condition to, if not a guarantee of, peaceful settlement; and it commended itself to certain members of the Council as a convenient device for keeping Soviet influence out of Palestine. The point that needs to be stressed is that the choice of machinery for checking compliance has in practice been determined at least as much by political as by technical considerations.

The combination in the same subsidiary organ of the functions of supervision and peaceful settlement has disadvantages, as evidenced especially by the Palestine experience in which, in the opinion of the acting mediator, the necessity of dealing with some problems of truce violation often arose at an inopportune time from the point of view of successful mediation. On the other hand, when separate machinery is provided, difficulties may arise unless the functions of the organs are clearly defined. The principal United Nations organ must act promptly to decide any questions of conflicting competence.

The establishment of a truce or armistice agreement and the creation of machinery to check on compliance do not, of course, end the responsibility of the Security Council, or of the General Assembly in case that organ has acted. Even when the subsidiary organ is given the power to deal directly with noncompliance when the fact is established, there still remain questions relating to its competence and failure to achieve compliance that require consideration by the principal United Nations organ.

Alleged violations and problems not covered by agreements between the parties have been brought before the Council by the parties themselves, by other states, and by the subsidiary organs. The Council has responded with varying degrees of insistence and definiteness, depending on such considerations as its estimate of the seriousness of the situation and the extent to which members are prepared to take supporting action.

In the armistice agreements concluded by Israel and the Arab states, provision was made for Mixed Armistice Commissions, headed by the Chief of Staff of the Palestine Truce Supervision Organization or one of his senior officers, to deal with alleged violation. The Council has taken the position that complaints regarding violations of these agreements should be handled by the procedures thus established and that it should not intervene unless the remedies provided by the agreements themselves have been exhausted.[47]

The effectiveness of provisional measures in achieving their purposes has been adversely affected by the weakness of the Council and the division among the major powers. If the permanent members of the Council had found it possible to co-operate more fully, and if, as a consequence, the Council had been able to take decisions when necessary and had acquired the authority and prestige that the authors of the Charter had hoped for, it would undoubtedly have been possible to use them more effectively. The Council would have been able in many cases to establish a firm and confident control of the situation, instead of being forced to rely on efforts at persuasion, too often unsupported by any capacity or willingness on the part of members to take effective implementing action, and, in fact, weakened by conflicts of interest and purpose among the permanent members of the Council. This division among the major powers has likewise, although to a lesser extent, lessened the effectiveness of such measures as the Assembly has adopted.

Nevertheless, even under the unfavorable world conditions that have existed since it began to function, the United Nations has had notable success in a number of cases in bringing hostilities to an end by agreement of the parties and without recourse to the measures specified in Articles 41 and 42 of the Charter. Although peaceful settlement or adjustment may not have been achieved in every case, at least it has been possible in most instances to prevent the further aggravation of disputes and situations and the use, or further use, of armed force.

[47] On handling of complaints under this procedure, see Jacob C. Hurewitz, "The Israeli-Syrian Crisis in the Light of the Arab-Israel Armistice System," *International Organization*, Vol. 5 (August 1951), pp. 459-79.

CHAPTER XVI

Advance Preparation of Collective Measures

THOSE who wrote the Charter definitely envisaged that the Security Council would have great freedom in determining the course it should follow when called upon to deal with a threat to the peace, breach of the peace, or act of aggression. If, however, it was confronted by a flagrant act of aggression, it was expected to take, without delay and to the extent required by the circumstances, measures of the kind described in Articles 41 and 42 of the Charter, in order to restore international peace and security.

By the terms of the "Uniting for Peace" resolution, the General Assembly resolved that in case the Security Council fails to exercise its "primary responsibility for the maintenance of international peace and security in any case where there appears to be a threat to the peace, breach of the peace, or act of aggression," the Assembly would consider the matter immediately with a view to making appropriate recommendations.[1] It is reasonable to assume that, under this resolution, the Assembly is expected to exercise a latitude of choice similar to that of the Council, and that in case of flagrant aggression the Assembly also is expected to recommend the necessary measures to suppress it.

If collective measures are to be effective, especially military measures, it is desirable and indeed necessary that there be some advance preparation. The Charter recognizes this, so far as action by the Security Council is concerned, by providing in Articles 43 and 45 for agreements by which Members undertake to place armed forces and facilities at the disposal of the Council. The "Uniting for Peace" resolution likewise recognizes the necessity by making provision for such advance planning in regard to measures initiated on recommendation of the Assembly.

The Need for Advance Preparation

By the terms of Article 16 of the Covenant, Members of the League of Nations agreed that, should any Member resort to war

[1] Pt. A, Sec. A(1). See App. F.

in violation of its obligations under the Covenant, Members of the League would immediately subject that Member to the severance of all trade and financial relations. Although there was no provision for the automatic application of military sanctions, it was declared to be the duty of the Council to recommend to the several governments what military, naval, and air forces they should contribute to "the armed forces to be used to protect the covenants of the League." In reporting to the Council of the League on a proposal that the Secretary-General had made for the study of the implementation of Article 16, Signor Tittoni of Italy observed: "It is obvious that all the measures to be taken, and the means of putting Article 16 into execution, must be considered in advance. If the line of action to be taken is considered in advance, without waiting for the moment when action becomes necessary, the measures to be taken will clearly be more efficacious, and will have a speedier effect."[2] Recognizing the soundness of this observation, the Assembly of the League, at its first session, established the International Blockade Committee, which carried out a thorough exploration of the problem. In its report, as well as in the subsequent action of the Assembly, three points in particular were stressed: (1) the impracticability of applying sanctions on the sweeping scale envisaged in the Covenant because of the lack of universality of the League; (2) the impossibility of stating in advance the particular measures to be applied, because different circumstances would call for different measures; and (3) the need of a co-ordinating agency, such as the Council of the League.

Failure of Members of the League to agree on steps to strengthen the League, together with the absence of any firm commitment on the part of Members to apply military sanctions, was largely responsible for the increasing reliance that many Members placed on treaties of mutual assistance concluded outside the League framework. These seemed to have the great advantage, among others, of being capable of more effective implementation in advance. When in October 1935 the occasion arose for the application of sanctions against Italy, special machinery of co-ordination had to be improvised and valuable time was lost in deciding on measures to be applied.[3] The desirability under any system of inter-

---

[2] League of Nations, *Official Journal*, No. 6 (1920), pp. 308 ff.
[3] See Royal Institute of International Affairs, *International Sanctions* (Oxford, 1938).

national sanctions of having detailed preparations made in advance to the greatest extent possible was fully demonstrated.

When the Charter of the United Nations was being drafted, account was taken of the experience of the League of Nations. Provision was made for the use of military as well as political, economic, and financial measures. The advance preparation of military measures was prescribed. What was considered most important of all, "primary responsibility" for applying such measures in case of a threat to the peace, breach of the peace, or act of aggression, was placed on the Security Council, with power to take decisions binding on Members. Members of the United Nations were to conclude special agreements with the Council by which they would undertake to make available, at the request of the Council, "armed forces, assistance, and facilities, including rights of passage."[4] These agreements were to have the advantage, from the point of view of the Members, of defining the limits of their obligation to provide such assistance, and, from the point of view of the Council, of defining the forces and facilities that would be at its disposal for discharging its "primary responsibility" for the maintenance of international peace and security. A Military Staff Committee, consisting of the chiefs of staff of the permanent members of the Council or their representatives, was to advise the Council on all matters relating to its military requirements for maintaining international peace and security, and on the employment and command of forces placed at its disposal.

Nature of Advance Preparation

To give maximum assurance that United Nations enforcement measures would be effective, preparation at two different levels was required. First, agreements must be concluded under Article 43 to the extent necessary to permit the Security Council to exercise its responsibilities under Article 42. It was never made clear, either at the San Francisco Conference or subsequently, how many of these agreements would have to be concluded before this condition would be met. Presumably, agreements with all Members of the United Nations would not be necessary. Would agreements with all permanent members of the Council be required? Inasmuch as, by the terms of Article 106, it was for the Council to decide when it was

[4] Art. 43(1).

able to begin the exercise of its responsibilities, it was possible for any permanent member to prevent any decision to that effect until it had concluded an agreement with the Council. But there was nothing in the Charter that explicitly required that agreements be concluded with all permanent members before the Council began the discharge of its responsibilities. Considering, however, that the agreements were to be concluded between the Security Council and individual Members or groups of Members, it was clear that there would have to be agreement among the permanent members of the Council on the principles governing the size, composition, organization, equipment, supply, and use of such forces and facilities as might be placed at the disposal of the Council.

Although the Charter made no explicit provision for advance preparation of political, economic, and financial measures, and although it might be reasonably assumed that no such detailed preparation was either feasible or desirable, the experience of the League of Nations had shown the desirability of advance study of the problems that might arise, the methods that might be used, and more particularly the machinery and procedures for achieving the necessary co-operation. The Charter made no provision for an economic and financial staff committee to assist the Council in this respect, but it was undoubtedly intended by the drafters of the Charter that the assistance given by the Economic and Social Council would include assistance of this nature.[5]

In addition to advance preparation by the organs of the United Nations, there was also need of preparations by the Members themselves for effective participation in the measures that might be ordered or recommended by United Nations organs, and more particularly for discharging the specific commitments that they might assume by the agreements concluded under Article 43. This preparation might take the form of legislative and administrative action, even constitutional revision if necessary, to make it possible for each Member, from the point of view of its internal constitutional and legal arrangements, to discharge its international commitments. This was not likely to present any serious problem to totalitarian regimes, but it might create serious difficulties for a state with a constitutional government, and especially for one organized according to the principle of the division of powers between the executive, legislative, and judicial branches.

[5] Art. 65.

Preparations by Members to Discharge Obligations under Chapter VII

From a practical point of view, the action taken by the United States is of principal concern because, among the permanent members of the Security Council, it alone has experienced internal constitutional difficulties in participating in international organizations. Although the Charter of the United Nations, according to the Constitution of the United States, became a part of "the supreme law of the land,"[6] its provisions relating to enforcement measures were directed to the appropriate constitutional authorities. In view of the legislative and financial powers of the Congress and its special war powers, it was necessary for Congress to enact legislation that would grant to the President authority to take the measures required to discharge the obligations of the United States under the Charter.

To prepare the way for United States participation in United Nations enforcement action, Congress enacted and the President signed the United Nations Participation Act of 1945, which provided in Section 5 (a) that:

> . . . Whenever the United States is called upon by the Security Council to apply measures which said Council has decided, pursuant to article 41 of said Charter, are to be employed to give effect to its decisions under said Charter, the President may, to the extent necessary to apply such measures, through an agency which he may designate, and under such orders, rules, and regulations as may be prescribed by him, investigate, regulate, or prohibit, in whole or in part, economic relations or rail, sea, air, postal, telegraphic, radio, and other means of communication between any foreign country or any national thereof or any person therein and the United States or any person subject to the jurisdiction thereof, or involving any property subject to the jurisdiction of the United States.[7]

Section 5 (b) of the act provided penalties for violation of orders or regulations made pursuant to this section. Section 6 authorized the President to negotiate agreements of the kind described in Article 43 of the Charter subject to congressional approval, and provided further that:

> The President shall not be deemed to require the authorization of the Congress to make available to the Security Council on its call in order to

[6] Art. VI(2).
[7] 59 Stat. 619-21.

take action under article 42 of said Charter and pursuant to such special agreement or agreements the armed forces, facilities, or assistance provided for therein: *Provided,* that nothing herein contained shall be construed as an authorization to the President by the Congress to make available to the Security Council for such purpose armed forces, facilities, or assistance in addition to the forces, facilities, and assistance provided for in such special agreement or agreements.[8]

It should be noted, however, that this authorization does not apply to action taken by the President in the absence of such an agreement or upon the basis of a recommendation made either by the Security Council or by the General Assembly. Justification for the President's action in sending armed forces to the assistance of the Republic of Korea, for example, was found in the President's powers as commander-in-chief of the armed forces.[9]

Failure to Conclude Agreements under Article 43

The Security Council, on February 16, 1946, directed the Military Staff Committee, as its first task, to examine from the military point of view the provisions of Article 43 of the Charter. The committee decided that, as a first step, it should formulate recommendations to the Council on the basic principles that should govern the organization of the forces to be made available to the Council under that article. Later, the General Assembly, in the course of its consideration of the general principles governing the regulation and reduction of armaments, during the second part of its first session, recognized that the organization of collective security was closely related. Consequently, in the resolution that the Assembly adopted, it recommended that the Council accelerate as much as possible "the placing at its disposal of the armed forces mentioned in Article 43 of the Charter."[10]

On February 13, 1947, the Council requested the Military Staff Committee to submit its recommendations not later than April 30. The report of the committee submitted on April 30 included recommendations on which the delegations were in agreement and others on which they were unable to agree.[11] Their agreements for the

---

[8] *Ibid.*

[9] See Memorandum of July 3, 1950, prepared by the U.S. Department of State on the authority of the President to repel the attack in Korea, *Military Situation in the Far East,* Hearings before the Senate Committee on Armed Services and the Committee on Foreign Relations, 82 Cong. 1 sess., Pt. 5, pp. 3373-81.

[10] Res. 41(I), Dec. 14, 1946.

[11] U.N. Security Council, Second Year, *Official Records,* Special Supplement No. 1, "Report of the Military Staff Committee."

most part were on propositions that were explicitly stated or clearly implied in the words of the Charter. Their disagreements were on questions of vital importance that had to be answered in order for the agreements to be concluded under Article 43. The Security Council examined the report between June 4 and July 15, 1947. But it was unable to resolve the deadlock that had developed in the Military Staff Committee over general principles. Moreover, the committee reported on July 2, 1948 that it could not make any progress in establishing levels of strength until it received guidance from the Council on general principles. Discussions thus came to a standstill, and it became apparent that agreements under Article 43 could not be concluded, in the absence of a definite improvement in the political atmosphere. The General Assembly subsequently urged the Security Council to make efforts to implement Article 43, but the deadlock continued.[12]

With respect to the strength and nature of armed forces to be made available to the Security Council, the views of the United Kingdom, France, and China appear to have been closer to those of the Soviet Union than to those of the United States; and from the discussions that took place in the Security Council, it was clear that a wide divergence existed between the views of the United States and the Soviet Union. The United States position was that since the problem facing the United Nations was that of enforcing peace "in all parts of the world, . . . the United Nations needs, first of all, a mobile force able to strike quickly at long range and to bring to bear, upon any given point in the world where trouble may occur, the maximum armed force in the minimum time."[13] The United States appeared unwilling to admit that the armed forces made available to the Security Council might not be used against a permanent member.[14] The estimates of strength that the United States delegation to the Military Staff Committee presented reflected an emphasis on mobile and striking weapons, such as air force and navy. Furthermore, the quantitative estimates were far in excess of those submitted by other delegations, especially the Soviet Union.[15]

The Soviet position, on the other hand, was that the armed forces

[12] See App. F, "Uniting for Peace" resolution.
[13] U.N. Security Council, Second Year, *Official Records*, No. 43, 138th Meeting (June 4, 1947), p. 956.
[14] *Ibid.*, No. 47, 142nd Meeting (June 18, 1947), p. 1026.
[15] See U.N. Doc. S/394 (June 30, 1947); U.N. Secretariat, Department of Public Information, *Yearbook of the United Nations, 1947-48*, p. 495.

made available to the Security Council need not be "excessively numerous," considering that the "aggressor bloc" in the last war had been defeated and that former enemy states had been placed "under the control of the Allies." "In the present situation," argued the Soviet representative "it would be sufficient for the Security Council to have at its disposal relatively small armed forces."[16] The United Kingdom, France, and China also favored small forces, largely, no doubt, because of their inability to make large contributions. The Soviet view derived a measure of support from the assumption quite generally made from the beginning that these forces, by virtue of Article 27(3), would not be used against a permanent member. Furthermore, it appeared to find support in Article 5 of the Report of the Military Staff Committee, one of the articles on which there was unanimous agreement, which emphasized "the moral weight and the potential power behind any decision to employ the Armed Forces made available" as a factor influencing the size of the forces required.

The composition of armed forces to be made available to the Security Council proved to be one of the basic issues on which the Soviet Union and the other permanent members were in disagreement.[17] The United States contended that in order to have a force of the mobility and striking power required, one utilizing the latest technical developments, it was necessary for each member to contribute those elements that it was best able to contribute. Said the United States representative, in the course of the discussion in the Council:

> We consider that the contributions of the permanent members of the Security Council can be properly balanced and rendered roughly comparable without prejudice to the interests of individual nations by arranging that those nations which make available a lesser proportion of the new mobile components could put up a larger portion of other components or other forms of assistance and facilities.[18]

Other members of the Council, with the exception of the Soviet Union and Poland, accepted this general view.

The Soviet position was that the contributions of the permanent members of the Council should be equal, both in over-all strength

[16] U.N. Security Council, Second Year, *Official Records*, No. 44, 139th Meeting (June 6, 1947), p. 968.

[17] "Report of the Military Staff Committee," Art. 11, and comment.

[18] U.N. Security Council, Second Year, *Official Records*, No. 43, 138th Meeting (June 4, 1947), p. 956.

and composition. "The principle of equality," the Soviet representative argued, "is based on the provisions of the United Nations Charter which place the main responsibility for the maintenance of international peace upon these States," and it "preserves the equal status of the permanent members in respect of the decision on this important question."[19] The principle of comparable contributions, he argued, would lead to a situation in which some members would enjoy "a predominant position as compared to others." It might lead to use of the armed forces "in the interest of individual powerful States and to the detriment of the legitimate interests of other countries."[20] Soviet support of the idea of a small force was, of course, closely related to its support of the equality principle, because if the principle of equality were applied in all categories, the size of the resulting force would of necessity be small, because of the inability of certain permanent members to make substantial contributions in some categories. However, as a minor concession to reality, the Soviet Union proposed that the Council might excuse a permanent member, at its request, from making an equal contribution.

The positions of the Soviet Union and other permanent members were also completely at variance on the implementation of Article 45 of the Charter. The position of the Soviet Union was that requirements "of national air-force contingents . . . immediately available" should be determined after the conclusion of agreements provided for in Article 43 and within the framework of those agreements. The other permanent members took the view that the total strength, composition, and readiness of national air force contingents to be made available to the Council under Article 43 agreements should be determined in part by the special obligations arising from Article 45.[21] This would justify a larger and more powerful force than the Soviet Union considered necessary.

All the permanent members of the Council were in agreement that initially they would contribute the major part of the armed forces to be made available to the Council. This would facilitate the early establishment of a force that would enable the Council to exercise its powers under Article 42.

In regard to the provision of Article 43 that members are to make

[19] *Ibid.*, No. 44, 139th Meeting (June 6, 1947), p. 966.
[20] *Ibid.*, p. 968.
[21] See "Report of the Military Staff Committee," Art. 25, and comment.

available to the Council, in addition to armed forces, "assistance, and facilities, including rights of passage," the Soviet Union insisted on an interpretation that would exclude the provision of bases. In addition to pointing out that the article in question contained no mention of bases, the Soviet representative in the Security Council argued that "the provision of bases inevitably affects the sovereignty of nations."[22] He claimed that "the acceptance of the proposal on bases would be utilized by some States as a means of exerting political pressure on other nations which provided such bases." The other permanent members, however, took the position that provision should be made in the agreements for the use of bases, and, with the exception of France, they felt that there should be "a general guarantee" of the use of such available bases of Member States as the armed forces operating under the direction of the Security Council might require.[23] The Soviet Union also objected to "a general guarantee of rights of passage."

On the location of armed forces, again, the argument of the Soviet Union was that the presence of such forces of one state within the territory of another, even on the basis of agreement, would constitute a means of political pressure. The Soviet representative proposed that such forces should be stationed within the frontiers of the contributing Member, except in cases envisaged in Article 107 of the Charter. The position of China, the United Kingdom, and the United States, on the other hand, was that armed forces available to the Security Council, when not employed by it, might "be based at the discretion of Member nations in any territories or waters to which they have legal right of access."[24] This was also in substance the French position.

On the question of the employment of armed forces, the members of the Military Staff Committee were in agreement that armed forces made available should be employed only by decision of the Security Council and only for the period necessary to fulfill the task envisaged in Article 42. It was also agreed that use of these forces, whenever possible, be initiated in time to forestall or to suppress promptly a breach of the peace or act of aggression.[25]

There was disagreement, however, on the principle governing

[22] U.N. Security Council, Second Year, *Official Records,* No. 44, 139th Meeting (June 6, 1947), p. 970.
[23] See "Report of the Military Staff Committee," Art. 26, and comment.
[24] *Ibid.,* Art. 32, and comment.
[25] *Ibid.,* Arts. 18 and 19.

withdrawal of the forces, once their mission had been completed. All the permanent members except the Soviet Union were of the opinion that, after the armed forces made available to the Council had completed their tasks, they should be withdrawn "as soon as possible" in accordance with the provisions of the agreements governing the location of forces.[26] This left considerable freedom of decision to the Council because the time and conditions of withdrawal were to be fixed by the Council. The Soviet Union objected, maintaining that strict time limits should be set for withdrawal. The Soviet argument was stated by the Soviet representative as follows:

The general formula providing for the withdrawal of armed forces "as soon as possible" is absolutely insufficient. It does not oblige the armed forces to leave the territories of other States when their presence is no longer necessary and when it is not called for in the interests of the maintenance of peace. This formula, if accepted, would be used as a pretext for the continuous presence of foreign troops in territories of other States, which is inadmissible from the point of view of the basic purposes of our Organization.[27]

Under the Soviet proposal, a decision of the Council would be required to delay withdrawal beyond a certain time rather than to fix the time of withdrawal.

On the question of logistical support, all the permanent members of the Council were in agreement that Members should provide their respective forces with necessary replacements in personnel and equipment and with all necessary supplies and transport,[28] and that they should maintain specified levels of reserves.[29] China, the United States, and the United Kingdom proposed that in case Members could not discharge their responsibilities as defined in Article 29 of the Report, they might invoke the assistance of the Council, which would negotiate with other appropriate Member nations for the necessary assistance. The Soviet Union and France, on the other hand, proposed that deviations be permitted only in individual instances at the request of the Member and by special decision of the Council.[30] Although the difference between the two positions does

[26] Ibid., Arts. 20 and 21 and comment.
[27] U.N. Security Council, Second Year, Official Records, No. 44, 139th Meeting (June 6, 1947), p. 975.
[28] "Report of the Military Staff Committee," Art. 29.
[29] Ibid., Art. 30
[30] Ibid., Art. 31 and comment.

not appear to have been great, the Soviet representative, in the discussion in the Council, professed to see in the majority proposal another indication that certain powerful nations were prepared to exploit the weakness of some Members "for political benefits and advantages."[31]

The divisions within the Military Staff Committee and the Security Council did not all follow the pattern indicated above. On the question whether national contingents might be used in case of self-defense and of national emergencies, France and China took an affirmative position, while the other three permanent members took a negative one. On the organization of command, China, the Soviet Union, and the United States favored a provision for an over-all commander, or over-all commanders, without any mention of service commanders, while the United Kingdom and France favored making provision for service commanders as well. These differences, however, were not of such a nature as to bar all possibility of agreement, as was true of the differences separating the Soviet Union and the other permanent members of the Council.

Failure of the Security Council to agree on principles governing the conclusion of agreements under Article 43 made it impossible for the Military Staff Committee to make any progress in establishing the levels of strength of the national contingents to be made available to the Council. This failure to reach decisions necessary to the implementation of Article 43 was not due primarily to technical difficulties. It was primarily the result of a political impasse. This was explicitly stated by the Soviet representative in the course of his argument for the principle of equal contributions when he said:

> . . . I should like to draw the Security Council's attention to the fact that the whole question of armed forces being made available to the Security Council by the United Nations under special agreements is not only, and not so much, a technical question as a political one. It is a political problem and should be decided as such. Obviously, in the settlement of this problem there will also arise a number of technical questions, which the Security Council will decide in the course of negotiations with the States which make armed forces available to the Security Council. I think, however, that no one will deny that, as I have pointed out, this whole question is political. If we bear this in mind, we cannot take such a light view of the Soviet proposal of equal contributions as certain representatives on the Council do.[32]

[31] U.N. Security Council, Second Year, *Official Records,* No. 44, 139th Meeting (June 6, 1947), p. 977.

[32] *Ibid.,* No. 50, 146th Meeting (June 25, 1947), p. 1099.

As a result of this impasse, the Council was never provided with armed forces that would enable it to discharge its responsibilities under Article 42 of the Charter. Futhermore, the fact that this had been a result of the inability of the permanent members of the Council to co-operate meant that there was little, if any, possibility of these same permanent members taking joint action under Article 106 to maintain or restore international peace and security.

Lessons of the Korean Experience

The North Korean attack on the Republic of Korea on June 25, 1950, clearly showed the weakness of the United Nations system of enforcement action so long as no preparations had been made in advance for placing armed forces at the disposal of the United Nations and for adequately training, equipping, organizing, and using these forces. This weakness was shown to exist quite apart from the paralysis that the Council was bound to suffer if the Soviet Union chose to exercise its veto. Fortunately, this weakness did not affect too seriously the operation of an improvised system of collective measures because the United States, the Member on whom the United Nations was primarily dependent for armed forces in this contingency, had substantial forces in Japan and the Western Pacific in close proximity to the area of North Korean military attack and was willing to use them. If it had not been for this special juxtaposition of circumstances, it is quite unlikely that assistance would have been rendered to the Republic of Korea in time to halt the North Korean attack. Experience with the application of sanctions by the League of Nations against Italy in 1935-36 suggested that once the aggressor had attained his military objective, plausible reasons would be advanced for recognizing the *fait accompli* and forgetting about the original aggression.

The importance of the readiness and willingness of the United States to dispatch effective aid immediately was shown by the slowness with which other Members of the United Nations made military assistance available. Small air and naval detachments were made available for the defense of the Republic of Korea by a few Members other than the United States with reasonable dispatch. But it was not until the end of August that the first ground force unit of a Member other than the United States—the United Kingdom—arrived in Korea. It was apparent that in a situation of equal urgency when no one state would be in a position to give immediate and adequate assistance, the time required for taking necessary political decisions, for equipping and transporting armed forces, and for organizing command relations would in all likelihood be fatal to the chances of stopping a powerful and determined aggressor.

A further lesson of the Korean experience was that when one state assumes a major responsibility initially for aiding the victim of aggression, largely on its own and not as part of a prepared plan of collective action, the whole operation fails to acquire a truly collective character, because the state bearing the major responsibility almost necessarily exercises a dominant control over the whole operation. The United Nations character of the collective military operation in Korea would undoubtedly have been greatly strengthened from the beginning if there had not been such a disparity between the military contributions of the United States and the other Members of the United Nations.[33]

The "Uniting for Peace" Resolution

One of the purposes of the "Uniting for Peace" resolution, adopted by the General Assembly on November 3, 1950, was "to eliminate any need for such improvisation as was necessary in Korea, by laying a basis for a program in which members will make adequate forces available to the United Nations without undue delay."[34] To this end the Assembly invited "each Member of the United Nations to survey its resources in order to determine the nature and scope of the assistance it may be in the position to render in support of any recommendations of the Security Council or the General Assembly for the restoration of international peace and security"; recommended that "each Member maintain within its national armed forces elements so trained, organized and equipped that they could promptly be made available in accordance with its constitutional processes, for service as a United Nations unit or units, upon recommendation by the Security Council or the General Assembly, without prejudice to the use of such elements in exercise of the right of individual or collective self-defence recognized in Article 51 of

[33] See below, Chap. XVIII, p. 460, for the ratio of contributions as of the end of 1951.

[34] U. S. Department of State, *United States Participation in the United Nations*, Report by the President to the Congress for the Year 1950, Publication 4178 (1951), p. 100.

the Charter"; invited Members to inform the Collective Measures Committee, established by the resolution, "as soon as possible of the measures taken in implementation" of this recommendation; and requested the Secretary-General to appoint, with the approval of the committee, "a panel of military experts who could be made available, on request, to Member States wishing to obtain technical advice regarding the organization, training, and equipment for prompt service as United Nations units of the elements" to be made available.[35] In addition, the Assembly directed the Collective Measures Committee:

> . . . in consultation with the Secretary-General and with such Member States as the Committee finds appropriate, to study and make a report to the Security Council and the General Assembly, not later than 1 September, 1951, on methods, including those in Section C of the present resolution, which might be used to maintain and strengthen international peace and security in accordance with the Purposes and Principles of the Charter, taking account of collective self-defence and regional arrangements (Articles 51 and 52 of the Charter).[36]

The "Uniting for Peace" resolution thus envisaged preparatory action along two distinct but complementary lines. In the first place, Members were encouraged to strengthen their own commitments to take favorable action on the basis of recommendations of the United Nations and to put themselves in the best possible position to act promptly and effectively in accordance with such recommendations. Appropriate United Nations assistance was to be provided to this end. In the second place, the Assembly, through a subsidiary organ, the Collective Measures Committee, was to undertake the preparation of basic principles and plans of action to guide and facilitate the application of collective measures, whether on the recommendation of the Assembly or the Council, should the occasion arise. The preparatory work of the committee was intended to supplement, not supplant, the work that the Security Council and the Military Staff Committee were supposed to do in implementation of Article 43. The Council was in fact urged to continue its efforts to implement Articles 43, 45, 46, and 47 of the Charter. Thus the

---

[35] Pt. A, Sec. C(7-10). See App. F.

The Collective Measures Committee consisted of fourteen Members: Australia, Belgium, Brazil, Burma, Canada, Egypt, France, Mexico, Philippines, Turkey, United Kingdom, United States, Venezuela, and Yugoslavia. The members of the Soviet bloc regarded the committee as illegal.

[36] Pt. A, Sec. D(11). See App. F.

work of the Collective Measures Committee was intended to be of assistance to the Council primarily in connection with recommendations of collective measures that it might make, as in the Korean case, under Article 39.

Preparations by Members Under the "Uniting for Peace" Resolution

At the request of the Collective Measures Committee, the Secretary-General addressed a letter to Member governments on April 16, 1951, calling attention to the provisions regarding availability of armed forces in paragraph 8, Section C of the "Uniting for Peace" resolution and asking for information on steps taken to implement it. The replies received did not evidence much willingness on the part of Members to undertake specific commitments for the future.[37] The Soviet Union and its satellites regarded Section C of the resolution as illegal, while some Members, including Argentina, India, Bolivia, Egypt, Indonesia, Mexico, and Sweden, were noncommittal or indicated lack of sympathy with the whole approach. The majority of the Members, however, indicated sympathy with the general purpose of the resolution and a willingness to consider how they might strengthen their capacities to take action pursuant to United Nations recommendations without, however, making specific commitments. Some Members referred to specific facts—such as their contributions to United Nations forces in Korea, their efforts to establish security in specific areas, such as Malaya and Indochina, and their commitments under regional security and collective self-defense agreements—to indicate their concrete support of collective action for the maintenance of international peace and security.

The United States in its reply to the letter from the Secretary-General stated that after the termination of hostilities in Korea and the withdrawal of armed forces opposing aggression there, "the extent to which the United States will maintain armed forces which could be made available for United Nations service will be reviewed." It further reported that it was maintaining substantial forces in Europe under the North Atlantic Treaty, and that these

---

[37] U.N. Doc. A/1822 and addenda. For summary of replies received as of Sept. 30, 1951, see U.N. General Assembly, Sixth Session, *Official Records*, Supplement No. 13, "Report of the Collective Measures Committee," Annex II. (Hereinafter cited as "First Report of the Collective Measures Committee.")

forces could, pursuant to the Treaty, the Charter, and due constitutional process, "participate in collective measures to maintain or restore peace and security in the North Atlantic area in support of United Nations action." Finally, it said that it would keep the matter of specific commitments under constant review in the light of changing circumstances and in furtherance of the United Nations policy to build up an effective collective security system.[38] A few Members, lesser powers such as Turkey, Greece, and Denmark, stated that they had established or intended to create special units that would be designated as United Nations units. Others, while noting that they were unable to take specific action, agreed to continue to examine and develop their capacity to contribute to collective security through the United Nations.

In the studies made by the Collective Measures Committee in connection with carrying out the assignment given it by the General Assembly, the committee was primarily concerned, as regards advance preparation by Members, with the implementation of the recommendation regarding availability of armed forces. This did not, however, constitute its sole concern, because it recognized the importance of advance preparation in connection with economic and financial measures that the United Nations might take, whether alone or concurrently with military measures. One of the guiding principles stressed by the committee was that: "Member States should in advance and as early as is practicable, examine their legal and administrative situations in order that they may be in a position to implement collective economic and financial measures expeditiously and efficiently in accordance with constitutional provisions."[39]

In considering the military measures that might be used to maintain and strengthen international peace and security, the Collective Measures Committee called attention to the variety of assistance that Members might give. In addition to maintaining in their armed forces specific elements "specially trained, organized and equipped," it was pointed out that Members might "pay special attention to organizing and training units in their forces so that such units could be more efficiently integrated into combined United Nations forces."[40] In addition, the committee emphasized the desirability of

[38] U.S. Department of State *Bulletin*, Vol. 24 (June 11, 1951), p. 959.
[39] "First Report of the Collective Measures Committee," p. 21.
[40] *Ibid.*, p. 23.

Members surveying their resources in order to determine the kinds of assistance and facilities they might be able to furnish in support of future collective military action by the United Nations. Members were asked to consider whether they might take any action in advance of a recommendation by the Council or Assembly to employ armed force "which would enable them to furnish such assistance and facilities more promptly and effectively if and when the need arises." The committee observed:

> In certain cases, the ability of Member States to furnish such assistance and facilities may be affected by their constitutional procedures. Member States might, therefore, examine their legislation and their administrative arrangements in order to remove any avoidable limitation on their ability to furnish prompt and effective support for United Nations action to deal with a breach of the peace or act of aggression. It is of particular importance that States should be in a position promptly to grant, in accordance with constitutional processes, rights of passage and related rights to United Nations forces employed as a result of a United Nations resolution to use armed force to resist a breach of the peace or act of aggression.[41]

The provisions of the "Uniting for Peace" resolution had recognized the right of Members of the United Nations to take into account the requirements of regional security and collective self-defense in determining the contributions that they would make to United Nations collective military action. Many Members, in their replies, alluded to their commitments under these arrangements as indicative of contributions that they were prepared to make to the cause of collective security. The Collective Measures Committee explicitly accepted the view that these replies appeared to suggest, that "collective self-defence and regional arrangements or agencies constitute an important aspect of the universal collective security system of the United Nations." The committee went even further. It proposed the utilization of such arrangements and agencies in making United Nations collective security action effective. Said the committee:

> If a breach of the peace or act of aggression involving the application, within the purposes and principles of the Charter, of the provisions of one of these collective self-defence or regional arrangements occurred, and if, to meet that situation, the United Nations resolved to undertake collective military measures for the restoration of international peace and security, there should be a mutually supporting relationship between the activities of such arrangements or agencies and the collective measures taken by the

[41] *Ibid.*

United Nations. Thus, collective self-defence and regional arrangements or agencies may, within the limits of their constitutional status, provide effective forces and facilities in their respective areas in order to carry out the Purposes and Principles of the Charter in meeting aggression. Also, the Security Council or the General Assembly might consider whether some or all of the States parties to such an arrangement in the area where the situation arose might, in certain cases, be invited to act jointly, within the limits of such arrangements, on behalf of the United Nations.[42]

From its study of measures that might be applied and procedures that might be followed in order to make United Nations collective action more effective, pending the conclusion of special agreements under Article 43, the committee recommended the following preparatory steps:

(i) States should take further action to maintain elements in their armed forces so trained, organized and equipped that they could promptly be made available, in accordance with their constitutional processes, for service as United Nations units;

(ii) States should take such steps as may be necessary to enable them to provide assistance and facilities for United Nations forces in support of collective military measures undertaken by the United Nations;

(iii) States should examine their legislation and administrative regulations to ensure that they can carry out, promptly and effectively, United Nations collective measures, in accordance with their constitutional processes;

(iv) States should continue to survey their resources to determine the nature and scope of the assistance that they may be able to render in support of United Nations collective measures.[43]

These, along with other recommendations contained in the report of the committee, were considered by the Assembly during its sixth session. It is significant that although all four of these recommendations were included in the resolution finally adopted by the Assembly, they were considerably modified and weakened in the process. During the course of consideration by the Assembly, it became clear that there was widespread sentiment in favor of further safeguarding the freedom of action of the Members of the United Nations. The resolution proposed by eleven Members,[44] introduced to implement the recommendations of the committee, although noting the report of the Collective Measures Committee and approving its conclusions, explicitly provided that the obligation to

[42] *Ibid.*, pp. 23-24.

[43] *Ibid.*, p. 33.

[44] U.N. Doc. A/C.1/676 (Dec. 1, 1951).

maintain elements specially trained, organized, and equipped for United Nations service did not prejudice "the use of such elements in exercise of the right of individual or collective self-defence recognized in Article 51 of the Charter." In the course of discussion in the First Committee, it became clear that the majority of Members would insist on further elucidation of the recommendations made by the Collective Measures Committee. It was emphasized that elements would be made available for United Nations service not only subject to constitutional processes but also on the basis of a judgment by each Member of its capacity to contribute. Furthermore, each Member was to be sole judge whether its internal security requirements prevented such forces being made available. Finally, with reference to the proposed recommendation of preliminary examination of legislation and administrative regulations with a view to ensuring prompt and effective action by Members, strong objection was registered to any such interference in an essentially domestic matter. The Mexican delegate stated this objection as follows:

> . . . The present text had the very serious drawback that it claimed to impose on Member States at least a moral obligation to review their legislation, both constitutional and ordinary, so as to ensure the prompt and effective implementation of the collective measures of the United Nations. The intention appeared to be that Member States should make ready to amend their laws with that object in view. Such an obligation could not be accepted by the Mexican Government which regarded the amendment of its laws as a sovereign right not liable to subordination or compromise of any sort.[45]

The resolution finally adopted by the Assembly did not contain an explicit approval of the conclusions of the Collective Measures Committee, and in some respects its provisions were weaker than the conclusions of the committee.[46] The resolution recognized that a Member which maintained in its armed forces elements specially organized, trained, and equipped for United Nations service might be guided, in its decision whether these elements should be made available for United Nations service on the recommendation of either the Security Council or the General Assembly, by its own judgment regarding its capacity to make such forces available. It explicitly recognized the right of each Member to use such units "in exercise of the right of individual or collective self-defence recog-

[45] U.N. General Assembly, Sixth Session, First Committee, *Official Records*, 480th Meeting (Jan. 4, 1952), p. 141.
[46] Res. 503(VI), Jan. 12, 1952.

nized in Article 51 of the Charter." It also asserted that the use of these units for purposes of internal security was in no way prejudiced. And it avoided any suggestion that Members modify their constitutions or their legislation in order that they might be in a position to carry out more promptly and effectively United Nations collective measures. Thus the recommendations addressed to Members were couched in general terms with meticulous care to safeguard the right of each Member to determine its course of action in the light of the circumstances of its particular situation and its special commitments under regional and limited security arrangements. The resolution contained an invitation to states not Members of the United Nations to take note of the report of the committee and consider ways and means by which they might most effectively contribute to United Nations collective measures. The Collective Measures Committee was directed to continue its studies for another year and report to the Assembly before its seventh session.

At the request of the Collective Measures Committee, the Secretary-General addressed a communication to Members in June 1952, in which he brought to their attention the recommendations contained in the resolution of the Assembly. Members were invited to give their views on these questions. To assist them in preparing their views, the communication was accompanied by three enclosures giving the results of studies of the committee.[47] A communication was also sent to states not Members of the Organization inviting them to send any information they might wish. The responses received did not provide the basis for any expectation that the resolution of the Assembly would have much effect in achieving its declared objective. Seven Members and six states not Members of the United Nations simply acknowledged the communication. Twelve Members reaffirmed their earlier assurances of support and of these, ten—Australia, Belgium, Canada, France, the Netherlands, New Zealand, Norway, the Philippines, the United Kingdom, and the United States—indicated that their legislative and administrative arrangements were such that by governmental action, in accordance with constitutional processes, they could participate in United Nations collective measures in appropriate circumstances.[48] It is significant that all of these ten Members were parties to collective self-defense

[47] U.N. General Assembly, Seventh Session, *Official Records,* Supplement No. 17, "Report of the Collective Measures Committee," pp. 19-20. (Hereinafter cited as "Second Report of the Collective Measures Committee.")
[48] *Ibid.,* p. 21.

arrangements under Article 51 and that the United States was a party to each of the arrangements in question.

It does not appear that the work of the Collective Measures Committee, and the discussions and resolutions of the Assembly have had any direct or immediate effect on preparatory measures taken by Members to strengthen "international peace and security in accordance with the Purposes and Principles of the Charter." The Members that have responded most favorably have not, as a matter of fact, indicated any intention of taking new steps on the basis of this initiative alone. Generally speaking, they have simply called attention to steps already taken either to meet specific situations such as Korea, Malaya, and Indochina or to implement their commitments under regional or collective self-defense arrangements such as the North Atlantic Treaty and the Inter-American Treaty of Reciprocal Assistance. Furthermore, the Latin-American Members, generally, have shown an intention to place the requirements of hemisphere defense ahead of those of United Nations collective security, and have not indicated much interest in collective action by the United Nations. The same is true of the members of the League of Arab States. Other Members, such as India, Burma, and Indonesia, which have sought to follow an independent course with respect to the cold war, have taken either a negative or a noncommittal attitude toward the efforts of the Collective Measures Committee and the Assembly to achieve more adequate preparation by Members for collective action on the basis of recommendations by the Assembly or the Council.

The United Nations Panel of Military Experts

The "Uniting for Peace" resolution had provided for a panel of military experts, to be appointed by the Secretary-General with the approval of the Collective Measures Committee, to "be made available, on request, to Member States wishing to obtain technical advice regarding the organization, training, and equipment" of units for prompt service with the United Nations. This panel was in no way conceived as a substitute for the Military Staff Committee as its functions were quite different from those of that committee. It was given no functions in connection with advising either the Security Council or the General Assembly. In fact, from the discussions in the Assembly as well as from the phraseology of the "Uniting for

Peace" resolution, it was clear that the panel was to have no functions as a panel. The individual military experts making up the panel were to be available to perform limited technical services for Members desirous of carrying out the advance preparations for participation in United Nations collective military action, which the "Uniting for Peace" resolution was intended to encourage.

The Collective Measures Committee limited itself to adopting a report prepared by its Working Group.[49] The report conceived the nature and functions of the Panel as follows:

The panel is not constituted as a body, but is a list of persons given a certain status in order to exercise certain functions. . . .

The members of the panel are in no sense representatives of their countries and will not be instructed by their governments, or report to them. . . .

The panel should include experts from land, sea and air forces. . . .

Members . . . should be selected from the personnel, either active or retired in good standing, of the national military services of Member States, on the basis of their individual qualifications, their professional standing and experience only.

Before nominating members . . . for the approval of the Collective Measures Committee, the Secretary-General should consult with governments of Member States which are able to make qualified candidates available.

Members . . . should be of sufficiently high rank to give effective advice at the top level. Therefore, it would be desirable for members . . . to hold the equivalent rank of general officer in their respective national services.

[Members will be assigned by the Secretary-General] in consultation with the Member States requesting the services of military experts.

Advice furnished . . . should pertain solely to units to be made available to the United Nations.

Technical advice should not include any competence for operational planning and direction. . . .

[Members of the panel] should not be authorized to furnish technical advice or to formulate opinions as a body.

As part of the action it took on the first report of the Collective Measures Committee, the Assembly, in its resolution in January 1952, requested that the Secretary-General appoint the members of the panel as soon as possible.[50] On the following April 15, the committee approved a list of military experts appointed by the Secretary-General.[51] In its second report to the Assembly, the committee expressed the opinion that, since the services of the members of the

[49] "First Report of the Collective Measures Committee," pp. 44-45.
[50] Res. 503(VI), Jan. 12, 1952.
[51] For list of Members, see "Second Report of the Collective Measures Committee," p. 19.

panel had not as yet been requested, the earlier report of the committee on the nature and functions of the panel "would constitute sufficient guidance in the initial stages."

Guiding Principles and Procedures of Collective Action

Once it became apparent that the provisions of Chapter VII of the Charter relating to the organization and conduct of enforcement action were inoperative because of the inability of the permanent members of the Council to co-operate, the United Nations system of collective security lost one feature that it was thought would make it an improvement over the League of Nations system. In fact, the United Nations system was in danger of becoming even weaker than the League system because the Charter does not provide for automatic sanctions, *i.e.*, does not obligate Members to apply sanctions or enforcement measures immediately against another Member that uses force in violation of the Charter. To fill the gap created by the failure of the Security Council to become an effective instrument of collective security, the proponents of the "Uniting for Peace" resolution sought to create a new system based on the power of the Assembly to discuss and make recommendations with respect to any questions and matters within the scope of the Charter.

The "Uniting for Peace" resolution directed the Collective Measures Committee to study and make a report on methods that might be used to maintain and strengthen international peace and security in accordance with the Purposes and Principles of the Charter. The basic premise of the study was stated by the committee in its first report in the following words: "Each Member has the duty to participate in accordance with the Charter in the maintenance of peace and security and to act collectively, if States are to be able to count on the security which the Charter is intended to provide."[52] The studies and conclusions of the committee were concerned primarily with "the preparedness of States" and "techniques, machinery and procedures relating to the co-ordination of national and international action in regard to collective measures."

The committee did not feel called upon to anticipate, nor did it attempt to anticipate, "any specific situation." This approach to the problem was stressed in the course of the discussion of the report

[52] "First Report of the Collective Measures Committee," p. 1.

of the committee that took place in the First Committee of the General Assembly during its sixth session. The Australian representative emphasized that the measures listed in the report were "United Nations measures in the fullest sense of the term. They were not designed for use against any particular State or group of States, and no particular set of circumstances calling for application of the measures had been envisaged. The union of strength of the peace-loving countries to achieve collective security against aggression would threaten nobody."[53]

The Collective Measures Committee envisaged collective measures falling into three categories: (1) political; (2) economic and financial; and (3) military. To quote its report:

> Political, economic and financial, and military collective measures may be applied singly or in combination. The measures which may be deemed appropriate will vary in different cases in accordance, on the one hand, with the circumstances giving rise to the threat to or breach of the peace and, on the other hand, with factors such as the geographical location of the offending State, its economic self-sufficiency or its sensitivity to moral pressure.[54]

Political Measures

Political measures were conceived by the Collective Measures Committee as taking a variety of forms, including collective denunciation, severance of diplomatic relations, suspension or expulsion of the Member concerned from the United Nations or a specialized agency, or non-recognition of changes brought about by the threat or use of force. The committee was of the opinion that some of these were especially suitable for preventive action and that, in general, they would depend for their effectiveness on moral factors. It emphasized the need of adapting the choice of particular measures to the circumstances of each case. Although various possibilities could be envisaged, advance planning was of little use, either with respect to the specific measures to be applied or the coordinating machinery to be used.

Economic and Financial Measures

The committee in analyzing the major problems that were likely

---

[53] U.N. General Assembly, Sixth Session, First Committee, *Official Records*, 480th Meeting (Jan. 4, 1952), pp. 121-22.
[54] "First Report of the Collective Measures Committee," p. 3.

to arise in connection with the application of collective economic and financial measures, kept in mind "that the problem of security must be considered as a whole, and that military, political and economic measures in any given situation are interrelated." The committee called attention to various factors determining the vulnerability of countries to economic and financial measures and emphasized the wide range of vulnerability that existed. It also called attention to the cost of collective economic and financial measures to the states applying them and the unequal incidence of this cost, to the consequent need for making adequate provision for sharing this cost, and to the need for special provision of aid to the victim of aggression.

The committee considered a wide variety of possible economic and financial measures, including total or selective blocking of the commodity trade of the aggressor, the total or selective banning of financial transactions, the interdiction of physical communication, and the blocking or vesting of funds or property. It analyzed the special problems arising in connection with each type of measure, and stressed the importance of universal application and the proper co-ordination of measures applied by Members.

The committee emphasized the responsibility resting on the Security Council or the General Assembly "to provide for the co-ordination, evaluation and general supervision of the measures against an aggressor."[55] To discharge this responsibility effectively, the committee recommended that "a co-ordinating committee should be established by the Council or the Assembly immediately upon a finding of a threat to or a breach of the peace or an act of aggression," the membership of the committee to vary according to the circumstances of each case.

In addition to its primary task of co-ordination, this committee would have the function of making specific recommendations to the Council or the Assembly regarding additions to, and amplification or modification of, such collective economic and financial measures as might have been initially decided on or recommended in the given situation by the Council or Assembly. This was, in fact, the course followed by the Assembly when it established the Additional Measures Committee to advise it on collective measures against the People's Republic of China at the same time that

[55] *Ibid.*, p. 15.

the Assembly found the People's Republic to have committed an act of aggression by its military intervention in Korea.

The functions of the proposed "co-ordinating committee" were defined as follows:

(i) Receive and study reports from co-operating States on action taken by them in implementing collective economic and financial measures decided upon or recommended by the Security Council or the General Assembly;

(ii) Co-ordinate action related to the adoption and application of economic and financial measures;

(iii) Arrange for the analysis and interchange of information;

(iv) Make such recommendations to the Security Council or the General Assembly and give such advice to States as may be appropriate regarding controls which might be applied;

(v) Define, when specifically requested, the scope of embargoes and other prohibitions;

(vi) Make recommendations, as appropriate, to the Security Council or the General Assembly, regarding additions to and amplifications or modifications of the measures imposed;

(vii) Report from time to time to the Security Council or the General Assembly with reference to the operation of the collective measures and to all related questions;

(viii) Perform such other functions as may be assigned to it.[56]

With respect to economic and financial measures of mutual assistance, whether in the form provided in Article 49 of the Charter or in the form of assistance to the victim of aggression, the Collective Measures Committee was less definite in its conclusions. After reviewing experience of the League of Nations with collective measures, the experience of the Second World War, and experience with collective measures in Korea, the committee concluded that as regards financial assistance and the provision of supplies "the respective roles of the United Nations and individual governments are by no means clear."[57] To meet the need which might arise as the result of a major aggression for the allocation of resources, the committee suggested that the General Assembly or the Security Council "might consider that there should be international machinery," and suggested the utilization of existing bodies or the creation of new bodies in specific cases. The "co-ordinating committee" above referred to would be made responsible for co-ordinating the activities of the various bodies. With respect to relief and refugee assistance, the committee was more definite. Obviously having the Korean experience in mind,

[56] *Ibid.*, pp. 15-16.
[57] *Ibid.*, p. 17.

it concluded: "Experience has demonstrated that relief and refugee assistance can be effectively undertaken by civilian organizations only after hostilities have ceased, in the area to be assisted, although the relief and refugee problem almost inevitably exists concurrently with hostilities. In these circumstances, measures to meet this situation must be taken by the armed forces in the area."[58]

Use of Specialized Agencies

The Charter had envisaged a role for the Economic and Social Council, its subsidiary organs, and the specialized agencies in the maintenance of international peace and security. Article 65 empowers the Economic and Social Council to furnish information to the Security Council and requires it to assist the Security Council on the request of the latter. Article 48(2) provides that decisions of the Security Council shall be carried out by Members "through their action in the appropriate international agencies of which they are members." Agreements between the United Nations and the specialized agencies provide for co-operation on the part of the specialized agencies with the Economic and Social Council in furnishing information and rendering assistance under Article 65.[59]

Neither the Charter nor the agreements concluded under Article 63 of the Charter made any provision for the co-operation of the specialized agencies in the carrying out of collective measures taken on the recommendation of the General Assembly. The "Uniting for Peace" resolution contained no provision for such co-operation. Nevertheless, during the twelfth session of the Economic and Social Council early in 1951, its Committee on Negotiations with Specialized Agencies submitted a resolution designed to promote this co-operation.[60] With slight amendment, this resolution was approved by the Economic and Social Council.[61] In the resolution adopted, the Economic and Social Council requested the Secretary-General to consult with the specialized agencies:

. . . as to the specific arrangements they might most appropriately make in order to provide for the furnishing by them of such information and

---

[58] *Ibid.,* p. 18.

[59] See, for example, Art. VI of the agreement between the United Nations and the Food and Agriculture Organization, U.N. Doc. A/78 (Sept. 30, 1946).

[60] U.N. Doc. E/1941 (Mar. 8, 1951).

[61] Res. 363(XII), Mar. 14, 1951.

for the rendering of such assistance in the maintenance or restoration of international peace and security as may be requested by the Security Council or the General Assembly, such arrangements to cover action on an emergency basis and within the constitutional and budgetary limitations of the agencies to meet urgent requests.

The specialized agencies were invited "to approve arrangements to this end as soon as possible."

The response of the specialized agencies to the Secretary-General's inquiries were varied. Generally speaking, they reflected a willingness to co-operate but little inclination to commit the agencies to specific courses of action. Only the International Bank for Reconstruction and Development and the International Monetary Fund were in the position, by virtue of being operating bodies, to make contributions of some importance to the implementation of collective measures. The other specialized agencies, established as they were to improve standards and provide technical advice and assistance, could be expected to make at most only limited contributions. The agreement between the Bank and United Nations, approved by the General Assembly in November 1947, provided that as a matter of policy the United Nations would refrain from making recommendations on specific loans. In the negotiation of the agreement between the Fund and the United Nations, it was understood that the same policy would be followed in relation to specific transactions of the Fund. In September 1951, the Bank and the Fund declared in identically worded resolutions that in the conduct of their activities they would have "due regard" for the recommendations of the Assembly made pursuant to the "Uniting for Peace" resolution. The Universal Postal Union had taken the position before the "Uniting for Peace" resolution was adopted, that it was not to be concerned with "the problem of sanctions."[62] Other agencies undertook to co-operate with the Assembly in providing assistance, leaving the form of such assistance to be determined by the agency in question in the light of circumstances.

The Collective Measures Committee considered the matter of the possible contributions of the specialized agencies in both its first and its second reports. Its second report was prepared after the Assembly had explicitly recommended to Members that they seek to obtain through international bodies of which they were members "all possible support for collective measures undertaken by the

[62] "Second Report of the Collective Measures Committee, p. 8.

United Nations."[63] On the basis of an examination of what the specialized agencies were in a position to do and had actually undertaken to do, the committee came to the following conclusions:

(a) The functional attributes and constitutional circumstances vary greatly from agency to agency, and none of them has been organized specifically with a view to the implementation of collective measures;

(b) The specialized agencies can, within their fields of competence, play a useful and important role in the application of collective measures. They have practically all expressed readiness to co-operate with the United Nations, although their respective constitutional positions may place limitations on their action;

(c) Among the chief means by which most of the specialized agencies might assist would be, on the one hand, positive measures of participation in programmes of assistance and, on the other hand, the more negative measures of withholding benefits and services or suspending membership rights where constitutionally possible;

(d) Each specialized agency must be regarded as responsible for deciding the nature and extent of its participation in collective measures;

(e) Members of the United Nations which are also members of the specialized agencies have an essential part to play in assuring ready co-operation and assistance on the part of those agencies in United Nations collective measures.[64]

From the reactions of the specialized agencies and from discussions both within the United Nations and in the specialized agencies, it appears that in spite of the willingness of the agencies to agree generally to co-operate with the United Nations in the application of collective measures on the recommendation of the General Assembly or the Security Council, they are not prepared to assume in advance any commitments that would contribute substantially to making more certain the effectiveness of collective measures. Both the agencies themselves and Members of the United Nations when cooperating through them are likely to be primarily concerned with achieving the special purposes for which the agencies were established. Although this will not prevent certain of the agencies from playing important and useful functions in rendering assistance in such matters as health, increased food production, and care of refugees, it is likely to stand in the way of any very active participation in the organization and implementation of collective measures applied against the aggressor. In the Korean case, only the United Nations Educational, Scientific and Cultural Organization aligned itself in a positive way in support of the collective measures directed against

[63] Res. 503(VI), Jan. 12, 1952.
[64] "Second Report of the Collective Measures Committee," p. 10.

the North Korean authorities and the People's Republic of China. Its activities were educational and public informational in character.

Military Measures

The "Uniting for Peace" resolution, under the influence of the Korean experience, was primarily concerned with developing ways of using collective military measures to fill the gap left by the inability of the Security Council to discharge its responsibilities under the Charter. Although the declared purpose of the resolution was to provide for collective military measures on the recommendation of either the Security Council or the General Assembly, it was quite obvious that in practice the second contingency was the one taken most seriously.

The approach of the Collective Measures Committee to the problem of co-ordinating military measures can best be described in its own words:

When the United Nations finds it necessary to adopt measures involving the use of armed force, there will inevitably be an urgent need to take many vital decisions. The basis on which these decisions should be taken should be agreed upon as far as possible beforehand, so as to avoid delays which could cause serious injury to the accomplishment of the purposes of the United Nations. Among essential decisions to be taken is the placing of responsibility for the conduct, on behalf of the Organization, of actual military operations. One of the vital first steps which can be taken beforehand is to agree upon the principle that an executive military authority should be designated for this purpose.

It should be possible to work out in advance certain general principles which cover the relationship of the executive military authority to the victim State and other States which are contributing forces to the United Nations. In addition, many other principles and procedures can be developed in advance of a determination by the United Nations to take military measures. It must, however, be recognized that circumstances may vary greatly in different cases, and it is impossible to make detailed or definite plans in advance. It is, therefore, essential that any methods or procedures worked out at the present stage should retain the maximum flexibility.[65]

The committee considered briefly the possible establishment of a United Nations force, internationally recruited and under an independent international command, but it was of the opinion that the creation of such a force was administratively, financially, and militarily impractical.[66]

[65] *Ibid.*, pp. 24-25.
[66] *Ibid.*, p. 12.

CHAPTER XVII

Initiation of Collective Measures

I F COLLECTIVE measures "for the prevention and removal of threats to the peace, and for the suppression of acts of aggression and other breaches of the peace" are to be "effective," it is obviously necessary that the states applying these measures should be in agreement regarding the circumstances in which they are to be applied and the procedures that are to be followed in their application. Once the occasion for their use arises, it is important that the states joining in the use of coercive measures act collectively, and not separately.

The League of Nations Experience

Under the Covenant of the League of Nations, Members undertook "to respect and preserve as against external aggression the territorial integrity and existing political independence of all Members of the League."[1] The Council of the League was to advise on how this obligation was to be fulfilled. Members also undertook, in case any Member resorted to war in violation of its covenants under Articles 12, 13, or 15, "immediately to subject it to the severance of all trade or financial relations, the prohibition of all intercourse between their nationals and the nationals of the covenant-breaking State and the prevention of all financial, commercial or personal intercourse between the nationals of the covenant-breaking State and the nationals of any other State, whether a Member of the League or not."[2] It was declared to be the duty of the Council of the League in any such case to recommend to the several governments what "effective military, naval or air force" they should contribute to the armed forces to be used to protect the covenants of the League.

The force of the obligations contained in Article 10 of the Covenant was largely destroyed by an interpretative resolution

[1] Art. 10.
[2] Art. 16(1).

424

that was almost unanimously approved by the Assembly of the League in 1923. It required the Council, when making a recommendation under Article 10, "to take account, more particularly, of the geographical situation and of the special conditions of each State." It also declared that it was "for the constitutional authorities of each Member to decide, in reference to the obligation of preserving the independence and the integrity of the territory of Members, in what degree the Member is bound to assure the execution of this obligation by employment of its military forces."[3]

The commitments set forth in Article 16 of the Covenant were cut down by a similar process of interpretation. Acting in accordance with recommendations of its International Blockade Committee, the Assembly of the League approved in 1921 four draft amendments to Article 16 and nineteen interpretative resolutions.[4] Although the draft amendments never entered into force, the action by the Assembly established the policy largely followed in the subsequent application of Article 16. The most important of the proposed changes were the following: (1) all sanctions, including economic and financial, were to be applied progressively and selectively; (2) any breach of the Covenant under Article 16 was to be brought to the Council of the League as a matter of urgency, and the Council was to make recommendations to Members regarding the action to be taken; and (3) the Council was to assume the responsibility of co-ordination, with such technical assistance as it might provide.

When sanctions were applied by the League of Nations against Italy in October 1935, the policy of selective sanctions was followed. The recommendation of measures to be applied and the time and other conditions of their application were made the responsibility of a specially constituted Coordination Committee consisting of all Members of the League joining in the application of sanctions. Five measures were put into operation. These included an embargo on the export of arms, munitions, and war materials to Italy, an embargo on loans and credits to Italy, a ban on the importation of goods made or grown in Italy, an embargo on the export to Italy of a selected list of goods of special usefulness in time of war, and mutual economic support. A few Members refused to participate;

---

[3] League of Nations, *Official Journal,* Special Supplement No. 11 (October 1923), p. 34.

[4] *Ibid.,* Special Supplement No. 6 (October 1921), pp. 14-15, 24-26.

others limited their application of the measures in question. In the case of the trade prohibitions, there was considerable delay in applying them. Thus in practice the automatic application of comprehensive economic and financial sanctions was never even attempted, and military measures were never applied.[5]

The Charter System

When the Charter of the United Nations was being prepared, special attention was given to remedying the demonstrated defects of the League of Nations system. The experience of the League appeared to suggest that economic and financial sanctions alone were not enough, and that some provision had to be made to ensure the use of military measures when necessary. The principle of the selective application of sanctions appeared sound provided there was some assurance that, if the measures initially selected proved to be ineffective, additional measures would be applied in time and on a scale adequate enough to be effective. The establishment of an international organ with competence to take necessary binding decisions with respect to measures to be applied seemed desirable. The course followed by Members of the League of Nations in applying sanctions against Italy, of improvising when the need arose, was open to serious criticism. It also seemed unrealistic to think that sanctions could be applied with equal success against either a large or a small nation. Obviously, it was desirable, if not essential, for the group of nations applying the sanctions to have a decisive superiority of power and that superiority could be most certainly achieved if the decision to apply sanctions was taken only with the concurrence of the major nations.

Considerations of this nature led to the incorporation in the Charter of the United Nations of a different approach to the problem of collective sanctions from that found in the Covenant of the League of Nations. The Security Council was made primarily responsible for the maintenance of international peace and security and was given the power to determine what coercive measures should be taken for maintaining or restoring international peace and security, once a threat to the peace, breach of the peace, or act

[5] See Royal Institute of International Affairs, *International Sanctions* (Oxford 1938).

of aggression had been determined to exist. The measures that might be taken under Articles 41 and 42 of the Charter might range from severance of diplomatic relations and a variety of economic and financial measures to the fullest use of air, sea, and land forces. Furthermore, the Council was empowered to decide what measures should be taken by individual Members, taking into account geographical circumstances and capacity. With respect to military measures, however, Members would be bound by decisions of the Council only to the extent that they had agreed to place forces and facilities at the disposal of the Council by agreements under Article 43 of the Charter. Pending the coming into force of such agreements as in the opinion of the Council would enable it to exercise its responsibilities, the permanent members of the Council were to consult together with a view to "such joint action on behalf of the Organization" as might be necessary to the maintenance of international peace and security.[6]

In addition to thus focusing responsibility and power of decision in the Council and its permanent members, the Charter placed the Member states under specific obligations. They were required to give the United Nations every assistance in any action taken "in accordance with the present Charter," and to refrain from giving assistance to any state "against which the United Nations is taking preventive or enforcement action."[7] They had to accept and carry out the decisions of the Council "in accordance with the present Charter."[8] They had to join "in affording mutual assistance in carrying out the measures decided upon by the Security Council."[9]

Competence of the Security Council and the General Assembly

The explicit provisions of the Charter with respect to the initiation of collective measures in case of a threat to the peace, breach of the peace, or act of aggression were found to be of limited value from the beginning because of the inability of the permanent members of the Security Council to co-operate and, more particularly, because of their failure to agree on the principles governing

[6] Art. 106.
[7] Art. 2(5).
[8] Art. 25.
[9] Art. 49.

the military agreements to be concluded under Article 43. As a result, it was necessary to develop alternative methods within the permissive limits of the Charter.

In addition to the express authority that the Council has under Articles 39, 41, and 42 to take binding decisions regarding measures to be applied, it has primary responsibility under Article 24 for maintaining international peace and security and, under Article 39, may make recommendations "to maintain or restore international peace and security." At the San Francisco Conference, the view was expressed and accepted by the responsible committee of the Conference that, in so far as the Council was making "recommendations" under Article 39 its action would be governed by the provisions of Chapter VI of the Charter.[10] In other words, the authority of the Council to make recommendations had special reference to the exercise of the function of peaceful settlement, while the authority to take binding decisions applied to collective measures taken under Articles 41 and 42 to maintain or restore international peace and security. The phraseology of Article 39 does not, however, preclude the recommendation by the Council of such collective measures. Therefore when the Council was considering the North Korean armed attack on the Republic of Korea, although it could not exercise its powers under Article 42 because no agreements under Article 43 were in force, it could and did adopt a resolution recommending that Members furnish assistance to the Republic of Korea. The Soviet Union and other members of the Soviet bloc argued that this resolution was invalid, not because the Council did not have authority to make this kind of recommendation, but because the resolution was not adopted in accordance with the provisions of Article 27.

The competence of the General Assembly with respect to collective measures was considered at some length in the discussions during the autumn of 1950 preceding the adoption of the "Uniting for Peace" resolution. The question had not been directly considered by the Assembly before this time, although certain inferences could have been drawn from earlier practice of the Assembly, especially in the Spanish and Greek cases.

In the Spanish case, after the Council had failed to agree on any course of action, either under Chapter VI or Chapter VII of the

[10] U.N. Information Organizations and U.S. Library of Congress, *Documents of the United Nations Conference on International Organization*, Vol. 12 (1945), p. 507.

Charter, several Members of the Organization asked the Assembly to consider the relations of Members with Spain. Some delegations questioned the right of the Assembly to recommend measures of the kind that the Council was expressly authorized to take under Chapter VII. But, in reply to those Members, it was pointed out that inasmuch as Members acting individually could adopt the proposed measures, the Assembly could recommend that such measures be taken collectively.

The Assembly finally adopted a resolution intended to bring limited pressure to bear on the Franco Government.[11] There was no assertion in the resolution of the competence of the Assembly to recommend collective measures for maintaining or restoring international peace and security. But the specific measures recommended—the withdrawal of heads of diplomatic missions and the exclusion of the Franco Government from membership in the specialized agencies and participation in conferences held under United Nations auspices—were of the nature of those measures the Council is expressly authorized to take under Article 41 for that purpose. The responses of Members to these recommendations disclosed no inclination openly to challenge the action of the Assembly.[12] Although the Assembly later revoked its 1946 recommendations, there is no evidence that this reflected a reversal of the original position of the Assembly with respect to its competence. Rather, it appears to have indicated a change of policy toward the Franco Government on the part of certain Members.

In the Greek case, the Assembly was also requested to take action following a deadlock in the Council. The situation that the Assembly was called upon to consider was quite different, however, from the Spanish case in that there was, according to the contention of one of the parties and in the view of a majority of the members of the Council, an actual threat to the peace. The first resolution of the Assembly, adopted on October 21, 1947, established a Special Committee on the Balkans to perform the functions of investigation, observation, and conciliation. When this committee reported its conclusion that aid was being given to the guerrillas with the knowledge of the governments of Albania, Bulgaria, and Yugoslavia and that, so long as the aid continued, a threat to the political inde-

---

[11] Res. 39(I), Dec. 12, 1946.

[12] U.N. General Assembly, Second Session, *Official Records*, Supplement No. 1, pp. 2-4.

pendence and territorial integrity of Greece would exist and international peace and security in the area would be endangered, the Assembly in its third session adopted a resolution of a more forceful nature. This resolution found that "continued aid" endangered peace in the Balkans, and recommended "to all Members of the United Nations and to all other States that their Governments refrain from any action designed to assist directly or through any other Government any armed group fighting against the Greek Government."[13]

Later, the Special Committee reported in 1949 that Albania and Bulgaria continued to give assistance to the Greek guerrillas, but aid from Yugoslavia appeared to be tapering off. At that time, the Assembly proceeded to take its strongest action and recommended to all Members and "to all other states": that they "refrain from any action designed to assist directly or through any other Government any armed group fighting against Greece"; that they refrain from direct or indirect provision of "arms or other materials of war to Albania and Bulgaria" until the Special Committee or another competent organ of the United Nations had determined that the unlawful assistance had ceased; and that they "take into account, in their relations with Albania and Bulgaria, the extent to which those two countries henceforth abide by the recommendations of the Assembly in their relations with Greece."[14] Thus the Assembly, even before the adoption of the "Uniting for Peace" resolution in November 1950, used its powers of recommendation to urge Members and states not Members of the United Nations to take collective measures—political and economic in character—to induce offending states to cease acts found by the Assembly to endanger international peace and security.

The Assembly in the "Uniting for Peace" resolution categorically asserted its competence to consider any case "where there appears to be a threat to the peace, breach of the peace, or act of aggression," with respect to which the Council "because of lack of unanimity of the permanent members, fails to exercise its primary responsibility." The Assembly would act with a view to making "appropriate recommendations" of collective measures to maintain or restore international peace and security, "including in the case of a breach of the

[13] Res. 193(III), Nov. 27, 1948.
[14] Res. 288(IV), Nov. 18, 1949.

peace or act of aggression the use of armed force when necessary."[15] In presenting the seven-power draft that was the basis of the resolution finally adopted, the United States delegate emphasized the broad powers of discussion and recommendation that the Assembly possessed under Article 10, qualified only by the provision of Article 12(1) that the Assembly could not make a recommendation with respect to a dispute or situation while the Council was exercising its functions.

The Soviet argument against this proposition stressed two principal points: (1) that the assumption by the General Assembly of the power to recommend collective measures was in violation of the principles of the primary responsibility of the Security Council and the unanimity of the great powers; and (2) that the proposal directly violated the provision of Article 11(2) of the Charter according to which the Assembly must refer to the Council, either before or after discussion, any question on which "action is necessary." The Soviet delegate maintained that the action there referred to was action of the kind that only the Council had the authority to take under Chapter VII of the Charter. "That was a very important prerogative," he said, "whose fulfillment might be fraught with dire consequences for the peace of the world since it related to the kind of action which required the concurring votes of the five permanent members of the Security Council."[16] He stated further that the Council alone was judge of what action was required and might decide that no action was necessary.[17]

To these arguments the supporters of the "Uniting for Peace" resolution responded that, although it was true that the primary responsibility for the maintenance of peace rested with the Security Council, the Members of the United Nations were none the less obliged to act collectively to keep the peace. It was admitted that, although the Assembly could not take "binding decisions," it could, under its broad powers, make recommendations that, if backed by large majorities, "would naturally carry considerable weight and would spur Member States to action."[18] One answer to the Soviet argument based on Article 11(2) was that this article did not limit

[15] Pt. A, Sec. A(1). See App. F.
[16] U.N. General Assembly, Fifth Session, First Committee, *Official Records*, 357th Meeting (Oct. 10, 1950), p. 85.
[17] *Ibid.*, 364th Meeting (Oct. 16, 1950), p. 133.
[18] *Ibid.*, 354th Meeting (Oct. 9, 1950), p. 66.

the powers of the Assembly under Article 10 because "action," as the word was used in Article 11, referred to enforcement action of the kind the Council could take under Articles 41 and 42, *i.e.* decisions committing Members to the use of particular measures. The Assembly, however, by the express terms of Article 10, was limited to making recommendations and therefore could not in any case take the kind of action referred to in Articles 41 and 42.[19] Another answer was that, even though "action" were interpreted to cover measures of the kind described in Articles 41 and 42, nothing in the Charter prevented the Assembly from making recommendations that such measures be applied, once the matter had been referred to the Council and the Council had ceased to exercise its functions with respect to it.[20] According to this view, if a dispute or situation claimed to be a threat to the peace, breach of the peace, or act of aggression, should initially be brought before the Assembly, the Assembly would be obligated first to refer it to the Council. If the Council was unable to take action, the Assembly would then be free to recommend collective measures.

There was agreement during the discussions that Article 12(1) constituted a limitation on the exercise of the powers of the Assembly, but as one delegate put it, this limitation affected not the competence of the Assembly "but the time when that competence could be exercised."[21] Neither the discussion nor the text of the resolution finally adopted made clear who should determine whether and when the Security Council had failed "to exercise its responsibility." Article 12(2) of the Charter implies that the decision must be taken by the Council, and this view has found support in the practice of the Council.

The General Assembly on February 1, 1951, approved a resolution proposed by the United States, finding that the People's Republic of China had engaged in aggression in Korea, calling upon states and authorities to give every assistance to the United Nations, and requesting a study of additional measures to meet the aggression. The Assembly exercised its authority under the "Uniting for Peace" resolution after the Council, which had been considering the "complaint of aggression against the Republic of Korea," voted to remove the item from its agenda. In the discussion preceding

[19] *Ibid.*, 363rd Meeting (Oct. 16, 1950), p. 127.
[20] *Ibid.*, 364th Meeting (Oct. 16, 1950), pp. 129-30.
[21] *Ibid.*, 360th Meeting (Oct. 12, 1950), p. 104.

this action, the British representative called attention to the fact that the Council had not "in effect, been exercising its functions in respect of this question" since the preceding November when the negative vote of the Soviet Union prevented the adoption of the resolution proposed by the six powers. "Nevertheless," he continued,

. . . the discussion which has since taken place in the General Assembly has ranged over a considerable field, and my own delegation, at any rate, feels that if the General Assembly were to adopt a resolution containing recommendations to Members and dealing with the question of Chinese intervention, or with the broader question of the complaint of aggression against the Republic of Korea, both questions having now become indistinguishable in practice, objections might then be raised that this would be an infringement of Article 12 of the Charter.[22]

When the report of the Additional Measures Committee, which had been established by the Assembly in its resolution of February 1, 1951, was being considered by the First Committee of the Assembly, the Soviet delegate repeated the contention of his Government that in view of the provisions of Articles 24 and 11(2) of the Charter, the Assembly had no competence to recommend the application of collective measures against the Government of China at Peiping. He refused to admit the competence of the Assembly, and announced that he would not participate in the discussion of measures to be taken. The Indian delegate also abstained, after calling attention to the fact that India had opposed the February 1 resolution. He did not, however, appear to deny the competence of the Assembly, but only the expediency of the proposed action. For the great majority of Members, the competence of the Assembly to recommend "additional measures" was taken for granted.

The Role of Member States

One of the main objectives of those who wrote the Charter of the United Nations was to limit, and in so far as practical to exclude, the possibility that one state or a small group of states should on their own initiative and without legal restraint use force or the threat of force to attain national ends. In line with this objective, an attempt was made to center in the United Nations itself respon-

[22] U.N. Security Council, Sixth Year, *Official Records*, 531st Meeting (Jan. 31, 1951), p. 8.

sibility for deciding when such force could be legitimately used. Furthermore, the primary responsibility was placed on the Security Council on the assumption that the great powers had special responsibilities and therefore should have corresponding authority.

Even on the assumption that the Council would be able to discharge this responsibility with reasonable success, it was found necessary to insert in the Charter certain provisions reserving the right of independent action by Member states in the use of armed force. Under the terms of Article 51, for example, "the inherent right of individual or collective self-defense" in case of armed attack upon a Member remains unimpaired until the Council takes the measures necessary to maintain international peace and security. By the terms of Article 53, although enforcement action cannot be taken under a regional arrangement or by a regional agency except on the authorization of the Council, this prohibition does not apply in the case of measures taken against an "enemy state," (any state which during the Second World War was an enemy of any signatory of the Charter) whether pursuant to Article 107 of the Charter or under "regional arrangements directed against renewal of aggressive policy on the part of any such state."

If the Security Council had been able to discharge its responsibility as the authors of the Charter had hoped, it is possible that in practice these exceptions would have been kept within narrow and relatively innocuous limits, because with its permanent members co-operating, the Council presumably would have been able to act promptly and decisively in case of any threat to or breach of the peace. Moreover, if such co-operation had been achieved, there would not have been the urgent necessity of considering what action should be taken to restrain aggression by a great power or a satellite of a great power. When co-operation among the permanent members broke down, or, more accurately, failed to materialize, and when as a consequence the Council was unable to perform its function of principal initiator of collective measures, it seemed necessary to many Members to make extensive use of the exceptions in the Charter.

By the terms of the collective self-defense arrangements concluded under Article 51 and the regional security arrangements directed against "enemy states" under Article 53, Members, individually and collectively, have assumed the right, subject to obligations under the Charter, to determine when and what collective measures of defense are to be applied in situations defined in the agreements.[23] These developments have greatly magnified the role of individual states and groups of states in determining when to initiate collective measures and the form that they should take. Even when the Security Council acts, as in the case of the North Korean attack on the Republic of Korea, the fact that it recommends and does not order leaves a wide range of discretion to each Member in determining the time and extent of its participation. The same is true in the case of a recommendation by the General Assembly. Furthermore, in view of the time required to follow the procedure prescribed by the "Uniting for Peace" resolution, it may appear necessary to Members that they act on their own initiative and take measures in advance of an anticipated recommendation by the United Nations in a situation where it is not strictly permissible for those Members to act under a collective self-defense arrangement or in the exercise of the right of individual or collective self-defense in case of armed attack against a Member.

This raises an important question regarding the extent to which Members may use force or the threat of force on their own responsibility to advance "the Purposes" of the United Nations. This question arose in connection with the military aid given by the United States to the Republic of Korea following the North Korean attack. Military measures, including the ordering of naval and air forces into action against the North Korean forces and the "neutralization" of Formosa by United States naval forces, were taken on June 26, 1950. The assistance to the Republic of Korea was justified as assistance given by the United States to the United Nations in the execution of the resolution of June 25, but although that resolution called upon Members to give every assistance in its execution, it did not contain any order or recommendation that Members use armed force to this end. It is true that the Council subsequently recommended on June 27 that assistance be given to the Republic of Korea, but the measures taken by the United States on June 26 went beyond the terms of the recommendation of the Council.

It is questionable whether this action of the United States in the Korean situation could be justified as an exercise of the right of collective self-defense within the limits defined by Article 51, inasmuch

---

[23] For detailed analysis of these agreements, see the volume in this Brookings series, *Regional Security and the United Nations.*

as the victim of the attack was not a Member.[24] Most Members of the United Nations viewed the action of the United States, in so far as assistance to the Republic of Korea was concerned, as necessary to the achievement of a major purpose of the United Nations, *i.e.* the restraint of aggression. There was also an inclination not to be overly concerned with technical points and a willingness to recognize that, as in certain circumstances a state may properly use armed force in self-defense, so in circumstances where time is of the essence, a Member of the United Nations can use armed force to assist in meeting an armed attack, which the Security Council has determined to have been committed, without waiting for an explicit decision or recommendation by a United Nations organ that such action should be taken.

Some Members of the United Nations found it more difficult, however, to justify the unilateral use by the United States of armed force in order to neutralize Formosa at a time when Communist China had not even been charged before the Council with being a party to the armed attack. The position of the United States was that "the occupation of Formosa by Communist forces would be a direct threat to the security of the Pacific area and to United States forces performing their lawful and necessary functions in that area."[25] This in effect was an assertion of the right of each Member to determine and to take measures considered necessary to the achievement of a United Nations purpose in circumstances that, in the opinion of many, did not require action in advance of a decision by the Security Council and in a situation in which other Members of the United Nations, especially those whose policies toward Communist China differed from those of the United States, were not in agreement. The exercise of such a broad right of independent action opens up dangerous possibilities of abuse and may become as serious a threat to the efficacy of collective action by the United Nations as the exercise of the historic right of individual self-defense. Although the Peiping Government charged the United States with having committeed an act of armed aggression in Formosa, which the United States denied, neither the Council nor the Assembly

[24] Although Article 51 characterizes the right of individual and collective self-defense as "inherent," it explicitly recognizes this right only in case of an armed attack upon a Member.

[25] U.N. Security Council, Fifth Year, *Official Records*, No. 16, 474th Meeting (June 27, 1950), p. 5.

ever took any decision on the complaint, which soon became over-shadowed by Chinese Communist intervention in support of the North Korean forces.

Under the Charter, a Member retains the right to use, in its discretion, measures intended to exercise a degree of compulsion on other states, including under certain circumstances force or the threat of force. One of the main purposes of the Charter, however, in addition to the limitation of this discretionary use of force, is to induce Members to take coercive measures in accordance with decisions of the United Nations for the common objective of maintaining or restoring international peace and security. Thus under the terms of Chapter VII of the Charter, the Security Council has the power to order Members to take political, economic, financial, and military measures to maintain or restore international peace and security, if a threat to the peace, breach of the peace, or act of aggression has been found to exist. Since the failure of the permanent members of the Council to co-operate has prevented this power from being used, efforts have been made to develop a sense of obligation to apply collective measures under other provisions of the Charter.

As has already been noted, the Council chose to recommend, not order, that Members give assistance to the Republic of Korea following the North Korean attack. In part, this was because agreements under Article 43 were not in force; in part, it was because of the importance of the time element. An order needed to be specific in its terms to have the desired effect, and this would have required more time, information, and advance preparation than circumstances permitted.

Notwithstanding the recommendatory language of the resolution of June 27, 1950, emphasis was placed on the duty of Members to comply with it. A number of Members, in reply to the cablegram of the Secretary-General informing them of the action by the Security Council, indicated an intention to fulfill the obligations incumbent on Members. On June 28, for example, the Council of the Organization of American States adopted a resolution that stated, after referring to the resolutions of the Security Council of June 25 and 27, that "all the States members of the Organization of American States are Members of the United Nations and are, therefore, obligated by the terms of those decisions and bound to comply with them."[26] However, in the course of discussion in the Security

[26] *Ibid.*, No. 17, 475th Meeting (June 30, 1950), pp. 6-7.

Council, following the first report on responses of Members to the resolution of June 27, it was made clear that Members were not legally obligated to accept and carry out the recommendation contained in it. The Egyptian representative, speaking as a Member that did not vote for the adoption of the resolution, stressed that it "does not order; it recommends." This meant that "each Government, according to its circumstances and its own judgment and in the light of the Charter and of international law, was free to decide how far it could go."[27] The British representative who had earlier provoked the Egyptian statement by a comment of his own, indicated his full agreement in the following words:

> Still less do I dispute, and still less would any of us here dispute, the complete right of Egypt to take any decision it desires to take. That is the main point I should like to make. Of course, under the resolution adopted, every Government is perfectly at liberty to accept or not to accept its recommendations. I should not dispute that for a moment and, if I suggested anything to the contrary, I withdraw it at once.[28]

In regard to recommendations of collective measures by the General Assembly, it is clear that they do not create legal obligations for Members. During the discussion leading up to the adoption of the "Uniting for Peace" resolution, the United States delegate argued that, although a recommendation of the Assembly did not have the obligatory force of a decision of the Council under Chapter VII, "the history of the Korean question had shown that the voluntary response to a recommendation could be even more effective than obedience to an order."[29] In its first report to the Assembly, the Collective Measures Committee established by that resolution stated that "each Member has the duty to participate in accordance with the Charter in the maintenance of peace and security and to act collectively, if States are to be able to count on the security which the Charter is intended to provide."[30] It is quite clear, however, that what the committee had in mind was not a legal duty, in the strict sense of the term, to carry out recommendations of the General Assembly or of the Security Council, but instead what might be called a moral duty to take collective action to maintain interna-

[27] *Ibid.*, p. 13.
[28] *Ibid.*, p. 15.
[29] U.N. General Assembly, Fifth Session, First Committee, *Official Records*, 354th Meeting (Oct. 9, 1950), p. 64.
[30] U.N. General Assembly, Sixth Session, *Official Records*, Supplement No. 13, p. 1.

tional peace and security. The recommendations of the Assembly and the Council were to be regarded as guides that should command great respect. The discussions leading up to the adoption of the resolution of the Assembly of May 18, 1951 recommending an embargo on the shipment of certain categories of strategic goods to North Korea and continental China and the responses of Members to it, indicated the considerable moral and political authority that such a recommendation has.[31] Nevertheless, in order to obtain the desired initial support for the resolution, it was made clear that each Member would determine for itself the specific articles to be embargoed and the procedures to be followed.

Considerations Affecting Initiation of Measures

Under the Charter, a determination by the Security Council of the existence of a threat to the peace, breach of the peace, or act of aggression places on that organ a duty to take necessary measures to maintain or restore international peace or security. But some members of the Council have been reluctant to agree to a determination of the existence of any one of these conditions if there were substantial reasons for believing that the permanent members would not be willing to co-operate in taking the measures necessary to maintain or restore international peace and security.

In the Palestine case, the Soviet Union was favorable to the use of collective measures, if necessary, to suppress any attempt to alter by force the plan of partition recommended by the General Assembly. This attitude was undoubtedly a result in large part of the Soviet desire to speed the withdrawal of the British from Palestine. The United Kingdom, however, was not willing to join in the exercise of coercion for this purpose, because of an unwillingness to antagonize the Arabs, special treaty relations with certain Arab states, and strong opposition to allowing the Soviet Union to get a foothold in the Eastern Mediterranean area. The United States, although favorable to partition and initially to the assumption by the Council of responsibility for preventing the use of force against the plan, later opposed for a time any determination by the Council that a threat to the peace existed as a result of Arab resistance. The United States also appears to have been motivated by a desire to

[31] Res. 500(V).

mollify the Arabs and keep Soviet influence out of the area. When it was finally decided in late May 1948 to address a strong demand to the parties for a cease-fire and for an undertaking not to bring in additional fighting personnel and war material, the members of the Council, with the exception of the Soviet Union, the Ukraine, and Syria, which abstained from voting, agreed to call upon all governments to assist in the implementation of this resolution. As a result, an embargo was imposed on a nondiscriminatory basis in support of the provisional measures that the parties were asked to accept and carry out. This involved none of the objectionable political consequences of overtly discriminatory action or joint military measures. Later, when fighting broke out in the Negeb between Egyptian and Israeli forces, and the Egyptian authorities were reluctant to agree to a cease-fire because of the unfavorable position of their forces, pressure was applied outside the Council in the form of a threat by the United Kingdom to invoke the Anglo-Egyptian treaty of 1936, which Egypt was anxious to terminate.

The action of the Council in dealing with the situation created by the first Netherlands "police action" in Indonesia was influenced by a variety of national attitudes. The original Australian draft resolution of August 1, 1948, called for action by the Council under Chapter VII of the Charter. The Soviet Union, for reasons of its own, including the desire to appear as the champion of the subject peoples and to eliminate Western European influence from the area, gave the Australian proposal strong support. The United States, the United Kingdom, and France, however, were reluctant to take any action of an openly coercive nature. The United States was willing to go further than either the United Kingdom or France in bringing pressure to bear on the Netherlands, but it was highly sensitive to the desirability of an orderly transition of authority, of avoiding too great a blow to Netherlands power and prestige, and of preventing Communist influence from gaining a foothold in the area. When the Council encountered difficulties in obtaining the acceptance by the Netherlands of its resolutions, following the second Netherlands "police action" in 1948, various pressures were applied. These included the withholding by the United States of economic aid from the Netherlands in Indonesia and other measures taken by certain Asian states independently and through the New Delhi Conference.

In Korea, on the other hand, although the fighting had certain of the aspects of a civil war, and although there were serious practical difficulties in the way of collective measures, the decision to recommend such measures was quickly taken. The United States even acted in advance of the specific recommendation by the Council that assistance be given the Republic of Korea.] The considerations explaining the difference between the course followed in Korea and that followed in Palestine and Indonesia include the following: (1) the clear-cut nature of North Korean aggression against a state that had in a sense been created by the United Nations, an attack certified by the United Nations Commission on the spot; (2) the conviction based on reports received from the commission that the North Korean authorities were in no mood to cease hostilities and negotiate; (3) the fact that this aggression was interpreted, especially in the United States, as an indication "that communism has passed beyond the use of subversion to conquer independent nations, and will now use armed invasion and war";[32] (4) the interest of the United States in the protection of the Republic of Korea and in making collective security work, together with the availability of the necessary armed forces and assistance to achieve these two ends; and (5) the willingness of other Members of the United Nations, especially members of the North Atlantic Treaty Organization, to take limited risks and assume limited responsibilities in view of the readiness of the United States to join in making collective security an operative reality. The members of the North Atlantic Treaty Organization, which were among the states giving strongest support to the United States initiative, had important special interests of their own that were being served: they were obtaining assurance that assistance by the United States under the North Atlantic Treaty and other special security arrangements could be expected in case of need; and the British and the French, in particular, were receiving new support in their fight against communism in their Asiatic territories.

When the United States proposed that Communist China be found guilty of aggression as a result of its intervention in Korea and that additional collective measures be taken against it, a variety of considerations influenced most Members of the United Nations to accept the proposal. But it was accepted only on condition that the application of "additional measures" should be delayed until further efforts had been made to achieve a cease-fire and a peaceful settle-

<hr/>

[32] U.N. Security Council, Fifth Year, *Official Records*, No. 16, 474th Meeting (June 27, 1950). Statement of President Truman, p. 5.

ment. Among the considerations that influenced Members to adopt this attitude were the following: (1) Certain Members, especially members of the North Atlantic Treaty Organization, were fearful that the defense of Western Europe would be weakened by the expansion of hostilities in Asia. (2) The view was frankly expressed that, although collective measures might be feasible against a small state, they could not be used with equal success against a great power, because the result would be a general war. (3) There was considerable feeling on the part of some Members that they were becoming involved in what they believed was essentially a power struggle between the great powers in east Asia. (4) There was a widespread conviction that collective measures, even if successful in defeating the aggression, would not contribute in the long run to the achievement of a durable political settlement in east Asia. The United States, on the other hand, took the position that additional measures should be promptly applied to deny the fruits of aggression, to establish a precedent for future collective security, and to prevent Communist expansion. The strong stand taken by the United States was by itself an important, if not decisive, consideration in causing many members to accept the proposal of the United States.

From the discussions and reports of the Additional Measures Committee and the discussions that took place in the First Committee of the General Assembly,[33] the following considerations appear to have determined the timing and nature of the recommendations by the Assembly on May 18 for the application of additional collective measures against Communist China and North Korea: (1) Although there was a strong desire to achieve a cease-fire and a peaceful settlement, and to do nothing that might in any way jeopardize the chances of achieving these ends, the launching of the spring offensives in April and early May 1951 by the Chinese Communist and North Korean forces had largely destroyed any hope that the Good Offices Committee might be successful and that the Chinese Communists would accept the United Nations proposals.[34] (2) There was a desire to localize the conflict and to prevent it from expanding into a large-scale war. Consequently, there was strong opposition to

[33] U.N. General Assembly, Fifth Session, First Committee, *Official Records*, Vol. II, 443-44th Meetings (May 17, 1951), pp. 629-38.
[34] The Good Offices Committee was established by the General Assembly resolution of Feb. 1, 1951.

collective measures that went substantially beyond those that were already being applied. Yet there was general agreement on the part of Members applying military and economic measures that measures already being taken should be as effective as possible and that any existing gaps should be filled in order to apply maximum pressure within these limits. (3) Those Members with armed forces in Korea were understandably anxious to withhold from the Chinese Communists and North Koreans all strategic materials that might be used against their armed forces. (4) As it was considered desirable to achieve the maximum degree of unity, it was not possible to make recommendations going much beyond the actual practice of states, or to limit the right of each Member to determine the materials to be subjected to the embargo or the methods to be followed.

Nature of Initiating Decisions

In no instance have collective measures been initiated by decision of the Security Council acting under Articles 41 and 42 of the Charter. In every case where collective measures have been adopted, the organ of the United Nations that has been responsible has recommended to Members that they apply them. In some cases, the organ has recommended specific measures to be taken; in others, the recommendation has been in general terms. When the General Assembly, for example, recommended collective political measures to be applied by Members with a view to weakening the position of the Franco Government in Spain, it indicated the specific measures to be taken.[35] Likewise, in indicating measures to be taken against Albania and Bulgaria in 1949, the Assembly recommended that Members and other States "refrain from the direct or indirect provision of arms or other materials of war."[36] By its resolution of February 1, 1951, the Assembly, after finding that Communist China had engaged in aggression by its action in Korea, called upon "all States and authorities to continue to lend every assistance to the United Nations action in Korea" and "to refrain from giving any assistance to the aggressors in Korea."[37] Later the same year, in its resolution of May 18, the Assembly specified in some detail the particular measures to be applied. It recommended that every State:

[35] Res. 39(I), Dec. 12, 1946.
[36] Res. 288(IV), Nov. 18, 1949.
[37] Res. 498(V).

(a) Apply an embargo on the shipment to areas under the control of the Central People's Government of the People's Republic of China and of the North Korean authorities of arms, ammunition and implements of war, atomic energy materials, petroleum, transportation materials of strategic value, and items useful in the production of arms, ammunition and implements of war;

(b) Determine which commodities exported from its territory fall within the embargo, and apply controls to give effect to the embargo;

(c) Prevent by all means within its jurisdiction the circumvention of controls on shipments applied by other States pursuant to the present resolution;

(d) Co-operate with other States in carrying out the purposes of this embargo;

(e) Report to the Additional Measures Committee, within thirty days and thereafter at the request of the Committee, on the measures taken in accordance with the present resolution.[38]

In dealing with the North Korean armed attack, the Security Council couched its initial resolution of June 25, 1950 in the broadest terms, leaving complete freedom to Members to determine the particular measures they would take. After calling for "the immediate cessation of hostilities" and the withdrawal of North Korean armed forces to the thirty-eighth parallel, the Council also called upon Members "to render every assistance to the United Nations in the execution of this resolution and to refrain from giving assistance to the North Korean authorities." By its resolution of June 27, the Council recommended that they "furnish such assistance to the Republic of Korea as may be necessary to repel the armed attack and to restore international peace and security in the area." The need for quick action was a principal reason for putting the recommendation in such general terms.

The resolution of the Assembly on May 18, 1951, providing for measures against Communist China, was the result of extensive study and consultation in advance, for the Assembly had provided in its resolution of February 1 for the consideration by a special committee of "additional measures" to be applied to meet the Chinese Communist aggression.[39] The specific recommendations that were made by the Additional Measures Committee were prepared initially by a subcommittee of five—Australia, France, the United Kingdom,

---

[38] Res. 500(V), May 18, 1951.

[39] The Additional Measures Committee was composed of the members of the Collective Measures Committe, see above, Chap. XVI, footnote 35. Two members, Yugoslavia and Burma, refused to serve.

the United States, and Venezuela. The United States took the initiative in the work of the committee and the subcommittee. It introduced the resolution, which the committee approved for presentation to the Assembly, and which, with one amendment, was adopted.

Response of Members to United Nations Recommendations

As the Security Council has not exercised its powers under Articles 41 and 42, there is no possibility of comparing the effectiveness, in terms of Member response, of decisions taken under those articles and recommendations made by the Council or the General Assembly under Articles 39 and 10, respectively. There is no conclusive evidence regarding the comparative effectiveness of recommendations by the Council and the Assembly. It might logically be expected, and there would appear to be some substantiation in practice, that a recommendation by the Assembly that has broad support, and to which the great majority of Members have committed themselves to the extent of voting for it, will receive as favorable a response in terms of compliance as a resolution by the Council. It must be borne in mind, however, that a recommendation does not legally commit Members to action, and that a variety of considerations may lead a Member state to vote for a particular resolution without providing equally strong motives for that state to comply fully with its provisions. Furthermore, it must be recognized that a broadly supported recommendation by the Assembly may not be easy to obtain. A great deal of patient negotiation may be required to overcome objections that may be raised and to achieve a text expressing a wide consensus.

The resolution of the Assembly of December 12, 1946, regarding Spain recommended that Members "immediately withdraw from Madrid their Ambassadors and Ministers plenipotentiary accredited there." The Secretary-General on December 20 sent a circular telegram to fifty-four Member governments requesting information on the action taken. Forty-five replies were received.[40] Three Members recalled their ambassadors or ministers as the result of the resolution. Nineteen had no ambassadors or ministers accredited at the

[40] U.N. General Assembly, Second Session, *Official Records*, Supplement No. 1, pp. 2-4.

time the resolution was adopted. Thirty Members had no diplomatic relations. One Member declared that it would adhere to the resolution. Another replied that proper consideration would be given to it. Another simply acknowledged receipt of the telegram and, contrary to the recommendation of the Assembly, proceeded to send an ambassador. The resolution also contained the recommendation that Spain be debarred from membership in international agencies brought into relation with the United Nations, and from participation in conferences sponsored by the United Nations and the specialized agencies. A number of specific acts were taken to implement this recommendation. Attempts to renew these recommendations failed, and the measure of compliance initially achieved was not maintained. In fact, as a result of the failure of the Assembly to reaffirm the recommendations during its second session, there was some question regarding their exact status until they were formally repealed in 1950.

The recommendation of the Assembly in 1949 that Members and "all other States" refrain from direct or indirect provision of "arms or others materials of war to Albania and Bulgaria" was apparently respected by all Members of the United Nations and other states outside the Soviet bloc. It was disregarded by the members of the Soviet bloc who took the view that it was not a proper exercise of the powers of the Assembly and therefore was invalid.

The resolutions of the Council of June 25 and 27, 1950, regarding the North Korean attack received a generally favorable response from Members, except for the Soviet Union and its associates, which refused to admit their validity. Nevertheless, there were such wide variations in the responses of particular Members that any attempt at generalization would be difficult, if not misleading.[41] Of course it was understandable that even concrete offers of assistance given at this early stage had to be general in nature. The United States Government adopted the view that fifty-three Members, including the United States, gave their support to the resolutions of the Council.[42] This figure, however, included Members who, in the replies of their governments to the Secretary-General's communication of June 29, 1950, indicated significant reservations regarding their inten-

[41] See U.N. Department of Public Information, *Yearbook of the United Nations, 1950*, pp. 224-25.
[42] U.S. Department of State, *United States Participation in the United Nations, Report by the President to the Congress, 1950*, Publication 4178, p. 35.

tions to take concrete measures. Lebanon and Syria, for example, took note only of the resolution of June 25, declaring that they would always refrain from giving aid to an aggressor. Mexico and Venezuela were prepared to co-operate within the limits of their resources, while Argentina reiterated its resolute support of the United Nations.

The United States did not even wait for the Security Council to recommend that assistance be given to the Republic of Korea before taking concrete measures. As early as the evening of June 25, after the Council had adopted its first resolution, President Truman, with the concurrence of his principal advisers, decided to move the Seventh Fleet from the Philippines to Formosan waters, to use naval and air forces to assist and protect the evacuation of American civilians from South Korea, and to furnish additional arms to Korea. On the evening of the 26th, after the President had received an urgent appeal from President Rhee of the Republic of Korea for "increasing support" and for "effective and timely aid in order to prevent this act of destruction of world peace," the President decided to support the Republic of Korea with naval and air forces, and to use the Seventh Fleet to neutralize Formosa. Orders to this effect were sent out that night. The President's statement of June 27, publicizing these decisions, was made several hours in advance of the meeting of the Council at which the resolution recommending assistance to the Republic of Korea was adopted.

During the critical period from the end of June to the middle of September, when the successful Inchon landing operation completely changed the military picture, the military forces of the United States and the Republic of Korea bore the brunt of the fighting and the contribution of the United States to the collective action completely overshadowed that of any other Member. Shortly after the June 27 resolution, naval and air units of certain Members,[43] which were based in the Far East, were put at the disposal of the United States Commander, General Douglas MacArthur. Because Commonwealth ground units were in Japan for occupational purposes, their size, nature, and equipment were not suitable for combat activity. It was not until August 27 that British ground forces, which were only of brigade strength, arrived in Korea; these were the first ground forces of a Member other than the United States to par-

[43] Australia, Canada, New Zealand, the United Kingdom, France, and the Netherlands.

ticipate. Australian and Philippine units arrived in the latter part of September, and Turkish ground forces arrived in October. The intervention of the Chinese Communists in late October increased the need for assistance if the new threat was to be successfully met, but at the same time it caused many Members to hesitate to make new military commitments because of the fear of a world war, concern over their own national security, or the feeling that the United States in exercising the duties of unified command had not shown proper restraint in the conduct of military operations north of the thirty-eighth parallel.

By the end of 1950, assistance in the form of military personnel, transport, commodities, supplies, funds, facilities, and other items had been offered by thirty-nine Members in addition to the United States, by one state not a Member of the United Nations and by nine organizations. Fifteen Members made offers of armed forces that were accepted, though in comparison with the contribution of the United States these military contributions were very small.[44]

It is clear that in terms of actual assistance rendered the response of Members to the June 27 resolution of the Security Council was quite uneven. Many Members failed to follow up their favorable verbal responses with concrete offers. Others made offers of modest size and in some instances only after considerable delay. Some offers were not accepted by the United States Government in the exercise of its function of unified command either because the military contingent offered was too small or because there was no provision for its supply and equipment. One offer, that of the Republic of China, was not accepted for reasons that were in part political. It is quite clear that, if it had not been for the initial response of the United States, the offers of Members of the United Nations would have been wholly inadequate for achieving their purpose. In fact, it is reasonably certain that they would not have been made. Moreover, the Members that made the most substantial contributions to the defense of the Republic of Korea were at the same time parties to collective defense arrangements to which the United States was a party or were in the position of being dependent on the United States for their security. Thus to these Members, a contribution was not only the honorable discharge of a United

---

[44] For further information on assistance offered by the end of 1950, see U.N. Department of Information, *Yearbook of the United Nations, 1950*, pp. 226-28. Assistance given by the United States is not included.

Nations duty but it was also a form of assurance that United States support would be given them in case of need. But it is significant that the Latin American Members, with the exception of Colombia, did not offer to make any significant military contributions. Perhaps the certainty of United States assistance to them in case of attack and the conviction that they did not need to pay a high price for any added assurance may have been factors of some importance in determining their courses of action.

The intervention of the Chinese Communists in Korea in late October caused the United States subsequently to propose the consideration of "additional measures" to be applied by Members. As most Members strongly felt that hostilities should not be extended to China, the view came to be accepted that these measures would have to be primarily economic in nature. The naval blockade of North Korean ports previously established by the United Nations Command had been generally effective. The United States had, during 1950, sharply reduced its exports to Communist China, prohibiting in particular the export of strategic items. This policy had not been generally followed by other Members supporting the United Nations collective action in Korea. After the Chinese Communists entered the Korean fighting, the United States in December 1950 prohibited the export of all items, whether strategic or nonstrategic, to Communist China. In addition United States ships were forbidden to call at Communist Chinese ports. During the period from November 1950 to May 1951, Members of the United Nations outside of the Soviet bloc progressively expanded controls over their exports of strategic goods to Communist China with the result that when the Assembly adopted its resolution on May 18, 1951 recommending to all states the application of an embargo, it was already largely in effect. In the months following, the effectiveness of the embargo was strengthened by improved definitions and procedures achieved through informal conferences of representatives of interested states. The only important breach in the embargo outside of the Communist states was the continued export of rubber by Ceylon, which was not a Member of the United Nations.[45]

---

[45] For detailed information on response of Members and the results of the embargo, see U.N. Doc. A/1841 of July 12, 1951, and addenda; and U.S. Foreign Operations Administration, Mutual Defense Assistance Control Act of 1951, *First Report to Congress*, January to July 1952; *Second Report to Congress*, January 1953; and *Third Report to Congress*, First Half of 1953.

In the practice of the United Nations, the method of initiating collective measures of coercion in a situation where such drastic action is deemed necessary has been quite different from that originally envisaged by the authors of the Charter. In fact, the practice that has developed is much closer to that of the League of Nations than to the system of the United Nations as initially conceived. Instead of centralization of responsibility and power in the Security Council, there has been limited centralization of the responsibility for deciding when such measures should be initiated, but very little centralization of the actual determination of what measures are to be applied. In fact, in the absence of any specific legal commitments such as existed under Article 16 of the Covenant of the League, it can be said that the United Nations system in practice is even looser than that of the League of Nations system, for not only has there been an absence of any central determination of measures that Members of the United Nations must take, but there is no legal duty placed on any Member to take any measures in the absence of such a determination. Consequently, the initiation of collective measures becomes dependent on the decisions of governments on what in the circumstances their best interests require, subject to such persuasive influence as a General Assembly or Security Council recommendation may have. This means in practice that Members of the United Nations are likely to follow the lead of the major nations to which they have special ties based on common interests and that are in the position and willing to provide strong leadership.

CHAPTER XVIII

Organization and Direction of
Collective Measures

WHEN COLLECTIVE measures are taken, whether for the purpose of maintaining peace when a "threat" exists in the sense of Article 39 or for the purpose of restoring international peace and security after a breach of the peace or act of aggression has been found to exist, the success of these measures may depend as much on the organization and direction of them as on their nature and scope. They must be organized and directed with a view to maximizing pressure toward the achievement of the declared purposes of the action, and reducing to a minimum and sharing equitably the losses and inconvenience suffered by those participating in the collective effort. The importance of these matters was fully recognized in the drafting of the Charter and has been amply demonstrated in the practice of the United Nations.

The League of Nations and the
United Nations Systems

Until the establishment of the League of Nations, the organization and direction of collective measures of coercion were treated largely from the point of view of the requirements of coalition warfare. Where states had entered into treaties of alliance, consultations were frequently held among staff officers, and agreements were reached regarding the practical details of combined military operations in the event the alliance should become operative. The problem of strategic direction and command of allied armed forces was never solved in a satisfactory manner during the First World War. When the League of Nations was established, one of its basic concepts was the organization and use of superior collective force to maintain international peace and security. The Covenant of the League did not, however, provide for a standing international force to be used for the purpose, nor did it commit members to make available to the organs of the League specific forces and facilities to be used in maintaining or restoring peace. It envisaged joint military action by Members and placed on the Council the duty of recommending the contributions that Members should make. Nevertheless, it left to each Member the decision regarding the particular measures it would take. During the numerous discussions that took place with respect to ways and means of implementing and strengthening the League system of collective security, attention was given to the organization and direction of collective military forces. Proposals were made for making armed forces available to serve the purposes of the League. No agreement was reached, however, on any practical plan of organization and direction.

More attention was given by the League of Nations to the organization and direction of nonmilitary sanctions. The Covenant made no express provision for the co-ordination of these measures by an organ of the League. As early as 1921, however, the Assembly of the League recognized the need for having a co-ordinating agency and accepted the recommendation of its International Blockade Committee that sanctions should be selectively and progressively applied, and that the Council of the League through its recommendations should undertake their proper co-ordination. When sanctions were applied against Italy in 1935-36, the Members of the League that participated joined in establishing a Co-ordination Committee, whose functions were to recommend initial measures to be applied, to examine their effectiveness, and to make further recommendations in the light of developments. But final decisions on measures to be applied were taken by Member governments. The Co-ordination Committee was assisted by a smaller Committee of Eighteen, which prepared proposals for its consideration. The League Secretariat provided secretarial and research assistance.

When the Charter of the United Nations was being formulated, the sponsoring governments agreed that specific provision should be made for the use of military as well as political, economic, and financial measures in support of international peace and security. Although it was decided not to establish an international force, recruited, organized, trained, and equipped under international direction and control, the decision was taken to go one step beyond a simple "alliance system" and provide for national contingents to be placed at the disposal and under the direction of an international organ, the Security Council. The Security Council, a political organ in which the great powers—those that provide the principal military forces—would have permanent membership and special voting privileges, was to be assisted in the organization and use of these forces by the Military Staff Committee, composed of the chiefs of staff of the permanent members of the Council. In this way, it was hoped that the effective organization and conduct of a collective military action for the maintenance or restoration of international peace and security would be assured.

With regard to nonmilitary measures—those of a political, economic, and financial nature—the Charter is equally specific in giving authority to the Council to decide what measures are to be employed, when, and by whom. Furthermore, Member states are required to carry out such decisions "directly and through their action in the appropriate international agencies of which they are members."[1] They have the right to consult the Council if confronted "with special economic problems arising from" the taking of enforcement measures.[2] The Economic and Social Council is required to assist the Security Council at its request,[3] and most of the agreements defining the relations between the specialized agencies and the United Nations contain a provision under which the agency concerned agrees to co-operate in rendering assistance to the Security Council "including assistance in carrying out decisions of the Security Council for the maintenance or restoration of international peace and security."[4]

Improvisation in Korea

Down to June 1950, no progress had been made in the conclusion of agreements for placing armed forces at the disposal of the Security Council, and no solution had been found for problems of organization and direction that might arise in any attempt that might be made to apply collective measures. In the Spanish case, the Secretary-General performed a limited co-ordinating function by requesting reports from Member states on action taken, by informing the specialized agencies of the measures they were expected to adopt, and by reporting to the General Assembly on the measure of implementation

[1] Art. 48 (2).
[2] Art. 50.
[3] Art. 65.
[4] See for example, Art. VI of the Agreement between the United Nations and the Food and Agriculture Organization. U.N. Doc. A/78 (Sept. 30, 1946).

achieved. Neither in the Greek nor in the Palestine case was an attempt made through any organ of the United Nations to co-ordinate the actions of Member states in applying an embargo on the shipment of arms and munitions. Each Member decided for itself what action it should take. The story of what the United Nations has done in the organization and direction—the co-ordination—of collective measures is therefore the story of what was done in Korea after June 25, 1950.

As the situation in Korea was found to call for prompt military action if the attack was to be repelled, the question of the organization of strategic direction and command also had to be considered rather promptly. The Charter provided that the Military Staff Committee should be responsible "under the Security Council for the strategic direction of any armed forces placed at the disposal of the Security Council,"[5] but questions of command were to be worked out subsequently. The Military Staff Committee was clearly unsuited for the performance of the task of strategic direction in Korea should the Soviet Union end its boycott of the Security Council, and the Soviet representative again participate in the work of the Military Staff Committee. With the responsibility, in fact, falling almost wholly on one member—the United States—and with no assurance that armed forces and facilities would be made available by other Member states in significant amounts, it was indeed questionable whether the Military Staff Committee was a suitable instrument for organizing strategic direction and command of the forces in Korea.

The first armed forces sent to the support of the Republic of Korea were United States naval and air units under General MacArthur's Far East Command. In accordance with President Truman's decision of June 26, announced on June 27, these forces went into action very shortly after the attack. Commonwealth naval and air units in the Pacific waters were shortly made available in response to the recommendation of the Council of June 27. These forces were placed under the operational control of the United States Far East Command at Tokyo. On July 1, the first United States ground forces arrived in Korea. This was the initial step in the rapid deployment there of major elements of the United States Eighth Army. At the time of the North Korean attack, and in fact since the completion of the

[5] Art. 47 (3).

withdrawal from Korea of United States military occupation forces at the end of June 1949, there had been a United States Military Advisory Group in Korea to assist in the development and training of the security forces of the Republic of Korea. Consequently, the Korean armed force, which initially faced the North Korean attack, had the assistance of United States military advisers and was to a certain extent in fact under United States military direction. Thus when, in response to the resolutions adopted by the Security Council on June 25 and 27, Members of the United Nations agreed to give assistance to the Republic of Korea, they were confronted by the fact that the United States had already established the basis for claiming dominant influence in the strategic direction and command of the collective military forces.

The Secretary-General and his advisers gave prompt consideration to the establishment of co-ordinating machinery. They prepared a draft resolution and circulated it on July 3 to the delegations of the United States, the United Kingdom, and France, and the President of the Council, Mr. Sunde, who was the representative of Norway. This resolution, if it had been approved, would have requested the United States to assume responsibility for organizing a United Nations command, would have authorized the armed forces placed under this command to fly the United Nations flag, and would have established a "Committee on Coordination of Assistance for Korea," composed of Australia, France, India, New Zealand, Norway, the United Kingdom, and the United States, with the Secretary-General as *rapporteur*, and with the Republic of Korea invited to send a representative. But the proposal was strongly opposed by the United States.[6] Therefore, presumably in recognition of the major contribution of the United States, the Security Council adopted on July 7 a resolution by which it recommended "that all Members providing military forces and other assistance pursuant to the aforesaid Security Council resolutions make such forces and other assistance available to a unified command under the United States," requested "the United States to designate the commander of such forces," authorized "the unified command at its discretion to use the United Nations flag in the course of operations against North Korean forces concurrently with the flags of the various nations participating," and requested "the United States to provide the Security Council with

[6] Trygve Lie, *In the Cause of Peace* (1954), pp. 333-34.

reports as appropriate on the course of action taken under the unified command."[7]

In submitting the draft resolution, the United Kingdom representative observed that inasmuch as the Security Council could only make recommendations to individual Members under Article 39 of the Charter, "it could not therefore be the United Nations or the Security Council which themselves appointed a United Nations commander. All the Security Council can do is recommend that one of its members should designate the commander of the forces which individual members have now made available."[8] In replying to the request contained in the resolution, the United States representative accepted on behalf of the United States the responsibility of unified command. He stated that "in spirit if not in word the resolution has been in effect since the very first resolution adopted on 25 June." He referred to the statement of the Prime Minister of the United Kingdom before the House of Commons on June 28 that United Kingdom naval forces in Japanese waters had been placed "at the disposal of the United States authorities to operate on behalf of the Security Council in support of South Korea."[9]

On July 8 President Truman announced that he had designated General Douglas MacArthur as "the commanding general of the military forces which the members of the United Nations place under the unified command of the United States pursuant to the United Nations' assistance to the Republic of Korea in repelling the unprovoked armed attack against it."[10] The United Nations Command, with General Headquarters at Tokyo, was formally established on July 25.[11] This was the instrumentality through which the

[7] U.N. Doc. S/1588 (July 7, 1950).

[8] U.N. Security Council, Fifth Year, *Official Records*, No. 18, 476th Meeting (July 7, 1950), pp. 3-4.

[9] *Ibid.*, pp. 10-11.

[10] *Military Situation in the Far East*, Hearings before the Senate Committee on Armed Services and the Committee on Foreign Relations, 82 Cong. 1 sess., Pt. 5, p. 3373. (Hereinafter referred to as *Military Situation in the Far East*.)

[11] General MacArthur's General Order No. 1, issued in his capacity as Commander-in-Chief, United Nations Command. For text, see *Military Situation in the Far East*, p. 3382.

"United Nations Command" refers to the command organization in the field with headquarters at Tokyo, initially under General MacArthur as Commander-in-Chief. "Unified command" is the term used to describe the authority vested in the United States Government and when capitalized refers to the United States Government itself, acting in the discharge of this responsibility.

United States discharged its responsibility of unified command, and the United States Government made its first report to the Security Council on that date.[12] Meanwhile, on July 15, President Rhee of the Republic of Korea had addressed a communication to General MacArthur in which he assigned to him "command authority over all land, sea, and air forces of the Republic of Korea during the period of the continuation of the present state of hostilities."[13]

The importance of the precedent thus set for the United Nations in the Korean situation was clearly shown later when the Collective Measures Committee, established by the "Uniting for Peace" resolution of the General Assembly, considered during 1951 the principles that should govern the strategic direction of collective military forces. The committee incorporated into its recommendations the substance of the Korean practice. It concluded that until such time as the Military Staff Committee could assume its responsibilities, the United Nations, when engaged in collective military measures, must provide some agency that will be responsible for the direction and conduct of its military operations and that will be empowered "to co-ordinate the efforts of individual States and to organize contributions of forces, assistance and facilities in order to initiate effective military operations against the aggressor in the shortest possible time."[14] The committee proposed that "the Organization should authorize a State or group of States to act on its behalf as executive military authority, within the framework of its policies and objectives as expressed through such resolutions as it may adopt at any stage of the collective action." The committee expressed the opinion that concrete arrangements must depend on the "political and military circumstances of the case." If the victim state should be able to conduct its own defense with only limited assistance from others, which had not been true in the case of the Republic of Korea, that state might be appointed.

[12] Such reports subsequently were made bimonthly. They summarized military operations under the United Nations Command for the periods covered. They did not, generally speaking, give information not already available in communiqués issued by the United Nations Command through U. S. Eighth Army headquarters in Korea.

[13] U. S. Department of State Bulletin, Vol. 23 (Aug. 7, 1950), p. 206.

[14] U.N. General Assembly, Sixth Session, Official Records, Supplement No. 13, "Report of the Collective Measures Committee," p. 25. (Hereinafter cited as the "First Report of the Collective Measures Committee.")

Procedure for Utilizing National Forces

Very shortly after the acceptance by the United States of the responsibility for establishing a unified command in Korea, a procedure was adopted for handling offers of military assistance. Under this procedure, Member states first communicated their offers to the Secretary-General who, in turn, communicated them to the United States representative at United Nations headquarters. Preliminary informal discussions on the nature of the offers between the Secretary-General and Member representatives at United Nations headquarters helped to ensure that governments would offer types of forces or materials that could actually be used by the United Nations Command. The United States representative then transmitted the offers received to Washington, and the United States Government, in the discharge of its responsibilities of unified command, entered into direct negotiations with the government of the Member state concerned regarding the details of the offer, its utilization, and other effective assistance which that government might be in a position to provide. Detailed arrangements for the utilization of assistance were made as the result of bilateral discussions, which were carried on first between the Unified Command and diplomatic and military representatives of the contributing state in Washington, and later in formal military staff conferences both in Washington and in the theatre of operations.

Two problems of considerable significance, from the point of view of future collective operations, arose in connection with the making of these arrangements: (1) the minimum strength of individual military contributions to be accepted; and (2) the organization of supplies for the national contingents. The Unified Command generally insisted that an army unit should at least be of the strength of a reinforced battalion (about 1200 men) with supporting artillery. Units such as engineers and ordnance should be of such size and organization as to be able to function as units. In addition, the Unified Command generally insisted that the contributing state should provide reinforcements adequate to maintain continuously the initial strength of the unit. This standard of minimum strength was not rigidly enforced, but some offers were declined on the ground of their inadequacy.

With respect to supplies, the Unified Command insisted that, for practical operational reasons, there should be only one logistical line of communication, with the one exception of the Commonwealth and those Members using British-type equipment. This made the United States the principal source of supply and created a variety of problems relating to the training of men in the use of new equipment, the equipping of them, and making payment for the equipment in question. It maximized the dependence of the participating Members on the United States but simplified shipping and front-line supply arrangements. Difficulties in the way of training and equipping personnel were minimized by the work already done under the Mutual Defense Assistance and other programs. The process of training and equipping personnel, if not completed by the time the units arrived in Korea, was concluded at the United Nations Reception Center in Korea.

Arrangements regarding payment for equipment and supplies were included in agreements between the United States and the participating states.[15] These agreements, in addition to containing detailed provisions regarding the accounting and payment for materials, supplies, and services furnished, contained an important provision bearing on the operational control of the armed forces contributed. Article 7 of the Netherlands agreement, for example, read as follows: "The Government of the Netherlands agrees that all orders, directives and policies of the Commander issued to the Netherlands Forces or its personnel shall be accepted and carried out by them as given and that in the event of disagreement with such orders, directives or policies, formal protest may be presented subsequently."

Here again, the precedents set for the United Nations by the experience in the Korean situation had an important bearing on subsequent developments for, generally speaking, the recommendations of the Collective Measures Committee under the "Uniting for Peace" resolution regarding procedures to be followed in the processing and utilization of national contributions by the executive military authority were based on the Korean practice.

Member Contributions to Collective Military Action

The arrangements for organizing and directing the national military forces in Korea were to a large extent determined by the great inequality of the contributions made. From the very beginning the

[15] See, for example, agreement between the Government of the United States and the Government of the Netherlands, signed May 15, 1952. U. S. Department of State Bulletin, Vol. 26 (May 26, 1952), pp. 831-32.

contribution of the United States so completely overshadowed the combined contributions of other Members that there was no serious thought of establishing any other than a United States command arrangement. Furthermore, the fact that contributions of other Members were quite generally at a minimal level placed them in a weak bargaining position when they sought to increase their effective participation in the strategic direction of the operation. In addition, the fact that only a small minority of the Members of the United Nations had participated in the military operation made the General Assembly, or a subsidiary organ of it, appear to many of the participants to be an inappropriate organ for undertaking that responsibility.

By the end of 1951, at a time when the Korean operation had become comparatively stabilized and truce negotiations had been initiated, only sixteen Members of the United Nations had armed forces in Korea. Of the total United Nations force in Korea, the United States had contributed 50.32 per cent of the ground force, 85.89 per cent of the naval force, and 93.38 per cent of the air force. The contributions of the Republic of Korea were 40.10 per cent, 7.45 per cent, and 5.65 per cent respectively. The remaining percentages were contributed by the other fifteen Members of the United Nations, the Commonwealth contributions being the major part in each category.[16] Casualties followed a similar pattern except that casualties of the Republic of Korea were proportionately much higher than those of the United States and other Members.[17]

From the inequality of the military contributions and sacrifices of Member states, one should not necessarily conclude that there was a widespread shirking of responsibilities or that the United States was forced to assume an inequitable burden. Various considerations need to be taken into account in assessing the relative burdens assumed by Members in the collective military action: the United States had initially brought the Korean question before the United Nations, had taken a leading part in determining United Nations policy in Korea, and for reasons of national interest, had voluntarily assumed a special responsibility for assisting the Republic of Korea.

---

[16] U.S. Department of State, *United States Participation in the United Nations*, Report by the President to the Congress for the Year 1951, Publication 4583 (1952), p. 288.

[17] See U.N. Department of Public Information, *Yearbook of the United Nations, 1951*, p. 258.

The United States was the only Member in a position, from the point of view of its available resources and mobilizable strength, to come to the assistance of the Republic quickly and effectively. Other Members, particularly Western European States, had responsibilities in Europe, or, as in the case of the United Kingdom and France, were engaged in major military operations elsewhere, which placed heavy demands on their resources.

Once the United States Government, using the structure of its military command in the Far East, had undertaken to organize a United Nations Command, United States military personnel, equipment, and supplies could be more efficiently used than those of other nations. Wide and substantial contributions by other Member governments became important more for psychological and political reasons than for reasons of military effectiveness. It was considered desirable by the United States Government to give the operation a collective character in the eyes of the world and to justify it as a United Nations operation before the American people. A number of offers of assistance were not accepted by the Unified Command for administrative reasons, or because, as in the case of the offer of Chinese Nationalist forces, acceptance was considered unwise for military and political reasons. It must also be recognized that, as a result of the gross inequality in power between states, a small state may frequently find it relatively more burdensome to make a small contribution to a collective effort than a great power to make a substantially larger contribution—particularly a power with the resources of the United States. Furthermore, the technological advances that have occurred in modern warfare preclude all but the more advanced industrial states from being able to contribute certain specialized units and equipment.

It must be emphasized also that the collective military action in Korea was directly supported by means other than the sending of armed forces, and in its first report to the General Assembly, the Collective Measures Committee stressed the importance of "ancillary support for any combined United Nations Military action."[18] In Korea, this ancillary support was of considerable importance and to some extent modified the picture of great inequality that the statistics on contributions of armed forces, taken by themselves, presented. For example, Norway contributed merchant ship tonnage and a surgical

[18] "First Report of the Collective Measures Committee," p. 23.

hospital unit, Panama, merchant ships, and India, a field ambulance unit.

Although these inequalities in Member contributions can be explained to some extent and the relative burdens made to appear more equal, it still remains true that, if collective action is to have its maximum significance, it must be based on the principle of the equal sharing of burdens as well as of advantages. This is necessary not only in order to achieve a fair distribution of sacrifices but also to provide a realistic basis for collective direction of the military operation. No effective procedure was developed, however, for achieving a more equitable sharing of the burdens of the Korean military action. The Security Council in its resolutions did not provide for a procedure to check on responses to, or to encourage favorable responses to, its recommendations of June 25 and 27, 1950. In practice, the Secretary-General assumed this responsibility in so far as the United Nations was concerned. On June 29, he sent a cable to all Member governments calling their attention to the recommendation of the Council of assistance to the Republic of Korea and adding that it would facilitate implementation of the resolution of the Council if all Members would give information on the type of assistance they could furnish. Later, on July 14, the Secretary-General cabled Members that the Unified Command was "in urgent need of effective military assistance" and asked each Government to consider "the possibility of such assistance including combat forces, particularly ground forces."[19] With the establishment of a unified command, the United States Government undertook the exercise of an independent initiative to obtain additional contributions to the collective action.

The question of methods by which military, financial, and other assistance in support of collective military action might be maximized was studied by the Collective Measures Committee at the request of the General Assembly. The committee accepted the general principle "that each State should contribute in accordance with its ability."[20] It recognized that contributions might take a variety of forms. One method that the committee recommended was "the establishment of an ad hoc negotiating committee to deal directly with States in respect to their contributions." This method had been used to obtain contributions for relief operations undertaken in

---

[19] *United Nations Bulletin,* Vol. 9 (Aug. 1, 1950), p. 94.
[20] U. N. General Assembly, Seventh Session, *Official Records,* Supplement No. 17, p. 11.

Korea and Palestine and for the Expanded Program of Technical Assistance.

The Collective Measures Committee described the purposes and operating procedures of the proposed committee as follows:

> The basic purpose of the *ad hoc* committee would be to obtain for the United Nations the forces, manpower, assistance, facilities, services and funds required for the effective conduct of the military operations. To carry out this purpose, the committee should obtain from the Executive Military Authority specifications of its requirements and seek by direct negotiations with States to elicit contributions from them to fulfill these requirements. The Committee should be authorized to carry on its activities in the manner which it deems most likely to be effective; it should in general act in private and through informal procedures designed to obtain the maximum support from both Members and non-member States. Detailed arrangements concerning the utilization of the contributions could then be made directly between the Executive Military Authority and the contributing States in the manner set forth in paragraphs 219 to 225 of the first report of the Collective Measures Committee. To an extent consistent with military security the *ad hoc* committee might keep the Members of the United Nations currently informed of the progress of its work and maintain for their use up-to-date lists of contributing States and the nature of their contributions.[21]

The Collective Measures Committee suggested that the Security Council or the General Assembly, when setting up such a committee and determining its composition, might take into account the following factors: the advisability of a committee of small size to facilitate the task of negotiation; the extent of participation in the United Nations action; the desirability of geographical representation; the advisability of representation of the state or states constituting the Executive Military Authority; and appropriate provision for consultation with the Secretary-General.

Relation of National Armed Forces to United Nations Command

The United Nations Command for the Korean operation that was set up in Tokyo under General MacArthur was practically identical with the Far East Command of the United States. General MacArthur was in charge of both. His chain of command was through the Chief of Staff of the Army to the Joint Chiefs of Staff,

[21] *Ibid.*

to the Secretary of Defense, to the President of the United States. From the common headquarters, General MacArthur commanded the Eighth Army, which included the ground forces of all the participating Members and the Republic of Korea, and the Far Eastern Air Force and the Seventh Fleet, which took in all air and naval forces respectively contributed by other states. Each service arm was under a United States service commander. Consequently, the organization of command down to the service level would have been no different if the military force had been a one-nation force.

It was at Eighth Army Headquarters in Korea that the multinational character of the United Nations Command became most apparent. This became the operating headquarters dealing with the ground forces of all participants, in addition to being an operating headquarters for the United States Eighth Army. It was later suggested that this headquarters be designated as that of the First United Nations army,[22] but the suggestion was never adopted. With the exception of the forces of the Republic of Korea, all ground forces were originally incorporated into United States divisions and brought under the operational command of United States divisional officers. The senior military representative of each Member state contributing forces was accorded the right of direct access to the United Nations Commander "on matters of major policy affecting the operational capabilities of the forces concerned."[23] After July 27, 1951, all units of members of the Commonwealth were combined into one Commonwealth division.

The forces of the Republic of Korea were treated in two ways. At first, the existing channels of command and communication were taken over with little change, the units of the Republic of Korea being simply brought under Eighth Army Command. In view of the confused and demoralized condition of many units of the Republic and the skeleton character of United States divisions, many Korean soldiers were later placed in American companies under a "buddy system." The plan finally adopted in late 1950 was the inclusion of Korean divisions in American corps, with the result that the identity of the Korean units was respected, and adequate logistical support for them was assured.

The incorporation of units of other Member states in United

---

[22] *New York Times* (May 30, 1951).
[23] "First Report of the Collective Measures Committee," p. 46.

States divisions and the close integration of divisions of the United States and those of other Member states was greatly facilitated by the fact that the countries concerned had previously received United States military equipment and advisers under the various foreign assistance programs. In no case, however, had training and re-equipping reached a point where units were completely combinable or interchangeable with United States units. Experience demonstrated, however, the soundness of the conclusion that "only similar organizations, similar units, and similar procedures, together with identical equipment and military doctrine, can permit the effective formation of joint forces for joint tasks and the full value of joint command."[24]

Numerous command peculiarities resulted from the incorporation of units of other Member states in a United States Army and a United States command system. For one thing, there was lack of uniformity in the ranks of officers in command at various levels. A British company might be under a major while a United States company was under a lieutenant. Units of battalions of regimental strength might be accompanied by higher ranking officers up to general, the purpose being to permit liaison with the higher commanders under whom the units served. The line of command was strictly American but in the issuance of orders a United States corps commander, for example, had to recognize the fact, that national practices differ. One of the principal devices for obtaining effective co-operation between different national units was the establishment of liaison arrangements. In spite of the obvious difficulties involved, General Marshall was able to report in the summer of 1951 that he was much impressed by the complete amalgamation of the various United Nations units into an integrated, co-ordinated, fighting force.[25]

Identification of United Nations Military Operation

In order to achieve maximum authority and support for the United Nations military operation in Korea and to impress on participating personnel its United Nations character, it was essential

[24] *Contributing to the Effective Maintenance of International Peace and Security,* H. Rept. 996, 80 Cong. 1 sess. (July 18, 1947), p. 7.

[25] U.S. Department of State, *Guide to the United Nations in Korea,* Publication 4299 (1951), p. 29.

that it be clearly and publicly identified. In proposing the draft resolution in the Security Council authorizing the use of the United Nations flag, the British representative stressed that it was important to emphasize "the unity of all those nations that are now banded together for a common purpose, and to indicate that they are acting in accordance with a higher law than one which is dictated merely by narrow national interests."[26] Also when President Truman designated General MacArthur as Commander-in-Chief of United Nations forces, he directed him to use the United Nations flag concurrently with the flags of the various participating states.

The United Nations character of the operations was further publicly identified from the time the Unified Command was established by use of the name of the United Nations in communiqués, public announcements, and reports, and by explanations of United Nations purposes in propaganda leaflets distributed to enemy forces.[27] Military observers attached to the United Nations Commission in Korea retained their national military uniforms but wore a United Nations armband when moving with United Nations military units or when on duty elsewhere. The secretarial staff of the commission and the members of the commission itself were not required to wear identifying insignia except for United Nations field personnel who wore the United Nations field service uniform at all times. All vehicles were required to fly the United Nations flag when used by personnel on duty. Members of relief teams attached to the United Nations Civil Assistance Command were required to wear a United Nations "arm flash." War correspondents accredited to the United Nations Command wore a "United Nations War Correspondent" arm flash.

In December 1950, the General Assembly requested the Secretary-General, in consultation with the Unified Command, to provide a "distinguishing ribbon or other insignia" for personnel participating in Korea "in the defence of the Principles of the Charter of the United Nations."[28] The Secretary-General through his representative in Korea had received similar suggestions from the United Nations Commander. Accordingly, arrangements were made for the award

[26] U.N. Security Council, Fifth Year, *Official Records,* No. 18, 476th Meeting (July 7, 1950), p. 4.
[27] U.N. Doc. S/1626 (July 25, 1950).
[28] Res. 483 (V), Dec. 12, 1950. The Sixth Committee had earlier recommended that such an award was legal.

of a United Nations service medal to all members of the armed forces designated by the Commander-in-Chief as having served the United Nations under his command. Regulations for the award were issued by the Secretary-General in late September 1951, and in the following December the United States authorized its forces to wear the medal and ribbon. However, the first ribbons in lieu of medals were given to Netherlands veterans at the Hague in October 1951. The first actual presentation of a medal at United Nations Headquarters was made by the Secretary-General to General Ridgway in May 1952, in the presence of delegates from the twenty-two countries that had armed forces or medical units in Korea.

The need in the future for identification of any United Nations operation was stressed by the Collective Measures Committee in its first report. The committee suggested that steps similar to those used in Korea be followed at every stage of the operation. Specifically, these included the use of the United Nations flag in the field; the issuance of all orders, reports, and instructions in the name of the United Nations Command; the provision of a United Nations service medal; and appropriate United Nations identification for non-military personnel and property. The committee also recommended that states see to it that their own laws permit their troops to fly the United Nations flag and that their nationals be permitted to receive United Nations awards.

Strategic Direction of Collective Military Operations

Under the terms of the Charter "the Military Staff Committee shall be responsible under the Security Council for the strategic direction of any armed forces placed at the disposal of the Security Council." The relationship between committee and Council that was envisaged presumably was similar to that of the Joint Chiefs of Staff to the President and his political advisers in the United States, or during the Second World War, of the Combined Chiefs of Staff to President Roosevelt and Prime Minister Churchill and their principal political advisers. As the British representative pointed out in submitting his proposal for the establishment of a unified command by the United States, this provision of the Charter was not applicable in the Korean case in view of the fact that the Security Council was not acting under Article 42. He also pointed out that all the Security Council could do was to recommend that one of its Members designate the commander of the forces that Members made available. He did not view the function of the Council as an operative one, but saw its role as limited to co-ordinating the activities of Members.[29] Although Secretary-General Lie had suggested that a committee on co-ordination be set up, the prevailing opinion in the Council appears to have been that additional machinery was unnecessary at this time because the United States would be submitting reports periodically, and the Council would be able to take any further action it considered necessary on the basis of these reports. With the end of the Soviet boycott of the Security Council and the return on August 1 of the Soviet representative to meetings of the Council, there was no possibility that the Council could take further action along this line because of the Soviet veto.

Objectives and General Principles

As previously noted, the resolution of the Security Council of June 27, 1950 had defined the purpose of assistance to the Republic of Korea to be "to repel the armed attack and to restore international peace and security in the area." Some light had been thrown on the meaning of these words by the request contained in the resolution of June 25 that the North Korean authorities withdraw their forces to the thirty-eighth parallel. Nevertheless, the resolution of June 27 said little more than the Charter itself and was likely to require further clarification.[30] The resolution of July 7, requesting the establishment of a unified command by the United States and recommending that Members place their forces under that command, could be interpreted as a delegation of authority to the command so established to use military force to achieve the objectives set forth in the Council resolutions and the Charter.[31] After August 1, the Council became incapable of giving even this limited amount of direction. There remained only the possibility, so far as the United Nations was concerned, of having the General Assembly take over the responsibility that the Council was no longer able to discharge.

[29] U.N. Security Council, Fifth Year, *Official Records*, No. 18, 476th Meeting (July 7, 1950), pp. 3-4.

[30] For further discussion on this point, see below, Chap. XIX.

[31] That was the view of the United States Government and of General Mac-Arthur. See *Military Situation in the Far East*, pp. 14, 1734, 1735. It was the view generally accepted.

Although the Assembly had no power to take decisions with respect to military operations that would be binding on Members, it did have the power under Article 10 to discuss any question or any matter within the scope of the Charter and make a recommendation regarding it, except as provided in Article 12. The fact that the complaint of North Korean aggression was on the agenda of the Council offered a technical difficulty, but certainly not one that was insuperable. More serious was the fact that by the time the Assembly convened in September 1950, the radical change in the military situation made a decision regarding the military objective urgent. United Nations forces, instead of being hard pressed in front of Pusan, were driving the North Korean forces in confusion to the north and were approaching the thirty-eighth parallel. It became necessary to decide whether to be satisfied with the attainment of a minimum military objective, *i.e.* driving the North Korean forces back to the thirty-eighth parallel, or to undertake a more ambitious program that might include an attempt to free all of North Korea from Communist control, thus facilitating the carrying out of the objective of the Assembly of a unified, independent, and democratic Korea as suggested in its resolution of November 1947.[32]

The view taken by the United States, and many other Members of the United Nations, appears to have been that the resolution approved by the Council on June 27, 1950 permitted the United Nations forces to cross the thirty-eighth parallel and to seek the destruction of North Korean forces if the latter refused to cease hostilities on acceptable terms. However, the United States Government was anxious to have a confirmation of this authority by the Assembly, presumably because of the advantage to be derived from having the United Nations character of the operation clearly established. Consequently, United Nations forces, other than Korean, were not ordered across the parallel until after the resolution of the Assembly of October 7 was adopted. This resolution, by implication, confirmed the authority of the United Nations Command to undertake the destruction of the North Korean forces by military operations north of the parallel and expressed approval of such a course. It recommended that "all appropriate steps be taken to ensure conditions of stability throughout Korea," that "all constituent acts be taken, including the holding of elections, under the auspices of the United Nations, for the establishment of a unified, independent and demo-

---

[32] Res. 112 (II) Nov. 14, 1947.

cratic government in the sovereign State of Korea," and that "United Nations forces should not remain in any part of Korea otherwise than so far as necessary" for achieving these objectives.[33]

Whatever the view taken on whether the United Nations Command needed this authorization by the Assembly before it could undertake military operations north of the thirty-eighth parallel, it is quite clear that the resolution of the Assembly was not regarded as laying down an inflexible course of action that United Nations forces had to pursue irrespective of circumstances that might arise. Nor was there any widespread feeling that the Assembly should assume the responsibility for strategic direction because it was not qualified to do this by composition, organization, or procedure. It was recognized by certain Members participating in the collective military operation, that a military advance north of the thirty-eighth parallel risked bringing Communist China or the Soviet Union into the fighting. But these Members appear to have been content with the assurance given by the United States that, in the discharge of the responsibilities of unified command, it would exercise, with caution and restraint, its authority to carry the fighting into North Korea.

Members of the Assembly, including some of the strongest supporters of the collective military action in Korea, were insistent, however, on having the Assembly, directly and through appropriate subsidiary organs, give guidance to and exercise some measure of control over the United Nations Command in connection with those operations directly related to the work of political and economic rehabilitation and reconstruction. Therefore, the resolution of October 7 also provided for the establishment of the United Nations Commission for the Unification and Rehabilitation of Korea to represent the United Nations in bringing about "the establishment of a unified, independent and democratic government of all Korea" and to "exercise such responsibilities in connexion with relief and rehabilitation in Korea as may be determined by the General Assembly." Pending the arrival of the commission in Korea, the governments of the states represented on the commission were to form an Interim Committee meeting at the seat of the United Nations "to consult with and advise the United Nations Unified Command in the light of the above recommendations."

The Interim Committee met on October 10, the day after United

---

[33] Res. 376 (V), Oct. 7, 1950.

Nations forces began to advance into North Korea, and, after obtaining the views of the Unified Command, adopted a resolution clearly intended to place definite limits on the discretionary authority of the Unified Command in the political reconstruction of North Korea. After recalling that no government had been recognized by the United Nations as having legal and effective control over North Korea, the committee advised the Unified Command "to assume provisionally all responsibilities for government and civil administration" in this area, "pending consideration by the United Nations Commission for the Unification and Rehabilitation of Korea of the administration of these territories," and recommended that the Unified Command "take immediate steps to associate with all authorities established for civilian administration in accordance with the present resolution, officers from the several forces of members of the United Nations serving under the Unified Command in Korea."[34]

The role of the Secretary-General in the Korean operation was primarily that of liaison officer between the Unified Command and the United Nations and its Members. The Secretary-General communicated to Members the actions of the Council, informed Members of the specific needs of the Unified Command, and transmitted the details of offers to it. The Secretary-General was represented at the United Nations Command by a personal representative, who with his staff assisted in the co-ordination of relief activities. In the performance of Secretariat activities directly bearing on military operations, the Secretary-General was embarrassed by the fact that the Assistant Secretary-General in charge of Security Council Affairs had from the beginning been a Soviet national. As a result, this work was concentrated in the Secretary-General's Executive Office under the direction of the executive assistant to the Secretary-General.

In general, the recommendations of the Collective Measures Committee to the General Assembly under the "Uniting for Peace" resolution followed the practice in the Korean case. In its recommendations the committee envisaged a similar role to that described above for the Secretary-General in case of collective military measures. It recommended that "in any future United Nations action to meet aggression, . . . the Secretary-General should immediately estab-

[34] U.N. General Assembly, Sixth Session, *Official Records*, Supplement No. 12, p. 13.

lish liaison with the executive military authority."[35] Referring to the relations between the Security Council and the General Assembly and the proposed executive military authority, which was to be the counterpart of the Unified Command in Korea, the committee laid down the following general principle, to be followed until such time as the provisions of Chapter VII of the Charter became fully applicable:

> The Security Council or the General Assembly, when it resolves to employ measures involving the collective use of armed force, will formulate the objectives and general policy of the United Nations. Within the framework so defined, or as developed subsequently by the appropriate United Nations body, the executive military authority should be responsible for the coordination and direction of the military operations.
>
> . . . .
>
> In the theatre of operations the executive military authority should have full responsibility for the co-ordination and strategic direction and control of the United Nations forces, within the framework of the policies and objectives as expressed through such resolutions as the United Nations may adopt at any stage of the collective action.[36]

Political-Military Questions

Although the Security Council and the General Assembly were able to lay down the broad objectives of collective military action in Korea, they were not able to provide continuous policy guidance in dealing with questions of a mixed political and military character that inevitably arose under the complex circumstances of the Korean operation. However, the need for such guidance was not at first apparent. The Members of the United Nations were generally in agreement that every effort should be made to drive the North Korean forces back to the thirty-eighth parallel, and they viewed with favor the destruction of North Korean forces as offering the best way to restore international peace and security on a sound basis. Nevertheless, the advantages of seeking the destruction of North Korean forces had to be weighed against the possible risks of extending the conflict by giving Communist China or the Soviet Union or both an excuse or reason for intervention, not just at the time the initial decision on a plan of action was taken but continuously and repeatedly as new circumstances unfolded in the carrying out of the plan. Consequently, from the time the Unified Command was confronted by

[35] "First Report of the Collective Measures Committee," p. 30.
[36] Ibid., pp. 25-26.

the necessity of deciding whether United Nations forces should proceed north of the thirty-eighth parallel, there were questions relating to the conduct of military operations that had serious political implications. The way in which they were decided might determine whether the collective action remained localized or became a major conflict involving the opposing armed forces of great powers.

The regular machinery of the United Nations provided no effective means for dealing with these questions. The Council itself was prevented from giving continuing guidance by the presence of the Soviet representative who wished to defeat the collective action, and the establishment by the Council of a subsidiary organ not including the Soviet Union for such guidance would have been difficult, if not impossible. The General Assembly, unsuited by its size for the direct performance of this function, could have established a small subsidiary organ for the purpose, but this solution was apparently not seriously considered, partly because it would have involved giving Members not active participants in the military operation a measure of influence that the more actively participating Members were unwilling to allow. In fact, there appeared to be only two possible alternatives: One was to give the United States, in the exercise of the responsibilities of Unified Command, full power to decide all questions of this kind; the other was to develop procedures of co-operation among the Members participating in the collective action in Korea that would permit some measure of participation by Members other than the United States in the decision of these questions. The first alternative was the one that appears to have been accepted, even as late as the discussions of the Assembly in September and early October 1950, although subject to the understanding that the power in question would be used with restraint and caution. When evidence began to accumulate indicating that restraint and caution were not always being displayed, there was an increasing body of opinion, official and unofficial, favoring some practical procedures by which the views of participating Members might more fully be taken into account in dealing with these borderline issues.

The problem came to have a dual aspect. No one denied that the United Nations Commander should receive his directives from and be subject to the undivided authority of the United States Government. Consequently, the effectiveness of any process by which other Members participated in resolving these questions depended not only on the extent to which there was real consultation between the United States Government and the governments of other Members, but also on the extent to which the United States Government was successful in getting the conclusions to which it had come after such consultations translated into action by the United Nations Commander. An agreement arrived at by consultation between interested governments might be nullified by the failure of the Commander to carry out the directive based upon it. A few examples of how such questions were handled and of the consequences that followed are given below.

Once the decision had been taken to carry military operations into North Korea, the question repeatedly arose whether certain limits should be placed on these in order to assure Communist China and the Soviet Union that the intentions of United Nations military action were not hostile to them. In line with this policy of restraint, which the United States Government had agreed to follow, a directive was sent to General MacArthur on September 27, 1950, by the United States Joint Chiefs of Staff stating that under no circumstances should his forces cross the Manchurian or Soviet borders, and that as a matter of policy no ground forces other than Korean should be used in the northeast provinces or in the area along the Manchurian border.[37] As United Nations forces advanced toward the Yalu River and the threat of Chinese Communist intervention became more real, there was increasing uneasiness on the part of some Member governments. Specific suggestions appear to have been made that the advance stop at the waist of Korea in the vicinity of the fortieth parallel. The United Kingdom and Canada through diplomatic channels counseled strongly against any advance to the Yalu River. Nevertheless, on October 24, presumably following increased resistance by the North Korean forces with Chinese Communist assistance, General MacArthur advised his field commanders that he was lifting restrictions imposed on the employment of United Nations forces in North Korea under the September 27 directive, although he cautioned that these forces should be withdrawn and replaced by Korean units as soon as feasible. He informed the Joint Chiefs of Staff to this effect. When they advised General MacArthur that these instructions were not in accordance with

[37] *Military Situation in the Far East*, p. 1230.

their previous directive and asked him for further information, they were informed that it was a matter of military necessity.[38]

Thus it appears that at a time when other Member governments were becoming concerned over the danger of Chinese Communist intervention and were making specific suggestions for the use of restraint, the United Nations Commander was permitted, for reasons of military necessity, to act contrary to instructions that were in line with such a course. No doubt General MacArthur's action was justified if the achievement of his military mission, which was to destroy the opposing forces in North Korea, was to be placed ahead of all other considerations. If, on the other hand, the prevention of the extension of the conflict was to be a major guiding consideration, as many Members desired, a strong case could be made for being satisfied with less than the complete fulfillment of the original mission. Although existing procedures of consultation appear to have been inadequate for achieving the balanced evaluation of alternative courses and their likely consequences in a situation of this kind, what was most apparent in this case was that the United States Government, in the discharge of its responsibility of unified command, did not effectively implement the policy that it had adopted both in an effort to meet the desires of its associates in the United Nations and on the basis of its own estimate of the situation.

With the intervention of organized Chinese Communist forces, a situation was created in which, in the estimate of the United Nations Commander, the forces opposing the United Nations had a "privileged sanctuary" in Manchuria. In these circumstances, on November 7, he requested that authority to pursue enemy aircraft two or three minutes flying time into Manchurian air space should be granted. The Department of State and the Joint Chiefs of Staff agreed that such authority should be granted, and, on November 13, the Department of State instructed United States embassies in five or six Member countries to take up with these governments the "hot pursuit" proposal. In all cases, the reactions from these governments were negative, and the United States Government, whether because of these replies or because there were subsequent doubts in the minds of the top military advisers regarding the wisdom of the proposed action, did not pursue the matter further.[39]

[38] *Ibid.*, p. 1240.
[39] *Ibid.*, pp. 1723-24.

It is significant that the consultations were limited, apparently for security reasons, to certain of the governments with forces in Korea. It is also significant that, even though the United States Government had a much larger stake in the success of military operations and the safety of the armed forces than other Members, it nevertheless appears to have been guided by the views of the associated governments consulted. This reflected a strong desire, apparently concurred in by the Joint Chiefs of Staff as well as the Department of State, to maintain a united front in Korea.

On March 30, 1951, after the Communist Chinese and North Korean forces had been driven back to the vicinity of the thirty-eighth parallel, the Joint Chiefs of Staff informed General MacArthur that negotiations with other governments were in process with a view to an announcement of possible bases for a cease-fire. Without any advance clearance, the United Nations Commander issued a statement from Tokyo emphasizing the hopelessness of the enemy position and threatening the extension of military operations to China.[40] This statement was widely viewed as effectively destroying, even if not so intended, any possibility of success for the proposed diplomatic initiative.[41] Its effect was to create the impression on the part of some of the other co-operating Members that Washington was not in effective control of the United Nations Command. It placed a strain on United Nations co-operation and was one reason given for the removal of General MacArthur on April 10.[42]

Informal Procedures for Consultation

The incidents mentioned above illustrate the difficulties that can arise in the direction of a collective military action when it involves matters "on the crucial border-line between operations and international politics."[43] They also indicate that such difficulties are increased when the contribution of one Member to the collective operation so completely outweighs the contributions of others as to produce among its people the feeling that, for all practical purposes,

[40] For text, see New York Times (Mar. 24, 1951).
[41] Military Situation in the Far East, pp. 1774-75.
[42] Ibid., pp. 1790-92.
[43] London Times (July 2, 1952).

the operation is maintained and supported by that state and should therefore be directed primarily in the national interest of that state. They become even more serious when the policies and attitudes of that Member toward problems within the area of co-operation do not command the complete support and confidence of some of the co-operating governments.

As has been noted, the other Members of the United Nations were willing, indeed insistent, that the United States should establish the Unified Command and name the Commander-in-Chief. They were also willing that the Commander so named should receive his directives through regular United States channels. Once the first stage of the operation was successfully completed and military decisions began to have possible serious political consequences, however, other Members began to feel, and the United States Government concurred, that their points of view should be taken more into account. Initially, such exchanges of views appear to have taken place through normal diplomatic channels on a selective basis and without any attempt being made to formalize the process. Toward the end of November 1950, after Chinese Communist intervention had become a fact and when other governments had become very much concerned over failure to avoid extension of the conflict, the United States Government initiated the practice of a weekly conference in Washington attended by its representatives and those of other Member governments contributing armed forces.

In these conferences, in which the Republic of Korea was not included, representatives of all Members contributing armed forces to the collective military operation took part. The group came to be referred to as "The Committee of Sixteen." A representative of the Department of Defense gave a briefing on current military operations. An intelligence summary was provided. Questions originating with the Unified Command on the political consequences of proposed military operations were discussed. In certain cases, Members were informed of impending military operations, provided the time interval between the briefing and the operation was so short as to preclude any possibility of a leak that might tip off the enemy. When information of this kind was given out in advance, it was customary to give it on a highly restricted basis to certain governments that were especially interested and whose security arrangements were dependable. The committee was not considered a policy-making body, but with the information thus obtained, governments were presumably in a better position to influence the decisions of the Unified Command through diplomatic channels.

This procedure did not prevent some serious misunderstandings from arising. In part, this was because of the fact that the initiative in informing other governments of proposed military plans and in deciding whether their possible political consequences justified security risks being taken lay with the Unified Command itself. That placed other governments in a position in which they were dependent on the understanding and efficiency of the United States Government to obtain the information they needed before they could determine whether some political initiative on their part might be desirable. Another important reason for misunderstandings, at least during the period when General MacArthur was United Nations Commander, was the failure of the United States Government to enforce effective control over the field commander, and what was probably equally serious, to give timely and clear political guidance to the commander in the field.

Back of these difficulties was the fact that the United States was engaged in carrying out policies in the Far East that did not command the full support and concurrence of other Members. The United States Government often found itself in the embarrassingly difficult position of having to defend positions taken largely in deference to strong domestic pressures. Reconciliation of these views with the attitudes of some co-operating governments was extremely difficult, and on occasion Washington appears to have preferred postponing a clear-cut decision to taking a decision bound to be unpopular in some influential quarter at home.

The Collective Measures Committee recognized the need for consultation but appears to have accepted the procedure developed in the Korean case as meeting the need. Thus in the first report of the committee to the General Assembly, the following recommendation appeared:

Although it is necessary to place responsibility on an executive military authority for the effective conduct of military operations on behalf of the United Nations, as a matter of principle as well as for practical reasons it is important that close relations should be established between that authority, the victim State, participating and contributing States and the Secretary-General. The executive authority should develop procedures for consultation on a regular basis with the State or States victims of aggression and other participating States, to ensure joint consideration of matters of common interest.[44]

The practice in Korea, as well as the recommendation of the Collective Measures Committee, leaves the final decision on border-line political questions to the Member or Members vested with executive military authority. Many regard this as far from satisfactory and consider that other participating Members, although their material contributions may be small, may have fully as much to lose from the extension or indefinite continuation of the fighting, or from other political consequences of a given decision, as the Member or Members who have made the major military contributions. For example, after the Yalu power plant bombing in June 1952, the following observation was made in the London *Times:*

Clearly neither the United Nations General Assembly nor a committee of countries directly concerned is competent to direct the Korean War. Yet equally clearly there is need, without impairing the American Command, for consultation and agreement on the objectives to be pursued and on the crucial border-line between operations and international politics.[45]

The insistence on "agreement" as well as "consultation" is to be noted. In an editorial appearing in the Paris *Le Monde* and reprinted in the London *Times,* the demand for a collective decision was even more strongly made. Referring to the bombings of the Yalu power plants, the editorial continued:

[It] raises once more the vital question which arose at the beginning of the Korean fighting and has never yet been resolved, to wit, the establishment rendered necessary by the ineffectualness in this matter of the United Nations General Assembly and its political committee, of a properly qualified organism, interested in the tasks of defining the policy of the United Nations in Korea and of ensuring its execution permanently. Without withholding the chief responsibilities from the country which bears almost the whole burden of this war, it has become necessary once and for all to define a practical means of giving other countries concerned—those who take part in the common effort and who would be most threatened if the conflict were generalized—a say in decision.[46]

The criteria of such a system of political guidance to collective military forces might be defined as follows: In the first place, the

[44] "First Report of the Collective Measures Committee," pp. 27-28.
[45] London *Times* (July 2, 1952).
[46] *Ibid.* (June 28, 1952).

political authority that directs the over-all military command must be realistically representative of all nations actively supporting the action. The representation need not be equal, but it should avoid the appearance that one nation is dictating to the others. Secondly, the political guidance furnished by the authority must be continuous, direct, strong, certain, and consistent. It must anticipate developments in the military situation that will require additional or changed directives to the military commander. Third, the military commander must keep the political authority completely informed of the military situation and his plans. He must keep his plans flexible and realize the necessity of changing his scheme of action, if necessary, because of political considerations.[47]

Co-ordination of Nonmilitary Measures

Proper co-ordination of nonmilitary measures to maintain or restore international peace and security in case of a threat to or breach of the peace may be of great importance if collective action is to be effective. When a policy of nonrecognition was adopted by the League of Nations Assembly as a collective measure to be used against Japan in Manchuria in 1932, an *Ad Hoc* Committee was set up to co-ordinate the actions of Members. Later, in 1935, when economic and financial measures were applied against Italy, a Co-ordination Committee was established.

It was implicit in the provision of Article 41 of the Charter of the United Nations that the Security Council should undertake directly or through a subsidiary organ the co-ordination of collective measures not involving the use of armed force. But such co-ordination was never undertaken up to the time of the North Korean attack. In the particular circumstances of this attack, the emphasis was from the beginning placed on military measures and down to the time of the Chinese Communist intervention, no special consideration needed to be given to nonmilitary measures. This was largely because of the fact that inasmuch as the People's Democratic Republic of Korea had been set up in disregard of the resolution of the General Assembly of November 14, 1947, Members of the United Nations other than the Soviet Union and its associates had

---

[47] See Frederick G. Bohannon, *Some Military Problems of Collective Enforcement Action* (Master's Essay, Columbia University, 1953).

not recognized the government of the People's Democratic Republic of Korea or developed significant trade relations with it. One of the first acts of the United States in coming to the aid of the Republic of Korea was the establishment of a naval blockade of North Korea, which was supported and respected by other Members except the members of the Soviet bloc.

When Communist China intervened in the Korean situation, however, Members faced a more complex situation. Many Members outside the Soviet bloc had recognized the Peiping Government and many more were carrying on trade with Communist China. Consequently, when the General Assembly on February 1, 1951, found Communist China to have committed aggression, it did not recommend that Members take any measures immediately other than "continue to lend every assistance to the United Nations action in Korea." By its resolution of May 18, however, the Assembly recommended that certain economic measures be taken against Communist China and North Korea, but it placed on each state the responsibility for determining what commodities fell within each category of embargoed goods and what specific controls were to be applied to give effect to the embargo. Recognizing the need of some central co-ordination, the Assembly also recommended that each state report to the Additional Measures Committee, established by the resolution of February 1, on measures taken. It requested this committee (1) to report to the Assembly on the effectiveness of the embargo and the desirability of continuing, extending, or relaxing it, and (2) to continue its consideration of "additional measures to be employed to meet the aggression in Korea," and to report thereon to the General Assembly. In accordance with the resolution of the Assembly, the committtee reported on the response of Members but discontinued its operations when armistice negotiations were initiated. It never made any recommendations regarding the effectiveness of measures being applied, the desirability of their being continued or strengthened, or the particular "additional measures" that should be applied.

The major responsibility for checking on effectiveness, suggesting ways of strengthening the measures being applied, and proposing additional measures appears to have been assumed by the United States Government as part of its responsibility for the direction of military operations in Korea and as the state making the major contribution to joint military action to restrain aggression. Efforts by the United States to get other Member governments to accept its policy of political boycott of the Peiping Government met with only limited success. Likewise its efforts to get these governments to move in the direction of a complete trade embargo were unsuccessful. However, the United States Government succeeded in obtaining a high degree of co-operation from other Member governments outside the Soviet bloc in subjecting Communist China to an embargo of strategic materials, even before the resolution of May 18 was adopted.

The machinery for the co-ordination of these economic measures was in process of development well before the North Korean attack. In 1948, the United States approached major recipients in Western Europe of aid under the Marshall Plan to obtain agreement on co-ordinated control of exports of strategic goods to Soviet-controlled countries. Early in 1950, these discussions were transferred to "an informal international committee . . . when experience showed that effective action required simultaneous agreement by all producer countries to control the export of a particular commodity."[48] The substantial expansion of agreed control lists following the North Korean attack was applied automatically to trade with Communist China. After Communist China was declared an aggressor by the Assembly, the participating governments applied much stricter security controls over exports to that country. Partly in response to approaches by the United States, similar controls were adopted by Japan and other countries outside the group receiving aid under the Marshall Plan. Thus the Foreign Ministers of the American Republics at their April 1951 conference agreed to co-operate in the adoption of effective measures of security control.

The enactment of the so-called Battle Act in October 1951 considerably strengthened the influence of the United States in persuading other countries to agree to its export control policies. By this act, it was declared to be the policy of the United States "that no military, economic, or financial assistance shall be supplied to any nation unless it applies an embargo on . . . shipments [of strategic goods as defined] to any nation or combination of nations threatening the security of the United States." It was also declared that the act should "be administered in such a way as to bring about the

---

[48] U S. Foreign Operations Administration, *Mutual Defense Assistance Control Act of 1951*, First Report to Congress (January to July 1952), pp. 8-9.

fullest support for any resolution of the General Assembly of the United Nations, supported by the United States, to prevent the shipment of certain commodities to areas under the control of governments engaged in hostilities in defiance of the United Nations."[49] The "informal international committee," which had earlier been set up in Europe to assist in the control of exports to Soviet controlled countries, was used in obtaining the co-operation required by the Battle Act. In the latter part of 1952, on the initiative of the United States, a special committee was set up with the specific task of improving the control of shipments to Communist China and North Korea. This committee, consisting of non-Communist states that were or had been important traders with the Communist mainland, was concerned "on a day-by-day basis, with improving the control of strategic items to Communist China and North Korea."[50]

Early in 1953, while the Korean armistice negotiations were deadlocked, the United States took further initiatives to increase the economic pressure on Communist China without making use of United Nations machinery for the purpose. On March 7, Foreign Secretary Eden, at the conclusion of a conference with Secretary of State Dulles, announced that his government had decided to introduce a new system of licensing vessels registered in the United Kingdom and its colonies and new bunkering regulations more effectively to prevent the shipment of strategic materials to China.[51] The French Government announced on March 28, that similar co-operative steps would be taken.[52]

Although the particular circumstances of the Korean case permitted the effective use of collective economic measures with the minimum of co-ordination by a United Nations agency, there can be little question that the pattern of co-ordination followed in practice was hardly adequate as a model for the future. The Collective Measures Committee in its first report to the General Assembly in 1951 recognized the need for the establishment by either the General Assembly or the Security Council of a committee "to provide for the co-ordination, evaluation and general supervision of the [economic and financial] measures against an aggressor." Conceivably the task

---

[49] Mutual Defense Assistance Control Act of 1951, 65 Stat. 644.
[50] U.S. Foreign Operations Administration, *Mutual Defense Assistance Control Act of 1951*, Second Report to Congress (January 1953) , p. 30.
[51] U.S. Department of State *Bulletin*, Vol. 28 (Mar. 16, 1953) , p. 396.
[52] *Ibid.* (Apr. 6, 1953), p. 491.

of co-ordination could be performed by the Member or Members constituting the "Executive Military Authority" in case military measures were being applied, but it would seem desirable that membership on such a committee should at least take account of the fact that Members not making military contributions may have important stakes in the consequences of collective economic measures. Furthermore, considering that there is a close interrelation between military and nonmilitary measures, that all measures should be evaluated in relation to their ultimate objective—the maintenance of international peace and security—and that all Members are interested in this objective, it can be strongly argued that the co-ordination committee that is established should be representative of the total membership of the Organization. Such representation need not, however, be on the basis of mathematical equality. It might properly take into account the particular interests of certain Members and their special contributions to the collective operation as well as their common interest in international peace and security.

Co-ordination of Relief and Rehabilitation Operations

In any situation where armed force is used in international relations, the need of assistance for relief and rehabilitation purposes on the part of one or more states is likely to arise. Especially if a state has been the victim of aggression or has suffered as the result of supporting a United Nations action, it should not be required to bear the burden alone. This principle was recognized by the League of Nations and is explicitly stated in the Charter of the United Nations. From the point of view of the Charter, this principle is equally valid whether the state that suffers is or is not a Member. If such assistance is to achieve maximum effectiveness, however, measures taken, whether by individual states or by an international agency, must be adequately co-ordinated to meet the requirements of the collective action as well as to ease the burdens of those who have suffered special losses.

As soon as the invasion of the Republic of Korea began, thousands of people became homeless. By September 1950 at least 360,000 refugees were in the area defended by United Nations forces, and as a result of the Chinese Communist intervention, the number of refugees was swollen to millions. In addition, homes as well as production, distribution, and transportation facilities were destroyed, and administration was disrupted. The Security Council in late June and early July 1950 recommended that assistance be given the Republic of Korea and that such assistance be made available to the Unified Command. By its resolution of July 31, the Council requested the Unified Command to exercise responsibility for determining the relief and support requirements of the civilian population and requested the Secretary-General to transmit offers to the Unified Command. The Secretary-General, the Economic and Social Council, other appropriate United Nations organs, the specialized agencies, and appropriate nongovernmental organizations were asked to provide such assistance as the Unified Command might request. On December 1, 1950, the General Assembly made a similar appeal.

By August 1950, a procedure had been worked out between the Secretary-General and the Unified Command for processing assistance from governments and other bodies. Under it, requests for assistance were made by the Unified Command to the Secretary-General, and transmitted by him to Member states, and, when appropriate, to specialized agencies and nongovernmental organizations. Replies and independent offers were made to the Secretary-General who transmitted them to the Unified Command. When the Unified Command accepted an offer, the Secretary-General informed the government or organization concerned, and the Unified Command corresponded directly with the government or organization to settle the details and to arrange for shipment.[53]

At first the responsibilities given the Unified Command were carried out principally by the United States Economic Cooperation Administration assisted in the field by the United Nations Command. In August, the Commander-in-Chief, United Nations Command, designated the Public Health and Welfare Section of his General Headquarters as the agency responsible for administering relief in Korea. A field agency was established to work with the competent authorities of the Republic and with the Economic Cooperation Administration. At the end of September, the Unified Command charged the United Nations Command with the provision of supplies and equipment to prevent disease, starvation, and unrest, and the provision of items of a civilian type to serve both

[53] U.N. General Assembly, Sixth Session, *Official Records*, Supplement No. 12 (1951), p. 32.

military and civilian interests. At the same time the Economic Co-operation Administration was charged with working out require-ments and plans for postwar rehabilitation and assisting the United Nations Command in an advisory capacity. The Commanding Gen-eral of the Eighth United States Army was made responsible for all civil assistance activities within Korea. He in turn allocated responsi-bility in the immediate combat zone to civil assistance sections of the various corps and divisions, and in all other zones to the United Nations Civil Assistance Command, Korea. At a fairly early stage, therefore, the responsibility for administering relief and rehabilita-tion in Korea was given to the military and as a result was sub-ordinated to military needs and policies. Although the United Na-tions Civil Assistance Command, Korea, worked in co-operation with the Korean authorities, the co-operation down to the time of the signing of the armistice was never among equals.

The role of the United Nations in respect to relief and recon-struction was considered by the General Assembly during its fifth session and by its resolution of October 7, 1950, the Assembly created the United Nations Commission for the Unification and Rehabilita-tion of Korea. The Assembly directed the commission to exercise such responsibilities in connection with relief and rehabilitation in Korea "as may be determined by the General Assembly after receiv-ing the recommendations of the Economic and Social Council." Two months later the Assembly adopted another resolution based on recommendations of the Economic and Social Council, establishing the United Nations Korean Reconstruction Agency under the di-rection of a United Nations Agent General.[54] The Agent General was to "be responsible to the General Assembly for the conduct, in accordance with the policies established by the General Assembly, and having regard to such general policy recommendations" as the Commission for the Unification and Rehabilitation of Korea might make, of the relief and rehabilitation program in Korea as de-termined from time to time by the Assembly. To this end, the com-mission, which was the instrument of the Assembly for carrying out its program for Korea, was given certain powers with respect to the operations of the Korean Reconstruction Agency. The commission could recommend policies considered necessary to the discharge of its responsibility for the establishment of a unified, independent,

[51] Res. 410 (V), Dec. 1, 1950.

and democratic government in Korea. It could determine the geographic areas within which the Agent General should operate. It could designate Korean authorities with which the Agent General might establish relations. It could consider reports of the Agent General, transmit comments to the Assembly and the Economic and Social Council, and ask for information. Thus the concept was elaborated and formalized of United Nations supervision and direction of the work of relief and rehabilitation. In practice, however, the concept was not to be realized during the period when military operations were being conducted.

The Reconstruction Agency, after having been authorized by the Commission for the Unification and Rehabilitation of Korea to do so, initiated discussions with the United Nations Command with a view to determining responsibility for relief and rehabilitation in Korea during the period of military operations. It was agreed that the United Nations Command should be responsible for relief and short-term economic aid until military operations permitted the transfer of this responsibility to the Agency, the date of transfer to be determined by agreement among the Unified Command, the commission, and the Agency. In order to make the eventual transfer as smooth as possible, the Agency was to be brought into the programs of the United Nations Command as they progressed. During the time when the United Nations Command had primary responsibility, the Agency was to have responsibility for long-range planning and high-level technical assistance to the Government of the Republic of Korea and for any program of economic aid in addition to the program of the United Nations Command that the military situation would allow to be carried out. It was agreed that when military considerations were involved, the United Nations Command retained "over-riding power."[55] This agreement was approved by the commission.

The principle was therefore established that during the period of military operations, the United Nations Command, and not the Korean Reconstruction Agency, was responsible for relief and rehabilitation in Korea. As a result, the agency did not undertake any programs apart from a limited number of agreed projects. Instead, it recruited international staff for seconding to the Civil Assistance Command, did some long-term planning and preparation, and

[55] U.N. General Assembly, Sixth Session, *Official Records*, Supplement No. 12, p. 39.

engaged in discussions with the military authorities and the Government of the Republic of Korea. Both the Commission for the Unification and Rehabilitation of Korea and the Korean Reconstruction Agency appear to have pressed, but without much success, for a larger role for the Agency during early 1952, especially in the field of education. In September 1952, however, as a result in part of the stabilization of battle lines and the reduction of fighting that had occurred after armistice negotiations were initiated, the United Nations Agent General was able to reach agreement with the United States Government in Washington and the United Nations Command in Tokyo that some of the reconstruction work, which by early agreements was to be postponed until the end of hostilities, might be undertaken immediately. Quite clearly at this time there was basic disagreement between the United Nations Command, which was thinking primarily in terms of military needs, and the United Nations civilian agencies, which attached greater importance than did the military to civilian morale in Korea and the need for demonstrating the constructive possibilities of United Nations action.

Responsibility for and organization of future relief and rehabilitation operations in areas where collective military measures are being taken by the United Nations were considered by the Collective Measures Committee of the Assembly in 1951. The committee agreed that relief and refugee assistance must be viewed as an essential part of any program of collective measures. It accepted the view that relief and refugee assistance can be effectively undertaken by civilian organizations only after hostilities have ceased in the area to be assisted, and that "in these circumstances, measures to meet this situation must be taken by the armed forces in the area."[56] This conclusion, however, did not give answers to some of the more important questions. Does it also follow that during a period of prolonged armistice negotiations, when hostilities still technically exist but when the military line is stabilized, that responsibility for relief and rehabilitation should rest with the armed forces? What is meant by the term "in the area"—the area immediately adjacent to the fighting, or the whole country in the case of Korea? Even though the military command must assume immediate responsibility for relief and rehabilitation, is it not possible to bring the military

[56] "First Report of the Collective Measures Committee," p. 18.

command under some over-all international civilian direction that will give better assurance that nonmilitary considerations will receive due attention? Basically, it must be recognized that effective relief and rehabilitation may be as important to the restoration of peace on a sound basis as successful military operations. The question is not whether a good or bad job was done in Korea but rather what is the pattern of organization most likely to facilitate a good result.

CHAPTER XIX

The Termination of Collective Measures

THE EFFECTIVENESS OF "collective measures for the prevention and removal of threats to the peace, and for the suppression of acts of aggression or other breaches of the peace" may depend as much on the conditions under which and the process by which these measures are terminated as on the manner in which they are initiated, organized, and directed. In fact, if the primary concern is the extent to which the measures achieve the declared purpose of the Charter, and not the extent to which they possess a collective character, the problem of their termination may become of most critical importance. It is therefore necessary to consider the conditions under which collective measures initiated by the United Nations have been brought to an end, the process by which this has been done, and the extent to which conditions achieved by the use of such measures constitute a fulfillment of the objectives of the United Nations.

Theory of the Charter

The Covenant of the League of Nations contained no provision explicitly defining the purposes of the sanctions that Members were to apply under Article 16 or the conditions under which these sanctions were to be terminated. It was, of course, assumed that their primary purpose was to defeat the aggression that led to their application. Presumably, either the Council or the Assembly of the League could recommend their termination, although Members were undoubtedly free to bring them to an end on their own responsibility, and either organ could exercise its general powers under the Covenant of the League in an effort to bring about some satisfactory adjustment of the situation resulting from their use. When sanctions were applied against Italy in 1935-36 on an extensive scale, they did not achieve their purpose of defeating Italian aggression. Furthermore, they were relaxed or brought to an end by Members on their own responsibility, in many cases without waiting for any guidance from an organ of the League.

Those who wrote the Charter of the United Nations thought a more effective system would be achieved by vesting primary responsibility for initiating, directing, and terminating collective measures in the Security Council. That organ was authorized, when it was confronted by a situation in which there was a threat to the peace, a breach of the peace, or an act of aggression, to choose, in the exercise of the wide discretion vested in it, the means best suited to achieve the purpose of maintaining or restoring international peace and security. If the Council should decide to use measures under Articles 41 and 42 of the Charter, it would subsequently have to decide under what conditions the enforcement measures should be terminated. In fact, the provisions of Article 5 of the Charter, according to which—following suspension of a Member—the exercise of the rights and privileges of membership might be restored by the Council, were clearly based on this assumption regarding the range of the responsibility and power of the Council.[1] The Council might, if it so desired, seek the advice of the General Assembly with respect to the conditions on which peace should be restored, but neither the Council nor the Members would be bound by the advice of the Assembly.

The provisions of the Charter were based on the assumption that the permanent members of the Security Council would find it in their interest to co-operate in the application of collective measures and in determining the conditions under which these measures would be terminated. Such conditions might, and most probably would, include not only arrangements governing the disposition and use of the armed forces involved but also the methods or terms of settlement of the dispute or situation that had given rise to the threat or use of armed force. Although the Council does not have the power under the Charter legally to obligate the parties to accept a particular settlement, terms proposed by the Council with the full agreement of the major powers would in all likelihood be accepted and carried out, because of the implied threat that refusal to accept them might be viewed as justification for the continued application of coercive measures. Small and weak states without major power support would find it fruitless, even though they might consider

[1] Article 5 provides that a Member against which preventive or enforcement action has been taken by the Security Council may be suspended from the exercise of the rights and privileges of membership by the General Assembly upon the recommendation of the Security Council.

their cause to be just, to continue to resist the combined will and power of the permanent members of the Council, supported as they would be by many of the smaller states.

Furthermore, the Council, in ordering collective measures and in recommending the conditions under which international peace and security would be restored, would be acting under the express terms of the Charter as the agent of the Members of the United Nations and thus would have authority derived from general consent as well as from predominant military power. The Council also would be required to act in accordance with "the Purposes and Principles of the United Nations."[2] Thus in performing its function of maintaining or restoring international peace and security by an appropriate combination of coercion and persuasion, the Council would be expected to have regard for both the principles of international law and justice and the interests of Member states.

Difficulties Created by Great Power Disagreement

The failure of the permanent members of the Security Council to co-operate largely eliminated the possibility of applying collective measures in the manner envisaged by the authors of the Charter. It encouraged the development of alternative methods of collective action, based on the principle of voluntary co-operation in carrying out recommendations of the United Nations. For the purposes of a voluntary system, the General Assembly has been recognized as having certain advantages over the Council as an initiating organ.

The development of what might be called "a voluntary system," under which collective measures are taken on the "recommendation" of a United Nations organ, has increased the likelihood that a situation will arise in which some Members of the United Nations apply collective measures, while others do not. Members may refuse to co-operate for a variety of reasons—because they do not recognize the proposed action as valid, because they do not consider it wise, or because they do not feel that their particular situation permits them to take any of the measures recommended. Under such circumstances, there may be Members whose attitude toward the collective action is either neutral or hostile, and yet who have not violated any legal obligation under the Charter. Another consequence of the

[2] Art. 24.

"voluntary system," in which collective measures are recommended by the Assembly, or by the Council as in the special circumstances of the Korean case, is that measures may be taken against a great power or a smaller state enjoying the support of a great power, with the result that there may not be the predominance of power on the side of the enforcing group or agency that the framers of the Charter originally envisaged.

If collective measures are taken in the name, or with the express approval of, the United Nations with only part of the Members participating and with other Members opposed to the action, or at least having a "neutral" attitude toward it, a different situation is created from that envisaged by the framers of the Charter in so far as the restoration of international peace and security is concerned. If, for example, there is no great preponderance of power on the side of the Members engaged in a particular collective action by the United Nations, and if a major war with all its objectionable consequences is to be avoided in the situation, it may become necessary, in order to limit the scope of military operations and eventually to achieve a peaceful settlement, to rely rather heavily on negotiations. It is also necessary to emphasize that collective military measures are being used for the limited purpose of denying to any state a possible gain from the use or threat of force and for creating conditions under which international peace and security will be at least as firmly established as before the threat or breach of the peace occurred. The possibility of dictating the conditions on which international peace and security are to be restored and of persuading the state or states against which collective measures are being taken to accept these conditions is greatly reduced.

Method and Conditions of Termination

The experience of the United Nations has shown the complexity of the problem of relating the termination of collective measures to the successful achievement of their objectives, under the conditions of stress and strain that have existed since the war. This problem has two important aspects that require consideration: (1) the substantive and (2) the procedural. The first relates to the conditions under which these measures will be terminated, especially in relation to the achievement of the major purpose of United Nations action—the maintenance or restoration of international peace and security. The second problem is the process by which collective measures, once they have been initiated, will be terminated. In considering these two aspects of the problem, the experience of the United Nations suggests the desirability of considering separately military and nonmilitary measures.

Military Measures

Not only does the Korean case offer the sole instance of the application of collective military measures under the Charter, but it also provides the sole experience with their termination. Furthermore, inasmuch as collective military measures were applied in Korea, following both the initial North Korean attack and the Communist Chinese intervention, and inasmuch as the opinion is widely held that the original objective of these measures was accomplished, it is important to analyze this experience with a view to ascertaining the conditions under which the collective military action was terminated and the relation of these conditions to the declared objectives of the enterprise.

The objective to be sought by joint military action in Korea was defined by Article 39 of the Charter to be the restoration of international peace and security. By its resolution of June 27, 1950, the Security Council stated the objective more concretely when it recommended that Members give assistance to the Republic of Korea "to repel the armed attack and to restore international peace and security in the area." This was followed two days later by a statement by the United States Secretary of State that the collective action was "solely for the purpose of restoring the Republic of Korea to its status prior to the invasion from the north and of reestablishing the peace broken by that invasion."[3] This statement appeared to express the view of other Members supporting the collective action, and from it the inference could be drawn that the Members of the United Nations, and the United States in particular, were prepared to accept the restoration of the *status quo ante* as the basis for terminating their joint military action.

Once the North Korean forces were in retreat to the north and the possibility opened up of obtaining a decisive military result, however, there appears to have been a change in the attitudes of many Members, especially the United States, regarding the conditions under which military action should be terminated. The view came

[3] U.S. Department of State *Bulletin*, Vol. 23 (July 10, 1950), p. 46.

to be widely accepted that the North Korean forces could, without undue risk and with ample justification, be destroyed as a fighting force, and that advantage could be taken of this decisive military result to carry out the program of the General Assembly for the establishment of an independent, democratic, and united Korea. This point of view was expressed by the United States Secretary of State in his address to the Assembly on September 20, 1950, in which he stated his "belief and every confidence that this challenge and defiance to the authority of the United Nations will be crushed as it deserves to be, and that thereafter the future of this small and gallant country may be returned where it belongs—to the custody of its own people under the guidance of the United Nations."[4] And, speaking in the First Committee of the Assembly on September 30, the United States representative gave expression to a more ambitious conception of United Nations objectives. After observing that "the forces of the United Nations stand on the threshold of military victory," he continued:

The opportunities for new acts of aggression, of course, should be removed. Faithful adherence to the United Nations objective of restoring international peace and security in the area counsels the taking of appropriate steps to eliminate the power and ability of the North Korean aggressor to launch future attacks. The aggressor's forces should not be permitted to have refuge behind an imaginary line because that would recreate the threat to the peace of Korea and of the world. Whatever ephemeral separation of Korea there was for purposes relating to the surrender of the Japanese was so volatile that nobody recognizes it. Let us not, at this critical hour and on this grave event, erect such a boundary. Rather, let us set up standards and means, principles and policies, according to the Charter, by which all Koreans can hereafter live in peace among themselves and with their neighbors.[5]

The Assembly resolution of October 7 defined in detail the "standards and means, principles and policies" by which an independent, united, and democratic Korea was to be brought into being, once "conditions of stability throughout Korea" had been established. The initial military steps to establish these "conditions" were General MacArthur's surrender demand of October 9, addressed to the North Korean Command, and the crossing of the thirty-eighth parallel by United Nations forces.[6]

---

[4] *Ibid.* (Oct. 2, 1950), p. 526.
[5] *Ibid.* (Oct. 9, 1950), pp. 579-80.
[6] *New York Times* (Oct. 9, 1950).

The view that collective military measures might be used to achieve "conditions of stability throughout Korea," thus permitting the carrying out of the program of the Assembly, was shared by most Members of the United Nations. In the course of consideration by the General Assembly of the Korean question in late September and early October, a number of significant statements were made in support of this position. The representative of the Philippines, for example, expressed the opinion that "the Security Council resolution of June 27 was broad enough to admit the continuation of military operations by the United Nations forces until international peace and security had been completely restored throughout Korea."[7] The representative of Australia was even more specific when he asserted:

The only logical interpretation of the Security Council resolution of 27 June was that the North Korean army, which was the aggressor, must be destroyed as a fighting force; that, by corollary, meant pursuing it across the parallel. Crossing of the 38th parallel would be for the sole object of putting an end to the present struggle and bringing about a unified Korea.[8]

The Norwegian representative also expressed the opinion that the stability of Korea was incompatible with the artificial division of the country and said:

By resorting to force and by disregarding both the United Nations appeal to cease hostilities and its call to surrender, the North Koreans had shown that no solution was possible until their final defeat. The unification of Korea was therefore closely linked with the maintenance of international peace and security in that part of the world and, as the artificial regime in existence at the outbreak of hostilities had collapsed, the United Nations must complete its task, if its efforts were not to be in vain.[9]

Some delegations, other than those of the Soviet bloc, which regarded the collective action in Korea as illegal, were of the opinion, however, that the proposal to make the establishment of conditions of stability throughout Korea the *sine qua non* of a cessation of military action was unwise. The representative of India, for example, thought the result of authorizing United Nations forces to enter North Korea "might be to intensify North Korean opposition and to increase the tension in that part of the world." Faith in

[7] U.N. General Assembly, Fifth Session, First Committee, *Official Records*, 347th Meeting (Sept. 30, 1950), p. 12.
[8] *Ibid.*, 350th Meeting (Oct. 3, 1950), p. 32.
[9] *Ibid.*, 351st Meeting (Oct. 3, 1950), p. 37.

the United Nations might be impaired if the Organization were even to "appear to authorize unification of Korea by the use of force against North Korea, after the Organization had resisted the attempt of North Korea to unify the country by force against South Korea."[10] And the representative of Yugoslavia expressed the view that a decision to cross the thirty-eighth parallel and to extend "the present regime to North Korea"

. . . would strike a serious blow at the prestige of the United Nations. For the question was whether it was capable of checking aggression without at the same time imposing on a country a specific political and social regime. It was by that test that the United Nations would be judged.

The aim of the Security Council's action had been to prevent the alteration by force of a given situation, and not to use armed force to change the *de facto* situation existing at the beginning of hostilities, which would establish such a precedent as to justify any intervention in a country's internal affairs.[11]

The threat, followed by the fact, of Chinese Communist military intervention in Korea produced a further change in the attitudes of many Members. At first an effort was made to maintain the policy of the resolution approved by the Assembly in October by giving assurances to Communist China that United Nations forces would not remain in any part of Korea "otherwise than so far as necessary for achieving the objectives" of the resolution and that it was the policy of the United Nations to respect the Chinese frontier and Chinese and Korean interests in the frontier zone.[12] When the proposal to this effect was vetoed by the Soviet Union in the Security Council, the question was brought before the General Assembly in early December, where a similar proposal was introduced. It soon became clear, however, that sentiment in the Assembly, under the influence of a deteriorating military situation and the threat of an extension of the fighting, had moved away from supporting any serious effort to pacify all of Korea by military means, and was now favorable to making every effort to bring the fighting to an end on terms consistent with the minimum requirements of the Charter and the resolutions of the Council and thus prevent the spread of the conflict.

Furthermore, the view gained wide acceptance that it was "the

[10] *Ibid.*, 350th Meeting (Oct. 3, 1950), p. 33.
[11] *Ibid.*, 351st Meeting (Oct. 3, 1950), p. 39.
[12] U.N. Doc. S/1894 (Nov. 10, 1950).

problem of Asia in general which was under consideration" and that the central need was to define the relations of China with the rest of the world on a satisfactory and mutually acceptable basis.[13] Those sympathizing with this view took the position that the specific objectives of collective military measures in Korea must be adapted to some extent to the requirements of international peace and security in the larger area. This was the approach of two draft resolutions introduced by the representative of India on December 12. The first of these proposals, which was sponsored by thirteen governments and to which priority was accorded, expressed the desire that immediate steps should be taken to prevent the spread of the conflict in Korea and that "further steps should then be taken for a peaceful settlement of existing issues in accordance with the purposes and principles of the United Nations."[14] To this end, it requested the President of the Assembly to constitute a group of three persons to determine the basis on which a satisfactory cease-fire in Korea could be arranged and to make recommendations to the Assembly. The second proposal, sponsored by twelve Members, called for a conference to make recommendations for "the peaceful settlement of existing issues."[15]

The adoption by the Assembly on December 14[16] of the resolution sponsored jointly by thirteen members represented for many members of the Assembly a retreat from their October position to the more modest stand that military action should be restricted to repelling aggression, that, once this condition had been achieved, military action at least should be terminated, and that the political conditions of peace and security in the area, including the unification of Korea, should be the subject of negotiations subsequent to the termination of hostilities.[17]

The efforts that were made by the so-called Group of Three, established by the resolution, were not successful in bringing about a cease-fire and subsequent negotiations for a peaceful settlement, but they did disclose the conditions that the Unified Command and many Members of the United Nations set for the termination

---

[13] Statement of Mr. Malik of Lebanon. U.N. General Assembly, Fifth Session, First Committee, *Official Records*, 413th Meeting (Dec. 11, 1950), pp. 421-24.

[14] U.N. Doc. A/C.1/641 (Dec. 12, 1950).

[15] U.N. Doc. A/C.1/642 (Dec. 12, 1950).

[16] Res. 384 (V).

[17] See U.N. General Assembly, Fifth Session, *Official Records*, 415th-17th Meetings (Dec. 12-13, 1950), pp. 436-53.

of collective military action. It should be borne in mind that at the time the Group of Three initiated its efforts, the United Nations forces in Korea were in retreat, and the Communist forces were approaching and were about to cross the thirty-eighth parallel. Immediately after the Group was constituted, it consulted with representatives of the Unified Command regarding a satisfactory basis for a cease-fire. The suggestions that emerged from this consultation and that "in the circumstances the Group felt constituted a reasonable basis for discussion," may be summarized as follows:[18]

1. All governments and authorities to order the cessation of all acts of armed force in all Korea.

2. Establishment of a demilitarized area across Korea approximately twenty miles in depth with the southern limit following generally the thirty-eighth parallel.

3. Disposition of and instructions to armed forces consistent with the above provisions.

4. Supervision of the cease-fire by a United Nations Commission whose members and observers would have free and unlimited access to the whole of Korea.

5. All governments and authorities promptly to cease introducing reinforcements, replacements, and additional war material and equipment into the area.

6. Exchange of prisoners of war on a one-for-one basis.

7. Appropriate provisions regarding security of forces, movement of refugees, and the handling of other specific problems.

8. Confirmation of arrangements by the General Assembly.

In explaining these proposals to the Peiping Government, the Group of Three affirmed its clear understanding, and also that of the twelve Asian states that had sponsored the proposed resolution for a conference, that once a cease-fire had been achieved, the negotiations envisaged in their draft resolution "should be proceeded with at once," and that the government of the People's Republic of China should be included in these negotiations.[19] The Peiping Government refused to accept the proposals as a basis for discussion, arguing that they were intended solely to provide time for United States forces to reorganize and not to prepare the way for a peaceful settlement.[20]

[18] U.N. Doc. A/C.1/643 (Jan. 2, 1951).
[19] Ibid., pp. 5-6.
[20] Ibid., Annex I.

In the discussions in the First Committee of the Assembly on the report of the Group, it was clear that Members were not willing to accept this failure as conclusive. Under pressure of the steadily worsening military situation and the increasing threat of an extension of the fighting, it was suggested that the Group of Three give consideration to principles that might be laid down as the basis for negotiations subsequent to a cease-fire.[21] On January 11, 1951, the Group of Three submitted a supplementary report in which it made proposals for both a cease-fire and negotiations for a peaceful settlement. The "five principles" formulated by the group, which were subsequently approved by the First Committee and communicated to the Peiping Government, constituted a definition of the conditions on which the First Committee recommended that collective military measures be ended. They were as follows:

1. In order to prevent needless destruction of life and property, and while other steps are being taken to retore peace, a cease-fire should be immediately arranged. Such an arrangement should contain adequate safeguards for ensuring that it will not be used as a screen for mounting a new offensive.

2. If and when a cease-fire occurs in Korea, either as a result of a formal arrangement or, indeed, as a result of a lull in hostilities pending some such arrangement, advantage should be taken of it to pursue consideration of further steps to be taken for the restoration of peace.

3. To permit the carrying out of the General Assembly resolution that Korea should be a unified, independent, democratic, sovereign State with a constitution and a government based on free popular elections, all non-Korean armed forces will be withdrawn, by appropriate stages, from Korea, and appropriate arrangements, in accordance with United Nations principles, will be made for the Korean people to express their own free will in respect of their future government.

4. Pending the completion of the steps referred to in the preceding paragraph, appropriate interim arrangements, in accordance with United Nations principles, will be made for the administration of Korea and the maintenance of peace and security there.

5. As soon as agreement has been reached on a cease-fire, the General Assembly shall set up an appropriate body which shall include representatives of the Governments of the United Kingdom, the United States of America, the Union of Soviet Socialist Republics, and the People's Republic of China with a view to the achievement of a settlement, in conformity with existing international obligations and the provisions of the United Nations Charter, of Far Eastern problems, including, among others,

[21] See statements by the Norwegian representative and the British representative, U.N. General Assembly, Fifth Session, First Committee, *Official Records*, 419th Meeting (Jan. 3, 1951), p. 461.

those of Formosa (Taiwan) and of representation of China in the United Nations.[22]

The discussion that occurred in the First Committee on this supplementary report of the Group of Three served further to clarify the positions of Members with respect to the conditions under which collective military measures should be terminated. Influential members of the Assembly expressed the view that, considering the danger of extension of the conflict and the destructive and unpredictable consequences of a third world war, every effort should be made "to arrive at an honorable and peaceful settlement. Such an effort should not be regarded as appeasement."[23] It was pointed out that "it was wholly consistent with the principles of the Charter that every effort should be made to achieve a peaceful settlement in the Far East before resort was had to additional collective measures."[24] Furthermore, it was pointed out that any solution of the Korean problem alone required an agreement with the neighbors of Korea, including the People's Republic of China.[25]

The refusal of the Peiping Government to accept the "five principles" resulted in further discussion of acceptable conditions of peace in Korea. The issue on which the majority of members of the General Assembly and the Peiping Government were in disagreement was the exact relation of the cease-fire to negotiations for a political settlement. The Peiping Government sought to use what it regarded as its favorable military position to extract political concessions and the Members of the United Nations—at least the great majority—were insistent that satisfactory arrangements for a cease-fire precede negotiations for the settlement, first of the Korean problem, and then of other Far Eastern questions.[26] It was made clear during the discussion in the First Committee that the cessation of hostilities could not be made dependent on "the prior granting of all the requests of the Peiping Government," as that would mean "that the United Nations would have to negotiate under duress."[27]

[22] U.N. Doc. A/C.1/645 (Jan. 11, 1951).
[23] U.N. General Assembly, Fifth Session, First Committee, *Official Records*, 422nd Meeting (Jan. 11, 1951), p. 475.
[24] *Ibid.*, 423rd Meeting (Jan. 12, 1951), p. 483.
[25] *Ibid.*, p. 484.
[26] See statement of the Canadian representative, *Ibid.*, 432nd Meeting (Jan. 26, 1951), pp. 553-56.
[27] Statement of the British representative, *Ibid.*, 426th Meeting (Jan. 18, 1951), p. 507.

It might be stated that by this time—the middle of January 1951—
the position of the United Nations forces in Korea had considerably
improved, the stabilization of the military line seemed in process
of being achieved, and the danger of extension of the fighting had
been somewhat reduced. During the discussions in the Assembly,
it became clear that most Members of the United Nations were not
prepared to use collective military measures to the extent necessary
to achieve a decisive military result and thus to make possible the
prompt attainment of Korean unification. The resolution that the
Assembly adopted on February 1, 1951, therefore affirmed "the
policy of the United Nations to bring about a cessation of hostilities
in Korea and the achievement of United Nations objectives in
Korea by peaceful means."[28]

The position of the United States Government, vested with the
responsibility of unified command, was of special importance. Somewhat reluctantly, it had accepted the "five principles." Although the
United States insisted that the Assembly find Communist China
guilty of aggression and take initial steps with a view to the application of "additional measures," in effect, it returned to its position of
June 1950 regarding the objectives of collective military action and
the conditions of its termination. Thus in testifying before the
Senate committees on June 1, 1951, the Secretary of State said:

> Our objective is to stop the attack, end the aggression on that Govern-
> ment [Republic of Korea], restore peace, providing against the renewal
> of aggression. Those are the military purposes for which, as we understand
> it, the United Nations troops are fighting. The United Nations has since
> 1947 and the United States has since 1943 or 1944 stood for a unified, free,
> and democratic Korea. That is still our purpose, and is still the purpose of
> the United Nations. I do not understand it to be a war aim. In other
> words, that is not sought to be achieved by fighting, but it is sought to be
> achieved by peaceful means, just as was being attempted before this aggres-
> sion.[29]

The failure of the Chinese Communist and North Korean forces
to drive the United Nations forces from Korea and the success of
the United Nations Command in stabilizing the military front and
driving the Communist forces back to a line in the vicinity of the
thirty-eighth parallel apparently were important factors in prompt-

[28] Res. 498 (V), Feb. 1, 1951.
[29] *Military Situation in the Far East,* Hearings before the Senate Committee on
Armed Services and Committee on Foreign Relations, 82 Cong. 1 sess., Pt. 3, p.
1729.

ing the broadcast of the Soviet representative to the United Nations on June 23, 1951, suggesting cease-fire and armistice negotiations. In preliminary exchanges with the Soviet Government, the United States made clear its view that the proposed armistice agreement should be limited "to strictly military matters without involving any political or territorial matters."[30] The agenda that was accepted by the respective military commands provided for limiting the discussion to military questions except for "recommendations which might be made to the governments concerned on both sides."[31] The United Nations Command, during these negotiations, insisted on the following requirements for an acceptable armistice:

1. A line of demarcation consistent with the United Nations objective of repelling aggression, based upon military realities, and affording defensible positions for the opposing forces;

2. Other provisions offering maximum reasonable assurance against a renewal of the aggression;

3. Appropriate arrangements for an exchange of prisoners of war;

4. Avoidance of political issues as not properly related to armistice negotiations.[32]

Although agreement on the agenda for the armistice negotiations was reached on July 26, 1951, it was not until two years later that the final armistice agreement was concluded. The terms of the agreement signed on July 27, 1953, in the names of the Commander-in-Chief, United Nations Command, on the one hand, and on the other hand, the Supreme Commander of the Korean People's Army and the Commander of the Chinese People's Volunteers, were in conformity with the conditions of termination that had been developed in the course of United Nations discussions and with the requirements that had been set by the United Nations Command.[33] The military demarcation line for which the armistice agreement provided was more favorable to the Republic of Korea than the thirty-eighth parallel had been. It involved some sacrifice of territory formerly under the jurisdiction of the Republic, but it removed a larger area of North Korean territory from Communist control, and it provided a more defensible line than the thirty-eighth parallel had been. The concrete arrangements for a cease-fire and an

[30] U.N. Doc. A/2228, (Oct. 18, 1952), p. 6.

[31] *Ibid.*, p. 7.

[32] *Ibid.*

[33] For text of the armistice, see *United Nations Bulletin*, Vol. 15 (Aug. 1, 1953), pp. 115-22.

armistice provided substantial assurance that the Republic of Korea would not again be subjected to an unprovoked military attack, even though not all the initial demands of the United Nations Command were met. This assurance was further strengthened by the declaration of the sixteen nations of July 27, 1953 that if there should be a renewal of the armed attack challenging again the principles of the United Nations, they would again be united and prompt to resist.

On the issue of prisoners of war, the armistice agreement went beyond the requirements imposed by the objectives of United Nations military action in Korea, in that it not only provided for the return of all prisoners held by the Communists who desired to return, but it also gave to prisoners held by the United Nations Command the right to refuse to be repatriated if they so desired. This latter provision, and the extent to which Chinese and North Koreans exercised their right not to return, were a source of considerable embarrassment to the Communists, and have been viewed as an important deterrent to the resumption of aggression.

The armistice agreement did not substantially advance the cause of Korean unity. By leaving Korea divided, and under the control of hostile military forces, the agreement did not remove what had been for years a serious threat to peace and security in the Far East. Originally, however, collective action had not been taken to achieve the settlement of the Korean question. In October 1950, under the influence of military success, Members of the United Nations were tempted to make that, in effect, their objective, but in the end they returned to the more modest goal.

It was recognized by the parties to the armistice agreement that political negotiations would be needed for a settlement of the Korean question. The military commands that were parties to the armistice agreement recommended "to the governments of the countries concerned on both sides" that a political conference be held to settle by negotiation the question of the withdrawal of all foreign forces from Korea, to achieve the peaceful settlement of the Korean question, "et cetera." The United Nations Command had made it clear, however, that the "et cetera" did not relate to matters outside of Korea. Thus it could not rightfully be said that the Peiping Government, as the result of its intervention, had obtained the promise on the part of the United Nations to consider certain questions such as Formosa and the seating of Chinese Communist representatives in the organs of the United Nations.

Nonmilitary Measures

The use by Members of nonmilitary measures of coercion is not prohibited under the Charter and consequently their use, whether individually or collectively, is permissible on recommendation of either the Security Council or the General Assembly, for purposes other than the removal of threats to the peace, the restraint of ag- gerssion, and the suppression of breaches of the peace. Inasmuch as the powers of recommendation of the Assembly are much broader than those of the Council, the Assembly can recommend nonmilitary measures for a greater variety of purposes and has full discretion to recommend their termination or not. Likewise, individual Members have wide discretion in regard to the application and termination of such measures.

In the Spanish case, the status of the collective measures recom- mended by the Assembly in December 1946 was in doubt for some time prior to the formal revocation in 1950 of the recommendation to withdraw ambassadors and ministers and to disbar Spain from the specialized agencies. A proposal made in 1947 that the Assembly re- affirm the recommendations contained in its 1946 resolution failed to receive the necessary two-thirds affirmative vote. The increasing disregard shown for the recommendation of the Assembly and the rapid decline in support for it from 1947 on were due to changes in the political attitudes of Member states toward the recommended measures, not to any success of the measures in question in achieving their declared objectives.

In the Greek case, the embargo on the export of arms and other war materials to Albania and Bulgaria, which the Assembly recom- mended in 1949, was to be operative until the Special Committee or another competent United Nations organ determined that the un- lawful assistance to the Greek guerrillas had ceased.[34] The Special Committee was dissolved in 1950, but no formal decision has been taken by any United Nations organ revoking the embargo. The Assembly, in dissolving the committee, recognized the continuing danger of the situation by asking the Peace Observation Commission to send a subcommittee on the Balkans. It should be noted, how- ever, that the arms embargo of the United Nations was never an important factor in dealing with the situation in the Balkans. The decisive factors in defeating the aggressive tactics of the northern

[34] See U.N. General Assembly, Fourth Session, Plenary, *Official Records,* 246th Meeting (Nov. 18, 1949), pp. 9-10.

neighbors of Greece were the military and economic assistance given to Greece by the United States, and the withdrawal of Yugoslavia from the Soviet bloc. Furthermore, an arms embargo was already in force, in so far as the principal non-Communist countries were concerned, as a result of co-operation between the United States and other Western powers in preventing the shipment of strategic goods to countries under Communist control. The Soviet Union and its satellites did not, of course, respect the embargo, and they were the principal suppliers of military goods.

The recommendation of an embargo on the export of arms and strategic materials to Communist China and North Korea, which the General Assembly made on May 18, 1951, was not revoked with the conclusion of the armistice agreement. At the time the embargo resolution was adopted by the Assembly, the Additional Measures Committee was authorized to make recommendations on the desirability of continuing, extending, or relaxing the embargo, but the committee has not done so.[35] The measures of economic coercion, in some cases initiated and in other cases developed and further perfected by Members, were primarily for the purpose of defeating the aggression of Communist China and forcing the acceptance of armistice terms consistent with the purposes and principles of the Charter. These measures were continued after the signing of the armistice, presumably in part with a view to inducing the Peiping Government to agree to United Nations terms for the unification of Korea and to refrain from expansionist activities, especially in Southeast Asia.

The Process of Termination

In considering the process by which collective measures have been terminated, two aspects of the matter should be kept in mind. (1) To what extent has the procedure followed been consistent with the collective character of the measures in question? (2) To what extent has the process been of such a nature as to contribute to the effectiveness of the measures in the achievement of their objectives?

In the Spanish case, as already noted, there was, after the first year, a general decline in respect for the 1946 recommendations of the General Assembly, and the 1950 revocation did little more than to recognize a factual situation. In the Greek case, there was no

[35] Res. 500 (V), May 18, 1951.

formal revocation of the embargo by the General Assembly or any other United Nations agency, and such measures as may have been taken in response to the recommendation have been continued as part of the cold war.

Only in Korea, in connection with the termination of military operations, has there developed a pattern of action. In this case, the basic principles with respect to the termination of military measures were largely developed by the United States Government. They were developed within the framework of the purposes and principles laid down in the Charter and the resolutions of United Nations organs, and under the influence of discussions in the Assembly and with other governments that had sent military forces to Korea. The return to limited military objectives in Korea was partly in response to the desire of other Members to avoid the risk of greatly expanded fighting. But it was in larger measure because the top civil and military officials of the United States were convinced that it was not in the interest of the United States to extend the fighting to the degree that would have been necessary to "win the war" in the traditional sense, and least of all, for the United States to proceed alone in doing so.

The predominant role of the United States in determining the conditions for the termination of collective military measures in Korea, was, to a certain extent, justifiable and understandable in the light of the leadership and the size of the contributions that the United States had provided. Nevertheless, the collective nature of the operation would have been given greater reality and many legitimate grounds of grievance could have been removed if circumstances had permitted the development of more effective machinery for consultation and decision.

In view of the fact that the purpose of the armistice negotiations was to establish conditions governing the cessation of hostilities, including the fixing of a military demarcation line, the establishment of adequate guarantees against the renewal of aggression, and appropriate arrangements for the exchange of prisoners of war, there was ample justification for the assumption by the United Nations Command of responsibility for conduct of the negotiations. But although the primary objective of an armistice agreement is to obtain a cessation of hostilities, many of the provisions inevitably have political implications.

The respective roles of the organs of the United Nations, the

Members of the United Nations with armed forces in Korea, and the United States Government in particular, in giving political guidance to the United Nations Command were not clearly defined. As in the conduct of hostilities, there were questions of a political or politico-military nature to be decided with respect to which Members of the United Nations, especially those with armed forces in Korea, might feel unwilling to accept the decision of the United State Government alone because of the far-reaching consequences of such a decision. Falling in this category were questions such as the withdrawal of troops, the establishment of a demarcation line, the establishment of rules governing the exchange of prisoners, and the extent to which specific armistice terms should be insisted on at the risk of failure to end the fighting and a possible extension of it. Furthermore, as military operations continued during the armistice negotiations, and as they might have the effect of endangering as well as promoting the success of negotiations, the decisions regarding particular military operations, for example, the bombing of the Yalu power plants in 1952, often acquired political significance.

The armistice negotiations were conducted by the United Nations Command under instructions prepared by the United States Government. Through meetings of the Committee of Sixteen[36] and other official contacts, governments with armed forces in Korea were kept fully informed of the course of these negotiations and, although not to the same extent, of positions that the United Nations Command was planning to take or of military measures that were under consideration. The United States Government appears to have taken certain of these governments more fully into its counsel than others, but even the more favored were not always satisfied with the measure of consultation and agreement.

The Security Council, apart from being technically the recipient of the reports of the United Nations Command, played no role in the political direction of the armistice negotiations. The Assembly had a role of some importance but a role not clearly defined. It had, through its First Committee, explored the possibilities of a cease-fire in December 1950 and January 1951, and again following the adoption of the resolution of February 1, 1951. By so doing, the Assembly informed the world of the terms on which the great majority of its members were prepared to accept the termination of military measures, and it helped to establish and gain acceptance of the

[36] See above, Chap. XVIII, pp. 477-78.

pattern of an armistice agreement that would meet the minimum requirements imposed by the purposes and principles of the United Nations.

From the time the armistice negotiations began in July 1951 until October 1952, the Assembly played no role in the conduct of them. During this period, the Assembly, in fact, refrained from considering the Korean question, and the majority of the Members supported the position of the United States that the Assembly should not take any step that might interfere with the conduct of the negotiations. Thus at its 1951 session, over the protests of the Soviet bloc, the Assembly did not consider the Korean question and decided that a special session would be convoked if an armistice was concluded, or "when other developments in Korea" made consideration of the Korean question "desirable."[37] In October 1952, however, the Assembly considered at length, on the basis of a report by the United Nations Command, the deadlock that had developed in the negotiations over the exchange of war prisoners. Two positions were taken with respect to the role of the Assembly: (1) that the Assembly should limit itself to approving the position taken by the United Nations Command, and (2) that the Assembly should attempt to find a way of obtaining agreement between the opposing sides that would permit the negotiations to be successfully concluded. The second view prevailed. The resolution finally adopted by the Assembly was not accepted by the Peiping Government and the North Korean authorities, but it made a substantial contribution to the final success of the truce negotiations.[38]

The Assembly did not again take a direct part in the armistice negotiations, but, in April 1953, it adopted a resolution noting the progress of the negotiations and again decided that it would resume consideration of the Korean question either on the notification of an armistice or "when in the view of the majority of Members, other developments in Korea" required consideration of the question by the Assembly.[39] The final armistice, which became effective on July 27, 1953, a month in advance of its approval by the General Assembly on August 28, was signed by the Commander-in-Chief of the United Nations Command and the Commanders of the Korean People's Army and the Chinese People's Volunteers.[40] To assist in the execu-

[37] Res. 507 (VI), Feb. 5, 1952.
[38] Res. 610 (VII), Dec. 3, 1952.
[39] Res. 705 (VII), Apr. 18, 1953.
[40] Res. 711 (VII), Aug. 28, 1953.

tion of the provisions of the agreement dealing with the cessation of hostilities and the exchange of prisoners, the two "sides" established machinery of their own choice.

Despite the fact that the Republic of Korea had the largest stake in the result of the collective military operation and, next to the United States, had made the largest contribution of men and resources, no special provision was made for ascertaining and taking into account the views of the Government of the Republic of Korea in the course of the armistice negotiations. An officer of the Republic of suitable rank was included in the delegation representing the United Nations Command, but there is no evidence that the Government of the Republic had any real part in the preparation of the directives or the taking of decisions that the delegation was expected to carry out. Clearly, the withdrawal from the armistice negotiations of the officer of the Republic of Korea, the action of President Rhee in ordering the freeing of Korean prisoners of war, and the execution of this order by the Korean armed forces were in violation of the agreement conferring operational control of such armed forces on the United Nations Command. These acts served the useful purpose, however, of calling attention to the basic inadequacy of an arrangement that failed to give to the Republic any effective voice in matters that concerned it directly. Furthermore, they pointed up the necessity of developing effective procedures for harmonizing the purposes and actions of the victim state with those of the United Nations, and, more particularly, of those Members actively taking part in the collective military action.

Collective Measures and the Political Settlement

The great majority of the Members of the United Nations, including the United States, were of the opinion that the political objective of the United Nations in Korea—the establishment of an independent, unified, and democratic state—as well as the adjustment of other problems of special concern to the People's Republic of China, should be sought by methods of negotiation, not by military means. At the beginning of the armistice talks, the United States Government took the position that the withdrawal of armed forces was not a subject that could appropriately be discussed in the armistice negotiations. It did, however, agree that the commanders of "both sides" should make a recommendation to the governments concerned for the holding of "a political conference of a higher level of both sides . . . by representatives appointed respectively to settle through negotiation the questions of the withdrawal of all foreign forces from Korea, the peaceful settlement of the Korean question, etc."[41] But the United Nations Command by its interpretation of "et cetera" made it quite clear that it did not agree to the discussion of matters "outside of Korea."

With the conclusion of the armistice agreement and the actual cessation of hostilities, attention was focused on the methods by which United Nations political objectives in Korea were to be achieved. In the armistice negotations, the United Nations Command had stated that the recommendation of a political conference would be made to the United Nations as well as to the governments concerned. The General Assembly had, on April 18, 1953, adopted a resolution calling for the reconvening of the Assembly to resume consideration of the Korean question on notification by the United Nations Command to the Security Council of the signing of an armistice.[42] Accordingly, on July 26, 1953, the date that the United States Government notified the Secretary-General of the signing of the armistice agreement, the President of the Assembly informed Member governments that the seventh session would reconvene on August 17 to resume consideration of the Korean question. Thus there was agreement among Members that the Assembly should play a role in the efforts to achieve a political settlement in Korea, as, indeed, it had been doing since September 1947.

When the Assembly reconvened, a number of proposals reflecting different approaches to the problem of political negotiation were submitted to it. A joint draft resolution submitted by fifteen of the sixteen Members with armed forces in Korea provided for a recommendation by the Assembly that "the side contributing armed forces" under the Unified Command should have as participants in the political conference those among the Member states contributing armed forces that desired to be represented, along with the Republic of Korea.[43] Each participating government would act independently and with full freedom of action. The United States Government would be authorized, after consultation with the other participating countries on its side, to arrange with "the other side" for the holding of the conference. The Soviet Union submitted a

[41] Armistice Agreement, *United Nations Bulletin,* Vol. 15 (Aug. 1, 1953), p. 120.
[42] Res. 705 (VII).
[43] U.N. Doc. A/L. 151/Rev. 1 (Aug. 17, 1953). The Union of South Africa did not join.

draft resolution recommending as participants in the political conference a list of states including a number of so-called neutrals.[44] This proposal was later revised to include fifteen states of which nine had not directly participated in the fighting in Korea. Of these, five were Arab-Asian states and three were members of the Soviet bloc. The amended proposal of the Soviet Union provided that the decisions of the conference were to be considered as "adopted" if they had the unanimous approval of the parties to the armistice agreement. By a joint proposal submitted by Australia and New Zealand, the Assembly would recommend that the Soviet Union participate if the other side desired it.[45] A joint resolution proposed by Australia, Canada, New Zealand, and the United Kingdom called for a recommendation that India participate.[46]

These proposals reflected different views regarding the function and composition of the political conference and the relation of the Assembly and the Members of the United Nations to it. Each, of course, reflected the special interests of those Members that most actively sponsored it. The proposal by the fifteen powers, which was strongly supported by the United States as adequate in itself, reflected the view that the Assembly had little more than a mechanical function to perform, that the composition of the conference had largely been settled by the armistice agreement, and that the task of negotiating a political settlement was one that the Members that had done the actual fighting were entitled to perform and best equipped to do. According to this conception, the political conference was in effect a peace conference. It should be noted that the attitude of the United States was strongly influenced by the belief that the contribution of the United States to the military effort had earned for it a corresponding major role in the peace negotiations, and by the strong opposition of President Rhee of the Republic of Korea to the participation of India. The Soviet proposal undoubtedly sought to capitalize on the view held by many Members that the Assembly should play a role of some importance in the organization of the conference and that among the states in the best position to make a major contribution to the success of the conference were those situated on the Asian continent that had a direct interest in the problems of that area. The proposal for the inclusion

[44] U.N. Doc. A/C. 1/1. 48 (Aug. 25, 1953).

[45] Denmark and Norway later joined in sponsoring it. U.N. Doc. A/L. 152 (Aug. 16, 1953).

[46] U.N. Doc. A/L. 153 (Aug. 16, 1953).

of the Soviet Union reflected a realistic conviction that no satisfactory settlement of the Korean question could be reached without the consent of that nation. The proposal to include India reflected the view that the "neutralist" Asian countries, and especially India, had an important contribution to make to the solution of the Korean question and any related problems that might be considered.

The resolution the Assembly finally adopted followed closely the proposal of the fifteen nations with the addition of the recommendation that the Soviet Union participate "provided the other side desires it."[47] Although a majority in the First Committee favored recommending the participation of India, the United States firmly opposed it, and as the necessary two-thirds support was not available, the Indian delegation requested that the proposal not be submitted to a vote in the Assembly. The Assembly also voted that the Secretary-General should communicate the recommendation and the records of the proceedings to the governments of the People's Republic of China and the People's Democratic Republic of Korea. These governments later informed the Secretary-General that they could not fully agree with the recommendation of the Assembly and hoped that the Assembly, when it met for its eighth session, would enlarge the composition of the conference to include the Soviet Union, India, Indonesia, Pakistan, and Burma as "invited neutral nations."

The initial efforts of the United States to arrange a conference were fruitless. Finally, after the Assembly had refused to include the question of the composition of the conference in the agenda of its eighth session, the Chinese Communist and North Korean representatives agreed to meet with a representative of the United States at Panmunjom on October 26. They agreed that the place and time of the proposed conference must be settled, but they insisted that the question of the composition of the conference must be further considered. The discussions finally broke down when on December 12, the representative of the United States left the meeting because of statements made by the Chinese representatives, which he termed "calculatedly rude, arrogant and insulting." These discussions were never resumed.

Efforts of India to convene the Assembly to consider the new situation were unsuccessful. At a meeting of the Foreign Ministers of France, the Soviet Union, the United Kingdom, and the United

[47] Res. 711 (VII), Aug. 28, 1953.

States held in Berlin, from January 15 to February 18, 1954, it was agreed that "the establishment, by peaceful means, of a united and independent Korea would be an important factor in reducing international tension and in restoring peace in other parts of Asia." To this end, the foreign ministers proposed:

That a conference of representatives of the United States, France, the United Kingdom, the Union of Soviet Socialist Republics, the Chinese People's Republic, the Republic of Korea, the People's Democratic Republic of Korea, and the other countries the armed forces of which participated in the hostilities in Korea, and which desire to attend, shall meet in Geneva on April 26 for the purpose of reaching a peaceful settlement of the Korean question.[48]

However, the discussions at Geneva on the Korean question ended in complete deadlock.

The experience of the United Nations in Korea suggests that the achievement of a satisfactory adjustment of a situation that has been the occasion for the use of collective military measures is a task that must be conceived in larger terms than the making of a peace by those who have been engaged in war. The fact that a Member has made material sacrifices in a collective military operation may give that Member a claim to participate in the political conference to follow, but this is by no means the only test to be applied. It is necessary also to take into account other contributions that Members may have made to the collective action, special interests that certain Members may have for geographic, cultural, or economic reasons, and the special contributions that certain Members may be in a position to make to the success of the negotiation.

Even though the United Nations has been incapable of functioning as orginially intended in the taking of enforcement measures, and, as a consequence, it has become necessary to improvise a "voluntary" system that permits a great and undesirable variation in the degree of participation, the Organization still is capable of performing its function of peaceful settlement in accordance with provisions of the Charter. In the opinion of many, this is its major responsibility and opportunity for useful work in the maintenance or restoration of international peace and security.

[48] U.S. Department of State *Bulletin,* Vol. 30 (Mar. 1, 1954), pp. 317-18. The text of the four-power communiqué was communicated by the United States Government to the Secretary-General, in accordance with the recommendation of the Assembly that Member states participating in the proposed political conference keep the United Nations informed regarding developments.

PART FIVE

THE REGULATION OF ARMAMENTS

CHAPTER XX

Background of United Nations Efforts

ALTHOUGH the principal emphasis of the Charter regarding the use of armed force is on the development of conditions and agreed procedures for its elimination, except in the common interest, the Charter is also concerned with the nature and level of armaments that individual states maintain. The nature and level of national armaments, including trained personnel, matériel, and facilities for the use of armed force, are not regarded exclusively as matters of national concern. The Charter recognizes an international interest in them that justifies consideration by the appropriate organs of the United Nations of the scale of armaments maintained as well as the conditions of their use.

National Armaments as an International Problem

Nations have in the past maintained armed forces for three principal purposes: to preserve internal order, to provide for national defense against external dangers, and to support their interests and policies abroad. The nature and level of these armaments have been determined by a variety of factors, including the state of technological development, geographical location, the extent of national resources, and the relations among states. The maintenance of adequate forces and facilities for the defense of national interests and to preserve internal order has been viewed historically as one of the unquestioned prerogatives of the sovereign state. When states, defeated in war, have been forced to accept dictated terms of peace, including the unilateral limitation of their armaments, their efforts to be re-accepted as equal members of the family of nations have customarily been centered on the termination of special armament limitations.

But although the right to possess armaments and freely to determine in the light of national requirements the nature and level of such armaments has been recognized in the past as the mark of a sovereign state, there has also been growing recognition that other

517

states have an interest in the nature and level of these armaments, as well as the uses to which they are put. A particular level of national armaments may be justified in terms of the requirements of national self-defense, but the concept of self-defense is an extremely flexible one, and action that may be viewed by one state as necessary to its defense may appear highly threatening to a neighboring state. This is especially true if relations between the two states are strained as the result of conflicts of interests, of fears and suspicions inherited from the past, or of ideological incompatibilities.

Accordingly, along with efforts that have been made with increasing frequency and insistence to prevent, or at least to limit, war, there have been intensified efforts in recent times to achieve international agreement on the limitation and reduction of national armaments. These efforts have stemmed from a variety of motives. There is first of all the belief that tensions between states are due in large part to competition in armaments and that, consequently, these tensions can be alleviated and the dangers of war reduced by the agreed limitation and reduction of national armaments. Then there is the view that even if the inevitability of war and armament rivalries is accepted, there are certain weapons the use of which should be restricted or prohibited on humanitarian grounds or because of their excessive destructiveness in relation to military objectives. Efforts to outlaw the use of poisonous gas and to eliminate or to limit strictly the use of the submarine after the First World War were based largely on such considerations.

Another commonly held view is that as a result of the increasing cost of armaments, especially in the light of modern technological developments, armament rivalry results in an excessive diversion of national resources to nonproductive purposes. This consideration has received growing recognition as governments and peoples have come to recognize the need of the more careful and intelligent use of available resources in order to meet the minimum human needs of the increasing population of the world, most of which still lives at a marginal or submarginal level of subsistence. Closely related is the uncertainty that has existed in many minds regarding the value for war purposes of certain relatively costly weapons, accompanied by doubts whether one country alone can run the risks that would be involved in scrapping them unilaterally. Thus at the end of the First World War, there was a conviction in many quarters, official and unofficial, that air power had rendered the

battleship obsolete. This uncertainty regarding the future value of
the battleship was undoubtedly one reason for the willingness of
the United States Government in 1922 to agree to a drastic limitation of battleship tonnage.

Another consideration encouraging efforts to limit and reduce
armaments by international agreement has been the desire of certain states to improve or at least to stabilize their security positions
by obtaining the agreement of other states to armament levels that
are more favorable than are likely to be achieved by free competition. Furthermore, even if a state fails in this endeavor, it is likely
to gain international prestige, especially with small countries. In
addition, the government in power may strengthen its position with
its people by having supported a generally popular cause. Finally,
most serious students of international affairs believe that international arrangements and procedures for the maintenance of international peace and security require for their maximum effectiveness not only that states agree to forego the use of force in their
international relations but also that they limit the nature and size
of their armed forces and armaments as well.

During the nineteenth century and down to the time of the
First World War, numerous efforts were made to achieve the limitation of national armed forces and armaments by international
agreement.[1] The Rush-Bagot agreement between the United States
and Great Britain in 1817 effectively limited naval armaments on
the Great Lakes. Agreements were also on occasion concluded for
the prohibition of the use of certain weapons. The Hague Declaration of 1899, for example, prohibited the "use of projectiles the sole
object of which is the diffusion of asphyxiating or deleterious
gases."[2] But major efforts to achieve the limitation of armaments,
such as the British initiative to get an Anglo-German agreement
on the limitation of naval armaments and the attempts at the
Hague Conferences of 1899 and 1907, ended in failure. Nevertheless,
there remained a strong conviction, not only among professional
peace advocates but on the part of responsible statesmen as well,
that rivalry in armaments among states was an important cause
of tension and ultimate armed conflict, and that every effort should
be made to end such rivalries by the agreed limitation and reduction of armaments.

[1] Merze Tate, *The Disarmament Illusion* (1942).
[2] A. P. Higgins, *The Hague Peace Conferences* (1909), p. 491.

Efforts During the Interwar Period[3]

With the rise of interest during the First World War in the establishment of a world peace organization, the movement for the international limitation of armaments gained further impetus. President Wilson included as the fourth of his Fourteen Points a provision for the reduction of national armaments to the lowest point consistent with the requirements of domestic safety. By the terms of the Hurst-Miller draft, which was submitted to the League of Nations Commission in Paris as the agreed Anglo-American proposal for "a general association of nations," members were to reduce their national armaments to the lowest point consistent with "domestic safety" and the enforcement by common action of international obligations. In the decisions of the commission, however, a concession was made to the French view that a necessary precondition of the limitation and reduction of national armaments was the effective organization of collective security and that the Covenant of the League of Nations as proposed did not adequately provide for such security. As the United States and Great Britain were not willing to accept the French proposal of an international general staff with an international force or designated national contingents under its command, they were forced to accept certain modifications of their agreed draft. Of special significance was the substitution of "national safety" for "domestic safety" as a criterion of reduction.

By Article 8 of the Covenant of the League, as finally adopted, the Members of the League recognized "that the maintenance of peace requires the reduction of national armaments to the lowest point consistent with national safety and the enforcement by common action of international obligations." Members furthermore undertook "to interchange full and frank information as to the scale of their armaments, their military, naval, and air programmes and the condition of such of their industries as are adaptable to warlike purposes." "In order to render possible the initiation of a general limitation of the armaments of all nations," the Treaty of Versailles imposed drastic limitations on the armaments of defeated Germany.[4] The other peace treaties contained comparable limitations on the armaments of Austria, Hungary, and Bulgaria.

[3] For stimulating and informative discussion, see Salvador de Madariaga, *Disarmament* (1929).
[4] Introduction to Pt. V of the Treaty of Versailles.

It is difficult to say what the generally accepted theory of the Covenant of the League was with respect to the place of disarmament[5] in the League system of war prevention, because the Covenant was to a considerable extent a compromise of opposing views, and agreement on a common text did not mean that basic differences of approach were necessarily resolved. Its phraseology often lent itself to different interpretations.

It soon became apparent as discussions in the League of Nations got under way that there was no basic agreement on the approach to be made to the problem of disarmament. Generally speaking, there were two major approaches to the problem, which for purposes of analysis can be referred to as the "direct" and the "indirect."[6] These corresponded roughly to the positions taken by the United States and Great Britain, on the one hand, and France, on the other, in the course of the discussions on the drafting of the Covenant.

Those who took the direct approach believed in general that rivalry in armaments was a direct cause of war, and that, consequently, any agreement reached that would end or at least limit this rivalry would contribute to more friendly relations among nations and to improving the prospects of peace. Those who thought such a direct approach possible naturally tended to emphasize the technical aspects of the problem, and were inclined to the view that, if agreement could be reached at the technical level on such questions as categories of armaments to be limited, methods of limitation, and ratios, national armaments could with good will be reduced with beneficial results, above all from the point of view of future international peace and security.

On the other hand, those who favored the indirect approach were inclined to the view that inasmuch as armaments were needed because of feelings of insecurity, there was not much point in attempting to limit and reduce armaments by international agreement until effective measures were taken to provide security by other means, for each state would insist on terms that would give it an advantage over any state or states with which its relations were such as to admit the possibility of war. Those who thought in such "realist" terms considered the problem of disarmament essentially a political one, which could be solved only by such an improvement in the

[5] The word "disarmament" was commonly used in discussions in the League to mean the agreed limitation and reduction of national armaments.
[6] See Salvador de Madariaga, *op. cit.*, especially pp. 97-98.

political relations between states as would make it possible for states to view their future security with confidence. This improvement might be achieved as a result of the peaceful settlement of specific differences, by the acceptance of procedures that would give assurance that future differences would be settled by such means, or by firm and dependable agreements that would ensure that in case of some threat to the security of the nation it would be able to rely with confidence on the assistance of other states.

In the discussions of the League of Nations, the leading proponents of the direct approach were Great Britain and the Dominions and the Scandinavian countries. France, Belgium, and the states of Eastern Europe that had come into existence or acquired additional territory as a result of the war—in general those members of the League that had most to fear from Soviet Russia and the irredentist activities on the part of the defeated central powers —were the ones who stressed most vigorously the indirect approach. It soon became clear that without compromise, there was no possibility of making any progress in carrying out the provisions of the Covenant. Subsequent events were to show that even with considerable willingness to compromise, the difficulties in the way of implementing the provisions of the Covenant regarding disarmament and the promises implicit in the peace treaties were insurmountable.

The first important step toward compromising opposing attitudes in the League was taken in 1922 when the British Government agreed to the general proposition, set forth in "Resolution XIV" of the Assembly of the League, that any substantial reduction in armaments must be preceded by satisfactory guarantees of national security.[7] In 1923 a second step was taken when the Conservative Government of Great Britain accepted the Draft Treaty of Mutual Assistance. That treaty went far to meet French insistence on specific assurances of collective assistance to the victim of aggression.[8] Although the first Labor Government under Ramsay MacDonald reversed this decision and refused to ratify the treaty, it found in the formula "arbitration, security, disarmament" a basis for cooperating with the new Herriot Government in France in drafting

[7] League of Nations, *Records of the Third Assembly*, Plenary Meetings, Vol. 1, p. 291.
[8] League of Nations, *Records of the Fourth Assembly*, Minutes of the Third Committee, pp. 203-06.

the famous Geneva Protocol of 1924.[9] By the terms of the Protocol, the Members of the League of Nations undertook to close the so-called "gaps" of the Covenant by prohibiting war except in self-defense, by further extending the obligations and procedures of peaceful settlement, and by strengthening the system of sanctions. Once these provisions were in effect, a general disarmament conference was to be held. When the Conservatives came back into power in Great Britain in late 1924 they refused to ratify the Protocol, but were willing to apply its basic principles on a more restricted territorial basis by agreeing to British participation in the Locarno Treaty of Mutual Guarantee of 1925. This was supplemented by a network of bilateral agreements, including agreements between Germany and its neighbors, intended to provide additional assurance of mutual assistance and the use of peaceful methods in the settlement of disputes.

Thus provided with additional guarantees of its security and that of its allies, France was finally willing to participate in preparatory work for the holding of a general disarmament conference. The experience of the Preparatory Commission, established by decision of the Council of the League in December 1925, as well as that of the General Disarmament Conference, which convened in February 1932, were not encouraging for those who regarded disarmament as a promising approach to the problem of international peace and security. Agreement was reached on some of the technical questions involved in the drafting of an international agreement for the limitation of armaments, but the rapid worsening of the world economic and political situation from 1931 on reduced the value of mutual security agreements. It increased international insecurity to the point where governments were inclined to question the adequacy of existing armaments rather than to consider their reduction to lower levels. The manifestation of increasingly aggressive attitudes by Japan, Germany, and Italy was a specific cause of unwillingness on the part of those states desirous of maintaining the *status quo* against change by force to consent to any substantial reduction or even limitation of their national armaments.

Although efforts of the League of Nations to achieve the general limitation and reduction of national armaments failed, limited success did attend efforts that were initiated by the United States

[9] League of Nations, *Records of the Fifth Assembly,* Text of the Debates, pp. 479-502.

and carried on outside the framework of the League to achieve limitation of armaments on a more restricted basis. At Washington in 1922 and at London in 1930, agreements were concluded that provided for the limitation and reduction of the naval armaments of the principal naval powers. These agreements were not, however, an unqualified victory for the "direct" method, then favored by the United States, because a prerequisite to their acceptance was the conclusion of certain agreements setting forth common policies and purposes in China and in the Pacific area. It is quite clear that had it not been for the nine-power treaty on China and the treaty providing for mutual respect by the signatories for certain insular possessions in the Western Pacific area, the United States, the United Kingdom, and Japan would not have been able to agree on the limitation and reduction of their naval armaments. The Washington and London naval agreements were viewed at the time with considerable favor as examples of the successful limitation and reduction of armaments, but there was an unfavorable reaction later in the United States when it came to be believed by many that it was in the shelter of these agreements that Japan was able to embark on its program of expansion and military aggression in Eastern Asia and the Pacific.

The United Nations Approach

The experience of the Second World War and the years immediately preceding somewhat dampened enthusiasm for disarmament as an approach to international peace and security. As a result, there was greater appreciation of the role of armed force in the organization of international peace and security, and recognition of the fact that so long as the possibility existed that some ambitious government might resort to the use of armed force to achieve its objectives, nations desiring peace had to be adequately prepared, whether acting alone or in co-operation with others, to take appropriate measures to restrain and suppress aggression. It was believed by many that such action was the responsibility of those nations that had taken the leading part in the defeat of the Axis powers in the Second World War, and which, if they had co-operated with equal vigor in the years preceding the war, would probably have been able to prevent it. Moved by such an interpretation of past experience, the architects of the Charter system gave priority to the effective organization of power in the interest of international peace and security.

Unlike the Covenant of the League of Nations, the Charter of the United Nations does not explicitly lay stress on the limitation and reduction of armaments by international agreement as an independent and immediate approach to the goal of international peace and security, although it recognizes the importance of the international regulation of armaments as an element in an effective international system for the maintenance of peace and security. Article 1 of the Charter specifies collective measures and peaceful settlement as means for achieving the maintenance of international peace and security, but it contains no mention of the international regulation of armaments. The General Assembly under Article 11 is empowered to consider "the general principles of co-operation in the maintenance of international peace and security, including the principles governing disarmament and the regulation of armaments." Under Article 26, the Security Council is directed: "In order to promote the establishment and maintenance of international peace and security with the least diversion for armaments of the world's human and economic resources," to formulate "plans . . . for the establishment of a system for the regulation of armaments."

Nowhere in the Charter is there any explicit affirmation of the principle set forth in Article 8 of the Covenant of the League "that the maintenance of peace requires the reduction of national armaments." Article 2(4) does, however, lay down the principle that Members shall refrain in their international relations from the threat or use of force in any manner inconsistent with the purposes of the United Nations. From this it might be inferred that Members also accept the principle of the limitation and reduction of their armaments, inasmuch as the maintenance of armaments of an especially menacing nature or size by one Member might be regarded by other Members as a threat of force.

The use of the term "regulation of armaments" in the Charter and other detailed provisions, together with views expressed at the time the Charter was being drafted and put into effect, tend to support the conclusion that the architects of the United Nations system were as much concerned with establishing a floor for national armaments as with fixing a ceiling. To be sure, they wished to avoid the unnecessary diversion of resources to armaments, but in establishing the level at which armaments should be maintained, they were especially concerned to have enough armaments available to keep the peace. In contrast to the Covenant of the League of Nations, the approach of the Charter to the armament problem might be phrased in these words: The Members of the United Nations recognize that national armaments should be brought under a system of international regulation at a level that ensures national safety and permits effective collective measures to prevent and suppress threats to and breaches of the peace, and at the same time prevents the unnecessary diversion to unproductive purposes of the human and economic resources of the world.

It is significant to note that the Charter does not require Members to make public information regarding the nature and size of their armaments. This, too, reflects a different approach to the question of armaments from that found in the Covenant of the League. Presumably it was believed, and the experience of the interwar period gave support to this view, that if the major powers were not inclined to co-operate for the maintenance of peace, such information as they might give would be of limited value. If they were prepared to co-operate in the manner described in the Charter, such information would become available to the extent necessary without any requirement in the Charter to that effect.

Under the Charter, the Security Council is responsible, with the assistance of the Military Staff Committee, for preparing plans "for the establishment of a system for the regulation of armaments." These plans are to be submitted to Members for their consideration. The Council is also made responsible for initiating negotiations with a view to the conclusion of agreements by which Members make available "armed forces, assistance, and facilities, including rights of passage, necessary for the purpose of maintaining international peace and security." Thus the primary responsibility is placed on the Council for initiating detailed arrangements for the limitation of national armaments, including the establishment of ceilings and prohibitions, and for providing assurance that necessary armaments will be available for United Nations purposes. The Military Staff Committee, consisting of the Chiefs of Staff of the permanent members of the Council or their representatives, advises the Council on all questions relating to the military requirements of the Council for the maintenance of international peace and security, "the regulation of armaments, and possible disarmament."[10]

Although the Security Council is made responsible for preparing a detailed system of armament regulation for approval by Mem-

[10] Art. 47(1).

bers, the General Assembly may consider the general principles governing "disarmament and the regulation of armaments," and may make recommendations with regard to such principles "to the Members or to the Security Council or to both."[11] Thus the role of the Assembly in dealing with problems in this area is much the same as was that of the Assembly of the League.

Advent of the Atomic Bomb

The Charter was drafted at a time when only a few people were aware of the work that was being done with a view to the development of atomic weapons, and no one was as yet sure that such weapons could be developed. It is possible that if knowledge of the destructive force of atomic weapons had been available at that time, certain of the provisions of the Charter would have been differently written, especially those relating to the regulation of armaments. This, however, is entirely speculative, and there is not much evidence to support the view that if the potentialities of atomic weapons had been fully known, a stronger organization would have been created, or that a fundamentally different approach to the problem of armaments regulation would have been taken.

The explosion of the two atomic bombs in Japan in early August 1945 not only was an important factor in the Japanese surrender but also produced widespread alarm over the possible consequences of atomic warfare in the future. In announcing on August 6 the explosion of an atomic bomb at Hiroshima, President Truman reminded the American public of the need for examining all "possible methods of protecting us and the rest of the world from the danger of sudden destruction."[12] The peril of the world was driven home by the opening statement of the President that this bomb "had more power than 20,000 tons of TNT." It was understandable that peoples and their representatives in many countries of the world should have become deeply concerned about the future possibility of survival and that tremendous pressures were generated to do something to avert complete destruction before it was too late. This sense of alarm and urgency was especially strong in the United States where it was recognized that the possession of the

[11] Art. 11(1).
[12] "Statement by the President," Press release, Aug. 6, 1945.

bomb provided no adequate guarantee of future security. As scientists were agreed that sooner or later the bomb would be developed by other countries, especially the Soviet Union, no decision of the United States that the bomb would not be used was sufficient to provide protection against future atomic warfare. Some form of international control was required.

The bomb made its appearance on the international scene at a time when the high hopes that had been raised of great power cooperation after the war were already being seriously dampened.[13] The unyielding attitude of the Soviet leaders in their relations with the West was undoubtedly encouraged by the drastic reduction of United States forces in Europe after the German surrender and the consequent serious weakening of the military strength of the Western powers. Soviet military strength, on the contrary, was maintained at a near-war level and Soviet armed forces remained in occupation of territories that they and other Allied forces had wrested from German military control. Under such circumstances, the Soviet leaders may well have believed that there was no need to make concessions and that with insistence and patience their immediate political objectives would be achieved.

This unyielding Soviet attitude and mounting evidence of Soviet bad faith and expansionist purposes put the United States and its friends in a difficult position in so far as the atomic bomb was concerned. Clearly there was a sincere desire on the part of the United States Government for some international arrangement that would give assurance that the atomic bomb would not be used in the future for military purposes. On the other hand, possession of the bomb was recognized as a powerful weapon in the hands of the United States, capable of being used to restore the balance of power between the Soviet Union and the Western democracies, and thus as a great deterrent to Soviet aggression. Yet there was reason to believe that the bomb was a wasting asset. Once the Soviet Union was able to develop a bomb of its own, the advantage of the West would be greatly reduced, if not completely lost. Then peoples on both sides of the Iron Curtain would be exposed to the destructive power of the atom.

Uncertainty regarding how long it would be before the Soviet Union acquired the bomb and the United States lost its monopoly position, and the unimaginable consequences of atomic warfare, led those responsible for determining the course of United States

[13] See above, Chap. II.

policy to take the view that time was of the essence. The threat of the atomic bomb was viewed as being so immediate and so overwhelming as to justify, if not require, consideration of the problem apart from that of the regulation of armaments in general. Thus it happened that under the impact of the explosion of the atomic bomb, the balanced approach to the regulation of armaments envisaged by the Charter was deferred, and priority was given to attempting to work out some acceptable system of international control of atomic energy.

A United Nations Approach to Control of Atomic Energy

It was recognized from the beginning by those primarily responsible for making United States policy that any effective international regulation of atomic weapons was dependent on agreement with the Soviet Union. There appear, however, to have been wide differences of opinion as to the best way to proceed. Henry L. Stimson, who as Secretary of War had had a major responsibility for the development of the atomic energy program, informed the President in September 1945 that the only promising course was, with British support, to approach the Soviet Union directly and without delay. He thought action by an international organization including many small states would not be taken seriously, and that an attempt to use the atomic bomb for bargaining purposes to obtain political advantages would arouse the suspicion and distrust of the Soviet leaders and result in an armament race of "a rather desperate character." He suggested to the President that such a direct approach to the Soviet Union:

. . . might more specifically lead to the proposal that we would stop work on the further improvement in, or manufacture of, the bomb as a military weapon, provided the Russians and the British would agree to do likewise. It might also provide that we would be willing to impound what bombs we now have in the United States provided the Russians and the British would agree with us that in no event will they or we use a bomb as an instrument of war unless all three Governments agree to that use. We might also consider including in the arrangement a covenant with the U.K. and the Soviets providing for the exchange of benefits of future developments whereby atomic energy may be applied on a mutually satisfactory basis for commercial and humanitarian purposes.[14]

[14] Henry L. Stimson and McGeorge Bundy, *On Active Service in Peace and War* (1947), p. 645.

In the course of a Cabinet meeting on September 11, 1945, other views were expressed regarding the best course to follow. Secretary of Commerce Wallace appears to have favored giving atomic information to the Russians in the belief that that was the only way to win their confidence and co-operation. Others would give nothing until the men in the Kremlin "demonstrated a willingness to work with us." Secretary of the Navy Forrestal favored United States trusteeship over the bomb on behalf of the United Nations, and an agreement limiting use of it to missions designated by the United Nations. It appears that the sense of the meeting was that the machinery of the United Nations should be employed in dealing with the problem, that information should be given to the Soviet Union only on a *quid pro quo* basis, and that the Soviet Union should be asked to accept adequate regulatory measures.[15]

By the end of October, the general lines of United States policy appear to have been determined. In his Navy Day address of October 27, President Truman expressed the view that "we must find the answer to the problems created by the release of atomic energy—as we must find the answers to the many other problems of peace—in partnership with all the peoples of the United Nations." He repeated the opinion expressed in his message to Congress in early October that consideration of the problem with other countries could not wait until the formal organization of the United Nations and stated that discussions "with Great Britain and Canada and later with other nations . . . looking toward a free exchange of fundamental scientific information" would begin in the near future.[16]

Discussions among the heads of the governments of the United States, the United Kingdom, and Canada resulted in the Agreed Declaration of November 15, 1945, that was explicit on the procedure to be followed. By this declaration, the three heads of government agreed:

In order to attain the most effective means of entirely eliminating the use of atomic energy for destructive purposes and promoting its widest use for industrial and humanitarian purposes, we are of the opinion that at the earliest practicable date a Commission should be set up under the United Nations Organization to prepare recommendations for submission to the Organization.

They also agreed that the commission should make specific proposals:

---

[15] Walter Millis (ed.), *The Forrestal Diaries* (1951), pp. 95-96.

[16] U.S. Department of State, *International Control of Atomic Energy: Growth of a Policy*, Publication 2702 (1946), p. 117.

(a) For extending between all nations the exchange of basic scientific information for peaceful ends,

(b) For control of atomic energy to the extent necessary to ensure its use only for peaceful purposes,

(c) For the elimination from national armaments of atomic weapons and of all other major weapons adaptable to mass destruction,

(d) For effective safeguards by way of inspection and other means to protect complying states against the hazards of violations and evasions.

The work of the commission was to proceed by separate stages "the successful completion of each one of which will develop the necessary confidence of the world before the next stage is undertaken."[17]

By this declaration, the three governments committed themselves to approach the problem of the control of atomic energy through the United Nations, but through a special organ not explicitly provided for in the Charter. Furthermore, by initiating the discussions leading to this agreement, the United States undertook to establish a common front with the United Kingdom and Canada before approaching the Soviet Union, which approach would be solely for the purpose of reaching agreement on general principles and procedure. Finally, from the terms of the agreement, as well as from previous discussions and statements of policy by officials of the governments concerned, it was clear that the approach to the Soviet Union was to be a cautious one. The declaration clearly expressed the basic assumption of the parties that Soviet good faith was not something to be taken for granted, but that effective safeguards were necessary.

Agreement was easily reached at the Moscow meeting of the Council of Foreign Ministers in December 1945 on the terms of a proposal to be presented to the General Assembly in London. This was a matter of some surprise as the United States Government at least had expected strong Soviet opposition to certain features of the Anglo-American-Canadian proposal. A Soviet proposal to place the Atomic Energy Commission under the Security Council was turned down, but a modified proposal, that made explicit the authority of the Council to issue directives to the commission in matters affecting security was accepted. Soviet Foreign Minister Molotov raised strong objection, as had been expected, to the provision that the work of the commission proceed by separate stages, arguing that this was a matter for the commission to decide. He withdrew his objection when the other foreign ministers in-

[17] *Ibid.*, pp. 118-20.

sisted on its retention.[18] The ease with which agreement was reached was not, however, a harbinger of future success, because it was quite possible, as later events seemed to confirm, that the Soviet Union did not take the constructive possibilities of the proposal too seriously.

When the General Assembly met in early January 1946, the permanent members of the Security Council and Canada joined in submitting the proposal on which agreement had been reached at Moscow. After limited debate, in the course of which the only serious objection raised was to the undue subordination of the commission to the Council, the Assembly unanimously approved the proposal on January 24, 1946.[19] The resolution provided for the establishment by the Assembly of a commission to deal with the problems raised by the discovery of atomic energy and other related matters. The commission was instructed to submit its reports and recommendations to the Council and be accountable to the Council for its work "in matters affecting security." The Council should, in appropriate cases, transmit these reports to the Assembly and Members of the United Nations. The commission was to be composed of one representative of each member of the Council and Canada. Its rules of procedure were to be subject to approval by the Council. Its terms of reference were defined in the language of the Agreed Declaration of November 1945. The commission was not to infringe on the responsibilities of any organ of the United Nations, but was to present recommendations for the consideration of these organs in the performance of their tasks under the United Nations Charter.

By their approval of this resolution, the Members of the United Nations, and more particularly the United States, the United Kingdom, and the Soviet Union, committed themselves to seek the international control of atomic energy within the framework of the United Nations. Although the establishment of the Atomic Energy Commission by action of the General Assembly might be viewed as an infringement on the special responsibilities of the Security Council and the Military Staff Committee under Article 26, the fact that this commission was to be concerned with all aspects of the development and use of atomic energy and their international control provided a justification for the initiative by the Assembly. It was obvious, however, that control of the bomb was the central

[18] James F. Byrnes, *Speaking Frankly,* (1947), pp. 267-68.
[19] Res. 1 (I), Jan. 24, 1946.

problem and that no progress could be made in dealing with this except by agreement of the United States and the Soviet Union.

The Atomic Energy Commission was in effect asked to prepare recommendations for the international control of atomic energy that would be acceptable to the United States and the Soviet Union at a time when their relations in different parts of the world were becoming increasingly strained, when mutual suspicion and distrust were mounting in the United States and the Soviet Union, and when the atomic bomb had already come to be accepted by many in the West as the great "equalizer," which, in effect, meant, and was interpreted by the Kremlin to mean, that it was regarded as the means by which Soviet power could be effectively countered. Thus the United Nations was invited to begin its consideration of the problem of armament regulation by exploring ways and means of bringing under effective international control a weapon that was generally recognized as playing a decisive role in the relations of the two most powerful nations in the world at a time when these relations were rapidly deteriorating. Certainly the United Nations was not being eased into the performance of its tasks in the field of armament regulation and the maintenance of international peace and security generally. Yet it is difficult to see how consideration of the problem could have been long delayed. If the initiative had not been taken by the Western powers, it would undoubtedly have been seized by the Soviet Union to advance its own particular purposes. Nor is it at all likely that, if the international control of atomic energy had been proposed as part of a comprehensive plan for the regulation of armaments, the result would have been significantly different.

CHAPTER XXI

Efforts of the United Nations
to Regulate Armaments

T HE United Nations began its efforts to regulate national armaments by seeking an acceptable plan for the international control of atomic energy. It was to discover, however, that this problem, which was mainly an armaments problem, could not be separated from the larger question of the limitation of armaments generally. Furthermore, it was to find, as had the League of Nations before it, that the limitation of armaments could not be realistically considered apart from other pressing problems of world politics, especially the relations of the great powers and the effectiveness of international machinery for ensuring peace and security.

Proposals for Controlling Atomic Energy

The Atomic Energy Commission, established by the resolution of the General Assembly on January 24, 1946, held its first meeting on the following June 14. In view of the unique position of the United States at the time as the only nation that possessed atomic bombs and the one that initiated the attempt to find a solution by the United Nations to the problem, it was natural that other members of the commission should look to the United States to take the lead in submitting proposals for the international control of atomic energy. The United States Government had recognized its special responsibility and had carefully prepared its position. Secretary of State James F. Byrnes had appointed a committee under the chairmanship of Assistant Secretary of State Dean Acheson which, with the aid of a Board of Consultants under David Lilienthal, then Chairman of the Tennessee Valley Authority, had prepared a report on the international control of atomic energy.[1] This report set forth basic findings and conclusions that were accepted by the Government as the basis of the United States position.

[1] U.S. Department of State, *A Report on the International Control of Atomic Energy*, Publication 2498 (1946).

At the first meeting of the commission, Bernard Baruch, the representative of the United States, presented the proposals of his Government.[2] Except for the proposal regarding the use of the veto, these were all set forth with supporting arguments in the so-called Acheson-Lilienthal Report, which had clearly defined the basic philosophy of the United States position in these words:

We have concluded unanimously that there is no prospect of security against atomic warfare in a system of international agreements to outlaw such weapons controlled *only* by a system which relies on inspection and similar police-like methods. The reasons supporting this conclusion are *not merely technical,* but primarily the inseparable political, social, and organizational problems involved in enforcing agreements between nations each free to develop atomic energy but only pledged not to use it for bombs. National rivalries in the development of atomic energy readily convertible to destructive purposes are the heart of the difficulty. So long as intrinsically dangerous activities may be carried on by nations, rivalries are inevitable and fears are engendered that place so great a pressure upon a system of international enforcement by police methods that no degree of ingenuity or technical competence could possibly hope to cope with them. We emphasize this fact of national rivalry in respect to intrinsically dangerous aspects of atomic energy because it was this fatal defect in the commonly advanced proposals for outlawry of atomic weapons coupled with a system of inspection that furnished an important clue to us in the development of the plan that we recommend later in this report.

We are convinced that if the production of fissionable materials by national governments (or by private organizations under their control) is permitted, systems of inspection cannot by themselves be made "effective safeguards . . . to protect complying states against the hazards of violations and evasions."[3]

The United States proposals provided for the establishment of an International Atomic Development Authority. The proposed authority would be entrusted with: (1) managerial control or ownership of all atomic energy activities "potentially dangerous to world security"; (2) the power to control, inspect, and license all other atomic activities; (3) the duty of fostering the beneficial use of atomic energy; and (4) research and development responsibilities of an affirmative character. The United States also proposed that, once an adequate system of control, including the renunciation of the atomic bomb as a weapon, had been agreed upon and put into

[2] U.N. Atomic Energy Commission, *Official Records,* No. 1, First Meeting (June 14, 1946), pp. 4-14.

[3] U.S. Department of State, *A Report on the International Control of Atomic Energy,* pp. 4-5.

effective operation, and suitable punishments for violation of the rules of control had been established, (1) the manufacture of atomic bombs should stop; (2) existing bombs should be disposed of; and (3) the proposed authority should be given possession of full information on the know-how for the production of atomic energy. It was an essential part of the plan, however, that this system of control should come into effect by successive stages, with the United States making information available and yielding control of activities to the extent necessary to the completion of each stage. The charter of the International Atomic Development Authority would determine the stages or at least establish the procedure by which they could be determined.

Furthermore, the United States proposals undertook to define what constituted violations of the control system. Penalties of a serious nature were to be fixed for:

. . . (1) illegal possession or use of an atomic bomb; (2) illegal possession or separation of atomic material suitable for use in an atomic bomb; (3) seizure of any plant or other property belonging to or licensed by the Authority; (4) willful interference with the activities of the Authority; (5) creation or operation of dangerous projects in a manner contrary to, or in the absence of, a license granted by the international control body.[4]

The United States insisted that there should be "no veto to protect those who violate their solemn agreements not to develop or use atomic energy for destructive purposes."[5]

The United States proposals and memoranda subsequently submitted made it clear that an important development and adaptation of the peace and security system of the United Nations was being suggested.[6] This was viewed as necessary because the question of the control and development of atomic energy was not considered in framing the Charter of the United Nations. None of the existing organs of the United Nations had the power that it was proposed to give to the International Atomic Development Authority. Consequently, under the Charter, these organs could neither exercise such power nor delegate it to subsidiary organs. Therefore, it was

[4] U.S. Department of State, *International Control of Atomic Energy: Growth of a Policy,* Publication 2702 (Aug. 6, 1945-Oct. 15, 1946), p. 53.

[5] *Ibid.*

[6] There were three memoranda submitted to Sub-Committee No. 1 of the Atomic Energy Commission that contained significant elaborations of the United States proposals. For texts, see, U.N. Atomic Energy Commission, First Year, *Official Records,* Special Supplement, *Report to the Security Council,* (1946), pp. 92-102, 106-11.

necessary to establish a new organ, the composition, functions, powers, and procedures of which would be determined by the basic atomic control agreement, and the relations of this new organ to other organs of the United Nations would be determined in like manner. As it was assumed that the authority would be "essentially non-political," would have personnel of "high caliber," and would need "wide discretion" to achieve its purposes, it was proposed that "great weight and a considerable degree of finality should be given to its determinations, orders and practices" and that these should be accepted by organs of the United Nations "unless clearly erroneous or beyond the scope of the authority's powers."[7]

The major organizational problem raised by the United States proposals and supporting memoranda was that of the relation of the proposed authority to the Security Council. The United States recognized in principle the primary responsibility of the Security Council for dealing with threats to the peace, breaches of the peace, and acts of aggression, including serious violations of the proposed system of atomic energy control. Nevertheless, it was insistent that the veto should not be used to prevent sanctions from being applied in case of such violation. To this end, it proposed the "voluntary relinquishment of the 'veto' on questions relating to a specific weapon previously outlawed by unanimous agreement because of its uniquely destructive character."[8] This, the United States contended, involved no "compromise of the principle of unanimity of action as applied to general problems or to particular situations not foreseeable and therefore not susceptible of advance unanimous agreement." The United States also took the position that inasmuch as an armed attack under Article 51 had assumed a different character as the result of the discovery of atomic weapons, it "would therefore seem to be both important and appropriate under present conditions that the treaty define 'armed attack' in a manner appropriate to atomic weapons and include in the definition not simply the actual dropping of an atomic bomb, but also certain steps in themselves preliminary to such action."[9] The effect of such a redefinition of "armed attack" would, of course, be to restrict still further the scope of the functions of the Security Council in

[7] *Ibid.*, pp. 106-07.
[8] *Ibid.*, p. 109.
[9] *Ibid.*, p. 110.

the discharge of its responsibilities under the Charter and under the voting procedure there prescribed.

On June 19, 1946, the Soviet representative presented the proposals of his Government.[10] These proposals did not appear to have been prepared with as much care or on the basis of as much scientific data as had the proposals of the United States. They were of a much simpler and less drastic nature. Citing as precedents past agreements for outlawing asphyxiating, poisonous, and other deleterious gases, and means of bacteriological warfare, the Soviet representative proposed a convention prohibiting the production and employment of weapons based on the use of atomic energy. Parties to this agreement would undertake "not to use atomic weapons in any circumstances whatsoever," "to prohibit the production and storing of weapons based on the use of atomic energy," and "to destroy, within a period of three months from the day of the entry into force of the present convention, all stocks of atomic energy weapons whether in a finished or an unfinished condition." This convention would enter into force following approval by the Security Council and ratification by half of the signatory states, including all the permanent members of the Council. The parties would within a period of six months from the entry into force of the convention pass legislation providing severe penalties "for violators of the statutes" of the proposed convention.

The Soviet representative made certain additional proposals for the organization of the work, which had significance for the light they threw on the Soviet approach to the problem of atomic energy control. He proposed the establishment of two committees: one to prepare recommendations concerning practical measures for organizing the exchange of scientific information, and the other to elaborate recommendations concerning the drafting of a convention for outlawing weapons based on atomic energy, "concerning the quest for and establishment of measures to prohibit" the production and use of atomic weapons, "concerning the measures, systems and organization of control over the use of atomic energy and over the observance of the terms of the above-mentioned international convention for the outlawing of atomic weapons," and "concerning the elaboration of a system of sanctions to be applied against the unlawful use of atomic energy."[11]

[10] U.N. Atomic Energy Commission, *Official Records*, No. 2, Second Meeting (June 19, 1946), pp. 23-30.

[11] *Ibid.*, p. 29.

It was fairly clear from the Soviet presentation that there would be great difficulty in harmonizing the two sets of proposals, because they reflected fundamentally divergent purposes and interests. The purpose of the United States proposals clearly was to achieve an effective system of international control of atomic energy that would give maximum assurance that atomic energy would not be produced and used except for peaceful purposes, but which would permit the United States, pending the establishment of such a system and proof of its effectiveness, to provide for its own security by continuing to manufacture atomic weapons, to have them in its possession, and to use them if necessary. The Soviet leaders, on the other hand, in seeking to achieve the immediate outlawry of the production, possession, and use of atomic weapons, apparently were influenced by the desire to improve the relative power position of the Soviet Union by destroying the great "equalizer" in the hands of the United States. The Soviet leaders may also have seen the possibilities of using their proposal for propaganda purposes and of continuing the discussion while Soviet scientists and engineers were busily engaged in developing and perfecting their own atomic bomb.

In the course of the discussions of the commission and its committees, it soon became clear that the United States proposals were acceptable, at least in their broad outlines and as a basis for discussion, to all the members of the commission except the Soviet Union and Poland. There were three principal points at which the Soviet position was opposed to that of the United States and the majority of the commission. First, the Soviet Union firmly maintained that a convention should be concluded, and forthwith made operative, prohibiting the manufacture, possession, and use of atomic weapons, without waiting for the establishment of an effective control system, while the United States insisted that prohibition should be a part of the control system and should not enter into force until the control system was in operation and shown to be effective. Second, the Soviet Union insisted that the development of atomic energy should be left to each state and that, subject to periodic inspections by the proposed international authority, each state should be given the responsibility for seeing that the terms of the convention on the use of atomic weapons were respected. The United States, on the other hand, insisted on a system of detailed international control, including ownership, management, supervision, leasing, licensing, and inspection, which the Soviet

Union regarded as unjustified interference with matters coming within its domestic jurisdiction. Third, the Soviet Union insisted that the international authority be organized within the framework of the Security Council and that no enforcement action be taken except by agreement of the permanent members of the Council, while the United States insisted that the provision regarding penalties to be applied against violators of the convention should not admit the possibility of a "veto" by a state not complying with it.

Although the Atomic Energy Commission made useful progress during its first year in clarifying the technical aspects of the problem and the areas of agreement and disagreement, no real progress was made in bringing the two major parties closer together on the basic issues that separated them. The Soviet Union refused to participate in the preparation of the first report of the commission to the Security Council. This report, which was adopted on December 30, 1946, by a vote of 10 to 0, with the Soviet Union and Poland abstaining, dealt with the scientific and technical aspects of the problem of control and the safeguards required to ensure the use of atomic energy for peaceful purposes only, and made general recommendations along the lines of the United States proposals for a system of international control.[12]

On the scientific and technical aspects of the problem, the commission recorded its approval of the unanimous conclusion of its Scientific and Technical Committee: "With regard to the question . . . 'whether effective control of atomic energy is possible,' we do not find any basis in the available scientific facts for supposing that effective control is not technologically feasible."[13] On the basis of its findings regarding safeguards necessary to ensure the use of atomic energy for peaceful purposes only, the commission recommended that "a strong and comprehensive international system of control and inspection aimed at attaining the objectives set forth in the Commission's terms of reference" should be established, and its scope and functions defined "by a treaty or convention in which all nations, Members of the United Nations, should be entitled to participate on fair and equitable terms." It also recommended that the treaty or convention should contain provisions that would: (1) establish an international control agency with rights, powers,

[12] U.N. Atomic Energy Commission, First Year, *Official Records*, Special Supplement, *Report to the Security Council* (1946).

[13] *Ibid.*, p. 11

and responsibilities clearly defined along the lines of the United States proposals, and with the "veto" excluded from its operations; (2) afford representatives of the proposed agency unimpeded rights of ingress, egress, and access for the performance of their duties within the territories of Member states; (3) prohibit the manufacture, possession, and use of atomic weapons; (4) provide for the disposal of existing stocks; (5) specify the means and methods of determining violations of its terms; and (6) establish the nature of measures of enforcement and punishment, the possibility of any "veto" being excluded. The commission observed that a violation might be of so grave a nature "as to give rise to the inherent right of self-defense recognized in Article 51 of the Charter of the United Nations." It further recommended that:

> The treaty or convention should embrace the entire programme for putting the international system of control and inspection into effect, and should provide a schedule for the completion of the transitional process over a period of time, step by step, in an orderly and agreed sequence leading to the full and effective establishment of international control of atomic energy. In order that the transition may be accomplished as rapidly as possible and with safety and equity to all, this Commission should supervise the transitional process, as prescribed in the treaty or convention, and should be empowered to determine when a particular stage or stages have been completed and subsequent ones are to commence.[14]

The General Assembly and the Problem of Armaments

The discussions in the Atomic Energy Commission during 1946 gave little encouragement to those who hoped that atomic weapons could be eliminated through a system of international control that would provide guarantees that atomic energy would be used only for peaceful purposes. In spite of the awesome nature of the atomic weapon and of the consequences of its future use, the Soviet Union appears to have been primarily motivated by a reluctance to accept any plan that would seem to ensure that the United States would have a dominant position in the development and use of atomic energy, and consequently a superiority of military power, and that would seem to subject the Soviet economy and political system to external influence and control, which would be incompatible with the objectives of the Soviet leaders. The United States, on the

[14] *Ibid.,* p. 19.

other hand, was not willing to forego the advantages of an atomic weapon monopoly, temporary though it might be, without definite guarantees that the Soviet Union would live up to its promises and accept an effective system of collective security.

As a result of a surprise initiative on the part of the Soviet Union, the whole question of the international regulation of armaments, including atomic and other weapons of mass destruction, was considered during the second part of the first session of the General Assembly, which lasted from October to December 1946, in a discussion that in its scope and substance was reminiscent of the debates in the Assembly of the League of Nations. Apparently, the Soviet leaders thought that by their initiative they would embarrass the United States, which was seemingly anxious that nothing should interfere with the consideration of its proposals for the international control of atomic energy. Furthermore, they apparently hoped to gain the propaganda initiative for themselves by shifting the focus of discussion from the highly concrete United States proposals on atomic energy to the more general topic of ways and means of reducing the burden of world armaments, in a discussion of which they would find more room for maneuver and better opportunity for propaganda. The Soviet leaders were not presumably unaware of specific advantages that the Soviet Union, with its highly developed techniques of subversion and large military reserves, would gain as the result of the reduction in the military strength of the United States and the other Western powers, and more especially by the withdrawal of United States armed forces from Western Europe and other areas in close proximity to Soviet frontiers.

The Soviet delegation introduced two proposals that led to a wide-ranging debate. The first of these was that Members should submit information on the location and size of armed forces maintained in the territory of other Members and in former enemy states, and on the location and personnel of air and naval bases similarly maintained.[15] The second proposal recognized "the necessity of a general reduction of armaments" and provided that "the implementation of the decision concerning the reduction of armaments should include as its primary objective the prohibition to produce and use atomic energy for military purposes."[16]

[15] U.N. Doc. A/C.1/62 (Nov. 20, 1946).
[16] U.N. Doc. A/Bur/42 (Oct. 30, 1946).

In the course of the debate that followed, the complexity of the problem of armament regulation and its essentially political nature were clearly confirmed. The Soviet delegation appeared as the leading protagonist of the direct approach. It was clear that in adopting this position the Soviet leaders were moved by the desire to achieve a military advantage and thus be in a relatively stronger position to further the interests of the Soviet state and the world communist movement. The directness of the Soviet approach was no doubt intended to gain psychological and propaganda advantages as well. The delegations of the United States and the United Kingdom on the other hand, made it clear that the reduction and limitation of armaments alone, whether they took the form of withdrawal of armed forces from other countries where they might be considered by the Soviet Union to be a threat, or the prohibition of the manufacture, possession, and use of atomic weapons, were not enough. According to the summary record of the committee meeting, the British representative, Sir Hartley Shawcross, speaking for the United Kingdom

. . . insisted on an effective system of collective security whose operation could not be prevented by any aggressive State and which could furnish aid to any State subject to attack. Disarmament and collective security must go hand in hand. Nor were collective security enforcement measures enough. There must be adequate control to assure that States were actually disarming and carrying out limitation agreements. . . . Such a system [of control] must not be subject to any "veto."[17]

During the discussion in the Assembly, a variety of specific approaches to the problem of armament regulation was considered. There was general agreement on certain principles, but when an attempt was made to give concrete expression to these principles, and to apply them to specific problems, basic conflicts of interests and objectives were quick to appear. There was general acceptance of the desirability of the limitation and reduction of national armaments, but only in the abstract. There was also general agreement on the desirability of making available factual information regarding national armed forces. The Soviet Union, however, wanted to begin with reporting on national armed forces stationed in foreign countries and was only willing to report on armed forces at home if the information given covered all armaments and armed

[17] U.N. General Assembly, First Session, Second Part. First Committee, *Official Records*, 30th Meeting (Nov. 28, 1946), pp. 184-85.

forces, including atomic weapons. The Western powers were not prepared to report information on forces stationed in foreign countries unless information was also made available regarding forces stationed in home territories, and they were not prepared to make available information regarding all armaments, especially atomic, without agreement on an effective system of international inspection and control.

There was agreement in principle on the desirability of eliminating from national armaments atomic weapons and weapons of mass destruction, but the Western powers qualified their acceptance of the principle by insisting that an effective international control system should first be put into operation. The Soviet Union professed to regard this as a maneuver to postpone indefinitely any effective prohibition. Although it declared that it accepted the principle of international control, and that it was willing to undertake the preparation of a plan, it would not agree to make prohibition dependent on the proved effectiveness of the control system.

There was also agreement in principle that effective safeguards by way of inspection and other means should be established to protect states complying with the terms of the limitation agreement against the hazards of violation. The Soviet Union, however, while willing to accept inspection in principle, in effect insisted that confidence must be placed in the good faith of governments. The United States and the United Kingdom insisted on a system of inspection and enforcement that would make it impossible for a great power to conceal a violation or protect itself against the penalties therefor. The Soviet Union did concede, however, that the principle of great power unanimity as expressed in the voting procedure of the Security Council did not prevent the interested states from agreeing by special convention to set up a special authority with power to take decisions by the vote therein specified. Nevertheless the right not to conclude such an agreement served the purpose of a "veto," and the Soviet Union made it clear that it would consent to no infringement on the responsibilities of the Council and the rights of its permanent members.

Furthermore, there was agreement in principle that the United Nations system of collective security should be fully implemented. But in the light of the basic disagreements between the Soviet Union and the other permanent members of the Security Council on the principles that should govern the provisions of the military agreements to be concluded under Article 43, there appeared to be little chance that the provisions of Chapter VII of the Charter would become fully operative in the near future.[18]

Finally, there was agreement in principle that an improvement of relations between the Soviet Union and the Western powers was desirable. The Soviet Union, however, took the position that the prohibition of atomic weapons and a reduction of armaments would contribute to such an improvement. It demanded the withdrawal of United States and United Kingdom forces from foreign countries and the relinquishment of bases in foreign countries, on the ground that they endangered international peace and security. The United States and the United Kingdom, on the other hand, argued that a reduction of the Soviet military establishment, which would be comparable to that already carried out by them, would be evidence of peaceful, nonaggressive purposes, and would result in a corresponding improvement of political relations, as would the conclusion of peace settlements and the solution of outstanding problems on the basis of the purposes and principles set forth in the Charter and other agreements concluded during the war.

The debate in the General Assembly was free of much of the bitterness and vituperation that was to characterize future discussions in that organ, and the principal parties showed a superficial willingness to make concessions in the interest of agreement, but the resolution on principles governing the general regulation and reduction of armaments, which the Assembly unanimously adopted on December 14, 1946, did not in fact resolve any of the basic differences between the Soviet Union and the Western powers.[19] It consisted of a series of carefully formulated propositions that covered underlying disagreements with the appearance of agreement. The Assembly recognized "the necessity of an early general regulation and reduction of armaments and armed forces." It recommended "that the Security Council give prompt consideration to formulating the practical measures, according to their priority, which are essential to provide for the general regulation and reduction of armaments and armed forces and to assure that such regulation and reduction . . . will be generally observed by all participants . . ."; and that, "as an essential step towards the urgent objective of prohibiting and elimi-

[18] See above, Chap. XVI.
[19] Res. 41(I), Dec. 14, 1946.

nating from national armaments atomic and all other major weapons adaptable now and in the future to mass destruction, and the early establishment of international control of atomic energy and other modern scientific discoveries and technical developments to ensure their use only for peaceful purposes," the Atomic Energy Commission should fulfill expeditiously its terms of reference. It also recommended that the Security Council expedite consideration of the reports of the Atomic Energy Commission and "of a draft convention or conventions for the creation of an international system of control and inspection, these conventions to include the prohibition of atomic and all other major weapons adaptable now and in the future to mass destruction and the control of atomic energy to the extent necessary to ensure its use only for peaceful purposes."

The Assembly furthermore recommended that the Council give prompt consideration "to the working out of proposals to provide . . . practical and effective safeguards" in connection with the general regulation and reduction of armaments and the control of atomic energy. To ensure the adoption of measures for the above-stated purposes, the Assembly resolved that "there shall be established, within the framework of the Security Council, which bears the primary responsibility for the maintenance of international peace and security, an international system . . . operating through special organs, which organs shall derive their powers and status from the convention or conventions under which they are established." "Regarding the problem of security as closely connected with that of disarmament," the Assembly recommended that the Council accelerate as much as possible the placing of armed forces at the disposal of the Council under Article 43 of the Charter, and that Members undertake "the progressive and balanced withdrawal," taking into account the needs of occupation, of armed forces stationed in former enemy territories, and the withdrawal without delay of armed forces stationed in the territories of Members without their consent. Finally, the Assembly recommended "a corresponding reduction of national armed forces, and a general progressive and balanced reduction of national armed forces." It was specifically stated that nothing in the resolution "shall alter or limit the resolution of the General Assembly passed on 24 January 1946, creating the Atomic Energy Commission."

In a separate resolution, reflecting the inability of Members to agree on any firm commitment to provide the United Nations with information regarding their armed forces, wherever located, the Assembly called upon the Security Council "to determine, as soon as possible, the information which the States Members of the United Nations should be called upon to furnish," in order to give effect to the main resolution.[20]

A Broader Approach to the Problem, 1947-50

The Security Council began its consideration of the resolutions of the General Assembly on January 9, 1947. It was the organ to which most of the recommendations of the Assembly were directed and the organ primarily responsible under the Charter for preparing plans for the regulation of armaments. After an extended discussion in the course of which various proposals were advanced, a resolution was finally formulated, which the Council approved on February 13 by a vote of 10 to 0 with the Soviet Union abstaining.[21] This resolution provided for (1) consideration by the Council "as soon as possible" of the first report of the Atomic Energy Commission, which had been submitted on December 31, 1946, and the taking of suitable decisions to facilitate the work of the commission; (2) the establishment of a Commission for Conventional Armaments[22] to prepare proposals "for the general regulation and reduction of armaments and armed forces" and "for practical and effective safeguards" in connection therewith, matters within the competence of the Atomic Energy Commission being excluded from the jurisdiction of the new commission; and (3) a request to the Military Staff Committee to submit to it "as soon as possible and as a matter of urgency" recommendations that it had been asked to give in pursuance of Article 43 of the Charter, and as a first step to submit not later than April 30 its recommendations regarding "the basic principles which should govern the organization of the United Nations Armed Force."

The decisions by which the major powers agreed to a broader and more comprehensive approach to the problem of armament regulation than had initially been adopted do not appear to have been based on any conviction that this approach would lead to agreement

---

[20] Res. 42(I), Dec. 14, 1946.

[21] U.N. Doc. S/268/Rev. 1 (Feb. 13, 1947).

[22] The commission was to consist of the members of the Security Council.

on the details of an acceptable plan. In fact, the United States appears to have entered this new phase of discussions in the United Nations with much reluctance and doubt regarding the wisdom of it, having in a sense been maneuvered during the session of the Assembly into accepting a basis of discussion that it had hoped to avoid. Once the discussion was under way, the United States saw no alternative but to make the best of it, and finally, in the spirit of compromise, agreed to formulas that did little to strengthen its position in the discussions that followed. Although the formulations contained in the resolution of the Assembly undoubtedly gave a more accurate picture of the complexity of the problem of armament regulation than did the more limited approach of the first resolution on atomic energy in January 1946, even this broader approach gave little promise of success, considering the current deterioration of political relations between the great powers, for it was a regrettable fact that at the very time that the Members of the United Nations were committing themselves to the new approach to the problem of armament regulation, relations between the Soviet Union and the Western nations were deteriorating at an alarming rate.[23] Under such conditions, more than a logically sound approach was required to ensure success.

International Control of Atomic Energy

The Security Council began its consideration of the first report of the Atomic Energy Commission on February 14, 1947. After extended discussion of the Soviet objections to the findings of the report, the Council transmitted the record of its consideration to the Atomic Energy Commission and urged the commission "in accordance with the General Assembly resolutions of 24 January and 14 December 1946, to continue its inquiry into all phases of the problem of international control of atomic energy and to develop as promptly as possible the specific proposals called for" in these resolutions, and "in due course to prepare and submit to the Security Council a draft treaty or treaties or convention or conventions incorporating its ultimate proposals."[24]

On March 19, the Atomic Energy Commission decided that its

[23] See above, Chap. II.
[24] U.N. Security Council, Second Year, *Official Records*, No. 24 (Mar. 10, 1947), pp. 487 ff.

Working Committee and its Committee 2, which had earlier been set up to study and report on safeguards, should consider the questions arising out of the resolution of the Council, "and in particular the questions relating to the establishment of international control of atomic energy on which agreement among its members has not yet been reached."[25] In the course of the spring and summer, the committees and the commission itself gave detailed consideration to: (1) points of disagreement with the first report of the commission raised by the Soviet representative in the course of discussions in the Security Council, (2) proposals submitted by the Soviet representative to the Atomic Energy Commission on June 11, 1947, and (3) the operational and developmental functions of the proposed international atomic authority.

The consideration of specific Soviet amendments to the first report of the commission led to the further clarification of the issues but did not result in any enlargement of the area of agreement. The main questions on which agreement was not possible were: (1) the extent to which the "veto" should be eliminated in connection with the enforcement and punishment provisions of the proposed plan; (2) the safeguards required for the strict international control of atomic energy; (3) the methods and the priorities by which the international control of atomic energy, including the prohibition of atomic weapons, was to be established; and (4) the right of the international control agency to conduct research in atomic weapons.[26]

The Soviet proposals of June 11 elaborated and expanded the Soviet position in important respects. They helped to clarify the Soviet concept of control and inspection, which was found to be quite different from that of the United States and the majority of the commission. Specifically, the Soviet proposals called for the establishment of an International Control Commission that would be composed of the representatives of states members of the Atomic Energy Commission. This commission would perform functions of control and inspection and would conduct research in the peaceful uses of atomic energy. Control, based on the assumption of national or private ownership and management of materials and facilities, included (1) inspection and investigation, (2) accounting, (3) the preparation of rules of technological control and observance of their

---

[25] U.N. Atomic Energy Commission, Second Year, *Official Records*, Special Supplement, p. 5.
[26] *Ibid.*, pp. 87-88.

operation, (4) the requesting of information from governments regarding activities of plants, and (5) the submitting of recommendations to governments and to the Security Council. Supervision, management, and licensing were wholly excluded as means of international control. Inspection was to be of "a periodic character, both in the general field and in the application to special cases," but this did not "necessarily imply the carrying out of inspection at regular intervals, fixed beforehand." Inspection might be carried out by "the decision of the International Control Commission in compliance with the necessity." "Necessity" appears to have been conceived in terms of discrepancies in government reports and formal complaints by governments. On the priority of prohibition and the safeguarding of the "veto," the Soviet proposals simply reaffirmed earlier positions. Although these proposals were, in certain respects, somewhat indefinite, they were much more detailed and specific than subsequent Soviet proposals on the regulation of armaments, including weapons of mass destruction, which were characterized by great vagueness.

The majority of the members of Committee 2 concluded that "these proposals as they now stand and the explanations given thereon do not provide an adequate basis for the development by the Committee of specific proposals for an effective system of international control of atomic energy."[27]

The conclusions to which the commission came on the operational and developmental functions of the proposed international control agency were along the lines of the original United States proposals and were unacceptable to the Soviet Union. The commission was of the opinion that these functions must include: (1) the ownership of nuclear fuel and source material; (2) the ownership, management, and operation of dangerous facilities, including the production of atomic fuel; (3) the licensing by the agency of non-dangerous facilities to be operated on a national basis; (4) inspection to prevent or detect clandestine activities; and (5) the conduct of research in the use of atomic energy for both peaceful and warlike purposes. "Far-reaching rights of entry into, movement and access within, and egress from national territories" were deemed essential to accomplish the purposes of effective international control.

In developing a plan of control, the commission made an effort to meet some of the objections that had been raised by the Soviet

[27] *Ibid.*, p. 95.

Union. It was proposed that a system of production quotas governing the amount of atomic fuel that might be produced in each country should be written into the treaty rather than left to the discretion of the control agency, and that the rights of the agency with respect to inspection should be strictly and carefully defined. Nevertheless, these concessions were not of sufficient importance to end the basic impasse that had developed.

The second report, adopted on September 11, 1947, by a vote of 10 to 1, the Soviet Union voting against it and Poland abstaining, was not formally considered by the Security Council. The commission recessed until the end of the year. In January 1948, it resumed its deliberations, but it soon became apparent that the commission was hopelessly deadlocked. By its third report, adopted on May 17, 1948, by a vote of 9 to 2, the Soviet Union and the Ukraine voting against it, the commission reported that it had reached an impasse.[28] It reaffirmed the view of the majority of the commission that an effective plan of international control was technically feasible but asserted that it required a substantial encroachment on traditional concepts of national sovereignty. As the Soviet Union was unwilling to accept such a plan and its co-operation was essential, the commission concluded that no useful purpose could be served "by carrying on negotiations at the commission level." It recommended consultations among the permanent members of the Council and Canada. A proposal introduced by the United States in the Security Council in June calling for approval of the findings and recommendations of the three reports of the commission was vetoed by the Soviet Union.

When the General Assembly met in Paris for its third session in September 1948, it was asked to consider various proposals relating to the international control of atomic energy and the regulation of armaments generally. The Soviet Union introduced a proposal calling for a one-third reduction of all land, naval, and air forces by the permanent members of the Council, the prohibition of atomic weapons, and the establishment within the framework of the Security Council of an international control body to supervise and control the implementation of the above measures. Canada submitted a proposal similar to the one that the United States had submitted in the Security Council, which had been vetoed by the

[28] U.N. Atomic Energy Commission, Third Year, *Official Records*, Special Supplement, *Third Report to the Security Council* (May 17, 1948).

Soviet Union. The Soviet Union proposed a resolution that modified its position on the timing of prohibition and control. It recommended the continuance by the Council and the Atomic Energy Commission of their activities, along the lines laid down in the two 1946 resolutions of the Assembly, and the preparation of two conventions, one on the prohibition of atomic weapons and the other on the establishment of effective international control, both conventions "to be signed and brought into operation simultaneously."[29] A resolution proposed by New Zealand provided for a request to the permanent members of the Atomic Energy Commission that they consult to determine when there existed any basis for agreement. An Indian proposal provided for the approval "in substance" of the general findings and recommendations of the first report and the specific proposals of the second report, while calling upon the Atomic Energy Commission to resume its work. In the course of discussions in the Assembly, there was evidence that many members felt the situation had become more hopeful since the time when the Atomic Energy Commission recommended the suspension of its work. There was strong opposition to suspending the work of the commission, and a reluctance to close any possible door to agreement among the major powers.

The Assembly finally adopted a resolution approving the "general findings" of the first report and the "specific proposals" of the second report regarding the operational and developmental functions of the proposed international agency, as constituting "the necessary basis for establishing an effective system of international control." It requested the five permanent members of the Council and Canada to meet together to "determine if there exists a basis for agreement on the international control of atomic energy" and to report to the Assembly not later than its next session. It called on the commission meanwhile to resume its sessions.[30] The Soviet proposal to combine prohibition of atomic weapons with the reduction of conventional weapons was defeated.

Neither further meetings of the Atomic Energy Commission nor the six-power discussions produced any break in the impasse. On July 29, 1949, the Atomic Energy Commission decided that no useful purpose could be served by its meeting again, and the six powers, which held talks from August until mid-October, were unable to

[29] U.N. Doc. A/C.1/310 (Oct. 2, 1948).
[30] Res. 191(III), Nov. 4, 1948.

reach any agreement. In early October, while the Assembly was again considering the matter, President Truman announced the Soviet explosion of an atomic device. The Assembly requested that the six powers continue their consultations. These talks were suspended, however, when the Soviet Union announced on January 19, 1950 that it would not accept the representative of the Nationalist Government on Formosa as representing China.

Regulation of Conventional Armaments

Along with attempts to break the impasse that had initially developed over the international control of atomic energy, parallel efforts were being made to carry out the directive of the General Assembly regarding the limitation of conventional armaments. The Commission for Conventional Armaments held its first meeting on March 24, 1947. One of its first tasks was to prepare a plan of work.

As in the case of the Atomic Energy Commission, the discussions in the Commission for Conventional Armaments centered around proposals submitted by the United States and the Soviet Union.[31] The plan proposed by the United States called for: (1) recommendations to the Security Council defining the armaments and armed forces that were within the jurisdiction of the commission; (2) the determination of general principles in connection with the regulation and reduction of armaments and armed forces; (3) consideration of practical and effective safeguards to be carried out under an international system of control operating through special agencies to protect complying states against the hazards of violation and evasion; (4) formulation of practical proposals for the regulation and reduction of armaments and armed forces; (5) extension of the foregoing principles and proposals to states not Members of the United Nations; and (6) submission of a report or reports to the Security Council, including, if possible, a draft convention. The Soviet plan linked the regulation and reduction of armaments with the prohibition of atomic weapons. It also included the regulation of war production, military bases, and means of production. The United States plan was adopted by the commission on June 18, and approved by the Council on July 8 by a vote of 9 to 0, with the Soviet Union and Poland abstaining.

[31] See U.N. Doc. S/C.3/12 (June 6, 1947).

The commission then established a Working Committee of the Whole, which had as its terms of reference the approved plan of work. The first question the committee considered was that of defining the armaments and armed forces that fell within the jurisdiction of the commission. The representative of the United States maintained that atomic weapons and weapons of mass destruction were excluded from the jurisdiction of the commission by the explicit words of the resolution of the Security Council. The Soviet representative, on the other hand, contended that such a separation was artificial, and would interfere with the preparation by the commission of practical proposals "for the general regulation and reduction of armaments and armed forces." The Working Committee on September 9, 1947 adopted a revised proposal of the United States by which it informed the commission

. . . that it considers that all armaments and armed forces, except atomic weapons and weapons of mass destruction, fall within its jurisdiction and that weapons of mass destruction should be defined to include atomic explosive weapons, radioactive material weapons, lethal chemical and biological weapons, and any weapons developed in the future which have characteristics comparable in destructive effect to those of the atomic bomb or other weapons mentioned above.[32]

The discussion on general principles to govern the regulation and reduction of armaments and armed forces was carried on for nearly a year and brought out a variety of points of view. The basic division was between the views of the United States and the United Kingdom and those of the Soviet Union. Generally speaking, the Anglo-American position was that an agreement for the general regulation and reduction of armaments and armed forces could be effected only under conditions of international confidence and security. Progress toward the establishment of such conditions could be made by setting up an effective system of international control of atomic energy, by the conclusion of peace treaties with Japan and Germany, and by implementing the collective security provisions of the Charter. The Soviet Union, on the other hand, took the position that a reduction in armaments and armed forces would help to create stability in international relations and to develop friendly relations between countries. A reduction in expenditure for armaments would result in lower taxes and greater material well-being for the peoples of the world. Although during the war great armies

[32] U.N. Doc. S/C.3/24 (July 28, 1948).

had been necessary, the decisions to demilitarize Germany and Japan removed the reasons for maintaining them. The Soviet argument was that the conditions laid down by the United States and the United Kingdom for the regulation and reduction of armaments were such as to postpone indefinitely the implementation of the resolution of the Assembly.

The Soviet position was given concrete expression in a resolution introduced in the Working Committee on July 26, 1948. This provided that the general regulation and reduction of armaments and armed forces should cover all countries and all kinds of armaments and armed forces, and that it should also provide for:

(a) Reduction of armies, naval and air forces both in respect to strength and armaments.

(b) Limitation of combat characteristics of certain kinds of armaments and the prohibition of separate kinds of armaments.

(c) Reduction of war budgets and state expenditures on production of armaments.

(d) Reduction of production of war materials.[33]

In addition, the proposed resolution would have provided for "the entire prohibition of production and use" of atomic and other weapons of mass destruction and the destruction of stocks of such weapons, and the establishment of "an international system of control . . . within the framework of the Security Council and as a component part of the plan for such regulation and reduction."

The Soviet proposal was defeated in the Working Committee, and instead a proposal made by the United Kingdom embodying amendments offered by the United States and Canada, was adopted.[34] This resolution was subsequently approved by the commission on August 12, 1948, by a vote of 9 to 2, the Soviet Union and the Ukraine voting against it. It listed the following principles that were to govern "the formulation of practical proposals for the establishment of a system for the regulation and reduction of armaments and armed forces:"

1. A system for the regulation and reduction of conventional armaments and armed forces should provide for the adherence of all states and initially must include all states "having substantial military resources."

2. The system could only be put into effect in an atmosphere of

[33] U.N. Doc. S/C.3/27 (Aug. 4, 1948).
[34] U.N. Doc. S/C.3/25 (July 28, 1948).

international confidence and security, though the establishment of such a system might increase confidence and so justify further regulation and reduction.

3. Examples of conditions essential to such confidence and security were (a) the establishment of an adequate system of agreements under Article 43 of the Charter, (b) the establishment of international control of atomic energy, and (c) the conclusion of peace settlements with Germany and Japan.

4. A system for the regulation and reduction of armaments and armed forces should provide for the least possible diversion for armaments of the human and economic resources of the world, and should limit armaments and armed forces to those "consistent with and indispensable to the maintenance of international peace and security" and "necessary for the implementation of Members' obligations and the protection of their rights under the Charter of the United Nations."

5. The system must include an adequate system of safeguards, including an agreed system of international supervision to ensure compliance with the treaty or convention. This system of safeguards must be technically feasible and practical, provide for the prompt detection of violations, and cause a minimum of interference with, and impose minimum burdens on, any aspect of the life of individual nations.

6. Provision must be made for effective enforcement in the event of violations.

The Soviet Union refused to accept the majority position as set forth in this resolution, and to agree to the proposed report of the commission to the Security Council. The commission never considered the other items of its plan of work.

When the General Assembly met in September 1948, it again considered the question of the general reduction of armaments. The Soviet delegation proposed a resolution that would tie the prohibition of atomic weapons to a one-third reduction of the conventional armaments and armed forces of the major powers. This was not acceptable to the majority of Members, mainly because existing levels of armaments would not be disclosed nor an effective check permitted. Instead, a resolution was adopted in which the Assembly, although recognizing that "the aim of the reduction of conventional armaments and armed forces can only be attained in an atmosphere of real and lasting improvement in international relations, which implies in particular the application of control of atomic energy involving the prohibition of the atomic weapon," expressed its trust that the Commission for Conventional Armaments, in carrying out its plan of work, would "devote its first attention to formulating proposals for the receipt, checking and publication, by an international organ of control within the framework of the Security Council, of full information to be supplied by Member States with regard to their effectives and their conventional armaments."[35] The Soviet Union regarded this as a delaying operation and resumed its advocacy of its plan in the Security Council when that organ considered the resolution of the Assembly. However, the Soviet Union did not attempt to veto a proposal of the United States to transmit the resolution of the Assembly to the Commission for Conventional Armaments.

When the commission met in February 1949, it instructed its Working Committee to undertake the implementation of the suggestion of the Assembly. The French representative submitted to the committee a paper on the collection, publication, and verification of information on military effectives and conventional armaments. This paper contained suggestions for the collection and verification of such data, and the structure and functions of the international organ of control. It was approved by the Working Committee and then by the commission by identical votes.[36] The Soviet Union opposed the plan on the grounds that it imposed preliminary conditions on the reduction of armaments and armed forces and that it did not provide for making information available regarding atomic weapons. In the absence of such provisions, the Soviet representatives maintained, any census would be meaningless and would serve only the purposes of military intelligence. Those who supported the proposal argued that it was a first and indispensable step toward the formulation of a real and workable plan for the regulation of armaments.

The census and verification proposals were considered by the Security Council, where a proposal of the United States to approve them was vetoed by the Soviet Union. The General Assembly, after considering the proposals during its fourth session, adopted a resolution noting the failure of the major powers to agree and requested the commission to continue its studies. In April 1950, however, the

[35] Res. 192(III), Nov. 19, 1948.
[36] U.N. S/C.3/40 (July 20, 1949). The vote was 8 to 3.

Soviet Union withdrew its representative from the commission and from that time on the work of the commission was for all practical purposes at an end.[37]

Other Approaches

The General Assembly in its resolution of December 14, 1946, had urged the Security Council to accelerate the conclusion of military agreements under Article 43, and the Council, by its resolution of February 13, 1947, requested the Military Staff Committee to submit a report by April 30 on principles that should govern the conclusion of such agreements. The Military Staff Committee reported,[38] however, that the permanent members of the Security Council were hopelessly deadlocked. Their agreements were for the most part limited to propositions that were explicitly stated or clearly implied in the provisions of the Charter. Their disagreements were on questions of fundamental importance, such as the size and composition of national contingents, which had to be resolved before military agreements under Article 43 could be concluded.[39]

The Security Council considered the report but was unable to resolve the impasse. The positions taken by representatives of members in the Council corresponded closely to positions taken by their counterparts on the Military Staff Committee. The committee informed the Council that it could make no further progress until it received additional guidance. By August 1948, discussions had come to a standstill. Although the Assembly subsequently urged the Council to make efforts to implement Article 43, the deadlock continued. It thus became apparent that efforts to provide assurance that national armed forces would be available to the Council in the interest of collective security could be no more successful than efforts to limit and reduce national armaments, so long as current tensions between the Soviet Union and the Western powers continued to exist.

New Efforts 1950-53

By the summer of 1950, it was clear that efforts to achieve the regulation and reduction of national armaments by international agreement within the framework of the resolutions of the Assembly

[37] The Working Committee continued ineffective discussions and reported again to the Security Council in August 1950.

[38] U.N. Doc. S/336 (Apr. 30, 1947).

[39] For extended treatment of these disagreements, see above, Chap. XVI.

of 1946, had completely failed and held little promise, at least for the immediate future. In the discussions that had taken place, a complete deadlock between the Soviet Union and the Western powers had developed. Furthermore, the Soviet Union had withdrawn from formal attempts to reach agreement following its refusal to recognize the right of the National Government to represent China. The North Korean attack on the Republic of Korea in June, 1950, which was widely viewed as having the full support of the Soviet Union, and which came within a year after the announcement that the Soviet Union had the secret of the atomic bomb, greatly increased the feeling of insecurity throughout the world and created an atmosphere hardly favorable to the international regulation of national armaments. In fact, in the months following, the emphasis in national policies was definitely on the strengthening of national armaments and, in the West, on the development of military strength for collective self-defense in order to meet the threat of Communist aggression. In these circumstances, it could hardly be expected that any proposals for the reduction and limitation of armaments would provide the basis for agreement between the major powers.

The initiative in suggesting a new approach to the problem of armament regulation was taken by the United States. In an address to the General Assembly on October 24, 1950, President Truman, after reviewing the activities of the United Nations, set forth the following three basic principles on which any successful plan of "disarmament" must rest:

First, the plan must include all kinds of weapons. Outlawing any particular kind of weapon is not enough. The conflict in Korea bears tragic witness to the fact that aggression, whatever the weapons used, brings frightful destruction.

Second, the plan must be based on unanimous agreement. A majority of nations is not enough. No plan of disarmament can work unless it includes every nation having substantial armed forces. One-sided disarmament is a sure invitation to aggression.

Third, the plan must be fool-proof. Paper promises are not enough. Disarmament must be based on safeguards which will insure the compliance of all nations. The safeguards must be adequate to give immediate warning of any threatened violation. Disarmament must be policed continuously and thoroughly. It must be founded upon free and open exchange of information across national borders.[40]

---

[40] U. S. Department of State, *United States Participation in the United Nations,* Report by the President to the Congress for the Year 1950, Publication 4178 (1951), p. 114.

Observing that much valuable work had been done by the Atomic Energy Commission and by the Commission for Conventional Armaments, the President expressed the belief that it would be useful to explore ways in which the work of the two commissions could be more closely brought together. He suggested as one possibility the establishment of "a new and consolidated disarmament commission."

The emphasis on "disarmament" in this initiative of the United States and in the discussions that followed had some significance. It suggested the increasing remoteness of the ideas that had been accepted at the time the Charter was written, especially that of the close interrelation of the regulation of armaments and the organization of collective security under the Security Council. In part this trend appears to have been due to the growing recognition by governments of the political advantages to be gained from "disarmament" proposals at a time when people everywhere were alarmed by the drift toward general war and were in a mood to welcome any suggestion that the trend might be reversed.

When the question was considered by the General Assembly, two proposals were introduced, one an eight-power draft resolution providing for the creation of a committee of twelve (the eleven members of the Security Council and Canada) to consider and report on the co-ordination of the work of the Atomic Energy Commission and the Commission for Conventional Armaments and on the advisability that their functions be merged and placed under a new consolidated disarmament commission. The other was a Soviet proposal that would have called upon the Atomic Energy Commission to prepare two draft conventions, one providing for the unconditional prohibition of the atomic weapon, and the other for the international control of atomic energy, the two to enter into force simultaneously. The Assembly on December 13 adopted the eight-power draft resolution with only the Soviet bloc voting against it.

Thus, although the deadlock continued, it assumed a somewhat different form. The United States, with the unanimous support of all Members outside of the Soviet bloc, was now apparently willing to discuss the reduction and regulation of atomic and conventional armaments together. The Soviet Union, while approving in principle the suggestion that the work of the two commissions should be combined, was insisting that priority be given to the immediate prohibition of atomic weapons. Several important considerations appear to have influenced the United States Government to change its earlier position that atomic and conventional weapons should be discussed separately. First, the explosion of an atomic device by the Soviet Union marked the end of the United States monopoly and therefore no longer permitted the use of this monopoly position for achieving the kind of international control system the United States had favored. Second, the Korean experience had demonstrated that aggression could be successfully undertaken by the use of conventional armaments alone, that superiority in atomic and other weapons of mass destruction did not provide security against aggression, and that, consequently, it was necessary in developing any system for the regulation and reduction of armaments to proceed from a broader base than the control of weapons of mass destruction. Also, the United States Government may have felt that it could embarrass the Soviet Union and, at the same time, gain additional support from other Members, by conceding a point that the Soviet Union had hitherto treated as of central importance. Finally, there was the belated recognition that the control of atomic energy and the prohibition of atomic weapons might contribute to a serious imbalance of power if other elements of armed strength, including especially the number of personnel in the armed forces, were not controlled and limited.

When the General Assembly met in Paris in early November 1951 for its sixth session, it had before it the report of the Committee of Twelve recommending the establishment of a new commission to carry forward the tasks assigned to the Atomic Energy Commission and the Commission for Conventional Armaments. In addition, the Assembly was asked by the governments of the United States, the United Kingdom, and France to consider the "regulation, limitation and balanced reduction of all armed forces and all armaments." The request was accompanied by a copy of a joint statement issued by these three governments on November 7, 1951 in which they expressed their belief "that if all governments sincerely join in the cooperative and effective regulation and limitation of armed forces and armaments, this would greatly reduce the danger of war and thus enhance the security of all nations." They proposed the disclosure and verification on a continuing basis and in successive stages of all armed forces and armaments "as an essential part of the program for regulation, limitation and balanced reduction of all armed forces and armaments to a level which would decrease substantially the possibility of a successful aggression and thereby decrease the chance that armed aggression would be used to further national objectives." They proposed that there should be criteria according to which the size of armed forces would be limited, the portion of national production used for military purposes would be restricted, and mutually agreed national military programs would be arrived at "within the prescribed limits and restrictions." It was suggested that the United Nations program for the international control of atomic energy continue to serve as the basis of the atomic energy aspects of the program unless and until a better plan could be devised. It was pointed out that such a general program could not be put into effect while United Nations forces were resisting aggression in Korea, and that concurrently with the entering into effect of such a program, major political issues would have to be settled.[41]

Discussions in the Assembly were largely based on a draft resolution submitted by France, the United Kingdom, and the United States, embodying the proposals contained in their joint statement and amendments submitted by the Soviet Union. In the course of its consideration by the Assembly, every effort was made to accommodate different points of view and to produce a resolution that would meet with general approval. The First Committee of the Assembly appointed a subcommittee consisting of the President of the Assembly, and representatives of France, the Soviet Union, the United Kingdom, and the United States to consider the various proposals and attempt to reconcile differences, but this subcommittee was forced to report that, although there were significant areas of agreement or possible agreement, there still remained points on which differences of opinion existed.

The resolution that the General Assembly finally adopted on January 11, 1952, was the original three-power proposal somewhat modified, but not to such an extent as to resolve the major points of disagreement.[42] The final vote was 41 to 6, with 8 abstentions, thus falling substantially short of the unanimous vote the resolution of December 14, 1946, had received. Consequently, the new resolution, although adopted by a large majority, did not provide any agreed basis for further discussions.

The new resolution affirmed the belief of the Assembly that a

[41] U. S. Department of State *Bulletin,* Vol. 25 (Nov. 19, 1951), p. 802.
[42] Res. 502 (VI), Jan. 11, 1952.

necessary means to the development of an effective collective security system was:

   . . . the development by the United Nations of comprehensive and co-ordinated plans, under international control, for the regulation, limitation and balanced reduction of all armed forces and all armaments, for the elimi-nation of all major weapons adaptable to mass destruction, and for the effec-tive international control of atomic energy to ensure the prohibition of atomic weapons and the use of atomic energy for peaceful purposes only.[43]

It established a Disarmament Commission "under the Security Council," with the same membership as the Atomic Energy Com-mission, to prepare proposals to be embodied in a draft treaty, or treaties. The commission was to be guided by the following prin-ciples:

   (a) In a system of guaranteed disarmament there must be progressive dis-closure and verification on a continuing basis of all armed forces—including para-military, security and police forces—and all armaments including atomic;

   (b) Such verification must be based on effective international inspection to insure the adequacy and accuracy of the information disclosed; this in-spection to be carried out in accordance with the decisions of the interna-tional control organ (or organs) to be established;

   (c) The Commission shall be ready to consider any proposals or plans for control that may be put forward involving either conventional arma-ments or atomic energy. Unless a better or no less effective system is devised, the United Nations plan for the international control of atomic energy and the prohibition of atomic weapons should continue to serve as the basis for the international control of atomic energy to insure the prohibition of atomic weapons and the use of atomic energy for peaceful purposes only;

   (d) There must be an adequate system of safeguards to insure observance of the disarmament programme, so as to provide for the prompt detection of violations while at the same time causing the minimum degree of inter-ference in the internal life of each country;

   (e) The treaty (or treaties) shall specifically be open to all States for signa-ture and ratification or adherence. The treaty (or treaties) shall provide what States must become parties thereto before the treaty (or treaties) shall enter into force.[44]

The commission was directed to formulate plans for the establish-ment of an international control organ "within the framework of the Security Council" to ensure the implementation of the treaty,

[43] *Ibid.*
[44] *Ibid.*

or treaties with the functions and powers of the organ to be defined by the treaty establishing it. The commission was also directed "to consider from the outset plans for progressive and continuing disclosure and verification, the implementation of which is recognized as a first and indispensable step in carrying out the disarmament programme." It was instructed "to determine how over-all limits and restrictions on all armed forces and all armaments can be calculated and fixed," and to consider methods by which states in negotiations among themselves can agree on the determination of these limits and "the allocation within their respective national military establishments of the permitted national armed forces and armaments." The commission was directed to report periodically, and provision was made for the convening of "a conference of all States" to consider proposals as soon as the commission should decide that "any part of its programme" was ready for submission.

By a separate resolution adopted on January 19, 1952, the General Assembly referred the Soviet proposals, together with the records of the discussions in the First Committee on these proposals, to the Disarmament Commission.[45] These proposals provided for: (1) a decision by the Assembly proclaiming the unconditional prohibition of atomic weapons and the establishment of strict international control, the two to be "put into effect simultaneously"; (2) the preparation by the Disarmament Commission and submission to the Security Council not later than June 1 of a draft convention to give effect to this decision; (3) a recommendation by the Assembly that the permanent members of the Council reduce their armaments and armed forces by one-third within a year; (4) a recommendation by the Assembly that forthwith, and not later than a month after the decision of the Assembly referred to above, all states should submit complete official data on their armaments and armed forces, "including data on atomic weapons and military bases in foreign territories"; (5) a recommendation by the Assembly for "the establishment within the framework of the Security Council of an international control organ"; (6) with a view to appropriate guarantees of observance, the granting to the control organ of "the right to conduct inspection on a continuing basis," but without the right "to interfere in the domestic affairs of States"; and (7) the calling within the shortest possible time, and in no case later than July 15, 1952, of a world disarmament conference.

[45] Res. 504 (VI), Jan. 19, 1952.

The discussions preceding the vote on these resolutions had disclosed limited areas of general agreement, but much more critical areas where the Soviet Union and the three Western powers—the United States, the United Kingdom, and France—were in disagreement. The Soviet Union was opposed to the principle advocated by the three Western powers of balanced reduction to levels adequate for defense, but not for offense, on the ground that it might mean an increase rather than a decrease in some instances, and that in any case the principle was not concrete. The proposal of the three nations for the prohibition of atomic weapons was opposed on the ground that it did not provide for immediate and unconditional prohibition, that it put control before prohibition, and that it gave no assurance that prohibition would ever become effective.

The Soviet Union also opposed the proposals for the international control of atomic energy for reasons stated many times before. It opposed the system of safeguards that the three powers would apply to conventional armaments as well as atomic weapons. It was opposed to the proposal for disclosure of armament information by stages on the ground that this would result in indefinite postponement of disclosure of information on the most destructive and dangerous weapons. It opposed the directives given the commission regarding the preparation of proposals on the over-all limits of armaments, and the allocation of armaments and armed forces within national military establishments.

On the other hand, the Western powers were unalterably opposed to the Soviet proposals for the prohibition of atomic weapons simultaneously with the establishment of a system of international control, the reduction by the major powers of existing armaments by one-third within a year, and the submission of complete data on all armaments and armed forces forthwith. One reason given, among others, was that these proposals contained no provisions that would ensure their observance. In the course of the debate, the Soviet delegation pointed to the current military preparations of the United States, the formation of what it claimed were aggressive blocs like the North Atlantic Treaty Organization, the establishment of military bases on the territory of other states, and the recent passage of the Mutual Security Act, as evidence of the chronic hostility of the United States toward the Soviet Union.

In the light of these basic disagreements and the failure of the major powers to make any progress in resolving them, no substantial progress was made subsequently in implementing the resolution of the Assembly. When the Disarmament Commission met, it set up two committees to function concurrently in carrying out its directives: one to consider the regulation of all armaments, and the other to deal with the matter of disclosure and verification.

At the first meeting of Committee 2 on April 5, 1952, the United States submitted detailed proposals for disclosure and verification, applicable to all armed forces and armaments, including atomic.[46] Five stages were envisaged, with the least sensitive information being first made available. For purposes of verification, inspectors would at all stages "have access to the entire national territory." The Soviet representative described the essence of the plan to be "the disclosure of armaments of other States and the concealment of information on the secret weapons of the United States and the atomic bomb," and repeated the Soviet proposals that had been previously introduced in the General Assembly. He insisted that they provided the most effective means of getting prompt and complete disclosure of armament data.

On April 24, in Committee 1, the United States introduced a proposal dealing with the essential principles of a disarmament program.[47] The proposal stressed that the "goal of disarmament is . . . to prevent war by relaxing the tensions and fears and making war inherently . . . impossible." To achieve this goal, states should cooperate to establish "an open and substantially disarmed world" in which "no state will be in a condition of armed preparedness to start a war" or "to undertake preparations for war without other states having knowledge of such preparations long before the offending state could start a war." This would require states to reduce their armed forces to levels and restrict their armaments to types and quantities necessary for "the maintenance of international security" and the "fulfillment of obligations of States to maintain peace and security in accordance with the United Nations Charter." The program envisaged would provide for "the progressive reduction of armed forces and permitted armaments to fixed maximum levels, radically less than present levels and balanced throughout the process of reduction, thereby eliminating mass armies and preventing any disequilibrium of power dangerous to peace," and "the

---

[46] U.N. Disarmament Commission, *Official Records,* Special Supplement No. 1, pp. 23-30.

[47] *Ibid.,* pp. 63-64.

elimination of all instruments adaptable to mass destruction." It would provide for effective safeguards including "an effective system of progressive and continuing disclosure and verification." In view of the completely negative attitude of the Soviet representative, there was a feeling that no useful purpose could be served by further debate on principles.

At a meeting of the Disarmament Commission on May 28, the United States, the United Kingdom, and France submitted proposals for establishing over-all numerical limitations on the size of the armed forces of all states.[48] The stated objective was to reduce the possibility and fear of successful aggression and to avoid a disequilibrium of power dangerous to international peace and security. It was emphasized that the proposal was intended to facilitate agreement on other essential parts of a comprehensive disarmament program. It was proposed that there should be fixed numerical ceilings for China, France, the Soviet Union, the United Kingdom, and the United States. It was tentatively suggested that the maximum ceilings for the Soviet Union, the United States, and China should be the same, between 1,000,000 and 1,500,000, and that the maximum ceilings for France and the United Kingdom should be the same, between 700,000 and 800,000. Ceilings for other states would be fixed in relation to these and should normally be less than 1 per cent of the population. It was made clear that these figures would cover personnel in all kinds of armed forces, including para-military and security forces. Suitable provision was to be made to prevent circumvention by building up large forces of trained reserves or militarily trained police.

In the course of the discussion in the commission, the United States representative made it clear that the proposed reductions depended on the settlement of the Korean conflict and some progress in establishing peaceful conditions throughout the world. The Soviet representative, however, denounced the proposal as hypocritical, and argued that it was intended to legalize the inflated armaments of its sponsors. He claimed that it did not deal with the distribution of armed forces among the various services or provide for the limitation of armaments or the prohibition of weapons of mass destruction.

In order to help resolve any honest disagreement that might exist regarding the order in which various substantive measures would be

[48] *Ibid.*, pp. 99-102.

put into effect, the French representative presented suggestions regarding scheduling and timing. His thought was that all decisions on limitation and prohibition should be subject to two conditions: (1) that there should be a definite sequence, and that each prohibition or limitation should be undertaken only after the previous one had been certified as achieved by a designated international organ, but should then follow automatically; and (2) that each limitation or prohibition should take place subject to the establishment in working order of the corresponding control mechanism. All operations would be classified into three groups: disclosure and verification, armed forces and conventional armaments, and atomic and other weapons of mass destruction. Three stages were suggested for putting into effect the complete system of regulation and limitation. In the first stage, there would be disclosure, verification, and limitation of armed forces and military expenditures, and the prohibition of the use of bacterial and chemical weapons. In the second, there would be disclosure, verification, and limitation of the main categories of conventional weapons, and of the manufacture of atomic weapons and of fissionable material in dangerous quantities. In the third period, there would be reduction of conventional weapons to agreed levels, followed by the prohibition of the use of atomic weapons and their destruction or conversion to peaceful uses.

In an effort further to meet the Soviet criticism, a supplemental clarifying proposal was submitted by the three powers on August 12, which stated that it was contemplated that any agreement for the limitation of armed forces would necessarily include (1) provisions to ensure that types and quantities of armaments bore a direct relation to amounts needed for permitted armed forces; (2) provisions regarding composition of permitted armed forces and armaments to prevent undue concentration; and (3) procedures "for the negotiation within over-all limitations of mutually agreed programmes of armed forces and armaments."[49] Suggestions were made with respect to procedures that might be followed. The Soviet representative claimed that these proposals did not involve concrete decisions on the reduction of armed forces and armaments simultaneously with a decision on the prohibition of the atom bomb and other weapons of mass destruction and the institution of controls, and therefore that they added no new elements to the discussion.

At the first meeting of the Disarmament Commission and again at

[49] *Ibid.*, pp. 130-31.

subsequent meetings of the commission and its committees, the Soviet Union raised the question of bacterial warfare, charging that United States forces in Korea had used bacterial weapons. This charge was vigorously denied. It was generally regarded by members of the commission as purely propagandistic in purpose, especially considering that the charge had no relevance to the subject of disarmament and that the Soviet Union was unwilling to agree to an impartial on-the-spot investigation. Nevertheless, the question of the prohibition of bacterial weapons was considered in connection with the work of the commission. The commission explicitly decided to include the question in its plan of work, although most of its members were of the opinion that it was already included in the category of weapons of mass destruction.

The United States had not ratified the Geneva Protocol of 1925 prohibiting the use of bacteriological methods of warfare, and the United States representative defended this action in the Disarmament Commission by citing the proven inadequacies of the Geneva Protocol.[50] He stated that his country "as a Member of the United Nations has committed itself, as have all other Members, to refrain from not only the use of poisonous gas and the use of germ warfare but the use of force of any kind contrary to the law. . . . Certainly there is no assurance that aggressors, which break their Charter obligations not to go to war, will keep their paper promises not to fight with certain weapons if they have them." Furthermore, he stated the view of his Government to be that bacterial weapons should be covered in "a comprehensive programme for the regulation, limitation and balanced reduction of all armed forces and armaments" and that such a program must be approached "from the point of view of preventing war and not from the point of view of regulating the armaments used in war or codifying the laws of war."[51]

The General Assembly again considered the question of regulation and limitation of armed forces and armaments in March 1953 during its seventh session. The Assembly had before it the report of the Disarmament Commission adopted on October 9, 1952, which covered the views and proposals that had been considered and the discussions on them. Statements made in the Assembly largely repeated the ideas that had been presented in the commission and brought out the same points of difference. The resolution the As-

[50] *Ibid.*, p. 144.
[51] *Ibid.*, p. 154.

sembly finally adopted took note of the report of the commission, requested that it report again not later than September 1, 1953, and expressed the hope that the members of the commission would co-operate "in efforts to produce constructive proposals likely to facilitate its task."[52] However, between the seventh and eighth sessions of the Assembly, the commission held only one meeting, on August 20, and that for the purpose of adopting its third report. In this it expressed the hope that recent international events[53] would create a more favorable atmosphere for the consideration of the disarmament question.

When the question was taken up by the Assembly in November 1953, during its eighth session, it was apparent that members generally were of the opinion that the ending of the hostilities in Korea and other indications of lessened international tension justified another major effort to resume the disarmament discussions. A draft resolution was submitted by fourteen members, including Canada, China, France, the United Kingdom, and the United States, and was considered at some length along with a number of proposed amendments. In the course of the discussion in the First Committee of the Assembly, the representative of France made suggestions along the lines of those made in the Disarmament Commission in the summer of 1952.

The General Assembly finally adopted a resolution on November 28, 1953 by a vote of 54 to 0, with the members of the Soviet bloc abstaining. This resolution reaffirmed the responsibility of the United Nations "for considering the problem of disarmament" and affirmed the need of providing for:

(a) The regulation, limitation and balanced reduction of all armed forces and armaments.

(b) The elimination and prohibition of atomic, hydrogen and other types of weapons of mass destruction.

(c) The effective international control of atomic energy to assure the prohibition of atomic weapons and the use of atomic energy for peaceful purposes only, the whole programme to be carried out under effective international control and in such a way that no State would have cause to fear that its security was endangered.[54]

The Assembly noted that progress in settling existing disputes was "vital to the attainment of peace and disarmament," that efforts to

[52] Res. 704 (VII), Apr. 8, 1953.
[53] The Korean armistice had been signed on July 27.
[54] Res. 715 (VIII), Nov. 28, 1953.

reach agreement on "a comprehensive and co-ordinated disarmament programme" should be made concurrently with progress in the settlement of international disputes, and that progress in one field could contribute to progress in the other. It recognized that competition in armaments "beyond what is necessary for the individual or collective security of Member States in accordance with the Charter of the United Nations is not only economically unsound but is in itself a grave danger to peace."

The Assembly also reaffirmed its earnest desire to reach agreement as early as possible on "a comprehensive and co-ordinated plan under international control for the regulation, limitation and reduction of all armed forces and armaments, for the elimination and prohibition of atomic, hydrogen, bacterial, chemical and all other weapons of war and mass destruction, and for the attainment of these ends through effective measures."[55] To this end, the Assembly requested the Disarmament Commission to continue its efforts to reach agreement on the problems before it, taking into consideration proposals made during the eighth session, and to report to it not later than September 1, 1954. It suggested that the commission study the desirability of establishing a subcommittee "consisting of the representatives of the powers principally involved, which should seek in private an acceptable solution, and report to the Disarmament Commission," and that this subcommittee hold its meetings "as appropriate in the different countries concerned with the problem."[56]

Meanwhile, in an effort to open up a fresh approach to the problem of international control of atomic energy, President Eisen-

[55] U.N. Doc. A./2562 (Nov. 20, 1953). Compare with corresponding provision of the Assembly resolution of Jan. 11, 1952 noted above.
[56] The Subcommittee of Five of the Disarmament Commission held 19 meetings in London from May 13 to June 22, 1954. For summary discussions, see U. S. Department of State, *The Record on Disarmament*, Publication 5581 (September 1954). See also United Nations, *Fourth Report of the Disarmament Commission*, U.N. Doc. DC/55 (July 29, 1954). A memorandum submitted by the United Kingdom and France on June 11 proposed a modification of earlier French proposals on the phasing and timing of a disarmament program. Although these suggestions were rejected by the Soviet Union at the time, later, when the subject of disarmament was again being considered by the General Assembly in its ninth session, the Soviet Union proposed that the Anglo-French proposals be accepted as a basis for further discussions by the Disarmament Commission. On November 4, a compromise resolution was unanimously adopted by the General Assembly requesting the Disarmament Commission to seek an acceptable solution of the problem before it, taking into account proposals made, and suggesting the reconvening of the Subcommittee of Five. *New York Times* (Nov. 5, 1954).

hower made a dramatic proposal to the General Assembly in the course of an address to it on December 8, 1953.[57] After calling attention to the fearful potentials of atomic and hydrogen weapons and reminding the Member states that the secrets of these weapons were no longer the monopoly of any one power, but were possessed by the Soviet Union as well as by the United States, the United Kingdom, and Canada, he announced that the United States Government was prepared, heeding the suggestion of the Assembly "to meet privately with such other countries as may be 'principally involved,' to seek 'an acceptable solution' to the atomic armaments race." He also proposed the establishment of an International Atomic Energy Agency, to which governments would contribute from "their stockpiles of normal uranium and fissionable materials," and the principal responsibility of which "would be to devise methods whereby this fissionable material would be allocated to serve the peaceful pursuits of mankind."[58]

[57] U. S. Department of State *Bulletin,* Vol. 29 (Dec. 21, 1953), pp. 847-51.

[58] This proposal was discussed through diplomatic channels during the months preceding the ninth session of the General Assembly in the autumn of 1954. In spite of basic differences in the approaches of the United States and the Soviet Union, unanimous agreement was reached in the Assembly on a resolution calling a technical conference to consider the matter. See U. S. Department of State *Bulletin,* Vol. XXXI (Dec. 13, 1954), p. 919.

CHAPTER XXII

Lessons of the United Nations Experience

T HE EFFORTS of the United Nations to regulate and reduce national armaments thus far have not been successful. National armed forces and armaments have been substantially increased both quantitatively and qualitatively during the past five years.

The experience of the United Nations has shown that efforts to develop a system for the international regulation of armaments encounter difficulties of both a political and a technical nature. Of these, the political difficulties have been the more important and the more decisive ones. In fact, it can be said that many of the so-called technical difficulties have a political motivation and would not arise in the absence of political factors. The Atomic Energy Commission concluded that there was nothing in the technological aspects of the problem of international control of atomic energy that stood in the way of the establishment of an effective system. The insurmountable difficulties were found to be political. Similarly, the discussions in the Commission for Conventional Armaments and the Disarmament Commission make it clear that political considerations were of paramount importance in explaining their failures.

The Political Obstacles to
Regulation of Armaments

A basic political obstacle is the general desire of states to achieve terms of armament limitation that will give them a favorable standing in power and prestige, especially in comparison with those states with which they are not on terms of mutual confidence. This, of course, is true of major powers whose interests are in conflict on many fronts and which have confidence in their ability, through their own strength and through special security arrangements, to maintain their prestige and power. The Soviet objection to the United States proposal for the international control of atomic energy was ostensibly based in part on unwillingness to accept inequality in atomic weapons with the United States during the period

573

when the system of international control was being set up and its effectiveness tested. On the other hand, the United States was unwilling to accept the repeated Soviet proposal for the immediate prohibition of atomic weapons and a one-third reduction in the armed forces and armaments of the permanent members of the Council partly because such a plan, if put into effect, would have placed the United States in a relatively less favorable power position and with no assurance that the Soviet Union would carry out its end of the bargain. One reason that the proposal for the numerical limitation of armed forces, which was jointly sponsored in 1952 by France, the United Kingdom, and the United States, received the support of the United States was that its acceptance by the Soviet Union would have required a greater proportional reduction of Soviet military strength, highly concentrated as it was in ground forces. The Soviet Union, on the other hand, professed to find the proposal unacceptable because it gave no assurance that a substantial reduction would be made in United States air and naval strength, particularly in the capacity of the United States to produce and deliver atomic bombs. Consequently, if the proposal were accepted, it would have had the effect in the Soviet view of altering the power relation between the Soviet Union and the Western powers in favor of the latter.

A second and closely related political obstacle to the international regulation and reduction of armaments is to be found in the divergent purposes, interests, and values of states. If the interests of states were always common ones, the problem of armament regulation, along with other international problems, would presumably present no great difficulties. But this unfortunately is not the case. Furthermore, it is not likely to be true of those states that, as the result of ample resources, great military strength, a militant ideology, or other factors, see the possibility or desirability of following independent policies and courses of action in the pursuit of particular objectives.

Since the Second World War, the Western powers, especially the United States, have gone far in identifying their purposes and values with those generally accepted by other nations, as has been evidenced by their participation in the United Nations and their cooperation in furthering its purposes and principles. The Soviet Union, on the other hand, largely because of the devotion of its leaders to Communist values and methods, has been unwilling to

co-operate in the furtherance of the purposes and principles of the
United Nations as those are understood by the Western democratic nations. Instead, it has pursued an essentially isolationist
course, characterized by distrust and obstruction, in efforts to achieve
its own purposes and advance its objectives.

The inability of the Soviet Union and the Western powers to agree
on the political reconstruction of areas occupied or controlled by
their armed forces at the close of the war or to adjust their mutual
power relations in these areas has been a special obstacle to agreement on the regulation of armaments. Although these powers had
agreed on the general principles to govern their action and future
relations in these areas, they soon found themselves at loggerheads
on the specific application of these principles. This was made clear
by the unwillingness of the Western powers to accept certain Soviet
dictated arrangements in Eastern Europe as definitive and by the
failure to agree on the future of Germany and Japan. These disagreements were hardly conducive to agreement on the regulation and
limitation of armed forces and armaments. Even the predictable consequences of atomic warfare have not caused the United States and
the Soviet Union to subordinate their differences to the common
purpose of preventing such a catastrophe.

Another political obstacle of considerable importance is the concept of national sovereignty and certain of its implications. Weaker
states may feel that for them the only alternative to intolerable insecurity and possible destruction is the creation of an international
authority that will be able to provide the protection and economic
benefits that by their own independent efforts they cannot hope to
achieve. Major powers, however, may regard the establishment of
such an authority as somewhat less urgent, especially if by participating in it they jeopardize the achievement of their particular objectives or subordinate unduly the functioning of their own political
and economic systems to decisions taken by others.

One reason the United States Government was willing to sponsor
the Baruch proposals for the international control of atomic energy
was that it believed that its interests would be adequately protected
under the provisions of the proposed plan. The conditions under
which the plan of control would be developed and the prohibition
of atomic weapons would finally become effective provided the
United States with an opportunity at successive stages to take deci-

sions protecting its own national interests. But it must be remembered that the plan was never submitted to Congress for its approval, and one can imagine strong opposition in that body to a plan that would have permitted inspectors representing the international authority, including Communist-controlled states, to travel freely in the United States and inspect military and industrial establishments.

The opposition of the Soviet Union to the control features of the atomic energy proposals made by the United States and the recommendations of the United Nations Atomic Energy Commission was ostensibly based in part on unwillingness to have an international agency over which it expected to have little effective control conduct important operations within Soviet territory, thereby allegedly seriously breaching the Soviet system of security and seriously endangering the independent development of its system of planned economy. In view of the irreconcilable objectives and motivations of the two principal world powers, it is difficult to see how either can agree to any important transference of sovereign powers to an international agency that it is not certain of controlling.

Role of the Security Council
and the General Assembly

By directing the Security Council to formulate plans for the regulation of armaments while authorizing the General Assembly to discuss "the general principles" governing disarmament and the regulation of armaments and to make recommendations to the Council and to Members, the Charter of the United Nations follows the experience of the League of Nations. Such a division of responsibility not only has historical precedent but also recognizes the special contribution that each organ is in the position to make by virtue of its composition and operating procedures.

Nevertheless, it must be recognized that principles cannot be divorced from actualities, and that consequently recommendations adopted by the Assembly by a two-thirds vote may, unless they are accepted by the major powers, have little value, except for the moral pressure they may exercise or the use they may have in furthering the interests of particular Member states. This has been recognized in the procedures of the Assembly, and special efforts have been made to obtain the agreement of the major powers in the preparation of resolutions. For example, in 1951 the First Committee of the Assembly created a subcommittee consisting of the President of the Assembly and representatives of France, the Soviet Union, the United Kingdom, and the United States to consider various proposals and to prepare an agreed draft of a resolution concerning armament regulation. Even the value of such an agreed draft may be illusive, however, if the agreement of the major powers is on the text of a resolution, the provisions of which are so phrased as to give the appearance of agreement without, however, resolving any of the basic conflicts. This is what happened in the first session of the General Assembly.

In view of the fact that no agreement has been reached among the major powers on any detailed plan for the international regulation of armaments, it is difficult to conclude that discussions and recommendations of the General Assembly have thus far made any appreciable contribution to the development of a system of international regulation of armaments. It must be recognized, however, that the Assembly may have made a contribution of some importance by giving expression to the widely held opinion that the consequences of an armament race and any war that may result therefrom are so serious that no effort should be spared to achieve international regulation and limitation of armaments and the easing of existing tensions. More specifically, the Assembly, by maintaining pressure on the major powers to come to some agreement, has conceivably helped to keep alive negotiations among them and thus has made it possible for full advantage to be taken of any favorable circumstance. There is no very satisfactory evidence up to the present, however, that this pressure has produced constructive results, although the repeated efforts of the major powers to achieve some measure of agreement in dealing with the disarmament problem may in some degree be due to the insistence of the Assembly that they keep talking. Some observers would indeed maintain that, inasmuch as political conditions have not been favorable to the reaching of any agreement, it would have been better if the matter had not been discussed at all, because under conditions that have prevailed, discussion may have served to sharpen differences and acerbate relations. In any case, they would maintain, discussion has been used for psychological warfare purposes more than for the purpose of achieving agreement on a program of disarmament.

Considering that an effective program for the regulation and limitation of armaments requires the participation of the major powers, especially the Soviet Union and the United States, the particular provisions of the Charter regarding the functions and procedures of organs for working out such a program would not appear to have critical importance. Although the dissent of the Soviet Union from proposals generally accepted by others has prevented any program from being put into operation, it does not seem that a useful result would be attained simply by amending the voting rules of the Security Council, by shifting formally the primary responsibility for preparing plans for the regulation of armaments from the Council to the Assembly, or by establishing a special organ to deal with disarmament matters. Even when the General Assembly has assumed a major role in the preparation of a program, it has found it necessary to recognize the special importance of co-operation and agreement among the major powers. If the key major powers are unwilling to co-operate in adopting and carrying out an agreed program under the Charter provisions as they stand, it does not appear likely that they will be willing to accept proposals that are prepared without their co-operation.

Principles and Methods of Armament Regulation

Discussions in, and decisions of, the General Assembly, the Security Council, and the subsidiary organs on the problem of the regulation of armaments have indicated general agreement on certain broad principles. These might be briefly summarized as follows: (1) there should be a full disclosure and verification of information on national armaments; (2) atomic weapons and other weapons of mass destruction should be prohibited; (3) other national armed forces and armaments should be limited and reduced to prevent excessive diversion of national resources, and to reduce tensions; (4) armed forces and armaments should be used only for the purposes and in accordance with the provisions of the Charter; (5) units of national armed forces and facilities should be made available to the Security Council by special agreement under Article 43 for use in accordance with the provisions of the Charter;[1] and (6) a system of international control should be established, including provision for inspection, to protect complying states against the dangers of noncompliance by other states. But once the discussions have gone beyond these generalities to the specific manner in which they are to

[1] See above, Chap. XVI.

be interpreted and applied and to the specific methods to be used to carry them out, insurmountable differences have appeared, especially between the Soviet Union and the United States. These differences have not proved susceptible of substantial alleviation by the methods of either public discussion or private conference, and it is difficult to conceive of any purely organizational or procedural device that will break the impasse.[2]

Disclosure and Verification

It is difficult to see how a system of international regulation of armaments can be developed without the disclosure, either preliminary to or as part of the basic agreement, of the size and character of national armed forces and armaments. The Covenant of the League of Nations required Members "to interchange full and frank information as to the scale of their armaments, their military, naval and air programs, and the condition of such of their industries as are adaptable to warlike purposes."[3] The information that Members made available was assembled in the *Armaments Yearbook,* a volume published annually by the Secretariat of the League.[4] With no means of checking the accuracy and completeness of information made available by Members, their good faith and self-interest provided the only assurance that they were living up to their obligations under the Covenant. Furthermore, important military powers were not Members of the League and, therefore, were under no obligation to report, and they did not do so.

No provision for reporting on armaments comparable to that in the Covenant was inserted in the Charter of the United Nations when it was written. Apparently, it was assumed that provision for such information would have to be included in any system later established for the regulation of national armaments, and from the very beginning of the discussions in the United Nations, efforts were made to achieve the disclosure of certain kinds of information. Under the conditions of distrust and tension that have existed since the war, however, the major powers have been unwilling to consent to the disclosure of information except on terms favorable to themselves.

[2] For analysis of differences that have arisen over the implementation of Art. 43 of the Charter, see above, Chap. XVI.

[3] Art. 8(6).

[4] The first volume was published in 1924 and the last in 1940. The information was drawn solely from official and public documents.

The policy of secrecy, based on the recognized value of keeping the enemy or the potential enemy in ignorance of one's capabilities and plans, has long been established military policy. Of the major powers, the Soviet Union has been most reluctant to accept detailed plans for the disclosure and verification of its armaments, in part because of its greater ability to keep information secret. The Western powers have had less to lose from disclosure and effective methods of verification because much information regarding the state of their armaments is publicly available owing to their governmental procedures, especially those that require parliamentary knowledge and approval of national defense plans and budgets.

The political context in which the problem of disclosure presents itself was indicated in the course of discussions and maneuvers during the second part of the first session of the General Assembly. The Soviet Union brought forward a proposal under which Member states would submit to the Secretary-General and to the Security Council information concerning (1) the points in the territory of states, not former enemies, at which armed forces of Member states were stationed and in what number; (2) the points in former enemy territories where such armed forces were stationed and in what number; and (3) the points in these territories where there were air and naval garrisons and the size of these garrisons. The declared purpose of this proposal was to assist in the implementation of Article 43. It was clear, however, that the real purpose of the Soviet Union was to embarrass the United States and the United Kingdom by drawing attention to forces and bases, maintained in such areas as North Africa, the Eastern Mediterranean, the Middle East, and China, as well as Germany and Japan, which the Soviet Union regarded as threats to its security and vital interests. The counterproposal made by the United States that the information cover all troops in active service throughout the world was not only logical in the context of the declared purpose of the Soviet proposal, but also served admirably the national interest of the United States in having as complete information as possible regarding the size of the Soviet military establishment. The reply of the Soviet Union that it would be willing to provide such information if extended to cover all armaments, including atomic weapons, could be logically justified as a prerequisite to the international regulation of armaments. In addition, the Soviet proposal admirably served the interest of the Soviet Union by requiring, if adopted, that information be given regarding the atomic weapons available to the United States at a time when the United States had a monopoly of them and when this monopoly was viewed as a serious threat to Soviet interests. To this, the rejoinder of the Western nations was that such general disclosure could only be agreed to as part of a comprehensive system of collective security. The resolution the Assembly finally adopted[5] resolved nothing in that it simply called upon the Security Council "to determine, as soon as possible, the information which the States Members of the United Nations should be called upon to furnish" in order to give effect to the resolution on general principles governing the regulation and reduction of armaments.[6]

The characteristic attitudes of the major nations toward proposals for the disclosure of armament information were further illustrated during the consideration of the problem of atomic energy control. The Soviet Union insisted on full and immediate exchange of information regarding atomic weapons and the development of atomic energy, while the United States, with the support of the great majority of United Nations Members, insisted that, until an international control system was in effective operation, there should not be any exchange, except as might be necessary for the establishment of such a system. The suggestion, approved by the Assembly in 1948, that the Commission on Conventional Armaments should devote its first attention to formulating proposals "for the receipt, checking and publication . . . of full information to be supplied by Member States with regard to their effectives and their conventional armaments"[7] was strongly opposed by the Soviet Union. In resisting the plan proposed by the French representative on the commission for carrying out this directive, the Soviet representative argued that it set unnecessary preliminary conditions for the reduction of armaments and armed forces, and furthermore avoided the issue of disclosure of information regarding atomic weapons.

The scope of disclosure is not the only aspect of the problem on which there has been disagreement. There has also been disagreement on the timing of disclosure, and the relation of disclosure to the establishment of effective arrangments for checking on the accuracy of the information disclosed and for providing other safeguards to national security that would take the place of advantages

[5] Res. 42(I), Dec. 14, 1946.
[6] Res. 41 (I), Dec. 14, 1946.
[7] Res. 192 (III), Nov. 19, 1948.

relinquished as the result of disclosure. The position consistently taken by the United States has been that full disclosure of information regarding armaments should accompany or follow the establishment of an effective system of control. The Soviet position has been that full information should be immediately disclosed, the good faith of states being relied on to ensure compliance with the undertaking. Although the Soviet Union has professed not to be opposed to the establishment of a control system, it has maintained that the full disclosure of armament information alone would improve relations among the great powers and facilitate the taking of further steps.

The debate over disclosure and verification was revived in the sixth session of the General Assembly and in the Disarmament Commission, following the submission by the United States in 1952, first, of a plan of work that gave priority to the progressive and continuing disclosure and verification of armed forces and armaments, and then of specific proposals for such disclosure and verification. The Soviet representative objected not to the fact that all information would not be immediately disclosed, but rather to the proposed system of priorities and stages, which would in his opinion result in the disclosure of information about Soviet ground forces before the United States disclosed information about its secret weapons, especially atomic weapons. Thus the impasse remained and continued into 1954.[8]

Prohibition of Certain Weapons and Methods of Warfare

In their efforts to develop a system for international regulation of armaments, the Members of the United Nations have been in agreement that certain weapons and methods of warfare should be prohibited, although they have been unable to agree on the detailed implementation of the principle. Efforts along this line have an extensive historical background. The Declaration of St. Petersburg of 1868 prohibited the use of explosive bullets weighing less than 400 grams. At the Hague Conference of 1899, declarations were adopted prohibiting the use of expanding bullets, the launching of projectiles and explosives from balloons, and the use of projectiles diffusing asphyxiating or deleterious gases. The Washington Conference

---

[8] It does not appear that the Soviet Union has modified its position in agreeing to accept the Anglo-French proposal of June 11, 1954, as a basis for drafting an international treaty.

of 1921-22 attempted unsuccessfully to achieve the prohibition of the use of the submarine and noxious gases. The Geneva Protocol of June 17, 1925, prohibited the use in war of asphyxiating, poisonous, or other gases, and of bacteriological methods of warfare. However, the record of compliance with such prohibitions as have been made legally operative has not been good. Under pressure of military necessity, good faith has proved a weak guarantee. During the First World War, both sides practiced gas warfare. During the Second World War, the belligerents abstained from its use, but it can be argued that this was primarily because neither side saw the possibility of gaining any decisive military advantage thereby.

Since the Second World War, and after experience with the use of the atomic bomb at Hiroshima and Nagasaki gave conclusive proof of the destructive force of atomic weapons, there has been general agreement among Members of the United Nations that the use of atomic weapons and other weapons of mass destruction should be prohibited. There has been some difficulty, however, in defining what is meant by weapons of mass destruction, and this difficulty has been greatly increased by the development of tactical atomic weapons. When the Commission for Conventional Armaments decided in 1947 to exclude atomic and other weapons of mass destruction from its consideration, the Soviet Union objected primarily on the ground that the separation thus made between these weapons and those of a more conventional nature was artificial. Later, when a proposal was made to define weapons of mass destruction as including "atomic explosive weapons, radioactive material weapons, lethal chemical and biological weapons, and any weapons developed in the future which have characteristics comparable in destructive effect to those of the atomic bomb or other weapons mentioned above," the Soviet Union objected to the definition as being too restrictive.[9]

The question of a definition was considered again in April 1952 in Committee 1 of the Disarmament Commission. The French representative pointed out that any conventional weapon, if used extensively, could be termed a weapon of mass destruction. He raised the question whether the characterization should be limited to a weapon "which produces a mass effect even with a single weapon."[10] He raised the further question whether the problem of humanizing war

---

[9] U.N. Doc. S/C.3/24 (July 28, 1948).

[10] U.N. Disarmament Commission, Committee 1, *Official Records*, 1st Meeting (Apr. 4, 1952), p. 7.

should be taken into account, which apparently had been a major consideration in determining weapons and methods of warfare to be prohibited in the years before the Second World War. He suggested that "weapons of mass destruction" might be defined as "those capable of destroying at one blow a number of human lives considerably higher, according to a ratio to be determined, than the number destroyed by conventional weapons when used singly" or as "those which dispose of the enemy otherwise than by the effect of metal or of explosives."[11]

The practicability of prohibiting the use of weapons of mass destruction is open to serious question. This has become increasingly true as science has developed the possibilities of adapting the destructive forces of atomic energy to tactical as well as strategic uses, for the development of tactical atomic weapons makes it more difficult to draw the line between weapons to be outlawed and those to be permitted. If nations go to war and men fight to kill, it is difficult to regulate the manner of killing or to give legal or moral justification to some forms of killing and not to others. When success in war is dependent on advanced technology and a complex industrial base, belligerents will not abstain from striking at the industrial and technological foundations of the strength of the enemy. The mass killings of civilians is an inevitable by-product, even if it is not used as a means of terrorization.

There is, of course, an additional difficulty in the way of prohibiting weapons of mass destruction. The experience of the United Nations has shown that the great majority of the Members are unwilling to accept the simple legal prohibition of the manufacture, possession, and use of such weapons without extensive safeguards for the purpose of protecting complying states. Because of the nature of certain of these weapons and the circumstances surrounding their production, these safeguards must, to be effective, encroach deeply on the domestic jurisdiction of states as that jurisdiction has been defined in the past. They can have important effects on the internal economy and political life of states, as well as on power relations. Efforts to reach agreement on a plan of atomic energy control showed the improbability of any agreement between the Soviet

[11] By its resolution of Nov. 28, 1953, the General Assembly affirmed its desire to eliminate and prohibit "atomic, hydrogen, bacterial, chemical and all such other weapons of war and mass destruction."

Union and the major Western nations. The United States has made clear that it will not be a party to the simple and unconditional outlawry of atomic and other weapons of mass destruction without adequate protection for a complying state against the dangers of noncompliance on the part of other states. Safeguards that the United States and the other Western powers consider necessary are claimed by the Soviet Union to constitute unwarranted interference in its domestic affairs.

Acknowledging the difficulties in the way of a completely effective plan for prohibiting the use of weapons of mass destruction, it can be argued that there is nevertheless an advantage in having an agreement not to use certain weapons especially in view of the devastating power of modern atomic and hydrogen weapons. It may be contended that, with agreement on the prohibition of the more destructive weapons, there will be a decline in fear, a better chance of constructive co-operation between states, and an improvement in political relations between the major protagonists in the cold war. Such agreement might help, moreover, to re-enforce a factual situation in which neither contending belligerent in war sees an advantage in the use of weapons of mass destruction, and to establish a general standard of conduct that each party would be expected to respect. However, it should be borne in mind that an agreement not to use certain particularly destructive weapons that is not a part of a general disarmament program may actually encourage a state with aggressive tendencies to go to war just because it feels secure from immediate attack by such weapons.

It is not to be assumed, of course, that, in the absence of an agreement prohibiting certain weapons and methods of warfare, these will necessarily be used in time of war. Without an agreement, it may happen in certain circumstances, as during the fighting in Korea, that neither side will see any over-all advantage in the use of certain weapons or methods of indiscriminate destruction, considering the possibilities of retaliation, the limited objectives being sought, and the possible unfavorable impact on world opinion. These considerations give support to the belief, entertained by some, that the possession of thermonuclear weapons by both the Soviet Union and the Western nations is, in the present disturbed state of the world, the greatest deterrent that exists to another world war. Whether this is true remains to be seen.

Methods of Limitation and Reduction

Any complete system for the regulation of national armaments requires the limitation of permitted armaments at agreed levels. These levels may or may not involve reduction in national armaments, although such reduction is commonly considered desirable. The question of methods is essentially a technical one, but it may come to have important political implications. Past experience, going back to the end of the First World War, would seem to indicate that when there is a real agreement at the political level to limit national armaments, the experts are able to agree on technical methods for its implementation. If, however, the agreement on limitation is in principle only and does not follow, or is not accompanied by, an accommodation of conflicting interests and policies, the question of methods becomes of the greatest political importance because the choices made may seriously affect the power positions and negotiating strength of the parties.

These conclusions are supported by the experience of the United Nations. In the absence of understandings among the major powers on their future political relations, their technicians have never been allowed to consider the methods of limitation in purely technical terms. In so far as the matter has been considered, possible power advantages have been a major concern. Thus the Soviet proposal in 1948 to reduce the land, naval, and air forces of the permanent members of the Security Council by one-third within a year was in effect an attempt to freeze the ratios of the major nations in all categories of armaments at a time when the relative power position of the Soviet Union was favorable. Apart from practical difficulties in carrying it out, the Soviet proposal would have permitted the Soviet Union to maintain the superiority of its land armies in Europe, while the Western powers would have been prevented from building up the military strength of their ground forces.

On the other hand, the proposal submitted to the Disarmament Commission by the United States, the United Kingdom, and France in May 1952, that provided for the over-all numerical limitation of armed forces, was clearly intended to achieve a balanced power relationship among the major nations that would reduce the advantage enjoyed by the Soviet Union and Communist China in ground forces and would make less likely any aggressive military attack by them. Earlier Soviet support of the principles of budgetary limitation and the limitation of the production of war materials reflected Soviet awareness of the greater technological development and war potential of the United States and the other Western nations.

During discussions in the United Nations, considerable attention of necessity has been given to factors entering into the determination of national levels. In the discussions of the Military Staff Committee and the Security Council on the principles that should govern the conclusion of military agreements under Article 43 of the Charter, the United States took the position that the military contributions of the permanent members of the Council should be determined by the ability of each to contribute to the United Nations force, while the Soviet Union insisted on applying the principle of absolute equality. The plan proposed in May 1952 by the United States, the United Kingdom, and France in the Disarmament Commission for the establishment of numerical limitations on the size of armed forces, contained the following comment on factors to be taken into account in determining national levels:

In fixing numerical limitations on the armed forces of States a number of factors, demographic, geographic, political and economic, have to be considered. The Charter responsibilities of States and the need of balanced power-relationships among States must also be taken into account. There is no one automatic formula which can inflexibly be applied in all cases. The objective must be to reduce the possibility and the fear of successful aggression and to avoid a disequilibrium of power dangerous to international peace and security.[12]

In the proposal submitted to Committee 1 of the Disarmament Commission on April 24, 1952, on principles governing a disarmament program, the United States stressed what might be called the functional approach to the determination of maximum national levels. It suggested that armed forces and armaments be reduced to levels necessary for "the maintenance of internal security," and the "fulfillment of obligations of States to maintain peace and security in accordance with the United Nations Charter."[13] This functional approach was developed in greater detail in some observations made by the French representative at an earlier meeting of the committee when he listed the following factors that needed to be taken into account:

[12] U.N. Disarmament Commission, *Official Records*, Special Supplement No. 1, p. 101.

[13] *Ibid.*, p. 63.

(i) The police units required for the security of the home country;

(ii) The units required for the security of the dependent territories of every State, geographically separated from that State and therefore involving problems of sending various reinforcements;

(iii) The forces to be kept in reserve for the two purposes just mentioned, in case of tension;

(iv) The forces to be placed at the disposal of the United Nations.[14]

From the discussions that have taken place in the United Nations, it is clear that the functional approach to the definition of national levels encounters the same difficulties as the League of Nations encountered. Agreement might be reached on the requirements of internal security, although the relatively greater demands of a police state would undoubtedly present serious difficulties. If agreements were concluded under Article 43, they would determine the minimum forces necessary to discharge United Nations obligations. Even on the assumption, a very large one indeed, that these two determinations are made, there would still remain the problem of determining what armed forces and armaments a Member needs for purposes of "individual and collective self-defense" under Article 51 and for the exceptional purposes specified in Article 53. Until the United Nations collective security system has developed the effectiveness that its authors envisaged, the forces necessary to satisfy the needs of major powers resulting from these exceptions to the "primary responsibility" of the Security Council will be as illusive and difficult to define in generally acceptable quantitative terms, as were the needs of France, for example, in the disarmament discussions of the League of Nations.

The Organization of Safeguards

A major obstacle to obtaining agreement on a program for the regulation and reduction of armaments has been the organization of adequate safeguards for complying states against the consequences of noncompliance by other states. This problem is of great importance and difficulty because the obligations that states must assume relate to vital matters of their national security. Generally speaking, states, in entering into international commitments, are willing, if only because no other guarantees are readily avail-

---

[14] U.N. Disarmament Commission, Committee 1, *Official Records*, 1st Meeting (Apr. 4, 1952), p. 10.

able, to rely on the good faith of other contracting parties so long as the agreement does not affect their national security too directly and possibilities exist of effective counteraction in case of noncompliance. But when it is a matter of providing for the security of the state against possible attack, governments have not usually been willing in the past to rely on paper guarantees or to put themselves in the position where they cannot, by readily available means, take such measures as they may consider necessary for their own defense. In the discussions in the United Nations, the United States and the other Western powers have taken the position that they are unwilling to rely on the good faith of the Soviet Union as a guarantee of compliance with agreements for the regulation and limitation of armaments.

The problem of organizing safeguards against the risks of noncompliance and evasion has been considered at great length in the United Nations. It has been discussed in connection with efforts to develop an effective system of international control of atomic energy and during consideration of principles governing the limitation and reduction of armaments in general and of conventional armaments in particular. The major aspects of the problem have been given special attention in the course of the discussions on control of atomic energy because: (1) the consequences of noncompliance with an agreement for the international control of atomic energy are likely to be more serious than those resulting from noncompliance with an agreement for the limitation of conventional armaments; and (2) up to a fairly advanced stage, the processes of producing atomic weapons and developing atomic energy for peaceful purposes are identical, thus creating many technical difficulties in operating any effective system of international control.

There are many possible safeguards that can be used to protect complying states. Discussions in the United Nations have been chiefly concerned with those methods that involve the establishment of an international agency or agencies with defined functions and powers. These functions and powers may include ownership of materials and facilities, management, supervision, licensing, leasing, inspection, determination of violations, and enforcement of penalties. Which of these safeguards are deemed necessary and in what combination depend in large part on the particular situation. To provide adequate safeguards against violation of an agreement not to produce, possess, or use atomic weapons, the whole range of possible safeguards has been considered necessary by the majority of United Nations Members. On the other hand, in the case of an agreement to limit naval armaments, a smaller number of safeguards might be considered as providing adequate protection.

The experience of the United Nations has shown, however, that the problem of organizing safeguards is one that cannot be handled solely on a technical level. The Atomic Energy Commission, for example, concluded that there was no reason to believe that a system of international control that would ensure the use of atomic energy solely for peaceful purposes was not technically feasible, but the Soviet Union took the view that the whole matter was essentially political. No doubt with the further development of atomic weapons, by the Soviet Union as well as by the United States, especially the hydrogen bomb and tactical atomic weapons, the technical aspects of international control have become more difficult and perhaps incapable of being handled with the same degree of assurance.

The problem of organizing safeguards has assumed two major aspects: (1) the establishment of the functions, powers, composition, and procedure of the control machinery; and (2) the timing or phasing of limitations and reductions of armed forces and armaments in relation to control arrangements. The experience of the United Nations indicates that the first presents the greater difficulty, perhaps only because agreement on the second is devoid of all practical significance without agreement on the machinery to be used.

Machinery of International Control

From the beginning, the position of the United States, supported in most respects by the other Western powers and the great majority of the Members of the United Nations, has been that an international control authority should be set up under the terms of the agreement for the limitation of armaments, and that such an authority should have substantial powers and be so constituted that it could function without the possibility of a veto by any state violating the terms of the agreement. Thus the United States originally proposed the establishment of an atomic energy authority, with powers of ownership, management, supervision, and inspection, and insisted that the authority should be able to make important decisions with respect to the determination of violations and of the measures to be taken without the possibility of a veto being exercised. Although recognizing that the principle of concurrence of the permanent members should continue to govern the substantive decisions of the Security Council, the United States argued that a special authority whose decisions would not be subject to the veto could be set up by agreement of the Members of the United Nations without in any way violating the terms of the Charter.

Later, when discussion of the problem of controlling atomic energy was merged with the consideration of other aspects of the problem of regulating armaments, the United States continued to insist on the establishment of an effective international control organ as an essential part of any program of armament regulation, but it was slow in advancing detailed suggestions for the constitution of such an authority.[15] The position of the United States appears to have been that the control organ should have important substantive powers, including the authority to carry out detailed on-the-spot inspections; to determine the details of the time and manner of reducing armed forces and armaments; to exercise a wide range of powers of the order suggested in the original United States proposals for the regulation of atomic energy; to determine violations of the disarmament agreement; and to order remedial measures, especially in case of any violation of the provisions of a treaty for the control of atomic energy. In case of the failure of a party to the treaty to take remedial action as prescribed by the authority, the authority would have the power to report the violation to the Security Council, the General Assembly, and to all other states. The authority, like the Disarmament Commission, would be composed of the members of the Security Council plus Canada and would be able to take decisions by a majority vote.

On the other hand, the Soviet Union, although agreeing in principle to the establishment of an international control authority, has favored granting the authority fewer powers and less independence of action. To begin with, it has insisted that the authority must be set up under the Security Council, which means that except as the parties to the treaty might give the authority power to exercise functions and to take decisions by a voting procedure other than that prescribed for the Security Council, the authority would be subject

---

[15] The United States representative submitted a working paper on the powers and constitution of such an organ during the meetings of the Subcommittee of Five of the Disarmament Commission in London, May 13 to June 22, 1954. For text of proposals, see U.N. Doc. DC/SC.1/5 (May 24, 1954); U.S. Department of State *Bulletin*, Vol. 31 (Aug. 2, 1954), pp. 179-81.

to the continuing control of the Council with the right of veto left intact. Furthermore, the Soviet Union has been unwilling to give the proposed authority any powers that would permit it or its instrumentalities to conduct independent operations within the territory of any state. The Soviet Union has accepted the principle of inspection on a continuing basis, but it has insisted that inspection be conducted without interference in the domestic affairs of states. The Soviet Union also has agreed that the control authority should supervise the observance of obligations, but has insisted that it do so by prescribing regulations and receiving and verifying reports by governments. Although the Soviet Union is willing to allow the authority to report and make recommendations to the Security Council, it is still unwilling to allow the authority itself to decide that violations have been committed and to order remedial measures.

Any attempt to harmonize these two approaches immediately runs up against the fundamental obstacle to agreement, the lack of mutual trust resulting from the irreconcilability of objectives, motivations, and methods, and the consequent difficulty of developing a field of common interest between the Soviet Union and the Western powers. The United States and the other Western powers are not prepared to rely on the good faith of the Soviet Union as a guarantee of compliance with its undertakings under a disarmament treaty, and consequently attach very little value to a control system that would be dependent for its effectiveness on Soviet good faith and co-operation. The Soviet Union, on the other hand, objects to a control system that would subject its acts and decisions in the field of security, and perhaps of economic development, to the control of an authority in which the Soviet Union believes it would be consistently outvoted on critical issues by those states whose interests and objectives are deemed inimical to those of the Soviet Union. It is difficult, therefore, to see what basis there is for compromise so long as relations between the Western powers and the Soviet Union continue on a "cold war" basis. An essential condition for the establishment of control machinery such as the Western powers demand is a substantive improvement in their relations with the Soviet Union that would provide the basis for a measure of mutual confidence. Paradoxically, once this improvement has taken place, the need for a control organ with such extensive authority as the Western powers now demand would not seem as great.

Phasing of Reduction and Control

An important question that has come up in the course of disarmament discussions has been the time relation between the setting up of effective controls and the carrying out of prescribed limitations, reductions, and prohibitions. Initially, the position of the United States was that the control system had to be in effective operation before the United States would give up the right to use atomic weapons, but in order that the control system could be set up, the United States was prepared progressively to give information and to submit to limitations necessary to implementing the whole plan by stages. The Soviet Union, on the other hand, insisted that prohibition must come first. It later agreed, however, that controls and prohibitions might become operative simultaneously, but the controls it found acceptable were not of the inclusive nature proposed by the United States.

Since the first discussions on the control of atomic energy, both major powers have moved considerable distances from their initial positions, and especially since the merging of the discussions on atomic energy and on conventional weapons there has appeared to be a narrowing of their differences. The program proposed by the United States, France, and the United Kingdom for carrying out limitation and reduction by stages was initially turned down by the Soviet Union allegedly because such a program postponed any real reduction of armaments. Later, however, the Soviet Union accepted as a basis for discussion an Anglo-French proposal for the phasing of steps in the reduction of armaments with the operations of the control authority.[16] This would suggest that the phasing problem may not be insoluble if agreement can be reached on the nature of the international control machinery, the levels of national armed forces and armaments to be allowed, and the weapons to be prohibited.

The Role of Armament Regulation in the Maintenance of Peace and Security

Past efforts to limit and reduce national armaments by international agreement have not produced encouraging results. Success has

[16] Proposal of June 11, 1954 in the Subcommittee of Five of the Disarmament Commission.

been achieved only in those instances where it has been possible for the nations involved to put their political relations on such a basis as to inspire mutual trust and confidence. The efforts of the United Nations thus far have fallen into the pattern of the past.

Does the development of weapons of destructive power hitherto unimagined alter the problem? Many think that it does. Nevertheless, it must be remembered that efforts in the past to achieve the limitation of armaments have also been made under the shadow of impending doom but without significant results. Furthermore, the development of the atomic bomb and the hydrogen bomb does not appear thus far to have made the major contestants in the cold war more willing to yield on the critical points that divide them in the disarmament discussions. It may be concluded that, although the development of new weapons has undoubtedly increased the urgency of effective action to prevent war, there is as yet no evidence that it has made governments more willing than formerly to give up any means of military action available to them that are considered necessary to the defense of vital national interests.

Although experience may suggest that there is little prospect of obtaining a general agreement on the regulation of national armaments in the absence of some improvement in the relations between the major powers, efforts to achieve a system of armament regulation should not necessarily be postponed until improvement is a fact. Such efforts may be one of many possible avenues to better understanding and closer co-operation among states. All avenues need to be explored, the difficulties in the way of agreement illuminated, and the alternatives clarified. Despite the unlikelihood that general agreement on the limitation and reduction of armaments can be achieved in isolation by what has been called the "direct" approach, some progress might be made by such efforts as part of a broad diplomatic attack on the many issues of tension that divide nations. The point to be emphasized is that the problem is essentially one of political adjustment, and although organs and procedures have their contributions to make, no quick or easy solution can be achieved by mechanical devices alone.

PART SIX

CONCLUSIONS

CHAPTER XXIII
Summary and Evaluation

T HE Charter of the United Nations reflected the desires
of its founders when it declared the primary purpose of the new
Organization to be the maintenance of international peace and
security. In the atmosphere prevailing toward the end of the Second
World War, the establishment of an international system for that
declared purpose seemed to be the foundation stone on which progress in the solution of all other international problems had to be
based. Without such a system, it appeared that little could be done
to improve the economic and social conditions of the peoples of the
world, to encourage wider respect for human rights and fundamental freedoms, and to assist the peoples of non-self-governing territories in achieving a larger measure of independence or self-
government.

The United Nations as an organization for the maintenance of international peace and security is a system of agreed procedures for
the peaceful settlement or adjustment of disputes and situations,
for the use of collective measures in dealing with threats to or
breaches of the peace, and for the development of arrangements for
the regulation of national armaments. The United Nations is fundamentally a voluntary association of states, with a set of organs and
procedures through which its Member states have agreed to co-operate, under stated conditions, for common purposes. Like the League
of Nations before it, the essence of the United Nations is that techniques previously used in international relations—the concert of
powers, the international conference, peaceful methods of settling
disputes—have been institutionalized and made part of the established and recognized process of conducting international affairs.

A comparison of the provisions of the Charter of the United Nations with the Covenant and practices of the League of Nations
clearly indicates that those who formulated the Charter drew heavily
on the experience of the League, and the Organization they planned
was, in fact, modeled in important respects on the League. The

United Nations, however, contained many features that were believed to represent a more realistic approach to the problem of
maintaining international peace and security. Most important of all,
an attempt was made in planning the United Nations to harness
responsibility to power and, therefore, to avoid the frustrating experience of the League of Nations in its efforts to achieve a purpose
beyond its resources. Furthermore, by emphasizing the political
rather than the legal approach to the problem, the planners of the
Charter reversed the emphasis in the Covenant of the League and
reverted to the practice of the nineteenth century, under which the
concert of powers—using extensive discretion in the choice and application of means—achieved considerable success in maintaining
international peace and security.

The nearly ten years of experience with the functioning of the
United Nations have now provided a basis for determining how
effective the new Organization has been as a means of achieving its
declared purpose of maintaining international peace and security.
A number of questions may be raised: To what extent does the
actual record of the United Nations justify the high confidence
that was placed in it, particularly in the United States, at the time
of its founding? What has the United Nations as an organization for
the maintenance of international peace and security come to be in
practice? How can it be made more effective as an important and
widely accepted means of preserving and strengthening international
peace and security?

Purposes and Principles of the United Nations

The purposes and principles set forth in Articles 1 and 2 of the
Charter have been of fundamental importance in the functioning of
the United Nations as an organization for the maintenance of international peace and security. This was anticipated by those who wrote
the Charter, for quite clearly they intended that these purposes and
principles should serve not only as limitations on the organs and
Members of the United Nations but also as a basis for developing
and expanding the activities of the Organization and for indicating
the general direction and scope of the co-operative efforts of its
Members.

Because it has been necessary to adapt the methods and processes
of the United Nations to the conditions existing in the postwar

world, especially the conflict between the Western powers and the Soviet Union, increased reliance has been placed on the purposes and principles as a basis for action. Had there been co-operation among the major powers, the detailed provisions of the Charter regarding the functions and powers of the Security Council would no doubt have been an adequate basis for United Nations action to maintain international peace and security. When, however, with the growing inability of the Council to act it seemed desirable to make greater use of the Assembly, Articles 1 and 2 of the Charter came to play an increasingly important role. Articles 10 and 14 provided the basis for the development of the role of the Assembly in the field of peace and security, because these articles empower the Assembly to discuss questions relating to the purposes and principles of the Organization and to make recommendations on them.

The purposes and principles have affected the functioning of the Organization in still another respect. There has been a definite tendency on the part of the principal organs, especially of the Security Council, to adopt and justify a particular course of action in terms of its effective contribution to advancing the purposes and principles of the Organization rather than on the ground that the action is in accordance with the detailed provisions of the Charter governing the powers and functions of the particular organ. Thus, in dealing with disputes and situations, the Security Council in practice has not considered itself rigidly bound by the detailed provisions of Chapters VI and VII of the Charter regarding the course of action to be followed. Rather the Council has adapted its course to the circumstances of each case, and in doing so, has been primarily concerned with bringing about "by peaceful means" the "adjustment or settlement" of particular disputes or situations, and with the taking of "effective collective measures for the prevention and removal of threats to the peace, and for the suppression of acts of aggression or other breaches of the peace."

Although the net effect of including "Purposes and Principles" in the Charter has been to provide a greater flexibility in adapting and expanding the activities of the United Nations, certain principles, especially Article 2(1), which asserts the sovereign equality of the Member states and Article 2(7), which protects their domestic jurisdiction, were intended to be limitations on the activities of the Organization. In practice, however, it is doubtful that they have produced this result to any appreciable extent. The principle of sovereign equality of Member states has been occasionally invoked. However, it is questionable whether the explicit statement of the principle in the Charter has had any far-reaching effects on the functioning of the Organization. The situation is much more complicated, however, with regard to the domestic jurisdiction principle.

There has been much confusion and lack of agreement regarding both the manner in which the principle of domestic jurisdiction should be invoked and the interpretation to be given to it. Neither the political organs of the United Nations nor the majority of the Member states have regarded the principle as a legal one to be interpreted by the International Court of Justice or by some other body of qualified jurists. The prevailing view in the Security Council and the General Assembly has been that the competence of the organs of the United Nations to deal with questions should be liberally interpreted and, consequently, that the principle of domestic jurisdiction should not be so construed as to prevent discussion in, or the adoption of a resolution by, an organ when such action might contribute to furthering the declared purposes of the United Nations. In those instances in which an organ has decided that a particular dispute or situation should not be discussed or that a proposed resolution should not be adopted, it has been usually because the contemplated action was deemed unwise or inexpedient rather than because the principle of domestic jurisdiction was considered applicable. Nevertheless, it is probably true that, because the principle is explicitly recognized in the Charter, many Member states have been encouraged to deny the right of the United Nations to take a particular course of action, or actively to resist the decision to take such a course.

The influence of the purposes and principles set forth in the Charter has by no means been limited to the United Nations, its organs, and the actions of Members within these organs. Quite clearly, their influence has extended over the whole range of policies and attitudes the Member states have adopted in their international relations. Although the degree of this influence may be debatable—and certainly would not be the same for all Members—there is no denying that governments frequently seek to justify their policies and courses of action in terms of the purposes and principles in the Charter. There may be profound disagreement over the interpretation to be given to the words in the Charter, but it is a fact of considerable importance that governments generally find it disadvantageous, if

not dangerous, to appear, either before their own people or before
the world, as openly hostile to the purposes and principles for which
the United Nations stands. The necessity of justifying national
policies and attitudes in terms of the Charter in all likelihood has
had a significant effect on the policies themselves.

Role of the United Nations in the Maintenance of International Peace and Security

When the Charter was being drafted, it was assumed that the postwar task of the United Nations in maintaining international peace
and security would be carried out within the framework of a world
order that would be largely based on the peace settlements to be
concluded at the end of the Second World War. The making of these
settlements was deemed to be the responsibility of the powers that had
played a major role in winning the war. It was assumed that these
powers would find it in their interest to co-operate in concluding
peace treaties, and that they would have a like interest in co-operating
through the United Nations in maintaining the peace they had
gained as military allies.

The co-operation among the major allies that was necessary for
making the peace settlements never materialized. Even before the
ending of hostilities, dissension over the terms of peace arose
and in threatening form, between the United States and the United
Kingdom on the one hand, and the Soviet Union on the other. Problems arising from the defeat of Germany and Japan, the major Axis
powers, remained unresolved and were the source of suspicion and
fear. With few exceptions, these problems have not been submitted
to the United Nations but have been dealt with by the traditional
methods of diplomacy, supplemented by modern techniques of psychological warfare.

The United Nations nevertheless has been called upon to consider
many problems affecting relations between the Soviet Union and the
Western powers. For the most part, however, these have been peripheral to the main areas of conflict. When states have brought such
problems before the Organization, they generally have regarded
possible action by the United Nations as a useful and valuable, but
not a decisive, supplement to their own efforts. It would, for example,
be misleading to assert that United Nations action in Greece determined the final outcome. And although the United States might

have taken military action in defense of the Republic of Korea in the absence of the United Nations, it is quite unlikely that, without the strong initiative on the part of the United States, the Members of the United Nations would have taken collective action. In these two cases, however, the action, in which the United States played a leading role, was more acceptable to other governments, received more general support, and was more effective as a result of having been taken within the framework of the United Nations.

In a number of cases, an appeal has been made to the United Nations solely for the purpose of mobilizing public sentiment and gaining some propaganda advantage. It could hardly have been expected, for example, that bringing before the General Assembly the complaints regarding the violation of human rights and fundamental freedoms in Bulgaria, Hungary, and Rumania would have any immediate effect in achieving greater respect for the treaty provisions in question. But these complaints publicized certain practices being followed by the accused states and were thought to serve the purposes of the free world in the cold war. The Soviet Union has used the forums of the United Nations in a somewhat similar manner for publicizing its charges against the Western powers. It is open to question, however, whether the submission of any of these matters to the United Nations has contributed to the maintenance of international peace and security.

But, although the role of the United Nations in dealing with the problems of the cold war has been limited and secondary, the United Nations has played a leading and significant part in facilitating the political adjustments that have had to be made as a result of the emergence of nationalism in Asia and Africa, and the demands of the peoples of these continents for political and racial equality. The Security Council had an important role in bringing to an end the hostilities in Palestine, in Kashmir, and in Indonesia and in achieving a political settlement in the latter case that opened the way to Indonesian independence. The General Assembly has provided the forum where representatives of the Asian and African countries have been able to plead the cause of the native peoples of Asia and Africa for equal and fair treatment, and where in specific cases they have been able to press claims for concrete steps toward independence and equality. The United Nations has not always been able to work out mutually acceptable accommodations of the conflicting interests and demands, but the availability of such a forum for mobilizing opinion and exercising political pressure has served to some extent to lessen tensions and to encourage the use of peaceful procedures instead of methods of violence.

The availability of the United Nations has not, however, precluded the use of other means for seeking a settlement of questions involving relations between the more advanced Western powers and the Asian and African peoples aspiring to independence and equality. For example, the disputes between the United Kingdom and Iran over petroleum rights and between the United Kingdom and Egypt over the Sudan and the Suez Canal, both of which were considered inconclusively by the Security Council, have been settled through regular diplomatic channels. The Indochinese question was never brought to the United Nations for settlement, and armed hostilities were finally brought to an end by agreements concluded after negotiations among the parties principally involved.

The importance of the United Nations in the maintenance of international peace and security cannot be considered, however, only in terms of the questions it has discussed, the recommendations it has made, or the extent of compliance with such recommendations. There is, of course, no way of measuring the influence that action by the United Nations has had on the policies followed by states outside the framework of the United Nations. Nor can one more than speculate regarding the extent to which such policies are influenced by the possibility of United Nations action. There is reason to presume, however, that the possibility of such action is a factor not lightly disregarded by states, and indeed may greatly influence the policies that they follow.

Respective Roles of the Principal Organs

In order to ensure prompt and effective action by the United Nations, the Charter vested in the Security Council the primary responsibility for the maintenance of international peace and security. The Council has not been able, however, to discharge this responsibility as had been hoped; in fact, in dealing with questions involving important interests of the major powers, the Council has been largely ineffective. In many cases, it has been unable to take any decision because of disagreement among its permanent members, and it is widely claimed that this failure has been a result of voting procedure under Article 27 of the Charter, which permits a permanent member of the Council to veto proposals not procedural in nature.

It is doubtful, however, whether the actual experience of the Council in dealing with the peaceful settlement of disputes and situations and with the regulation of armaments can be fairly interpreted as supporting the conclusion that the veto has prevented a satisfactory solution from being achieved in many of the cases in which it has been employed. For example, the Soviet veto in the Syrian-Lebanese case did not prevent the United Kingdom and France from accepting the proposal supported by the majority of the Council. If there had been no possibility of a Soviet veto and the Council had been able to undertake an investigation of the Communist *coup d'etat* in Czechoslovakia in 1948, it is unlikely that more than a possible propaganda advantage would have been gained because there was little, if any, chance of altering the *de facto* political situation except by the use of armed force. Approval of the reports of the Atomic Energy Commission by majorities of the Council that did not include the Soviet Union would not have brought the world any nearer to the regulation of atomic armaments because if a control system for that purpose were to be established, it could not be effective without the agreement and participation of the Soviet Union.

Quite possibly, in certain circumstances, the Security Council would be able to contribute to the peaceful settlement or adjustment of a dispute or situation if it were able to adopt a recommendation by a majority of seven that did not include the concurring votes of its permanent members. But there is little evidence that the Council would have been much more effective in dealing with the disputes and situations that have actually come before it had this possibility existed. It can, of course, be argued that a recommendation adopted under such a voting procedure would have an important psychological effect and might provide a basis for concerted political action to obtain its acceptance. Even now, however, when a permanent member prevents the adoption of a proposal by the exercise of its right of veto, those members of the Council that support the conclusions of the majority are free to use their influence to obtain the acceptance of those conclusions by the interested parties.

The frequent use of the veto is, after all, simply a reflection of the current and basic conflicts of interest among the major powers. Until there is a definite improvement in this situation, there is little hope that any voting procedure can be devised that will strengthen the Security Council to the point where it will, in fact, effectively discharge its primary responsibility for the maintenance of international peace and security. To the extent that relations among the major powers improve, the possibility exists of developing the role of the Council along the lines laid down in the Charter.

The decline in the importance of the Security Council has been paralleled by a marked increase in the importance and influence of the General Assembly and the assumption by it of those responsibilities for the maintenance of international peace and security that the Council had been expected to discharge. This shift was probably inevitable in any case, for such had been the experience of the League of Nations. Furthermore, at the San Francisco Conference, the smaller powers had on numerous occasions sought to strengthen the role of the Assembly, and on certain issues they had been restrained only by the fact that they were confronted by the strong opposition of the major powers, whose participation in the proposed organization was accepted by the smaller powers as being essential to its success.

The broad and flexible nature of the powers given to the General Assembly by the Charter favored their further development and expansion. As soon as differences among the major powers made it seem to their advantage to use the Assembly to further their particular purposes, the stage was set for a substantial enlargement of the importance and prestige of the Assembly. Any such initiative on the part of the major powers was likely to command wide support from the smaller states. This first occurred in connection with the problem of armament regulation. The Assembly was assigned a central role in the consideration of this problem from the outset. By the agreement of the major powers, it was asked in early 1946 to establish the Atomic Energy Commission and to approve the directives under which it was to operate. Thereafter, the Assembly fully utilized its broad powers to discuss and recommend principles of international co-operation and became the generally accepted forum for discussing not only the pressing problem of international control of atomic energy but also the whole problem of the limitation and reduction of armaments in all its ramificatons.

The General Assembly has also from the beginning been the forum to which individual states and groups of states have brought disputes and situations, and this has been increasingly the case as the cold war developed and as the Asian and African peoples became more vocal in expressing their nationalist aspirations. Member states resorted to the Assembly because of a variety of reasons: the inability of the Security Council to function effectively; the broad nature of the competence of the Assembly; the possibilities that the Assembly offered for obtaining the backing of a wide section of the international community; and the superiority of the Assembly as a propaganda forum. In thus making use of the Assembly, Member states have customarily sought to supplement efforts being made through other channels.

The second session of the Assembly, held in 1947, marked the decisive point in the shift of emphasis from the Council to the Assembly. At that session, the Assembly took up the situation in the Balkans, after the Security Council had reached a deadlock as a result of Soviet opposition, and also began considering the problem of Korean independence, which was submitted to it after direct negotiations between the United States and the Soviet Union had failed. The increasing activity of the Assembly in the peace and security field made necessary the consideration of methods by which it might discharge its functions more effectively. Accordingly, at its second session the Assembly also established the Interim Committee to assist in its work.

Down to 1950, the General Assembly, in dealing with disputes and situations, confined itself to recommending procedures and terms for settlement and the measures, short of the use of armed force, that might be taken to prevent the aggravation of a situation or to contribute to the achievement of a final satisfactory settlement. When, however, the Soviet representative, after a temporary absence, returned to the Security Council in August 1950, and the Council was no longer able to discharge its responsibilities in dealing with the situation in Korea, the Assembly adopted the "Uniting for Peace" resolution. In this resolution, the Assembly asserted its right to consider any threat to the peace, breach of the peace, or act of aggression and to recommend the application by Member states of appropriate measures, including the use of armed force in the case of a breach of the peace or act of aggression. The Assembly thereby assumed the major responsibility within the United Nations for dealing with the more serious threats to and breaches of the peace, and it proceeded to exercise this authority following the Communist Chinese intervention in Korea.

Although actions of the Assembly under the "Uniting for Peace" resolution are subject, because of the provisions of the Charter, to a number of limitations that do not apply to actions of the Security Council, for all practical purposes these limitations have had little significance. It is true, of course, that the Assembly can only *recommend* the application of collective military measures, whereas the Council has the power to *order* the application of such measures. But the Council has never used this power, and, if the generally accepted interpretation of the relevant provisions of the Charter continues to prevail, cannot use it so long as the agreements envisaged by Article 43 are not concluded. Moreover, the limitations imposed on the Assembly by Articles 11 and 12, which were designed to ensure the primacy of the Council in peace and security matters, had ceased to be of great importance even before the adoption of the "Uniting for Peace" resolution.

So long as the major powers remain divided, the role that the General Assembly has gradually assumed in the maintenance of international peace and security is not likely to be substantially altered. Even if they again achieve the degree of unity that they ostensibly displayed at the San Francisco Conference, it is doubtful whether the developments that have occurred in the respective roles of the Security Council and the General Assembly since the Charter was written can be reversed. If the major powers do succeed, however, in demonstrating their ability to co-operate in accordance with the purposes and principles of the Charter, the Security Council may again assume important responsibilities, in part due to the deficiencies of the General Assembly in dealing with situations in which the use of collective measures may be necessary in order to prevent or suppress a threat to or a breach of the peace. Irrespective, however, of the future role of the Council, the additional responsibilities the Assembly has assumed require consideration of the manner in which its organization and procedures can be better adapted to the performance of its new functions.

The Security Council and the General Assembly are not the only organs to which the Charter assigns responsibilities in connection with the maintenance of international peace and security. The Secretary-General and the International Court of Justice are also given important functions to perform.

The Charter not only establishes the Secretary-General as the chief administrative officer of the Organization but also gives him important political powers. The possibilities for the effective exercise of these powers have been drastically reduced, however, because of the tensions in the postwar world, especially the far-reaching conflicts of interest among the leading Members of the Organization. The efforts of the first Secretary-General to provide some political leadership and to give direction and guidance to the political organs were generally unsuccessful. His opinions on the handling by the Security Council of the Iranian complaint against the Soviet Union and on the issue of Chinese representation in the United Nations were not accepted by the majority. Likewise, his efforts to achieve some lessening of tension between the Western powers and the Soviet Union failed.

From the experience of the Organization thus far, it appears that the Secretary-General is likely to be more successful in advancing the interests and purposes of the United Nations when he exercises his influence behind the scenes in confidential exchanges with governments and their representatives. Public manifestations of support for the particular positions of governments, although perhaps admirable in principle, may indeed greatly weaken, if not destroy, the effectiveness of the Secretary-General as an intermediary and as a servant of common purposes and interests.

The Charter explicitly recognizes the International Court of Justice as the principal judicial organ of the United Nations. Yet in practice the Court has not played as important a part in the work of the United Nations as the Permanent Court of International Justice did in the work of the League of Nations. This has been largely due to the nature of the conflicts that have arisen in the postwar world and to the fact that the states involved often have not accepted international law, with the Court as an impartial interpreter, as a standard to be applied in the settlement of these conflicts. The Soviet Union, for example, refuses to accept international law as it has developed in the Western world during the past few centuries. Nor are the countries of Asia and Africa willing to accept legal standards and judicial procedures, developed by advanced Western countries, for deciding disputes resulting from their demands that existing political and economic arrangements be modified. Consequently, major disputes have not usually been decided by the Court, nor have legal questions that have arisen in connection with the consideration of disputes and situations by the Security Council or the General Assembly been referred to the Court for its opinion.

So long as relations between states remain in a condition of instability and flux, it is unlikely that the Court will be called upon to play a very important part in the maintenance of international peace and security. Only when these relations have been stabilized on the basis of general consent will it be possible for the Court to play the role that the advocates of the judicial process have long envisaged.

Process of Peaceful Settlement and Adjustment

The Charter contains detailed provisions regarding the steps to be taken by the Security Council in the peaceful settlement and adjustment of disputes and situations, but it is less specific regarding those to be taken by the General Assembly. In practice, however, both organs have adopted a highly practical approach, preferring to adapt their methods and procedures to the requirements of the particular dispute or situation.

In the case of the Council, practices have been followed that in some instances are difficult to harmonize with the detailed provisions of the Charter. Generally, the Council has liberally construed its authority to consider disputes and situations and has not, in advance of its consideration of means of settlement, determined whether the continuance of the dispute or situation is "likely to endanger the maintenance of international peace and security." As a rule, it has treated the mere submission of a question by a Member as being sufficient to justify a detailed consideration of the question with a view to recommending procedures or terms of settlement. Furthermore, the Council has not been inclined to determine whether the matter before it is a dispute or a situation and, consequently, has made little consistent effort to apply either the proviso of Article 27 (3) concerning abstention from voting by a party to a dispute or the provisions of Article 32 concerning the participation in the discussion relating to a dispute of a party thereto that is not represented on the Council. Nor has the Council attempted to differentiate between its powers under Article 36 to recommend "appropriate procedures or methods of adjustment" and its powers under Article 37 to recommend "terms of settlement."

It is difficult to escape the conclusion that the actual practices of the Council bear little relation to most of the refinements and details of method and procedure prescribed in the Charter, especially in Chapter VI. In retrospect, a more realistic approach to the whole question of the powers and procedures of the Council would seem to have been to give the Council wide discretion in dealing with any dispute or situation in which there is alleged to be a threat to peace or to friendly relations among nations, and to permit it to develop its own standards for determining when its action would be helpful and its own procedures for seeking a peaceful settlement or adjustment of the question. In any event, this has been the manner in which the Council has exercised its authority.

Neither the Security Council nor the General Assembly has been inclined to take a narrow view of its competence to consider disputes and situations with a view to their peaceful settlement or adjustment. In particular, neither organ has been willing to admit that the question of competence is one to be decided on strictly legal grounds or on the basis of an opinion by the International Court of Justice. This is a sound position inasmuch as the question whether a particular dispute or situation is of such a nature as to endanger international peace and security or to impair friendly relations among nations is essentially a political one, to be decided by the organ to which the matter has been submitted on the basis of its evaluation of the circumstances of the particular case. The result almost inevitably has been a liberal construction of the powers of the two organs under the Charter. This, however, does not of necessity mean that either organ must use its power to the full in every dispute or situation submitted to it, because each has discretion under the Charter regarding the extent to which it shall use its powers. What is needed is greater restraint by these organs in the use of their powers, guided by a preliminary judgment regarding the contribution that either can make toward the fulfillment of the purposes of the Charter.

In certain circumstances, although either the Council or the Assembly has the competence to act, it may find that conditions are not favorable to its intervention and that eventual agreement will be furthered by allowing the interested parties to continue negotiations. At times, the cause of peace may be more effectively advanced by allowing time for passions to cool and realities to be faced than by exercising pressure in order to have a dispute promptly settled. In the recent practice of both the Council and the Assembly, there has been a growing tendency to postpone consideration of certain questions in order to allow the interested parties more time to discuss matters among themselves and to attempt to work out acceptable arrangements of their own. There can be no doubt that under certain circumstances such a course of action best serves the interests of international peace and security. At the same time, however, it is necessary to guard against the use of such an approach purely as a device for avoiding consideration of legitimate grievances on which Members, for their own particular reasons, are reluctant to take positions.

In the practice of both the Council and the Assembly, free public discussion has generally been accepted as a useful means of furthering the aims of the United Nations, and each organ has, with few exceptions, recognized the right of a Member to have its complaint fully and publicly discussed. From the beginning, the role of the General Assembly as the "town meeting of the world" has been stressed. This emphasis has increased as use has been made of the Assembly in the cold war.

Experience to date does not suggest, however, that free and public discussion is in all cases the best way to promote the spirit of compromise and accommodation necessary to agreement on controversial issues. To be sure, on many questions, especially those arising in connection with the cold war, there may be little possibility of agreement, even under favorable conditions for negotiation, and the only service the United Nations organ can render may well be to give support to the party best able to justify its position under the provisions of the Charter. Nevertheless, there are other cases where a more cautious and less publicized approach may yield better results. The Council of the League of Nations, for example, used to considerable advantage the devices of preliminary private discussion and of appointing a *rapporteur* authorized to carry out private talks and report to the full Council. More ingenuity in the development of comparable procedures and greater willingness to use them and to resist the temptations of public debate might increase the effectiveness of United Nations action, even under the tense conditions of the cold war.

Both the Council and the Assembly, as well as the Members of the United Nations, have been reluctant to use the procedures of arbitration and judicial settlement for the settlement of disputes and the advisory procedure of the International Court for clarifying questions of law. To a considerable extent, this has been, as previously noted, because of the basic political conflicts of the postwar period, which have further narrowed the area in which parties to a dispute are prepared to accept the decision of a tribunal bound to apply the rules of international law. In addition, the emphasis of the Charter on the importance of the political approach in the organization of international peace and security has not encouraged the use of judicial organs and processes even in situations where the issues are of a justiciable nature. In fact, a comparison of the discussions in the League of Nations Assembly and in the United Nations General Assembly shows how far the world has moved in discounting the value of international law, and the procedures for settling disputes on the basis of law, as approaches to international peace and security.

Some observers believe that the United States has gone too far in strongly emphasizing the political as against the legal approach. It is quite possible that consideration should be given to greater use of the Court for the settlement of disputes, especially by wider acceptance of its compulsory jurisdiction over legal disputes, without the attachment of crippling conditions, and for assisting the Council and the Assembly in the clarification of legal aspects of disputes and situations. Both these steps can be taken without the necessity of any amendment of the Charter of the United Nations as it stands. It must be recognized, however, that they are not likely to be taken until all nations, especially the major powers, are in greater agreement on the rules of law that are to govern their relations with each other.

The provisions of the Charter that authorize the Security Council and the General Assembly to make decisions on substantive matters by specified majorities of those members voting were widely regarded, when the Charter was written, as an advance of considerable importance over the provisions of the Covenant of the League of Nations, which required such decisions to be made by unanimous vote. This view has not been wholly confirmed by experience. The unanimity rule had the undoubted merit of emphasizing the importance of achieving agreement among the states chiefly concerned, even though it frequently resulted in the adoption of resolutions so watered down as to be largely meaningless. It recognized that resolutions adopted without the full concurrence of the interested parties often would be of doubtful value, especially if a major power was among the parties dissenting. In many cases, resolutions adopted by the General Assembly or the Security Council with a view to the peaceful settlement or adjustment of disputes or situations have had little effect because they have not had the support of states whose co-operation was necessary to their implementation. When it is possible for a decision of the Council or the Assembly to be implemented without the co-operation of the dissenting states, the decision can be effective. Generally speaking, however, if recommendations of United Nations organs for the settlement or adjustment of disputes or situations are to be effective, they must win the acquiescence, whether by formal vote or otherwise, of the interested parties.

If the Security Council or the General Assembly is to achieve maximum effectiveness as an instrument of peaceful settlement and adjustment, the Member states must bear in mind, when they are drafting proposals and voting on recommendations, that a principal function of the organ is not to make a finding but to obtain the acceptance by the parties of the recommended methods or terms of settlement or adjustment. If such acceptance cannot be obtained, majority recommendations may, of course, have some value as means of moral and psychological pressure because they will frequently represent the views of the preponderant part of the world community. But cognizance must also be taken of the fact that recommendations adopted by a two-thirds vote of the General Assembly will not always reflect the views of governments representing the greater part of the population of the world or even the greater part of its wealth and power. Furthermore, the limitations, even the dangers, must be recognized in any attempts to apply moral and psychological pressures through recommendations by the Assembly. A state, when confronted by a recommendation supported by a large majority of the Members of the United Nations, may become more stubborn and recalcitrant in its opposition instead of more pliant and willing to compromise. On the other hand, there may be situations in which, for domestic political reasons, the government of a state will find it easier to accept particular terms of settlement if some outside pressure is applied.

Once the United Nations organ has adopted its recommendation or decision for the settlement or adjustment of a particular dispute or situation, there remains the problem of implementation. Under the Charter only very limited measures are available to the United Nations for ensuring the implementation of such recommendations and decisions. The Charter does not authorize the use of collective measures to enforce compliance with recommendations of the Security Council or the General Assembly or with even a judgment of the International Court of Justice.

There is usually a minimum of difficulty in obtaining full implementation if the parties to a dispute or situation have agreed in advance to accept the proposals or decisions of a third party or of an international organ. This especially has been the experience of the International Court, although in the Corfu Channel case and in the Iranian Oil case difficulties arose over the claim of one party that the Court had no jurisdiction. Only a minimum of difficulty is also likely to occur when the states chiefly concerned agree in advance to accept and carry out the decision of the General Assembly or the Security Council, as in the case of the recommendations by the Assembly regarding the disposition of the former Italian colonies. But when recommendations are made by the Council or the Assembly without any advance agreement by the interested parties to carry them out, the problem of implementation becomes more difficult because the Charter itself imposes no legal obligation in this connection on Member states.

It is true, of course, that Member states are obligated by the Charter to refrain in their international relations from the threat or use of force, and this obligation extends to any action of such a nature as they might take in order to prevent the implementation of recommendations by the United Nations. This obligation is scarcely adequate, however, to ensure in most circumstances that a solution endorsed by the United Nations will be executed. In the Palestine case, for example, the Council refused to take prompt and effective action to prevent armed force from being used to frustrate the implementation of the recommendation by the Assembly. In certain conditions, action taken to prevent or suppress the use of armed force may contribute to the implementation of a recommendation of the Assembly or the Council, but it cannot be said that implementation by coercive measures is a normally permissible procedure under the Charter or one that Members have viewed favorably. Furthermore, it would not be realistic, given present conditions, to expect that states would be willing to vest in any international authority the power to impose a settlement in disputes and situations where important national interests are in conflict. Certainly there is little likelihood of the major powers agreeing to such limitation on their freedom of action.

All of the foregoing emphasizes how important it is that, in dealing with a dispute or situation, the Security Council or the General Assembly should use every available means to clarify the issues, to widen the area of agreement, to convince the parties that their

interests can best be served by peaceful settlement, and to assist the
parties in carrying out the terms of their agreements. In performing
their tasks of peaceful settlement, both the Council and the Assembly have found that subsidiary organs with limited membership and
capable of great mobility, flexibility, and continuity of action have
been invaluable in clarifying the facts and issues, in keeping the
parties in contact with each other, in exploring possible bases of
agreement, in encouraging the parties to agree to specific proposals,
and in supervising the implementation of agreements. Such an approach also serves the purpose of emphasizing the interest of the
United Nations in achieving a peaceful settlement and affords some
means of maintaining a measure of control by the United Nations
over developments. The creation and use of such subsidiary organs,
adapted to the circumstances in each case, illustrate the flexibility
of procedure that is required if the function of peaceful settlement
is to be successfully performed by the United Nations.

Collective Measures to Maintain or Restore Peace

When a dispute or situation is claimed to constitute a threat to the
peace, or an actual breach of the peace or an act of aggression, the
organ of the United Nations to which the matter is brought is
allowed wide discretion in the evaluation of the situation and the
choice of the course of action to be followed. In so far as the Security Council is concerned, this discretion is explicitly recognized
in the provisions of Articles 39 and 40 of the Charter. For the General Assembly, the discretion is implicit in the general terms that
are used to define the functions and powers of that organ. In practice, this discretion has proved to be of the greatest value in the
efforts made to maintain or restore international peace and security.

The Charter authorizes the Security Council to follow three general courses of action in dealing with threats to or breaches of the
peace or acts of aggression. These courses, which can be pursued
either singly or in combination, and either consecutively or concurrently, are: (1) to seek the peaceful settlement or adjustment of
the dispute or situation by appropriate recommendations; (2) to
call upon the parties to take provisional measures to prevent the
situation from deteriorating further or to bring hostilities to an end;
and (3) to recommend or order collective measures to maintain or
restore international peace and security.

It was basic to the initial concept of the peace and security system provided by the Charter that the major powers—the permanent members of the Council—would be willing to co-operate, because their support would be indispensable for the adoption and successful carrying out of any of the collective measures authorized by the Charter. Of necessity, such willingness depended on the acceptance by the major powers of common purposes, on mutual trust and confidence among them, and on a common belief that the adjustment of any conflicts of interest and attitudes that might arise among them would be equally advantageous to all and could be achieved without vital sacrifices on the part of any of them. So far, however, these conditions for major power co-operation have not existed in the postwar period, at least in the relations between the Soviet Union and the Western powers. Consequently, the Security Council has been effective only in special circumstances where a measure of agreement among the major powers has been possible or where the fact of their disagreement could momentarily be circumvented. For example, in dealing with hostilities in Palestine there was sufficient agreement among the major powers to enable the Council to achieve a cease-fire and armistice agreements. Moreover, in the cases of Indonesia and Kashmir, such agreement enabled the Council to play a significant role in bringing fighting to an end. In dealing with the Korean question, however, the Council was able to act initially only because of the absence of the Soviet representative. But in dealing with Chinese Communist intervention in Korea, the Council was completely deadlocked because of disagreement among the major powers.

Not only has the effectiveness of the Security Council been reduced by the inability of the major powers to agree on measures to be taken in dealing with a particular situation, but also the Council has been unable to take necessary steps to prepare itself militarily for effective action. In the Military Staff Committee and in the Council, a hopeless deadlock arose over the principles that were to govern the military agreements to be concluded under Article 43 of the Charter. Without military forces at its disposal, the Council has not been in a good position to use the lesser measures provided for under Article 41. Furthermore, the measures of a provisional nature that the Council may take are not likely to command the respect they otherwise would if the Council had military power available to it. And finally, because of lack of co-operation among the major powers, the provisions of Article 106, which were intended to

provide the basis for necessary enforcement action pending the conclusion of agreements under Article 43, have been ineffective.

To many, the most serious set-back of the United Nations has
been the failure of the major powers to co-operate in giving effect
to the Charter system of enforcement action. This, in turn,
has weakened the authority of the United Nations organs in achieving the peaceful settlement or adjustment of disputes and situations,
because the inability of the United Nations promptly to put an end
to, or to prevent, the use of force has encouraged states not to accept
proposals for peaceful settlement so long as they see any possibility
of obtaining more advantageous terms by independent action. Member states consequently have been deprived of the security they had
hoped to achieve through the Organization.

The increasing inability of the Security Council to act led directly
to the use of other provisions of the Charter under which the individual Member states might achieve their collective security, with
the result that since 1947 there has been a proliferation of regional
security and collective defense arrangements. These arrangements
have been based for the most part on agreements that utilize the
right of individual and collective self-defense that Member states
have reserved under Article 51. Thus, the agreements concluded by
the Western powers—the Rio Treaty, the Brussels Pact, the North
Atlantic Treaty, the Anzus Pact, the treaties between the United
States and the Philippines, the Republic of Korea, and Japan, and
the more recent Southeast Asia Treaty—are all based on the principle of collective self-defense. They provide for mutual assistance
among the parties in the event of an armed attack, reserving to each
party the right to decide whether an armed attack has been committed. All of these agreements declare that the parties to them are
motivated by a desire to support the purposes and principles of the
Charter, and that the obligations imposed by the agreements on the
parties are subordinate to their commitments under the Charter.
The agreements provide that the Security Council will be informed
of any measures taken under them in dealing with an armed attack.

It is beyond the scope of this volume to appraise the role and effectiveness of these security and defense arrangements for the maintenance of international peace and security.[1] But the extent to which

---

[1] The bilateral mutual assistance agreements among the Soviet Union and its
satellites have been concluded under the exception contained in Art. 53 of the
Charter. For detailed discussion and appraisal of arrangements entered into
under Arts. 51 and 53, see the volume in this Brookings series, *Regional Security
and the United Nations*.

the existence of these special arrangements can influence the manner in which collective military measures are carried out when taken under the authority of a United Nations resolution was clearly shown by the experience in Korea. Almost all Member states that joined with the United States in taking military measures in Korea were parties to collective defense agreements to which the United States was a party, or were dependent in a special way on United States military assistance. There is little doubt that the prior existence of such agreements greatly facilitated the organization of the collective military effort in Korea.

The experience in Korea was of great significance in the development of the United Nations system of collective security. When military attack occurred in June 1950, the Security Council—despite the lack of armed forces at its disposal—was able to initiate collective measures under its authority by recommending that the Member states use armed force to repel the North Korean attack.

It seemed obvious, however, that, although fortuitous circumstances had made it possible to use the Security Council for initiating collective measures to meet the North Korean attack, there was little prospect that the Council would be able to perform this function successfully in the future, especially if an act of aggression were to be encouraged or supported by a permanent member of the Council. The "Uniting for Peace" resolution, therefore, provided for extensive use of the General Assembly in order to mobilize and direct the collective efforts of Member states in dealing with any alleged threat to the peace, breach of the peace, or act of aggression. The basic approach to the problem that the resolution took was, in a real sense, similar to that of the League of Nations. There was a difference, however, in that the Charter, in contrast to the Covenant of the League, does not obligate Member states immediately to take measures against an aggressor. But this difference is more of form than of substance because Member states that join in supporting a recommendation by the General Assembly are probably as likely to take collective measures as if bound to do so by a legal commitment the application of which they alone determine.

Efforts made thus far to implement the "Uniting for Peace" resolution do not provide an adequate basis for making a final judgment on whether an effective system of collective security can be constructed around the General Assembly, or whether the Assembly, by using a combination of persuasion, exhortation, and coercion, can be made as efficient an organ for dealing with threats to and breaches of the peace as the Security Council was supposed to be. The experience of the Assembly in dealing with Chinese Communist intervention in Korea indicates that it is not likely to take the prompt, decisive action that may be required to meet effectively a carefully planned aggression. The Assembly is clearly better suited because of its structure and procedures to serve the functions of informing and developing opinion and of seeking ways and means for peaceful settlement than to organizing and directing measures of coercion and suppression.

The Collective Measures Committee, established by the "Uniting for Peace" resolution, has of course been giving extensive consideration to the problem of how the General Assembly can best organize and maintain armed forces sufficient to enable it to discharge the responsibilities it has assumed under the resolution. So far, however, the studies and recommendations of the committee have not pointed to a satisfactory solution. If any threat to the peace or violation of the peace originating with or encouraged by a great power is to be effectively headed off or brought to an end without the terrible consequences of another world war, it is necessary in the first instance to have in being, or to be able to mobilize quickly for use, forces—military, economic, and spiritual—that will convince the state intending to use, or already using, force that its action does not and will not pay. Furthermore, there must be flexible machinery and procedures available for preventing the aggravation of any situation involving a threat to or breach of the peace, for bringing an end to hostilities if they have occurred, and for achieving the peaceful adjustment of the basic difficulty. In other words, the problem fundamentally is that of creating effective material and spiritual deterrents to the unilateral use of force while providing acceptable procedures for peaceful settlement.

It would appear, however, that, given its present powers and functions, the General Assembly can make only a limited contribution to the mobilization of such force. It can, through its discussions and resolutions giving expression to the sentiments of the Member states, assist in the creation of a general opinion that even great powers would hesitate to disregard. Also, it can assist in the mobilization of various political and economic pressures intended to deter or bring to an end any use of force. But when it comes to the actual mobilization and use of armed force, it would seem that the role of the Assembly must be a limited one.

Member states are not likely to be willing to enter into serious commitments to place armed forces at the disposal of the Assembly, nor are they likely to be guided in their choice and use of measures by recommendations of the Assembly, except as such recommendations may be in accord with their interests and their commitments under collective defense or other mutual assistance agreements. This reluctance is due basically to the unwillingness of Members to commit themselves in advance to use their armed forces in a future contingency when they may not be certain that their national interests will require such action. Furthermore, Member states that are not committed either to one or the other of the major antagonists in the cold war, by defense or assistance agreements or, in the absence of such formal agreements, by the fact of their substantial dependence on one of the antagonists, will, in all likelihood, be hesitant to take action in accordance with a recommendation by the Assembly when such action requires taking sides in a great power struggle or increases the risk of involvement in a major armed conflict.

In looking to the foreseeable future, therefore, it would seem that Members of the United Nations will have to rely primarily on their national armed forces and the forces that are made available under special defense agreements permitted by the Charter to meet major military attacks. Under regional and collective defense arrangements, which are restricted to a limited number of Members and usually envisage action in fairly specific situations, advanced detailed planning becomes possible and Member states can usually—although not always—be depended on to take action in accordance with their commitments because these have been defined in terms of recognized national interests. In those situations in which such arrangements do not apply, the United Nations provides a framework within which individual Members, especially the major powers, can take necessary initiatives in accordance with their rights and responsibilities under the Charter and their national interests.

If principal reliance is to be placed in the future on regional security and collective defense arrangements and on the independent action of great powers to provide the military means to meet the illicit use of force by a great power, would it not be desirable that the decision for the collective use of such force should be taken by the General Assembly? There are two considerations that need to be taken into account in giving an answer. In the first place, the procedure of discussion and recommendation by the Assembly is too slow and cumbersome to meet effectively any deliberately planned military attack by or with the encouragement of a great power. In order for the requisite speed of action to be achieved, it is necessary that the use of military force be contingent on the decision of its possessors and on the basis of their judgment that the circumstances justify it. Secondly, to place on the Assembly the responsibility for making this decision might have the effect of weakening, if not destroying, its effectiveness as a means subsequently for achieving the cessation of hostilities and a peaceful settlement. By not being directly involved in the initiation and direction of collective measures, particularly military measures, the General Assembly can be in a stronger position to exercise a useful restraining influence and thus to prepare the way for negotiations leading to the settlement of differences. This does not, however, exclude the possibility that the General Assembly may play a useful supplementary role in connection with the application of collective measures by mobilizing wider support for measures initially taken and by recommending the application of additional measures if the state or states primarily responsible for the breach of the peace or act of aggression are unwilling to accept reasonable proposals for the termination of hostilities.

Although the importance of the availability and use of adequate collective force to deter or suppress the improper use of force should not be minimized, it remains true that, in dealing with a critical situation resulting from the threat or use of force by or with the encouragement of a great power, it is of the greatest importance that every possible action consistent with the purposes and principles of the United Nations should be taken to prevent the situation from deteriorating into a major conflict. Consequently, from the time the Assembly is asked to consider such a situation, it should emphasize two objectives: (1) the cessation of hostilities and the prevention of any deterioration of the situation; and (2) the achievement of a political settlement. In the choice of steps to be taken to these ends, the Assembly should be accorded the utmost freedom of decision. Each step must necessarily be taken on the basis of a total evaluation of the situation. The effectiveness of action by the Assembly in

preventing the deterioration of the situation or in achieving a cessation of hostilities will depend more on the confidence it is able to
inspire, the reasonableness of its proposals, and the extent to which
its recommendations appear to reflect an alert and aroused world
opinion, than on any legal force they may technically have.

In dealing with an alleged threat to or breach of the peace or an
act of aggression, the natural inclination of the Assembly is to direct
its action primarily toward encouraging the interested parties to
agree to cease hostilities, refrain from provocative acts, and settle
their differences by negotiation. This emphasis on pacification as
against enforcement action is not only likely but also desirable, for
it is the approach that the General Assembly is best suited to take
in view of the diversity in interests and attitudes of its members.
Furthermore, the General Assembly clearly is the best qualified of
all the principal organs to serve as a center for harmonizing the
conflicting policies of nations, which is recognized by the Charter
to be one of the major functions of the United Nations.

Regulation of Armaments

The Charter correctly recognizes that the regulation of national
armaments is an essential feature of any effective system for the
maintenance of international peace and security. It also correctly
recognizes that such regulation must form a part of an integrated
system and cannot be successfully undertaken until those conditions
in international relations are created that will make the maintenance of high levels of national armaments, and freedom in determining their nature and use, no longer appear to states as necessary for the preservation of their national security.

Nevertheless, for the reasons noted earlier in this volume, the
Members of the United Nations from the outset undertook to deal
with the regulation of armaments as a problem capable of being
treated, in large measure, in isolation from other major problems
bearing directly on the maintenance of international peace and security. An important reason for this approach was that the establishment of some effective international control of atomic energy
seemed to be vitally urgent. The efforts of the United Nations to
achieve first of all the international control of atomic weapons and
other weapons of mass destruction, and then later the control of all
weapons, have been without apparent success, however, because of
the conflicting postions of the Soviet Union and the Western powers.

During the course of the debates in the United Nations, every opportunity has been used by both sides to score propaganda victories and to discredit the motives and intentions of the other side, but the world appears to be no nearer now to an effective international control of national armaments than it was in 1945.

From this experience, some have drawn the conclusion that the best way of providing a system for the regulation of armaments is through the establishment of an international authority with power to maintain international peace and security and to enforce limitations on national armaments. A proposal of this kind, which involves the creation of a supranational authority with real power, raises serious problems—how the international authority will be created, what its structure will be, and what are to be its functions and operating procedures. So long as relations between the Western powers and the Soviet Union continue to be characterized by fear and distrust, it is difficult to see how such an authority could be created on the basis of voluntary agreement.

Past experience, including that of the United Nations, would seem to point to the conclusion that, no matter how serious the possible consequences may be of the use of national armaments for purely national purposes, the effective international control of such armaments cannot be achieved until favorable international political conditions exist. Certainly it would also seem that no effective system of international control can be established under present circumstances that does not include all the major powers, especially the United States and the Soviet Union. This conclusion indicates that, for the immediate future, emphasis must be placed on improving relations among the major powers in the hope that they will develop sufficient mutual confidence in the intentions and good faith of each other to make it possible to reach agreements regulating the nature, levels, and use of their national armaments. Such a view of the problem, however, does not preclude the possibility that continued discussions, especially among the major powers themselves, of the issues involved in any effective regulation of armaments may provide a valuable means of ascertaining the intentions of the various parties and the areas of political relationships in which negotiations might be most fruitful.

There are, of course, those who entertain the belief that the Charter of the United Nations has been outmoded by the development of atomic weapons. It would appear, however, that there is little in the experience of the United Nations, or for that matter in the records of the discussions leading up to the conclusion of the Charter, to justify the view that the Charter is a pre-atomic document in the sense that a radically different United Nations would have been organized if at the time of the San Francisco Conference the whole world had known and had already seen the destructive power of atomic weapons. The Charter of the United Nations has not been an obstacle to the international regulation of atomic energy. Rather it has provided the framework within which the major powers could agree on a plan for the effective control of atomic energy, and thus avoid the consequences of atomic warfare, if they had regarded the destructive potentialities of atomic weapons to be so great as to require the establishment of a supranational authority or the imposition of other limitations on their national sovereignties. The fact that so far they have not done so gives some indication of what their attitudes might have been in the spring of 1945 during the final drafting of the Charter even if the destructive potentialities of atomic weapons had then been widely known. It is quite possible that the major powers, or at least certain of them, would have insisted on more, instead of less, explicit and extensive reservations in the Charter regarding their freedom of action. Article 51 might indeed have been made a larger exception and the United Nations might have been a weaker organization than it is now.

General Conclusion

The record of the United Nations in maintaining international peace and security cannot of course be viewed with complete satisfaction or optimism. Admittedly the Organization has been less effective than was generally expected when the Charter was signed in 1945. But from the record to date, it is not clear that the Organization would have been more effective if the machinery of the United Nations had been different or if certain provisions of the Charter had been differently phrased. Nevertheless, the failures of the United Nations and disappointment with its record have caused some people to give considerable attention to the ways in which the Organization might be strengthened and made more effective.

Some of the most drastic proposals currently being advanced for "strengthening" the United Nations system for the maintenance of international peace and security contemplate the complete recasting of the system into some kind of world government or other form of supranational authority. A detailed analysis and appraisal of the implications of such proposals, which are dealt with in detail in another volume in this series,[2] has been beyond the scope of the present study, but one point should be made here. It is difficult to believe, on the basis of an analysis of the record of the United Nations in maintaining peace and security, that Member states would be willing to accept the more stringent obligations and limitations on their national sovereignties that would be necessary under a world government or some other form of supranational authority when they have so frequently been unwilling to fulfill the obligations and abide by the limitations imposed by the present Charter.

Another set of current proposals that would basically affect the nature of the United Nations system rests on the premise that the system could and should be reorganized to exclude the Soviet Union and its satellites. It is widely believed that the failure of the United Nations to be as effective as it was hoped it would be in maintaining international peace and security can be attributed primarily to the objectives and policies of the Soviet Union. The view is also widely held that pursuit by the Soviet leaders of objectives and policies designed to promote world revolution and encourage the spread of international communism by violent means is the chief threat to the peace and security of every nation of the free world. There are, however, many who accept these views who do not believe that the United Nations should be transformed into an alliance of the free world against the Communist-controlled states.

Even in those countries that are most firmly aligned against Communist expansionism, especially the countries of Western Europe, there is widespread unwillingness on the part of governments and peoples to accept the thesis that war between the Western powers and the Soviet Union is inevitable and, consequently, that there is no possibility of reducing existing tensions between them and of establishing the basis for increased, though perhaps limited, co-operation. To many who hold this view, a major value of the United Nations as presently constituted is that it keeps alive contacts between the Western powers and the Soviet Union and provides opportunities and means by which tensions may be reduced, co-operative relations may be established, and some firmer basis for peace and security may be achieved than is provided by military alliances and armament rivalry. The United Nations not only provides the

---

[2] See the volume in this Brookings series, *Proposals for Changes in the United Nations*.

means of easy contact between representatives of the great powers but it also brings these relations under the moderating and harmonizing influence of the agreed purposes and principles of the United Nations and of the mediatory action of other states not directly involved in the great power conflict but deeply committed to the avoidance of war and the advancement of general peace and welfare.

Moreover, proposals to reorganize the United Nations so as to direct it against the Communist powers are unacceptable to governments and peoples in other parts of the world who refuse to align themselves either with Moscow and Peiping or with Washington, London, and Paris. Since the Second World War, a number of new Asian and African states have emerged that do not identify themselves with Western culture and are not prepared to align themselves unreservedly with either communism or Western capitalist democracy. If confronted by the necessity of choosing between a United Nations organized as an anti-Communist alliance and withdrawal from the Organization, these Asian and African states would probably choose the latter. Because of the importance of these countries to the welfare and security of the Western world, it would seem absolutely essential, from the point of view of the true interests of the West, that the United Nations should continue to be the kind of organization in which these new nations will find membership attractive. To command the support of the people and governments of these states, it would appear obvious that the United Nations cannot be a mere alliance against communism; it must provide practical assistance to the peoples of the underdeveloped areas of the world in furthering their political, economic, and social development.

If the United Nations is to remain a voluntary association of sovereign national states, open to the membership of states of divergent ideologies, and concerned as much with harmonizing national policies as with organizing collective security, the need is to preserve and strengthen the Charter system for the maintenance of international peace and security. There are two main aspects of this problem: (1) whether there are important changes in the structure and functioning of the Organization that are desirable at this time in order to make it more effective in the maintenance of international peace and security; and (2) how these changes can best be brought about.

From an analysis of the work of the United Nations, it is apparent that the Organization is in a state of flux, that important changes in its methods and processes have occurred or are in progress, and that others may be desirable in the future. It is also clear that the most important obstacle in the way of a more effective organization is the political climate that has prevailed. The Organization has displayed a remarkable capacity for adaptation and growth within the limits of the Charter as initially written. In the light of these considerations, the question may well be raised whether the wiser course in the long run might not be to allow a little more time for improvement in the political atmosphere, especially in the relations among the major powers, and for the Organization further to develop and adapt itself to the conditions of the times and the demands made on it.

The wisdom of allowing the United Nations more time to develop and adapt itself to conditions is confirmed by the experience with the development of other political institutions. The Charter of the United Nations, although open to much justifiable criticism of its details, has generally shown a remarkable flexibility in practice and a capacity for being interpreted and applied in such a manner as to remedy its inherent weaknesses and deficiencies and to provide the basis for healthy institutional development. No doubt a more realistic Charter could now be written that would describe more accurately what the United Nations has become as an organization for the maintenance of international peace and security. It is less certain, however, that the Charter could be rewritten so as to make the United Nations a more effective organization in the achievement of its primary purpose. That result can be achieved only through better co-operation among the Member states in dealing with practical problems of day-to-day concern, a co-operation that must be grounded in the firm acceptance of the purposes and principles of the United Nations and the application of understanding, tolerance, and good faith in carrying them out.

APPENDIXES

APPENDIX A

Covenant of the League of Nations (Excerpts)[1]

THE HIGH CONTRACTING PARTIES,

In order to promote international co-operation and to achieve international peace and security

by the acceptance of obligations not to resort to war,

by the prescription of open, just and honourable relations between nations,

by the firm establishment of the understandings of international law as the actual rule of conduct among Governments, and

by the maintenance of justice and a scrupulous respect for all treaty obligations in the dealings of organised peoples with one another,

Agree to this Covenant of the League of Nations.

* * * *

Article 3

1. The Assembly shall consist of Representatives of the Members of the League.

2. The Assembly shall meet at stated intervals and from time to time as occasion may require at the Seat of the League or at such other place as may be decided upon.

3. The Assembly may deal at its meetings with any matter within the sphere of action of the League or affecting the peace of the world.

4. At meetings of the Assembly each Member of the League shall have one vote, and may have not more than three Representatives.

Article 4

1. The Council shall consist of Representatives of the Principal Allied and Associated Powers[2] together with Representatives of four other Members of the League. These four Members of the League shall be selected by the Assembly from time to time in its discretion. Until the appointment of the Representatives of the four Members of the League first selected by the Assembly, Representatives of Belgium, Brazil, Spain and Greece shall be members of the Council.

2. With the approval of the majority of the Assembly, the Council may name additional Members of the League whose Representatives shall always be members of the Council;[3] the Council with like approval may increase the number of Members of the League to be selected by the Assembly for representation on the Council.[4]

2 bis. *The Assembly shall fix by a two-thirds majority the rules dealing with the election of the non-permanent members of the Council, and particularly such regulations as relate to their term of office and the conditions of re-eligibility.*

3. The Council shall meet from time to time as occasion may require, and at least once a year, at the Seat of the League, or at such other place as may be decided upon.

4. The Council may deal at its meetings with any matter within the sphere of action of the League or affecting the peace of the world.

5. Any Member of the League not represented on the Council shall be invited to send a Representative to sit as a member at any meeting of the Council during the consideration of matters specially affecting the interests of that Member of the League.

[1] Source: Text as given in League of Nations, *Report on the Work of the League, 1942-1943* (Geneva, September 1943), pp. 87-99. Portions of text in italics indicate amendments to the original Covenant that were in force when the League was dissolved. The numbering of the paragraphs is in accordance with the resolution adopted by the League Assembly on September 21, 1926.

[2] These were the following: the United States, the United Kingdom, France, Italy, and Japan. The United States did not join the League, and both Italy and Japan later withdrew from it.

[3] By virtue of this provision, Germany was made a permanent member of the Council in September 1926 and the Union of Soviet Socialist Republics was made a permanent member in September 1934. Later, Germany withdrew from the League, and the Soviet Union was expelled from it.

[4] Under this provision, the number of members of the Council selected by the Assembly was subsequently increased from four to eleven.

6. At meetings of the Council, each Member of the League represented on the Council shall have one vote, and may have not more than one Representative.

****

Article 8

1. The Members of the League recognise that the maintenance of peace requires the reduction of national armaments to the lowest point consistent with national safety and the enforcement by common action of international obligations.

2. The Council, taking account of the geographical situation and circumstances of each State, shall formulate plans for such reduction for the consideration and action of the several Governments.

3. Such plans shall be subject to reconsideration and revision at least every ten years.

4. After these plans shall have been adopted by the several Governments, the limits of armaments therein fixed shall not be exceeded without the concurrence of the Council.

5. The Members of the League agree that the manufacture by private enterprise of munitions and implements of war is open to grave objections. The Council shall advise how the evil effects attendant upon such manufacture can be prevented, due regard being had to the necessities of those Members of the League which are not able to manufacture the munitions and implements of war necessary for their safety.

6. The Members of the League undertake to interchange full and frank information as to the scale of their armaments, their military, naval and air programmes and the condition of such of their industries as are adaptable to war-like purposes.

Article 9

A permanent Commission shall be constituted to advise the Council on the execution of the provisions of Articles 1 and 8 and on military, naval and air questions generally.

Article 10

The Members of the League undertake to respect and preserve as against external aggression the territorial integrity and existing political independence of all Members of the League. In case of any such aggression or in case of any threat or danger of such aggression the Council shall advise upon the means by which this obligation shall be fulfilled.

Article 11

1. Any war or threat of war, whether immediately affecting any of the Members of the League or not, is hereby declared a matter of concern to the whole League, and the League shall take any action that may be deemed wise and effectual to safeguard the peace of nations. In case any such emergency should arise, the Secretary-General shall on the request of any Member of the League forthwith summon a meeting of the Council.

2. It is also declared to be the friendly right of each Member of the League to bring to the attention of the Assembly or of the Council any circumstance whatever affecting international relations which threatens to disturb international peace or the good understanding between nations upon which peace depends.

Article 12

1. The Members of the League agree that if there should arise between them any dispute likely to lead to a rupture, they will submit the matter either to arbitration *or judicial settlement* or to inquiry by the Council, and they agree in no case to resort to war until three months after the award by the arbitrators *or the judicial decision* or the report by the Council.

2. In any case under this Article the award of the arbitrators *or the judicial decision* shall be made within a reasonable time, and the report of the Council shall be made within six months after the submission of the dispute.

Article 13

1. The Members of the League agree that whenever any dispute shall arise between them which they recognise to be suitable for submission to arbitration *or judicial settlement*, and which cannot be satisfactorily settled by diplomacy, they will submit the whole subject-matter to arbitration *or judicial settlement*.

2. Disputes as to the interpretation of a treaty, as to any question of international law, as to the existence of any fact which if established would constitute a breach of any international obligation, or as to the extent and nature of the reparation to be made for any such breach, are declared to be among those which are generally suitable for submission to arbitration *or judicial settlement.*

3. *For the consideration of any such dispute, the court to which the case is referred shall be the Permanent Court of International Justice, established in accordance with Article 14, or any tribunal agreed on by the parties to the dispute or stipulated in any convention existing between them.*

4. The Members of the League agree that they will carry out in full good faith any award *or decision* that may be rendered, and that they will not resort to war against a Member of the League which complies therewith. In the event of any failure to carry out such an award *or decision,* the Council shall propose what steps should be taken to give effect thereto.

Article 14

The Council shall formulate and submit to the Members of the League for adoption plans for the establishment of a Permanent Court of International Justice. The Court shall be competent to hear and determine any dispute of an international character which the parties thereto submit to it. The Court may also give an advisory opinion upon any dispute or question referred to it by the Council or by the Assembly.

Article 15

1. If there should arise between Members of the League any dispute likely to lead to a rupture, which is not submitted to arbitration *or judicial settlement* in accordance with Article 13, the Members of the League agree that they will submit the matter to the Council. Any party to the dispute may effect such submission by giving notice of the existence of the dispute to the Secretary-General, who will make all necessary arrangements for a full investigation and consideration thereof.

2. For this purpose the parties to the dispute will communicate to the Secretary-General, as promptly as possible, statements of their case with all the relevant facts and papers, and the Council may forthwith direct the publication thereof.

3. The Council shall endeavour to effect a settlement of the dispute, and if such efforts are successful, a statement shall be made public giving such facts and explanations regarding the dispute and the terms of settlement thereof as the Council may deem appropriate.

4. If the dispute is not thus settled, the Council either unanimously or by a majority vote shall make and publish a report containing a statement of the facts of the dispute and the recommendations which are deemed just and proper in regard thereto.

5. Any Member of the League represented on the Council may make public a statement of the facts of the dispute and of its conclusions regarding the same.

6. If a report by the Council is unanimously agreed to by the members thereof other than the Representatives of one or more of the parties to the dispute, the Members of the League agree that they will not go to war with any party to the dispute which complies with the recommendations of the report.

7. If the Council fails to reach a report which is unanimously agreed to by the members thereof, other than the Representatives of one or more of the parties to the dispute, the Members of the League reserve to themselves the right to take such action as they shall consider necessary for the maintenance of right and justice.

8. If the dispute between the parties is claimed by one of them, and is found by the Council, to arise out of a matter which by international law is solely within the domestic jurisdiction of that party, the Council shall so report, and shall make no recommendation as to its settlement.

9. The Council may in any case under this Article refer the dispute to the Assembly. The dispute shall be so referred at the request of either party to the dispute, provided that such request be made within fourteen days after the submission of the dispute to the Council.

10. In any case referred to the Assem-

bly, all the provisions of this Article and of Article 12 relating to the action and powers of the Council shall apply to the action and powers of the Assembly, provided that a report made by the Assembly, if concurred in by the Representatives of those Members of the League represented on the Council and of a majority of the other Members of the League, exclusive in each case of the Representatives of the parties to the dispute, shall have the same force as a report by the Council concurred in by all the members thereof other than the Representatives of one or more of the parties to the dispute.

Article 16

1. Should any Member of the League resort to war in disregard of its covenants under Articles 12, 13 or 15, it shall *ipso facto* be deemed to have committed an act of war against all other Members of the League, which hereby undertake immediately to subject it to the severance of all trade or financial relations, the prohibition of all intercourse between their nationals and the nationals of the covenant-breaking State, and the prevention of all financial, commercial or personal intercourse between the nationals of the covenant-breaking State and the nationals of any other State, whether a Member of the League or not.

2. It shall be the duty of the Council in such case to recommend to the several Governments concerned what effective military, naval or air force the Members of the League shall severally contribute to the armed forces to be used to protect the covenants of the League.

3. The Members of the League agree, further, that they will mutually support one another in the financial and economic measures which are taken under this Article, in order to minimise the loss and inconvenience resulting from the above measures, and that they will mutually support one another in resisting any special measures aimed at one of their number by the covenant-breaking State, and that they will take the necessary steps to afford passage through their territory to the forces of any of the Members of the League which are co-operating to protect the covenants of the League.

4. Any Member of the League which has violated any covenant of the League may be declared to be no longer a Member of the League by a vote of the Council concurred in by the Representatives of all the other Members of the League represented thereon.

Article 17

1. In the event of a dispute between a Member of the League and a State which is not a Member of the League, or between States not Members of the League, the State or States not Members of the League shall be invited to accept the obligations of membership in the League for the purposes of such dispute, upon such conditions as the Council may deem just. If such invitation is accepted, the provisions of Articles 12 to 16 inclusive shall be applied with such modifications as may be deemed necessary by the Council.

2. Upon such invitation being given the Council shall immediately institute an inquiry into the circumstances of the dispute and recommend such action as may seem best and most effectual in the circumstances.

3. If a State so invited shall refuse to accept the obligations of membership in the League for the purposes of such dispute, and shall resort to war against a Member of the League, the provisions of Article 16 shall be applicable as against the State taking such action.

4. If both parties to the dispute when so invited refuse to accept the obligations of membership in the League for the purposes of such dispute, the Council may take such measures and make such recommendations as will prevent hostilities and will result in the settlement of the dispute.

* * * *

Article 19

The Assembly may from time to time advise the reconsideration by Members of the League of treaties which have become inapplicable and the consideration of international conditions whose continuance might endanger the peace of the world.

APPENDIX B

Charter of the United Nations [1]

WE THE PEOPLES OF THE UNITED NATIONS
DETERMINED

to save succeeding generations from the scourge of war, which twice in our life-time has brought untold sorrow to mankind, and

to reaffirm faith in fundamental human rights, in the dignity and worth of the human person, in the equal rights of men and women and of nations large and small, and

to establish conditions under which justice and respect for the obligations arising from treaties and other sources of international law can be maintained, and

to promote social progress and better standards of life in larger freedom,

AND FOR THESE ENDS

to practice tolerance and live together in peace with one another as good neighbors, and

to unite our strength to maintain international peace and security, and

to ensure, by the acceptance of principles and the institution of methods, that armed force shall not be used, save in the common interest, and

to employ international machinery for the promotion of the economic and social advancement of all peoples,

HAVE RESOLVED TO COMBINE OUR EFFORTS
TO ACCOMPLISH THESE AIMS.

Accordingly, our respective Governments, through representatives assembled in the city of San Francisco, who have exhibited their full powers found to be in good and due form, have agreed to the present Charter of the United Nations and do hereby establish an international organization to be known as the United Nations.

[1] Source: Photographic reproduction of the text given in *Charter of the United Nations and Statute of the International Court of Justice*, U.S. Department of State Publication 2368 (1945), pp. 1-20, which is a facsimile of the Charter agreed to at the San Francisco Conference.

CHAPTER I

PURPOSES AND PRINCIPLES

Article 1

The Purposes of the United Nations are:

1. To maintain international peace and security, and to that end: to take effective collective measures for the prevention and removal of threats to the peace, and for the suppression of acts of aggression or other breaches of the peace, and to bring about by peaceful means, and in conformity with the principles of justice and international law, adjustment or settlement of international disputes or situations which might lead to a breach of the peace;

2. To develop friendly relations among nations based on respect for the principle of equal rights and self-determination of peoples, and to take other appropriate measures to strengthen universal peace;

3. To achieve international cooperation in solving international problems of an economic, social, cultural, or humanitarian character, and in promoting and encouraging respect for human rights and for fundamental freedoms for all without distinction as to race, sex, language, or religion; and

4. To be a center for harmonizing the actions of nations in the attainment of these common ends.

Article 2

The Organization and its Members, in pursuit of the Purposes stated in Article 1, shall act in accordance with the following Principles.

1. The Organization is based on the principle of the sovereign equality of all its Members.

2. All Members, in order to ensure to all of them the rights and benefits resulting from membership, shall fulfil in good faith the obligations assumed by them in accordance with the present Charter.

3. All Members shall settle their international disputes by peaceful means in such a manner that international peace and security, and justice, are not endangered.

4. All Members shall refrain in their international relations from the threat or use of force against the territorial integrity or political independence of any state, or in any other manner inconsistent with the Purposes of the United Nations.

5. All Members shall give the United Nations every assistance in any action it takes in accordance with the present Charter, and shall refrain from giving assistance to any state against which the United Nations is taking preventive or enforcement action.

6. The Organization shall ensure that states which are not Members of the United Nations act in accordance with these Principles so far as may be necessary for the maintenance of international peace and security.

7. Nothing contained in the present Charter shall authorize the United Nations to intervene in matters which are essentially within the domestic jurisdiction of any state or shall require the Members to submit such matters to settlement under the present Charter; but this principle shall not prejudice the application of enforcement measures under Chapter VII.

CHAPTER II

MEMBERSHIP

Article 3

The original Members of the United Nations shall be the states which, having participated in the United Nations Conference on International Organization at San Francisco, or having previously signed the Declaration by United Nations of January 1, 1942, sign the present Charter and ratify it in accordance with Article 110.

Article 4

1. Membership in the United Nations is open to all other peace-loving states which accept the obligations contained in the present Charter and, in the judgment of the Organization, are able and willing to carry out these obligations.

2. The admission of any such state to membership in the United Nations will be effected by a decision of the General Assembly upon the recommendation of the Security Council.

Article 5

A Member of the United Nations against which preventive or enforcement action has been taken by the Security Council may be suspended from the exercise of the rights and privileges of membership by the General Assembly upon the recommendation of the Security Council. The exercise of these rights and privileges may be restored by the Security Council.

Article 6

A Member of the United Nations which has persistently violated the Principles contained in the present Charter may be expelled from the Organization by the General Assembly upon the recommendation of the Security Council.

CHAPTER III
ORGANS

Article 7

1. There are established as the principal organs of the United Nations: a General Assembly, a Security Council, an Economic and Social Council, a Trusteeship Council, an International Court of Justice, and a Secretariat.

2. Such subsidiary organs as may be found necessary may be established in accordance with the present Charter.

Article 8

The United Nations shall place no restrictions on the eligibility of men and women to participate in any capacity and under conditions of equality in its principal and subsidiary organs.

CHAPTER IV
THE GENERAL ASSEMBLY

Composition
Article 9

1. The General Assembly shall consist of all the Members of the United Nations.

2. Each Member shall have not more than five representatives in the General Assembly.

Functions and Powers
Article 10

The General Assembly may discuss any questions or any matters within the scope of the present Charter or relating to the powers and functions of any organs provided for in the present Charter, and, except as provided in Article 12, may make recommendations to the Members of the United Nations or to the Security Council or to both on any such questions or matters.

Article 11

1. The General Assembly may consider the general principles of cooperation in the maintenance of international peace and security, including the principles governing disarmament and the regulation of armaments, and may make recommendations with regard to such principles to the Members or to the Security Council or to both.

2. The General Assembly may discuss any questions relating to the maintenance of international peace and security brought before it by any Member of the United Nations, or by the Security Council, or by a state which is not a

Member of the United Nations in accordance with Article 35, paragraph 2, and, except as provided in Article 12, may make recommendations with regard to any such questions to the state or states concerned or to the Security Council or to both. Any such question on which action is necessary shall be referred to the Security Council by the General Assembly either before or after discussion.

3. The General Assembly may call the attention of the Security Council to situations which are likely to endanger international peace and security.

4. The powers of the General Assembly set forth in this Article shall not limit the general scope of Article 10.

Article 12

1. While the Security Council is exercising in respect of any dispute or situation the functions assigned to it in the present Charter, the General Assembly shall not make any recommendation with regard to that dispute or situation unless the Security Council so requests.

2. The Secretary-General, with the consent of the Security Council, shall notify the General Assembly at each session of any matters relative to the maintenance of international peace and security which are being dealt with by the Security Council and shall similarly notify the General Assembly, or the Members of the United Nations if the General Assembly is not in session, immediately the Security Council ceases to deal with such matters.

Article 13

1. The General Assembly shall initiate studies and make recommendations for the purpose of:
   a. promoting international cooperation in the political field and encouraging the progressive development of international law and its codification;

b. promoting international cooperation in the economic, social, cultural, educational, and health fields, and assisting in the realization of human rights and fundamental freedoms for all without distinction as to race, sex, language, or religion.

2. The further responsibilities, functions, and powers of the General Assembly with respect to matters mentioned in paragraph 1(b) above are set forth in Chapters IX and X.

Article 14

Subject to the provisions of Article 12, the General Assembly may recommend measures for the peaceful adjustment of any situation, regardless of origin, which it deems likely to impair the general welfare or friendly relations among nations, including situations resulting from a violation of the provisions of the present Charter setting forth the Purposes and Principles of the United Nations.

Article 15

1. The General Assembly shall receive and consider annual and special reports from the Security Council; these reports shall include an account of the measures that the Security Council has decided upon or taken to maintain international peace and security.

2. The General Assembly shall receive and consider reports from the other organs of the United Nations.

Article 16

The General Assembly shall perform such functions with respect to the international trusteeship system as are assigned to it under Chapters XII and XIII, including the approval of the trusteeship agreements for areas not designated as strategic.

Article 17

1. The General Assembly shall consider and approve the budget of the Organization.

2. The expenses of the Organization shall be borne by the Members as apportioned by the General Assembly.

3. The General Assembly shall consider and approve any financial and budgetary arrangements with specialized agencies referred to in Article 57 and shall examine the administrative budgets of such specialized agencies with a view to making recommendations to the agencies concerned.

Voting

Article 18

1. Each member of the General Assembly shall have one vote.

2. Decisions of the General Assembly on important questions shall be made by a two-thirds majority of the members present and voting. These questions shall include: recommendations with respect to the maintenance of international peace and security, the election of the non-permanent members of the Security Council, the election of the members of the Economic and Social Council, the election of members of the Trusteeship Council in accordance with paragraph 1(c) of Article 86, the admission of new Members to the United Nations, the suspension of the rights and privileges of membership, the expulsion of Members, questions relating to the operation of the trusteeship system, and budgetary questions.

3. Decisions on other questions, including the determination of additional categories of questions to be decided by a two-thirds majority, shall be made by a majority of the members present and voting.

Article 19

A Member of the United Nations which is in arrears in the payment of its financial contributions to the Organization shall have no vote in the General Assembly if the amount of its arrears equals or exceeds the amount of the contributions

due from it for the preceding two full years. The General Assembly may, nevertheless, permit such a Member to vote if it is satisfied that the failure to pay is due to conditions beyond the control of the Member.

Procedure

Article 20

The General Assembly shall meet in regular annual sessions and in such special sessions as occasion may require. Special sessions shall be convoked by the Secretary-General at the request of the Security Council or of a majority of the Members of the United Nations.

Article 21

The General Assembly shall adopt its own rules of procedure. It shall elect its President for each session.

Article 22

The General Assembly may establish such subsidiary organs as it deems necessary for the performance of its functions.

CHAPTER V

THE SECURITY COUNCIL

Composition

Article 23

1. The Security Council shall consist of eleven Members of the United Nations. The Republic of China, France, the Union of Soviet Socialist Republics, the United Kingdom of Great Britain and Northern Ireland, and the United States of America shall be permanent members of the Security Council. The General Assembly shall elect six other Members of the United Nations to be non-permanent members of the Security Council, due regard being specially paid, in the first instance to the contribution of Members of the

United Nations to the maintenance of international peace and security and to the other purposes of the Organization, and also to equitable geographical distribution.

2. The non-permanent members of the Security Council shall be elected for a term of two years. In the first election of the non-permanent members, however, three shall be chosen for a term of one year. A retiring member shall not be eligible for immediate re-election.

3. Each member of the Security Council shall have one representative.

Functions and Powers
Article 24

1. In order to ensure prompt and effective action by the United Nations, its Members confer on the Security Council primary responsibility for the maintenance of international peace and security, and agree that in carrying out its duties under this responsibility the Security Council acts on their behalf.

2. In discharging these duties the Security Council shall act in accordance with the Purposes and Principles of the United Nations. The specific powers granted to the Security Council for the discharge of these duties are laid down in Chapters VI, VII, VIII, and XII.

3. The Security Council shall submit annual and, when necessary, special reports to the General Assembly for its consideration.

Article 25

The Members of the United Nations agree to accept and carry out the decisions of the Security Council in accordance with the present Charter.

Article 26

In order to promote the establishment and maintenance of international peace and security with the least diversion for armaments of the world's human and economic resources, the Security Council shall be responsible for formulating, with the assistance of the Military Staff Committee referred to in Article 47, plans to be submitted to the Members of the United Nations for the establishment of a system for the regulation of armaments.

Voting
Article 27

1. Each member of the Security Council shall have one vote.

2. Decisions of the Security Council on procedural matters shall be made by an affirmative vote of seven members.

3. Decisions of the Security Council on all other matters shall be made by an affirmative vote of seven members including the concurring votes of the permanent members; provided that, in decisions under Chapter VI, and under paragraph 3 of Article 52, a party to a dispute shall abstain from voting.

Procedure
Article 28

1. The Security Council shall be so organized as to be able to function continuously. Each member of the Security Council shall for this purpose be represented at all times at the seat of the Organization.

2. The Security Council shall hold periodic meetings at which each of its members may, if it so desires, be represented by a member of the government or by some other specially designated representative.

3. The Security Council may hold meetings at such places other than the seat of the Organization as in its judgment will best facilitate its work.

Article 29

The Security Council may establish such subsidiary organs as it deems necessary for the performance of its functions.

Article 30

The Security Council shall adopt its own rules of procedure, including the method of selecting its President.

Article 31

Any Member of the United Nations which is not a member of the Security Council may participate, without vote, in the discussion of any question brought before the Security Council whenever the latter considers that the interests of that Member are specially affected.

Article 32

Any Member of the United Nations which is not a member of the Security Council or any state which is not a Member of the United Nations, if it is a party to a dispute under consideration by the Security Council, shall be invited to participate, without vote, in the discussion relating to the dispute. The Security Council shall lay down such conditions as it deems just for the participation of a state which is not a Member of the United Nations.

CHAPTER VI

PACIFIC SETTLEMENT OF DISPUTES

Article 33

1. The parties to any dispute, the continuance of which is likely to endanger the maintenance of international peace and security, shall, first of all, seek a solution by negotiation, enquiry, mediation, conciliation, arbitration, judicial settlement, resort to regional agencies or arrangements, or other peaceful means of their own choice.

2. The Security Council shall, when it deems necessary, call upon the parties to settle their dispute by such means.

Article 34

The Security Council may investigate any dispute, or any situation which might lead to inter-national friction or give rise to a dispute, in order to determine whether the continuance of the dispute or situation is likely to endanger the maintenance of international peace and security.

Article 35

1. Any Member of the United Nations may bring any dispute, or any situation of the nature referred to in Article 34, to the attention of the Security Council or of the General Assembly.

2. A state which is not a Member of the United Nations may bring to the attention of the Security Council or of the General Assembly any dispute to which it is a party if it accepts in advance, for the purposes of the dispute, the obligations of pacific settlement provided in the present Charter.

3. The proceedings of the General Assembly in respect of matters brought to its attention under this Article will be subject to the provisions of Articles 11 and 12.

Article 36

1. The Security Council may, at any stage of a dispute of the nature referred to in Article 33 or of a situation of like nature, recommend appropriate procedures or methods of adjustment.

2. The Security Council should take into consideration any procedures for the settlement of the dispute which have already been adopted by the parties.

3. In making recommendations under this Article the Security Council should also take into consideration that legal disputes should as a general rule be referred by the parties to the International Court of Justice in accordance with the provisions of the Statute of the Court.

Article 37

1. Should the parties to a dispute of the nature referred to in Article 33 fail to settle it by the means indicated in that Article, they shall refer it to the Security Council.

2. If the Security Council deems that the continuance of the dispute is in fact likely to endanger the maintenance of international peace and security, it shall decide whether to take action under Article 36 or to recommend such terms of settlement as it may consider appropriate.

Article 38

Without prejudice to the provisions of Articles 33 to 37, the Security Council may, if all the parties to any dispute so request, make recommendations to the parties with a view to a pacific settlement of the dispute.

CHAPTER VII

ACTION WITH RESPECT TO THREATS TO THE PEACE, BREACHES OF THE PEACE, AND ACTS OF AGGRESSION

Article 39

The Security Council shall determine the existence of any threat to the peace, breach of the peace, or act of aggression and shall make recommendations, or decide what measures shall be taken in accordance with Articles 41 and 42, to maintain or restore international peace and security.

Article 40

In order to prevent an aggravation of the situation, the Security Council may, before making the recommendations or deciding upon the measures provided for in Article 39, call upon the parties concerned to comply with such provisional measures as it deems necessary or desirable. Such provisional measures shall be without prejudice to the rights, claims, or position of the parties concerned. The Security Council shall duly take account of failure to comply with such provisional measures.

Article 41

The Security Council may decide what measures not involving the use of armed force are to be employed to give effect to its decisions, and it may call upon the Members of the United Nations to apply such measures. These may include complete or partial interruption of economic relations and of rail, sea, air, postal, telegraphic, radio, and other means of communication, and the severance of diplomatic relations.

Article 42

Should the Security Council consider that measures provided for in Article 41 would be inadequate or have proved to be inadequate, it may take such action by air, sea, or land forces as may be necessary to maintain or restore international peace and security. Such action may include demonstrations, blockade, and other operations by air, sea, or land forces of Members of the United Nations.

Article 43

1. All Members of the United Nations, in order to contribute to the maintenance of international peace and security, undertake to make available to the Security Council, on its call and in accordance with a special agreement or agreements, armed forces, assistance, and facilities, including rights of passage, necessary for the purpose of maintaining international peace and security.

2. Such agreement or agreements shall govern the numbers and types of forces, their degree of readiness and general location, and the nature of the facilities and assistance to be provided.

3. The agreement or agreements shall be negotiated as soon as possible on the initiative of the Security Council. They shall be concluded between the Security Council and Members or between the Security Council and groups of Members and shall be subject to ratification by the signatory states in accordance with their respective constitutional processes.

Article 44

When the Security Council has decided to use force it shall, before calling upon a Member not represented on it to provide armed forces in fulfillment of the obligations assumed under Article 43, invite that Member, if the Member so desires, to participate in the decisions of the Security Council concerning the employment of contingents of that Member's armed forces.

Article 45

In order to enable the United Nations to take urgent military measures, Members shall hold immediately available national air-force contingents for combined international enforcement action. The strength and degree of readiness of these contingents and plans for their combined action shall be determined, within the limits laid down in the special agreement or agreements referred to in Article 43, by the Security Council with the assistance of the Military Staff Committee.

Article 46

Plans for the application of armed force shall be made by the Security Council with the assistance of the Military Staff Committee.

Article 47

1. There shall be established a Military Staff Committee to advise and assist the Security Council on all questions relating to the Security Council's military requirements for the maintenance of international peace and security, the employment and command of forces placed at its disposal, the regulation of armaments, and possible disarmament.

2. The Military Staff Committee shall consist of the Chiefs of Staff of the permanent members of the Security Council or their representatives. Any Member of the United Nations not permanently represented on the Committee shall be invited by the Committee to be associated with it when the efficient discharge of the Committee's responsibilities requires the participation of that Member in its work.

3. The Military Staff Committee shall be responsible under the Security Council for the strategic direction of any armed forces placed at the disposal of the Security Council. Questions relating to the command of such forces shall be worked out subsequently.

4. The Military Staff Committee, with the authorization of the Security Council and after consultation with appropriate regional agencies, may establish regional subcommittees.

Article 48

1. The action required to carry out the decisions of the Security Council for the maintenance of international peace and security shall be taken by all the Members of the United Nations or by some of them, as the Security Council may determine.

2. Such decisions shall be carried out by the Members of the United Nations directly and through their action in the appropriate international agencies of which they are members.

Article 49

The Members of the United Nations shall join in affording mutual assistance in carrying out the measures decided upon by the Security Council.

Article 50

If preventive or enforcement measures against any state are taken by the Security Council, any other state, whether a Member of the United Nations or not, which finds itself confronted with special economic problems arising from the carrying out of those measures shall have the right to consult the Security Council with regard to a solution of those problems.

Article 51

Nothing in the present Charter shall impair the inherent right of individual or collective self-defense if an armed attack occurs against a Member of the United Nations, until the Security Council has taken the measures necessary to maintain international peace and security. Measures taken by Members in the exercise of this right of self-defense shall be immediately reported to the Security Council and shall not in any way affect the authority and responsibility of the Security Council under the present Charter to take at any time such action as it deems necessary in order to maintain or restore international peace and security.

CHAPTER VIII

REGIONAL ARRANGEMENTS

Article 52

1. Nothing in the present Charter precludes the existence of regional arrangements or agencies for dealing with such matters relating to the maintenance of international peace and security as are appropriate for regional action, provided that such arrangements or agencies and their activities are consistent with the Purposes and Principles of the United Nations.

2. The Members of the United Nations entering into such arrangements or constituting such agencies shall make every effort to achieve pacific settlement of local disputes through such regional arrangements or by such regional agencies before referring them to the Security Council.

3. The Security Council shall encourage the development of pacific settlement of local disputes through such regional arrangements or by such regional agencies either on the initiative of the states concerned or by reference from the Security Council.

4. This Article in no way impairs the application of Articles 34 and 35.

Article 53

1. The Security Council shall, where appropriate, utilize such regional arrangements or agencies for enforcement action under its authority. But no enforcement action shall be taken under regional arrangements or by regional agencies without the authorization of the Security Council, with the exception of measures against any enemy state, as defined in paragraph 2 of this Article, provided for pursuant to Article 107 or in regional arrangements directed against renewal of aggressive policy on the part of any such state, until such time as the Organization may, on request of the Governments concerned, be charged with the responsibility for preventing further aggression by such a state.

2. The term enemy state as used in paragraph 1 of this Article applies to any state which during the Second World War has been an enemy of any signatory of the present Charter.

Article 54

The Security Council shall at all times be kept fully informed of activities undertaken or in contemplation under regional arrangements or by regional agencies for the maintenance of international peace and security.

CHAPTER IX

INTERNATIONAL ECONOMIC AND SOCIAL COOPERATION

Article 55

With a view to the creation of conditions of stability and well-being which are necessary for peaceful and friendly relations among nations based on respect for the principle of equal rights and self-determination of peoples, the United Nations shall promote:

a. higher standards of living, full employment, and conditions of economic and social progress and development;

b. solutions of international economic, social, health, and related problems; and international cultural and educational cooperation; and

c. universal respect for, and observance of, human rights and fundamental freedoms for all without distinction as to race, sex, language, or religion.

Article 56

All Members pledge themselves to take joint and separate action in cooperation with the Organization for the achievement of the purposes set forth in Article 55.

Article 57

1. The various specialized agencies, established by intergovernmental agreement and having wide international responsibilities, as defined in their basic instruments, in economic, social, cultural, educational, health, and related fields, shall be brought into relationship with the United Nations in accordance with the provisions of Article 63.

2. Such agencies thus brought into relationship with the United Nations are hereinafter referred to as specialized agencies.

Article 58

The Organization shall make recommendations for the coordination of the policies and activities of the specialized agencies.

Article 59

The Organization shall, where appropriate, initiate negotiations among the states concerned for the creation of any new specialized agencies required for the accomplishment of the purposes set forth in Article 55.

Article 60

Responsibility for the discharge of the functions of the Organization set forth in this Chapter shall be vested in the General Assembly and, under the authority of the General Assembly, in the Economic and Social Council, which shall have for this purpose the powers set forth in Chapter X.

CHAPTER X

THE ECONOMIC AND SOCIAL COUNCIL

Composition

Article 61

1. The Economic and Social Council shall consist of eighteen Members of the United Nations elected by the General Assembly.

2. Subject to the provisions of paragraph 3, six members of the Economic and Social Council shall be elected each year for a term of three years. A retiring member shall be eligible for immediate re-election.

3. At the first election, eighteen members of the Economic and Social Council shall be chosen. The term of office of six members so chosen shall expire at the end of one year, and of six other members at the end of two years, in accordance with arrangements made by the General Assembly.

4. Each member of the Economic and Social Council shall have one representative.

Functions and Powers

Article 62

1. The Economic and Social Council may make or initiate studies and reports with respect to international economic, social, cultural, educational, health, and related matters and may make recommendations with respect to any such matters to the General Assembly, to the Members of the United Nations, and to the specialized agencies concerned.

2. It may make recommendations for the purpose of promoting respect for, and observance of, human rights and fundamental freedoms for all.

3. It may prepare draft conventions for submission to the General Assembly, with respect to matters falling within its competence.

4. It may call, in accordance with the rules prescribed by the United Nations, international conferences on matters falling within its competence.

Article 63

1. The Economic and Social Council may enter into agreements with any of the agencies referred to in Article 57, defining the terms on which the agency concerned shall be brought into relationship with the United Nations. Such agreements shall be subject to approval by the General Assembly.

2. It may coordinate the activities of the specialized agencies through consultation with and recommendations to such agencies and through recommendations to the General Assembly and to the Members of the United Nations.

Article 64

1. The Economic and Social Council may take appropriate steps to obtain regular reports from the specialized agencies. It may make arrangements with the Members of the United Nations and with the specialized agencies to obtain reports on the steps taken to give effect to its own recommendations and to recommendations on matters falling within its competence made by the General Assembly.

2. It may communicate its observations on these reports to the General Assembly.

Article 65

The Economic and Social Council may furnish information to the Security Council and shall assist the Security Council upon its request.

Article 66

1. The Economic and Social Council shall perform such functions as fall within its competence in connection with the carrying out of the recommendations of the General Assembly.

2. It may, with the approval of the General Assembly, perform services at the request of Members of the United Nations and at the request of specialized agencies.

3. It shall perform such other functions as are specified elsewhere in the present Charter or as may be assigned to it by the General Assembly.

Voting

Article 67

1. Each member of the Economic and Social Council shall have one vote.

2. Decisions of the Economic and Social Council shall be made by a majority of the members present and voting.

Procedure

Article 68

The Economic and Social Council shall set up commissions in economic and social fields and for the promotion of human rights, and such other commissions as may be required for the performance of its functions.

Article 69

The Economic and Social Council shall invite any Member of the United Nations to participate, without vote, in its deliberations on any matter of particular concern to that Member.

Article 70

The Economic and Social Council may make arrangements for representatives of the specialized agencies to participate, without vote, in its deliberations and in those of the commissions established by it, and for its representatives to participate in the deliberations of the specialized agencies.

Article 71

The Economic and Social Council may make suitable arrangements for consultation with non-governmental organizations which are concerned with matters within its competence. Such arrangements may be made with international organizations and, where appropriate, with national organizations after consultation with the Member of the United Nations concerned.

Article 72

1. The Economic and Social Council shall adopt its own rules of procedure, including the method of selecting its President.

2. The Economic and Social Council shall meet as required in accordance with its rules, which shall include provision for the convening of meetings on the request of a majority of its members.

CHAPTER XI

DECLARATION REGARDING NON-SELF-GOVERNING TERRITORIES

Article 73

Members of the United Nations which have or assume responsibilities for the administration of territories whose peoples have not yet attained a full measure of self-government recognize the principle that the interests of the inhabitants of these territories are paramount, and accept as a sacred trust the obligation to promote to the utmost, within the system of international peace and security established by the present Charter, the well-being of the inhabitants of these territories, and, to this end:

a. to ensure, with due respect for the culture of the peoples concerned, their political, economic, social, and educational advancement, their just treatment, and their protection against abuses;

b. to develop self-government, to take due account of the political aspirations of the peoples, and to assist them in the progressive development of their free political institutions, according to the particular circumstances of each territory and its peoples and their varying stages of advancement;

c. to further international peace and security;

d. to promote constructive measures of development, to encourage research, and to cooperate with one another and, when and where appropriate, with specialized international bodies with a view to the practical achievement of the social, economic, and scientific purposes set forth in this Article; and

e. to transmit regularly to the Secretary-General for information purposes, subject to such limitation as security and constitutional considerations may require, statistical and other information of a technical nature relating to economic, social, and educational conditions in the territories for which they are respectively responsible other than those territories to which Chapters XII and XIII apply.

Article 74

Members of the United Nations also agree that their policy in respect of the territories to which this Chapter applies, no less than in respect of their metropolitan areas, must be based on the general principle of good-neighborliness, due account being taken of the interests and well-being of the rest of the world, in social, economic, and commercial matters.

CHAPTER XII

INTERNATIONAL TRUSTEESHIP SYSTEM

Article 75

The United Nations shall establish under its authority an international trusteeship system for the administration and supervision of such territories as may be placed thereunder by subsequent individual agreements. These territories are hereinafter referred to as trust territories.

Article 76

The basic objectives of the trusteeship system,

in accordance with the Purposes of the United
Nations laid down in Article 1 of the present Charter, shall be:

    a. to further international peace and se-
curity;

    b. to promote the political, economic, social,
and educational advancement of the inhabitants
of the trust territories, and their progressive
development towards self-government or independence as may be appropriate to the particular circumstances of each territory and its
peoples and the freely expressed wishes of the
peoples concerned, and as may be provided by
the terms of each trusteeship agreement;

    c. to encourage respect for human rights
and for fundamental freedoms for all without
distinction as to race, sex, language, or religion,
and to encourage recognition of the interde-
pendence of the peoples of the world; and

    d. to ensure equal treatment in social, eco-
nomic, and commercial matters for all Members
of the United Nations and their nationals, and
also equal treatment for the latter in the administration of justice, without prejudice to the
attainment of the foregoing objectives and subject to the provisions of Article 80.

Article 77

1. The trusteeship system shall apply to
such territories in the following categories as may
be placed thereunder by means of trusteeship
agreements:

    a. territories now held under mandate;

    b. territories which may be detached from
enemy states as a result of the Second World
War; and

    c. territories voluntarily placed under the
system by states responsible for their administration.

2. It will be a matter for subsequent agreement
as to which territories in the foregoing categories
will be brought under the trusteeship system and
upon what terms.

Article 78

The trusteeship system shall not apply to territories which have become Members of the United
Nations, relationship among which shall be based
on respect for the principle of sovereign equality.

Article 79

The terms of trusteeship for each territory to
be placed under the trusteeship system, including
any alteration or amendment, shall be agreed upon
by the states directly concerned, including the
mandatory power in the case of territories held
under mandate by a Member of the United Nations, and shall be approved as provided for in
Articles 83 and 85.

Article 80

1. Except as may be agreed upon in individual
trusteeship agreements, made under Articles 77,
79, and 81, placing each territory under the trusteeship system, and until such agreements have
been concluded, nothing in this Chapter shall be
construed in or of itself to alter in any manner
the rights whatsoever of any states or any peoples
or the terms of existing international instruments
to which Members of the United Nations may respectively be parties.

2. Paragraph 1 of this Article shall not be interpreted as giving grounds for delay or postponement of the negotiation and conclusion of agreements for placing mandated and other territories
under the trusteeship system as provided for in
Article 77.

Article 81

The trusteeship agreement shall in each case
include the terms under which the trust territory
will be administered and designate the authority
which will exercise the administration of the trust
territory. Such authority, hereinafter called the

administering authority, may be one or more states or the Organization itself.

Article 82

There may be designated, in any trusteeship agreement, a strategic area or areas which may include part or all of the trust territory to which the agreement applies, without prejudice to any special agreement or agreements made under Article 43.

Article 83

1. All functions of the United Nations relating to strategic areas, including the approval of the terms of the trusteeship agreements and of their alteration or amendment, shall be exercised by the Security Council.

2. The basic objectives set forth in Article 76 shall be applicable to the people of each strategic area.

3. The Security Council shall, subject to the provisions of the trusteeship agreements and without prejudice to security considerations, avail itself of the assistance of the Trusteeship Council to perform those functions of the United Nations under the trusteeship system relating to political, economic, social, and educational matters in the strategic areas.

Article 84

It shall be the duty of the administering authority to ensure that the trust territory shall play its part in the maintenance of international peace and security. To this end the administering authority may make use of volunteer forces, facilities, and assistance from the trust territory in carrying out the obligations towards the Security Council undertaken in this regard by the administering authority, as well as for local defense and the maintenance of law and order within the trust territory.

Article 85

1. The functions of the United Nations with

regard to trusteeship agreements for all areas not designated as strategic, including the approval of the terms of the trusteeship agreements and of their alteration or amendment, shall be exercised by the General Assembly.

2. The Trusteeship Council, operating under the authority of the General Assembly, shall assist the General Assembly in carrying out these functions.

CHAPTER XIII
THE TRUSTEESHIP COUNCIL

Composition

Article 86

1. The Trusteeship Council shall consist of the following Members of the United Nations:

   a. those Members administering trust territories;

   b. such of those Members mentioned by name in Article 23 as are not administering trust territories; and

   c. as many other Members elected for three-year terms by the General Assembly as may be necessary to ensure that the total number of members of the Trusteeship Council is equally divided between those Members of the United Nations which administer trust territories and those which do not.

2. Each member of the Trusteeship Council shall designate one specially qualified person to represent it therein.

Functions and Powers

Article 87

The General Assembly and, under its authority, the Trusteeship Council, in carrying out their functions, may:

   a. consider reports submitted by the administering authority;

b. accept petitions and examine them in consultation with the administering authority;

c. provide for periodic visits to the respective trust territories at times agreed upon with the administering authority; and

d. take these and other actions in conformity with the terms of the trusteeship agreements.

Article 88

The Trusteeship Council shall formulate a questionnaire on the political, economic, social, and educational advancement of the inhabitants of each trust territory, and the administering authority for each trust territory within the competence of the General Assembly shall make an annual report to the General Assembly upon the basis of such questionnaire.

Voting

Article 89

1. Each member of the Trusteeship Council shall have one vote.

2. Decisions of the Trusteeship Council shall be made by a majority of the members present and voting.

Procedure

Article 90

1. The Trusteeship Council shall adopt its own rules of procedure, including the method of selecting its President.

2. The Trusteeship Council shall meet as required in accordance with its rules, which shall include provision for the convening of meetings on the request of a majority of its members.

Article 91

The Trusteeship Council shall, when appropriate, avail itself of the assistance of the Economic and Social Council and of the specialized agencies in regard to matters with which they are respectively concerned.

CHAPTER XIV
THE INTERNATIONAL COURT OF JUSTICE

Article 92

The International Court of Justice shall be the principal judicial organ of the United Nations. It shall function in accordance with the annexed Statute, which is based upon the Statute of the Permanent Court of International Justice and forms an integral part of the present Charter.

Article 93

1. All Members of the United Nations are *ipso facto* parties to the Statute of the International Court of Justice.

2. A state which is not a Member of the United Nations may become a party to the Statute of the International Court of Justice on conditions to be determined in each case by the General Assembly upon the recommendation of the Security Council.

Article 94

1. Each Member of the United Nations undertakes to comply with the decision of the International Court of Justice in any case to which it is a party.

2. If any party to a case fails to perform the obligations incumbent upon it under a judgment rendered by the Court, the other party may have recourse to the Security Council, which may, if it deems necessary, make recommendations or decide upon measures to be taken to give effect to the judgment.

Article 95

Nothing in the present Charter shall prevent Members of the United Nations from entrusting the solution of their differences to other tribunals by virtue of agreements already in existence or which may be concluded in the future.

Article 96

1. The General Assembly or the Security Council may request the International Court of Justice to give an advisory opinion on any legal question.

2. Other organs of the United Nations and specialized agencies, which may at any time be so authorized by the General Assembly, may also request advisory opinions of the Court on legal questions arising within the scope of their activities.

CHAPTER XV

THE SECRETARIAT

Article 97

The Secretariat shall comprise a Secretary-General and such staff as the Organization may require. The Secretary-General shall be appointed by the General Assembly upon the recommendation of the Security Council. He shall be the chief administrative officer of the Organization.

Article 98

The Secretary-General shall act in that capacity in all meetings of the General Assembly, of the Security Council, of the Economic and Social Council, and of the Trusteeship Council, and shall perform such other functions as are entrusted to him by these organs. The Secretary-General shall make an annual report to the General Assembly on the work of the Organization.

Article 99

The Secretary-General may bring to the attention of the Security Council any matter which in his opinion may threaten the maintenance of international peace and security.

Article 100

1. In the performance of their duties the Secretary-General and the staff shall not seek or receive instructions from any government or from any other authority external to the Organization. They shall refrain from any action which might reflect on their position as international officials responsible only to the Organization.

2. Each Member of the United Nations undertakes to respect the exclusively international character of the responsibilities of the Secretary-General and the staff and not to seek to influence them in the discharge of their responsibilities.

Article 101

1. The staff shall be appointed by the Secretary-General under regulations established by the General Assembly.

2. Appropriate staffs shall be permanently assigned to the Economic and Social Council, the Trusteeship Council, and, as required, to other organs of the United Nations. These staffs shall form a part of the Secretariat.

3. The paramount consideration in the employment of the staff and in the determination of the conditions of service shall be the necessity of securing the highest standards of efficiency, competence, and integrity. Due regard shall be paid to the importance of recruiting the staff on as wide a geographical basis as possible.

CHAPTER XVI

MISCELLANEOUS PROVISIONS

Article 102

1. Every treaty and every international agreement entered into by any Member of the United Nations after the present Charter comes into force shall as soon as possible be registered with the Secretariat and published by it.

2. No party to any such treaty or international agreement which has not been registered in accordance with the provisions of paragraph 1 of

this Article may invoke that treaty or agreement before any organ of the United Nations.

Article 103

In the event of a conflict between the obligations of the Members of the United Nations under the present Charter and their obligations under any other international agreement, their obligations under the present Charter shall prevail.

Article 104

The Organization shall enjoy in the territory of each of its Members such legal capacity as may be necessary for the exercise of its functions and the fulfillment of its purposes.

Article 105

1. The Organization shall enjoy in the territory of each of its Members such privileges and immunities as are necessary for the fulfillment of its purposes.

2. Representatives of the Members of the United Nations and officials of the Organization shall similarly enjoy such privileges and immunities as are necessary for the independent exercise of their functions in connection with the Organization.

3. The General Assembly may make recommendations with a view to determining the details of the application of paragraphs 1 and 2 of this Article or may propose conventions to the Members of the United Nations for this purpose.

CHAPTER XVII

TRANSITIONAL SECURITY ARRANGEMENTS

Article 106

Pending the coming into force of such special agreements referred to in Article 43 as in the opinion of the Security Council enable it to begin the exercise of its responsibilities under Article 42, the parties to the Four-Nation Declaration, signed at Moscow, October 30, 1943, and France, shall, in accordance with the provisions of paragraph 5 of that Declaration, consult with one another and as occasion requires with other Members of the United Nations with a view to such joint action on behalf of the Organization as may be necessary for the purpose of maintaining international peace and security.

Article 107

Nothing in the present Charter shall invalidate or preclude action, in relation to any state which during the Second World War has been an enemy of any signatory to the present Charter, taken or authorized as a result of that war by the Governments having responsibility for such action.

CHAPTER XVIII

AMENDMENTS

Article 108

Amendments to the present Charter shall come into force for all Members of the United Nations when they have been adopted by a vote of two thirds of the members of the General Assembly and ratified in accordance with their respective constitutional processes by two thirds of the Members of the United Nations, including all the permanent members of the Security Council.

Article 109

1. A General Conference of the Members of the United Nations for the purpose of reviewing the present Charter may be held at a date and place to be fixed by a two-thirds vote of the members of the General Assembly and by a vote of any seven members of the Security Council. Each Member of the United Nations shall have one vote in the conference.

2. Any alteration of the present Charter recommended by a 'wo-thirds vote of the conference shall take effect when ratified in accordance with their respective constitutional processes by two thirds of the Members of the United Nations including all the permanent members of the Security Council.

3. If such a conference has not been held before the tenth annual session of the General Assembly following the coming into force of the present Charter, the proposal to call such a conference shall be placed on the agenda of that session of the General Assembly, and the conference shall be held if so decided by a majority vote of the members of the General Assembly and by a vote of any seven members of the Security Council.

CHAPTER XIX

RATIFICATION AND SIGNATURE

Article 110

1. The present Charter shall be ratified by the signatory states in accordance with their respective constitutional processes.

2. The ratifications shall be deposited with the Government of the United States of America, which shall notify all the signatory states of each deposit as well as the Secretary-General of the Organization when he has been appointed.

3. The present Charter shall come into force upon the deposit of ratifications by the Republic of China, France, the Union of Soviet Socialist Republics, the United Kingdom of Great Britain and Northern Ireland, and the United States of America, and by a majority of the other signatory states. A protocol of the ratifications deposited shall thereupon be drawn up by the Government of the United States of America which shall communicate copies thereof to all the signatory states.

4. The states signatory to the present Charter which ratify it after it has come into force will become original Members of the United Nations on the date of the deposit of their respective ratifications.

Article 111

The present Charter, of which the Chinese, French, Russian, English, and Spanish texts are equally authentic, shall remain deposited in the archives of the Government of the United States of America. Duly certified copies thereof shall be transmitted by that Government to the Governments of the other signatory states.

IN FAITH WHEREOF the representatives of the Governments of the United Nations have signed the present Charter.

DONE at the city of San Francisco the twenty-sixth day of June, one thousand nine hundred and forty-five.

Statute of the International Court of Justice [1]

Article 1

THE INTERNATIONAL COURT OF JUSTICE established by the Charter of the United Nations as the principal judicial organ of the United Nations shall be constituted and shall function in accordance with the provisions of the present Statute.

CHAPTER I

ORGANIZATION OF THE COURT

Article 2

The Court shall be composed of a body of independent judges, elected regardless of their nationality from among persons of high moral character, who possess the qualifications required in their respective countries for appointment to the highest judicial offices, or are jurisconsults of recognized competence in international law.

Article 3

1. The Court shall consist of fifteen members, no two of whom may be nationals of the same state.

2. A person who for the purposes of membership in the Court could be regarded as a national of more than one state shall be deemed to be a national of the one in which he ordinarily exercises civil and political rights.

Article 4

1. The members of the Court shall be elected by the General Assembly and by the Security Council from a list of persons nominated by the national groups in the Permanent Court of Arbitration, in accordance with the following provisions.

2. In the case of Members of the United Nations not represented in the Permanent Court of Arbitration, candidates shall be nominated by national groups appointed for this purpose by their governments under the same conditions as those prescribed for members of the Permanent Court of Arbitration by Article 44 of the Convention of The Hague of 1907 for the pacific settlement of international disputes.

3. The conditions under which a state which is a party to the present Statute but is not a Member of the United Nations may participate in electing the members of the Court shall, in the absence of a special agreement, be laid down by the General Assembly upon recommendation of the Security Council.

Article 5

1. At least three months before the date of the election, the Secretary-General of the United Nations shall address a written request to the members of the Permanent Court of Arbitration belonging to the states which are parties to the present Statute, and to the members of the national groups appointed under Article 4, paragraph 2, inviting them to undertake, within a given time, by national groups, the nomination of persons in a position to accept the duties of a member of the Court.

2. No group may nominate more than four persons, not more than two of whom shall be of their own nationality. In no case may the number of candidates nominated by a group be more than double the number of seats to be filled.

Article 6

Before making these nominations, each national group is recommended to consult its highest court of justice, its legal faculties and schools of law, and its national academies and national sections of international academies devoted to the study of law.

Article 7

1. The Secretary-General shall prepare a list

[1] Source: Photographic reproduction of the text given in *Charter of the United Nations and Statute of the International Court of Justice*, U.S. Department of State Publication 2368 (1945), pp. 21-30, which is a facsimile of the Statute agreed to at the San Francisco Conference.

in alphabetical order of all the persons thus nominated. Save as provided in Article 12, paragraph 2, these shall be the only persons eligible.

2. The Secretary-General shall submit this list to the General Assembly and to the Security Council.

Article 8

The General Assembly and the Security Council shall proceed independently of one another to elect the members of the Court.

Article 9

At every election, the electors shall bear in mind not only that the persons to be elected should individually possess the qualifications required, but also that in the body as a whole the representation of the main forms of civilization and of the principal legal systems of the world should be assured.

Article 10

1. Those candidates who obtain an absolute majority of votes in the General Assembly and in the Security Council shall be considered as elected.

2. Any vote of the Security Council, whether for the election of judges or for the appointment of members of the conference envisaged in Article 12, shall be taken without any distinction between permanent and non-permanent members of the Security Council.

3. In the event of more than one national of the same state obtaining an absolute majority of the votes both of the General Assembly and of the Security Council, the eldest of these only shall be considered as elected.

Article 11

If, after the first meeting held for the purpose of the election, one or more seats remain to be filled, a second and, if necessary, a third meeting shall take place.

Article 12

1. If, after the third meeting, one or more seats still remain unfilled, a joint conference consisting of six members, three appointed by the General Assembly and three by the Security Council, may be formed at any time at the request of either the General Assembly or the Security Council, for the purpose of choosing by the vote of an absolute majority one name for each seat still vacant, to submit to the General Assembly and the Security Council for their respective acceptance.

2. If the joint conference is unanimously agreed upon any person who fulfils the required conditions, he may be included in its list, even though he was not included in the list of nominations referred to in Article 7.

3. If the joint conference is satisfied that it will not be successful in procuring an election, those members of the Court who have already been elected shall, within a period to be fixed by the Security Council, proceed to fill the vacant seats by selection from among those candidates who have obtained votes either in the General Assembly or in the Security Council.

4. In the event of an equality of votes among the judges, the eldest judge shall have a casting vote.

Article 13

1. The members of the Court shall be elected for nine years and may be re-elected; provided, however, that of the judges elected at the first election, the terms of five judges shall expire at the end of three years and the terms of five more judges shall expire at the end of six years.

2. The judges whose terms are to expire at the end of the above-mentioned initial periods of three and six years shall be chosen by lot to be drawn by the Secretary-General immediately after the first election has been completed.

3. The members of the Court shall continue to

discharge their duties until their places have been filled. Though replaced, they shall finish any cases which they may have begun.

4. In the case of the resignation of a member of the Court, the resignation shall be addressed to the President of the Court for transmission to the Secretary-General. This last notification makes the place vacant.

Article 14

Vacancies shall be filled by the same method as that laid down for the first election, subject to the following provision: the Secretary-General shall, within one month of the occurrence of the vacancy, proceed to issue the invitations provided for in Article 5, and the date of the election shall be fixed by the Security Council.

Article 15

A member of the Court elected to replace a member whose term of office has not expired shall hold office for the remainder of his predecessor's term.

Article 16

1. No member of the Court may exercise any political or administrative function, or engage in any other occupation of a professional nature.

2. Any doubt on this point shall be settled by the decision of the Court.

Article 17

1. No member of the Court may act as agent, counsel, or advocate in any case.

2. No member may participate in the decision of any case in which he has previously taken part as agent, counsel, or advocate for one of the parties, or as a member of a national or international court, or of a commission of enquiry, or in any other capacity.

3. Any doubt on this point shall be settled by the decision of the Court.

Article 18

1. No member of the Court can be dismissed unless, in the unanimous opinion of the other members, he has ceased to fulfil the required conditions.

2. Formal notification thereof shall be made to the Secretary-General by the Registrar.

3. This notification makes the place vacant.

Article 19

The members of the Court, when engaged on the business of the Court, shall enjoy diplomatic privileges and immunities.

Article 20

Every member of the Court shall, before taking up his duties, make a solemn declaration in open court that he will exercise his powers impartially and conscientiously.

Article 21

1. The Court shall elect its President and Vice-President for three years; they may be re-elected.

2. The Court shall appoint its Registrar and may provide for the appointment of such other officers as may be necessary.

Article 22

1. The seat of the Court shall be established at The Hague. This, however, shall not prevent the Court from sitting and exercising its functions elsewhere whenever the Court considers it desirable.

2. The President and the Registrar shall reside at the seat of the Court.

Article 23

1. The Court shall remain permanently in session, except during the judicial vacations, the dates and duration of which shall be fixed by the Court.

2. Members of the Court are entitled to peri-

odic leave, the dates and duration of which shall be fixed by the Court, having in mind the distance between The Hague and the home of each judge.

3. Members of the Court shall be bound, unless they are on leave or prevented from attending by illness or other serious reasons duly explained to the President, to hold themselves permanently at the disposal of the Court.

Article 24

1. If, for some special reason, a member of the Court considers that he should not take part in the decision of a particular case, he shall so inform the President.

2. If the President considers that for some special reason one of the members of the Court should not sit in a particular case, he shall give him notice accordingly.

3. If in any such case the member of the Court and the President disagree, the matter shall be settled by the decision of the Court.

Article 25

1. The full Court shall sit except when it is expressly provided otherwise in the present Statute.

2. Subject to the condition that the number of judges available to constitute the Court is not thereby reduced below eleven, the Rules of the Court may provide for allowing one or more judges, according to circumstances and in rotation, to be dispensed from sitting.

3. A quorum of nine judges shall suffice to constitute the Court.

Article 26

1. The Court may from time to time form one or more chambers, composed of three or more judges as the Court may determine, for dealing with particular categories of cases; for example, labor cases and cases relating to transit and communications.

2. The Court may at any time form a chamber for dealing with a particular case. The number of judges to constitute such a chamber shall be determined by the Court with the approval of the parties.

3. Cases shall be heard and determined by the chambers provided for in this Article if the parties so request.

Article 27

A judgment given by any of the chambers provided for in Articles 26 and 29 shall be considered as rendered by the Court.

Article 28

The chambers provided for in Articles 26 and 29 may, with the consent of the parties, sit and exercise their functions elsewhere than at The Hague.

Article 29

With a view to the speedy despatch of business, the Court shall form annually a chamber composed of five judges which, at the request of the parties, may hear and determine cases by summary procedure. In addition, two judges shall be selected for the purpose of replacing judges who find it impossible to sit.

Article 30

1. The Court shall frame rules for carrying out its functions. In particular, it shall lay down rules of procedure.

2. The Rules of the Court may provide for assessors to sit with the Court or with any of its chambers, without the right to vote.

Article 31

1. Judges of the nationality of each of the parties shall retain their right to sit in the case before the Court.

2. If the Court includes upon the Bench a judge of the nationality of one of the parties, any other party may choose a person to sit as judge. Such person shall be chosen preferably from among

those persons who have been nominated as candidates as provided in Articles 4 and 5.

3. If the Court includes upon the Bench no judge of the nationality of the parties, each of these parties may proceed to choose a judge as provided in paragraph 2 of this Article.

4. The provisions of this Article shall apply to the case of Articles 26 and 29. In such cases, the President shall request one or, if necessary, two of the members of the Court forming the chamber to give place to the members of the Court of the nationality of the parties concerned, and, failing such, or if they are unable to be present, to the judges specially chosen by the parties.

5. Should there be several parties in the same interest, they shall, for the purpose of the preceding provisions, be reckoned as one party only. Any doubt upon this point shall be settled by the decision of the Court.

6. Judges chosen as laid down in paragraphs 2, 3, and 4 of this Article shall fulfil the conditions required by Articles 2, 17 (paragraph 2), 20, and 24 of the present Statute. They shall take part in the decision on terms of complete equality with their colleagues.

Article 32

1. Each member of the Court shall receive an annual salary.

2. The President shall receive a special annual allowance.

3. The Vice-President shall receive a special allowance for every day on which he acts as President.

4. The judges chosen under Article 31, other than members of the Court, shall receive compensation for each day on which they exercise their functions.

5. These salaries, allowances, and compensation shall be fixed by the General Assembly. They may not be decreased during the term of office.

6. The salary of the Registrar shall be fixed by the General Assembly on the proposal of the Court.

7. Regulations made by the General Assembly shall fix the conditions under which retirement pensions may be given to members of the Court and to the Registrar, and the conditions under which members of the Court and the Registrar shall have their traveling expenses refunded.

8. The above salaries, allowances, and compensation shall be free of all taxation.

Article 33

The expenses of the Court shall be borne by the United Nations in such a manner as shall be decided by the General Assembly.

CHAPTER II

COMPETENCE OF THE COURT

Article 34

1. Only states may be parties in cases before the Court.

2. The Court, subject to and in conformity with its Rules, may request of public international organizations information relevant to cases before it, and shall receive such information presented by such organizations on their own initiative.

3. Whenever the construction of the constituent instrument of a public international organization or of an international convention adopted thereunder is in question in a case before the Court, the Registrar shall so notify the public international organization concerned and shall communicate to it copies of all the written proceedings.

Article 35

1. The Court shall be open to the states parties to the present Statute.

2. The conditions under which the Court shall be open to other states shall, subject to the special provisions contained in treaties in force, be laid

down by the Security Council, but in no case shall such conditions place the parties in a position of inequality before the Court.

3. When a state which is not a Member of the United Nations is a party to a case, the Court shall fix the amount which that party is to contribute towards the expenses of the Court. This provision shall not apply if such state is bearing a share of the expenses of the Court.

Article 36

1. The jurisdiction of the Court comprises all cases which the parties refer to it and all matters specially provided for in the Charter of the United Nations or in treaties and conventions in force.

2. The states parties to the present Statute may at any time declare that they recognize as compulsory *ipso facto* and without special agreement, in relation to any other state accepting the same obligation, the jurisdiction of the Court in all legal disputes concerning:

   a. the interpretation of a treaty;

   b. any question of international law;

   c. the existence of any fact which, if established, would constitute a breach of an international obligation;

   d. the nature or extent of the reparation to be made for the breach of an international obligation.

3. The declarations referred to above may be made unconditionally or on condition of reciprocity on the part of several or certain states, or for a certain time.

4. Such declarations shall be deposited with the Secretary-General of the United Nations, who shall transmit copies thereof to the parties to the Statute and to the Registrar of the Court.

5. Declarations made under Article 36 of the Statute of the Permanent Court of International Justice and which are still in force shall be deemed, as between the parties to the present Statute, to be acceptances of the compulsory jurisdiction of the International Court of Justice for the period which they still have to run and in accordance with their terms.

6. In the event of a dispute as to whether the Court has jurisdiction, the matter shall be settled by the decision of the Court.

Article 37

Whenever a treaty or convention in force provides for reference of a matter to a tribunal to have been instituted by the League of Nations, or to the Permanent Court of International Justice, the matter shall, as between the parties to the present Statute, be referred to the International Court of Justice.

Article 38

1. The Court, whose function is to decide in accordance with international law such disputes as are submitted to it, shall apply:

   a. international conventions, whether general or particular, establishing rules expressly recognized by the contesting states;

   b. international custom, as evidence of a general practice accepted as law;

   c. the general principles of law recognized by civilized nations;

   d. subject to the provisions of Article 59, judicial decisions and the teachings of the most highly qualified publicists of the various nations, as subsidiary means for the determination of rules of law.

2. This provision shall not prejudice the power of the Court to decide a case *ex aequo et bono*, if the parties agree thereto.

CHAPTER III

PROCEDURE

Article 39

1. The official languages of the Court shall be French and English. If the parties agree that the

case shall be conducted in French, the judgment shall be delivered in French. If the parties agree that the case shall be conducted in English, the judgment shall be delivered in English.

2. In the absence of an agreement as to which language shall be employed, each party may, in the pleadings, use the language which it prefers; the decision of the Court shall be given in French and English. In this case the Court shall at the same time determine which of the two texts shall be considered as authoritative.

3. The Court shall, at the request of any party, authorize a language other than French or English to be used by that party.

Article 40

1. Cases are brought before the Court, as the case may be, either by the notification of the special agreement or by a written application addressed to the Registrar. In either case the subject of the dispute and the parties shall be indicated.

2. The Registrar shall forthwith communicate the application to all concerned.

3. He shall also notify the Members of the United Nations through the Secretary-General, and also any other states entitled to appear before the Court.

Article 41

1. The Court shall have the power to indicate, if it considers that circumstances so require, any provisional measures which ought to be taken to preserve the respective rights of either party.

2. Pending the final decision, notice of the measures suggested shall forthwith be given to the parties and to the Security Council.

Article 42

1. The parties shall be represented by agents.

2. They may have the assistance of counsel or advocates before the Court.

3. The agents, counsel, and advocates of par-

ties before the Court shall enjoy the privileges and immunities necessary to the independent exercise of their duties.

Article 43

1. The procedure shall consist of two parts: written and oral.

2. The written proceedings shall consist of the communication to the Court and to the parties of memorials, counter-memorials and, if necessary, replies; also all papers and documents in support.

3. These communications shall be made through the Registrar, in the order and within the time fixed by the Court.

4. A certified copy of every document produced by one party shall be communicated to the other party.

5. The oral proceedings shall consist of the hearing by the Court of witnesses, experts, agents, counsel, and advocates.

Article 44

1. For the service of all notices upon persons other than the agents, counsel, and advocates, the Court shall apply direct to the government of the state upon whose territory the notice has to be served.

2. The same provision shall apply whenever steps are to be taken to procure evidence on the spot.

Article 45

The hearing shall be under the control of the President or, if he is unable to preside, of the Vice-President; if neither is able to preside, the senior judge present shall preside.

Article 46

The hearing in Court shall be public, unless the Court shall decide otherwise, or unless the parties demand that the public be not admitted.

Article 47

1. Minutes shall be made at each hearing and signed by the Registrar and the President.
2. These minutes alone shall be authentic.

Article 48

The Court shall make orders for the conduct of the case, shall decide the form and time in which each party must conclude its arguments, and make all arrangements connected with the taking of evidence.

Article 49

The Court may, even before the hearing begins, call upon the agents to produce any document or to supply any explanations. Formal note shall be taken of any refusal.

Article 50

The Court may, at any time, entrust any individual, body, bureau, commission, or other organization that it may select, with the task of carrying out an enquiry or giving an expert opinion.

Article 51

During the hearing any relevant questions are to be put to the witnesses and experts under the conditions laid down by the Court in the rules of procedure referred to in Article 30.

Article 52

After the Court has received the proofs and evidence within the time specified for the purpose, it may refuse to accept any further oral or written evidence that one party may desire to present unless the other side consents.

Article 53

1. Whenever one of the parties does not appear before the Court, or fails to defend its case, the other party may call upon the Court to decide in favor of its claim.

2. The Court must, before doing so, satisfy itself, not only that it has jurisdiction in accordance with Articles 36 and 37, but also that the claim is well founded in fact and law.

Article 54

1. When, subject to the control of the Court, the agents, counsel, and advocates have completed their presentation of the case, the President shall declare the hearing closed.
2. The Court shall withdraw to consider the judgment.
3. The deliberations of the Court shall take place in private and remain secret.

Article 55

1. All questions shall be decided by a majority of the judges present.
2. In the event of an equality of votes, the President or the judge who acts in his place shall have a casting vote.

Article 56

1. The judgment shall state the reasons on which it is based.
2. It shall contain the names of the judges who have taken part in the decision.

Article 57

If the judgment does not represent in whole or in part the unanimous opinion of the judges, any judge shall be entitled to deliver a separate opinion.

Article 58

The judgment shall be signed by the President and by the Registrar. It shall be read in open court, due notice having been given to the agents.

Article 59

The decision of the Court has no binding force except between the parties and in respect of that particular case.

Article 60

The judgment is final and without appeal. In the event of dispute as to the meaning or scope of the judgment, the Court shall construe it upon the request of any party.

Article 61

1. An application for revision of a judgment may be made only when it is based upon the discovery of some fact of such a nature as to be a decisive factor, which fact was, when the judgment was given, unknown to the Court and also to the party claiming revision, always provided that such ignorance was not due to negligence.

2. The proceedings for revision shall be opened by a judgment of the Court expressly recording the existence of the new fact, recognizing that it has such a character as to lay the case open to revision, and declaring the application admissible on this ground.

3. The Court may require previous compliance with the terms of the judgment before it admits proceedings in revision.

4. The application for revision must be made at latest within six months of the discovery of the new fact.

5. No application for revision may be made after the lapse of ten years from the date of the judgment.

Article 62

1. Should a state consider that it has an interest of a legal nature which may be affected by the decision in the case, it may submit a request to the Court to be permitted to intervene.

2. It shall be for the Court to decide upon this request.

Article 63

1. Whenever the construction of a convention to which states other than those concerned in the case are parties is in question, the Registrar shall notify all such states forthwith.

2. Every state so notified has the right to intervene in the proceedings; but if it uses this right, the construction given by the judgment will be equally binding upon it.

Article 64

Unless otherwise decided by the Court, each party shall bear its own costs.

CHAPTER IV

ADVISORY OPINIONS

Article 65

1. The Court may give an advisory opinion on any legal question at the request of whatever body may be authorized by or in accordance with the Charter of the United Nations to make such a request.

2. Questions upon which the advisory opinion of the Court is asked shall be laid before the Court by means of a written request containing an exact statement of the question upon which an opinion is required, and accompanied by all documents likely to throw light upon the question.

Article 66

1. The Registrar shall forthwith give notice of the request for an advisory opinion to all states entitled to appear before the Court.

2. The Registrar shall also, by means of a special and direct communication, notify any state entitled to appear before the Court or international organization considered by the Court, or, should it not be sitting, by the President, as likely to be able to furnish information on the question, that the Court will be prepared to receive, within a time limit to be fixed by the President, written statements, or to hear, at a public sitting to be held for the purpose, oral statements relating to the question.

3. Should any such state entitled to appear before the Court have failed to receive the special communication referred to in paragraph 2 of this Article, such state may express a desire to submit a written statement or to be heard; and the Court will decide.

4. States and organizations having presented written or oral statements or both shall be permitted to comment on the statements made by other states or organizations in the form, to the extent, and within the time limits which the Court, or, should it not be sitting, the President, shall decide in each particular case. Accordingly, the Registrar shall in due time communicate any such written statements to states and organizations having submitted similar statements.

Article 67

The Court shall deliver its advisory opinions in open court, notice having been given to the Secretary-General and to the representatives of Members of the United Nations, of other states and of international organizations immediately concerned.

Article 68

In the exercise of its advisory functions the Court shall further be guided by the provisions of the present Statute which apply in contentious cases to the extent to which it recognizes them to be applicable.

CHAPTER V
AMENDMENT
Article 69

Amendments to the present Statute shall be effected by the same procedure as is provided by the Charter of the United Nations for amendments to that Charter, subject however to any provisions which the General Assembly upon recommendation of the Security Council may adopt concerning the participation of states which are parties to the present Statute but are not Members of the United Nations.

Article 70

The Court shall have power to propose such amendments to the present Statute as it may deem necessary, through written communications to the Secretary-General, for consideration in conformity with the provisions of Article 69.

APPENDIX D

Provisional Rules of Procedure of The Security Council (Excerpts)[1]

CHAPTER I. MEETINGS

****

Rule 3

The President shall call a meeting of the Security Council if a dispute or situation is brought to the attention of the Security Council under Article 35 or under Article 11(3) of the Charter, or if the General Assembly makes recommendations or refers any question to the Security Council under Article 11(2), or if the Secretary-General brings to the attention of the Security Council any matter under Article 99.

****

CHAPTER II. AGENDA

Rule 6

The Secretary-General shall immediately bring to the attention of all representatives on the Security Council all communications from States, organs of the United Nations, or the Secretary-General concerning any matter for the consideration of the Security Council in accordance with the provisions of the Charter.

Rule 7

The Provisional Agenda for each meeting of the Security Council shall be drawn up by the Secretary-General and approved by the President of the Security Council.

Only items which have been brought to the attention of the representatives on the Security Council in accordance with Rule 6, items covered by Rule 10, or matters which the Security Council has previously decided to defer, may be included in the Provisional Agenda.

****

Rule 9

The first item of the Provisional Agenda for each meeting of the Security Council shall be the adoption of the Agenda.

Rule 10

Any item of the Agenda of a meeting

of the Security Council, consideration of which has not been completed at that meeting, shall, unless the Security Council otherwise decides, automatically be included in the Agenda of the next meeting.

****

CHAPTER VI. CONDUCT OF BUSINESS

****

Rule 37

Any Member of the United Nations which is not a member of the Security Council may be invited, as the result of a decision of the Security Council, to participate, without vote, in the discussion of any question brought before the Security Council when the Security Council considers that the interests of that Member are specially affected, or when a Member brings a matter to the attention of the Security Council in accordance with Article 35(1) of the Charter.

Rule 38

Any member of the United Nations invited in accordance with the preceding Rule or in application of Article 32 of the Charter to participate in the discussions of the Security Council may submit proposals and draft resolutions. These proposals and draft resolutions may be put to a vote only at the request of a representative on the Security Council.

Rule 39

The Security Council may invite members of the Secretariat or other persons, whom it considers competent for the purpose, to supply it with information or to give other assistance in examining matters within its competence.

Rule 40

Voting in the Security Council shall be in accordance with the relevant Articles of the Charter and of the Statute of the International Court of Justice.

[1] Source: U. N. Doc. S/96/Rev. 4 (July 29, 1952).

664

APPENDIX E

Rules of Procedure of the General Assembly (Excerpts)[1]

I. SESSIONS

****

SPECIAL SESSIONS

****

SUMMONING ON REQUEST FROM THE SECURITY COUNCIL OR MEMBERS

Rule 8

(a) Special sessions of the General Assembly shall be held within fifteen days of the receipt by the Secretary-General of a request for such a session from the Security Council, or of a request from a majority of the Members of the United Nations, or of the concurrence of a majority of Members as provided in rule 9.

(b) Emergency special sessions pursuant to General Assembly resolution 377 A (V) shall be convened within twenty-four hours of the receipt by the Secretary-General of a request for such a session from the Security Council, on the vote of any seven members thereof, or of a request from a majority of the Members of the United Nations expressed by vote in the Interim Committee or otherwise, or of the concurrence of a majority of Members as provided in rule 9.

REQUEST BY MEMBERS

Rule 9

(a) Any member of the United Nations may request the Secretary-General to summon a special session. The Secretary-General shall immediately inform the other Members of the United Nations of the request and inquire whether they concur in it. If within thirty days of the date of the communication of the Secretary-General a majority of the Members concur in the request, a special session of the General Assembly shall be summoned in accordance with rule 8.

(b) This rule shall apply also to a request by any Member for an emergency special session pursuant to resolution 377 A (V). In such a case the Secretary-General shall communicate with the other Members by the most expeditious means of communication available.

****

II. AGENDA

REGULAR SESSIONS

PROVISIONAL AGENDA

Rule 12

The provisional agenda for a regular session shall be drawn up by the Secretary-General and communicated to the Members of the United Nations at least sixty days before the opening of the session.

Rule 13

The provisional agenda of a regular session shall include:

(a) Report of the Secretary-General on the work of the Organization;

(b) Reports from the Security Council, the Economic and Social Council, the Trusteeship Council, the International Court of Justice, the subsidiary organs of the General Assembly, specialized agencies (where such reports are called for under agreements entered into);

(c) All items the inclusion of which has been ordered by the General Assembly at a previous session;

(d) All items proposed by the other principal organs of the United Nations;

(e) All items proposed by any Member of the United Nations;

(f) All items pertaining to the budget for the next financial year and the report on the accounts for the last financial year;

(g) All items which the Secretary-General deems it necessary to put before the General Assembly; and

(h) All items proposed under Article 35, paragraph 2, of the Charter by States not Members of the United Nations.

---

[1] Source: U. N. Doc. A/520/Rev. 3 (July 1954). Figures indicated between brackets in sections dealing with rules for plenary meetings refer to identical or corresponding rules for committee meetings, and vice versa.

Rule 14

Any Member or principal organ of the United Nations or the Secretary-General may, at least thirty days before the date fixed for the opening of a regular session, request the inclusion of supplementary items in the agenda. These items shall be placed on a supplementary list, which shall be communicated to the Members of the United Nations at least twenty days before the date fixed for the opening of the session.

ADDITIONAL ITEMS

Rule 15

Additional items of an important and urgent character, proposed for inclusion in the agenda less than thirty days before the opening of a regular session or during a regular session, may be placed on the agenda, if the General Assembly so decides by a majority of the Members present and voting. No additional item may be considered until seven days have elapsed since it was placed on the agenda, unless the General Assembly, by a two-thirds majority of the Members present and voting, decides otherwise, and until a committee has reported upon the question concerned.

SPECIAL SESSIONS

PROVISIONAL AGENDA

****

Rule 17

The provisional agenda for a special session shall consist only of those items proposed for consideration in the request for the holding of the session.

SUPPLEMENTARY ITEMS

Rule 18

Any Member or principal organ of the United Nations or the Secretary-General may, at least four days before the date fixed for the opening of a special session, request the inclusion of supplementary items in the agenda. Such items shall be placed on a supplementary list which shall be communicated to the Members of the United Nations as soon as possible.

ADDITIONAL ITEMS

Rule 19

During a special session items on the supplementary list and additional items may be added to the agenda by a two-thirds majority of the Members present and voting. During an emergency special session additional items concerning the matters dealt with in resolution 377 A (V) may be added to the agenda by a two-thirds majority of the Members present and voting.

REGULAR AND SPECIAL SESSIONS

EXPLANATORY MEMORANDA

Rule 20

All items proposed for inclusion in the agenda shall be accompanied by an explanatory memorandum and, if possible, by basic documents or by a draft resolution.

APPROVAL OF THE AGENDA

Rule 21

At each session the provisional agenda and the supplementary list, together with the report of the General Committee thereon, shall be submitted to the General Assembly for approval as soon as possible after the opening of the session.

****

DEBATE ON INCLUSION OF ITEMS

Rule 23

Debate on the inclusion of an item in the agenda, when that item has been recommended for inclusion by the General Committee, shall be limited to three speakers in favor of and three against the inclusion. The President may limit the time to be allowed to speakers under this rule.

****

VI. GENERAL COMMITTEE

COMPOSITION

Rule 38

The General Committee shall comprise the President of the General Assembly, who shall preside, the seven Vice-Presidents, the Chairmen of the six Main Committees and the Chairman of the Ad Hoc Political Committee when one is established. No two members of the General Committee shall be members of the same delegation, and it shall be so constituted as to ensure its representative character. Chairmen of other committees upon which all Members have the right to be represented and which are established by the General Assembly to meet during the session, shall be entitled to attend meetings of the General Committee and may participate without vote in the discussions.

****

FUNCTIONS

Rule 40

The General Committee shall, at the beginning of each session, consider the provisional agenda, together with the supplementary list, and shall make recommendations to the General Assembly with regard to each item proposed, concerning its inclusion in the agenda, the rejection of the request for inclusion, or the inclusion of the item in the provisional agenda of a future session. It shall, in the same manner, examine requests for the inclusion of additional items in the agenda, and shall make recommendations thereon to the General Assembly. In considering matters relating to the agenda of the General Assembly, the General Committee shall not discuss the substance of any item, except in so far as this bears upon the question whether the General Committee should recommend the inclusion of the item in the agenda, the rejection of the request for inclusion, or the inclusion of the item in the provisional agenda of a future session, and what priority should be accorded to an item the inclusion of which has been recommended.

Rule 41

The General Committee shall make recommendations to the General Assembly concerning the closing date of the session. It shall assist the President and the General Assembly in drawing up the agenda for each plenary meeting, in determining the priority of its items, and in the co-ordination of the proceedings of all committees of the General Assembly. It shall assist the President in the general conduct of the work of the General Assembly which falls within the competence of the President. It shall not, however, decide any political question.

Rule 42

The General Committee shall meet periodically throughout each session to review the progress of the General Assembly and its committees and to make recommendations for furthering such progress. It shall also meet at such other times as the President deems necessary or upon the request of any other of its members.

****

PARTICIPATION BY REPRESENTATIVES OF MEMBERS REQUESTING THE INCLUSION OF ITEMS IN THE AGENDA

Rule 43

A Member of the General Assembly which has no representative on the General Committee, and which has requested the inclusion of an item in the agenda, shall be entitled to attend any meeting of the General Committee at which its request is discussed, and may participate, without vote, in the discussion of that item.

****

XII. PLENARY MEETINGS

CONDUCT OF BUSINESS

****

REPORT OF THE SECRETARY-GENERAL

Rule 66

Proposals to refer any portion of the report of the Secretary-General to one of the Main Committees without debate shall be decided upon by the General Assembly without previous reference to the General Committee.

REFERENCE TO COMMITTEES

Rule 67

The General Assembly shall not, unless it decides otherwise, make a final decision upon any item on the agenda until it has received the report of a committee on that item.

****

PRECEDENCE

Rule 71 [112]

The Chairman and the Rapporteur of a committee may be accorded precedence for the purpose of explaining the conclusion arrived at by their committee.

****

PROPOSALS AND AMENDMENTS

Rule 80 [121]

Proposals and amendments shall normally be introduced in writing and handed to the Secretary-General, who shall circulate copies to the delegations. As a general rule, no proposal shall be discussed or put to the vote at any meeting of the General Assembly unless copies of it have been circulated to all delegations not later than the day preceding the meeting. The President may, however, permit the discussion and consideration of amendments, or of motions as to procedure, even though these amendments and motions have not been circulated or have only been circulated the same day.

****

VOTING
****

TWO-THIRDS MAJORITY
****

Rule 86

Decisions of the General Assembly on amendments to proposals relating to important questions, and on parts of such proposals put to the vote separately, shall be made by a two-thirds majority of the Members present and voting.

****

ELECTIONS
****

Rule 95 [133]

When only one person or Member is to be elected and no candidate obtains in the first ballot the majority required, a second ballot shall be taken which shall be restricted to the two candidates obtaining the largest number of votes. If in the second ballot the votes are equally divided, and a majority is required, the President shall decide between the candidates by drawing lots. If a two-thirds majority is required, the balloting shall be continued until one candidate secures two-thirds of the votes cast; provided that, after the third inconclusive ballot, votes may be cast for any eligible person or Member. If three such unrestricted ballots are inconclusive, the next three ballots shall be restricted to the two candidates who obtained the greatest number of votes in the third of the unrestricted ballots, and the following three ballots thereafter shall be unrestricted, and so on until a person or Member is elected. These provisions shall not prejudice the application of rules 144, 145, 147 and 149.

****

EQUALLY DIVIDED VOTES

Rule 97 [134]

If a vote is equally divided on matters other than elections, a second vote shall be taken at a subsequent meeting which shall be held within forty-eight hours of the first vote, and it shall be expressly mentioned in the agenda that a second

vote will be taken on the matter in question. If this vote also results in equality, the proposal shall be regarded as rejected.

XIII. COMMITTEES

CREATION, OFFICERS, ETC.

CREATION

Rule 98

The General Assembly may set up such committees as it deems necessary for the performance of its functions.

****

CONDUCT OF BUSINESS
****

POINTS OF ORDER

Rule 114 [73]

During the discussion of any matter, a representative may rise to a point of order, and the point of order shall be immediately decided by the Chairman in accordance with the rules of procedure. A representative may appeal against the ruling of the Chairman. The appeal shall be immediately put to the vote and the Chairman's ruling shall stand unless overruled by a majority of the members present and voting. A representative rising to a point of order may not speak on the substance of the matter under discussion.

****

ORDER OF PROCEDURAL MOTIONS

Rule 120 [79]

Subject to rule 114, the following motions shall have precedence in the following order over all other proposals or motions before the meeting:

(a) To suspend the meeting;
(b) To adjourn the meeting;
(c) To adjourn the debate on the item under discussion.
(d) For the closure of the debate on the item under discussion.

****

RECONSIDERATION OF PROPOSALS

Rule 124 [83]

When a proposal has been adopted or rejected it may not be reconsidered at the same session unless the committee, by a two-thirds majority of the members present and voting, so decides. Permission to speak on a motion to reconsider shall be accorded only to two speakers opposing the motion, after which it shall be immediately put to the vote.

APPENDIX F

"Uniting for Peace" Resolution[1]

Approved by the General Assembly at its 302nd plenary meeting, Nov. 3, 1950

377 (V). Uniting for peace
A

The General Assembly,

Recognizing that the first two stated Purposes of the United Nations are:

"To maintain international peace and security, and to that end: to take effective collective measures for the prevention and removal of threats to the peace, and for the suppression of acts of aggression or other breaches of the peace, and to bring about by peaceful means, and in conformity with the principles of justice and international law, adjustment or settlement of international disputes or situations which might lead to a breach of the peace", and

"To develop friendly relations among nations based on respect for the principle of equal rights and self-determination of peoples, and to take other appropriate measures to strengthen universal peace",

Reaffirming that it remains the primary duty of all Members of the United Nations, when involved in an international dispute, to seek settlement of such a dispute by peaceful means through the procedures laid down in Chapter VI of the Charter, and recalling the successful achievements of the United Nations in this regard on a number of previous occasions,

Finding that international tension exists on a dangerous scale,

Recalling its resolution 290 (IV) entitled "Essentials of peace", which states that disregard of the Principles of the Charter of the United Nations is primarily responsible for the continuance of international tension, and desiring to contribute further to the objectives of that resolution,

Reaffirming the importance of the exercise by the Security Council of its primary responsibility for the maintenance of international peace and security, and the duty of the permanent members to seek unanimity and to exercise restraint in the use of the veto,

Reaffirming that the initiative in negotiating the agreements for armed forces provided for in Article 43 of the Charter belongs to the Security Council, and desiring to ensure that, pending the conclusion of such agreements, the United Nations has at its disposal means for maintaining international peace and security,

Conscious that failure of the Security Council to discharge its responsibilities on behalf of all the Member States, particularly those responsibilities referred to in the two preceding paragraphs, does not relieve Member States of their obligations or the United Nations of its responsibility under the Charter to maintain international peace and security,

Recognizing in particular that such failure does not deprive the General Assembly of its rights or relieve it of its responsibilities under the Charter in regard to the maintenance of international peace and security,

Recognizing that discharge by the General Assembly of its responsibilities in these respects calls for possibilities of observation which would ascertain the facts and expose aggressors; for the existence of armed forces which could be used collectively; and for the possibility of timely recommendation by the General Assembly to Members of the United Nations for collective action which, to be effective, should be prompt,

A

1. *Resolves* that if the Security Council, because of lack of unanimity of the permanent members, fails to exercise its primary responsibility for the maintenance of international peace and security in any case where there appears to be a threat to the peace, breach of the peace, or act of aggression, the General Assembly shall consider the matter immediately with a view to making appropriate recommendations to Members for collective measures, including in the case of a breach of the peace or act of aggression the use of armed force when necessary, to maintain or restore international peace and security. If not in session at the time, the General Assembly may meet in emergency special session within twenty-four hours of the request therefor. Such emergency special session shall be called if requested by the Security Council on the vote of any seven members, or by a majority of the Members of the United Nations;

2. *Adopts* for this purpose the amendments to its rules of procedure set forth in the annex to the present resolution;

B

3. *Establishes* a Peace Observation Commission which, for the calendar years 1951 and 1952, shall be composed of fourteen Members, namely: China, Colombia, Czechoslovakia, France, India, Iraq, Israel, New Zealand, Pakistan, Sweden, the Union of Soviet Socialist Republics, the United Kingdom of Great Britain and Northern Ireland, the United States of America and Uruguay, and which could observe and report on the situation in any area where there exists international tension the continuance of which is likely to endanger the maintenance of international peace and security. Upon the invitation or with the consent of the State into whose territory the Commission would go, the General Assembly, or the Interim Committee when the Assembly is not in session, may utilize the Commission if the Security Council is not exercising the functions assigned to it by the Charter with respect to the matter in question. Decisions to utilize the Commission shall be made on the affirmative vote of two-thirds of the members present and voting. The Security Council may also utilize the Commission in accordance with its authority under the Charter;

4. *Decides* that the Commission shall have authority in its discretion to appoint sub-commissions and to utilize the services of observers to assist it in the performance of its functions;

5. *Recommends* to all governments and authorities that they co-operate with the Commission and assist it in the performance of its functions;

[1] Source: Photographic reproduction of the text given in U. N. General Assembly, Fifth Session, *Official Records*, Supplement No. 20, pp. 10-12.

6. *Requests* the Secretary-General to provide the necessary staff and facilities, utilizing, where directed by the Commission, the United Nations Panel of Field Observers envisaged in General Assembly resolution 297 B (IV);

C

7. *Invites* each Member of the United Nations to survey its resources in order to determine the nature and scope of the assistance it may be in a position to render in support of any recommendations of the Security Council or of the General Assembly for the restoration of international peace and security;

8. *Recommends* to the States Members of the United Nations that each Member maintain within its national armed forces elements so trained, organized and equipped that they could promptly be made available, in accordance with its constitutional processes, for service as a United Nations unit or units, upon recommendation by the Security Council or the General Assembly, without prejudice to the use of such elements in exercise of the right of individual or collective self-defence recognized in Article 51 of the Charter;

9. *Invites* the Members of the United Nations to inform the Collective Measures Committee provided for in paragraph 11 as soon as possible of the measures taken in implementation of the preceding paragraph;

10. *Requests* the Secretary-General to appoint, with the approval of the Committee provided for in paragraph 11, a panel of military experts who could be made available, on request, to Member States wishing to obtain technical advice regarding the organization, training, and equipment for prompt service as United Nations units of the elements referred to in paragraph 8;

D

11. *Establishes* a Collective Measures Committee consisting of fourteen Members, namely: Australia, Belgium, Brazil, Burma, Canada, Egypt, France, Mexico, Philippines, Turkey, the United Kingdom of Great Britain and Northern Ireland, the United States of America, Venezuela and Yugoslavia, and directs the Committee, in consultation with the Secretary-General and with such Member States as the Committee finds appropriate, to study and make a report to the Security Council and the General Assembly, not later than 1 September 1951, on methods, including those in section C of the present resolution, which might be used to maintain and strengthen international peace and security in accordance with the Purposes and Principles of the Charter, taking account of collective self-defence and regional arrangements (Articles 51 and 52 of the Charter);

12. *Recommends* to all Member States that they co-operate with the Committee and assist it in the performance of its functions;

13. *Requests* the Secretary-General to furnish the staff and facilities necessary for the effective accomplishment of the purposes set forth in sections C and D of the present resolution;

E

14. *Is fully conscious* that, in adopting the proposals set forth above, enduring peace will not be secured solely by collective security arrangements against breaches of international peace and acts of aggression, but that a genuine and lasting peace depends also upon the observance of all the Principles and Purposes es-

tablished in the Charter of the United Nations, upon the implementation of the resolutions of the Security Council, the General Assembly and other principal organs of the United Nations intended to achieve the maintenance of international peace and security, and especially upon respect for and observance of human rights and fundamental freedoms for all and on the establishment and maintenance of conditions of economic and social well-being in all countries; and accordingly

15. *Urges* Member States to respect fully, and to intensify, joint action, in co-operation with the United Nations, to develop and stimulate universal respect for and observance of human rights and fundamental freedoms, and to intensify individual and collective efforts to achieve conditions of economic stability and social progress, particularly through the development of under-developed countries and areas.

ANNEX

The rules of procedure of the General Assembly are amended in the following respects:

1. The present text of rule 8 shall become paragraph (*a*) of that rule, and a new paragraph (*b*) shall be added to read as follows:

"Emergency special sessions pursuant to resolution 377 A (V) shall be convened within twenty-four hours of the receipt by the Secretary-General of a request for such a session from the Security Council, on the vote of any seven members thereof, or of a request from a majority of the Members of the United Nations expressed by vote in the Interim Committee or otherwise, or of the concurrence of a majority of Members as provided in rule 9."

2. The present text of rule 9 shall become paragraph (*a*) of that rule and a new paragraph (*b*) shall be added to read as follows:

"This rule shall apply also to a request by any Member for an emergency special session pursuant to resolution 377 A (V). In such a case the Secretary-General shall communicate with other Members by the most expeditious means of communication available."

3. Rule 10 is amended by adding at the end thereof the following:

". . . In the case of an emergency special session convened pursuant to rule 8 (*b*), the Secretary-General shall notify the Members of the United Nations at least twelve hours in advance of the opening of the session."

4. Rule 16 is amended by adding at the end thereof the following:

". . . The provisional agenda of an emergency special session shall be communicated to the Members of the United Nations simultaneously with the communication summoning the session."

5. Rule 19 is amended by adding at the end thereof the following:

". . . During an emergency special session additional items concerning the matters dealt with in resolution 377 A (V) may be added to the agenda by a two-thirds majority of the Members present and voting."

6. There is added a new rule to precede rule 65 to read as follows:

"Notwithstanding the provisions of any other rule and unless the General Assembly decides otherwise, the Assembly, in case of an emergency special session, shall convene in plenary session only and proceed directly to consider the item proposed for consideration in the request for the holding of the session, without previous reference to the General Committee or to any other Committee; the President and Vice-Presidents for such emergency special sessions shall be, respectively, the Chairman of those delegations from which were elected the President and Vice-Presidents of the previous session."

B

For the purpose of maintaining international peace and security, in accordance with the Charter of the United Nations, and, in particular, with Chapters V, VI and VII of the Charter,

The General Assembly

Recommends to the Security Council:

That it should take the necessary steps to ensure that the action provided for under the Charter is taken with respect to threats to the peace, breaches of the peace or acts of aggression and with respect to the peaceful settlement of disputes or situations likely to endanger the maintenance of international peace and security;

That it should devise measures for the earliest application of Articles 43, 45, 46 and 47 of the Charter of the United Nations regarding the placing of armed forces at the disposal of the Security Council by the States Members of the United Nations and the effective functioning of the Military Staff Committee;

The above dispositions should in no manner prevent the General Assembly from fulfilling its functions under resolution 377 A (V).

C

The General Assembly,

Recognizing that the primary function of the United Nations Organization is to maintain and promote peace, security and justice among all nations,

Recognizing the responsibility of all Member States to promote the cause of international peace in accordance with their obligations as provided in the Charter,

Recognizing that the Charter charges the Security Council with the primary responsibility for maintaining international peace and security,

Reaffirming the importance of unanimity among the permanent members of the Security Council on all problems which are likely to threaten world peace,

Recalling General Assembly resolution 190 (III) entitled "Appeal to the Great Powers to renew their efforts to compose their differences and establish a lasting peace",

Recommends to the permanent members of the Security Council that:

(a) They meet and discuss, collectively or otherwise, and, if necessary, with other States concerned, all problems which are likely to threaten international peace and hamper the activities of the United Nations, with a view to their resolving fundamental differences and reaching agreement in accordance with the spirit and letter of the Charter;

(b) They advise the General Assembly and, when it is not in session, the Members of the United Nations, as soon as appropriate, of the results of their consultations.

APPENDIX G
Membership of the United Nations[1]

ORIGINAL MEMBER STATES

Argentina
Australia
Belgium
Bolivia
Brazil
Byelorussian Soviet Socialist Republic
Canada
Chile
China
Colombia
Costa Rica
Cuba
Czechoslovakia
Denmark
Dominican Republic
Ecuador
Egypt
El Salvador
Ethiopia
France
Greece
Guatemala
Haiti
Honduras
India
Iran
Iraq
Lebanon
Liberia
Luxembourg
Mexico
Netherlands
New Zealand
Nicaragua
Norway
Panama
Paraguay
Peru
Philippines
Poland
Saudi Arabia
Syria
Turkey
Ukrainian Soviet Socialist Republic
Union of South Africa
Union of Soviet Socialist Republics
United Kingdom of Great Britain and Northern Ireland
United States of America
Uruguay
Venezuela
Yugoslavia

STATES SUBSEQUENTLY ADMITTED TO MEMBERSHIP[2]

Afghanistan (November 9, 1946)
Burma (April 19, 1948)
Iceland (November 9, 1946)
Indonesia (September 28, 1950)
Israel (May 11, 1949)
Pakistan (December 30, 1947)
Sweden (November 9, 1946)
Thailand (December 15, 1946)
Yemen (December 30, 1947)

STATES PARTIES TO ONLY THE STATUTE OF THE INTERNATIONAL COURT OF JUSTICE[3]

Japan (April 2, 1954)
Liechtenstein (March 29, 1950)
San Marino (February 18, 1954)
Switzerland (July 28, 1948)

[1] As of December 31, 1954.

[2] Dates given are those on which the General Assembly approved the admission of the state to membership.

[3] All Member states are *ipso facto* parties to the Statute, but states that are not Members of the United Nations can become parties to the Statute in accordance with the provisions of Article 93(2) of the Charter. Dates given are those on which the state deposited with the Secretary-General its instrument of accession to the Statute.

INDEX

Index

Aaland Islands dispute, 160
Abstention, practice of, 92-93, 231-32, 609
Acheson, Dean, 494, 495, 502, 534, 535
Acheson-Lilienthal Report (1946), on international control of atomic energy, 534, 535
Additional Measures Committee, 418-19, 433, 442, 444, 481, 506
African-Asian states (see also Arab-Asian states), 608, 626; nationalism, 4, 40-42, 43, 49, 51-52, 53, 58-64, 83, 324, 338, 602, 605-06
Agenda of U.N. organs, 98-127; evaluation of practices, 126-27
 factors influencing decision to consider a question, 113-26; Art. 2(7), application of (see also Domestic jurisdiction), 115-17; Art. 107, application of, 118-20; attitudes of major groups, 124-26; "dispute," question of existence of, 117-18; exclusion of items because of other means of settlement, 120-21; full discussion, benefits of, 122-23; hearing, right of, 114-15; validity of charges, 121-22
 procedures for inclusion of questions, 98-107; additional items, 100, 100n, 101n; agenda committees, proposals for, 106-07; discussion, limitation on scope, 104-06; discussion, participation in, by non-Members, 102-04; General Assembly, procedures, 74-75, 98, 100-02, 103-07, 126-27; priority of items on agenda, 99, 103, 147-48; provisional agenda, 74-75, 76, 98, 99, 100, 100n, 127; Security Council, procedures, 75, 98-99, 102-04, 106, 126-27; states not Members, questions submitted by, 74-75; supplementary list, 100, 101n
 significance of inclusion of items, 107-13; Art. 12, relevance of, 109-11, 431; competence, issue of, 108-09; merit of complaint, 108-09
Aggression, act of. See Threat to the peace, breach of the peace, or act of aggression

Aggression, act of, definition of term, 357-60
Aggression, Special Committee on the Definition of, 360
Agreed Declaration (1945), 530-31, 532
Albania, Corfu Channel dispute with United Kingdom (see Corfu Channel dispute); Greek charges of attempts to overthrow government (see Greece, frontier incidents); Monetary Gold case, 325-26, 337-38
Aliens, treatment behind Iron Curtain, 83
Allied Control Council, 39
Ambatielos case, United Kingdom and Greece, 88, 163n, 326, 334
American republics. See Latin American states
Anglo-Egyptian question, 52, 62, 80, 91, 269, 270, 272-73, 274, 280-81, 290, 335, 603
Anglo-Egyptian treaty (1936), 440
Anglo-Iranian oil dispute. See under Iran
Anzus Pact, 617
Apartheid question. See under South Africa, Union of
Arab Higher Committee, 134, 140, 156
Arab League, 84, 375, 414
Arab Refugees, Palestine, 140
Arab-Asian states, International Court of Justice, reluctance to use, 92; Korean armistice, contribution toward, 57; membership of Arab-Asian bloc, 57n; nationalism (see Nationalism); position on collective measures by United Nations, 414; on disposal of Italian colonies, 243, 244; on inclusion of items in agenda, 73, 124-25; on Moroccan and Tunisian questions (see Morocco and Tunisia); on Palestine question (see also Palestine situation), 101, 112, 189, 196, 245, 246, 247, 254-55, 268, 304, 309, 314, 317; on racial policies of Union of South Africa, 211; relations with Western powers, 282-83, 290, 608, 626
Arbitral Procedure, Draft on, 325, 326